DP-300: Administering Relational Databases on Microsoft Azure

Study Guide with Practice Questions & Labs

First Edition

www.ipspecialist.net

Document Control

Proposal Name	:	Azure Database Administrator – Associate
Document Edition	:	First
Document Release Date	:	24th January 2022
Reference	:	DP-300

Registered in England and Wales
Company Registration No: 10883539
Registration Office at: Office 32, 19-21 Crawford Street, London W1H 1PJ, United Kingdom
www.ipspecialist.net

Feedback:
If you have any comments regarding the quality of this book, or otherwise alter it to better suit your needs, you can contact us through email at info@ipspecialist.net
Please make sure to include the book's title and ISBN in your message.

About IPSpecialist

IPSPECIALIST LTD. IS COMMITTED TO EXCELLENCE AND DEDICATED TO YOUR SUCCESS.

Our philosophy is to treat our customers like family. We want you to succeed, and we are willing to do everything possible to help you make it happen. We have the proof to back up our claims. We strive to accelerate billions of careers with great courses, accessibility, and affordability. We believe that continuous learning and knowledge evolution are the most important things to keep re-skilling and up-skilling the world.
Planning and creating a specific goal is where IPSpecialist helps. We can create a career track that suits your visions as well as develop the competencies you need to become a professional Network Engineer. We can also assist you with the execution and evaluation of your proficiency level, based on the career track you choose, as they are customized to fit your specific goals.
We help you STAND OUT from the crowd through our detailed IP training content packages.

Course Features:

- Self-Paced Learning
  - Learn at your own pace and in your own time
- Covers Complete Exam Blueprint
  - Prep-up for the exam with confidence
- Case Study Based Learning
  - Relate the content with real-life scenarios
- Subscriptions that Suits You
  - Get more and pay less with IPS subscriptions
- Career Advisory Services
  - Let the industry experts plan your career journey
- Virtual Labs to test your skills
  - With IPS vRacks, you can evaluate your exam preparations
- Practice Questions
  - Practice questions to measure your preparation standards
- On Request Digital Certification
  - On request digital certification from IPSpecialist LTD.

About the Authors:

This book has been compiled with the help of multiple professional engineers. These engineers specialize in different fields, e.g. Networking, Security, Cloud, Big Data, IoT, etc. Each engineer develops content in its specialized field that is compiled to form a comprehensive certification guide.

About the Technical Reviewers:

Nouman Ahmed Khan

AWS-Architect, CCDE, CCIEX5 (R&S, SP, Security, DC, Wireless), CISSP, CISA, CISM is a Solution Architect working with a major telecommunication provider in Qatar. He works with enterprises, mega-projects, and service providers to help them select the best-fit technology solutions. He also works closely as a consultant to understand customer business processes and helps select an appropriate technology strategy to support business goals. He has more than 14 years of experience working in Pakistan/Middle-East & UK. He holds a Bachelor of Engineering Degree from NED University, Pakistan, and an M.Sc. in Computer Networks from the UK.

Abubakar Saeed

Abubakar Saeed has more than twenty-five years of experience, Managing, Consulting, Designing, and implementing large-scale technology projects, extensive experience heading ISP operations, solutions integration, heading Product Development, Presales, and Solution Design. Emphasizing adhering to Project timelines and delivering as per customer expectations, he always leads the project in the right direction with his innovative ideas and excellent management.

Dr. Fahad Abdali

Dr. Fahad Abdali is a seasoned leader with extensive experience managing and growing software development teams in high-growth start-ups. He is a business entrepreneur with more than 18 years of experience in management and marketing. He holds a Bachelor's Degree from NED University of Engineering and Technology and Doctor of Philosophy (Ph.D.) from the University of Karachi.

Mehwish Jawed

Mehwish Jawed is working as a Senior Research Analyst. She holds a Master's and Bachelors of Engineering degree in Telecommunication Engineering from NED University of Engineering and Technology. She also worked under the supervision of HEC Approved supervisor. She has more than three published papers, including both conference and journal papers. She has a great knowledge of TWDM Passive Optical Network (PON). She also worked as a Project Engineer, Robotic Trainer in a private institute and has research skills in the field of communication networks. She has both technical knowledge and industry-sounding information, which she utilizes effectively when needed. She also has expertise in cloud platforms, as AWS, GCP, Oracle, and Microsoft Azure.

Kulsoom Khan

Kulsoom Khan has started her professional career as a Technical Content Writer. She has completed her Bachelor's Degree in Computer Science from the University of Karachi. She has a sound knowledge of Networking, Machine Learning, IoT, SQL, Computers, Network Security, development Platform and also knows multiple programming languages. She also has expertise in cloud platforms, as in Google Cloud and Microsoft Azure.

Hareem Khan

Hareem Khan is currently working as a Technical Content Developer, having command over networking and security. She has completed training in CCNA and Cybersecurity. She holds a BE in Telecommunications Engineering from NED University of Engineering and Technology. She has strong knowledge of all the basics of IP and Security Networks and Routing and Switching Protocols.

Free Resources:

For Free Resources: Please visit our website and register to access your desired Resources Or contact us at: helpdesk@ipspecialist.net

Career Report: This report is a step-by-step guide for a novice who wants to develop his/her career in the field of computer networks. It answers the following queries:

- What are the current scenarios and future prospects?
- Is this industry moving towards saturation, or are new opportunities knocking at the door?
- What will the monetary benefits be?
- Why get certified?
- How to plan, and when will I complete the certifications if I start today?
- Is there any career track that I can follow to accomplish the specialization level?

Furthermore, this guide provides a comprehensive career path towards being a specialist in networking and highlights the tracks needed to obtain certification.

IPS Personalized Technical Support for Customers: Good customer service means helping customers efficiently, in a friendly manner. It is essential to be able to handle issues for customers and do your best to ensure they are satisfied. Providing good service is one of the most important things that can set our business apart from the others of its kind.

Excellent customer service will result in attracting more customers and attain maximum customer retention.

IPS offers personalized TECH support to its customers to provide better value for money. If you have any queries related to technology and labs, you can simply ask our technical team for assistance via Live Chat or Email.

Our Products

Study Guides

IPSpecialist Study Guides are the ideal guides to developing the hands-on skills necessary to pass the exam. Our workbooks cover the official exam blueprint and explain the technology with real-life case study-based labs. The content covered in each workbook consists of individually focused technology topics presented in an easy-to-follow, goal-oriented, step-by-step approach. Every scenario features detailed breakdowns and thorough verifications to help you completely understand the task and associated technology.

We extensively used mind maps in our workbooks to visually explain the technology. Our workbooks have become a widely used tool to learn and remember information effectively.

vRacks

Our highly scalable and innovative virtualized lab platforms let you practice the IPSpecialist Study Guide at your own time and place at your convenience.

Exam Cram

Our Exam Cram notes are a concise bundling of condensed notes of the complete exam blueprint. It is an ideal and handy document to help you remember the most important technology concepts related to the certification exam.

Practice Questions

IP Specialists' Practice Questions are dedicatedly designed from a certification exam perspective. The collection of these questions from our Study Guides is prepared keeping the exam blueprint in mind, covering not only important but necessary topics. It is an ideal document to practice and revise your certification.

Content at a glance

Table of Contents

Microsoft Certifications

Microsoft Azure Certifications are industry-recognized credentials that validate your technical Cloud skills and expertise while assisting you in your career growth. These are one of the most valuable IT certifications right now since Azure has established an overwhelming growth rate in the public cloud market. Even with the presence of several tough competitors such as Amazon Web Services, Google Cloud Engine, and Rackspace, Azure is going to be the dominant public cloud platform today, with an astounding collection of proprietary services that continues to grow.

In this certification, we will discuss cloud concepts where we will learn the core benefits of using Azure like high availability, scalability, etc. We will talk about the Azure Architecture in which cloud resources are put together to work at best; Azure Compute, where you will learn how to run applications in Azure; Networking in which the discussion is on how Azure resources communicate with each other; Storage, where you put all of your data and have different ways of storing it. We will also cover databases used for data storage, its efficient retrieval as per demand, and ensuring that the users have the right access to the resources. Also, we will counter some complex scenarios with their solutions. We will have discussions on important topics like; Security, which makes Azure the best secure choice for your applications and functions; Privacy, Compliance, and Trust that make sure how services ensure privacy and how you stay compliant with standards; As well as, Pricing in Azure to stay ahead on cost.

AZ-900 is the first certification of Microsoft Azure, which is the foundational certificate in Azure. After this certification, you can prove to the world that you are proficient and have the credibility to reach the highest point of your professional life.

Value of Azure Certifications

Microsoft places equal emphasis on sound conceptual knowledge of its entire platform and hands-on experience with the Azure infrastructure and its many unique and complex components and services.

For Individuals

- Demonstrate your expertise in designing, deploying, and operating highly available, cost-effective, and secured applications on Microsoft Azure.
- Gain recognition and visibility of your proven skills and proficiency with Azure.
- Earn tangible benefits such as access to the Microsoft Certified Community, get invited to Microsoft Certification Appreciation Receptions and Lounges, obtain Microsoft Certification Practice Exam Voucher and Digital Badge for certification validation, Microsoft Certified Logo usage.
- Foster credibility with your employer and peers.

For Employers

- Identify skilled professionals to lead IT initiatives with Cloud technologies.
- Reduce risks and costs to implement your workloads and projects on the Azure platform.
- Increase customer satisfaction.

Types of Certification

Role-based Certification

- ***Fundamental*** - Validates overall understanding of the Azure Cloud.
- ***Associate***- Technical role-based certifications. No pre-requisite required.
- ***Expert***- Highest level technical role-based certification.

About Microsoft Certified: Azure Database Administrator Associate

Exam Questions	**Case study, short answer, repeated answer, MCQs**
Number of Questions	140-160
Time to Complete	120 minutes
Exam Fee	165 USD

The Microsoft Certified: Database administrators and data management specialists who handle on-premises and cloud relational databases developed with SQL Server and Azure Data Services are candidates for this test.

The Azure Database Administrator is responsible for implementing and managing cloud native and hybrid data platform solutions based on Azure Data Services and SQL Server. To accomplish day-to-day operations, and Azure Database Administrator employs a range of methodologies and technologies, including the usage of T-SQL for administrative management.

This position is in charge of managing, securing, and optimizing modern relational database solutions in terms of availability, security, and performance. This role collaborates with the Azure Data Engineer role to manage operational elements of data platform solutions.

This exam measures your ability to accomplish the following technical tasks:

- Plan and implement data platform resources (15-20%)
- Implement a secure environment (15-20%)
- Monitor and optimize operational resources (15-20%)
- Optimize query performance (5-10%)
- Perform automation of tasks (10-15%)

- Plan and implement a High Availability and Disaster Recovery (HADR) environment (15-20%)
- Perform administration by using T-SQL (10-15%)

Recommended Knowledge

- Deploy resources by using manual methods
- Recommend an appropriate database offering based on specific requirements
- Configure resources for scale and performance
- Evaluate a strategy for moving to Azure
- Implement a migration or upgrade strategy for moving to Azure
- Configure database authentication by using platform and database tools
- Configure database authorization by using platform and database tools
- Implement security for data at rest
- Implement security for data in transit
- Implement compliance controls for sensitive data
- Monitor activity and performance
- Implement performance-related maintenance tasks
- Identify performance-related issues
- Configure resources for optimal performance
- Configure a user database for optimal performance
- Review query plans
- Evaluate performance improvements
- Review database table and index design
- Create scheduled tasks
- Evaluate and implement an alert and notification strategy
- Manage and automate tasks in Azure
- Recommend an HADR strategy for a data platform solution
- Test an HADR strategy by using platform, OS, and database tools
- Perform backup and restore a database by using database tools
- Configure HA/DR by using OS, platform, and database tools
- Examine system health
- Monitor database configuration by using T-SQL
- Perform backup and restore a database by using T-SQL
- Manage authentication by using T-SQL
- Manage authorization by using T-SQL

All the required information is included in this certification course.

	Domain	Percentage
Domain 1	Plan and implement data platform resources	15-20%
Domain 2	Implement a secure environment	15-20%
Domain 3	Monitor and optimize operational resources	15-20%
Domain 4	Optimize query performance	5-10%
Domain 5	Perform automation of tasks	10-15%
Domain 6	Plan and implement a High Availability and Disaster Recovery (HADR) environment	15-20%
Domain 7	Perform administration by using T-SQL	10-15%

Chapter 01: Azure SQL Fundamentals

Introduction

In this chapter and throughout the activities, you will study how to deploy and configure Azure SQL. By studying the pre-deployment planning guidance and best practices, you will be more willing to deploy Azure SQL Database or Azure SQL Managed Instance. In addition, you will get practical knowledge and will learn about the deployment process through the Azure portal.

After deployment, you look into running verification checks and configuring Azure SQL to meet your scenario's requirements.

When securing Azure SQL, you must first consider your network and identity access, permitting only connections and access from the right places, people, and applications, depending on your organization and infrastructure. Additionally, you can encrypt and cover sensitive data and apply security management tools, such as those available in the Advanced Data Security suite.

To provide consistent performance, you need monitoring and troubleshooting capabilities. This module will teach you several methods and tools to monitor and troubleshoot performance with practical activities for a CPU scaling scenario. You will also study how to develop CPU scaling for your workload without any migration required for your database.

Introduction to Azure SQL

There has been a major trend of moving present systems to the cloud, building new applications quickly, and removing some on-premises costs.

This module will start with a brief history of Azure SQL. You will then study the several deployment options and service tiers, including what to use for your organization and when.

Azure SQL History

Software and services for relational databases have been a large part of the products provided by Microsoft over the years. Before you study Azure SQL, let us study where it started.

Launch of Windows Azure

In 2008, Ray Ozzie declared the new cloud computing operating system: Windows Azure. One of the five critical components of the Azure Services Platform launch was

Microsoft SQL Services. From the commencement, SQL has been a huge part of Azure. SQL Azure was built to provide a cloud-hosted version of SQL Server.

Evolution of database services on Azure

Let us look at an early explanation of Azure SQL from 2010:

Azure SQL is a cloud database offering which Microsoft offers as the amount of the Azure cloud computing platform. You do not want to architect a database installation for scalability, high availability, or disaster recovery, as the service offers these features automatically. Any application that uses Azure SQL needs Internet access to the link of the database.

This explanation remains valid, but the capabilities around security, performance, availability, and scale have improved. Azure SQL has changed over the years to include Azure virtual machines, managed instances, and a few options for databases. There are now multiple deployment options that have the flexibility to scale to your requirements. There have been more than 7 million deployments of some form of Azure SQL.

Azure SQL Deployment Options

There are many deployment options and selections that you have to do to meet your requirements. These options offer you the flexibility to get and pay for exactly what you want. The deployment options briefed here include SQL Server on virtual machines, Azure SQL Managed Instance, Azure SQL Database, Azure SQL Managed Instance pools, and Azure SQL Database elastic database pools.

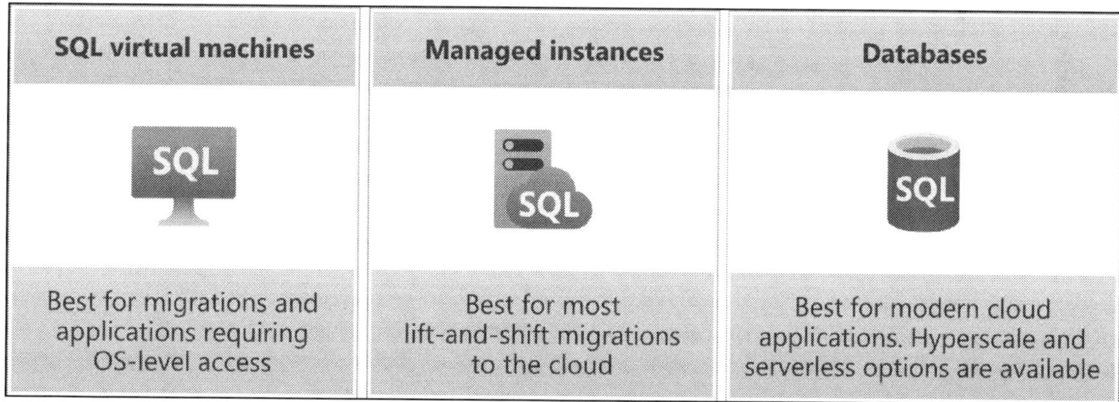

Figure 01-01: Azure SQL Deployment Options

SQL Server on Azure Virtual Machines

It is just SQL Server, so all your SQL Server skills must directly transfer; however, Azure can help automate backups and security patches. SQL Server on an Azure virtual machine is stated as *infrastructure as a service (IaaS)*. You are accountable for updating and patching the OS and SQL Server, apart from critical SQL Server security patches.

Here are a few points for deploying and managing SQL Server:

- Deploy specific SQL Server and operating system versions from preinstalled Azure gallery images. Assume you self-install SQL Server on an Azure VM, in which case, you can have the advantage of the SQL Server IaaS Agent Extension for licensing flexibility and for enabling automatic backups and updates
- Use the proper storage configuration and take advantage of Azure Blob storage read caching
- Add your virtual machines to on-premises networks
- Have the advantage of automated backups, backups to Azure Blob Storage, and integration with Azure Backup
- Always On Failover Cluster Instances is maintained with Azure premium file share
- Always On availability groups are sustained, including Cloud Witness

Companies around the world have used SQL Server on virtual machines. One example is Allscripts. Allscripts is required to move to Azure quickly to transform its applications and host them securely and reliably. The company used Azure Site Recovery to migrate tons of acquired applications running on virtual machines to Azure.

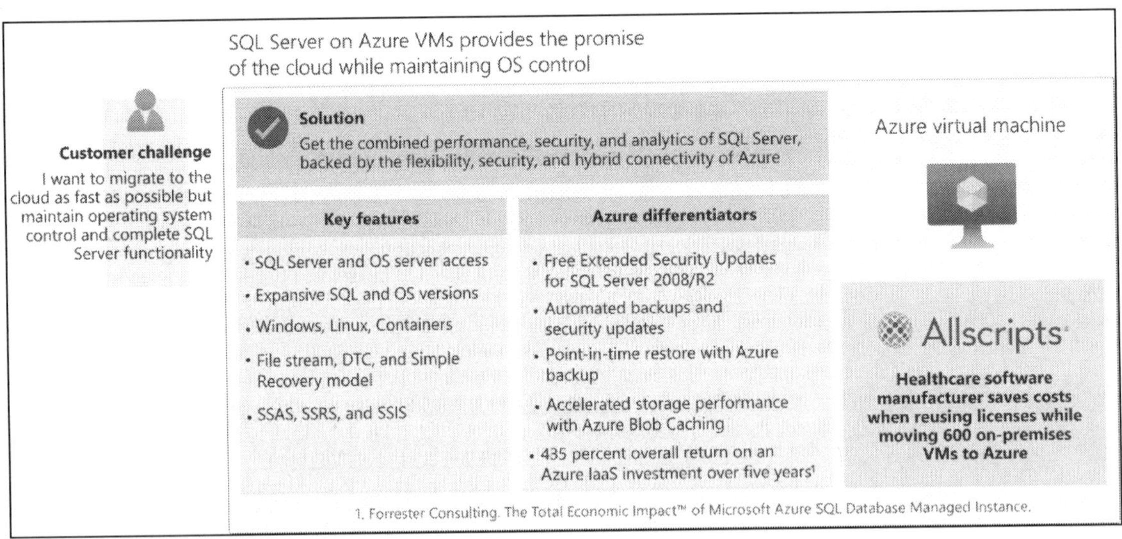

Figure 01-02: SQL Server on Azure Virtual Machines

IaaS vs. PaaS

SQL Server on a virtual machine is known as IaaS. The other choices in the Azure SQL platform, Azure SQL Managed Instance, and Azure SQL Database, are platform as a service (PaaS) deployments. Here are some key features of SQL Managed Instance and SQL Database:

- **High availability** guarantees your databases are up and running 99.99% of the time. No need to concern about maintenance or downtimes

- **Automated backups** are formed and use Azure read-access geo-redundant storage (RA-GRS) to offer geo-redundancy
- **Long-term backup retention** allows you to store specific complete databases for up to 10 years
- **Geo-replication** generates readable replicas of your database in the same datacenter (region) or a different one
- **Scalability**. You can easily add more resources (CPU, memory, storage) without long provisioning
- **Network security** features safeguard your data over the network. These features include firewalls to restrict connectivity, Azure Private Link to make sure your data is not exposed to the internet, and integration with virtual networks for connectivity to on-premises environments
- **Advanced security** identifies threats and vulnerabilities in your databases and enables you to secure your data
- **Automatic tuning** analyzes your workload. It offers recommendations that can optimize the performance of your applications by adding indexes, removing unused indexes, and automatically fixing query plan problems
- **Built-in monitoring** capabilities allow you to get insights into the performance of your databases and workload and troubleshoot performance problems
- **Built-in intelligence** automatically recognizes potential problems in your workload and offers recommendations to help you fix those problems

Versionless Database Services

Another major difference between IaaS and PaaS is *versionless SQL*. As a consumer of the service, you do not require control over these updates, and the result of @@VERSION would not line up with a specific SQL Server version. However, versionless SQL allows for worry-free patching of both the underlying OS and SQL Server and Microsoft to provide you with the latest bits.

SQL Managed Instance

It offers you an instance of SQL Server but eliminates much of the overhead of managing a virtual machine. This option is best for customers who need to move to Azure without re-architecting their applications.

SQL Managed Instance lets you access instance-scoped features. However, you do not need to worry about, nor do you have access to, the OS or the infrastructure underneath.

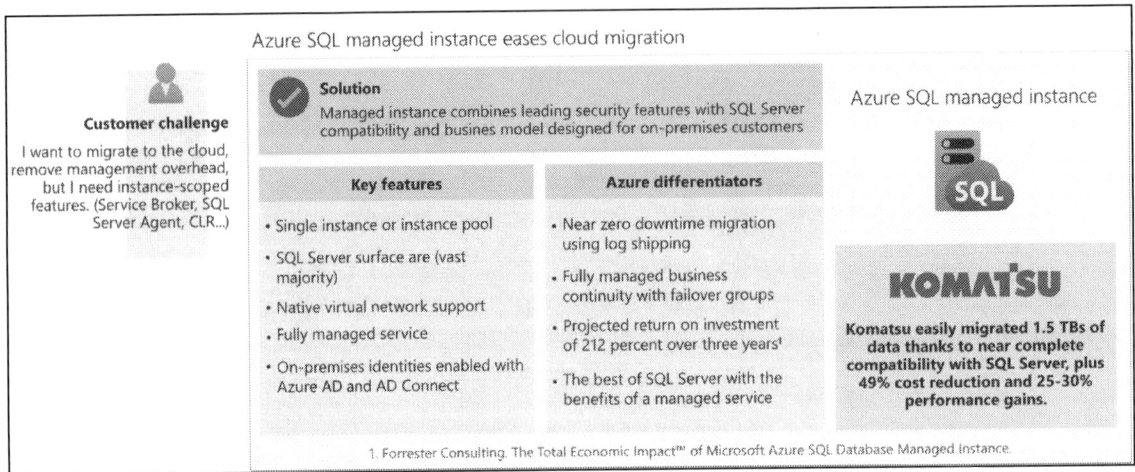

Figure 01-03: AzureSQL Managed Instances

Let us look at another industry scenario, this one from Komatsu. It is a manufacturing company that creates and sells heavy equipment for construction. The company had multiple mainframe applications for various types of data. Komatsu needed to consolidate these applications to get an overall view. Additionally, Komatsu required a way to decrease overhead. The company uses a large surface area of SQL Server features; thus, the IT decision-makers decided to move to Azure SQL Managed Instance. After migrating, Komatsu reported about 49% cost reduction and 25-30% performance gains.

SQL Database

SQL Database is a PaaS deployment selection of Azure SQL that removes both the OS and the SQL Server instance away from users. SQL Database is also the only deployment choice that gives scenarios that need unlimited database storage (hyperscale) and autoscaling for unpredictable workloads (serverless).

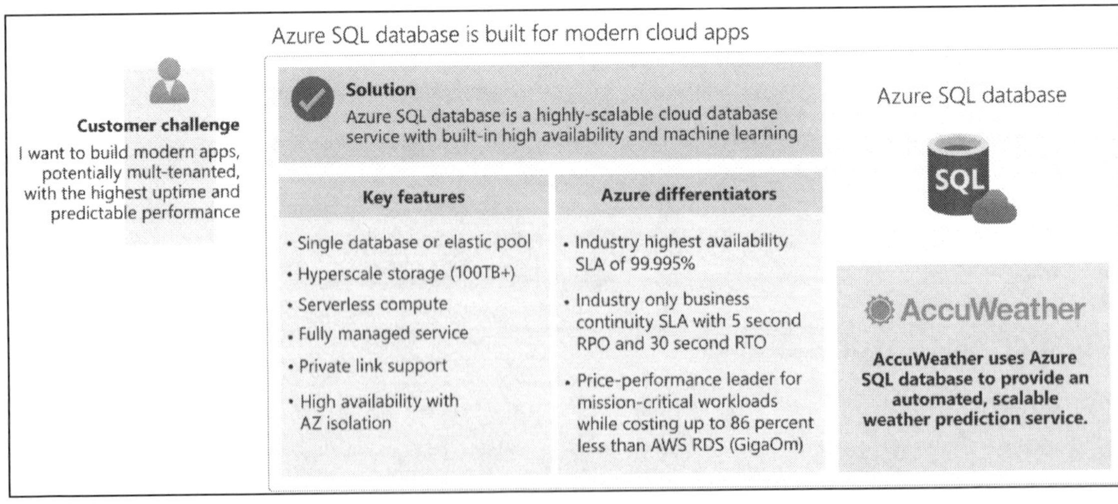

Figure 01-04: Azure SQL Database

AccuWeather offers a great example of using SQL Database. It has been analyzing and predicting the weather for more than 55 years. The company required access to Azure

for its big data, machine learning, and AI capabilities. AccuWeather needs to focus on building new models and applications, not on managing databases.

Elastic Database Pool

There are other options for SQL Database and SQL Managed Instance if you have many instances or databases. These options are denoted as *elastic database pools*. Elastic database pools permit you to share resources between multiple instances and databases and improve your costs.

- **SQL Database Elastic pools** permit you to host many databases. This option is best for a software as a service (SaaS) application or provider because you can control and monitor performance in a simplified way for many databases
- **SQL Managed Instance pools** lets you host multiple managed instances and share resources. You can pre-provision compute resources

Paychex is an outstanding example of a company that uses SQL Database elastic database pools. Paychex required a way to separately manage the time and pay management for its customers and cut costs. The company selected SQL Database elastic database pools, which simplify management and allow resource sharing between separate databases to lower costs.

Azure SQL Deployment Options

The following image reviews the deployment options for Azure SQL.

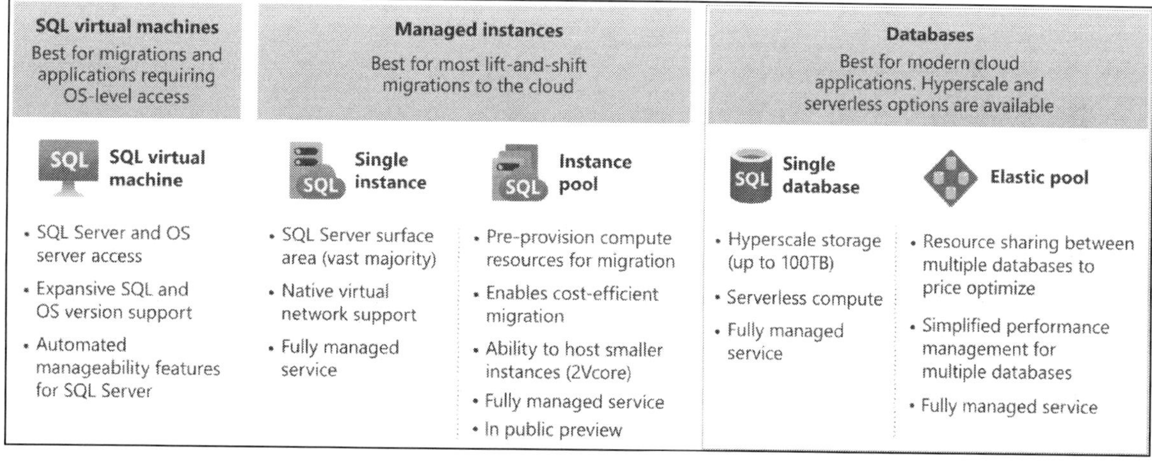

Figure 01-05: Azure SQL Deployment Options

Purchasing Models, Service Tiers, and Hardware Choices

After you have an idea of which deployment option is most suitable for your desires, you have to determine the purchasing model, service tier, and hardware.

Purchasing Model

The Azure SQL purchasing model offers two options:

- Based on virtual cores (vCore-based)
- Based on database transaction units (DTU- based)

In the vCore model, you compensate:

- Compute resources. (The service tier + the total of vCores and the memory + the generation of hardware)
- The kind and amount of data and log storage

The vCore model allows you to use Azure Hybrid Benefit for SQL Server and reserved capacity (pay in advance) to save money.

Service Tier

Next, you want to choose a service tier for performance and availability. It is recommended that you start with the General Purpose tier and adjust as required. Three tiers are present in the vCore model:

- **General Purpose**: Appropriate for most business workloads
- **Business Critical**: Appropriate for business applications with low-latency response requirements
- **Hyperscale**: Appropriate for business workloads with highly scalable storage (100 TB+) and read-scale requirements. From a performance and cost viewpoint, this tier falls between General Purpose and Business Critical. Hyperscale is currently accessible only for single databases in Azure SQL Database

Compute Tier

You have a decision to make regarding the compute tier:

- **Provisioned compute** is destined for more regular usage patterns with higher average compute utilization over time. Provisioned compute gives a fixed amount of resources over time to ensure optimal performance and is billed for those resources irrespective of usage. In provisioned compute, you have to manage the sizing of computing resources for your workload
- **Serverless computing** is for usage with lower average compute utilization over time. Serverless provides automatic computed scaling to improve performance management, and it is billed only for the quantity used

Hardware

The default hardware generation is referred to as *Gen5* hardware. If you choose General Purpose within SQL Database and need to use the serverless compute tier, Gen5 hardware is currently the only option. It can now scale up to 40 vCores.

> **EXAM TIP:** The purchasing model service tier and hardware selections you make will significantly influence your deployment's performance availability and cost.

Management Interfaces for Azure SQL

You will use numerous interfaces and tools as you deploy, use, and manage Azure SQL resources. This unit will look at the available tools, their capabilities, and when to use them.

Azure Portal

The Azure portal offers a comprehensive set of features for Azure SQL resources. You can deploy, administer, and even link to databases and run queries through the Azure portal.

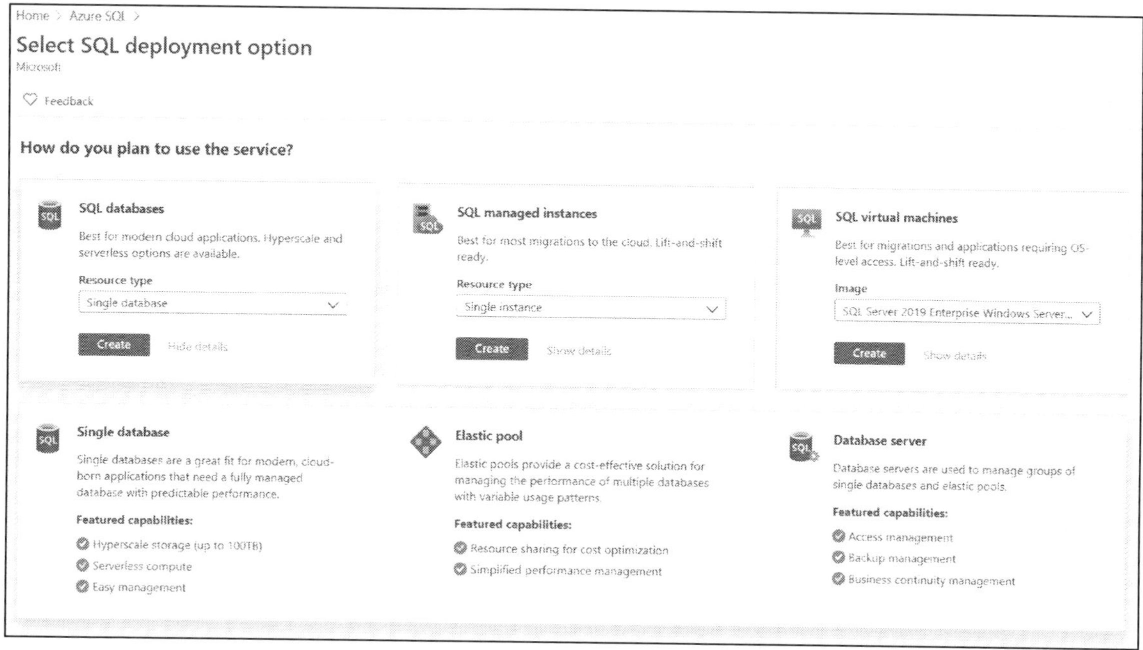

Figure 01-06: Azure Portal

SQL Server Management Studio

SQL Server Management Studio (SSMS) is used for SQL Server in the world. SSMS is integrated to envision and work with Azure SQL, including SQL Server in virtual machines, SQL managed instances, and SQL databases.

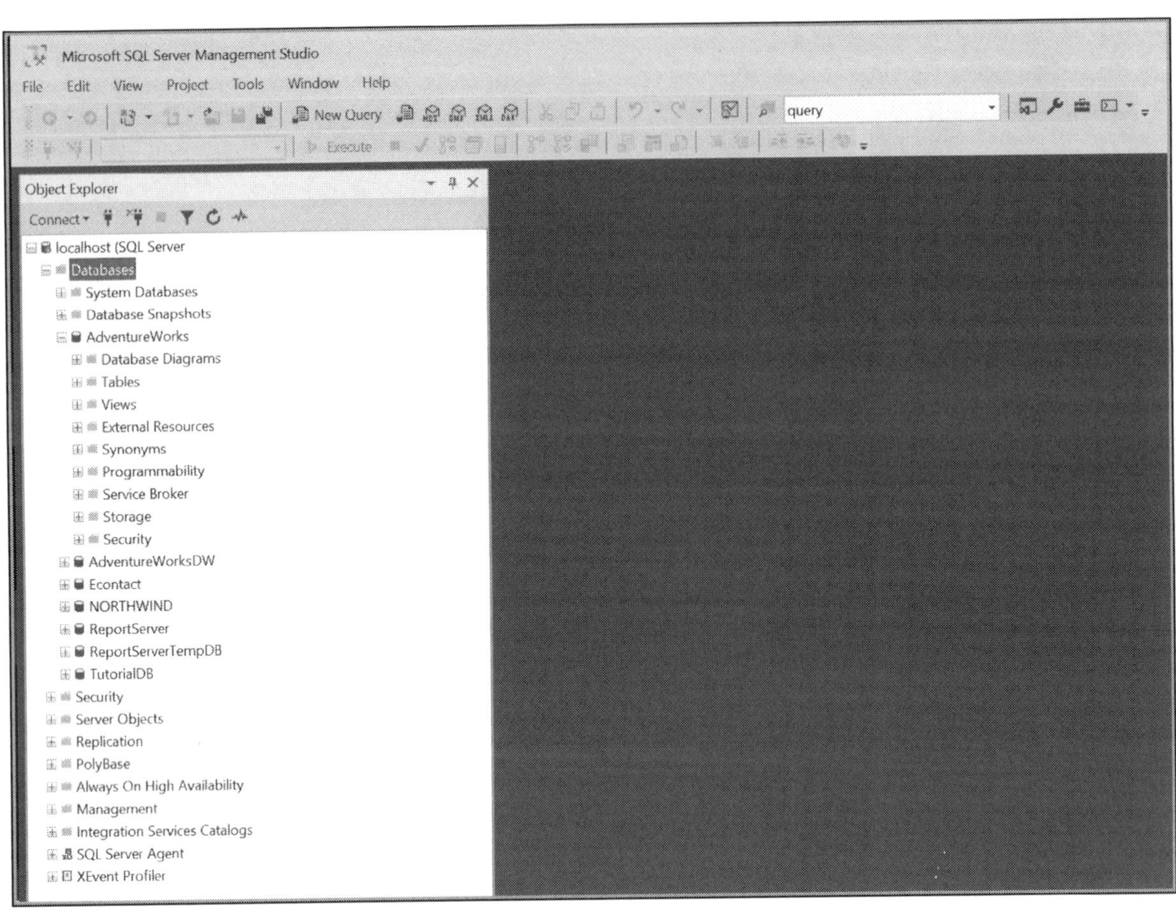

Figure 01-07: SQL Server Management Studio

Azure Data Studio

Azure Data Studio provisions a powerful tool called *notebooks*. You can save the results.

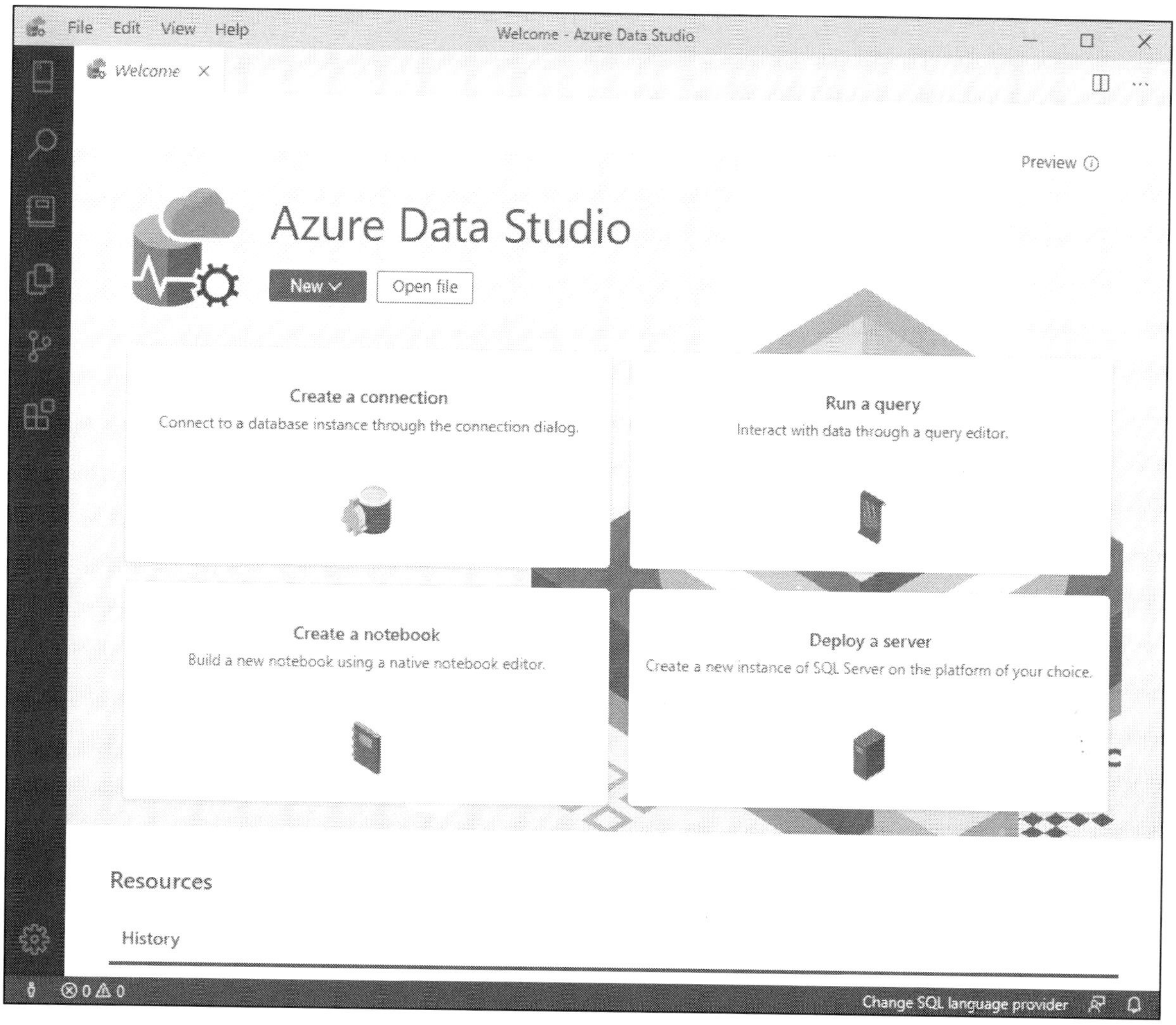

Figure 01-08: Azure Data Studio

Languages and APIs

All Azure SQL services are based on the SQL Server engine; thus, Azure SQL offers the Transact-SQL (T-SQL) language and the Tabular Data Stream (TDS) protocol. So all drivers that generally work with SQL Server work with Azure SQL.

Azure SQL also provides REST APIs for the management of SQL-managed instances and SQL databases.

Command-line Interfaces

Popular command-line interfaces like sqlcmd and BCP are supported with Azure SQL services. All these CLIs are held across Windows, macOS, and Linux clients.

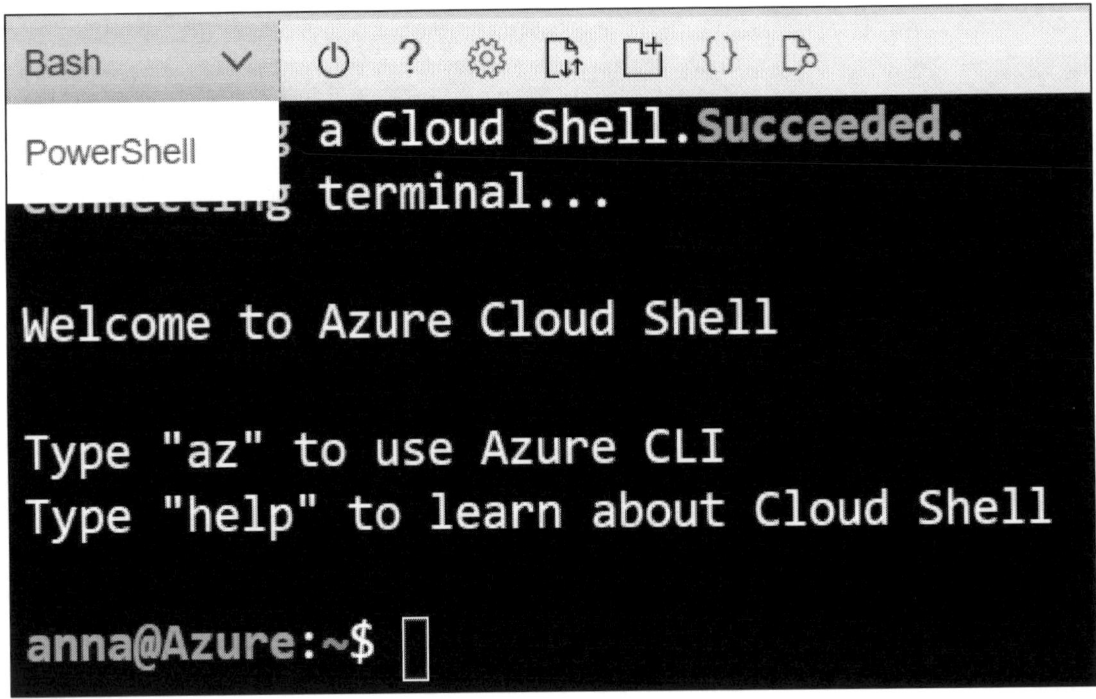

Figure 01-09: Command-line Interfaces

What to Use When

There are several interfaces you can use to interact with Azure SQL. Many capabilities are available in all the interfaces. Which one you select will depend on a combination of preference and what you are trying to accomplish. Throughout this learning path, you will use many of the interfaces described here.

Deploy Databases for Azure SQL

Managing and handling data is a crucial element of any company. In particular, relational databases and Microsoft SQL Server have been the most common data handling tools for many years. If you need to manage your data using the cloud, you commonly use Azure virtual machines to host your own Microsoft SQL Server instance. Although it is a perfectly good approach, Microsoft Azure provides you with another great platform that is more cost-effective and much easier to provide. Azure SQL database is a Platform-as-a-Service (PaaS) offering which provides you the responsibility to manage and maintain fewer infrastructure overheads.

You need to make a simple prototype of something to share with your staff. A database for holding driver, customer, and order details will be contained within your prototype. The foundation for your production app will be your prototype, so the technological decisions you make now can carry over to what your team is delivering.

Plan your Azure SQL Database

To help you manage all types of data, from highly structured relational data to unstructured data, Azure provides Platform as a Service (PaaS) services.

Why Choose Azure SQL Database?

Convenience

You want to know about hardware and software requirements when configuring SQL Server on a VM or physical hardware. You would have to understand the current best practices in security and regularly manage operating system and SQL Server patches. You will have to manage backup and data retention issues yourself.

Azure SQL Database controls the hardware, software updates, and OS patches for you. All you specify is your database name and a couple of choices. You will have a SQL database running in a matter of minutes.

Azure SQL Database instances can be set up and down for your convenience. Azure SQL Database is quick and easy to configure. You should concentrate less on software configuration and more on making your app successful.

Cost

There are no systems for you to buy, supply power for, or otherwise maintain, while Azure runs everything for you.

There are several pricing options for Azure SQL Database. These pricing options let you balance performance against cost. You can start for only a few dollars a month.

Scale

When your desires change, you can adjust the output and size of your database on the go with Azure SQL Database.

Security

Azure SQL Database comes with a firewall designed to limit internet connections automatically. You are permitted to access the unique IP addresses you trust. Visual Studio, SQL Server Management Studio, or some other Azure SQL database management tool will help you achieve this.

Two options are considered for your database:

On-premises Host SQL Server: The IT team runs a small in-house data center to support the finance department and a few other departments. To host a SQL Server deployment in their data center, you can work with IT.

Host Azure SQL Cloud Database: Based on SQL Server, the Azure SQL Database provides the relational database features you require.

Azure SQL Database and Managed Instance

It has been verified that your deployment was successful, and you know what resources are available. Now you need to configure your SQL managed instance, SQL database, or databases within a managed instance. These are termed *managed databases*.

Azure SQL Managed Instance

Azure SQL Managed Instance is a managed SQL Server instance. You have options available around tempdb, model, and master. In addition, you have control over your network connectivity and configuration, which will be discussed later on in the chapter.

Database Configuration

Managed databases in Azure SQL Managed Instance Database, you have selections available with the ALTER DATABASE command. In Azure SQL Managed Instance, you can accomplish file maintenance.

Additionally, the following default options are set to **ON**:

- SNAPSHOT_ISOLATION_STATE
- READ_COMMITTED_SNAPSHOT
- FULL RECOVERY
- CHECKSUM
- QUERY_STORE
- TDE
- ACCELERATED_DATABASE_RECOVERY

Job Management

SQL Server Agent offers a configuring and scheduling system for SQL Server users. You can accomplish equivalent functionality in Azure SQL through the following options:

SQL Agent in SQL Managed Instance

SQL Agent jobs are opted only for T-SQL and SQL Server Integration Services job steps. Command shell steps are not supported.

Elastic Jobs for SQL Database

You can use the Elastic Job Agent service in Azure to form and schedule jobs. Jobs are T-SQL scripts that you can execute against many databases, including parallel execution.

Azure Automation

You can use the Azure Automation service to orchestrate processes through a concept called a runbook.

Storage Management

For Azure SQL Managed Instance, possible maximum storage size is permitted for the instance based on your chosen SLO. You choose maximum storage, for instance, up to this possible maximum size. You can modify the size and the number of files, but you do not have control over their physical location.

Load Data into Azure SQL

The next part is to bring in data after a database or instance is deployed, verified, and configured.

Options

Many options are available for loading data into Azure SQL. Some overlap with what is available on-premises. This unit calls out a few.

Bulk Copy Program

Bulk Copy Program is a tool for linking to Azure SQL from on-premises and from an Azure virtual machine.

Bulk Insert

Bulk insert operations are related to what is available in SQL Server on-premises. However, instead of loading data from a file (or multiple files) on your machine, you load data from Azure Blob storage.

SSIS Packages

In Azure SQL, you can use packages to link with SQL Server Integration Services (SSIS) on-premises. You can host an SSIS database.

Other Options

Other options include using technologies like Spark or Azure Data Factory to load data into Azure SQL Database, or Azure SQL Managed Instance. In Azure SQL Managed Instance, you can use T-SQL commands to reestablish a database natively from a URL.

Considerations for Loading Data

The main difference between loading data on-premises and loading data into Azure SQL is that the data you need to load should be hosted in Azure. This strategy will also enhance your efficiency in loading your files and setting up ETL jobs. Due to the full recovery mode and limits around log throughput, you might be influenced by log governance as you are loading data.

Secure your Data with Azure SQL

Security Capabilities and Tasks

SQL Server and Azure SQL services have been recognized for their importance on security, specifically enterprise-class.

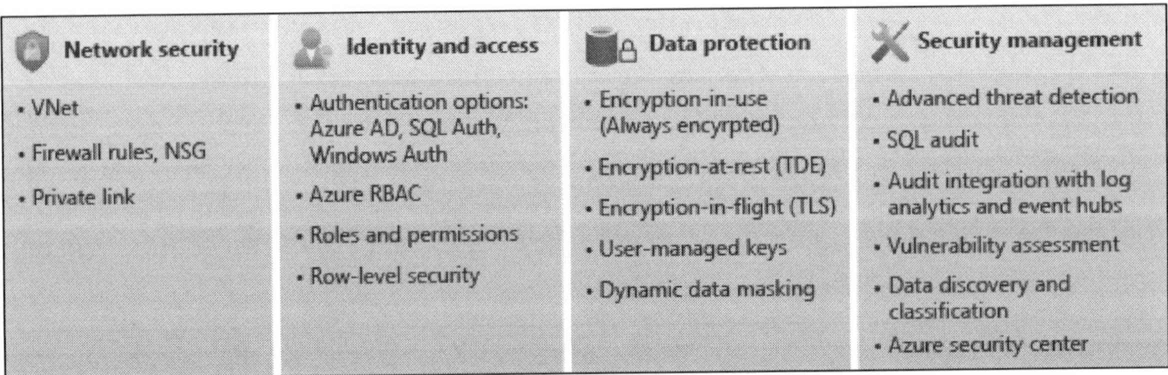

Figure 01-10: Security Capabilities and Tasks

Network Security

The first layer of security includes the network. The networking capabilities and tasks differ between Azure SQL Database and Azure SQL Managed Instance, so they will be discussed separately.

Azure SQL Database

When you are securing your network for Azure SQL Database, you have four main selections:

- Allow access to Azure services
- Use firewall rules
- Use virtual network rules
- Use Azure Private Link

In addition to these main options, you have the opportunity to block all public access (only with Private Link) and the option to force a minimum Transport Layer Security (TLS) version. The least secure method, but the easiest to configure, is to let access to Azure services. The most secure method is to use Private Link.

Allow Access to Azure Services

During the deployment of Azure SQL Database, you have the option to set **Allow Azure services and resources access to this server** to **Yes**. If you select this option, you are permitting any resource from any region or subscription, the possibility to access your resource. This option makes it easier to get up, execute and get Azure SQL Database connected to other services, such as Azure Virtual Machines, Azure App Service, or even Azure Cloud Shell, because you permit anything that comes through Azure to have the option to connect.

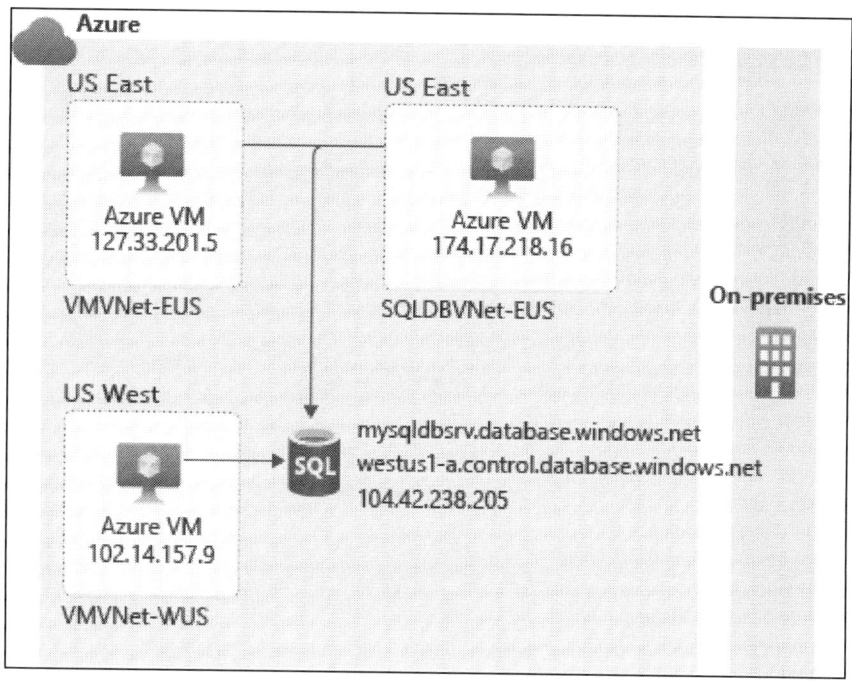

Figure 01-11: Allow Access to Azure Resources

However, letting access to Azure services does not permit anything outside of Azure (for example, your on-premises environment) to have access.

If you can switch **Allow Azure services and resources access to this server** to **No**, it is the secure configuration of the public endpoint. It blocks all connections and networks, apart from ones you have explicitly added, with the various options that are discussed in the following sections.

Firewall Rules

Your next option is to apply firewall rules. Your results may be similar to those of **Allow Azure services and resources access to this server** except that, for each service to link (in the following image, a virtual machine [VM]), you will have to add a unique firewall rule to let the VM connect. Firewall rules also allow you on-premises environment because you can add the rules for machines and applications in your on-premises environment.

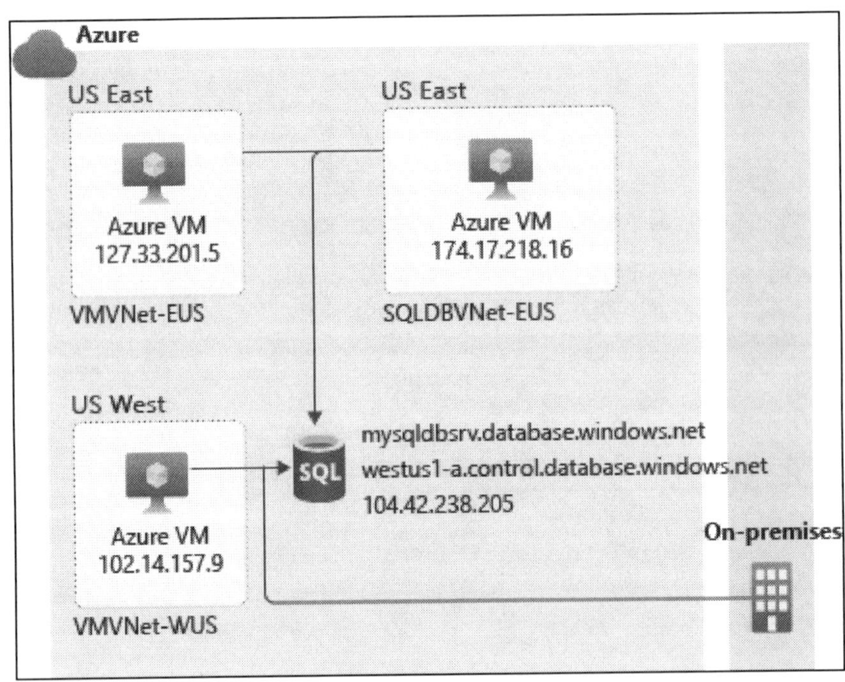

Figure 01-12: Firewall Rules

You can also access Azure services and then add firewall rules for on-premises connectivity only to get connectivity in Azure. **Allowing Azure services and resources access to this server** is not as secure because it permits all Azure traffic.

Virtual Network Rules

If you need to use only firewall rules, setting this up can be complicated. It means that you will have to specify a range of IP addresses for all your connections, which can sometimes have dynamic IP addresses. A much easier substitute is to use virtual network rules to create and manage access from specific networks that contain VMs or other services that want to access the data.

If you configure access from a virtual network with a virtual network rule, any resource in that virtual network can access the Azure SQL Database logical server. This can simplify the challenge of configuring access to all static and dynamic IP addresses that want to access the data. You can apply virtual network technologies to link networks across regions in both Azure and on-premises.

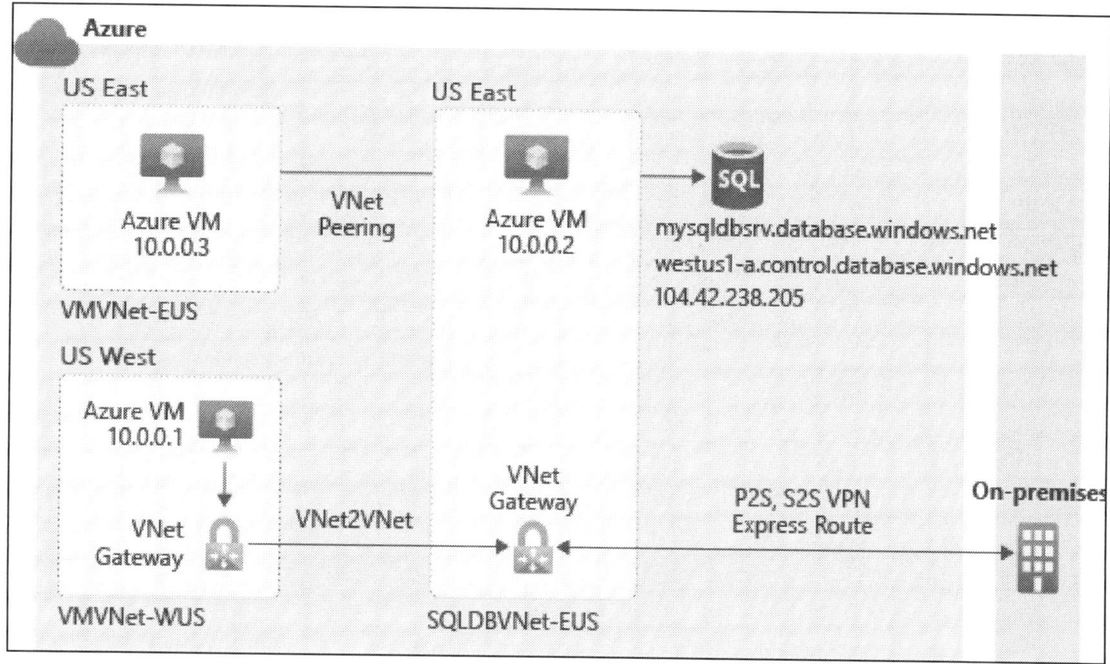

Figure 01-13: Virtual Network Rules

Another common strategy for analyzing your connection is to observe the Domain Name System (DNS) hierarchy. In the same Azure VM, in a command prompt, you can run the following command:

nslookup aw-server.database.windows.net

```
Server:  UnKnown
Address:  192.168.0.1
```

Figure 01-14(a): Commands

Non-authoritative answer:

```
Non-authoritative answer:
Name:    cr3.eastus1-a.control.database.windows.net
Address:  40.79.153.12
Aliases:  aw-server.database.windows.net
          dataslice6.eastus.database.windows.net
          dataslice6eastus.trafficmanager.net
```

Figure 01-14(b): Commands

Under the non-authoritative answer are some essential things to look at:

- **Name**: The endpoint is part of the public DNS hierarchy
- **Address**: The IP address reverted here should match the public IP address of your Azure VM
- **Aliases**: Aliases are numerous points within the DNS hierarchy

Although the connection through T-SQL comes through the private IP address of the Azure VM, you are still ultimately involved through a public endpoint.

Private Link for an Azure SQL Database Instance

You have understood how to configure the most secure network by using your database in Azure SQL Database with the public endpoint, similar to how your Azure SQL managed instance is deployed. With Private Link, you can link to your database in SQL Database and numerous other platforms as a service offered by using a private endpoint. This means that it has a private IP address within a specific virtual network.

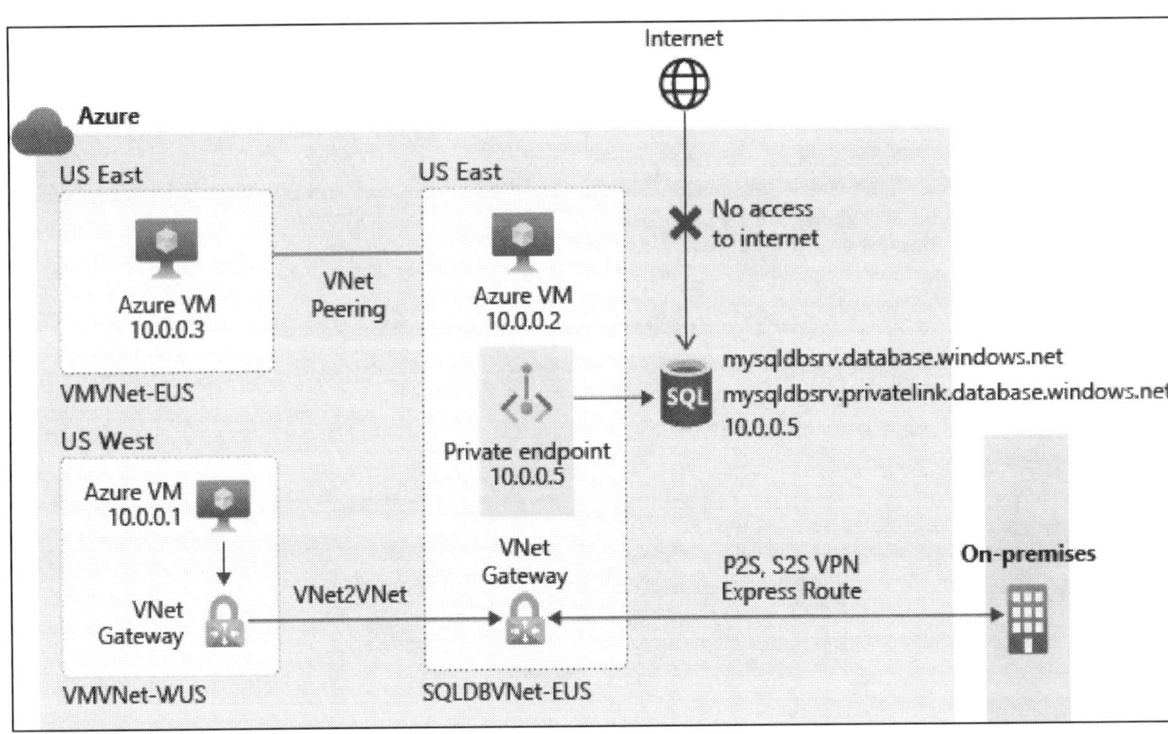

Figure 01-15: Private Link for an Azure SQL Database

In the preceding example, you will see that the general networking infrastructure did not change, and you can still apply the virtual network connectivity strategies from the virtual network rules.

An Azure SQL Managed Instance

Although deploying an Azure SQL managed instance varies from deploying a database in SQL Database, it is easy to translate networking functionality at a high level from one to the other. For an Azure SQL managed instance, either before or during deployment, you need to create a specific subnet, or logical grouping within a virtual network, with some requirements to host the managed instances. After they are deployed, they are already configured similar to a private endpoint in a database in SQL Database. You have to enable access to the virtual network where the managed instance lives by using

standard networking practices. By default, you have a private endpoint and a relatively private DNS hierarchy.

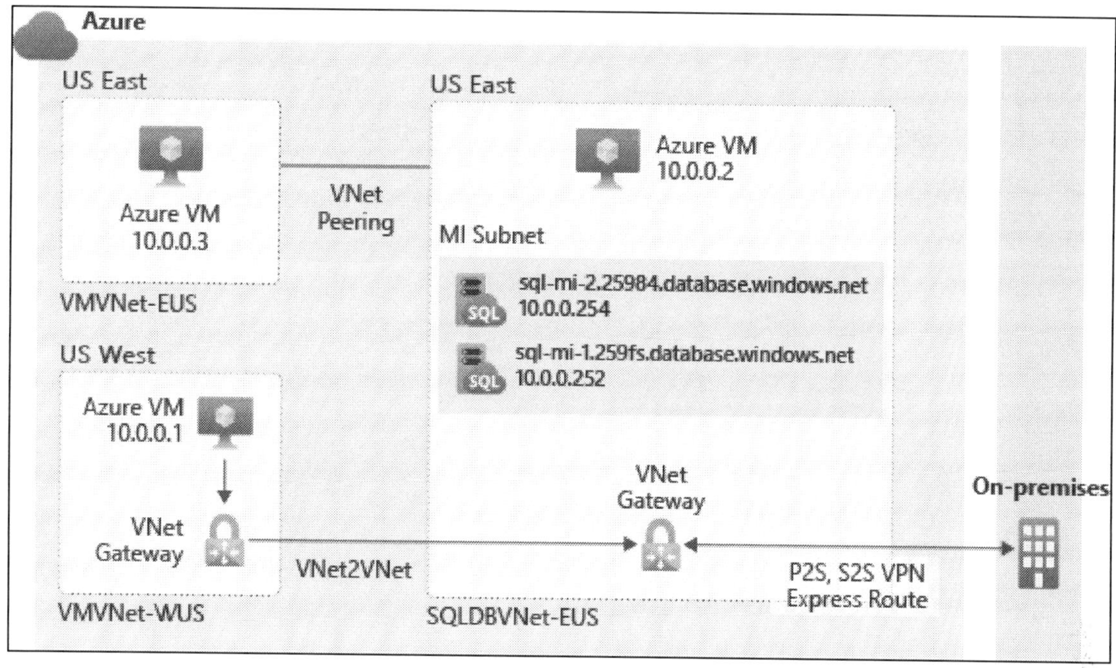

Figure 01-16: Azure SQL Managed Instance

If you go through the Azure portal flow for deployment, the virtual network and subnet can be deployed for you.

Identity and Access

After you have observed the networking access, the next layer to consider is identity and access.

Role-based Access Control

All Azure kinds of operations for Azure SQL are organized through role-based access control (RBAC). The rights apply to operations in the Azure portal, the Azure CLI, and Azure PowerShell.

Built-in roles are available to decrease the requirement for higher-level RBAC roles such as Owner or Contributor. You can use these roles effectively to have specific individuals deploy Azure SQL resources (or manage security policies) but grant other users actual access to use or manage the instance or database. The built-in roles include:

- **SQL DB Contributor**: Can form and manage databases but cannot access them
- **SQL Managed Instance Contributor**: Can form and manage managed instances but cannot access them
- **SQL Security Manager**: Can handle security policies for databases and instances (such as auditing) but cannot access them

➢ **SQL Server Contributor**: Can handle servers and databases but cannot access them

Authentication

If you are migrating a workload that requires Windows Authentication or your organization uses Azure Active Directory (Azure AD), you can use Azure AD.

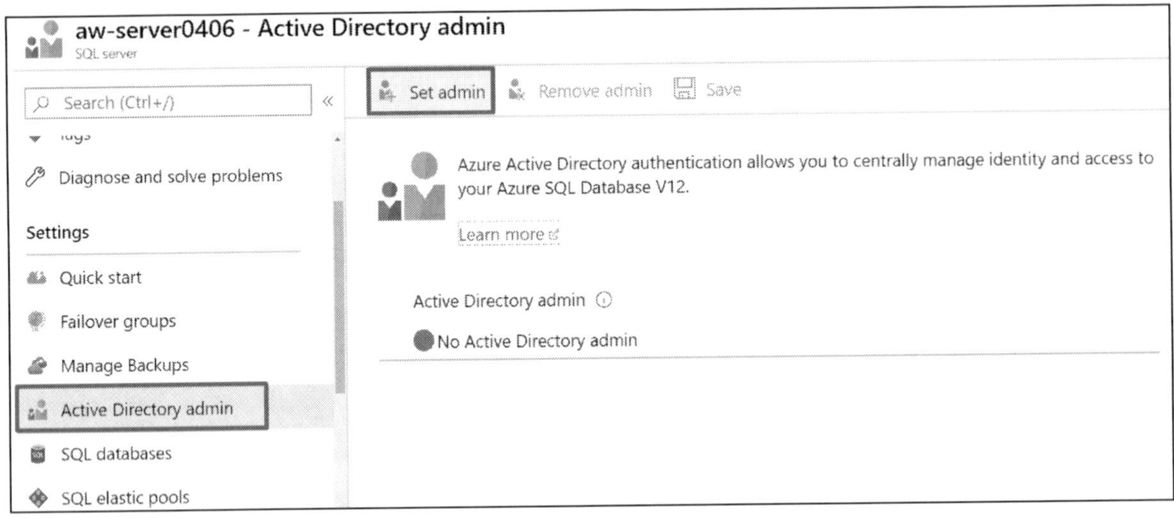

Figure 01-17: Authentication

You can connect to it by using any of the following three methods (for example, in SSMS):

➢ **Azure Active Directory - Integrated**: A non-interactive way you can use if you are signed in to Windows with your Azure credentials

➢ **Azure Active Directory - Password**: A method that allows you to connect with an Azure AD principal name using the Azure AD-managed domain From the documentation:

➢ **Azure Active Directory - Universal with Multi-Factor Authentication**: An interactive method that safeguards access to data while meeting an organization's demand for a single sign-in process with Azure AD Multi-Factor Authentication

For an Azure SQL managed instance, the method is similar to that for SQL Server: you can have SQL or Azure AD logins, database users, and contained database users.

Although the server admin for Azure SQL Database essentially has sysadmin rights, you can create limited admins by using database-level roles in the master of the Azure SQL Database logical server. Two roles are available:

➢ **Login Manager**: A database-level role that allows members to create logins for the database server

- **DB Manager**: A database-level role that allows members to create and delete databases for the database server

Finally, when you set up and configure authentication and authorization, you have four guidelines to follow:

- Deploy with a server admin
- Create other admins as necessary
- Admins can create users
- Grant access just like you would work in SQL Server

Protect your Data

Now that your network and identity access are configured and secure, let us consider how to protect your data, whether it is at rest, in motion, or viewed by users and admins.

Data Encryption

It can be configured for all deployment options via a switch in the Azure portal, as shown here:

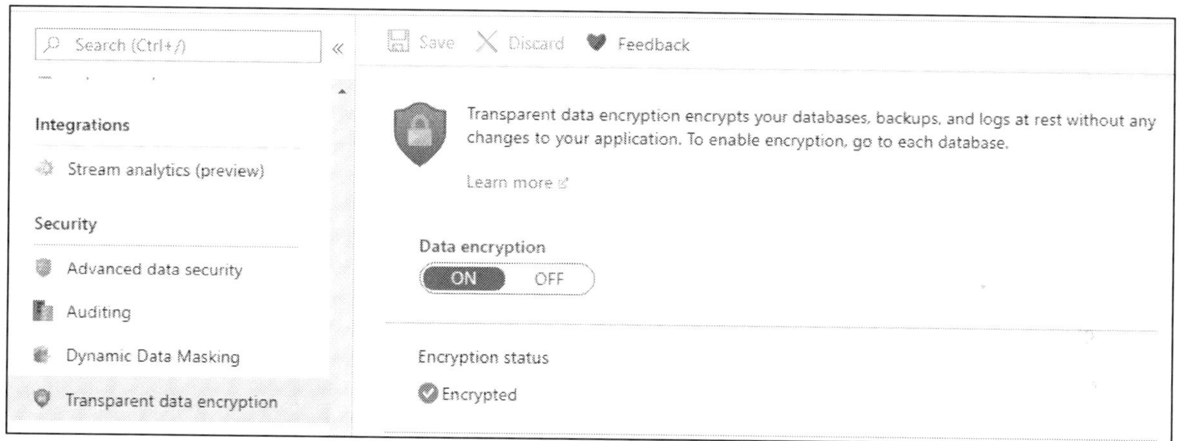

Figure 01-18: Data Encryption

You can also use a service-managed key or Bring Your Own Key (BYOK) at the server or instance level. You have seen how to do this with the Azure portal; however, you can also use Azure PowerShell, the Azure CLI, Transact-SQL (T-SQL), or REST APIs.

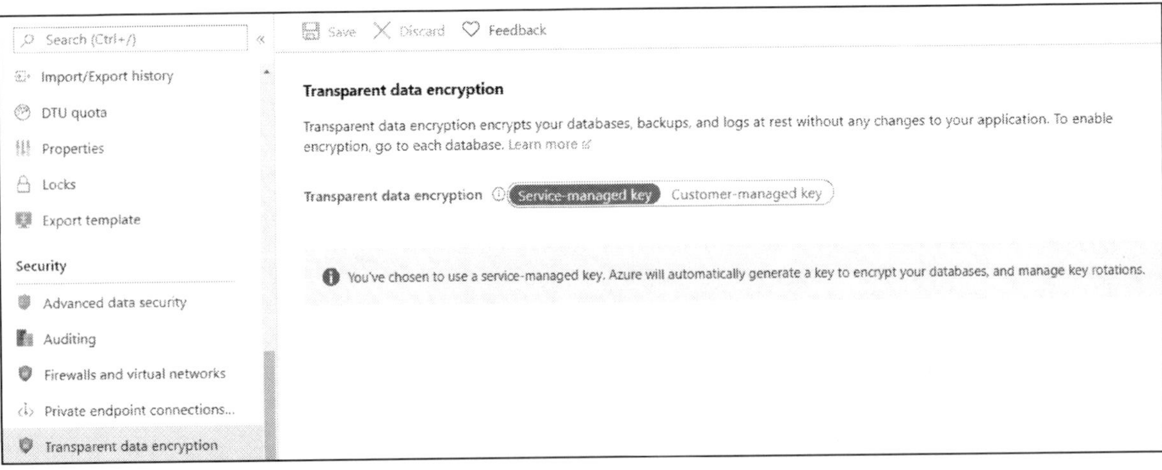

Figure 01-19: Transparent Data Encryption

You can, alternately, use BYOK and take advantage of an Azure key vault. In this scenario, you are responsible for and in complete control of crucial lifecycle management (essential creation, rotation, and deletion), key usage permissions, and auditing operations on keys.

You can also take advantage of column-level encryption, supported in Azure SQL, just as it is in SQL Server. Similarly, the Always Encrypted feature is supported just as it is in SQL Server. This process involves using client-side encryption of sensitive data, which uses keys never given to the database system.

Dynamic Data Masking

On occasions, you will need to mask or modify specific data so that non-privileged users cannot see it, but they can still perform queries that contain that data. This capability is supported just as it is in SQL Server. However, the Azure portal has additional capabilities and views that let you see recommendations of fields to mask.

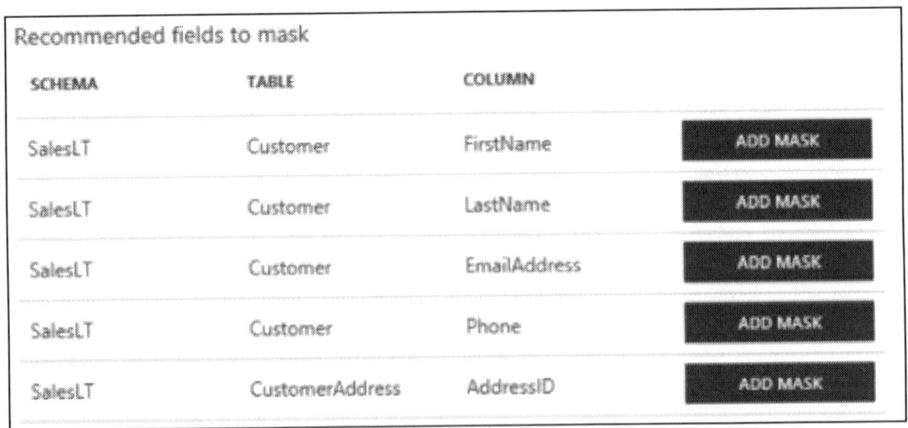

Figure 01-20: Dynamic Data Masking

Tasks for Data Protection

- Make sure that your applications force connection encryption

- Evaluate and enable TDE
- Take advantage of Dynamic Data Masking
- For advanced protection, you can form the Always Encrypted feature

Manage your Security

After your Azure SQL Database instance or Azure SQL managed instance is secured on the networking, authentication, and data protection levels, the last step is to understand how you will manage security on an ongoing basis. Managing security contains auditing, monitoring, data classification, and, in the case of Azure SQL, Azure Defender.

Auditing

Auditing can help you keep regulatory compliance. Traditional SQL Server auditing using Transact-SQL (T-SQL) is available, with some alterations, only in an Azure SQL managed instance.

As an alternative to SQL Server audit, Azure SQL Database has *Azure SQL auditing*. It writes events to an audit log in Azure Blob storage, Azure Monitor logs (also called Log Analytics), or an event hub.

Monitoring

There are two features to monitoring and managing security: the Azure level and the database or server level. In Azure, you can apply tools such as activity logs and role-based access control auditing.

In your Azure SQL managed instance, you can configure SQL Server audit, and the engine can track the failed and successful logins. Failed logins for the Azure SQL managed instance are also tracked in the ERRORLOG. Microsoft suggests that you configure Azure Defender for both services, including setting up alerts for Advanced Threat Protection.

Data Discovery & Classification

The service is aimed at protecting the data and not just the database. The portal view is available only for Azure SQL, but SQL Server supports similar functionality through a SQL Server Management Studio wizard.

Azure Defender

It provides a single go-to location for enabling and managing two main capabilities:

- Vulnerability Assessment
- Advanced Threat Protection

Advanced Threat Protection

With Advanced Threat Protection, you can detect and respond to potential threats as they occur by receiving security alerts on anomalous activities. Advanced Threat

Protection applies advanced monitoring and machine learning technologies to detect whether any of the following threats have occurred:

- SQL injection
- SQL injection vulnerability
- Data exfiltration
- Unsafe action
- Brute force attempt
- Anomalous client login

Deliver Consistent Performance with Azure SQL

Performance Capabilities

As Azure SQL Database and Azure SQL Managed Instance are based on the SQL Server database engine, most of the capabilities with SQL Server are also available with Azure SQL. There are a few capabilities that impact the performance of your databases that you should consider when you are deploying and configuring Azure SQL.

Memory, CPU, and I/O Capacities

Choosing the proper deployment and service tier for Azure SQL Database or SQL Managed Instance can be necessary for performance. In the second module, you learned about the various deployment options for Azure SQL.

In-memory OLTP

Online transaction processing (OLTP) processes data from transactions in real-time. In-memory OLTP is a capability for transaction latency-sensitive applications, such as applications involving a high number of concurrent users modifying data.

- Memory-optimized tables are only available in Business Critical tiers
- When a database is created, the memory-optimized FILEGROUP is pre-created in Azure SQL Database and SQL Managed Instance (even for general purpose tiers)
- The amount of memory for memory-optimized tables is a percentage of the vCore dependent memory limit

SQL Server 2019 Performance Enhancements

Many of the performance features in SQL Server 2019, such as intelligent query processing, are also available in Azure SQL. However, there are some exceptions. For example, tempdb metadata optimization is not yet available for Azure SQL.

Configure and Maintain Performance

Understanding the capabilities of Azure SQL is essential for delivering consistent performance. It is also essential to understand the options and restrictions you have to configure in Azure SQL Managed Instance and Azure SQL Database that can affect performance. This includes the following:

- Topics of the tempdb database
- Configuring databases
- Configuring files and filegroups
- Configuring max degree of parallelism
- Using Resource Governor
- Maintaining indexes and statistics

Tempdb

Tempdb is a vital shared resource used by applications. Ensuring the proper configuration of tempdb can affect your ability to deliver consistent performance.

The database option MIXED_PAGE_ALLOCATION is set to OFF, and AUTOGROW_ALL_FILES is set to ON. This cannot be configured; however, as with SQL Server, they are the recommended defaults.

Database Configuration

For performance, one option that you cannot change is the recovery model of the database. The default is total recovery.

Files and Filegroups

Azure SQL Database has one file (Hyperscale typically has several), and the maximum size is configured through Azure interfaces. Azure SQL Managed Instance allows adding database files and configuring sizes but not the physical placement of files. The total number of files and file sizes for SQL Managed Instance can be used to improve I/O performance. In addition, user-defined filegroups are supported for SQL Managed Instance for manageability purposes.

Resource Governor

Resource Governor is an option in SQL Server that you can control resource usage for workloads through I/O, CPU, and memory. Note that Resource Governor is supported for SQL Managed Instance for user-defined workload groups and pools but not for Azure SQL Database.

Index Maintenance

Index formation and maintenance for Azure SQL is the same as that for SQL Server. For example, creating, rebuilding, and reorganizing indexes is fully supported, as with SQL Server. This includes online and resumable indexes.

Monitor and Troubleshoot Performance

Monitoring and troubleshooting are crucial elements to deliver consistent performance. This includes features like dynamic management views (DMVs), extended events, and Azure Monitor.

Tools and Capabilities to Monitor Performance

Azure SQL offers monitoring and troubleshooting capabilities in the Azure system and familiar tools with SQL Server. The following sections briefly describe these.

Azure Monitor

You can visualize Azure Monitor data in the Azure portal; applications can access this data through Azure Event Hubs or APIs. Much like Windows Performance Monitor, Azure Monitor helps you access resource usage metrics for Azure SQL without using SQL Server tools.

Dynamic Management Views

Azure SQL offers a similar DMV infrastructure as SQL Server, with a few differences. For example, you can see queries, resource usage, query plans, and resource wait types.

Extended events

Azure SQL offers the extended event's infrastructure as SQL Server, with a few changes. Extended events allow you to trace key execution events within SQL Server that powers Azure SQL.

Lightweight Query Profiling

You use lightweight query profiling to examine the query plan and running state of an active query. This is a crucial feature to debug query performance for statements as they are running. This capability reduces the time for you to solve performance problems compared to using tools like extended events to trace query performance. You access lightweight query profiling through DMVs, and it is on by default for Azure SQL as it is for SQL Server 2019.

Query Store

Query Store is scheduled by default for Azure SQL and provides automatic plan correction and automatic tuning capabilities. SQL Server Management Studio (SSMS) reports for the store are also available for Azure SQL.

> **Note:** It is not possible to use SSMS to view operational data for Azure SQL Database.

Extended events for Azure SQL Managed Instance

Keep these essential ideas in mind when forming extended event sessions:

- All events, targets, and actions are maintained

- File targets are held with Azure Blob storage because you do not access the underlying operating system disks
- Some specific events are added for SQL Managed Instance to trace events specific to the management and execution of the instance

Common Performance Scenarios

The below diagram displays a decision tree to determine if a SQL Server performance issue is running or waiting.

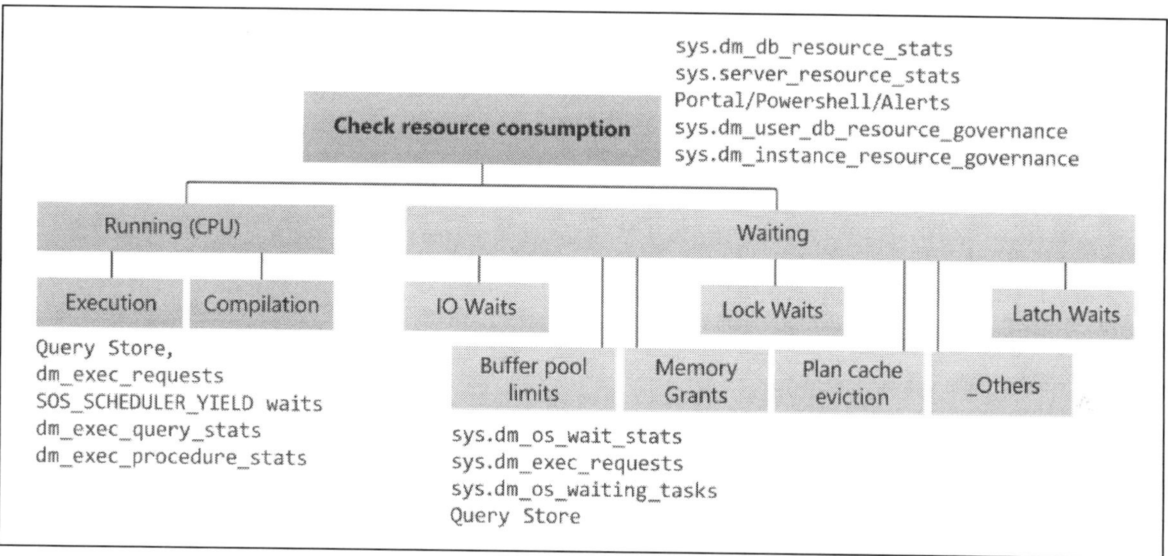

Figure 01-21: Common Performance Scenarios

Waiting

If a query does not seem to be high CPU resource usage, it might be that the performance problem involves waiting on a resource. Scenarios involving waiting on resources include:

- I/O waits
- Lock waits
- Latch waits
- Buffer pool limits
- Memory grants
- Plan cache eviction

> EXAM TIP: You can use extended events for any running or waiting for scenarios. To do so, you need to set up an extended event session to trace queries. This method to debug a performance problem can be considered heavy.

Scenarios Specific to Azure SQL

There are a few performance scenarios, all running and waiting, that are specific to Azure SQL. These include log governance, worker limits, waits encountered for Business Critical service tiers, and waits specifically to a Hyperscale deployment.

Log Governance

Azure SQL can use log rate governance to enforce resource limits on transaction log usage. You might need this enforcement to ensure resource limits and to meet promised SLA.

Business Critical HADR Waits

Even though waits might not slow down your application, you might not be expecting to see these. They are generally specific to using an Always On availability group. Business Critical tiers use availability group technology to implement SLA and availability features of a Business Critical service tier, so these wait types are expected. Note that long wait times might indicate a bottleneck such as I/O latency or replica behind.

> **Note:** Azure SQL Managed Instance scaling can take significant time but does not require any migration.

Increase Memory or Workers

Having enough memory or workers might be essential to your application and deployment. For Azure SQL Database, scale-up vCores for higher memory limits or workers. For SQL Managed Instance, scale-up vCores for higher memory limits. Currently, SQL Managed Instance also supports increasing workers with "max worker threads."

A Tune like it is SQL Server

Azure SQL is still SQL Server. There is rarely a substitute for ensuring you tune your SQL Server queries, and look at the following:

- Proper index design
- Using batches
- Using stored procedures
- Parameterizing queries to avoid too many cached *ad hoc* queries
- Processing results in your application quickly and correctly

Intelligent Query Processing

Intelligent query processing (IQP) is a group of new capabilities made into the query processor. You enable it by using the latest database compatibility level. Applications can gain performance by simply using the latest database compatibility level. There are no code changes required. However, a unique aspect of automatic tuning for Azure SQL Database is automatic indexing.

> **EXAM TIP:** Automatic indexing is not currently available in SQL Managed Instance.

Remember that automatic tuning for index recommendations does not account for any overhead performance an index can cause on your operations, such as inserts, updates, or deletes.

Example of Indexes with Automatic Tuning in Azure SQL Database

The following is an example from the Azure portal, in which indexes are recommended for a database based on workload analysis over time.

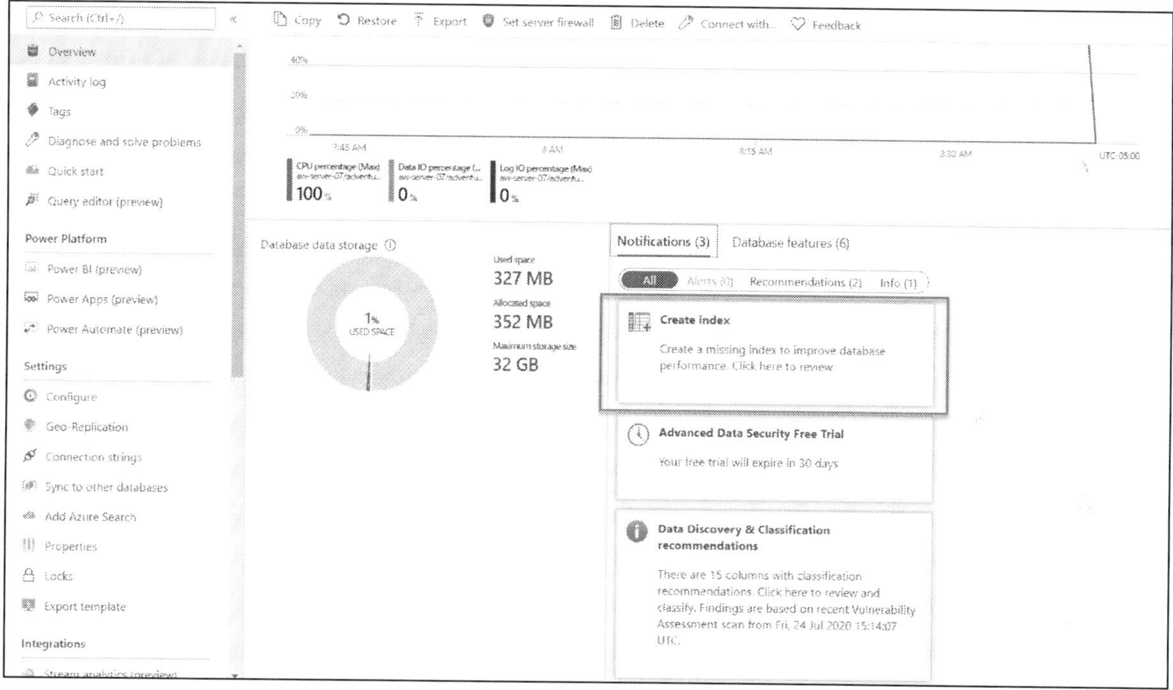

Figure 01-22: Example of Indexes with Automatic Tuning in Azure SQL Database

In the Azure portal, in **Performance Overview**, you can see performance information for the top 5 resource-consuming queries, as found in the Query Store. There is also a recommendation.

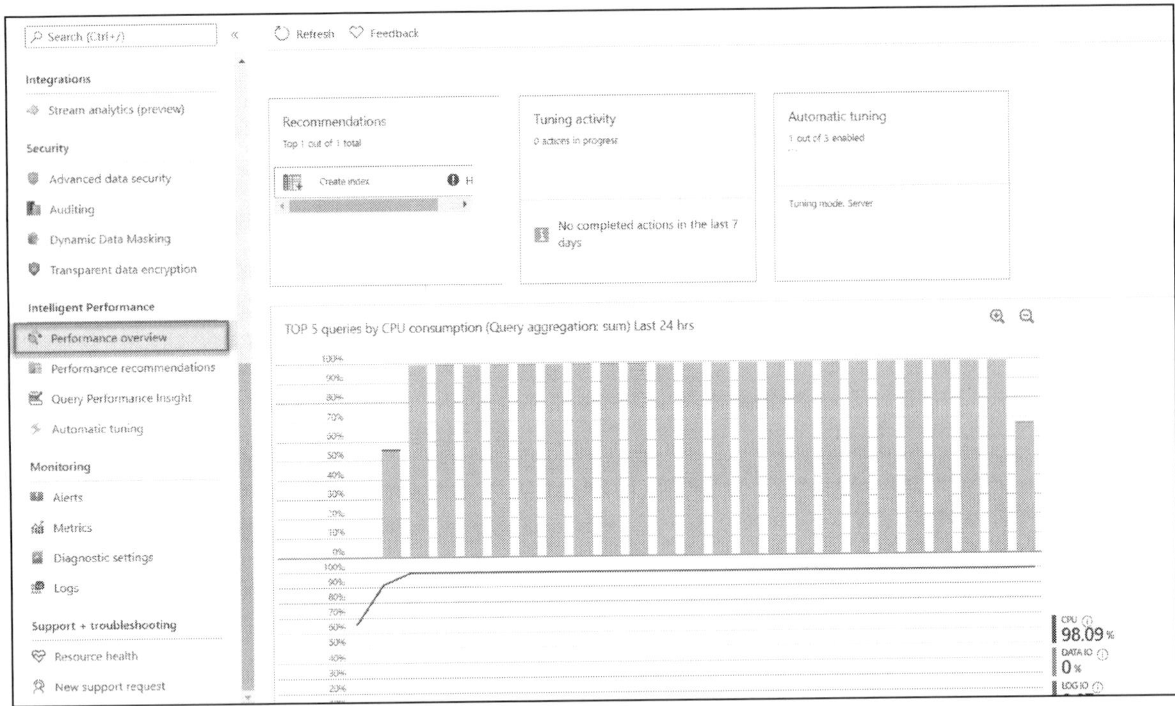

Figure 01-23: Performance Overview

The Azure portal also offers Query Performance Insights, a visual reporting tool based on the Query Store. In this example, Query Performance Insights show the specific query consuming the most resources and advises how to improve query performance.

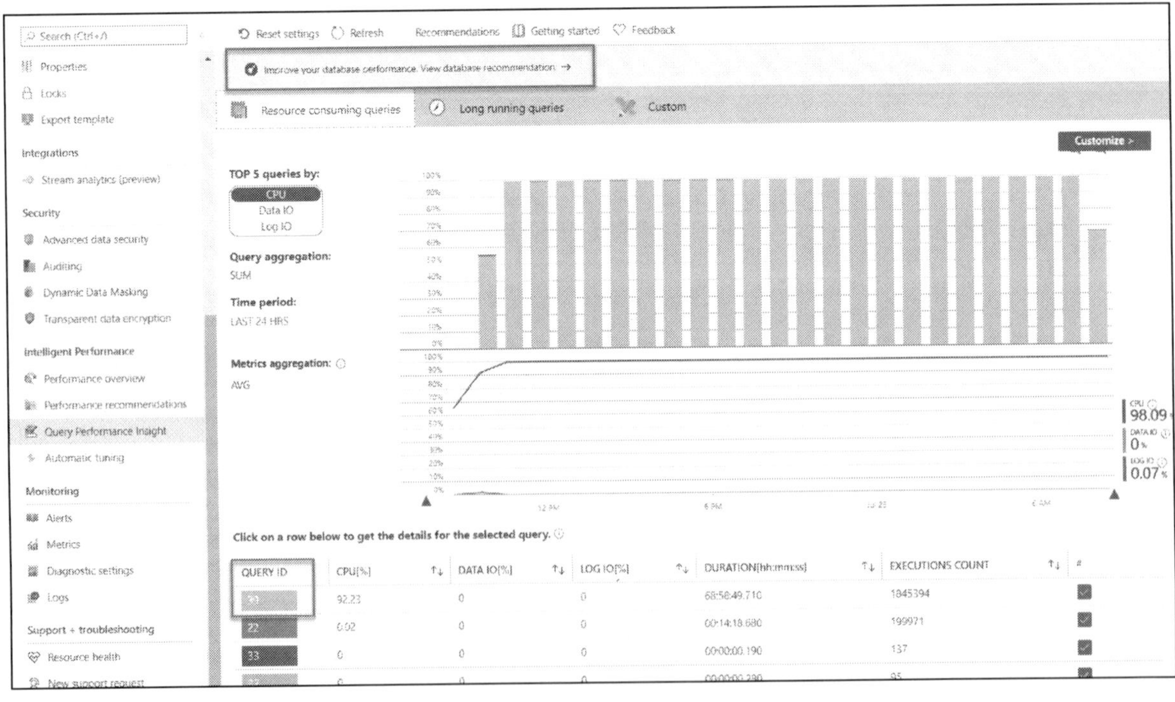

Figure 01-24: Query Performance Overview

The Azure portal also provides a direct way to see any performance recommendations.

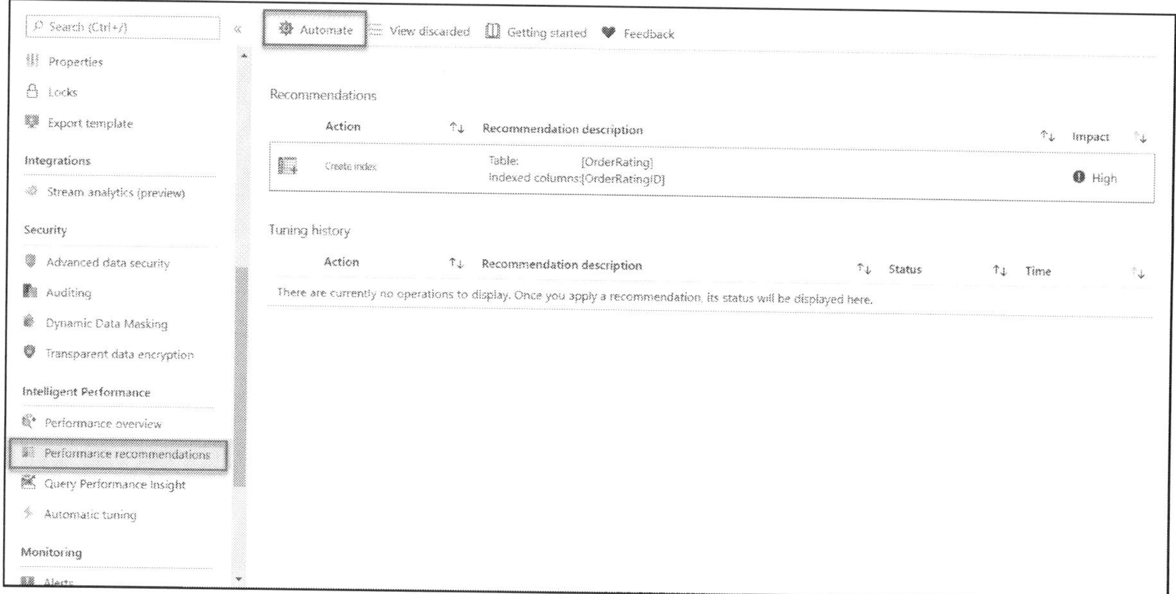

Figure 01-25: Performance Recommendations

The Automate option enables automatic tuning. In this view, you see specific recommendations.

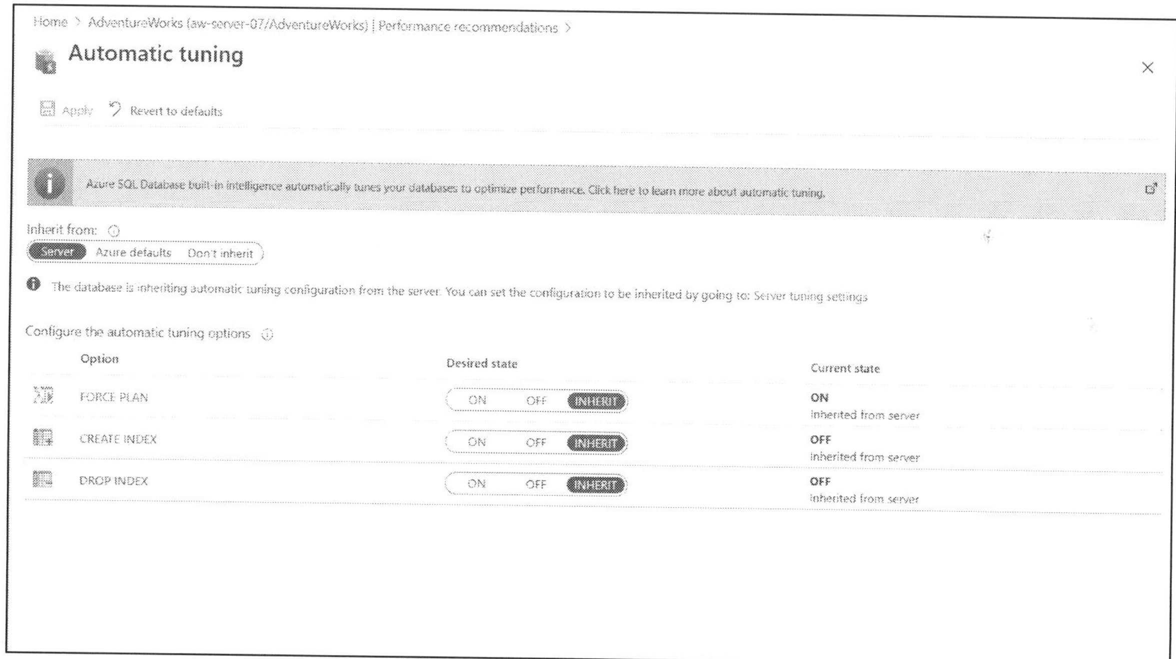

Figure 01-26: Automatic Tuning

You can set automatic tuning options at the database server or database level. If you had enabled automatic tuning in this scenario, the index would be automatically created.

EXAM TIP: Recommendations and automation are unavailable for indexes and parameter-sensitive plans for Azure SQL Managed Instance or SQL Server. Automatic plan correction is available.

If you select the recommended index, you get more details about the specific index.

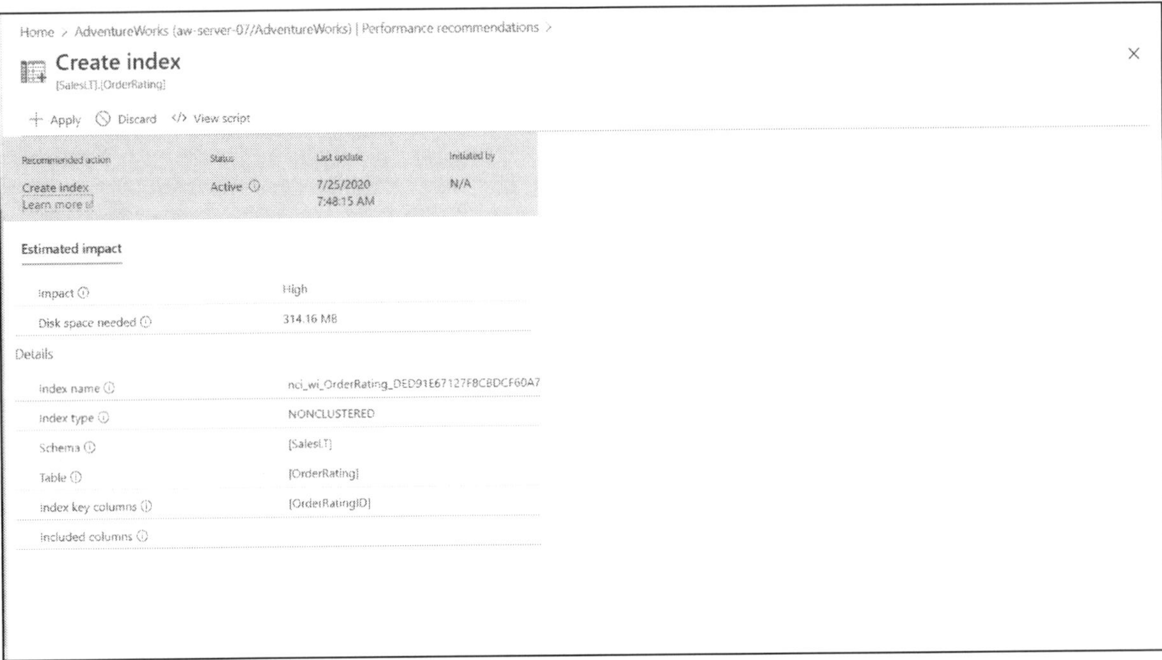

Figure 01-27: Recommended index

You will see details about the index, table, and space required. You can apply the recommended index or view a T-SQL script that applies the index.

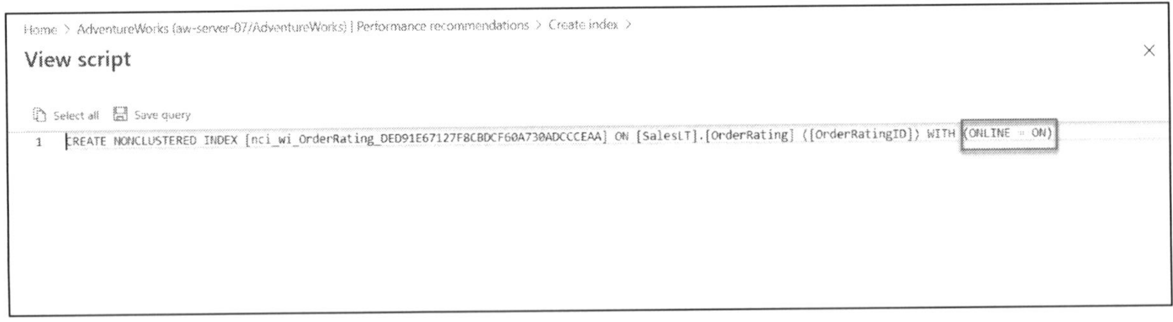

Figure 01-28: T-SQL Script

Deploy Solutions using Azure SQL

Backup and Restore

In large or small organizations, accidents and incidents can happen, which is why you always need to plan how to restore your systems if they are disrupted. In SQL Server, if

you want to restore a database to a point in time, you can do that only if you are running in the full recovery model.

As Azure SQL manages your backups and runs in the full recovery model, it can restore your database to any point in time. You can even restore a deleted database within the configured retention policy. Microsoft also automatically encrypts your backups if TDE is enabled on the logical server or instance.

Create a Backup Strategy for Azure SQL Managed Instance and Azure SQL Database

It is still essential to understand how backups are stored and processed and your options for retention and restoration. Ultimately, you are still responsible for the overall strategy for point-in-time restore.

Point in Time Restore

You can perform a self-service restore. You can choose the exact point in time to which you want to restore and start the process by using the Azure portal, the PowerShell/Azure CLI, or REST APIs. You must rename both the original and the new database to return to a working condition. However, you would not need to update connection strings.

Long-term Retention

If 35 days is not long enough to meet your organization's needs or compliance requirements, you can choose long-term retention (LTR). This option enables you to automatically create full database backups stored in RA-GRS, ZRS, or LRS storage for up to 10 years.

Geo-restore

You are protected if an entire region goes down and your databases or managed instances are in that region. Geo-restore can be a bit overdue for the primary because it takes time to duplicate the Azure blob to another region. You can efficiently perform a geo-restore using the Azure portal, the PowerShell/Azure CLI, or REST APIs.

General Purpose

Databases and managed instances in this service tier need the same availability architecture. Using the following figure as a guide, first, consider the *application* and *control ring*. The application connects to the server name, which then connects to a gateway (GW) that points the application to the server to connect to, running on a VM. With General Purpose, the primary replica uses locally attached SSD for the tempdb. In other words, it is globally redundant storage (with copies in multiple regions).

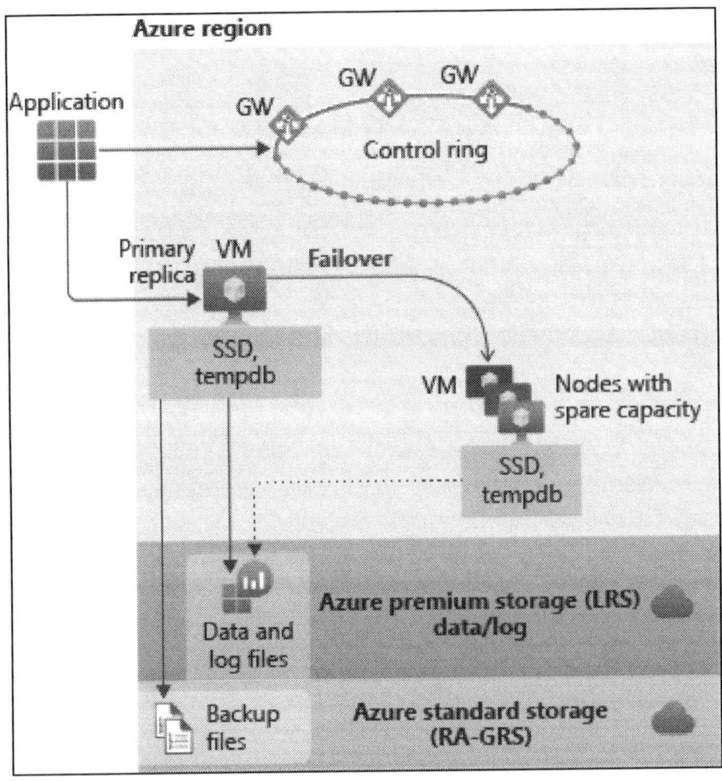

Figure 01-29: Azure Region General Purpose

Business Critical

The following service tier to consider is Business Critical.

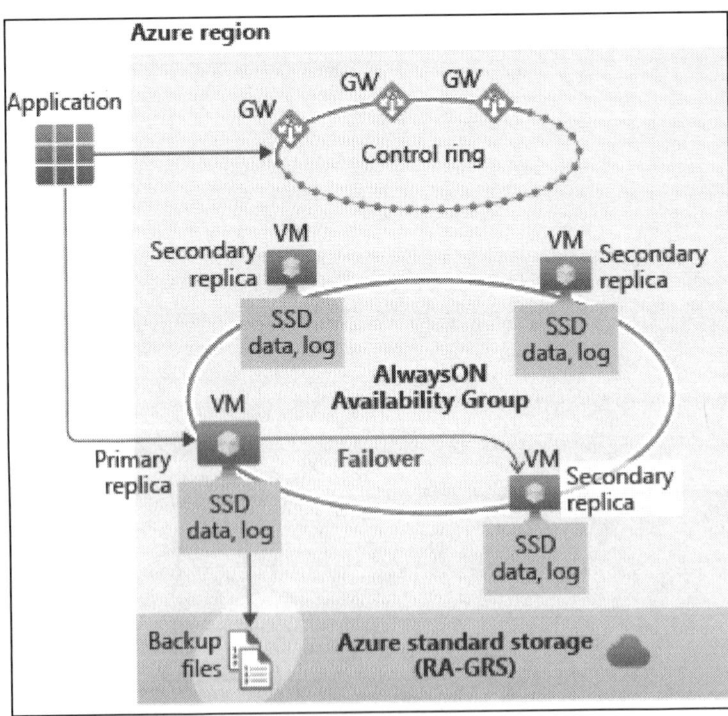

Figure 01-30: Azure Region Business Critical

Using Business Critical is like deploying an Always On availability group (AG) behind the scenes. Unlike in the General Purpose tier, in Business Critical, the data and log files are all running on direct-attached SSD, which significantly reduces network latency.

Hyperscale

The Hyperscale service tier is available only for Database. This service tier has a great architecture because it uses a tiered layer of caches and page servers to expand the ability to access database pages without accessing the data file directly.

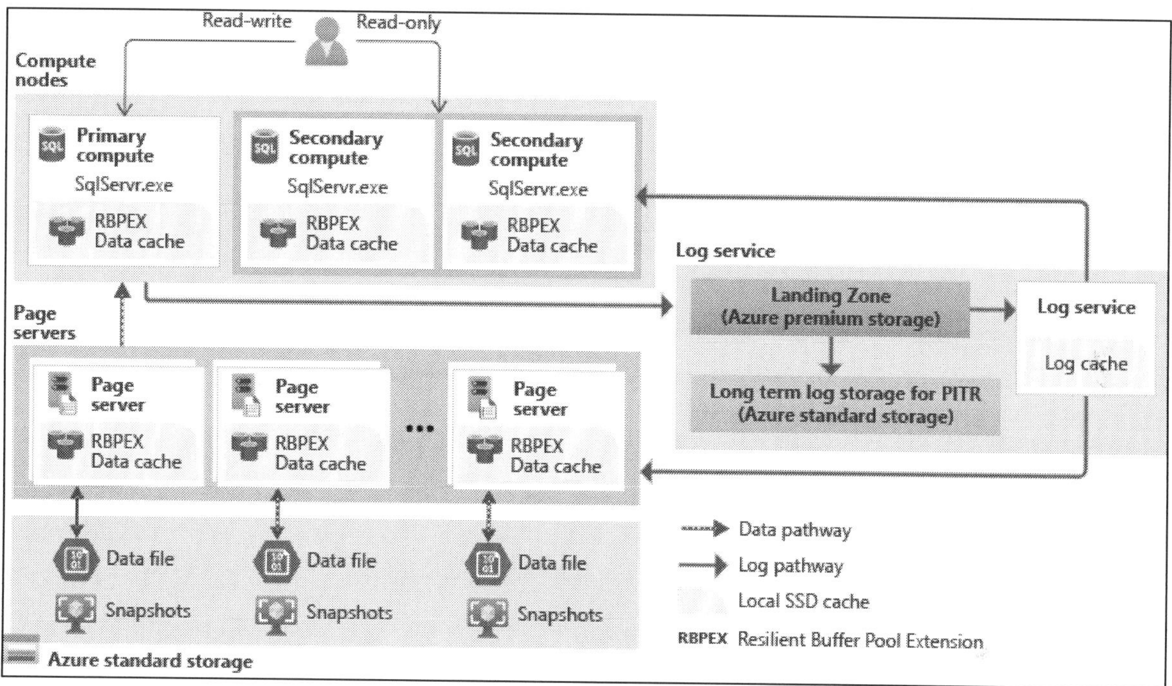

Figure 01-31: Hyperscale

Because this architecture uses paired page servers, you can scale horizontally to put all the data in caching layers. This new architecture also lets Hyperscale support databases as large as 100 TB. As it uses snapshots, nearly instantaneous database backups can occur regardless of size.

Going further with the Availability

Azure offers great availability options by default in the various service tiers. In this unit, you will see how you can go further with various options for availability in Azure SQL.

Availability Zones

An Availability Zone is a separate data center within a given region. There is always a physical separation between Availability Zones. This capability protects against catastrophic failures that might occur to a data center in a region.

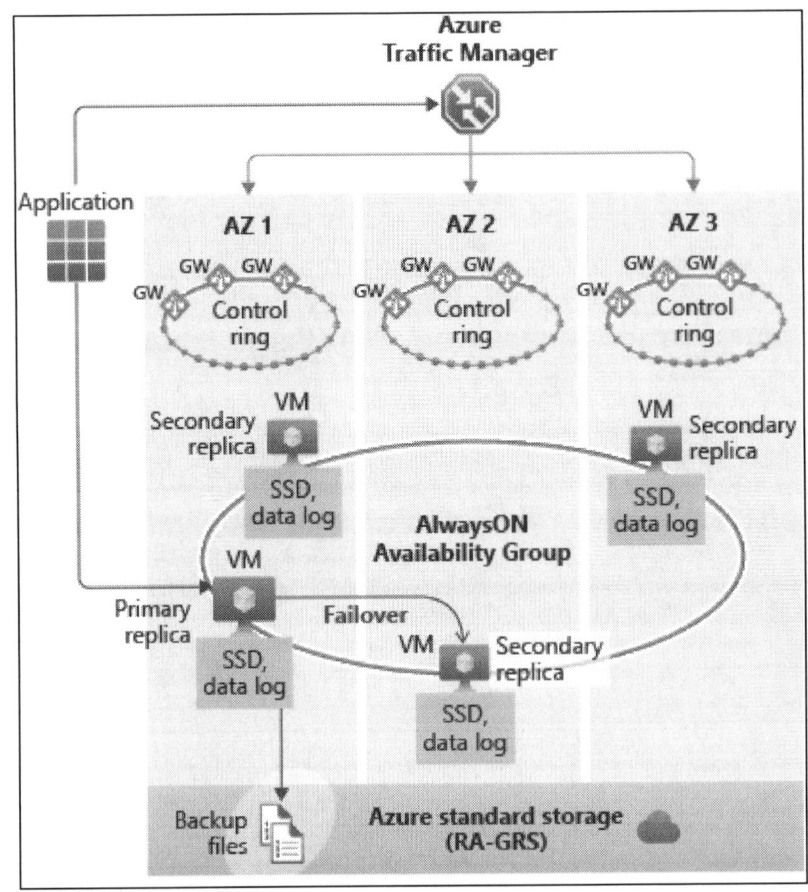

Figure 01-32: Availability Zones

There might be a slight increase in network latency from a performance standpoint because your AG is now spread across datacenters that have some distance between them. For this reason, Availability Zones are not turned on by default. You can choose to use what is commonly called a "Multi-Az" or a "Single-Az" deployment. Configuring this option is as simple as adding a parameter to a PowerShell/Azure CLI command or selecting a check box in the portal.

Azure SQL SLA

Azure SQL maintains a service-level agreement (SLA) that offers financial backing to accomplish and maintain service levels.

Remember that you choose how many replicas you have in Hyperscale. If you do not have any, the failover behavior is similar to that of General Purpose. If you have replicas, the failover behavior is similar to that of Business Critical. Here are the SLAs, based on the number of replicas:

- 0 replicas: 99.5%
- 1 replica: 99.9%
- 2 or more replicas: 99.99%

Geo-replication and Auto-failover Groups

After you choose a service tier (and consider Availability Zones as applicable), you can consider some other options for getting read-scale or the capability to failover to another region: geo-replication and auto-failover groups.

The cloud, and Azure SQL specifically, have made this process easier. For both geo-replication and auto-failover groups, you can get configured with a few clicks in the Azure portal or a few commands in the PowerShell/Azure CLI.

Here are some points to help you decide if geo-replication or auto-failover groups are best for your scenario:

GEO-REPLICATION AND AUTO-FAILOVER GROUPS		
	Geo-replication	**Failover groups**
Automatic failover	No	Yes
Failover multiple databases simultaneously	No	Yes
User must update connection string after failover	Yes	No
SQL Managed Instance support	No	Yes
It can be in the same region as the primary	Yes	No
Multiple replicas	Yes	No
Supports read-scale	Yes	Yes

Table 01-01: Geo-Replication and Auto-Failover Groups

Availability and Consistency

If you have some background working with SQL Server, you might know how to manage database availability and consistency. In this unit, you will learn about performing those tasks in Azure SQL.

Database Availability

You cannot fix a database state to OFFLINE or EMERGENCY. If you think about it, OFFLINE does not make sense because you cannot attach databases. Because you cannot use EMERGENCY, you cannot do emergency mode repair. Accelerated Database Recovery (ADR) is built into the engine.

Database Consistency

Multiple copies of your data and backups occur locally and across regions. Regularly, backup and restore integrity checks run. Detection for *lost write* and *close read* is also in place. You can run DBCC CHECKDB (no repair), and CHECKSUM is on by default. Automatic page repair will occur in the back end, and data integrity error alert monitoring will also occur.

Configure and Monitor the Availability

Now that you know about all the possibilities, you need to create a strategy for the specific workload that your Azure SQL database or Azure SQL managed instance is a part of.

Make the Right Choices

A large part of creating a strategy is stepping back and thinking about the requirements of your workload. You need to make sure your database is meeting your availability requirements. But you also need to be sure your application is meeting those requirements. Additionally, you need to ensure the connectivity between the data and the applications meets your requirements. For example, if your application and database are in different regions, that placement will increase network latency. Place your application and data as close together as possible. Throughout this module, you have also seen how crucial implementing retry logic in your applications is for maintaining availability.

Monitor Availability

Azure SQL provides several tools and capabilities to monitor certain aspects of availability. These tools include the Azure portal, T-SQL, and interfaces like PowerShell, az CLI, and REST APIs.

The following sections describe some examples of using these tools to monitor availability.

Region and Datacenter Availability

The availability of regions and datacenters is critical for a managed instance or a database deployment. *Azure status* and *Azure Service Health* are vital to understanding any data center or region outages, including specific services like Azure SQL.

Azure status is a dashboard that shows any service that is causing problems in any Azure global region. You can use an RSS feed to get notifications of changes to Azure status.

You can view Azure Service Health in the Azure portal. Azure Service Health provides information about service problems, planned maintenance events, health advisories, and health history.

Instance, Server, and Database Availability

In addition to Azure service events, you can also view the availability of your Azure SQL Managed Instance or Azure SQL Database databases in the Azure portal.

One way to view a possible reason for a managed instance or database to be unavailable is to examine resource health by using the Azure portal or REST APIs.

You can always use standard SQL Server tools like SQL Server Management Studio to connect to a managed instance or database server and check the status of these resources. You can use the tool or T-SQL queries.

Backup and Restore History

Standard backup history is unavailable, but you can view long-term backup retention history using the Azure portal or CLI interfaces. Also, in Azure SQL Managed Instance, you can use XEvents to track backup history.

Any database restore that uses point in time restore creates a new database. You can use the Azure Activity Log to view operations that create databases.

Replica Status

Replicas are used for Business-critical service tiers. You can view the status of a replica by using the DMV **sys.dm_database_replica_states**.

Failover Causes

To determine the cause of a failover event for an Azure SQL Managed Instance or database deployment, check the resource health by using the Azure portal or REST APIs.

System Center Management Pack for Azure SQL

System Center provides management packs to monitor Azure SQL Managed Instance and Azure SQL Database. See the management pack documentation for requirements and details.

Putting it all together with Azure SQL

Scenario 1 - Architect Global Scale and Secure Access

In the following two units, you will review two business scenarios. You can work on this yourself, but it might be interesting to brainstorm with others if possible.

Process for Developing Solutions

Your goal, in these scenarios and likely in the real world, is to understand:

- The problem that the company needs to solve
- Any requirements and constraints that go along with a result

This goal is often in the form of a problem statement. It is a formal set of paragraphs that clearly define the circumstances, present condition, and desired outcomes. At this point, it is acceptable to have unrealistic constraints.

In production, there are usually six phases to create a solution. Developing the problem statement is just the beginning.

1. **Discovery**: The new statement of the problem from the customer
2. **Envisioning**: A "blue sky" description of what success in the project would look like. It is often phrased as *"I can..."* statements
3. **Architecture Design Session**: A primary layout of the technology options and choices for a preliminary solution
4. **Proof of Concept**: After the optimal technologies and processes are selected for the solution, a POC is set up with a small representative example of what a solution might look like. If a currently running solution in a parallel example is available, you can use that
5. **Implementation**: Executing a phased-in rollout of the completed solution based on findings from the previous phases
6. **Handoff**: A postmortem on the project with a discussion of future enhancements

Scenario Details

Your customer has requested your assistance in building a system that can handle thousands of writes per second to what is essentially an operational data mart.

The customer is also trying to determine which authentication methods to use in its hybrid environment. Although the leading solution and application will live in Azure, the customer also needs to accommodate the following:

- An older application would not allow the change of the driver or connection string on a non-Azure machine
- Multiple users run reports from SQL admin tools (SQL Server Management Studio, Azure Data Studio, PowerShell) on non-Azure machines that are not domain-joined

Wherever possible, the customer wants to eliminate hard-coding passwords or secrets in the connection strings and app configuration files. It also wants to eliminate using passwords in SQL tools or find a way to improve that authentication.

Scenario Guidance

- Start with the Azure SQL deployment option that is well-suited with the current solution and available now

- How will the customer scale over multiple regions with multiple queries happening simultaneously while isolating read workloads from write workloads
- Which authentication methods would you suggest for the interaction paths described in the scenario

After you have a preliminary solution in mind, the following step is to present it to the larger team (or customer or leadership, depending on the scenario). You will need to assemble and present your solution to share the project goals and constraints and how your solution addresses those items.

Scenario 1 Explanation - Architect Global Scale and Secure Access

In the previous unit, you worked through a scenario about the global scale for a content delivery network. In this unit, you will review one potential solution and some items to consider.

Often, more than one correct solution exists for any problem, but there are always tradeoffs. As you review, you should compare the provided solution to the one you developed in the previous unit. Which items in your solution differ from the proposed one? Is there anything in your solution you might want to rethink? Is there anything in the provided solution that you think is addressed more thoroughly in your solution?

Deployment Option and Configuration

The first decision to consider is which deployment option of Azure SQL you should select. Although SQL Server in an Azure virtual machine (VM) would work, a platform as a service (PaaS) offering might provide a better fit with less management overhead.

The customer is using auto-failover groups; thus, whether or not it needs the Business Critical service tier will depend on how many read-only endpoints its analytics workload requires. With an auto-failover group in the Business Critical service tier, the customer would get three readable endpoints:

- One secondary replica from the primary region's availability group
- The secondary of the failover group (which is the primary replica of the database in the secondary region)
- The secondary replica from the secondary region's availability group

If the analytics workload does not need all these readable replicas, using General Purpose might be a more cost-effective solution.

Selecting the most Appropriate Authentication Methods

The other piece of this scenario involves determining the best way for each application or person to connect to the solution, given the need to create and use the most secure

technologies possible. If you break down the scenario, four separate clients will need access to Azure SQL Managed Instance:

- An application running on an Azure VM
- An application running on a non-Azure machine that is domain-joined
- DBAs or other users of SQL admin tools (SQL Server Management Studio, Azure Data Studio, PowerShell) from a non-Azure machine that is not domain-joined
- Older applications running on a non-Azure machine where you cannot change the driver or connection string

An Application Running on an Azure VM

Managed identities for Azure resources are, in general, the recommended form of password-less authentication for applications running on Azure virtual machines.

An Application Running on a non-Azure Machine that is Domain-joined

For non-Azure machines, using managed identities is not an option. Integrated authentication via Azure Active Directory (Azure AD) is the recommended authentication method for apps running on domain-joined machines outside Azure, assuming that the domain has been federated with Azure AD.

Older Applications Running On A Non-Azure Machine Where You Cannot Change the Driver or Connection String

In scenarios where the driver or connection string cannot be changed, an option for eliminating passwords does not exist today. You might consider diving deeper into the restrictions and how they can be lifted to use a more secure and safeguarded approach for authenticating applications.

Scenario 2 - Mission-critical Application

In the last unit, you analyzed a solution with global scale requirements, isolating read and write workloads and determining the most secure authentication methods depending on the client. These are common themes that occur in many scenarios. Like in the last unit, you will review an additional business scenario focused on mission-critical applications.

Scenario Details

You are hired to build a mission-critical cloud application that requires 99.995 percent availability because downtime might be life-threatening. 911 dispatch, notifications about stolen credit cards, or corporate security reporting are examples of such applications.

In this case, you will focus on a 911 dispatch system. High performance is required because any delay in response carries a high risk and can be life-threatening. Given the

sensitivity of the collected personal information, data sovereignty must be guaranteed. Your primary mission is to ensure that the app is designed and deployed with the appropriate data redundancy and fault resilience to meet the availability and data sovereignty goals.

At the same time, DBAs need to troubleshoot performance by using the Azure portal, SQL Server Management Studio, and Azure Data Studio. They also need to create new contained database users who must be mapped to Azure AD principles.

Scenario Guidance

- Start by selecting the Azure SQL deployment option, service tier, and configuration that create the highest availability for the 911 dispatch system
- Consider geo-redundancy
- Think about what role colocation plays in your solution
- Determine a security strategy for meeting the data sensitivity requirements

Scenario 2 Solution - Mission-critical Application

Often, more than one correct solution exists for any problem, but there are always tradeoffs. As you review, you should compare the provided solution to the one you developed in the previous unit. Which items in your solution differ from the proposed one? Is there anything in your solution you might want to rethink? Is there anything in the provided solution that you think is addressed more thoroughly in your solution?

Deployment Option and Configuration

The first selection in addressing a scenario is often to identify which Azure SQL deployment option will potentially be the best fit. If you consider service-level agreement (SLA) alone, the requirement is for an SLA of 99.995 percent, which only Azure SQL Database can provide. To get this SLA, you must deploy the Business Critical service tier and enable availability zones.

In this configuration, it is also essential to think about the role that colocation plays. Your application needs to be as close to your database as possible to maintain high availability, certainly in the same region. You would want to make sure your application is deployed in both regions of the auto-failover group, so a redundant copy of the application (for example, a web app) exists. If there is a failover, you can use Azure Traffic Manager to reroute traffic to the application in the secondary region.

DBAs and Sensitive Data

The 911 dispatch system coordinators have expressed concern about protecting sensitive data (like health history and other personal information) while allowing DBAs to do their jobs.

To ensure that DBAs cannot see sensitive data stored in specific columns and that all access to tables that contain sensitive data is monitored, you can use a few Azure SQL technologies. Using SQL Audit is a best practice to monitor access, but DBAs will still see the data. Classifying the sensitive data using Data Classification will help because it will be labeled, and you can track it with SQL Audit. However, with these implemented, DBAs can still view sensitive data. You can use dynamic data masking to help mask sensitive data, but it is impossible to keep a db_owner from viewing user data with permissions only.

DBAs need to have sensitive data masked, but they still need to troubleshoot performance using the Azure portal and SQL Server Management Studio or Azure Data Studio. Also, they need to be able to create new contained database users who must be mapped to Azure Active Directory (Azure AD) principles.

One solution is to create an Azure AD group called SQL DBA for the DBAs on each instance. Then, assign the group to the Azure role-based access control (RBAC) role of SQL Server Contributor. Finally, you can set the group to be the Azure AD admin on the logical server.

Opportunities in Azure

You now know how to get a workload or application up and to run with Azure SQL. You also know how to configure it according to what you have learned in the learning path related to security, performance, and availability.

Azure SQL is the world's database

Satya Nadella, the Microsoft CEO, once claimed that Azure is the world's computer. With the combination of stability and innovation from the SQL Server and Azure SQL platform, Azure SQL has become the world's database. After you are on Azure SQL, you can connect and integrate with other services in Azure, as well as to your on-premises environment.

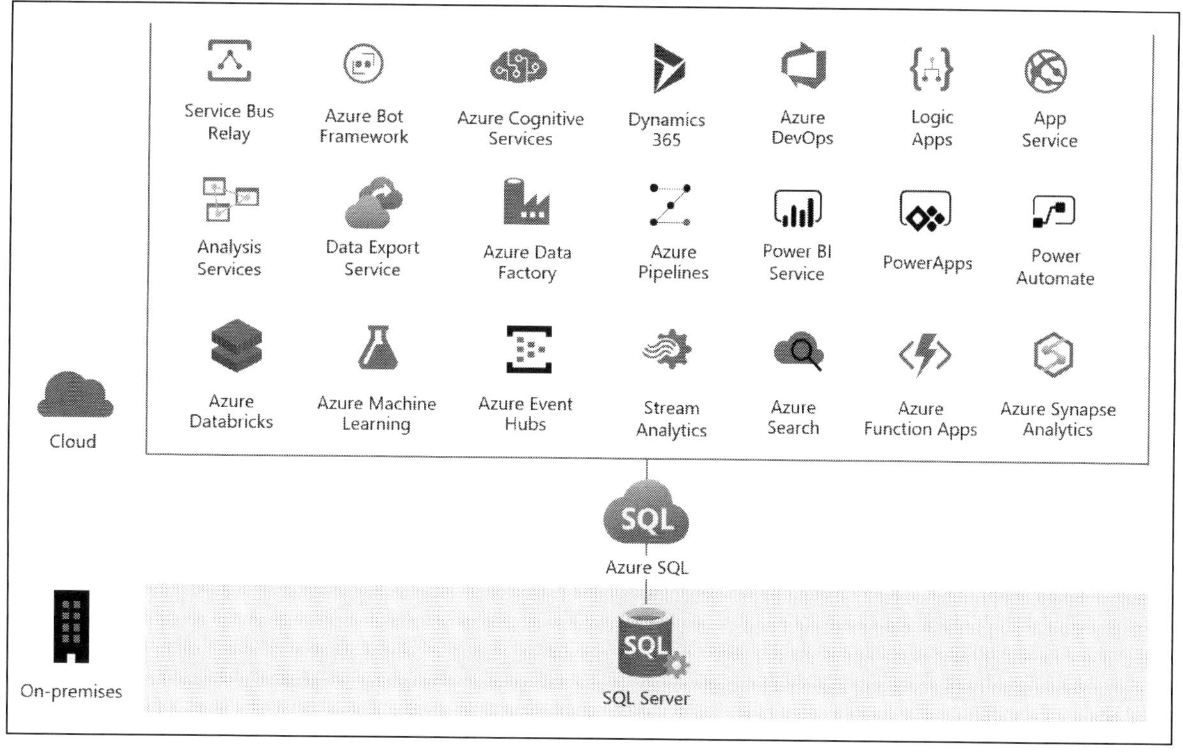

Figure 01-33: Azure SQL

Integration with Other Services

Azure SQL Database, for example, integrates with many other services. For example, the integration of Azure SQL Database with Microsoft Power Platform can make it easier for you to:

- Connect to SQL data with Power BI (such as through DirectQuery)
- Build no-code applications with Power Apps
- Create automated workflows across apps and services with Power Automate

Microsoft Power Platform is just one example of how you can go beyond Azure SQL. There are also integrations and connectors around Azure Cognitive Search and Azure Stream Analytics. Even services with no specific integrations are built on the Azure backbone (largely Azure Service Fabric). You can configure them to talk to each other efficiently.

Extension of on-premises

For your workloads that remain on-premises, there are many technologies and strategies for making the communication with SQL Server on-premises (for example) fast and effective. Technologies like Azure ExpressRoute, which gives you a direct line to Azure, can help you be successful wherever you are in your Azure journey.

Lab 01-01: Secure your Data with Azure SQL

Introduction

SQL Database provides predictable performance with multiple resource types, service tiers, and compute sizes. These capabilities let you focus on rapid app development and accelerate your time-to-market rather than managing virtual machines and infrastructure.

Problem

Many companies have an aging or under-engineered data platform strategy. There has been a major trend of moving existing systems to the cloud, building new applications quickly by using the cloud, and offloading some on-premises costs. You want a plan for how to move some workloads to the cloud.

Solution

In this lab, you will start with Microsoft-built Azure SQL. These options include Azure SQL Database, Azure SQL Managed Instance, and SQL Server in an Azure virtual machine. You must understand how to set up your organization for success. You also have to understand the role of a database administrator (DBA).

Step 01: Deploy an Azure SQL Database

1. From the Azure portal, click on + **"Create a Resource"** in the left side navigation bar.

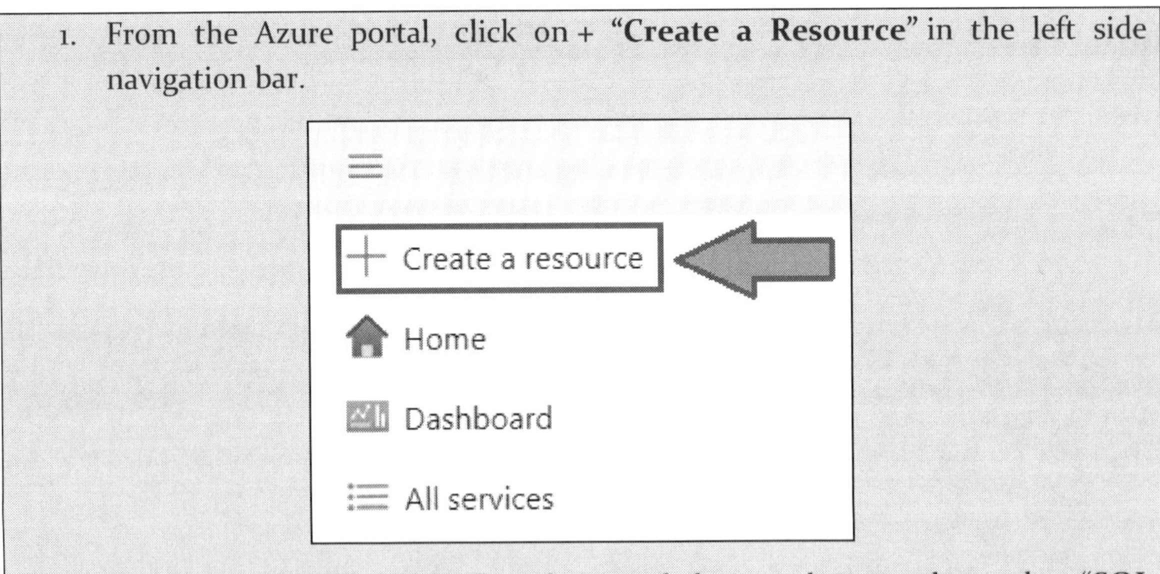

2. Search for **"SQL Database"** in the search box at the top, then select **"SQL Database"** from the list of options.

sql database

Services See all

SQL databases
SQL Server stretch databases
Dedicated SQL pools (formerly SQL DW)
Azure Database for MySQL servers
Reservations
Azure SQL
Azure Database for MySQL flexible servers
Azure Database for PostgreSQL flexible servers
Azure Database for PostgreSQL server groups
Azure Database for PostgreSQL servers

Resources

No results were found.

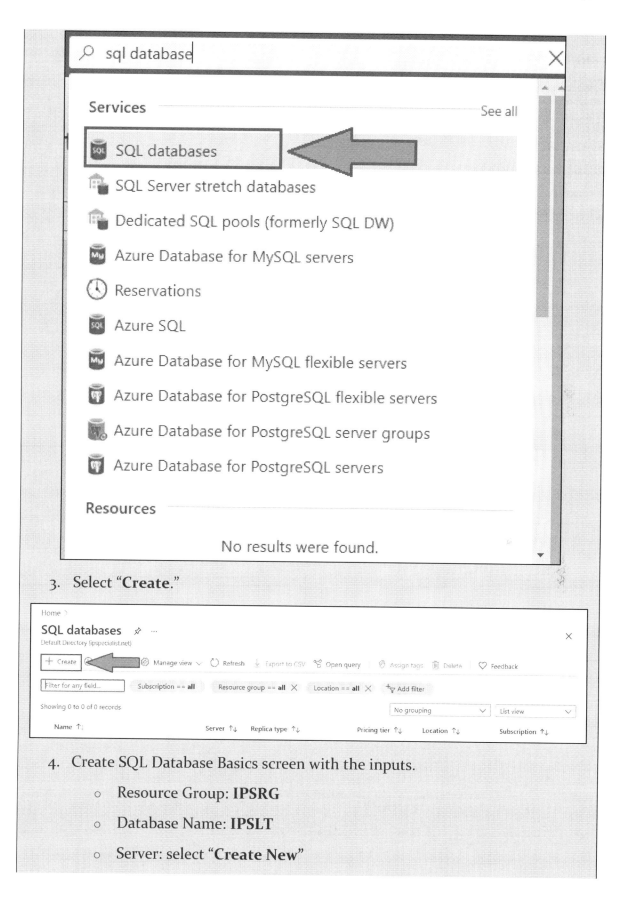

3. Select "**Create.**"

Home >
SQL databases
Default Directory (ipspecialist.net)
+ Create | Manage view | Refresh | Export to CSV | Open query | Assign tags | Delete | Feedback
Filter for any field... | Subscription == all | Resource group == all | Location == all | Add filter
Showing 0 to 0 of 0 records. | No grouping | List view
Name | Server | Replica type | Pricing tier | Location | Subscription

4. Create SQL Database Basics screen with the inputs.
   - Resource Group: **IPSRG**
   - Database Name: **IPSLT**
   - Server: select "**Create New**"

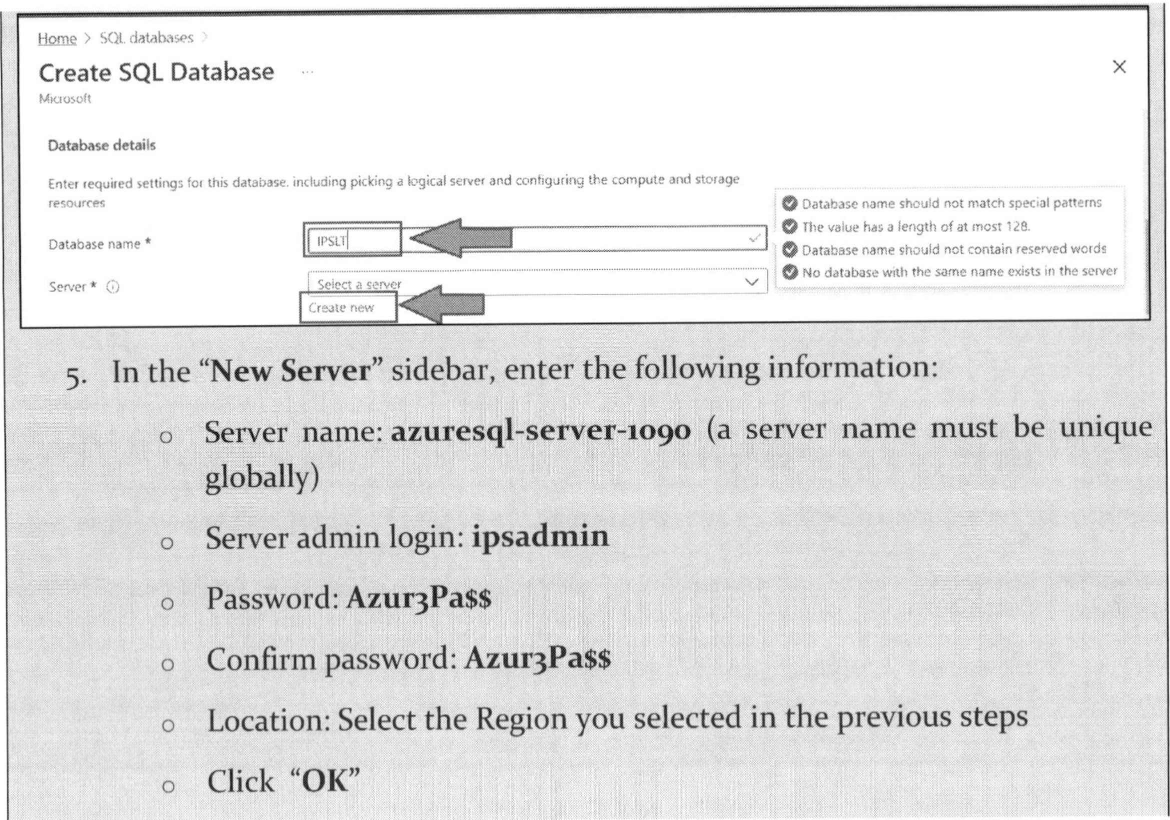

5. In the "**New Server**" sidebar, enter the following information:
    - Server name: **azuresql-server-1090** (a server name must be unique globally)
    - Server admin login: **ipsadmin**
    - Password: **Azur3Pa$$**
    - Confirm password: **Azur3Pa$$**
    - Location: Select the Region you selected in the previous steps
    - Click "**OK**"

New server
Microsoft

Server name *
azuresql-server-1090
.database.windows.net

Server admin login *
ipsadmin

Password *
•••••••••

Confirm password *
•••••••••

Location *
(US) East US

OK

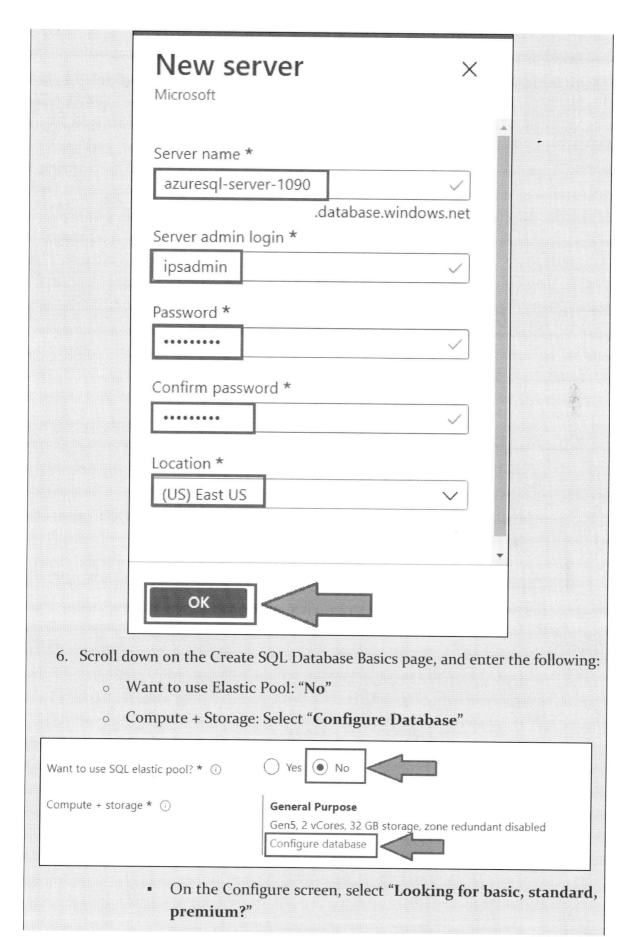

6. Scroll down on the Create SQL Database Basics page, and enter the following:
   - Want to use Elastic Pool: "**No**"
   - Compute + Storage: Select "**Configure Database**"

Want to use SQL elastic pool? * Yes No

Compute + storage * General Purpose
Gen5, 2 vCores, 32 GB storage, zone redundant disabled
Configure database

- On the Configure screen, select "**Looking for basic, standard, premium?**"

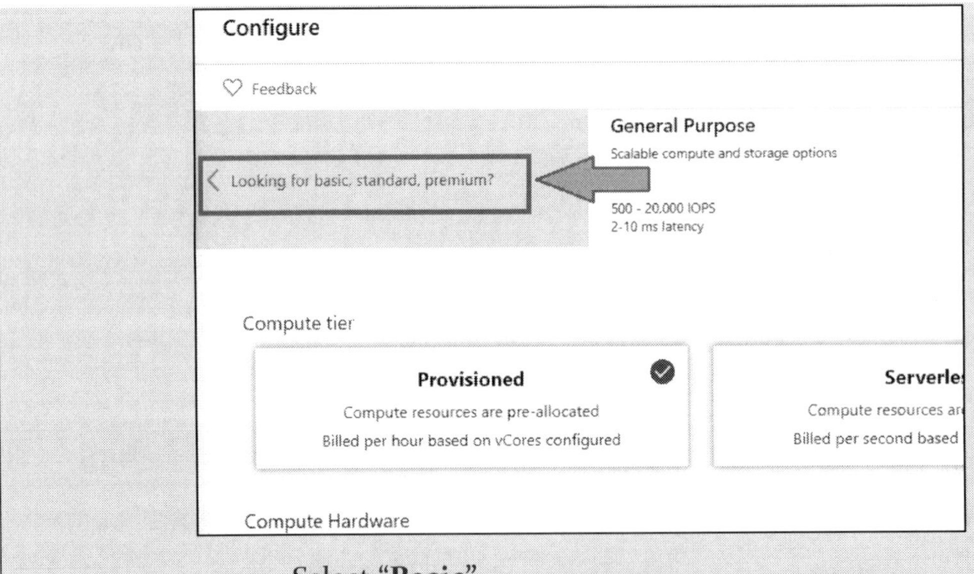

- Select "**Basic**"
- -Click on the "**Apply**" button

7. Review settings and then select "**Next: Networking.**"

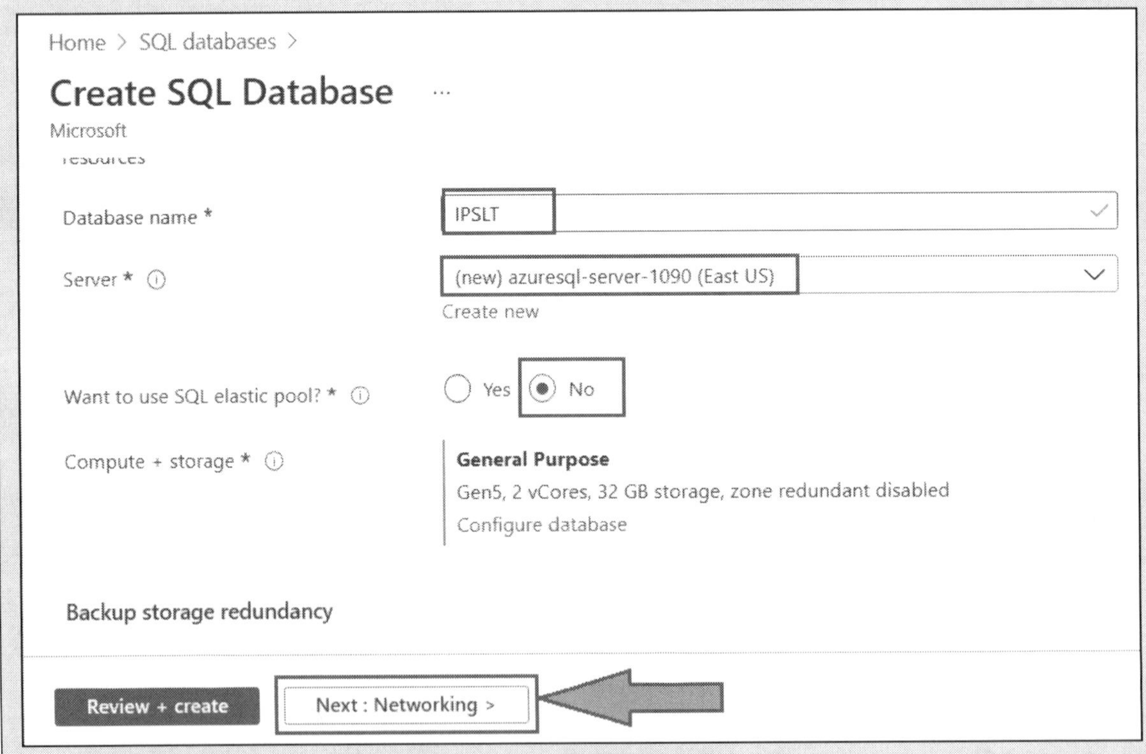

8. On the Networking screen, for the Connectivity method, select the "**Private Endpoint**" radio button.

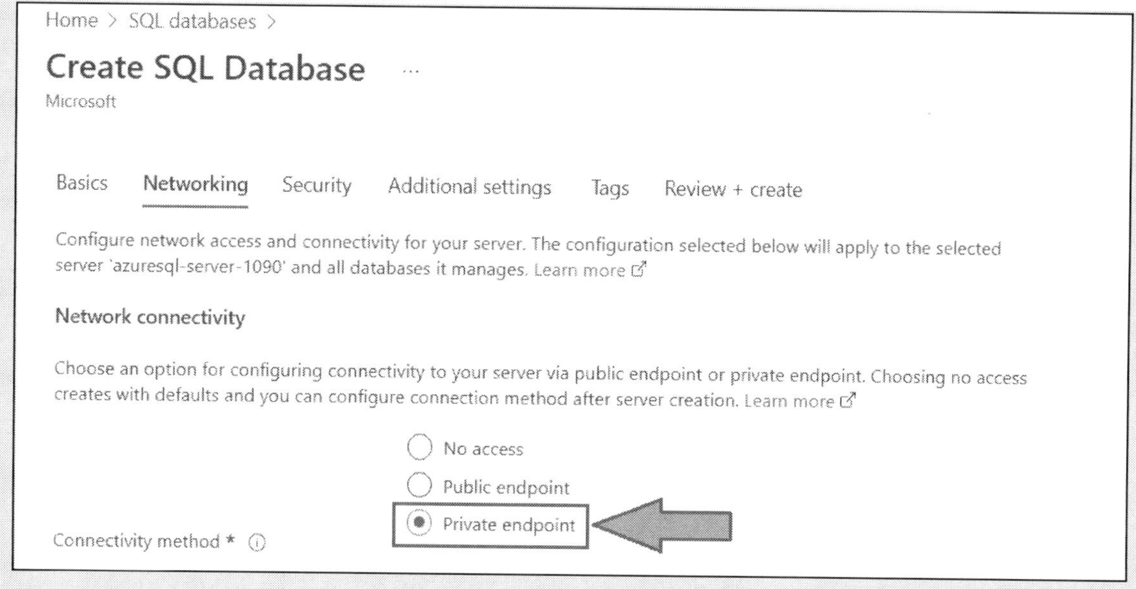

9. Click "**Review + Create**."

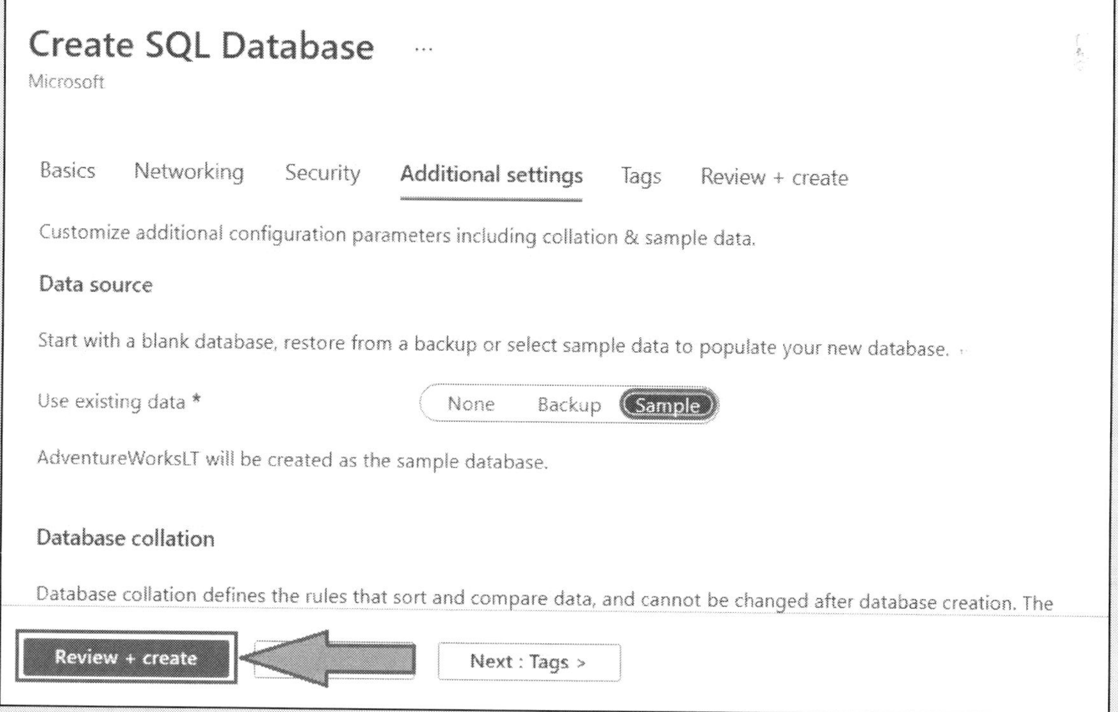

10. Review the settings before clicking on "**Create**."
11. Click on "**Go to the Resource**."

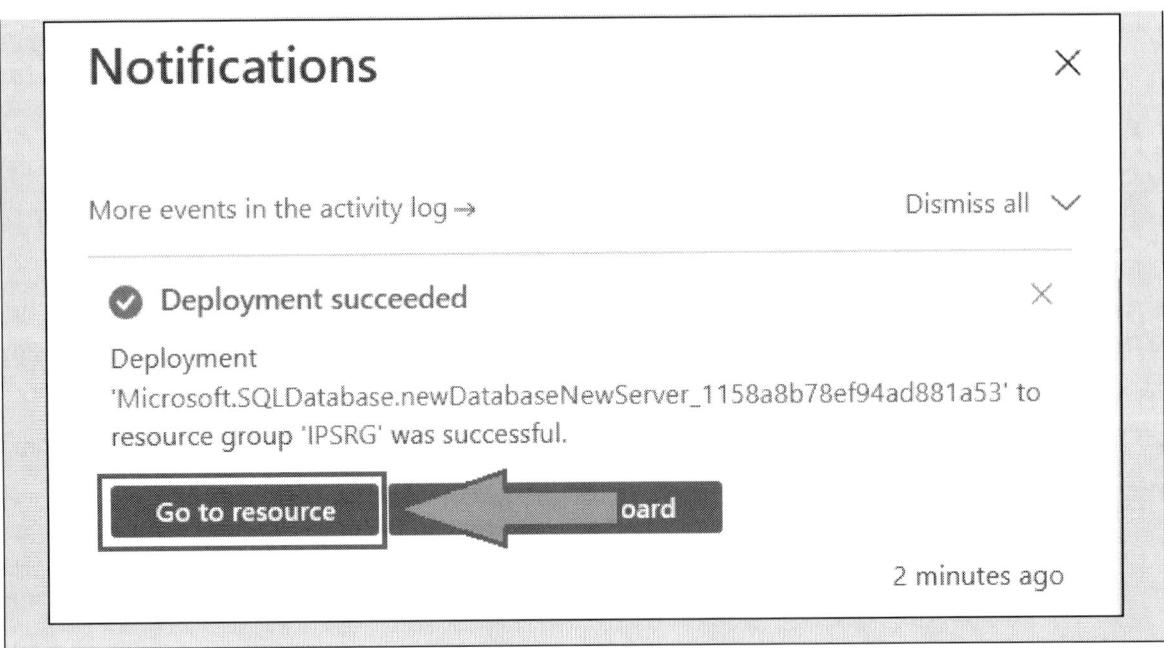

Set the Server Firewall

1. From the Home screen, select the menu, and select "**SQL Databases**."

sql database

Services — See all

SQL databases
SQL Server stretch databases
Dedicated SQL pools (formerly SQL DW)
Azure Database for MySQL servers
Reservations
Azure SQL
Azure Database for MySQL flexible servers
Azure Database for PostgreSQL flexible servers
Azure Database for PostgreSQL server groups
Azure Database for PostgreSQL servers

Resources

No results were found.

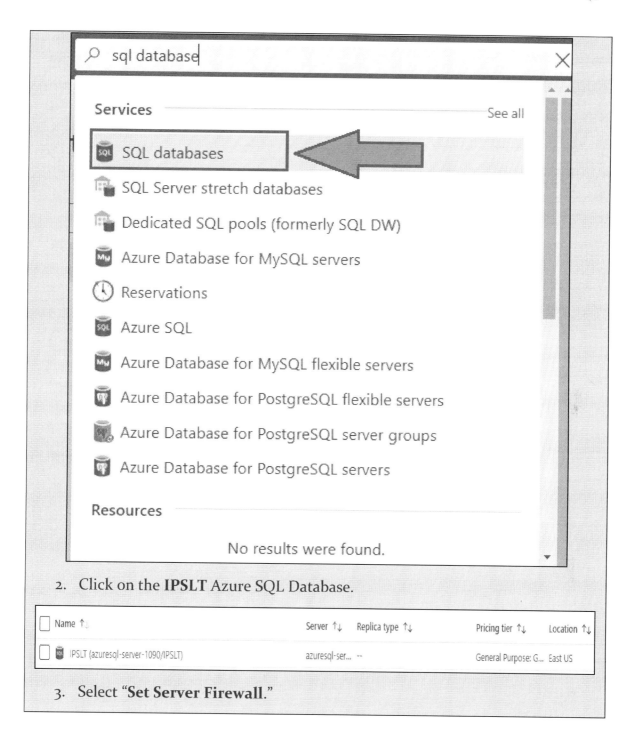

2. Click on the **IPSLT** Azure SQL Database.

Name ↑↓	Server ↑↓	Replica type ↑↓	Pricing tier ↑↓	Location ↑↓
IPSLT (azuresql-server-1090/IPSLT)	azuresql-ser...	--	General Purpose: G...	East US

3. Select "**Set Server Firewall**."

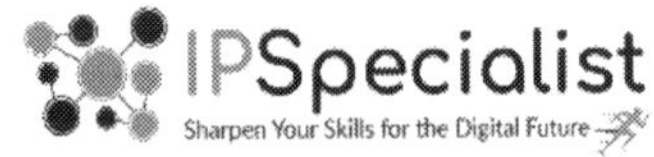

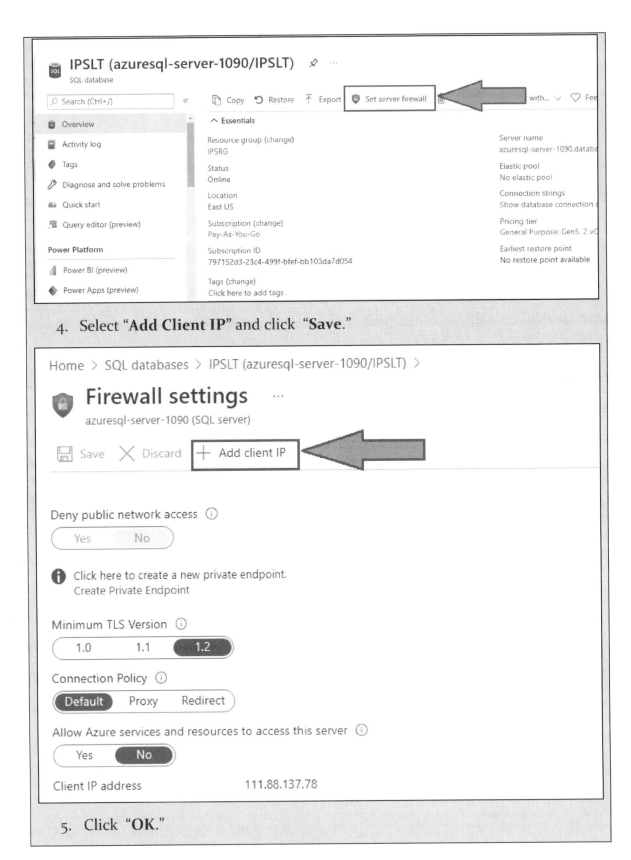

4. Select "**Add Client IP**" and click "**Save**."

5. Click "**OK**."

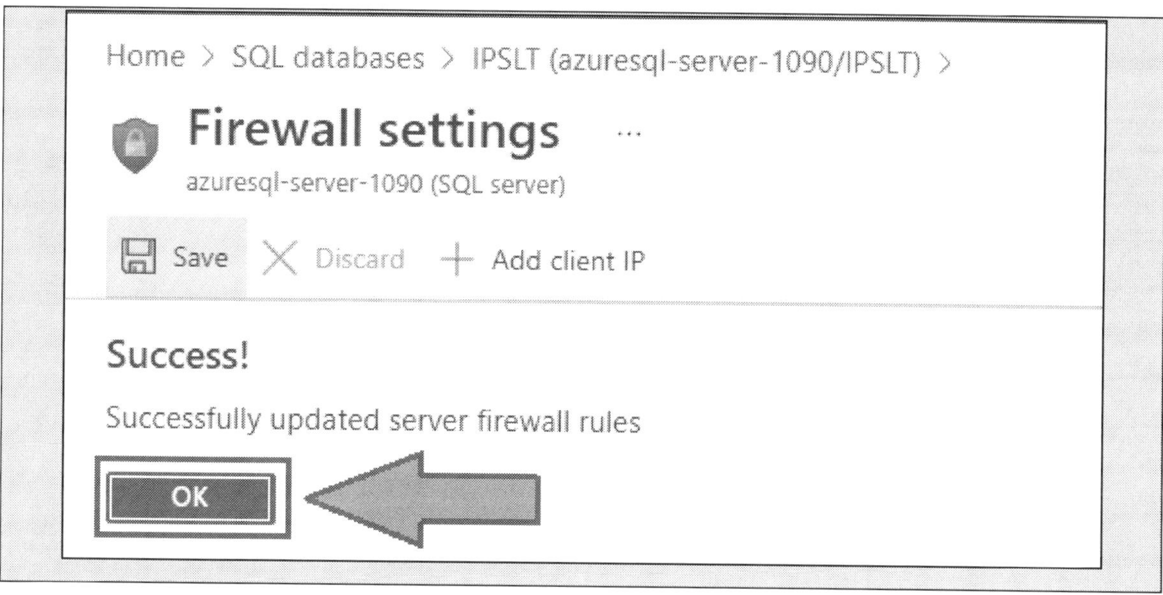

Configure Azure SQL Database

In this exercise, you will use Cloud Shell. It already includes the Azure CLI and Azure PowerShell modules.

Connecting with Azure Cloud Shell and the Azure CLI

You will run all of the commands by using the integrated Cloud Shell instance to your right. You can easily copy them and then press Shift + Insert to paste into the terminal.

1. Configure a default resource group and an Azure SQL Database logical server.

```
$resourceGroup = "Sandbox resource group name"
$server = Get-AzSqlServer -ResourceGroupName $resourceGroup
$logical_server = $server.ServerName
$databaseName = Get-AzSqlDatabase `
                    -ResourceGroupName $resourceGroup `
                    -ServerName $logical_server `
                    | Where DatabaseName -like IPSLT*
$databaseName = $databaseName.DatabaseName
```

```
PS /home/ipslabs> $resourceGroup = "Sandbox resource group name"
PS /home/ipslabs> $server = Get-AzSqlServer -ResourceGroupName $resourceGroup
```

```
PS /home/ipslabs> $logical_server = $server.ServerName
PS /home/ipslabs> $databaseName = $databaseName.DatabaseName
```

```
PS /home/ipslabs> $databaseName = $databaseName.Da
```

2. Set the defaults in Cloud Shell to specify your default resource group and Azure SQL Database logical server.

```
az configure --defaults group=$resourceGroup sql-server=$logical_server
```

```
PS /home/ipslabs> az configure --defaults group=$resourceGroup sql-server=$logical_server
```

3. Run the following command:

```
az configure --list-default
```

```
PS /home/ipslabs> az configure --list-defaults
```

4. Run the following command to show all databases:

```
PS /home/ipslabs> az sql db list
```

5. Run the following command if you just want to see specifics for the database:

```
PS /home/ipslabs> az sql db show --name $databaseName
```

6. Run the following command to determine database size and usage:

```
PS /home/ipslabs> az sql db list-usages --name $databaseName
```

Manage Connection Policies with Azure CLI

You might use the Azure CLI or Azure PowerShell commands for updating the connection policy.

1. See what the current policy is by using the Azure CLI.

```
PS /home/ipslabs> az sql server conn-policy show
```

The results tell you the connection type is Default.

2. Set the connection policy to Proxy and determine the round-trip time.

```
# update policy
az sql server conn-policy update --connection-type Proxy
# confirm update
az sql server conn-policy show
```

```
PS /home/ipslabs> # update policy
PS /home/ipslabs> az sql server conn-policy update --connection-type Proxy
```

```
PS /home/ipslabs> # confirm update
PS /home/ipslabs> az sql server conn-policy show
```

3. To test round-trip time, you can connect with SSMS.

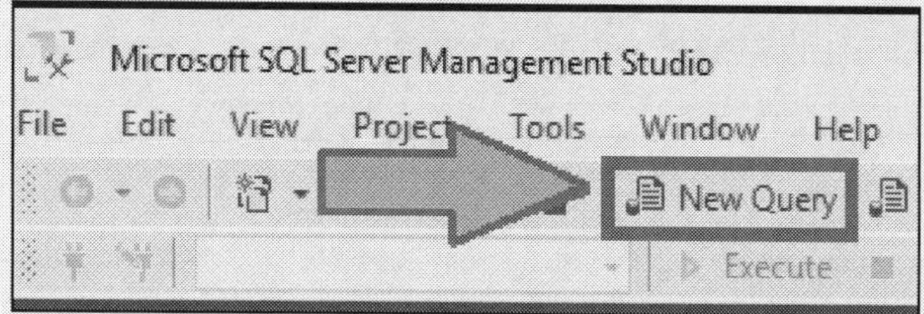


```
-- Proxy
SELECT * FROM SalesLT.Product
GO 10
```

After ten trials, an average wait time on server replies might be something like 46.6000. Make a note of the time that you observe.

4. Update the connection policy.

```
# update policy
az sql server conn-policy update --connection-type Redirect
# confirm update
az sql server conn-policy show
```

```
PS /home/ipslabs> # update policy
PS /home/ipslabs> az sql server conn-policy update --connection-type Redirect
```

```
PS /home/ipslabs> # confirm update
PS /home/ipslabs> az sql server conn-policy show
```

5. Create a new query by using the following text:

```
-- Redirect
SELECT * FROM SalesLT.Product
GO 10
```

After ten trials, an average wait time on server replies might be around 25.8000, almost half of the proxy connection policy.

6. Set the policy back to default.

```
# update policy
az sql server conn-policy update --connection-type Default
# confirm update
az sql server conn-policy show
```

```
PS /home/ipslabs> # update policy
PS /home/ipslabs> az sql server conn-policy update --connection-type Proxy
```

```
PS /home/ipslabs> # confirm update
PS /home/ipslabs> az sql server conn-policy show
```

Load Data into Azure SQL Database

In this exercise, you will explore one scenario for bulk loading data from Azure Blob storage by using T-SQL and shared access signatures into Azure SQL Database.

sqlcmd in Azure Cloud Shell

1. You first need to change the terminal mode by running the following command:

TERM=dumb

```
PS /home/ipslabs> TERM=dumb
```

2. Run the following command:

```
sqlcmd -S <server name>.database.windows.net -P <password> -U cloudadmin -d IPSLT
```

```
PS /home/ipslabs> sqlcmd -S <server name>.database.windows.net -P <password> -U cloudadmin -d IPSLT
```

3. Run the following script in the terminal:

```
IF SCHEMA_ID('DataLoad') IS NULL
EXEC ('CREATE SCHEMA DataLoad')
CREATE TABLE DataLoad.store_returns
(
    sr_returned_date_sk             bigint,
    sr_return_time_sk               bigint,
    sr_item_sk                      bigint
    sr_customer_sk                  bigint,
    sr_cdemo_sk                     bigint,
    sr_hdemo_sk                     bigint,
    sr_addr_sk                      bigint,
    sr_store_sk                     bigint,
    sr_reason_sk                    bigint,
    sr_ticket_number                bigint
    sr_return_quantity              integer,
    sr_return_amt                   float,
    sr_return_tax                   float,
    sr_return_amt_inc_tax           float,
    sr_fee                          float,
    sr_return_ship_cost             float,
    sr_refunded_cash                float,
    sr_reversed_charge              float,
    sr_store_credit                 float,
    sr_net_loss                     float
);
GO
```

4. Next, create a master key.

```
CREATE MASTER KEY
ENCRYPTION BY PASSWORD='MyComplexPassword00!';
GO
```

5. A master key is required to create a "**DATABASE SCOPED CREDENTIAL**" value.

```
CREATE DATABASE SCOPED CREDENTIAL [https://azuresqlworkshopsa.blob.core.windows.net/data/]
WITH IDENTITY = 'SHARED ACCESS SIGNATURE',
SECRET = 'st=2020-09-28T22%3A05%3A27Z&se=2030-09
-29T22%3A05%3A00Z&sp=rl&sv=2018-03-28&sr=c&sig
=52WbuSIJCWyjS6IW6W0ILfIpqh4wLMXmOlifPyOetZI%3D';
GO
```

```
CREATE DATABASE SCOPED CREDENTIAL [https://azuresqlworkshopsa.blob.core.windows.net/data/]
WITH IDENTITY = 'SHARED ACCESS SIGNATURE',
SECRET = 'st=2020-09-28T22%3A05%3A27Z&se=2030-09-29T22%3A05%3A00Z&sp=rl&sv=2018-03-28&sr=c&sig=52WbuSIJCWyjS6IW6W0IL
GO
```

6. Create an external data source for the container.

```
CREATE EXTERNAL DATA SOURCE dataset
WITH
(
    TYPE = BLOB_STORAGE,
    LOCATION = 'https://azuresqlworkshopsa.blob.core.windows.net/data',
    CREDENTIAL = [https://azuresqlworkshopsa.blob.core.windows.net/data/]
);
GO
```

7. Run the following script:

```
SET NOCOUNT ON -- Reduce network traffic by stopping the message that
shows the number of rows affected
BULK INSERT DataLoad.store_returns -- Table you created in step 3
FROM 'dataset/store_returns/store_returns_1.dat' -- Within the container, the location of the file
WITH (
DATA_SOURCE = 'dataset' -- Using the external data source from step 6
,DATAFILETYPE = 'char'
,FIELDTERMINATOR = '\|'
,ROWTERMINATOR = '\|\n'
,BATCHSIZE=100000 -- Reduce network traffic by inserting in batches
, TABLOCK -- Minimize number of log records for the insert operation
);
GO
```


```
SET NOCOUNT ON -- Reduce network traffic by stopping the message that shows the number of rows affected
BULK INSERT DataLoad.store_returns -- Table you created in step 3
FROM 'dataset/store_returns/store_returns_1.dat' -- Within the container, the location of the file
WITH (
DATA_SOURCE = 'dataset' -- Using the external data source from step 6
,DATAFILETYPE = 'char'
,FIELDTERMINATOR = '\|'
,ROWTERMINATOR = '\|\n'
,BATCHSIZE=100000 -- Reduce network traffic by inserting in batches
, TABLOCK -- Minimize number of log records for the insert operation
);
GO
```


8. Check how many rows were inserted into the table.

```
SELECT COUNT(*) FROM DataLoad.store_returns;
GO
```

If you want to run through the exercise again, run the following code to reset what you have done:

```
DROP EXTERNAL DATA SOURCE dataset;
DROP DATABASE SCOPED CREDENTIAL [https://azuresqlworkshopsa.blob.core.windows.net/data/];
DROP TABLE DataLoad.store_returns;
DROP MASTER KEY;
GO
```


```
DROP EXTERNAL DATA SOURCE dataset;
DROP DATABASE SCOPED CREDENTIAL [https://azuresqlworkshopsa.blob.core.windows.net/data/];
DROP TABLE DataLoad.store_returns;
DROP MASTER KEY;
GO
```


Step 02: Configure Auditing

Use Scripts to Deploy Azure SQL Database

1. Start by obtaining your local IP address.

2. Run the following commands in Cloud Shell:

```
$adminSqlLogin = "cloudadmin"
$password = Read-Host "Your username is 'cloudadmin'.
Enter a password for your Azure SQL Database server that meets the password requirements"
# Prompt for local ip address
$ipAddress = Read-Host "Disconnect your VPN, open PowerShell on your machine and run
'(Invoke-WebRequest -Uri "https://ipinfo.io/ip").Content'.
Enter the value (include periods) next to 'Address': "
# Get resource group and location and random string
$resourceGroup = Get-AzResourceGroup | Where ResourceGroupName -like "Sandbox resource group name"
$resourceGroupName = "Sandbox resource group name"
$uniqueID = Get-Random -Minimum 100000 -Maximum 1000000
$storageAccountName = "mslearnsa"+$uniqueID
$location = $resourceGroup.Location
# The logical server name has to be unique in the system
$serverName = "aw-server$($uniqueID)"
```

```
PS /home/ipslabs> $adminSqlLogin = "cloudadmin"
PS /home/ipslabs> $password = Read-Host "Your username is 'cloudadmin'. Please enter a password for your Azure SQL Database server that

Your username is 'cloudadmin'. Please enter a password for your Azure SQL Database server that meets the password requirements: hareem
PS /home/ipslabs> # Prompt for local ip address
PS /home/ipslabs> $ipAddress = Read-Host "Disconnect your VPN, open PowerShell on your machine and run '(Invoke-WebRequest -Uri "https:/
 enter the value (include periods) next to 'Address': "
Disconnect your VPN, open PowerShell on your machine and run '(Invoke-WebRequest -Uri  https://ipinfo.io/ip).Content'. Please enter the
```

```
'Address': : 1
PS /home/ipslabs> # Get resource group and location and random string
PS /home/ipslabs> $resourceGroup = Get-AzResourceGroup | Where ResourceGroupName -like "Sandbox resource group name"
PS /home/ipslabs> $resourceGroupName = "Sandbox resource group name"
PS /home/ipslabs> $uniqueID = Get-Random -Minimum 100000 -Maximum 1000000
PS /home/ipslabs> $storageAccountName = "mslearnsa"+$uniqueID
PS /home/ipslabs> $location = $resourceGroup.Location
PS /home/ipslabs> # The logical server name has to be unique in the system
PS /home/ipslabs> $serverName = "aw-server$($uniqueID)"
```

3. Output and store in a text file the information you will need throughout the module by running the following code in Cloud Shell.

```
Write-Host "Your unique ID for future exercises in this module:" $uniqueID
Write-Host "Your resource group name is:" $resourceGroupName
Write-Host "Your resources were deployed in the following region:" $location
Write-Host "Your server name is:" $serverName
```

```
PS /home/ipslabs> Write-Host "Please note your unique ID for future exercises in this module:"
Please note your unique ID for future exercises in this module:
PS /home/ipslabs> Write-Host $uniqueID
249990
PS /home/ipslabs> Write-Host "Your resource group name is:"
Your resource group name is:
PS /home/ipslabs> Write-Host $resourceGroupName
Sandbox resource group name
PS /home/ipslabs> Write-Host "Your resources were deployed in the following region:"
Your resources were deployed in the following region:
PS /home/ipslabs> Write-Host $location

PS /home/ipslabs> Write-Host "Your server name is:"
Your server name is:
PS /home/ipslabs> Write-Host $serverName
aw-server249990
```

Remember to note your password, unique ID, and region. You will use them throughout the module.

4. Run the script to deploy an Azure SQL Database instance.

```
# The logical server name has to be unique in the system
$serverName = "aw-server$($uniqueID)"
# The sample database name
$databaseName = "AdventureWorks"
# The storage account name has to be unique in the system
$storageAccountName = $("sql$($uniqueID)")
# Create a new server with a system wide unique server name
$server = New-AzSqlServer -ResourceGroupName $resourceGroupName `
    -ServerName $serverName `
    -Location $location `
    -SqlAdministratorCredentials $(New-Object -TypeName System.Management.Automation.
    PSCredential -ArgumentList $adminSqlLogin,
    $(ConvertTo-SecureString -String $password -AsPlainText -Force))
# Create a server firewall rule that allows access from the specified IP range
```

```
and all Azure services
$serverFirewallRule = New-AzSqlServerFirewallRule `
    -ResourceGroupName $resourceGroupName `
    -ServerName $serverName `
    -FirewallRuleName "AllowedIPs" `
    -StartIpAddress $ipAddress -EndIpAddress $ipAddress
$allowAzureIpsRule = New-AzSqlServerFirewallRule `
    -ResourceGroupName $resourceGroupName `
    -ServerName $serverName `
    -AllowAllAzureIPs
# Create a database
$database = New-AzSqlDatabase  -ResourceGroupName $resourceGroupName `
    -ServerName $serverName `
    -DatabaseName $databaseName `
```

```
    -SampleName "AdventureWorksLT" `
    -Edition "GeneralPurpose" -Vcore 2 -ComputeGeneration "Gen5"
# Enable Advanced Defender
$azureDefender = Enable-AzSqlServerAdvancedDataSecurity `
    -ResourceGroupName $resourceGroupName `
    -ServerName $serverName
# Create a storage account
$storageAccount = New-AzStorageAccount -ResourceGroupName $resourceGroupName `
    -AccountName $storageAccountName `
    -Location $location `
    -Type "Standard_LRS"
```

```
PS /home/ipslabs> $server = New-AzSqlServer -ResourceGroupName $resourceGroupName `
>>     -ServerName $serverName `
>>     -Location $location `
>>     -SqlAdministratorCredentials $(New-Object -TypeName System.Management.Automation.PSCredential -ArgumentList $adminSqlLogin, $(ConvertTo-SecureString -String $pas
sword -AsPlainText -Force))
```

```
PS /home/ipslabs> # Create a server firewall rule that allows access from the specified IP range and all Azure services
PS /home/ipslabs> $serverFirewallRule = New-AzSqlServerFirewallRule `
>>     -ResourceGroupName $resourceGroupName `
>>     -ServerName $serverName `
>>     -FirewallRuleName "AllowedIPs" `
```

```
PS /home/ipslabs> # Create a database
PS /home/ipslabs> $database = New-AzSqlDatabase  -ResourceGroupName $resourceGroupName `
>>     -ServerName $serverName `
>>     -DatabaseName $databaseName `
>>     -SampleName "AdventureWorksLT" `
>>     -Edition "GeneralPurpose" -Vcore 2 -ComputeGeneration "Gen5"
WARNING: Upcoming breaking changes in the cmdlet 'New-AzSqlDatabase' :

- The output type 'Microsoft.Azure.Commands.Sql.Database.Model.AzureSqlDatabaseModel' is changing
- The following properties in the output type are being deprecated : 'BackupStorageRedundancy'
- The following properties are being added to the output type : 'CurrentBackupStorageRedundancy' 'RequestedBackupStorageRedundancy'
- The change is expected to take effect from the version : '3.0.0'
Note : Go to https://aka.ms/azps-changewarnings for steps to suppress this breaking change warning, and other information on breaking changes in Azure PowerShell.
```

```
PS /home/ipslabs> # Enable Advanced Defender
PS /home/ipslabs> $azureDefender = Enable-AzSqlServerAdvancedDataSecurity `
>>     -ResourceGroupName $resourceGroupName `
>>     -ServerName $serverName
```

```
PS /home/ipslabs> # Create a storage account
PS /home/ipslabs> $storageAccount = New-AzStorageAccount -ResourceGroupName $resourceGroupName `
>>     -AccountName $storageAccountName `
>>     -Location $location `
>>     -Type "Standard_LRS"
```

5. Change the authentication to "**SQL Server Authentication**."

Connect to Server

SQL Server

Server type: Database Engine
Server name:
Authentication: SQL Server Authentication
Login:
Password:
Remember password

Connect | Cancel | Help | Options >>

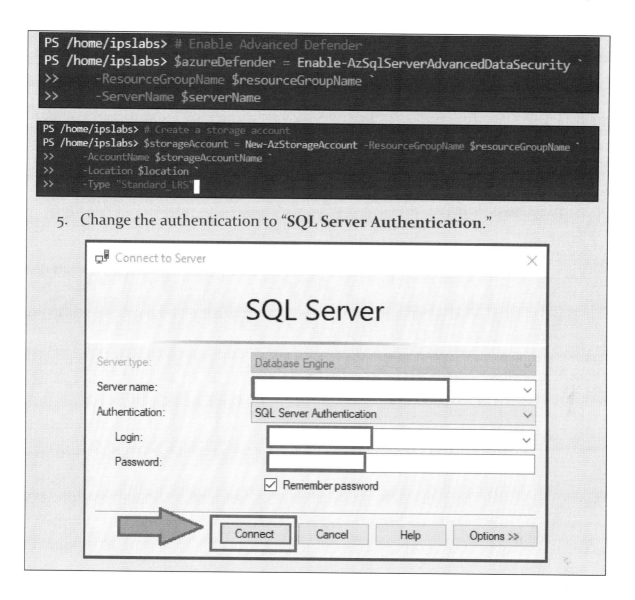

Configure Auditing

1. In the Azure portal, in the search bar, type "**Log Analytics**," and under *Marketplace*, select "**Log Analytics Workspace**." Select your subscription, resource group, and provide a name like "**Azure SQL-la**."

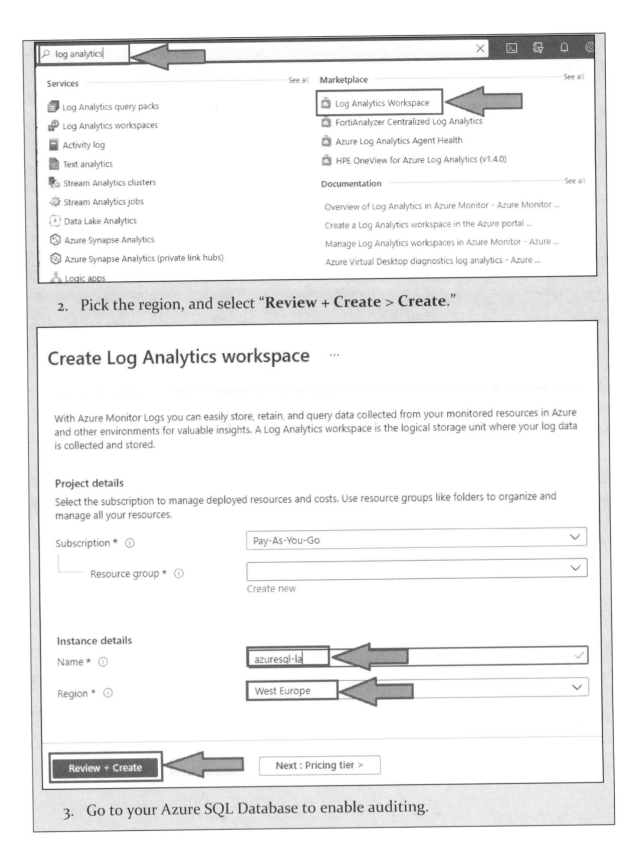

2. Pick the region, and select "**Review + Create > Create**."

3. Go to your Azure SQL Database to enable auditing.

Search (Ctrl+/) « Copy Restore Export Set server firewall Delete Connect with... Feedback

Overview
Activity log
Tags
Diagnose and solve problems
Quick start
Query editor (preview)

Essentials

JSON View

Resource group (change) : cloud-shell-storage-westeurope
Status : Online
Location : East US
Subscription (change) : Pay-As-You-Go
Subscription ID : 797152d3-23c4-499f-bfef-bb103da7d054
Tags (change) : Click here to add tags

Server name : aw-server4064.database.windows.net
Elastic pool : No elastic pool
Connection strings : Show database connection strings
Pricing tier : General Purpose: Gen5, 2 vCores
Earliest restore point : No restore point available

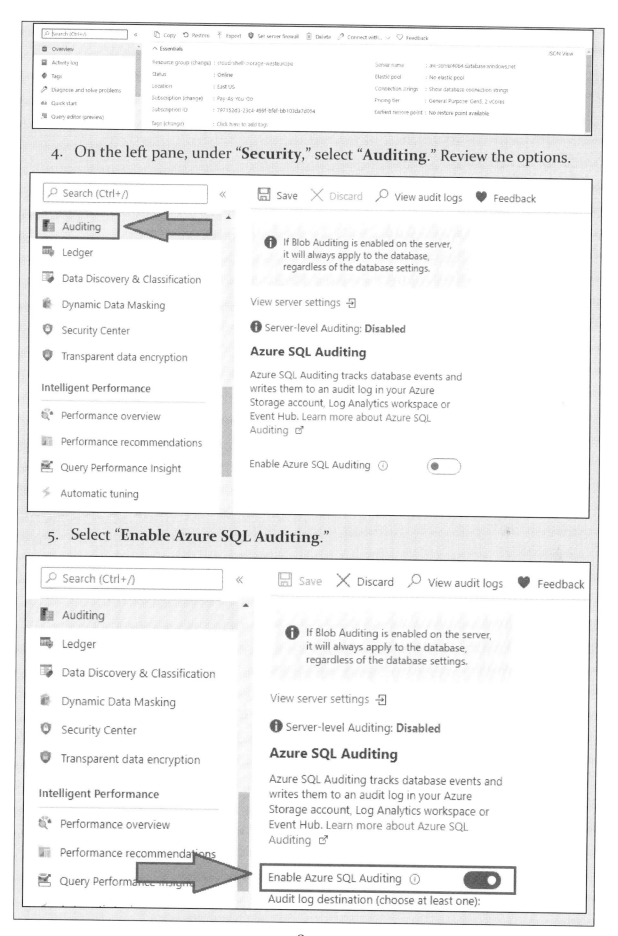

4. On the left pane, under “**Security**,” select “**Auditing**.” Review the options.

Search (Ctrl+/) « Save Discard View audit logs Feedback

Auditing
Ledger
Data Discovery & Classification
Dynamic Data Masking
Security Center
Transparent data encryption

Intelligent Performance

Performance overview
Performance recommendations
Query Performance Insight
Automatic tuning

If Blob Auditing is enabled on the server, it will always apply to the database, regardless of the database settings.

View server settings

Server-level Auditing: **Disabled**

Azure SQL Auditing

Azure SQL Auditing tracks database events and writes them to an audit log in your Azure Storage account, Log Analytics workspace or Event Hub. Learn more about Azure SQL Auditing

Enable Azure SQL Auditing

5. Select “**Enable Azure SQL Auditing**.”

Search (Ctrl+/) « Save Discard View audit logs Feedback

Auditing
Ledger
Data Discovery & Classification
Dynamic Data Masking
Security Center
Transparent data encryption

Intelligent Performance

Performance overview
Performance recommendations
Query Performance Insight

If Blob Auditing is enabled on the server, it will always apply to the database, regardless of the database settings.

View server settings

Server-level Auditing: **Disabled**

Azure SQL Auditing

Azure SQL Auditing tracks database events and writes them to an audit log in your Azure Storage account, Log Analytics workspace or Event Hub. Learn more about Azure SQL Auditing

Enable Azure SQL Auditing

Audit log destination (choose at least one):

6. Select "**Log Analytics**," and under Log Analytics, select the workspace you created.

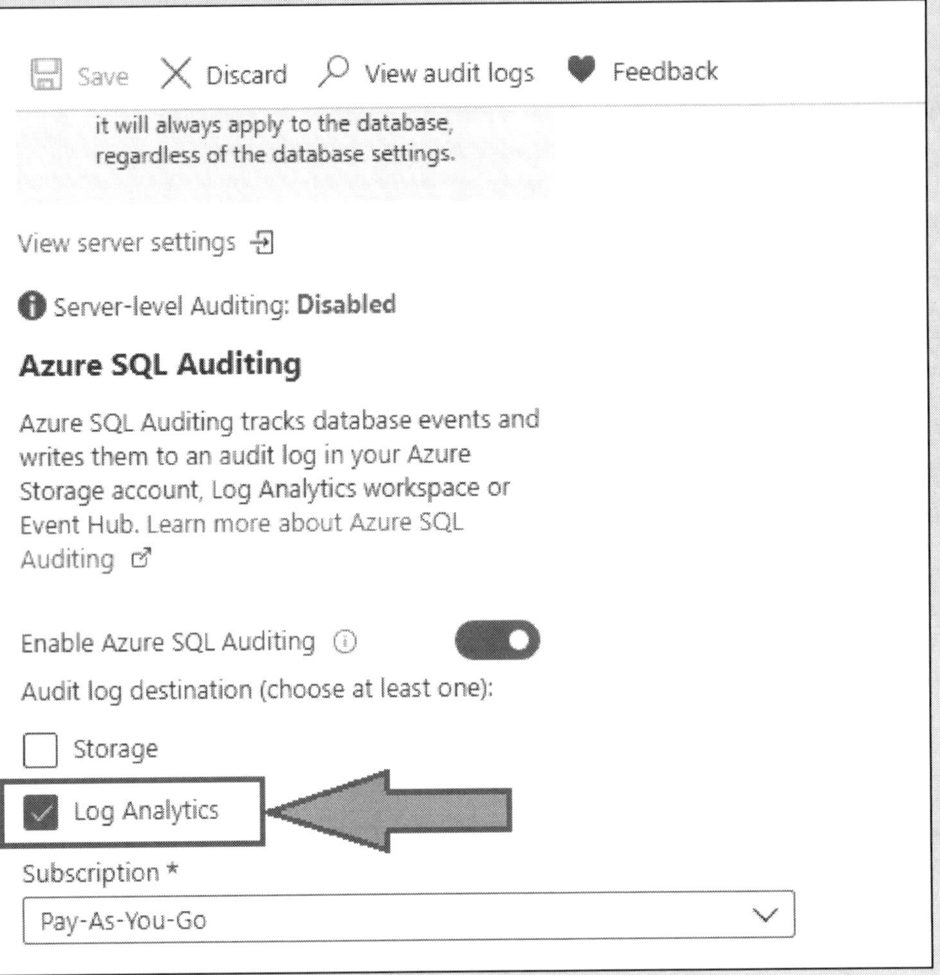

7. Select "**Storage**," and under Storage account, select the storage account that contains *sqlva* and *a random string of letters and numbers*.

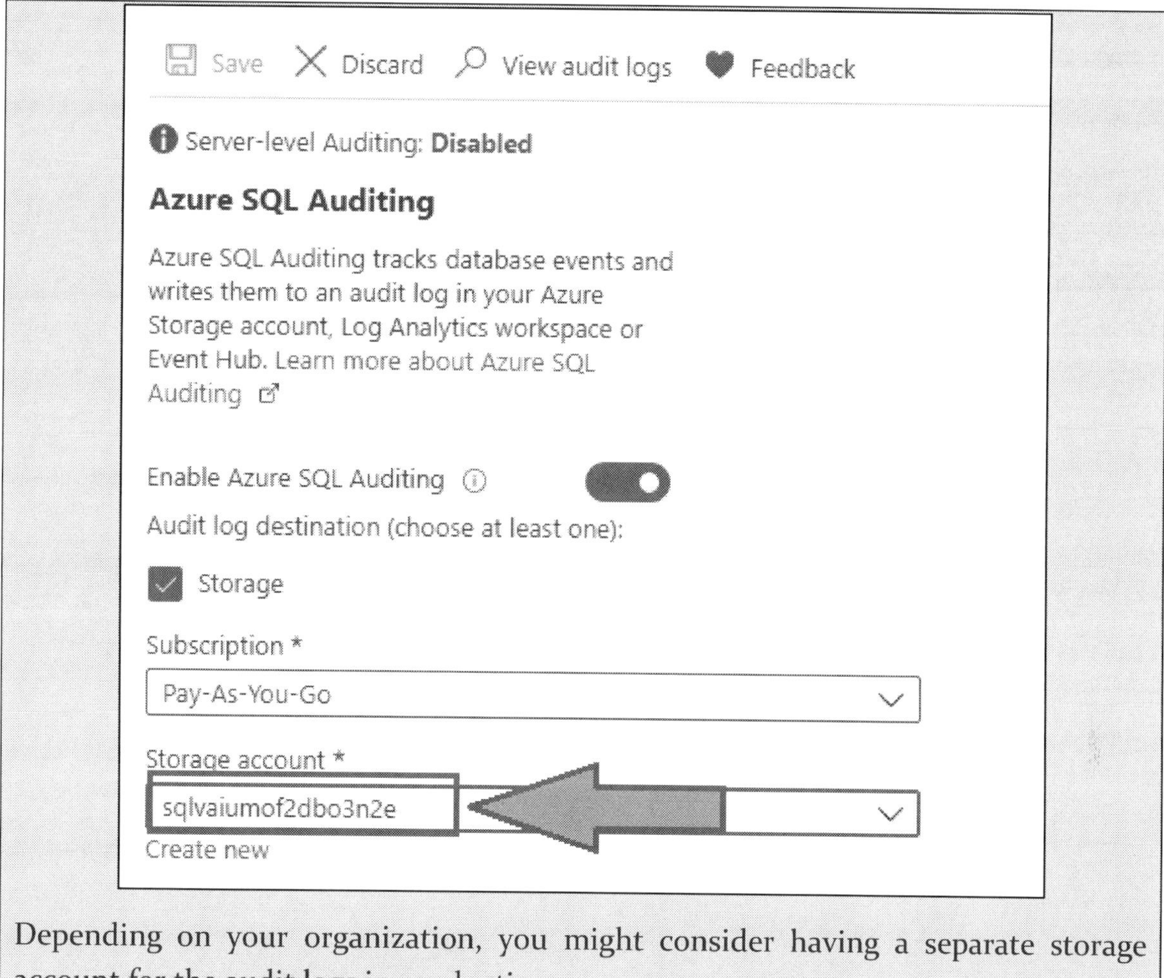

Depending on your organization, you might consider having a separate storage account for the audit logs in production.

8. Under Advanced properties, for "**Retention (Days)**," enter 7, and for a "**Storage Access Key**, select "**Primary**."

Event Hub. Learn more about Azure SQL Auditing

Enable Azure SQL Auditing

Audit log destination (choose at least one):

Storage

Subscription *

Pay-As-You-Go

Storage account *

sqlvaiumof2dbo3n2e

Create new

Advanced properties

Retention (Days)

7

Storage access key

Primary Secondary

9. Click "**Save**."

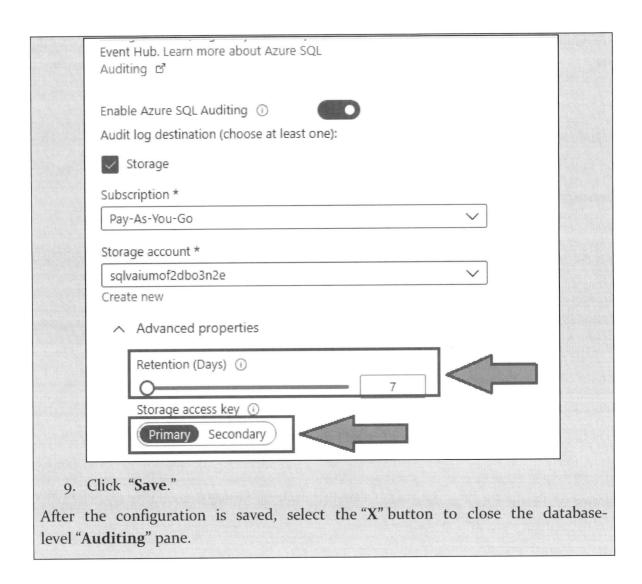

After the configuration is saved, select the "**X**" button to close the database-level "**Auditing**" pane.

Step 03: Secure your Network

Secure the Network

When you deployed your database in Azure SQL Database, the script you ran configured "**Allow Azure services and resources access to this server**" to "**Yes**."

Manage Firewall Rules in the Azure Portal

1. Go to the Azure portal, and find your Azure SQL Database logical server.

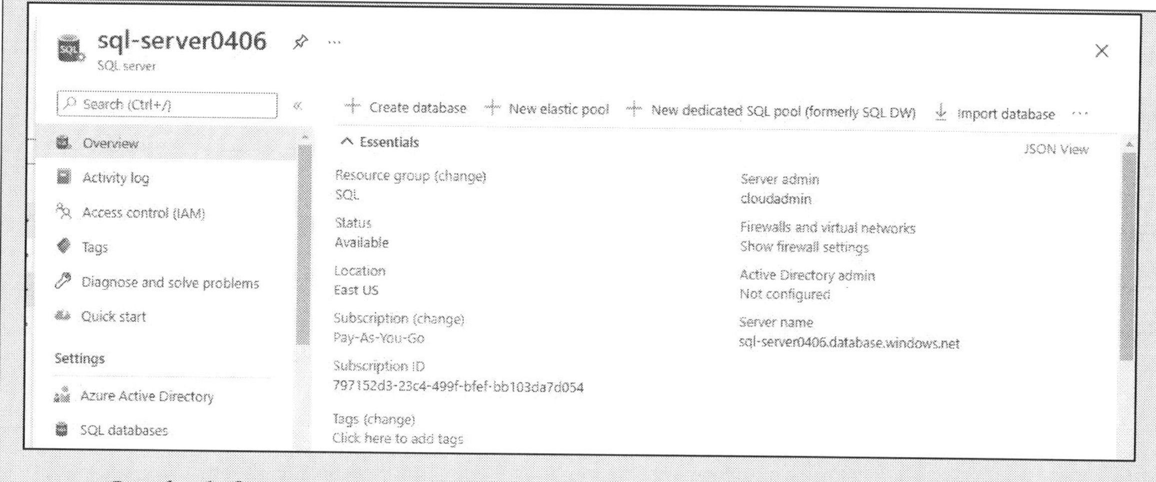

2. On the left pane, under "**Security**," select "**Firewalls and Virtual Networks**."

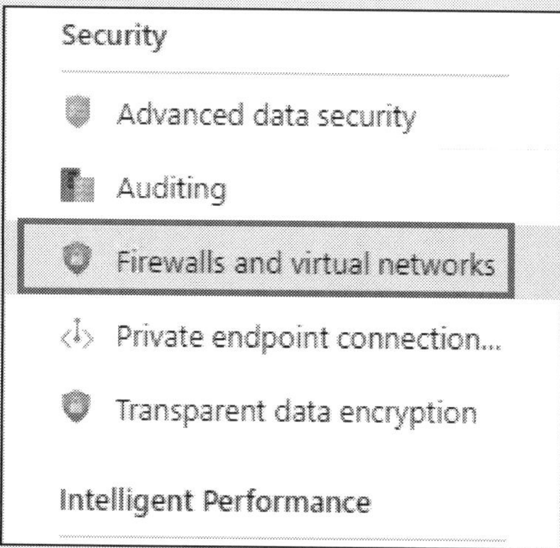

3. Select "**No**" for "**Allow Azure services and resources to access this server**."

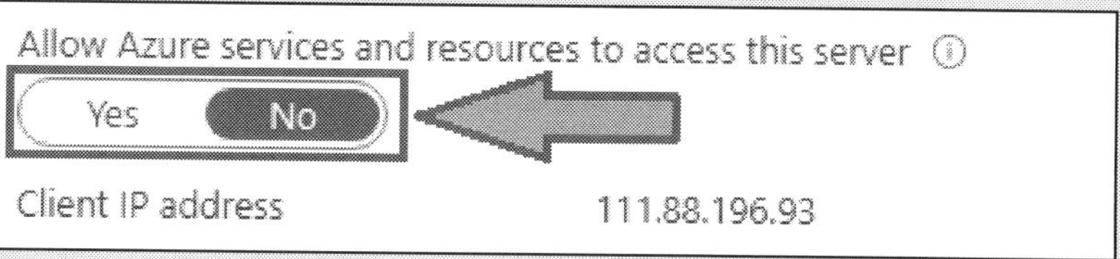

4. Click "**Save**. "
5. To confirm that you still have access from your local machine, go to SQL Server Management Studio (SSMS) and refresh your connection.

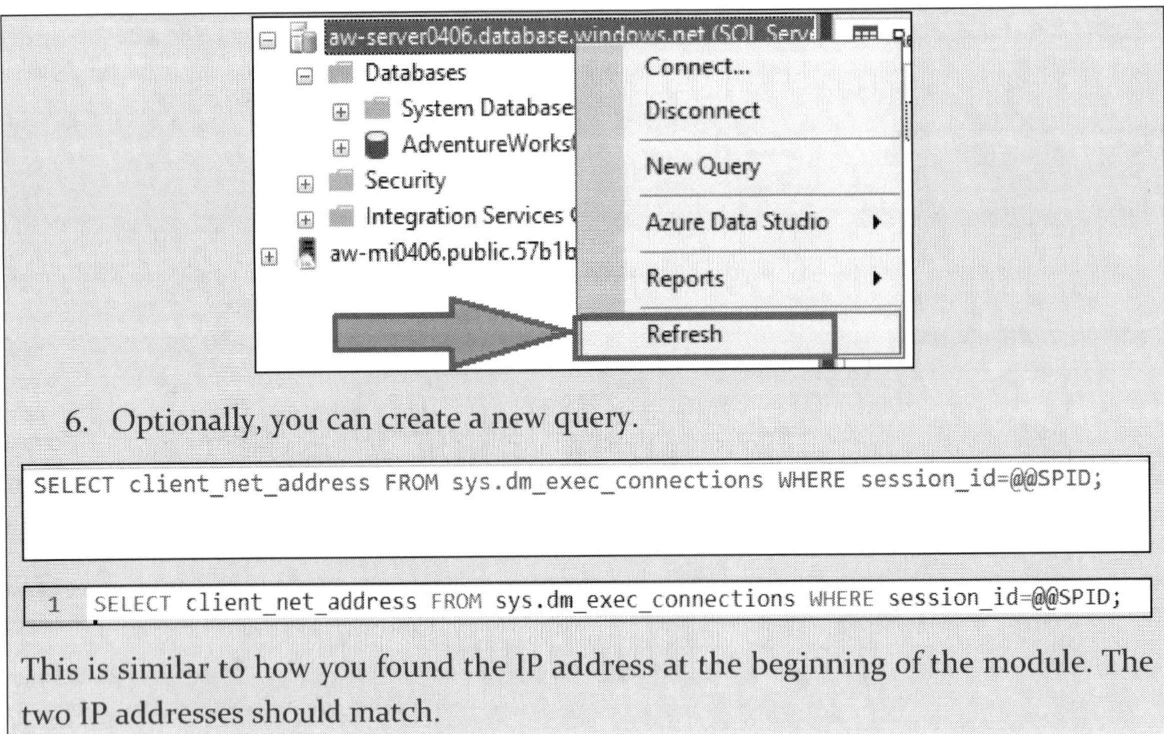

6. Optionally, you can create a new query.

```
SELECT client_net_address FROM sys.dm_exec_connections WHERE session_id=@@SPID;
```

```
1  SELECT client_net_address FROM sys.dm_exec_connections WHERE session_id=@@SPID;
```

This is similar to how you found the IP address at the beginning of the module. The two IP addresses should match.

Manage Firewall Rules with Azure Cloud Shell

You can use the Azure CLI through your Azure virtual machine (VM) or a PowerShell notebook.

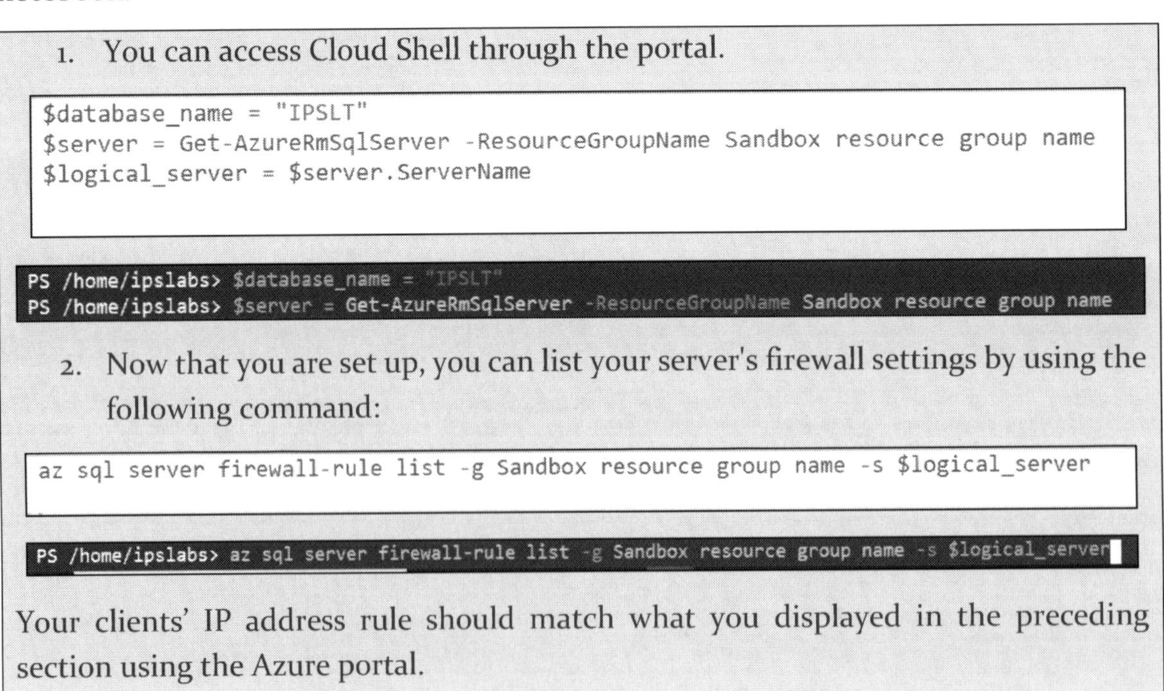

1. You can access Cloud Shell through the portal.

```
$database_name = "IPSLT"
$server = Get-AzureRmSqlServer -ResourceGroupName Sandbox resource group name
$logical_server = $server.ServerName
```

```
PS /home/ipslabs> $database_name = "IPSLT"
PS /home/ipslabs> $server = Get-AzureRmSqlServer -ResourceGroupName Sandbox resource group name
```

2. Now that you are set up, you can list your server's firewall settings by using the following command:

```
az sql server firewall-rule list -g Sandbox resource group name -s $logical_server
```

```
PS /home/ipslabs> az sql server firewall-rule list -g Sandbox resource group name -s $logical_server
```

Your clients' IP address rule should match what you displayed in the preceding section using the Azure portal.

Step 04: Configure Authentication

In this exercise, you will create logins, users, and admins, and you will grant Azure Active Directory (Azure AD) users access to the database, as you would for regular users in SQL Server.

1. Connect to your database.

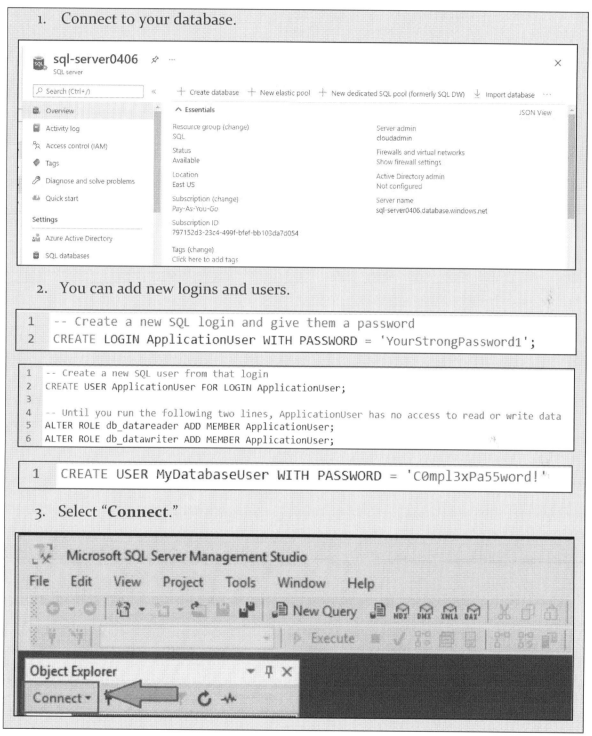

2. You can add new logins and users.

```
-- Create a new SQL login and give them a password
CREATE LOGIN ApplicationUser WITH PASSWORD = 'YourStrongPassword1';
```

```
-- Create a new SQL user from that login
CREATE USER ApplicationUser FOR LOGIN ApplicationUser;

-- Until you run the following two lines, ApplicationUser has no access to read or write data
ALTER ROLE db_datareader ADD MEMBER ApplicationUser;
ALTER ROLE db_datawriter ADD MEMBER ApplicationUser;
```

```
CREATE USER MyDatabaseUser WITH PASSWORD = 'C0mpl3xPa55word!'
```

3. Select "**Connect.**"

Step 05: Manage Security and Azure Defender

In this exercise, you will confirm that Advanced-Data Security is enabled, and you will explore some of the features within each of the capabilities mentioned in the previous unit.

Configure Azure Defender

1. In the Azure Portal, go to your "**Azure SQL Database**" logical server.

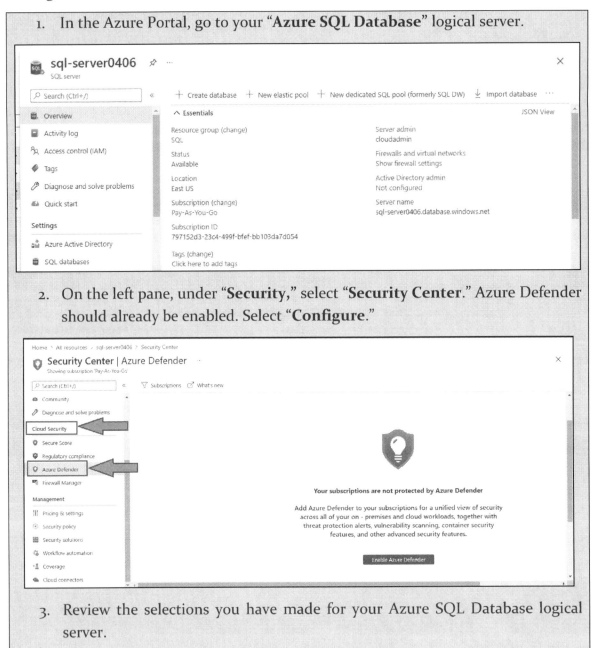

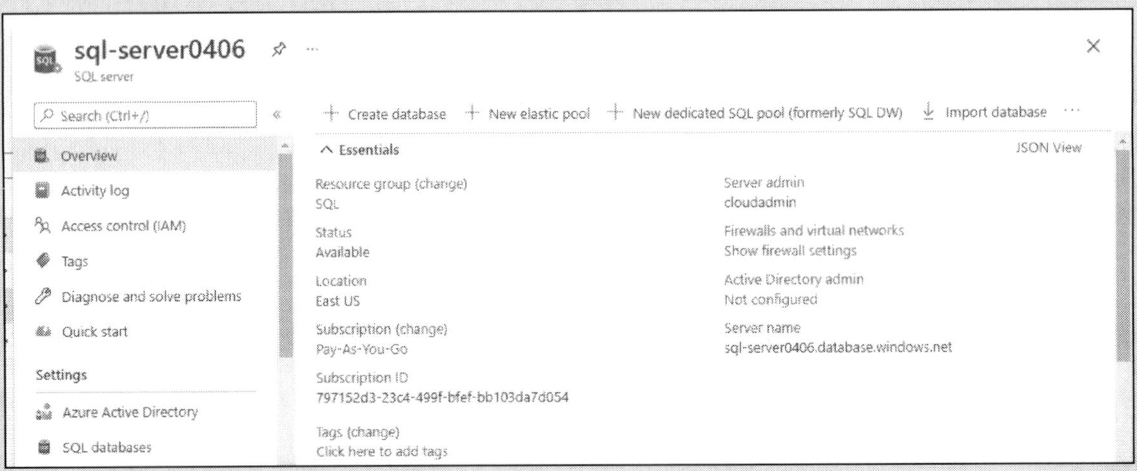

2. On the left pane, under "**Security,**" select "**Security Center**." Azure Defender should already be enabled. Select "**Configure**."

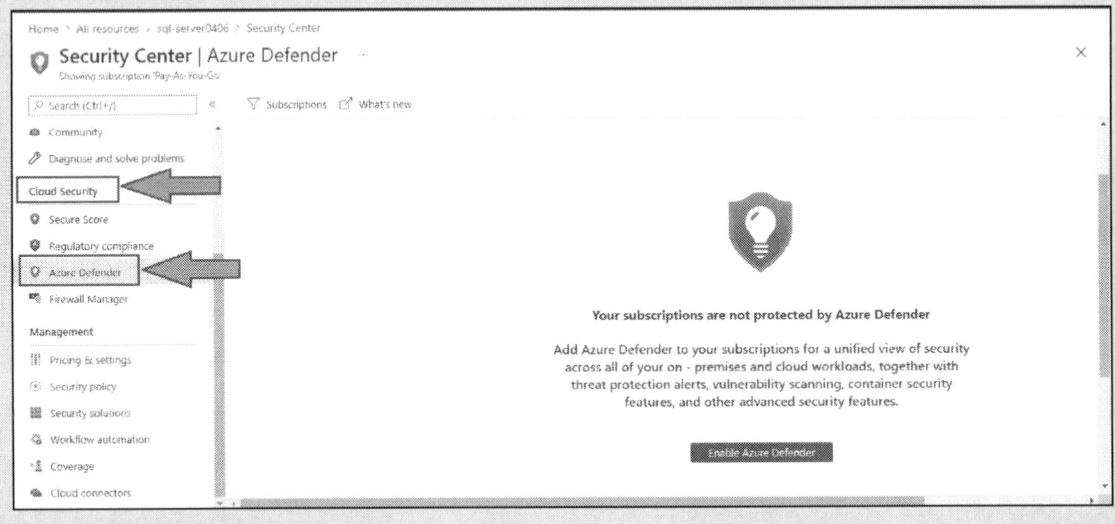

3. Review the selections you have made for your Azure SQL Database logical server.

Data Discovery & Classification

1. On the left pane, under "**Security,**" select "**Data Discovery & Classification.**"

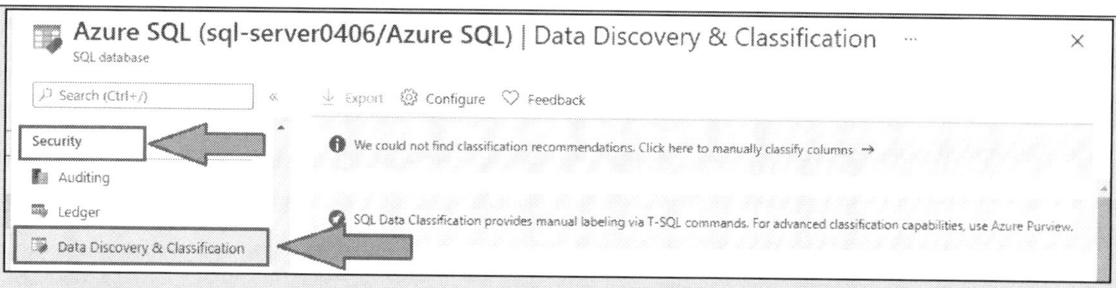

2. Review "**Data Discovery & Classification.**"
3. Click on "**Overview.**"

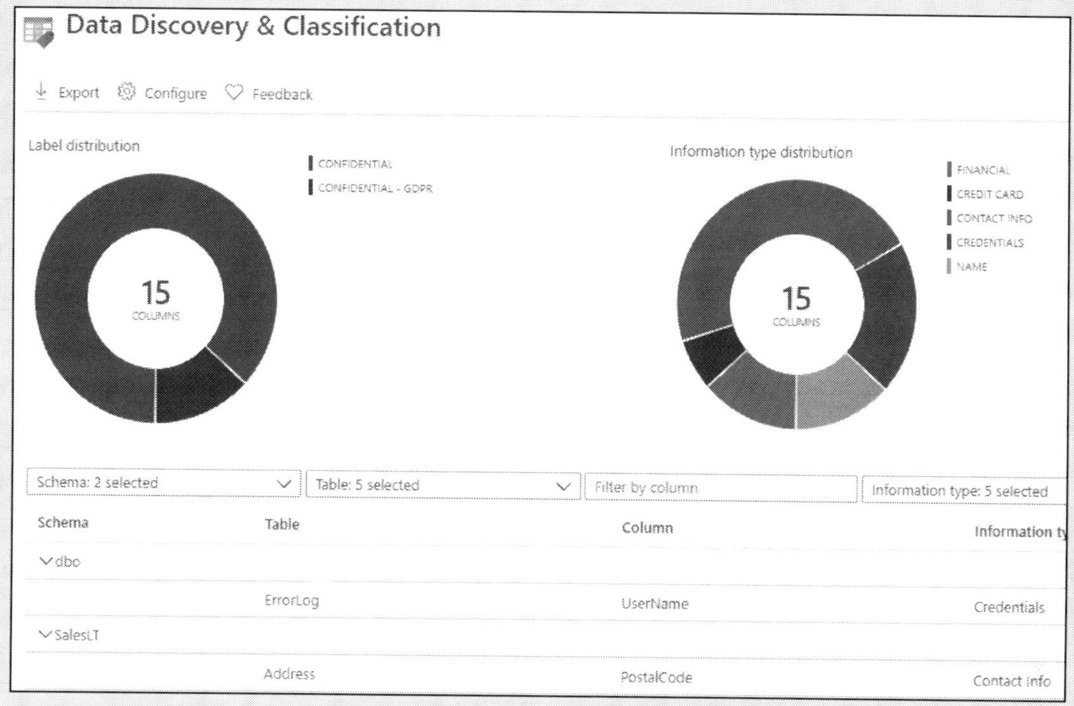

Vulnerability Assessment

1. Select the "**Security Center**" tab under Security to view the "**Security Center**" dashboard for your SQL Database.

2. To begin reviewing the Vulnerability Assessment capabilities, select "**View Additional Findings in Vulnerability Assessment**."

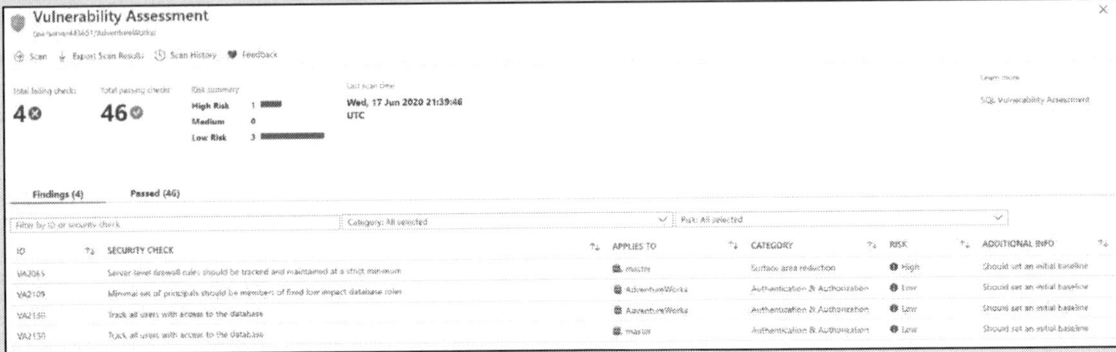

3. Every security risk has a risk level.

If "**VA2065**" does not fail, you can perform a similar exercise later, depending on any failed security checks.

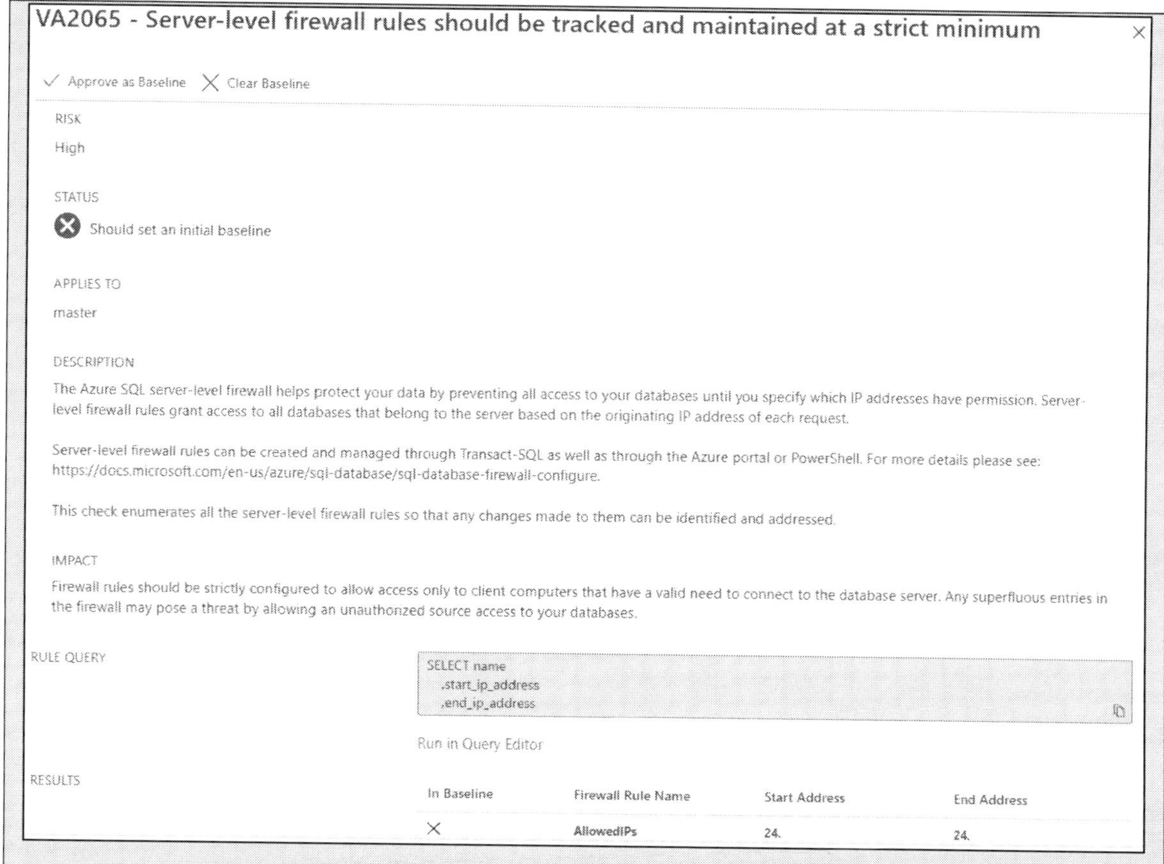

In this image, the Vulnerability Assessment suggests that you configure a baseline of the set firewall rules.

4. You can then complete another scan by selecting "**Scan**."

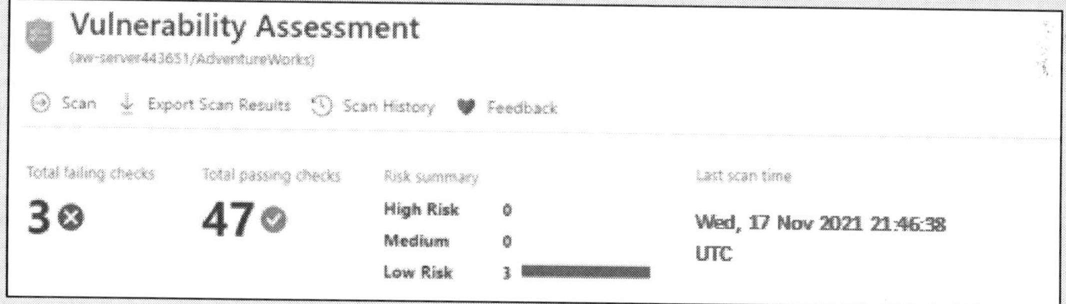

If you click into the preceding passed security check, you should see the baseline you configured.

Advanced Threat Protection

1. In SSMS, select **File** > **New** > **Database Engine Query** to create a query by using a new connection.

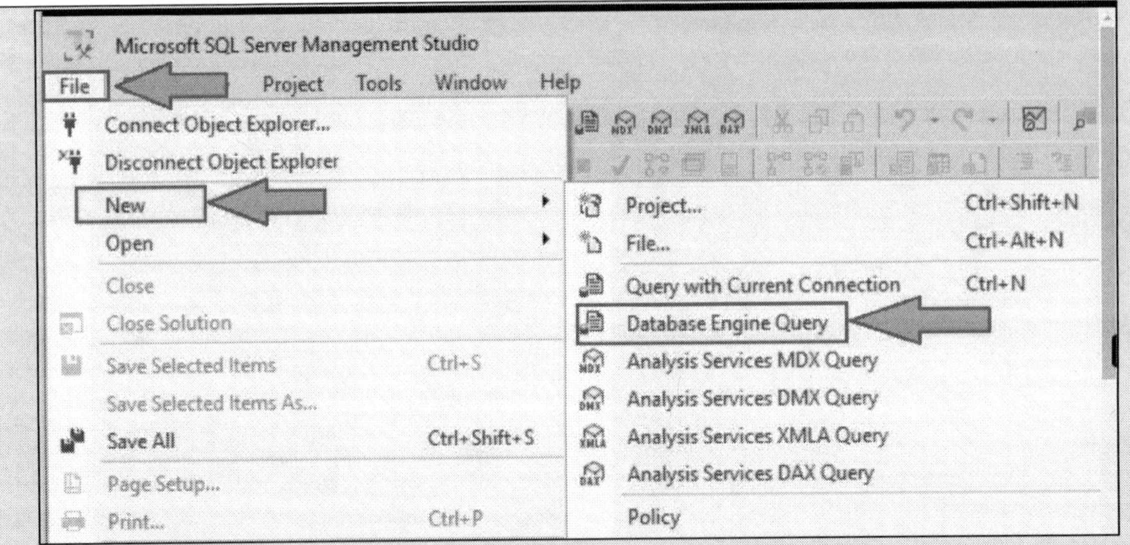

2. In the main login window, log in to the database with SQL authentication.

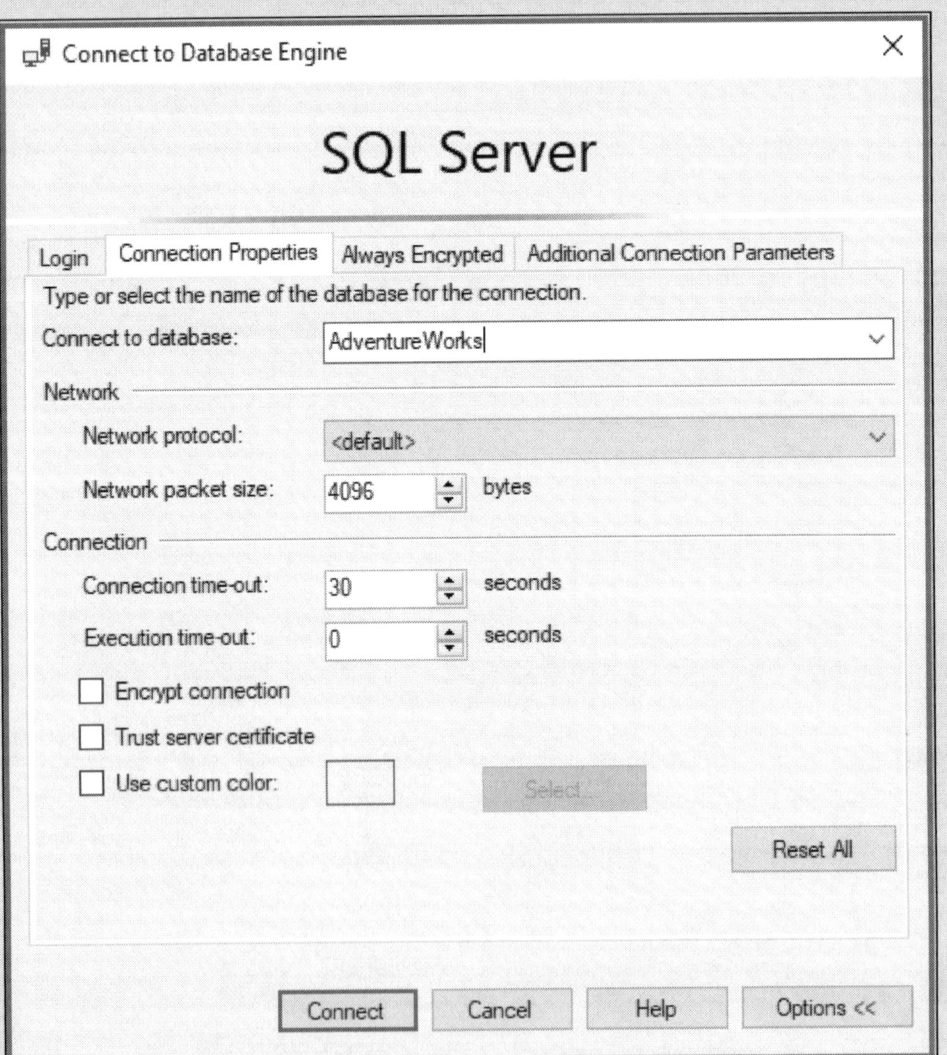

3. Select the "**Additional Connection Parameters**" tab, and then insert the following connection string in the text box.

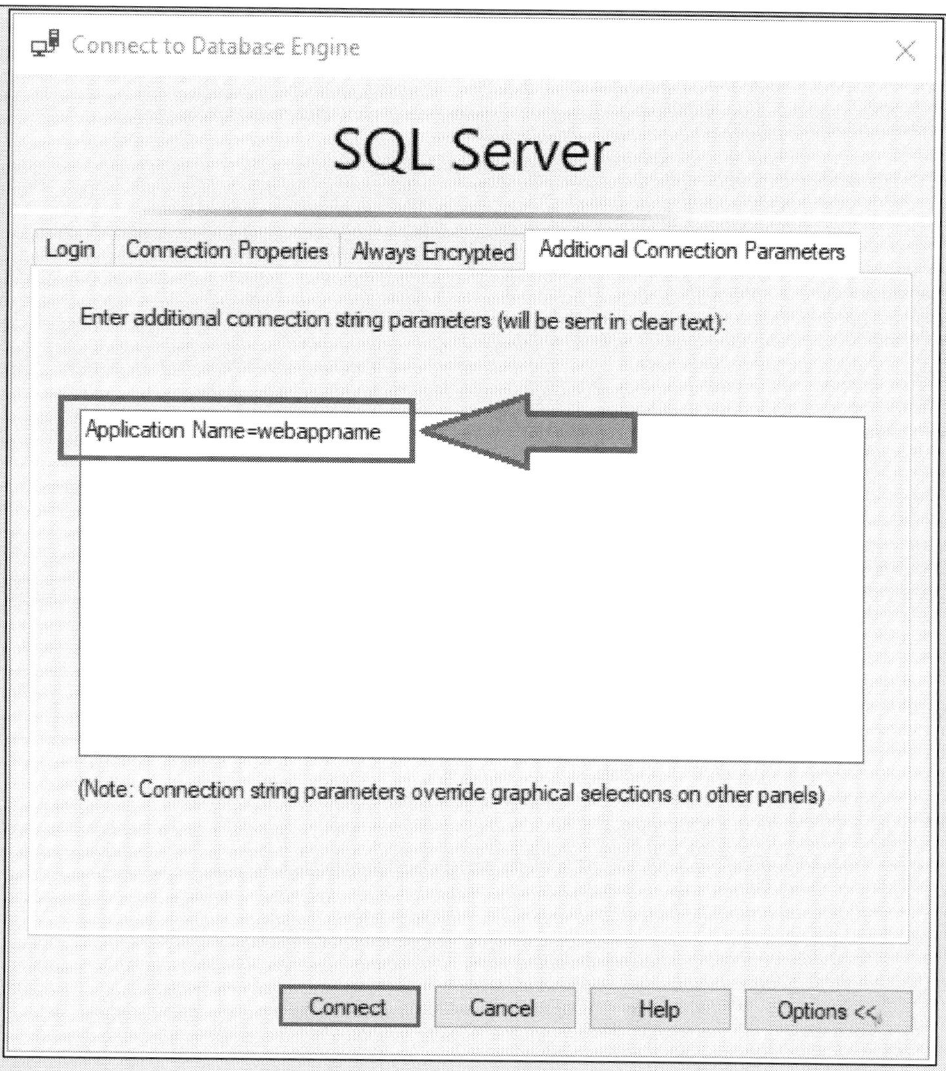

Connect to Database Engine

SQL Server

Login | Connection Properties | Always Encrypted | Additional Connection Parameters

Enter additional connection string parameters (will be sent in clear text):

Application Name=webappname

(Note: Connection string parameters override graphical selections on other panels)

Connect | Cancel | Help | Options <<

4. Select "**Connect**."

Connect to Database Engine

SQL Server

Login | Connection Properties | Always Encrypted | Additional Connection Parameters

Enter additional connection string parameters (will be sent in clear text):

Application Name=webappname

(Note: Connection string parameters override graphical selections on other panels)

Connect | Cancel | Help | Options <<

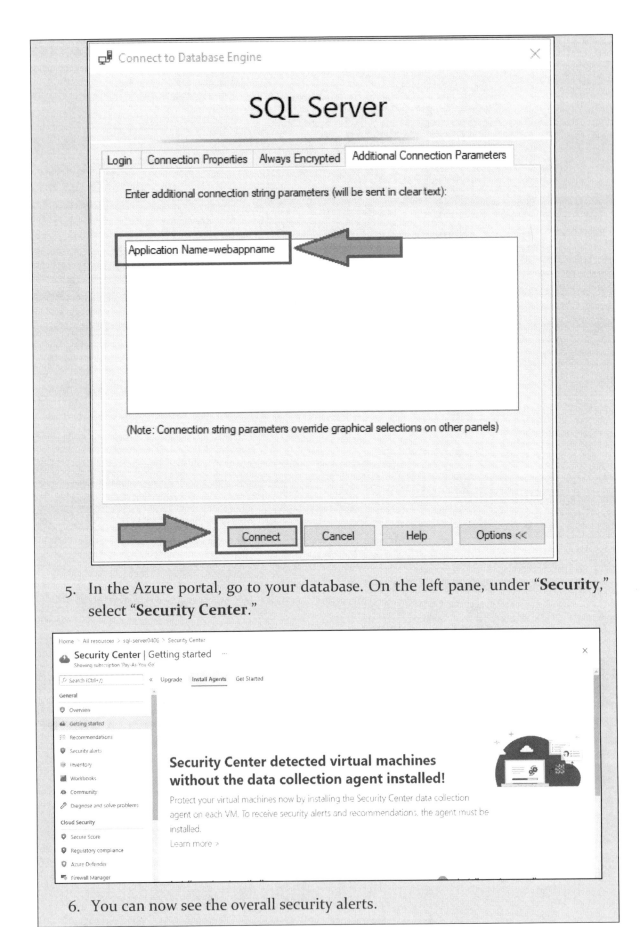

5. In the Azure portal, go to your database. On the left pane, under "**Security**," select "**Security Center**."

Security Center | Getting started

Security Center detected virtual machines without the data collection agent installed!

Protect your virtual machines now by installing the Security Center data collection agent on each VM. To receive security alerts and recommendations, the agent must be installed.

Learn more >

6. You can now see the overall security alerts.

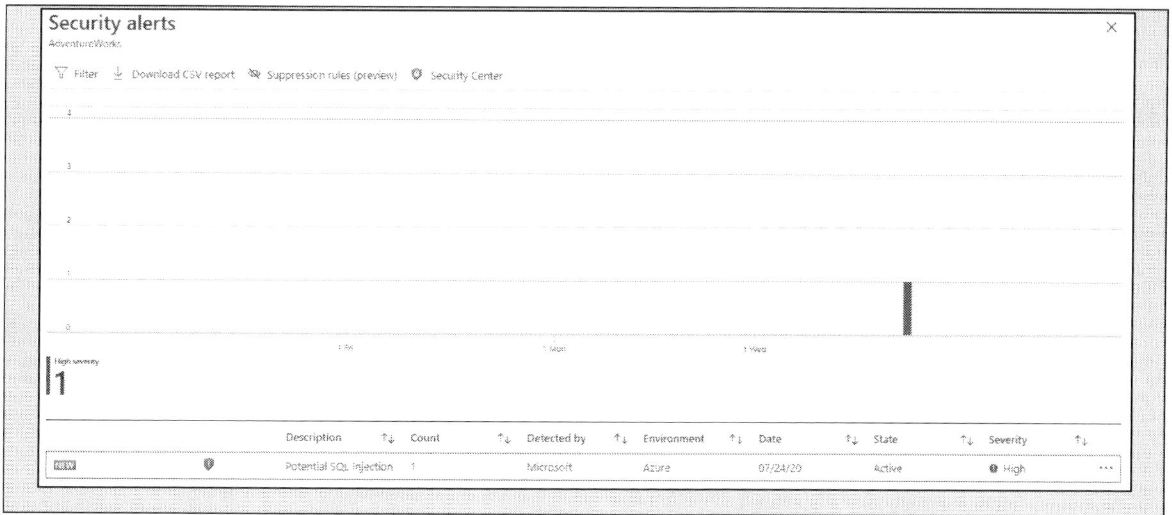

Step 06: Data Classification, Dynamic Data Masking, and SQL Audit

This exercise combines several things you have already learned about in the module: data protection, auditing, and Azure Defender.

Configure Data Classification and Masking

1. In the Azure portal, go to your Azure SQL Database instance (not logical server).

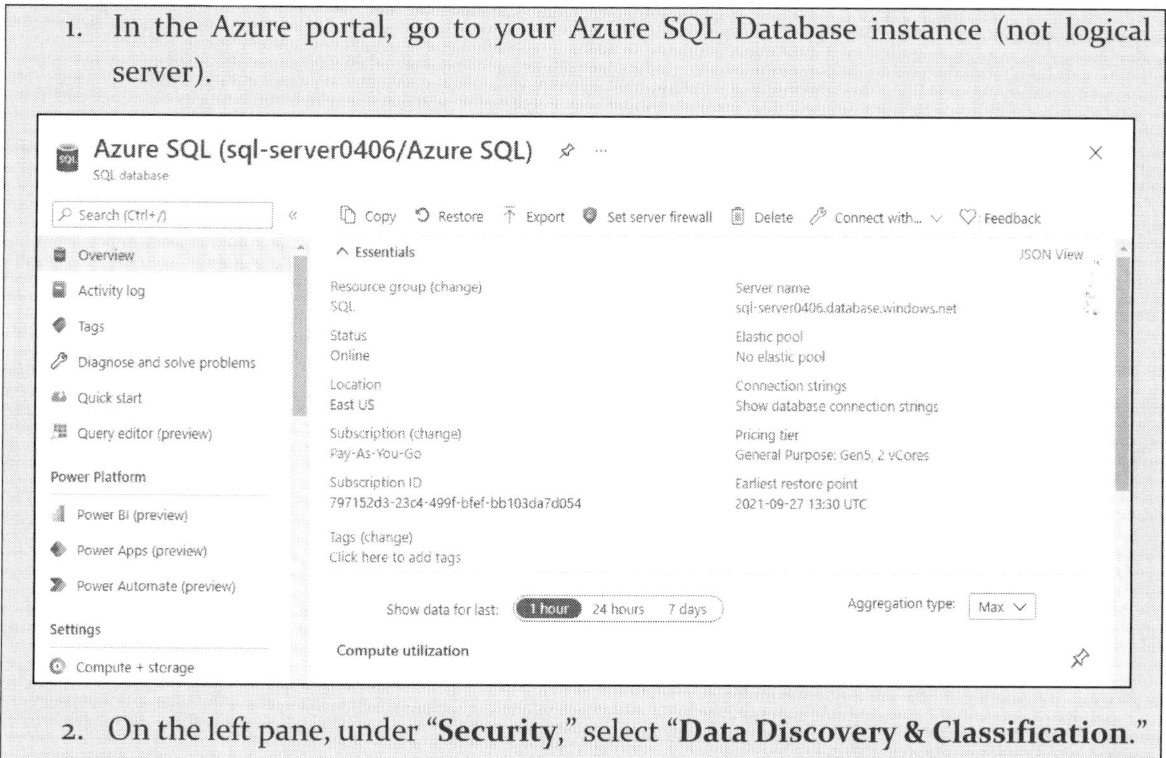

2. On the left pane, under "**Security**," select "**Data Discovery & Classification**."

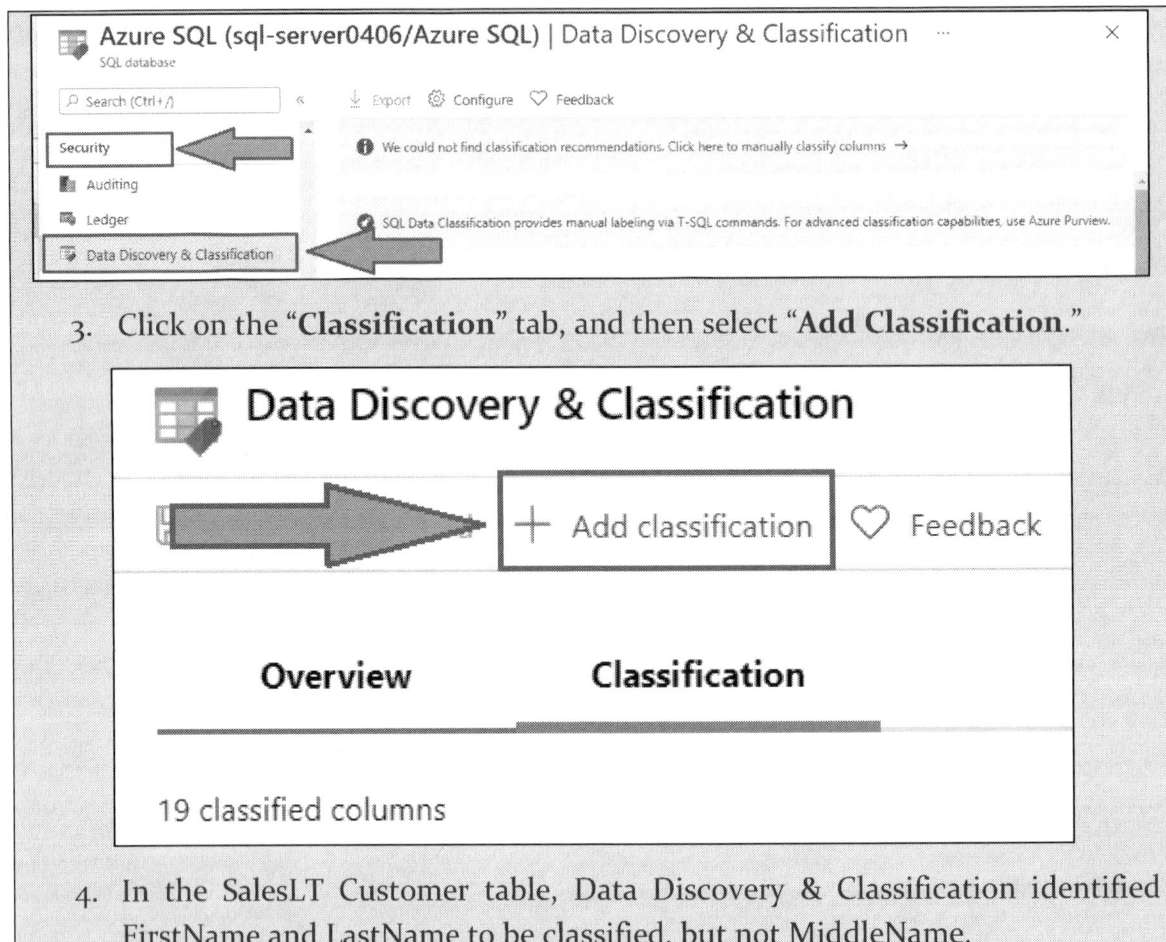

3. Click on the "**Classification**" tab, and then select "**Add Classification**."

4. In the SalesLT Customer table, Data Discovery & Classification identified FirstName and LastName to be classified, but not MiddleName.

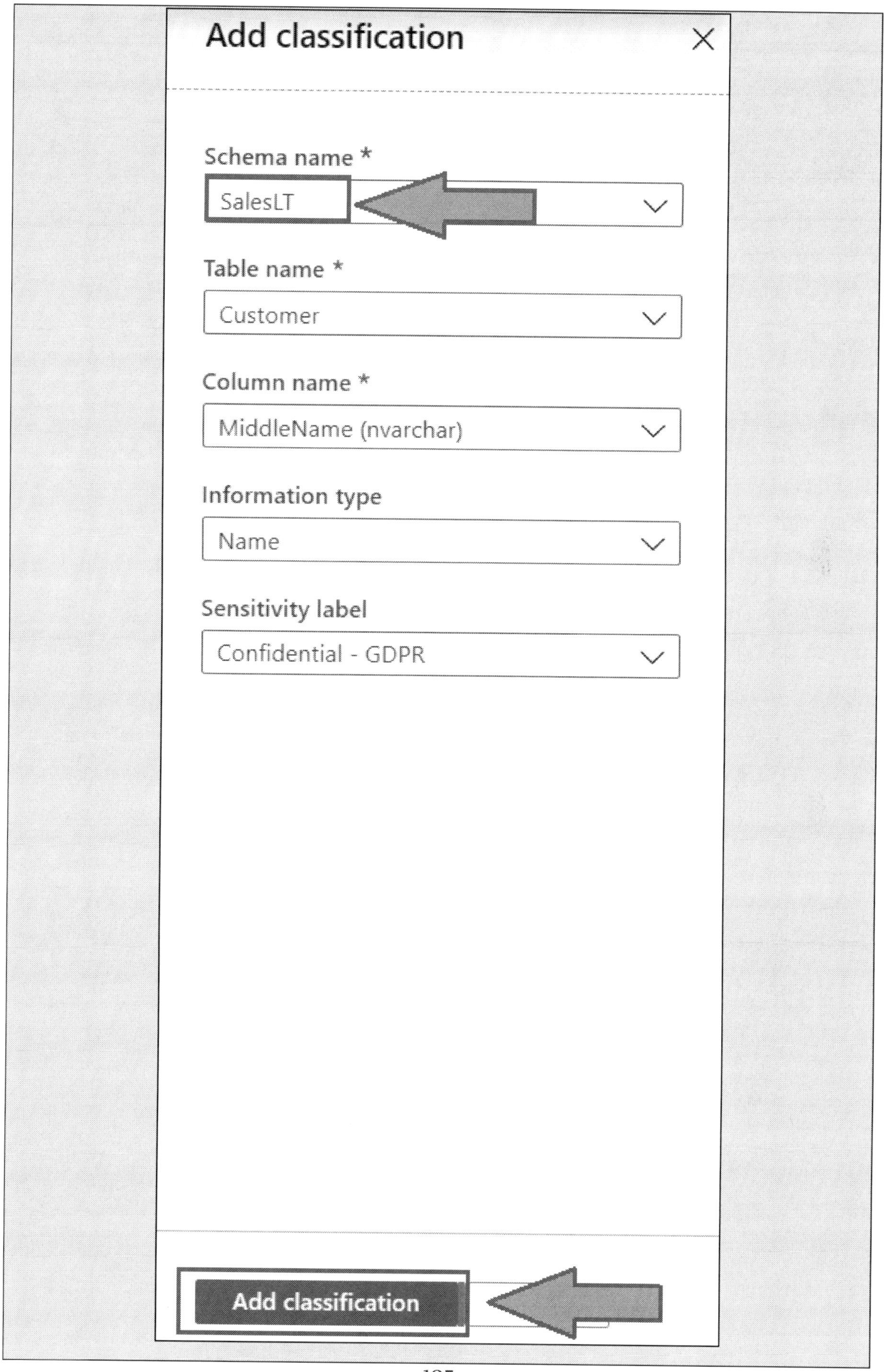

Add classification

Schema name *

SalesLT

Table name *

Customer

Column name *

MiddleName (nvarchar)

Information type

Name

Sensitivity label

Confidential - GDPR

Add classification

5. Select "**Save.**"
6. In the drop-down lists, select the "**SalesLT**" schema, "**Customer**" table, and "**FirstName**" column. Select "**Add**" to add the masking rule.

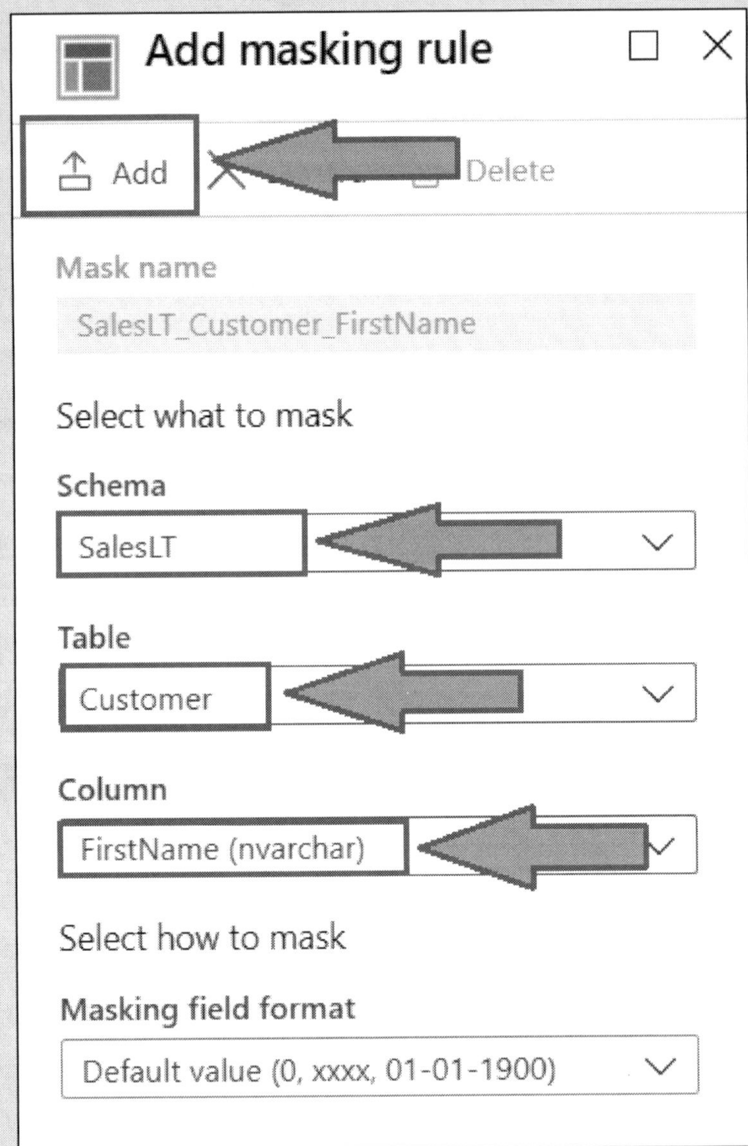

7. Repeat the previous steps for both "**MiddleName**" and "**LastName**" in that table.

You now have three masking rules similar to those shown here:

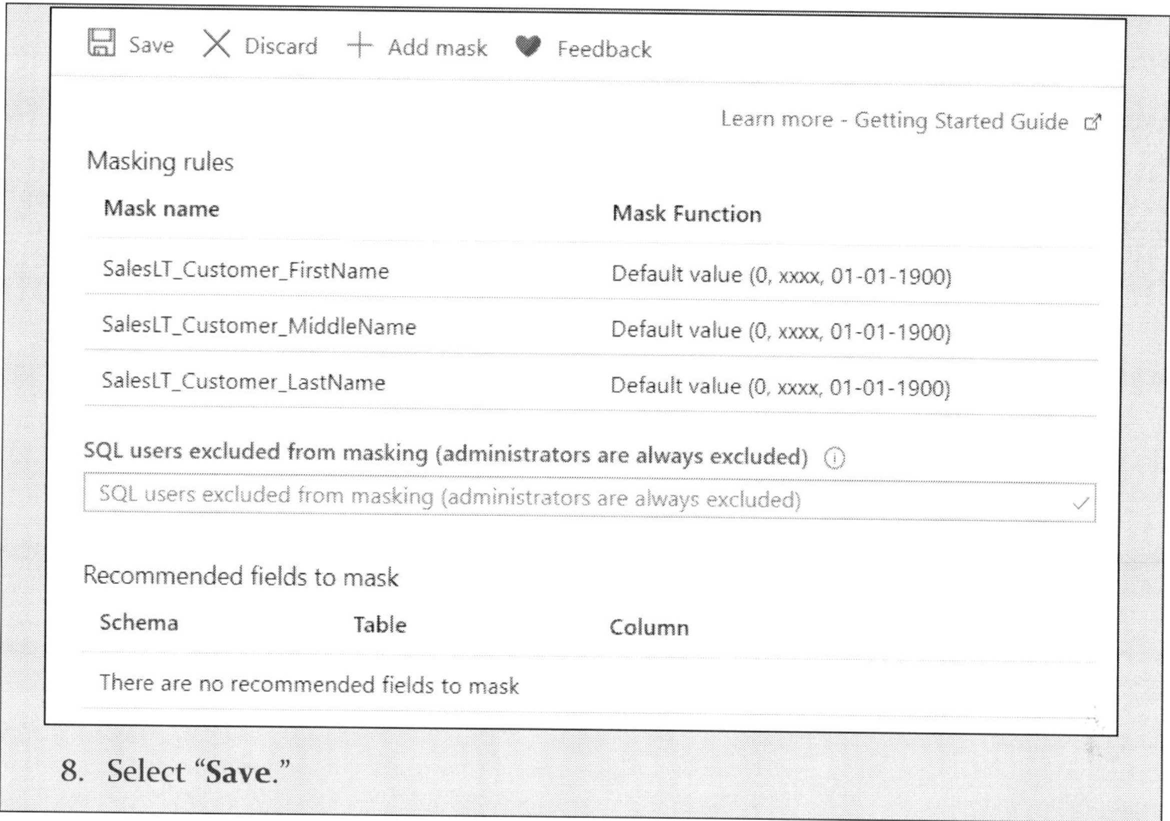

8. Select "**Save**."

Retrieve Data that is Classified and Masked

Next, you simulate someone querying the classified columns and explore Dynamic Data Masking in action.

1. Go to SQL Server Management Studio (SSMS).
2. To create a new query in your database, right-click the database and select "**New Query**."

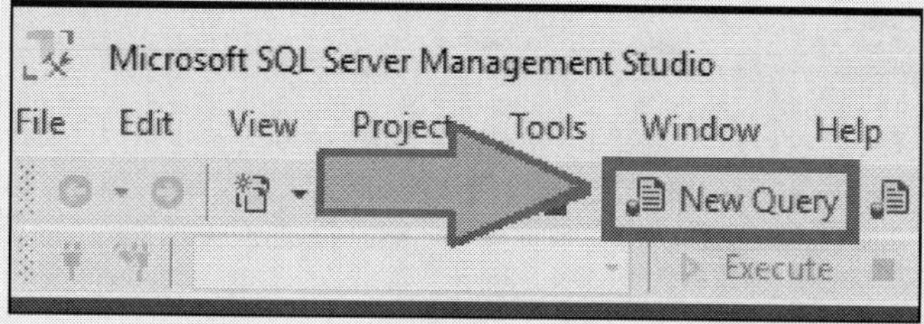


```
SELECT TOP 10 FirstName, MiddleName, LastName
FROM SalesLT.Customer;
```

Your result should display the first ten names, with no masking applied.

	FirstName	MiddleName	LastName
1	Orlando	N.	Gee
2	Keith	NULL	Harris
3	Donna	F.	Carreras
4	Janet	M.	Gates
5	Lucy	NULL	Harrington
6	Rosmarie	J.	Carroll
7	Dominic	P.	Gash
8	Kathleen	M.	Garza
9	Katherine	NULL	Harding
10	Johnny	A.	Caprio

```
-- Create a new SQL user and give them a password
CREATE USER Bob WITH PASSWORD = 'c0mpl3xPassword!';

-- Until you run the following two lines, Bob has no access to read or write data
ALTER ROLE db_datareader ADD MEMBER Bob;
ALTER ROLE db_datawriter ADD MEMBER Bob;

-- Execute as our new, low-privilege user, Bob
EXECUTE AS USER = 'Bob';
SELECT TOP 10 FirstName, MiddleName, LastName
FROM SalesLT.Customer;
REVERT;
```

The result should now display the first ten names.

	FirstName	MiddleName	LastName
1	xxxx	xxxx	xxxx
2	xxxx	NULL	xxxx
3	xxxx	xxxx	xxxx
4	xxxx	xxxx	xxxx
5	xxxx	NULL	xxxx
6	xxxx	xxxx	xxxx
7	xxxx	xxxx	xxxx
8	xxxx	xxxx	xxxx
9	xxxx	NULL	xxxx
10	xxxx	xxxx	xxxx

```
GRANT UNMASK TO Bob;
EXECUTE AS USER = 'Bob';
SELECT TOP 10 FirstName, MiddleName, LastName
FROM SalesLT.Customer;
REVERT;
```

Your results must include the names in full.

	FirstName	MiddleName	LastName
1	Orlando	N.	Gee
2	Keith	NULL	Harris
3	Donna	F.	Carreras
4	Janet	M.	Gates
5	Lucy	NULL	Harrington
6	Rosmarie	J.	Carroll
7	Dominic	P.	Gash
8	Kathleen	M.	Garza
9	Katherine	NULL	Harding
10	Johnny	A.	Caprio

```
-- Remove unmasking privilege
REVOKE UNMASK TO Bob;

-- Execute as Bob
EXECUTE AS USER = 'Bob';
SELECT TOP 10 FirstName, MiddleName, LastName
FROM SalesLT.Customer;
REVERT;
```

Your results should include the masked names.

	FirstName	MiddleName	LastName
1	xxxx	xxxx	xxxx
2	xxxx	NULL	xxxx
3	xxxx	xxxx	xxxx
4	xxxx	xxxx	xxxx
5	xxxx	NULL	xxxx
6	xxxx	xxxx	xxxx
7	xxxx	xxxx	xxxx
8	xxxx	xxxx	xxxx
9	xxxx	NULL	xxxx
10	xxxx	xxxx	xxxx

Review Audit Logs in SSMS

As an admin, you might want to review and audit who is accessing the databases and, specifically, the classified data.

1. Select **File** > **Open** > **Merge Audit Files**.

2. Select "**Add**."

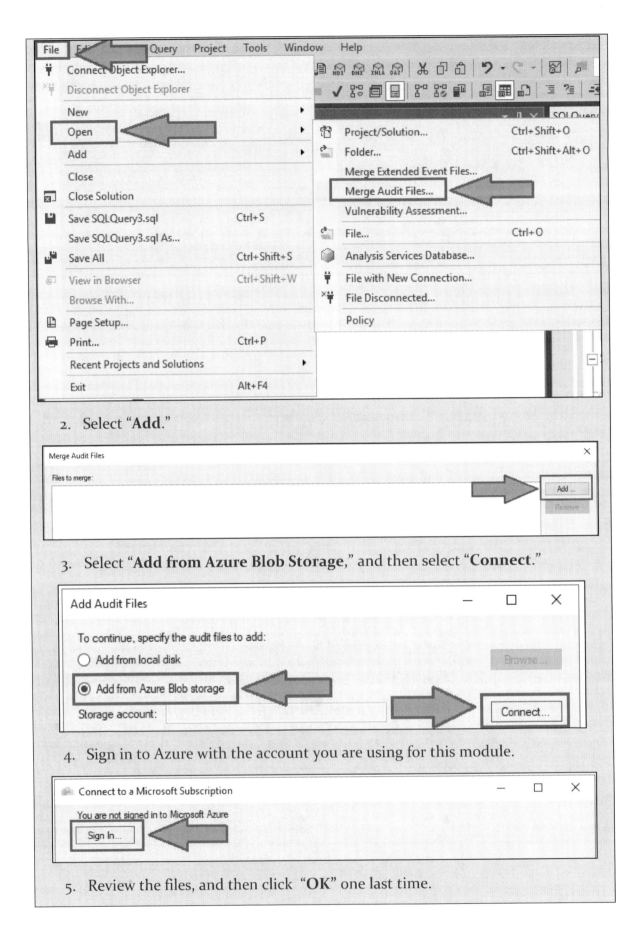

3. Select "**Add from Azure Blob Storage**," and then select "**Connect**."

4. Sign in to Azure with the account you are using for this module.

5. Review the files, and then click "**OK**" one last time.

Review Audit Logs in the Azure portal

This section will expose you to querying security logs in the Azure portal with Log Analytics.

1. In the Azure portal, go to your Azure SQL Database instance. On the left pane, under "**Security**," select "**Auditing > View Audit Logs**."

Azure SQL (sql-server0406/Azure SQL) | Auditing

SQL database

Search (Ctrl+/)

Save Discard View audit logs Feedback

Security

Auditing

Ledger

If Blob Auditing is enabled on the server, it will always apply to the database, regardless of the database settings.

Audit records

Refresh Filter Log Analytics View dashboard

Click here to learn more about methods for viewing & analyzing audit records.

Audit source

Server audit Database audit

Showing audit records up to Mon, 27 Jan 2020 23:49:19 UTC.

Run in Query Editor

Event time (UTC)	Principal name	Event type	Action status
1/27/2020 11:07:25 PM		BATCH COMPLETED	Succeeded
1/27/2020 11:07:25 PM		DATABASE AUTHENTICATION SUCCEEDED	Succeeded
1/27/2020 11:07:25 PM		BATCH COMPLETED	Succeeded
1/27/2020 11:07:25 PM		BATCH COMPLETED	Succeeded
1/27/2020 11:07:12 PM		RPC COMPLETED	Succeeded
1/27/2020 11:07:12 PM		RPC COMPLETED	Succeeded
1/27/2020 11:07:12 PM		BATCH COMPLETED	Succeeded
1/27/2020 11:07:12 PM		DATABASE AUTHENTICATION SUCCEEDED	Succeeded
1/27/2020 11:07:12 PM		BATCH COMPLETED	Succeeded
1/27/2020 11:07:12 PM		RPC COMPLETED	Succeeded

Load more

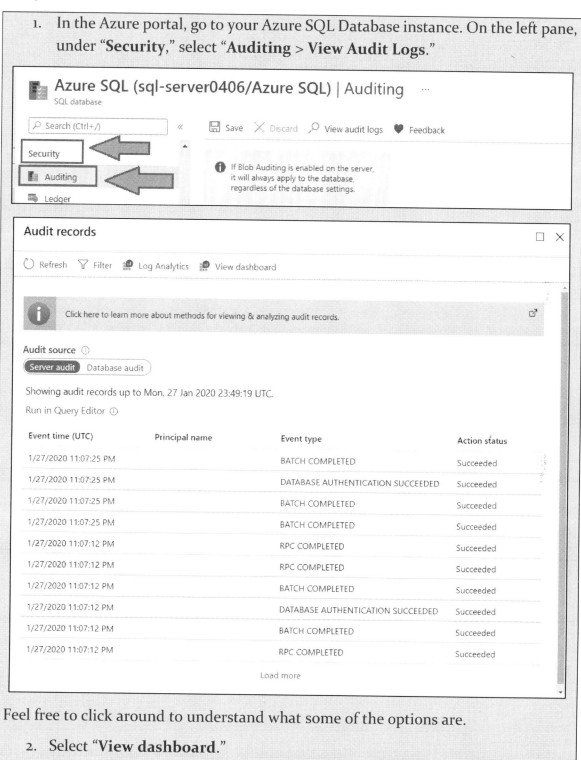

Feel free to click around to understand what some of the options are.

2. Select "**View dashboard**."

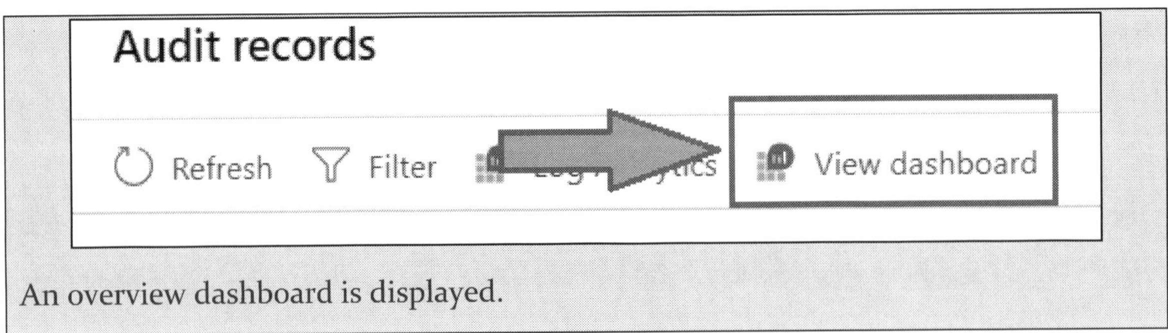

An overview dashboard is displayed.

Step 07: Monitor and Troubleshoot Performance

This exercise will teach you how to monitor and troubleshoot a performance problem with Azure SQL by using familiar and new tools and capabilities.

Use the Query Store for Analysis

1. Open the Query Store folder using the Object Explorer in SSMS to find the Top Resource Consuming Queries report.

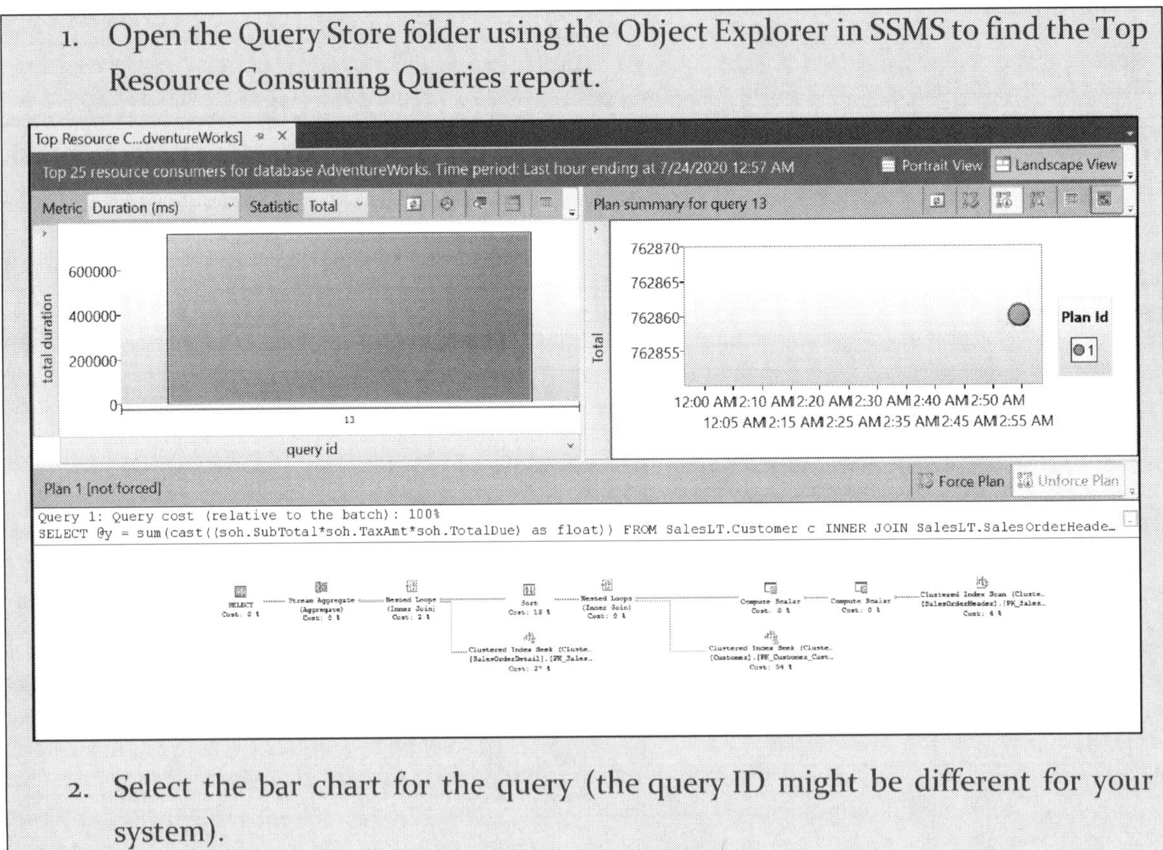

2. Select the bar chart for the query (the query ID might be different for your system).

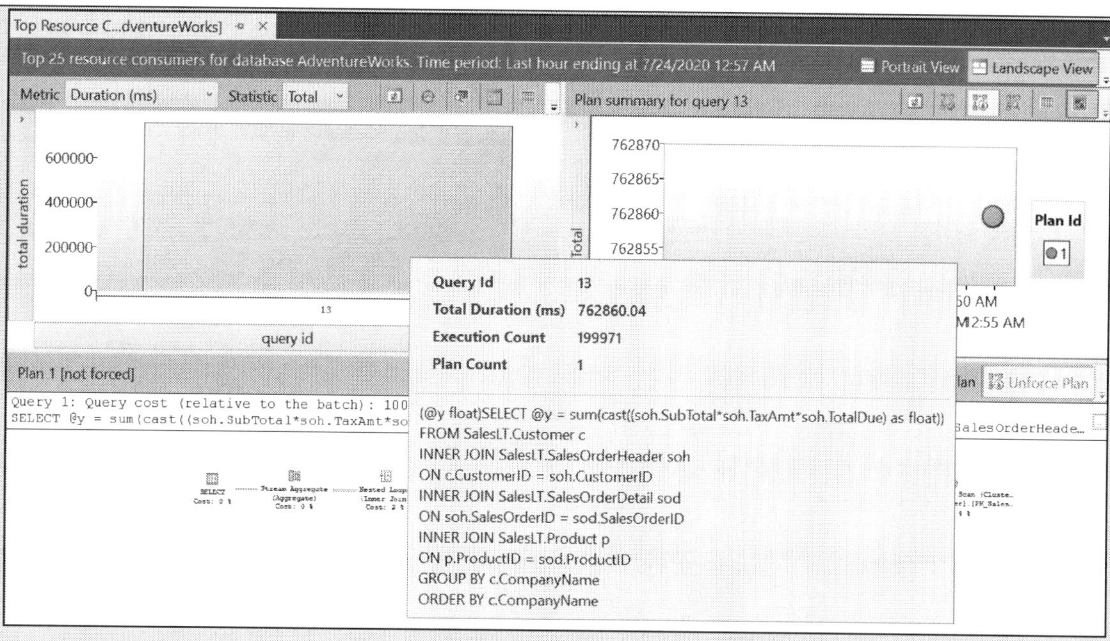

You can see the duration of the text.

3. Go over the dot associated with the plan.

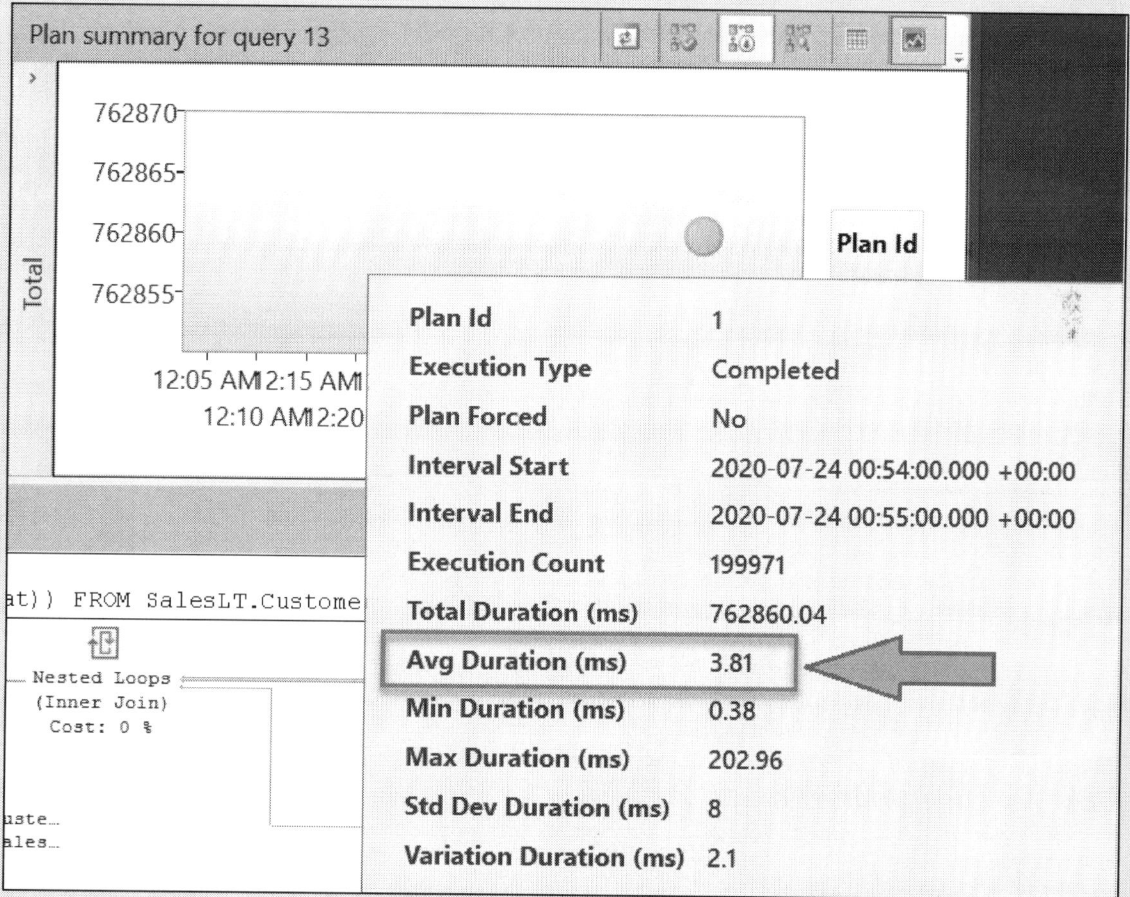

4. The last component is the visual query plan.

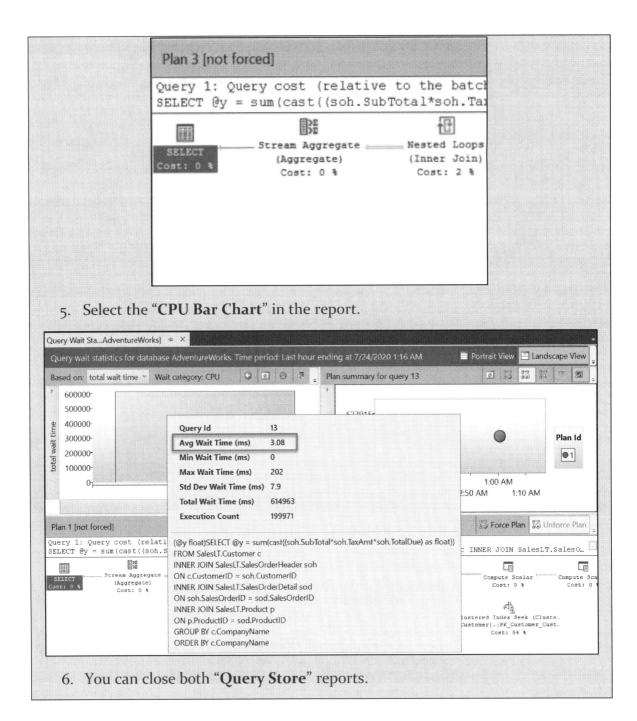

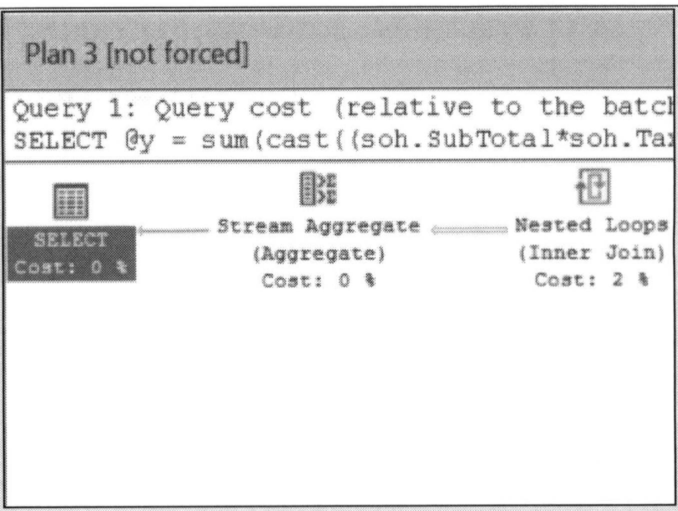

5. Select the "**CPU Bar Chart**" in the report.

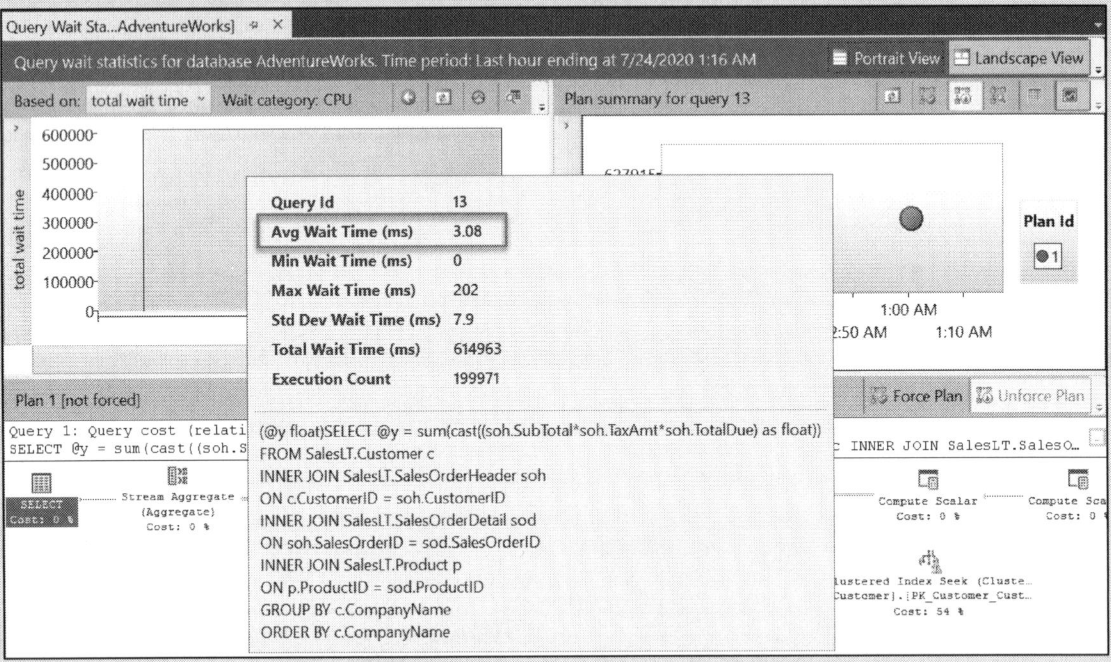

6. You can close both "**Query Store**" reports.

Observe Performance with Azure Monitor

Now use one other method to view the resource usage of our workload. Azure Monitor provides performance metrics that you can view in various ways, including the Azure portal.

1. On the "**Overview**" for a database, the default view in the "**Monitoring**" pane is called "**Compute Utilization.**"

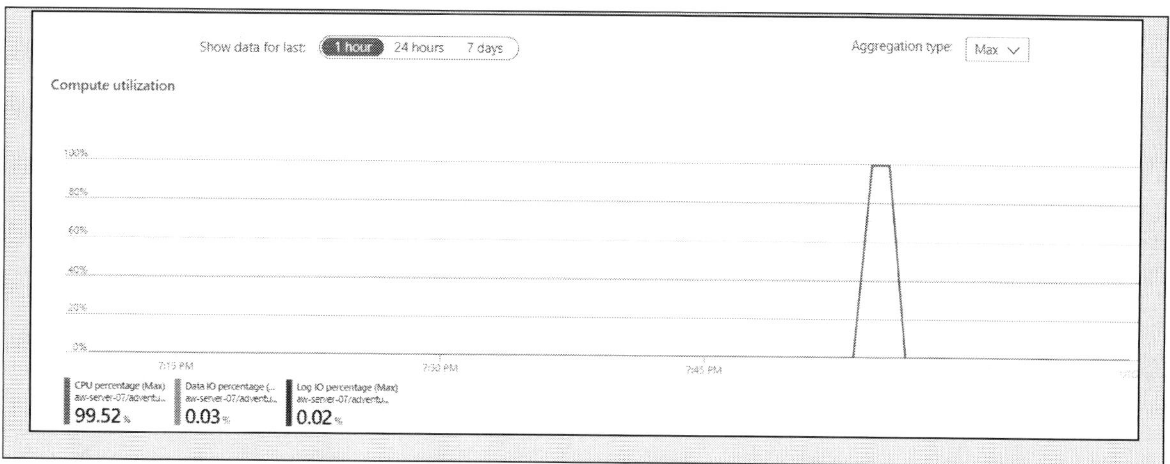

Step 08: Scale the Performance of your Workload

In this exercise, you will take the problem you encountered in the first exercise and improve performance by scaling more CPUs for Azure SQL Database.

Scale-up Azure SQL Performance

To scale performance for a problem that appears to be a CPU capacity problem, you should decide your options and then scale CPUs using provided interfaces for Azure SQL.

1. Decide how to scale performance.
2. Using the Azure portal, you can see options for how you can scale for more CPU resources.

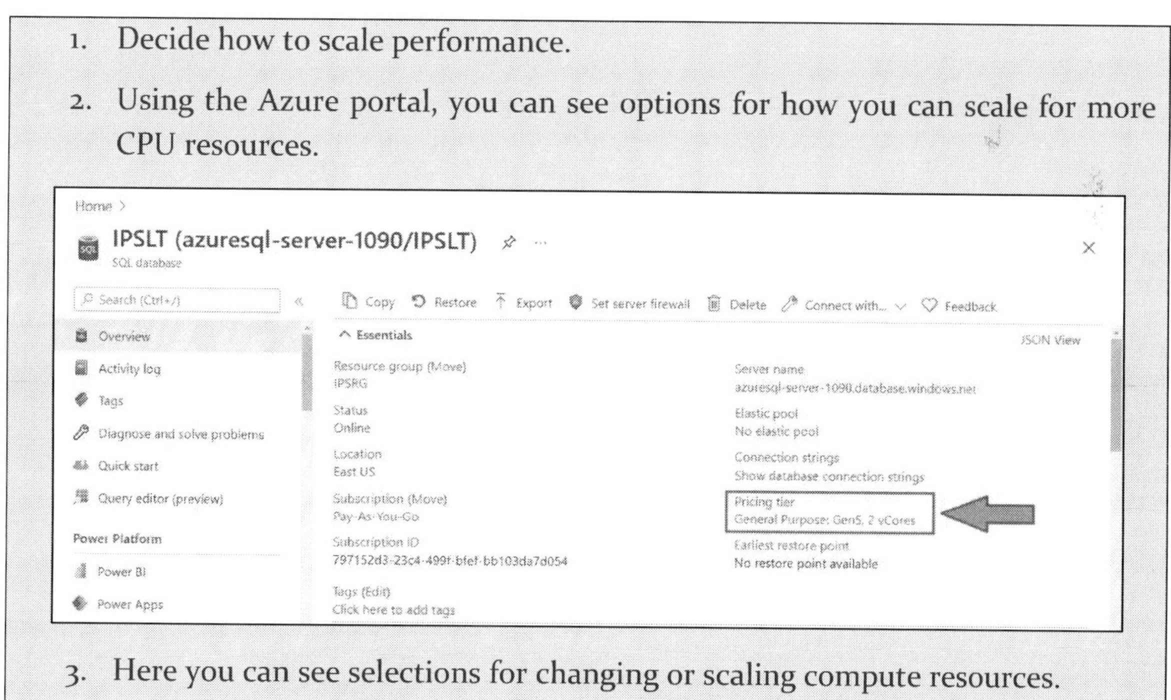

3. Here you can see selections for changing or scaling compute resources.

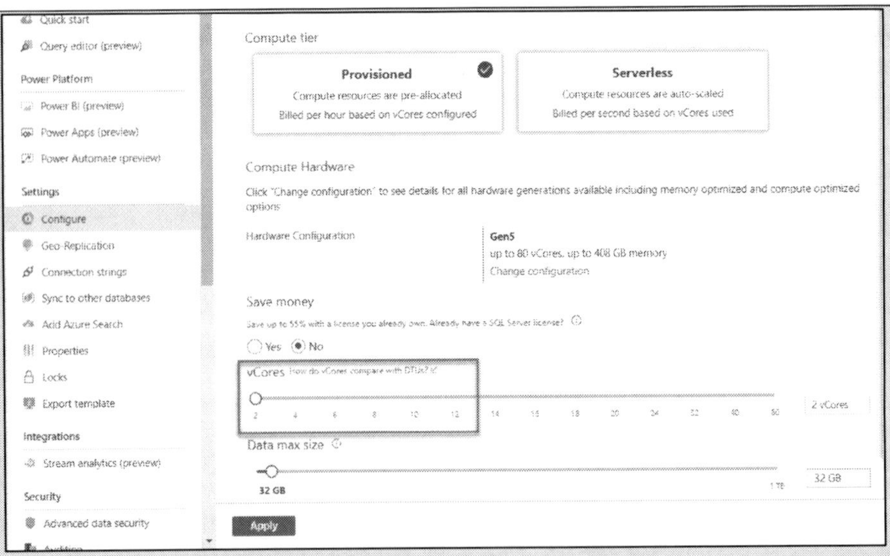

You can also use a different method to scale your workload.

5. Open the script "**modify_service_objective.sql**" in SSMS, and run the T-SQL batch.

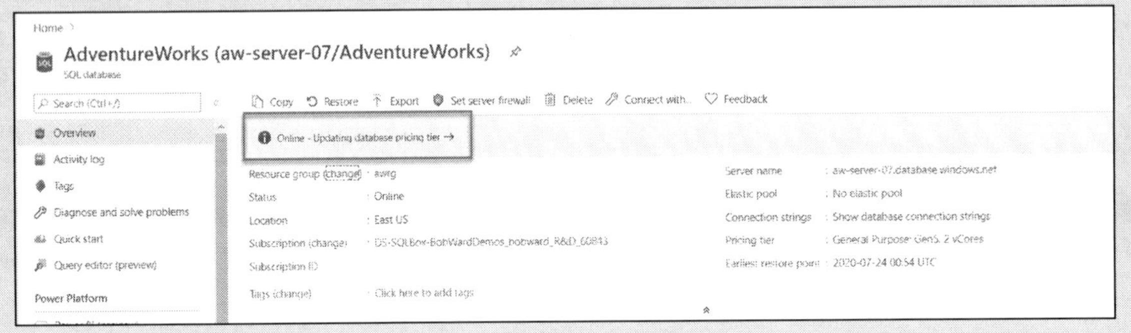

Observe Query Store Reports

Now, look at the same Query Store reports as we did in the previous exercise.

1. Using the same techniques as the first exercise in this module, at the "**Top Resource Consuming Queries**" report from SSMS.

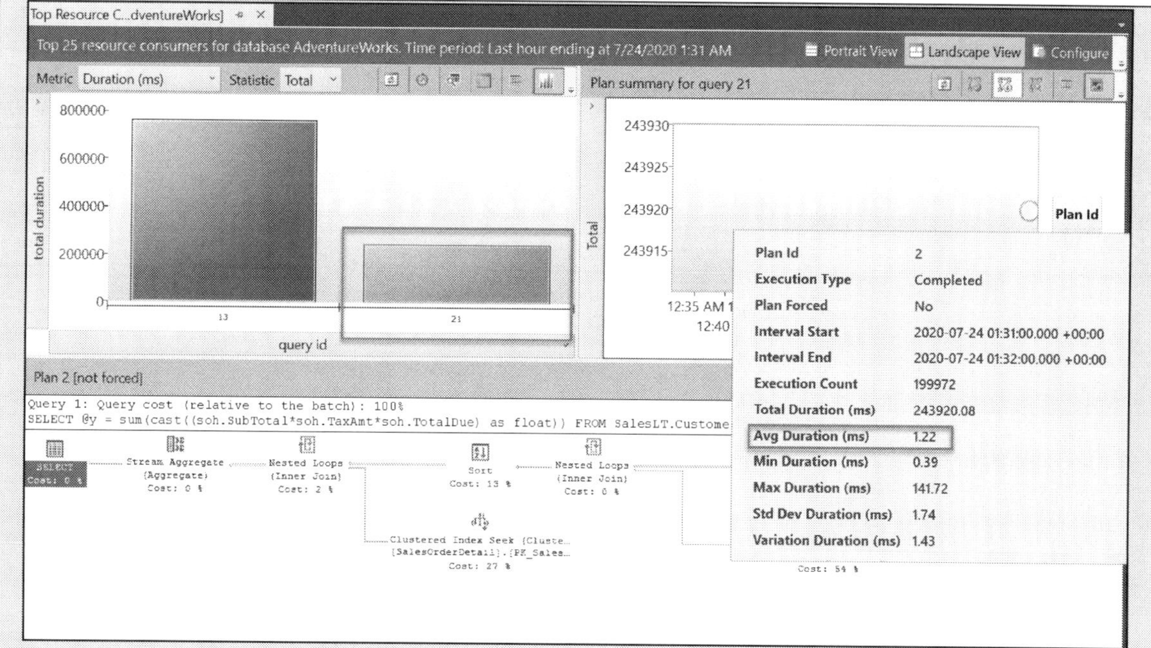

You will now see two queries (query_id).

2. Also, view the "**Query Wait Statistics**" report as you did in the previous exercise.

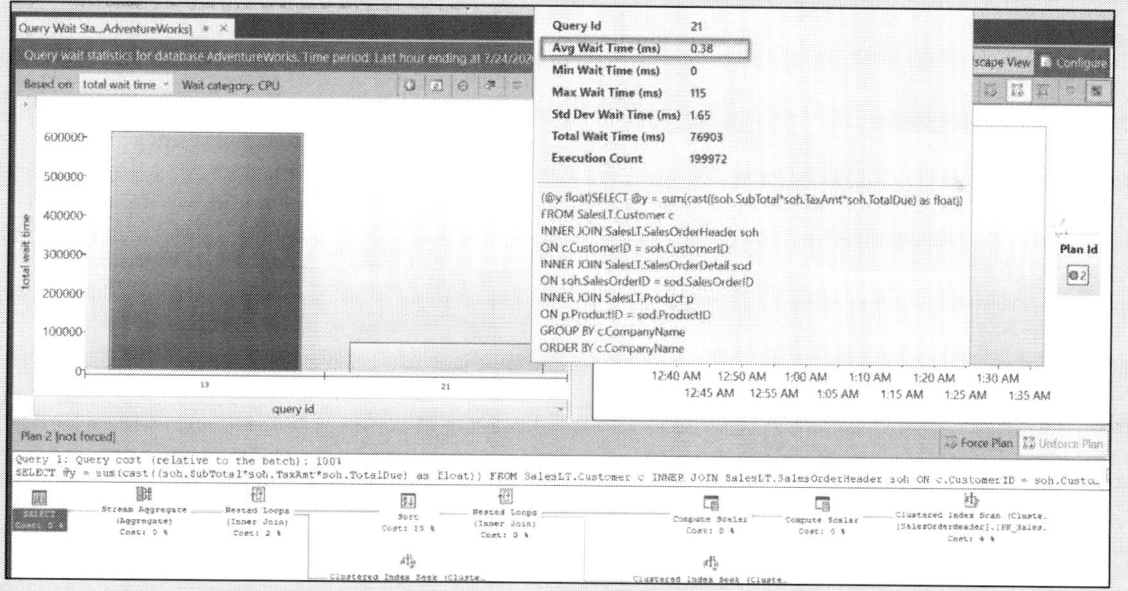

3. You can close out all reports and query editor windows. Leave SSMS connected because you will need this in the next exercise.

Observe Changes from Azure Metrics

1. Go to the database in the Azure portal, and look at the "**Overview**" pane again for "**Compute Utilization.**"

Notice that the duration is shorter for high CPU utilization, which means an overall drop in the CPU resources is required to run the workload.

2. This chart can be somewhat misleading. From the "**Resource**" menu, use "**Azure Metrics**." The CPU comparison chart looks more like the following:

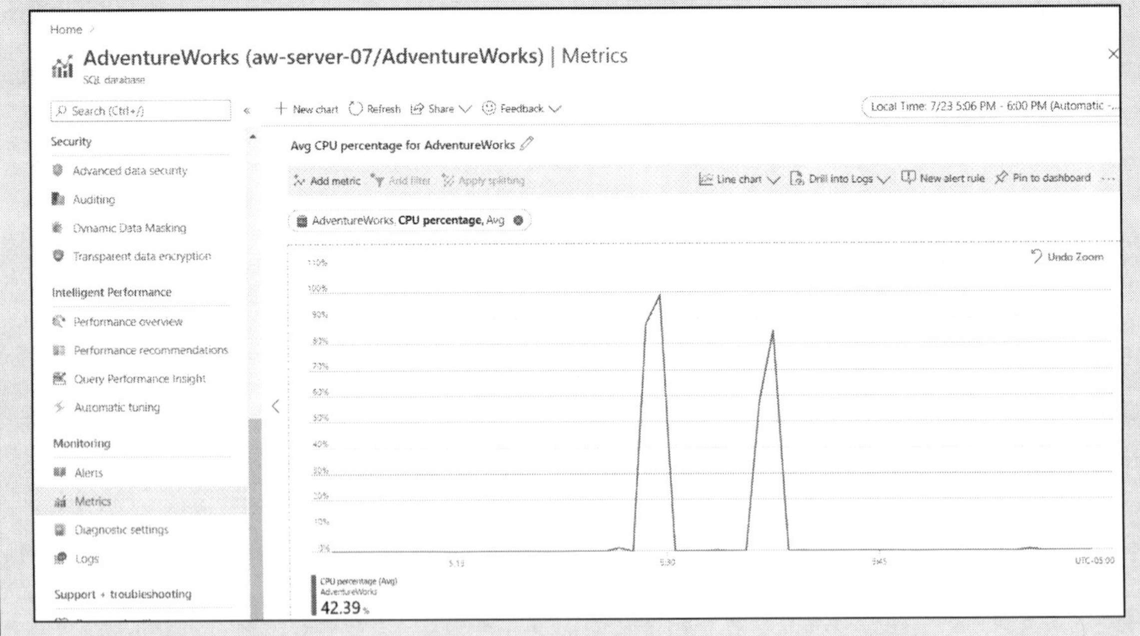

Step 09: Optimize Application Performance

In this exercise, you observe a new performance scenario and resolve it by optimizing the application and queries.

Optimize Application performance with Azure SQL

Create a New Table for the Application

```
DROP TABLE IF EXISTS SalesLT.OrderRating;
GO
CREATE TABLE SalesLT.OrderRating
(OrderRatingID int identity not null,
SalesOrderID int not null,
OrderRatingDT datetime not null,
OrderRating int not null,
OrderRatingComments char(500) not null);
GO
```

Load Queries to Monitor Query Execution

Now load some T-SQL queries for dynamic management views (DMVs) to observe query performance.

1. Run the following query:

```
SELECT er.session_id, er.status, er.command, er.wait_type,
er.last_wait_type, er.wait_resource, er.wait_time
FROM sys.dm_exec_requests er
INNER JOIN sys.dm_exec_sessions es
ON er.session_id = es.session_id
AND es.is_user_process = 1;
```

```
SELECT er.session_id, er.status, er.command, er.wait_type, er.last_wait_type, er.wait_resource, er.wait_time
FROM sys.dm_exec_requests er
INNER JOIN sys.dm_exec_sessions es
ON er.session_id = es.session_id
AND es.is_user_process = 1;
```

2. Run the below code:

```
SELECT * FROM sys.dm_os_wait_stats
ORDER BY waiting_tasks_count DESC;
```

3. Run the code.

```
SELECT io_stall_write_ms/num_of_writes as avg_tlog_io_write_ms, *
FROM sys.dm_io_virtual_file_stats
(db_id('IPSLT'), 2);
```

Prepare the Workload Script for Execution

Edit the workload script "**order_rating_insert_single.cmd**."

Run the Workload

1. From a command prompt, change to the directory for the following module activity:

```
cd c:<base directory>\04-Performance\tuning_applications
```

```
PS /home/ipslabs> cd c:<base directory>\04-Performance\tuning_applications
```

2. Run the workload with the following command:

```
PS /home/ipslabs> .\order_rating_insert_single.cmd
```

Observe DMVs and Workload Performance

Now run the SQL Server Management Studio (SSMS) queries that you previously loaded to observe performance.

Step 10: Restore to a Point in Time

In this exercise, you will see how you can recover from a common error by using point-in-time restore (PITR).

Setup: Use Scripts to Deploy Azure SQL Database

1. Run the following script in Azure Cloud Shell.

```
$adminSqlLogin = "cloudadmin"
$password = Read-Host "Your username is 'cloudadmin'.
Please enter a password for your Azure SQL Database server
that meets the password requirements"
# Prompt for local IP address
$ipAddress = Read-Host "Disconnect your VPN,
open PowerShell on your machine and run
'(Invoke-WebRequest -Uri "https://ipinfo.io/ip").Content'.
Please enter the value (include periods) next to 'Address': "
```

```
# Get resource group and location and random string
$resourceGroup = Get-AzResourceGroup |
Where ResourceGroupName -like "Sandbox resource group name"
$resourceGroupName = "Sandbox resource group name"
$uniqueID = Get-Random -Minimum 100000 -Maximum 1000000
$storageAccountName = "mslearnsa"+$uniqueID
$location = $resourceGroup.Location
# The logical server name has to be unique in the system
$serverName = "aw-server$($uniqueID)"
```

```
PS /home/ipslabs> $adminSqlLogin = "cloudadmin"
PS /home/ipslabs> $password = Read-Host

Your username is 'cloudadmin'. Please enter a password for your Azure SQL Database server that meets the password requirements: hareem
PS /home/ipslabs>
PS /home/ipslabs> $ipAddress = Read Host                    https://ipinfo.io/ip").Content'. Please
 enter the value (include periods) next to 'Address': "
Disconnect your VPN, open PowerShell on your machine and run '(Invoke-WebRequest -Uri  https://ipinfo.io/ip).Content'. Please enter the value (include periods) next to
'Address': : 1
PS /home/ipslabs>
PS /home/ipslabs> $resourceGroup = Get-AzResourceGroup | Where ResourceGroupName
PS /home/ipslabs> $resourceGroupName
PS /home/ipslabs> $uniqueID   Get-Random          100000          1000000
PS /home/ipslabs> $storageAccountName            +$uniqueID
PS /home/ipslabs> $location   $resourceGroup.Location
PS /home/ipslabs>
PS /home/ipslabs> $serverName            $($uniqueID)
```

2. Output and store (in a text file or similar location) the information.

```
Write-Host "Please note your unique ID for future exercises in this module:"
Write-Host $uniqueID
Write-Host "Your resource group name is:"
Write-Host $resourceGroupName
Write-Host "Your resources were deployed in the following region:"
Write-Host $location
Write-Host "Your server name is:"
Write-Host $serverName
```

3. Run the following script to deploy an Azure SQL database and logical server:

```
# The logical server name has to be unique in the system
$serverName = "aw-server$($uniqueID)"
# The sample database name
$databaseName = "AdventureWorks"
# The storage account name has to be unique in the system
$storageAccountName = $("sql$($uniqueID)")
# Create a new server with a system-wide unique server name
$server = New-AzSqlServer -ResourceGroupName $resourceGroupName `
    -ServerName $serverName `
    -Location $location `
    -SqlAdministratorCredentials $(New-Object -TypeName System.Management.Automation
    .PSCredential -ArgumentList $adminSqlLogin,
    $(ConvertTo-SecureString -String $password -AsPlainText -Force))
# Create a server firewall rule that allows access from the specified IP range
```

```
and all Azure services
$serverFirewallRule = New-AzSqlServerFirewallRule `
    -ResourceGroupName $resourceGroupName `
    -ServerName $serverName `
    -FirewallRuleName "AllowedIPs" `
    -StartIpAddress $ipAddress -EndIpAddress $ipAddress
$allowAzureIpsRule = New-AzSqlServerFirewallRule `
    -ResourceGroupName $resourceGroupName `
    -ServerName $serverName `
    -AllowAllAzureIPs
# Create a database
$database = New-AzSqlDatabase  -ResourceGroupName $resourceGroupName `
    -ServerName $serverName `
    -DatabaseName $databaseName `
```

```
    -SampleName "AdventureWorksLT" `
    -Edition "GeneralPurpose" -Vcore 2 -ComputeGeneration "Gen5"
# Enable Azure Defender
$azureDefender = Enable-AzSqlServerAdvancedDataSecurity `
    -ResourceGroupName $resourceGroupName `
    -ServerName $serverName
# Create a storage account
$storageAccount = New-AzStorageAccount -ResourceGroupName $resourceGroupName `
    -AccountName $storageAccountName `
    -Location $location `
    -Type "Standard_LRS"
```

```
PS /home/ipslabs> # The logical server name has to be unique in the system
PS /home/ipslabs> $serverName = "server$($uniqueID)"
PS /home/ipslabs> # The sample database name
PS /home/ipslabs> $databaseName = "AdventureWorks"
PS /home/ipslabs> # The storage account name has to be unique in the system
PS /home/ipslabs> $storageAccountName = $("sql$($uniqueID)")
PS /home/ipslabs> # Create a new server with a system-wide unique server name
PS /home/ipslabs> $server = New-AzSqlServer -ResourceGroupName $resourceGroupName `
>>     -ServerName $serverName `
>>     -Location $location `
>>     -SqlAdministratorCredentials $(New-Object -TypeName System.Management.Automation.PSCredential -ArgumentList $adminSqlLogin, $(ConvertTo-SecureString -String $pas
sword -AsPlainText -Force))
```

```
PS /home/ipslabs> # Create a server firewall rule that allows access from the specified IP range and all Azure services
PS /home/ipslabs> $serverFirewallRule = New-AzSqlServerFirewallRule `
>>     -ResourceGroupName $resourceGroupName `
>>     -ServerName $serverName `
>>     -FirewallRuleName "AllowedIPs" `
>>     -StartIpAddress $ipAddress -EndIpAddress $ipAddress
```

```
PS /home/ipslabs> # Create a database
PS /home/ipslabs> $database = New-AzSqlDatabase  -ResourceGroupName $resourceGroupName `
>>     -ServerName $serverName `
>>     -DatabaseName $databaseName `
>>     -SampleName "AdventureWorksLT" `
>>     -Edition "GeneralPurpose" -Vcore 2 -ComputeGeneration "Gen5"
WARNING: Upcoming breaking changes in the cmdlet 'New-AzSqlDatabase' :

- The output type 'Microsoft.Azure.Commands.Sql.Database.Model.AzureSqlDatabaseModel' is changing
- The following properties in the output type are being deprecated : 'BackupStorageRedundancy'
- The following properties are being added to the output type : 'CurrentBackupStorageRedundancy' 'RequestedBackupStorageRedundancy'
- The change is expected to take effect from the version : '3.0.0'
Note : Go to https://aka.ms/azps-changewarnings for steps to suppress this breaking change warning, and other information on breaking changes in Azure PowerShell.
```

```
PS /home/ipslabs> # Enable Azure Defender
PS /home/ipslabs> $azureDefender = Enable-AzSqlServerAdvancedDataSecurity `
>>     -ResourceGroupName $resourceGroupName `
>>     -ServerName $serverName
```

```
PS /home/ipslabs> # Create a storage account
PS /home/ipslabs> $storageAccount = New-AzStorageAccount -ResourceGroupName $resourceGroupName `
>>     -AccountName $storageAccountName `
>>     -Location $location `
>>     -Type "Standard_LRS"
```

4. On your local computer, open SSMS and create a new connection to your logical server.

Simulate Deletion of Data

First, confirm that the table you will *accidentally* delete exists and has data in it. Now, look at some of the values in SalesLT.OrderDetail.

1. Go to SSMS and check/update your connection.

Connect to Server

SQL Server

Login | Connection Properties | Always Encrypted | Additional Connection Parameters

Type or select the name of the database for the connection.

Connect to database: <default>

Network

Network protocol: <default>

Network packet size: 4096 bytes

Connection

Connection time-out: 30 seconds

Execution time-out: 0 seconds

☑ Encrypt connection

☑ Trust server certificate

☐ Use custom color: Select...

Reset All

Connect | Cancel | Help | Options <<

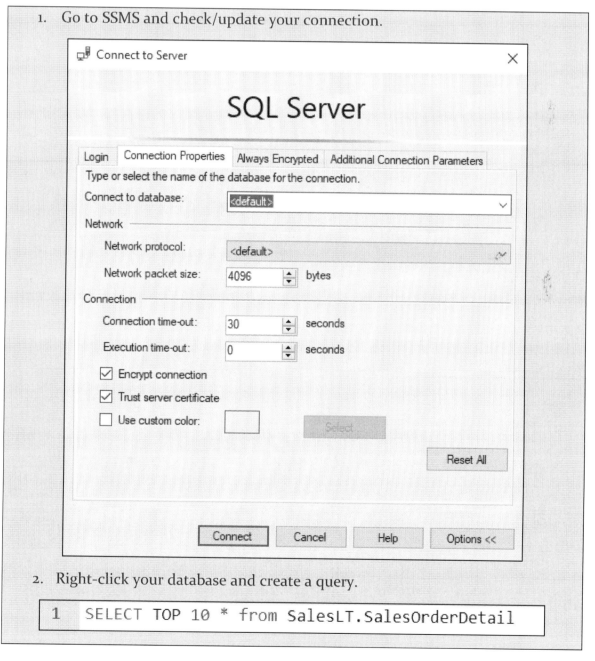

2. Right-click your database and create a query.

```
SELECT TOP 10 * from SalesLT.SalesOrderDetail
```

	SalesOrderID	SalesOrderDetailID	OrderQty	ProductID	UnitPrice	UnitPriceDiscount	LineTotal	rowguid	ModifiedDate
1	71774	110562	1	836	356.898	0.00	356.898000	E3A1994C-7A68-4CE8-96A3-77FDD3BBD730	2008-06-01 00:00:00.000
2	71774	110563	1	822	356.898	0.00	356.898000	5C77F557-FDB6-43BA-90B9-9A7AEC55CA32	2008-06-01 00:00:00.000
3	71776	110567	1	907	63.90	0.00	63.900000	6DBFE398-D15D-425E-AA58-88178FE360E5	2008-06-01 00:00:00.000
4	71780	110616	4	905	218.454	0.00	873.816000	377246C9-4483-48ED-A5B9-E56F005364E0	2008-06-01 00:00:00.000
5	71780	110617	2	983	461.694	0.00	923.388000	43A54BCD-536D-4A1B-8E69-24D083507A14	2008-06-01 00:00:00.000
6	71780	110618	6	988	112.998	0.40	406.792800	12706FAB-F3A2-48C6-B7C7-1CCDE4081F18	2008-06-01 00:00:00.000
7	71780	110619	2	748	818.70	0.00	1637.400000	B12F0D3B-5B4E-4F1F-B2F0-F7CDE99DD826	2008-06-01 00:00:00.000
8	71780	110620	1	990	323.994	0.00	323.994000	F117A449-039D-44B8-A4B2-B12001DACC01	2008-06-01 00:00:00.000
9	71780	110621	1	926	149.874	0.00	149.874000	92E5052B-72D0-4C91-9A8C-42591803667E	2008-06-01 00:00:00.000
10	71780	110622	1	743	809.76	0.00	809.760000	8BD33BED-C4F6-4D44-84FB-A7D04AFCD794	2008-06-01 00:00:00.000

3. Simulate the loss of data by dropping a table in the database.
4. Run the following code in Azure Cloud Shell:

```
$resourceGroup = Get-AzResourceGroup |
Where ResourceGroupName -like Sandbox resource group name
$server = Get-AzureRmSqlServer -ResourceGroupName $resourceGroup.ResourceGroupName
$logical_server = $server.ServerName
$resource_group = $resourceGroup.ResourceGroupName
# Specify your default resource group and Azure SQL Database logical server
az configure --defaults group=$resource_group sql-server=$logical_server
# Confirm the defaults are set
az configure --list-defaults
```

```
PS /home/ipslabs> $logical_server = $server.ServerName
PS /home/ipslabs> $resource_group = $resourceGroup.ResourceGroupName
PS /home/ipslabs>
PS /home/ipslabs> # Specify your default resource group and Azure SQL Database logical server
PS /home/ipslabs> az configure --defaults group=$resource_group sql-server=$logical_server
PS /home/ipslabs>
PS /home/ipslabs> # Confirm the defaults are set
PS /home/ipslabs> az configure --list-defaults
```

The group and sql-server parameters returned should match the names of your Microsoft Learn resource group and your Azure SQL Database logical server.

Identify the Time to Restore the Database

You will restore before the bad transaction but after the last good one.

The way to determine the drop time is by looking at the completion time of the DROP statement.

Restore the Database and Confirm Missing Data

1. Run the following script in the terminal on the right side of this window:

```
# Restore the database to a time before the database was deleted
az sql db restore --dest-name "AdventureWorks-copy" --name "AdventureWorks"
--time $before_error_time --verbose
```

```
PS /home/ipslabs> # Restore the database to a time before the database was deleted
PS /home/ipslabs> az sql db restore --dest-name "AdventureWorks-copy" --name "AdventureWorks" --time $before_error_time --verbose
```

2. You can check the status by refreshing your view of databases in SSMS.

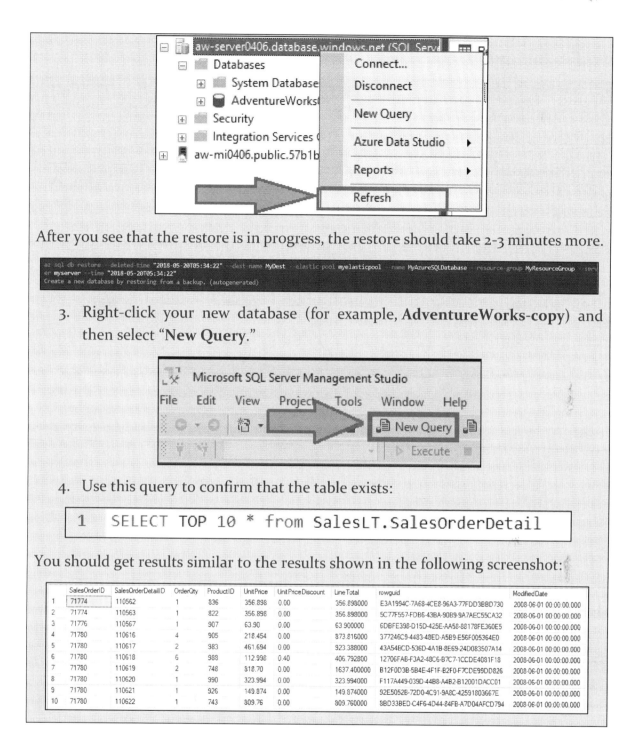

After you see that the restore is in progress, the restore should take 2-3 minutes more.

```
az sql db restore --deleted-time "2018-05-20T05:34:22" --dest-name MyDest --elastic-pool myelasticpool --name MyAzureSQLDatabase --resource-group MyResourceGroup --server myserver --time "2018-05-20T05:34:22"
Create a new database by restoring from a backup. (autogenerated)
```

3. Right-click your new database (for example, **AdventureWorks-copy**) and then select "**New Query**."

4. Use this query to confirm that the table exists:

```
1  SELECT TOP 10 * from SalesLT.SalesOrderDetail
```

You should get results similar to the results shown in the following screenshot:

	SalesOrderID	SalesOrderDetailID	OrderQty	ProductID	UnitPrice	UnitPriceDiscount	LineTotal	rowguid	ModifiedDate
1	71774	110562	1	836	356.898	0.00	356.898000	E3A1994C-7A68-4CE8-96A3-77FDD3BBD730	2008-06-01 00:00:00.000
2	71774	110563	1	822	356.898	0.00	356.898000	5C77F557-FDB6-43BA-90B9-9A7AEC55CA32	2008-06-01 00:00:00.000
3	71776	110567	1	907	63.90	0.00	63.900000	6DBFE398-D15D-425E-AA58-88178FE360E5	2008-06-01 00:00:00.000
4	71780	110616	4	905	218.454	0.00	873.816000	377246C9-4483-48ED-A5B9-E56F005364E0	2008-06-01 00:00:00.000
5	71780	110617	2	983	461.694	0.00	923.388000	43A54BCD-536D-4A1B-8E69-24D083507A14	2008-06-01 00:00:00.000
6	71780	110618	6	988	112.998	0.40	406.792800	12706FAB-F3A2-48C6-B7C7-1CCDE4081F18	2008-06-01 00:00:00.000
7	71780	110619	2	748	818.70	0.00	1637.400000	B12F0D3B-5B4E-4F1F-B2F0-F7CDE99DD826	2008-06-01 00:00:00.000
8	71780	110620	1	990	323.994	0.00	323.994000	F117A449-039D-44B8-A4B2-B12001DACC01	2008-06-01 00:00:00.000
9	71780	110621	1	926	149.874	0.00	149.874000	92E5052B-72D0-4C91-9A8C-42591803667E	2008-06-01 00:00:00.000
10	71780	110622	1	743	809.76	0.00	809.760000	8BD33BED-C4F6-4D44-84FB-A7D04AFCD794	2008-06-01 00:00:00.000

Step 11: General Purpose High Availability

In this exercise, you will use the ostress tool you might have used in the previous module to create a workload.

Run the Ostress Workload

The first step is to create a long-running workload.

1. Open a new Command Prompt window on your local computer. Use cd to go to the directory in the repository you cloned or downloaded earlier that contains the availability module. For example, you can use this command:

```
cd C:\Users\username\mslearn-azure-sql-fundamentals\05-Availability
```

```
C:\Users\I.T>cd C:\Users\username\mslearn-azure-sql-fundamentals\05-Availability
```

2. Use the following ostress script to run the workload:

```
.\ostress.exe -S"serverName.database.windows.net"
-Q"SELECT COUNT(*) FROM SalesLT.Customer" -U"cloudadmin"
-d"AdventureWorks" -P"password" -n1 -r50000
```

```
C:\Users\I.T>.\ostress.exe -S"serverName.database.windows.net" -Q"SELECT COUNT(*) FROM SalesLT.Customer" -U"cloudadmin"
-d"AdventureWorks" -P"password" -n1 -r50000
```

If you want to run the workload again, you can run the command again.

Use PowerShell in Azure Cloud Shell to Initiate a Failover and Observe the Results

1. In the Azure Cloud Shell terminal, run the code.

```
$resourceGroup = "Sandbox resource group name"
$database = "AdventureWorks"
$server = Get-AzureRmSqlServer -ResourceGroupName $resourceGroup
$server = $server.ServerName
# Specify your default resource group and Azure SQL Database logical server
az configure --defaults group=$resourceGroup sql-server=$server
# Confirm the defaults are set
az configure --list-defaults
```

```
PS /home/ipslabs> $resourceGroup = "Sandbox resource group name"
PS /home/ipslabs> $database = "AdventureWorks"
PS /home/ipslabs> $server = Get-AzureRmSqlServer -ResourceGroupName $resourceGroup
```

```
PS /home/ipslabs> $server = $server.ServerName
PS /home/ipslabs>
PS /home/ipslabs> # Specify your default resource group and Azure SQL Database logical server
PS /home/ipslabs> az configure --defaults group=$resourceGroup sql-server=$server
PS /home/ipslabs>
PS /home/ipslabs> # Confirm the defaults are set
PS /home/ipslabs> az configure --list-defaults
```

2. Run the following code in the terminal:

```
# Create a failover
Invoke-AzSqlDatabaseFailover -ResourceGroupName $resourceGroup `
    -ServerName $server `
    -DatabaseName $database
```

```
PS /home/ipslabs> az configure --list-defaults# Create a failover
```

```
PS /home/ipslabs> Invoke-AzSqlDatabaseFailover -ResourceGroupName $resourceGroup `
>>     -ServerName $server `
>>     -DatabaseName $database
```

3. Run the following command to try another failover:

```
# Create a failover again
Invoke-AzSqlDatabaseFailover -ResourceGroupName $resourceGroup `
    -ServerName $server `
    -DatabaseName $database
```

```
PS /home/ipslabs> # Create a failover again
PS /home/ipslabs> Invoke-AzSqlDatabaseFailover -ResourceGroupName $resourceGroup `
>>     -ServerName $server `
>>     -DatabaseName $database
```

4. You can now stop the workload in the Command Prompt window by selecting the window and then clicking **Ctrl+C**.

Step 12: Business-critical High Availability

You will use the ostress tool you used in the previous exercise to create a workload.

Deploy the Same Database in the Business Critical tier

1. In the Azure Cloud Shell terminal, run the following PowerShell script to configure your environment:

```
$resourceGroup = "Sandbox resource group name"
$database = "AdventureWorks-bc"
$server = Get-AzureRmSqlServer -ResourceGroupName $resourceGroup
$server = $server.ServerName
# Specify your default resource group and
Azure SQL Database logical server
az configure --defaults group=$resourceGroup sql-server=$server
# Confirm the defaults are set
az configure --list-defaults
```

```
PS /home/ipslabs> $resourceGroup = "Sandbox resource group name"
PS /home/ipslabs> $database = "AdventureWorks-bc"
PS /home/ipslabs> $server = Get-AzureRmSqlServer -ResourceGroupName $resourceGroup
```

```
PS /home/ipslabs> $server = $server.ServerName
PS /home/ipslabs>
PS /home/ipslabs> # Specify your default resource group and Azure SQL Database logical server
PS /home/ipslabs> az configure --defaults group=$resourceGroup sql-server=$server
PS /home/ipslabs>
PS /home/ipslabs> # Confirm the defaults are set
PS /home/ipslabs> az configure --list-defaults
```

2. Run the following command to create a database in the Business Critical service tier:

```
az sql db create --name $database `
--edition BusinessCritical `
--family Gen5 `
--capacity 2 `
--sample-name AdventureWorksLT `
--read-scale Enabled `
--zone-redundant false
```

```
PS /home/ipslabs> az sql db create --name $database `
>> --edition BusinessCritical `
>> --family Gen5 `
>> --capacity 2 `
>> --sample-name AdventureWorksLT `
>> --read-scale Enabled `
>> --zone-redundant false
```

3. Another way to check the service tier is to go to your database in the Azure portal.

Run the Ostress Workload

As in the previous exercise, you will use ostress to query your Azure SQL database repeatedly.

1. Open a new Command Prompt window on your local computer. Use cd to go to the directory in the repository you cloned or downloaded earlier that

contains the availability module. For example, you might use the following command:

```
cd C:\Users\username\mslearn-azure-sql-fundamentals\05-Availability
```

```
C:\Users\I.T>cd C:\Users\username\mslearn-azure-sql-fundamentals\05-Availability
```

2. Use the following ostress script to run the workload.

```
.\ostress.exe -S"serverName.database.windows.net"
-Q"SELECT COUNT(*) FROM SalesLT.Customer" -U"cloudadmin"
-d"AdventureWorks-bc" -P"password" -n1 -r50000
```

```
C:\Users\I.T>.\ostress.exe -S"serverName.database.windows.net" -Q"SELECT COUNT(*) FROM SalesLT.Customer" -U"cloudadmin"
-d"AdventureWorks" -P"password" -n1 -r50000
```

If you want to run the workload again, you can run the command again.

Initiate a Failover and View the Results

1. Run the following code in the Azure Cloud Shell terminal:

```
# create a failover
Invoke-AzSqlDatabaseFailover -ResourceGroupName $resourceGroup `
    -ServerName $server `
    -DatabaseName $database
```

```
PS /home/ipslabs> # create a failover
PS /home/ipslabs> Invoke-AzSqlDatabaseFailover -ResourceGroupName $resourceGroup `
>>     -ServerName $server `
>>     -DatabaseName $database
```

2. While this command is running, you should observe any changes that appear in the terminal.

Connect to the Read-only Replica

To access the read-only replica in applications, you just have to add this parameter to your connection string for a database:

```
1   ApplicationIntent=ReadOnly;
```

1. In SSMS, create a new query connection. (Select **File** > **New** > **Database Engine Query**.)

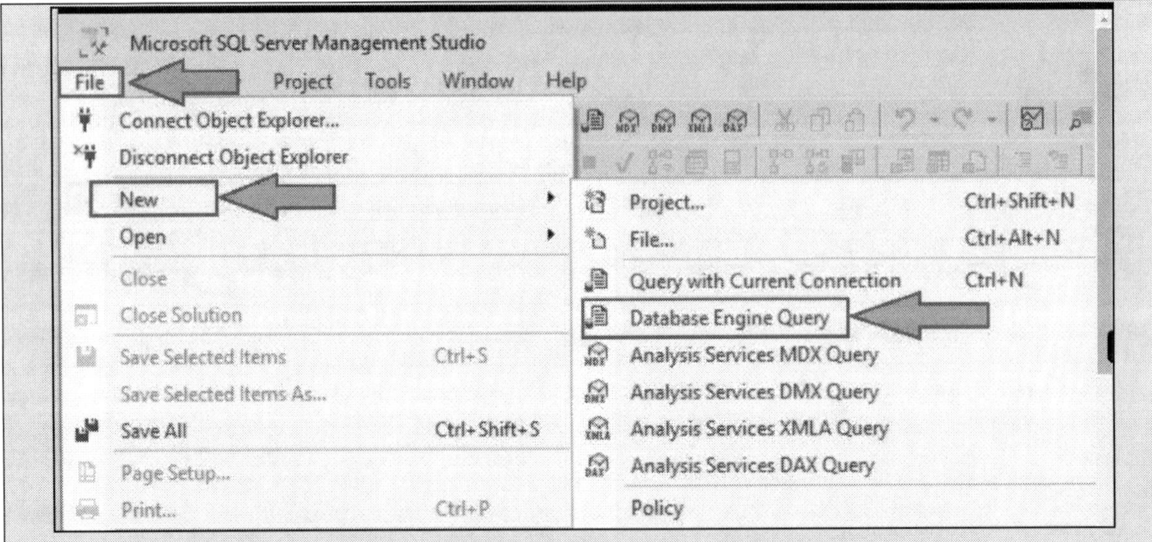

2. Select "**Connection Properties**," and then select "**Reset All**."
3. Select "**Additional Connection Parameters**" and write the text displayed in the following image into the text box. Select **Connect**.

SQL Server

Login | Connection Properties | Always Encrypted | Additional Connection Parameters

Enter additional connection string parameters (will be sent in clear text):

ApplicationIntent = Readonly;

(Note: Connection string parameters override graphical selections on other panels)

Connect | Cancel | Help | Options <<

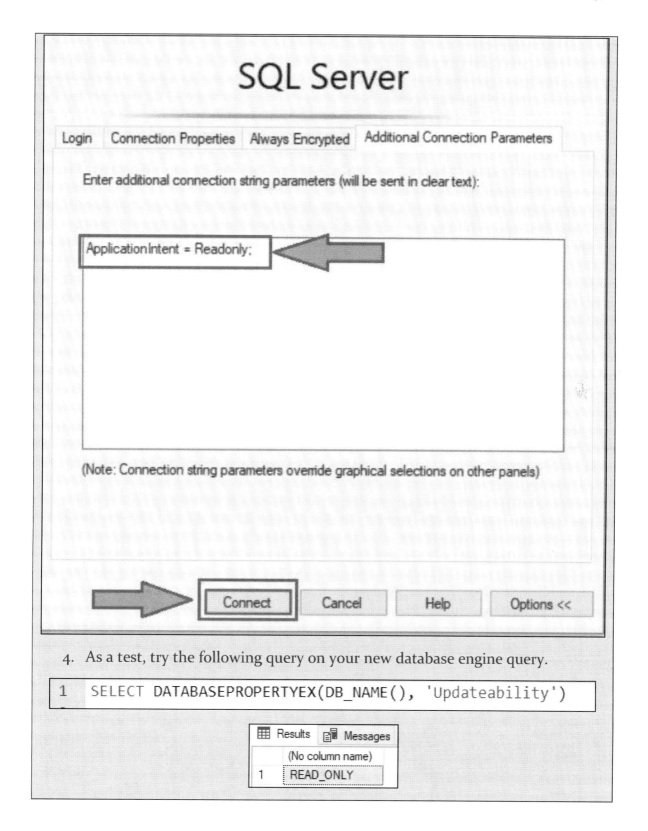

4. As a test, try the following query on your new database engine query.

```
SELECT DATABASEPROPERTYEX(DB_NAME(), 'Updateability')
```

Results | Messages

	(No column name)
1	READ_ONLY

Step 13: Geo-distributed Auto-failover Groups with Read-scale

In this exercise, you will configure auto-failover groups for your Azure SQL database. You will then initiate a failover and view the results.

Configure the Environment

1. Run this script in Azure Cloud Shell.

```
$admin = "cloudadmin"
$resourceGroup = Get-AzResourceGroup |
Where ResourceGroupName -like Sandbox resource group name
$location = $resourceGroup.Location
$resourceGroup = $resourceGroup.ResourceGroupName
$database = "IPSLT"
$server = Get-AzureRmSqlServer -ResourceGroupName $resourceGroup
$server = $server.ServerName
$drServer = "$($server)-dr"
$failoverGroup = "$($server)-fg"
$firewallRule = "AllowMyIp"
Write-Host "Variables Received"
```

```
PS /home/ipslabs> $admin = "cloudadmin"
PS /home/ipslabs> $resourceGroup = Get-AzResourceGroup | Where ResourceGroupName -like Sandbox resource group name
```

```
PS /home/ipslabs> $location = $resourceGroup.Location
PS /home/ipslabs> $resourceGroup = $resourceGroup.ResourceGroupName
PS /home/ipslabs> $database = "IPSLT"
PS /home/ipslabs> $server = Get-AzureRmSqlServer -ResourceGroupName $resourceGroup
```

```
PS /home/ipslabs> $server = $server.ServerName
PS /home/ipslabs> $drServer = "$($server)-dr"
PS /home/ipslabs> $failoverGroup = "$($server)-fg"
PS /home/ipslabs> $firewallRule = "AllowMyIp"
PS /home/ipslabs> Write-Host "Variables Received"
Variables Received
```

2. Create an empty Azure SQL Database server in the failover region.

```
# Create a backup server in the failover region
New-AzSqlServer -ResourceGroupName $resourceGroup `
    -ServerName $drServer `
    -Location $drLocation `
    -SqlAdministratorCredentials $(New-Object -TypeName System.Management.Automation.
    PSCredential `
    -ArgumentList $admin, $(ConvertTo-SecureString -String $password -AsPlainText -Force))
Write-Host "New Azure SQL Database logical server Created in the different region."
```

```
PS /home/ipslabs> # Create a backup server in the failover region
PS /home/ipslabs> New-AzSqlServer -ResourceGroupName $resourceGroup `
>>     -ServerName $drServer `
>>     -Location $drLocation `
>>     -SqlAdministratorCredentials $(New-Object -TypeName System.Management.Automation.PSCredential `
>>     -ArgumentList $admin, $(ConvertTo-SecureString -String $password -AsPlainText -Force))
```

```
PS /home/ipslabs> Write-Host "New Azure SQL Database logical server Created in different region"
```

3. Create a failover group between the servers.

```
# Create a failover group between the servers
New-AzSqlDatabaseFailoverGroup -ResourceGroupName $resourceGroup `
    -ServerName $server `
    -PartnerServerName $drServer `
    -FailoverGroupName $failoverGroup
Write-Host "New auto-failover group created between the two Azure SQL Database logical servers."
```

```
PS /home/ipslabs> Write-Host "New Azure SQL Database logical server Created in different region"
New Azure SQL Database logical server Created in different region
PS /home/ipslabs> # Create a failover group between the servers
PS /home/ipslabs> New-AzSqlDatabaseFailoverGroup -ResourceGroupName $resourceGroup `
>>     -ServerName $server `
>>     -PartnerServerName $drServer `
>>     -FailoverGroupName $failoverGroup
```

```
PS /home/ipslabs> Write-Host "New auto-failover group created between the two Azure SQL Database logical servers"
New auto-failover group created between the two Azure SQL Database logical servers
```

4. Configure the network by running the following script in Azure Cloud Shell:

```
# Add a firewall rule that gives your VM access to the new server
New-AzSqlServerFirewallRule -ResourceGroupName $resourceGroup `
    -ServerName $drServer `
    -FirewallRuleName $firewallRule `
    -StartIpAddress $ipAddress `
    -EndIpAddress $ipAddress;
```

```
PS /home/ipslabs> # Add a firewall rule that gives your VM access to the new server
PS /home/ipslabs> New-AzSqlServerFirewallRule -ResourceGroupName $resourceGroup `
>>     -ServerName $drServer `
>>     -FirewallRuleName $firewallRule `
>>     -StartIpAddress $ipAddress `
>>     -EndIpAddress $ipAddress;
```

5. Add one or more databases to the failover group by running the following script in Azure Cloud Shell:

```
# Add the database or databases to the failover group
Get-AzSqlDatabase -ResourceGroupName $resourceGroup `
    -ServerName $server -DatabaseName $database | `
    Add-AzSqlDatabaseToFailoverGroup -ResourceGroupName $resourceGroup `
    -ServerName $server `
    -FailoverGroupName $failoverGroup
Write-Host "IPSLT database added to the auto-failover group"
```

```
PS /home/ipslabs> # Add the database or databases to the failover group
PS /home/ipslabs> Get-AzSqlDatabase -ResourceGroupName $resourceGroup `
>>     -ServerName $server -DatabaseName $database | `
>>     Add-AzSqlDatabaseToFailoverGroup -ResourceGroupName $resourceGroup `
>>     -ServerName $server `
>>     -FailoverGroupName $failoverGroup
```

```
PS /home/ipslabs> Write-Host "IPSLT database added to the auto-failover group"
IPSLT database added to the auto-failover group
```

It will take some time for this script to run.

Configure your Command Prompt Applications

In this section, you will use two ostress workloads to check the Update ability (whether a database is in a ReadWrite or ReadOnly state) of the primary and secondary servers in your failover group.

1. Open two separate Command Prompt windows. Set up the windows to see this window (the browser) and both Command Prompt windows.
2. In both Command Prompt windows, use this command.

```
cd C:\Users\username\mslearn-azure-sql-fundamentals\05-Availability
```



```
cd C:\Users\username\mslearn-azure-sql-fundamentals\05-Availability
```


3. Run the following command using your server name and password:

```
.\ostress.exe -S"<server-name>-fg.database.windows.net"
-Q"SELECT DATABASEPROPERTYEX(DB_NAME(),'Updateability')"
-U"cloudadmin" -d"AdventureWorks" -P"password" -n1 -r5000 -oprimary
```

```
ostress.exe -S"<server-name>-fg.database.windows.net" -Q"SELECT DATABASEPROPERTYEX(DB_NAME(),'Updateability')"
-U"cloudadmin" -d"AdventureWorks" -P"password" -n1 -r5000 -oprimary
```

4. Run the following command using your server name and password:

```
ostress.exe -S"<server-name>-fg.secondary.database.windows.net"
-Q"SELECT DATABASEPROPERTYEX(DB_NAME(),'Updateability')"
-U"cloudadmin" -d"AdventureWorks" -P"password" -n1 -r5000 -osecondary
```

```
ostress.exe -S"<server-name>-fg.secondary.database.windows.net" -Q"SELECT DATABASEPROPERTYEX(DB_NAME(),'Updateability')"
-U"cloudadmin" -d"AdventureWorks" -P"password" -n1 -r5000 -osecondary
```

Initiate a Failover and View the Results

1. Use the Azure Cloud Shell terminal on the right side of the following page to check the status of the secondary server:

```
(Get-AzSqlDatabaseFailoverGroup -FailoverGroupName $failoverGroup `
    -ResourceGroupName $resourceGroup -ServerName $drServer).
    ReplicationRole
```

```
PS /home/ipslabs> (Get-AzSqlDatabaseFailoverGroup -FailoverGroupName $failoverGroup `
>>     -ResourceGroupName $resourceGroup -ServerName $drServer).ReplicationRole
```

2. You can now see what happens when a failover occurs.

```
Switch-AzSqlDatabaseFailoverGroup -ResourceGroupName $resourceGroup `
 -ServerName $drServer -FailoverGroupName $failoverGroup
```

```
PS /home/ipslabs> Switch-AzSqlDatabaseFailoverGroup -ResourceGroupName $resourceGroup `
>>  -ServerName $drServer -FailoverGroupName $failoverGroup
```

3. Check the status of the secondary server by running the following script in Azure Cloud Shell:

```
(Get-AzSqlDatabaseFailoverGroup -FailoverGroupName $failoverGroup `
    -ResourceGroupName $resourceGroup -ServerName $drServer).
    ReplicationRole
```

```
PS /home/ipslabs> (Get-AzSqlDatabaseFailoverGroup -FailoverGroupName $failoverGroup `
>>     -ResourceGroupName $resourceGroup -ServerName $drServer).ReplicationRole
```

This server should now be in the primary role.

4. Failback by running the following script in Azure Cloud Shell:

```
Switch-AzSqlDatabaseFailoverGroup -ResourceGroupName $resourceGroup `
 -ServerName $server -FailoverGroupName $failoverGroup
```

```
PS /home/ipslabs> Switch-AzSqlDatabaseFailoverGroup -ResourceGroupName $resourceGroup `
>>  -ServerName $server -FailoverGroupName $failoverGroup
```

5. Lastly, you can view the status of the secondary server yet again.

```
(Get-AzSqlDatabaseFailoverGroup -FailoverGroupName $failoverGroup `
    -ResourceGroupName $resourceGroup -ServerName $drServer).
    ReplicationRole
```

```
PS /home/ipslabs> (Get-AzSqlDatabaseFailoverGroup -FailoverGroupName $failoverGroup `
>>     -ResourceGroupName $resourceGroup -ServerName $drServer).ReplicationRole
```

6. You can now close both Command Prompt windows and maximize the Microsoft Learn browser window.

Mind Map

- Azure SQL Fundamentals
  - Introduction to Azure SQL
    - Management interfaces for Azure SQL
    - Azure SQL deployment options
    - SQL Database
    - Versionless database services
    - SQL Server on Azure Virtual Machines
    - Evolution of database services on Azure
    - Azure SQL history
    - Launch of Windows Azure
    - Azure SQL deployment options
    - IaaS vs. PaaS
    - SQL Managed Instance
    - Elastic database pool
    - Purchasing models, service tiers, and hardware choices
  - Deploy highly available solutions by using Azure SQL
    - Configure and monitor the availability
    - Availability and consistency
    - Long-term retention (LTR)
    - Backup and restore
    - Point in time restore (PITR)
    - High availability by service tier
    - Availability Zones
  - Deliver consistent performance with Azure SQL
    - Monitor and troubleshoot performance
    - Performance capabilities
    - Configure and maintain performance
  - Putting it all together with Azure SQL
    - Mission-critical application
    - Architect global scale and secure access
    - An application running on an Azure VM
    - Opportunities in Azure
  - Secure your data with Azure SQL
    - Authentication
    - Identity and access
    - Private Link for an Azure SQL Database instance
    - Firewall rules
    - Azure SQL Database
    - Security capabilities and tasks
    - Network security
    - Allow access to Azure services
    - Virtual network rules
    - An Azure SQL managed instance
    - Role-based access control

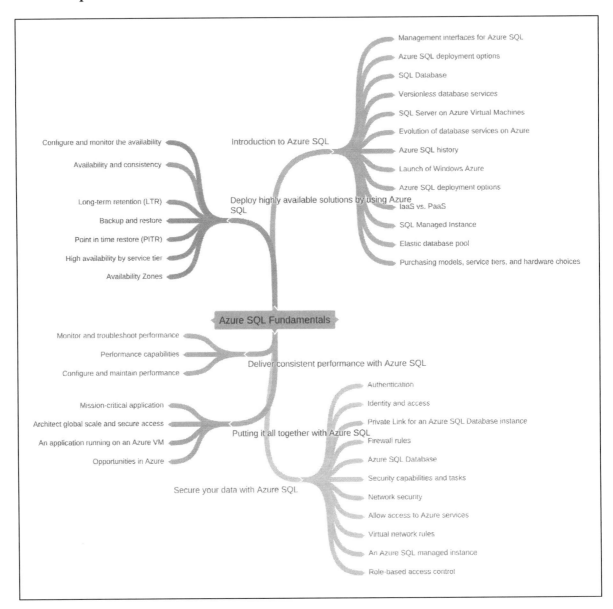

Figure 01-34: Mind Map

Practice Questions

1. Consider this scenario: you need to migrate to the cloud, but you use a third-party application that requires access to the operating system (OS). Which option will you choose?

A. SQL Server in an Azure virtual machine

B. Azure SQL Managed instance

C. Azure SQL Database, single database

D. Azure SQL Database, elastic database pool

2. Consider this scenario: you need to migrate to the cloud and remove some of the management associated with SQL Server, but your application uses CLR and Service Broker capabilities from SQL Server. Which option will you pick?

A. SQL Server in an Azure virtual machine

B. Azure SQL Managed instance

C. Azure SQL Database, single database

D. Azure SQL Database, elastic database pool

3. You are moving an application and database to Azure, but your database is currently 62 TB and will continue to grow. You do not currently use any instance-scoped features. Which option will you choose?

A. SQL Server in an Azure virtual machine

B. Azure SQL Managed instance

C. Azure SQL Database, single database

D. Azure SQL Database, elastic database pool

4. Imagine having Azure SQL Database with the serverless compute tier database deployed and an auto-pause delay of two hours. After two hours of no activity, what occurs to your database and incurred charges?

A. Azure will break your database to stop compute costs and charge you only for storage.

B. Database resources are reduced to a lower service tier to reduce costs.

C. Both of the above

D. None of the above

5. Which of the options have limits depending on your deployment option and service tier?

A. Size of tempdb

B. Max log size

C. Backup retention

D. All of the above

6. For verifying deployments, some new queries are specific to Azure SQL Database and Azure SQL Managed Instance. Which of the queries are available only for the Azure SQL platform as a service (PaaS)?

A. SELECT * FROM sys.dm_os_schedulers

B. SELECT * FROM sys.dm_user_db_resource_governance

C. SELECT * FROM sys.dm_exec_requests

D. SELECT * FROM sys.dm_os_process_memory

7. If Data max size in Azure SQL Database is 10 GB, what is the maximum transaction log size?

A. 1 GB

B. 3 GB

C. 5 GB

D. 10 GB

8. What is the default connection policy for Azure SQL Database and Azure SQL Managed Instance?

A. Proxy for all connections

B. Redirect for all connections

C. Proxy for connections within Azure and redirect for connections outside Azure

D. Proxy for connections outside Azure and redirect for connections within Azure

9. Which Azure SQL deployment options support natively restoring a database?

A. SQL Server on an Azure VM

B. Azure SQL Managed Instance

C. Azure SQL Database

D. SQL Server on an Azure VM and Azure SQL Managed Instance

10. What is not an example of how you can load data into Azure SQL Database and Azure SQL Managed Instance more efficiently?

A. Use clustered column store indexes

B. Use batching with appropriately sized batches

C. Use simple recovery mode

D. All of the above will help in Azure SQL Database and Azure SQL Managed Instance

11. What is the recommended, most secure way to protect your network for Azure SQL Database?

A. Allow access to Azure services

B. Firewall rules

C. Virtual network rules

D. Private Link

12. Which of the following are ways that you can monitor security-related events for Azure SQL Database?

A. Azure SQL auditing

B. DMVs

C. Azure Metrics and Alerts

D. All of the above

13. The number of files for tempdb is configurable for Azure SQL Database by which method?

A. The T-SQL ALTER DATABASE statement

B. File properties in SQL Server Management Studio (SSMS)

C. Increasing the number of vCores through the Azure portal

D. All of the above

14. You can configure I/O Performance for Azure SQL Database by which method?

A. Place database files on Azure Premium Storage

B. Choose a deployment option that meets your I/O requirements

C. Place specific tables and indexes on different filegroups

D. None of the above

15. How do you maintain indexes with Azure SQL?

A. You can create, rebuild, and reorganize indexes in Azure SQL just like SQL Server

B. Use a specific deployment option that supports rebuilding indexes

C. Use an offline index rebuild because online index rebuilds are not supported on Azure SQL

D. None of the above

Chapter 02: Plan and Implement Data Platform Resources

Introduction

Azure provides a great deal of flexibility for deploying SQL Server to an Azure virtual machine. The hybrid licensing options reduce your cost and allow additional protection for high availability and disaster recovery as part of your software assurance benefits. Azure Resource Manager offers several ways to deploy your resources in both a programmatic and graphical fashion. Azure and SQL Server include several tools that help migrate your data.

You will learn about the platform as a service option for SQL Server on Azure. Azure SQL Database is a flexible platform, well suited for software as service applications. It has several platform options for large databases, multiple databases, or development environments that do not need to be online 24x7. Azure SQL Database Managed Instance is a PaaS version of SQL Server that allows you to quickly move on-premises environments into a managed service. Managed Instance also supports many server-level capabilities that are not available on Azure SQL Database.

The open-source offerings on the Azure Database for MariaDB, MySQL, and PostgreSQL platforms cover the most popular open-source offerings while offering value-added services like built-in high availability and backups. These offerings also help in easily scaling up and down, offering flexibility that an application needs.

Deploy SQL Server In A Virtual Machine

The most common advantage for deploying SQL Server in an Azure Virtual Machine (VM) is that it is an easy and straightforward method to migrate an existing on-premises SQL Server into the cloud. Understanding the options and methods for deploying SQL Server in an Azure VM is critical for a successful migration. Infrastructure as a Service (IaaS) allows for greater flexibility in configuration. This flexibility means that a database administrator must plan his configuration carefully. Choosing the proper VM sizing, storage, and networking options are crucial for ensuring adequate performance for workloads.

The upcoming part will focus on ways to provision and deploy Microsoft SQL Server into an Azure virtual machine. It will also provide factual information about the various options for performing a migration.

Deploying SQL Server in Azure

Many applications will require a VM running SQL Server. Some reasons for this option include:

- **Older versions of SQL Server**—If an application requires an older version of SQL Server for vendor support, running inside a VM is the best option for these applications because it allows the application to be supported by that vendor.
- **Use of other SQL Server services**— Analysis Services, and to an extent, Integration Services (through the use of Azure Data Factory) are available as PaaS offerings; allowing many users to maximize their licensing by running SQL Server Analysis Services, Integration Services, or Reporting Services on the same machine as the database engine.
- **General application incompatibility**—This reason is somewhat of a catch-all. For example, Azure SQL Database does not support cross-database querying, but managed instance does. Some applications may require additional services to be co-located with the database instance in a manner that is not compatible with a PaaS offering.

Infrastructure as a Service (IaaS) allows the administrator to have more granular access over specific settings of the underlying infrastructure than the other Azure offerings. While the Azure platform manages the underlying server and network hardware, you still have access to the virtual storage, networking configuration, and any additional software you may want to install within the virtual machine. This includes Microsoft SQL Server.

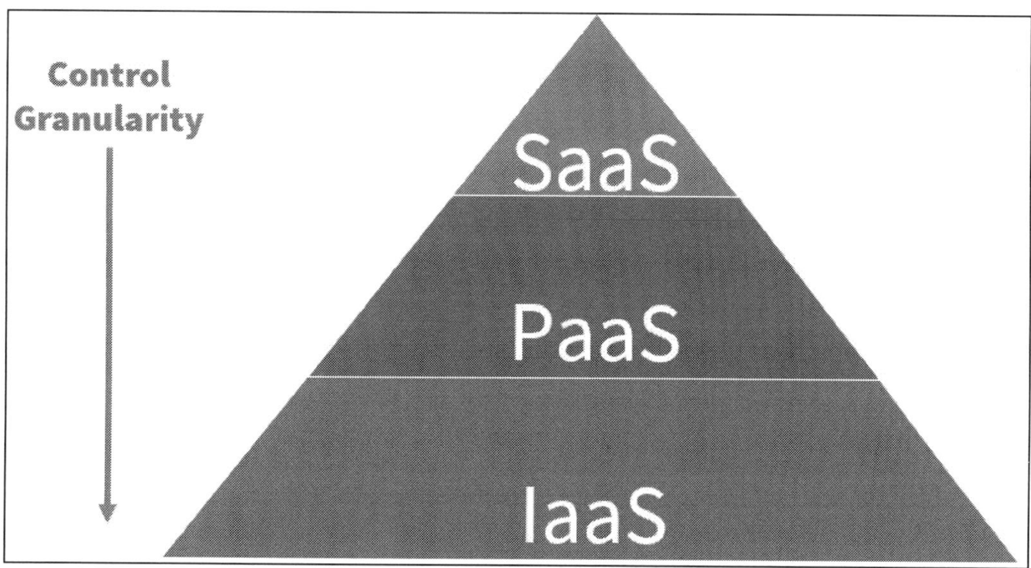

Figure 02-01: Increased Control of using IaaS

The image above illustrates the increased control you have using IaaS compared to the other Azure SQL offerings. While the exact configuration options vary between service

offerings, the administrator is typically responsible only for user security and possibly data management in SaaS offerings. When using PaaS services, the cloud provider manages the operating system (OS) and other software. An excellent example of this is the Azure Database platform, where Microsoft installs and configures the operating system and RDBMS, allowing you to start building database applications quickly. IaaS solutions are the most open-ended as you are responsible for OS patching as well as the optimal configuration of your network and storage options. With an IaaS deployment, you are also responsible for software configuration.

For IaaS solutions running in Azure, Microsoft will manage any resource below the operating system, including the physical servers, storage, and physical networking. The database administrator is responsible for the configuration of your SQL Server instances running on the operating system.

Some of your applications may not be suited for other Azure offerings, such as Azure SQL Database, because they require specific operating conditions. These conditions could include a specific combination of SQL Server and Windows versions for vendor support purposes or additional software that needs to be installed alongside SQL Server. SQL Server paired with the Azure IaaS platform provides the required control options for many organizations, regardless of specific features like CLR, replication, or Active Directory (as opposed to Azure Active Directory) authentication. Another requirement is that some applications install software alongside SQL Server that requires direct access to the underlying operating system. However, direct access to the OS is not supported in a PaaS model. These organizations and their applications can benefit from moving to a cloud service without losing their organization's critical capabilities.

SQL Server IaaS Agent Extension

When you deploy an SQL Server VM from the Azure Marketplace, part of the process installs the IaaS Agent Extension.

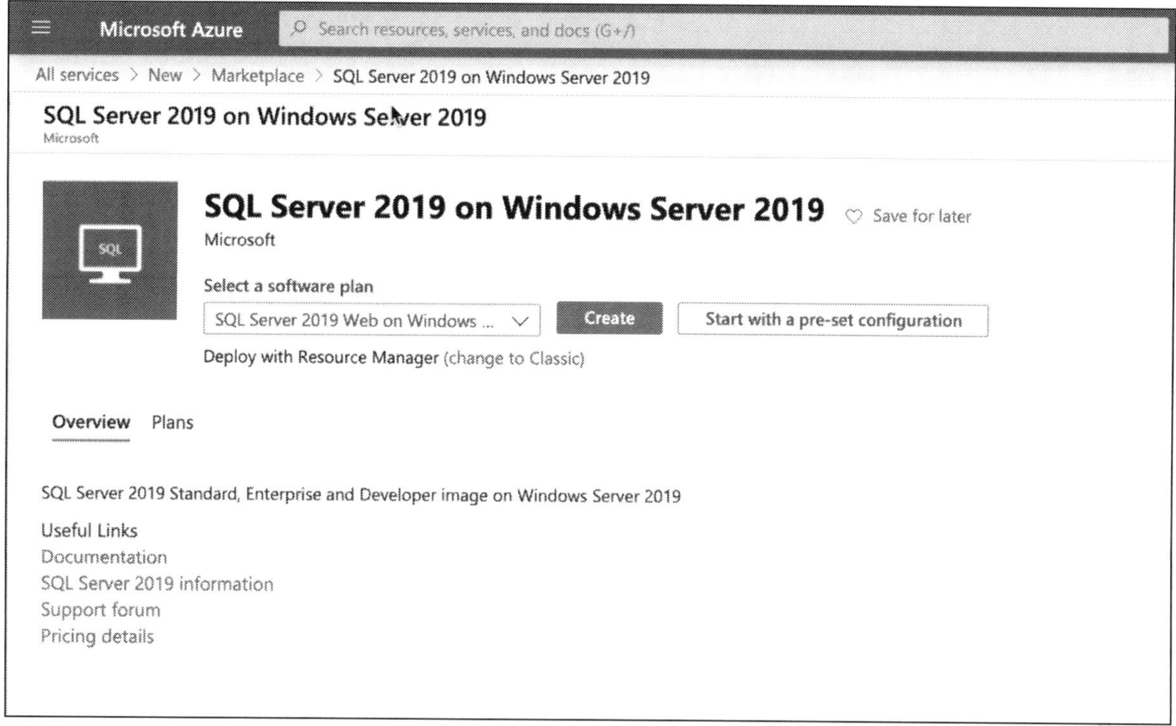

Figure 02-02: SQL Server

Extensions are codes that are executed on your VM post-deployment, typically to perform post-deployment configurations. Some examples are installing anti-virus features or Windows features. The SQL Server IaaS Agent Extension provides three key features that can reduce your administrative overhead.

- **SQL Server automated backup**
- **SQL Server automated patching**
- **Azure Key Vault integration**

In addition to these features, the extension allows you to view information about your SQL Server's configuration and storage utilization.

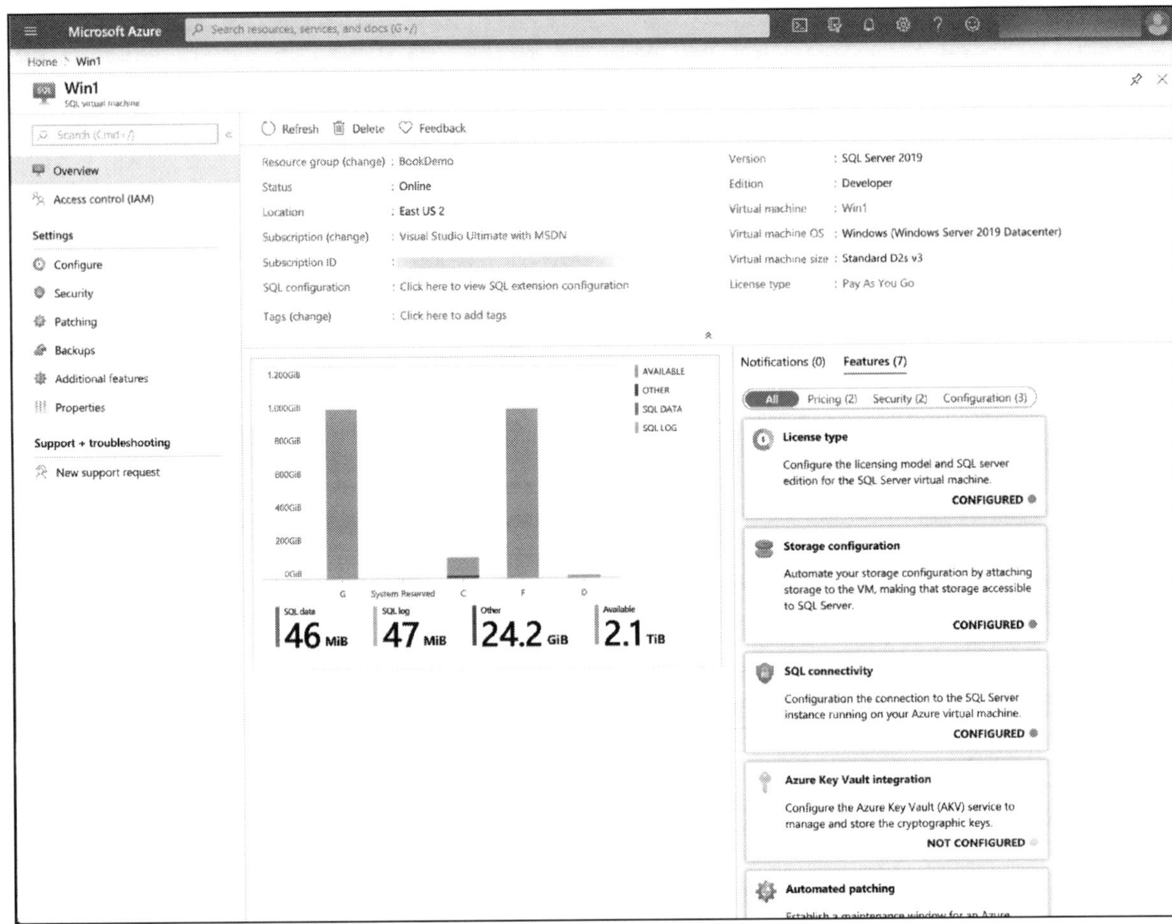

Figure 02-03: SQL Server IaaS Agent Extension

SQL Server Licensing Models

There are several different options related to how SQL Server is licensed when using the Azure IaaS offering.

Suppose you are not participating in the Microsoft Software Assurance (SA) program. In this case, you can deploy an image from the Azure Marketplace containing a preconfigured SQL Server and pay-per-minute for the use of SQL Server. This option is referred to as the Pay As You Go model, and the cost of the SQL Server license is included with the cost of the virtual machine.

However, if you are participating in the Microsoft Software Assurance (SA) program, you have more flexibility in how you license your SQL Server:

- You can use the previous method and pay-per-minute by deploying a virtual machine image containing a SQL Server from the Azure Marketplace
- You can Bring Your License (BYOL) when deploying the virtual machine that does not contain a preconfigured SQL Server instance. This option is possible when you have already purchased a valid SQL Server license for your on-premises infrastructure. This license can be applied to the virtual machine to

ensure that you are correctly licensed. You must report the usage of licenses to Microsoft by using the License Mobility verification form within ten days of implementing the virtual machine.

When choosing this method, you can manually install SQL Server through the media you have obtained, or you can choose to upload a virtual machine image to Azure.

In addition to flexible licensing options for SQL Server, Windows Server licensing options can be beneficial. These Windows Server options are known as the Azure Hybrid Benefit (AHB). Just as applying for a SQL Server license you already have purchased, you can take advantage of Windows Server licenses you already own.

Reserving a virtual machine for one to three years provides another cost-saving option. This commitment does not require an upfront payment and can be billed monthly. Using the reservation option can be beneficial if you know the workloads are going to be persistent. Hence, the cost savings can be significant, especially for larger VMs.

Virtual Machine Families

When deploying to an Azure virtual machine, several series or "families" of virtual machine sizes can be selected. Each series is a combination of memory, CPU, and storage that meets the specific requirements. For example, the series that are compute-optimized have a higher CPU to memory ratio. Having multiple options allows you to select an appropriate hardware configuration for the expected workload. The following six series have various sizes available, the details of which are fully described in the Azure portal when you choose the option to select your VM size.

General-purpose - These VMs provide a balanced ratio of CPU to memory. This VM class is ideal for testing and development of small to medium-sized database servers and low to medium-traffic web servers.

Compute-optimized - Compute-optimized VMs have a greater CPU-to-memory ratio and are well-suited for web servers with an average amount of traffic, network appliances, batch processes, and application servers. These VMs can also support machine learning workloads that cannot benefit from GPU-based VMs.

Memory-optimized - These VMs provide a high memory-to-CPU ratio. These VMs cover a comprehensive range of CPU and memory options (up to 4 TB of RAM) and are suitable for most database workloads.

Storage optimized - Storage optimized VMs provide fast, local, NVMe storage that is ephemeral. It is possible to use them with SQL Server; however, since the storage is temporary, you need to ensure you configure data protection using a feature like Always On Availability Groups or Log Shipping.

GPU - Azure VMs with GPUs are targeted at two primary workloads. These include naturally graphics processing operations like video rendering and processing as well as massively parallel machine learning workloads that can take advantage of GPUs.

High-performance computing - High Performance Compute workloads support applications that can scale horizontally to thousands of CPU cores. This maintenance is offered by high-performance CPU and Remote Direct Memory Access (RDMA) networking that offers low latency communications between VMs.

The easiest way to see the sizing options within each series is through the Azure portal. From the blade for creating a VM, you can click the option to "Select Size" and see a list.

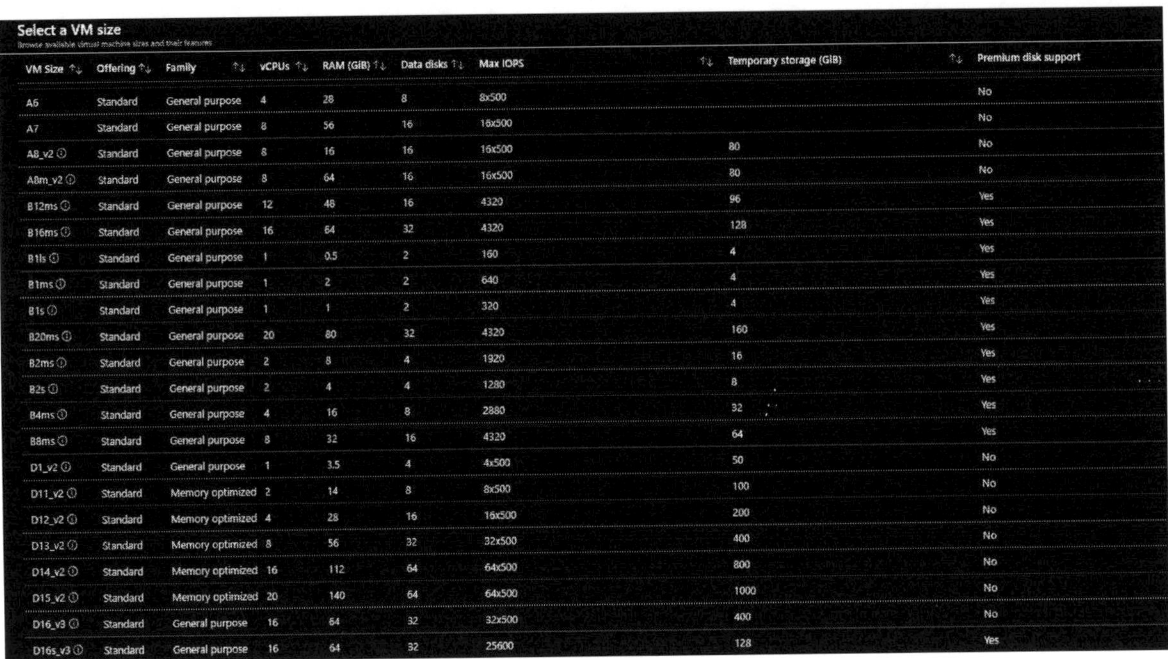

Select a VM size

VM Size	Offering	Family	vCPUs	RAM (GiB)	Data disks	Max IOPS	Temporary storage (GiB)	Premium disk support
A6	Standard	General purpose	4	28	8	8x500		No
A7	Standard	General purpose	8	56	16	16x500		No
A8_v2	Standard	General purpose	8	16	16	16x500	80	No
A8m_v2	Standard	General purpose	8	64	16	16x500	80	No
B12ms	Standard	General purpose	12	48	16	4320	96	Yes
B16ms	Standard	General purpose	16	64	32	4320	128	Yes
B1ls	Standard	General purpose	1	0.5	2	160	4	Yes
B1ms	Standard	General purpose	1	2	2	640	4	Yes
B1s	Standard	General purpose	1	1	2	320	4	Yes
B20ms	Standard	General purpose	20	80	32	4320	160	Yes
B2ms	Standard	General purpose	2	8	4	1920	16	Yes
B2s	Standard	General purpose	2	4	4	1280	8	Yes
B4ms	Standard	General purpose	4	16	8	2880	32	Yes
B8ms	Standard	General purpose	8	32	16	4320	64	Yes
D1_v2	Standard	General purpose	1	3.5	4	4x500	50	No
D11_v2	Standard	Memory optimized	2	14	8	8x500	100	No
D12_v2	Standard	Memory optimized	4	28	16	16x500	200	No
D13_v2	Standard	Memory optimized	8	56	32	32x500	400	No
D14_v2	Standard	Memory optimized	16	112	64	64x500	800	No
D15_v2	Standard	Memory optimized	20	140	64	64x500	1000	No
D16_v3	Standard	General purpose	16	64	32	32x500	400	No
D16s_v3	Standard	General purpose	16	64	32	25600	128	Yes

Figure 02-04: Virtual Machine Families

The image above shows just a small set of the series and size possibilities. For each option, you can see the number of virtual CPUs, the amount of RAM, the number of Data disks, the Max IPS, the temporary storage provided, and whether Premium storage is supported.

High Availability

One of the most significant benefits of cloud computing is that high platform availability is part of the architecture. Azure provides a high level of built hardware, storage, and networking redundancy. High availability for a system is typically measured as a percentage of uptime per year. In the table below, you can see what those numbers translate into in terms of time.

HIGH AVAILABILITY	
Availability %	Downtime per Year

99%	3.65 days
99.5%	1.83 days
99.9%	8.77 hours
99.95%	4.38 hours
99.99%	52.60 minutes
99.995%	26.30 minutes
99.999%	5.26 minutes

Table 02-01: High Availability

A single Azure Virtual Machine provides three nines (99.9%) of high availability when used with Azure-managed storage. Three nines mean that the service guarantees the availability of the virtual machine up to 99.9% of the time, which translates into a downtime of no more than 8.77 hours each year.

In addition to the default number of nines, there are additional features that you can include with your SQL Server in Azure virtual machine to achieve the maximum amount of uptime.

Azure Platform Availability

Beyond its built-in high availability, the Azure platform offers two options for providing higher levels of availability for VM and some PaaS workloads. These include Availability Zones and Availability Sets that protect your workloads from planned maintenance activity and potential hardware failures.

Availability Zones

Availability Zones are physical locations inside a region. Each zone comprises one or more data centers equipped with independent power, cooling, and networking. Within Azure regions that support Availability Zones, you can specify which zone you want the virtual machine to reside when using available Zones during VM creation. There are three Availability Zones within each supported Azure region that provide high availability against datacenter failures when you deploy multiple VMs into different zones. In addition, they also provide a means for Microsoft to perform maintenance (using a grouping called An update domain) within each region by only updating one zone at any given time. Utilizing Availability Zones in conjunction with your Azure virtual machines raises your uptime to four nines (99.99%) which equates to a maximum of 52.60 minutes of downtime per year. If Availability Zones are available in your region and your application can support minimal cross-zone latency, Availability Zones will provide the highest level of availability for your application.

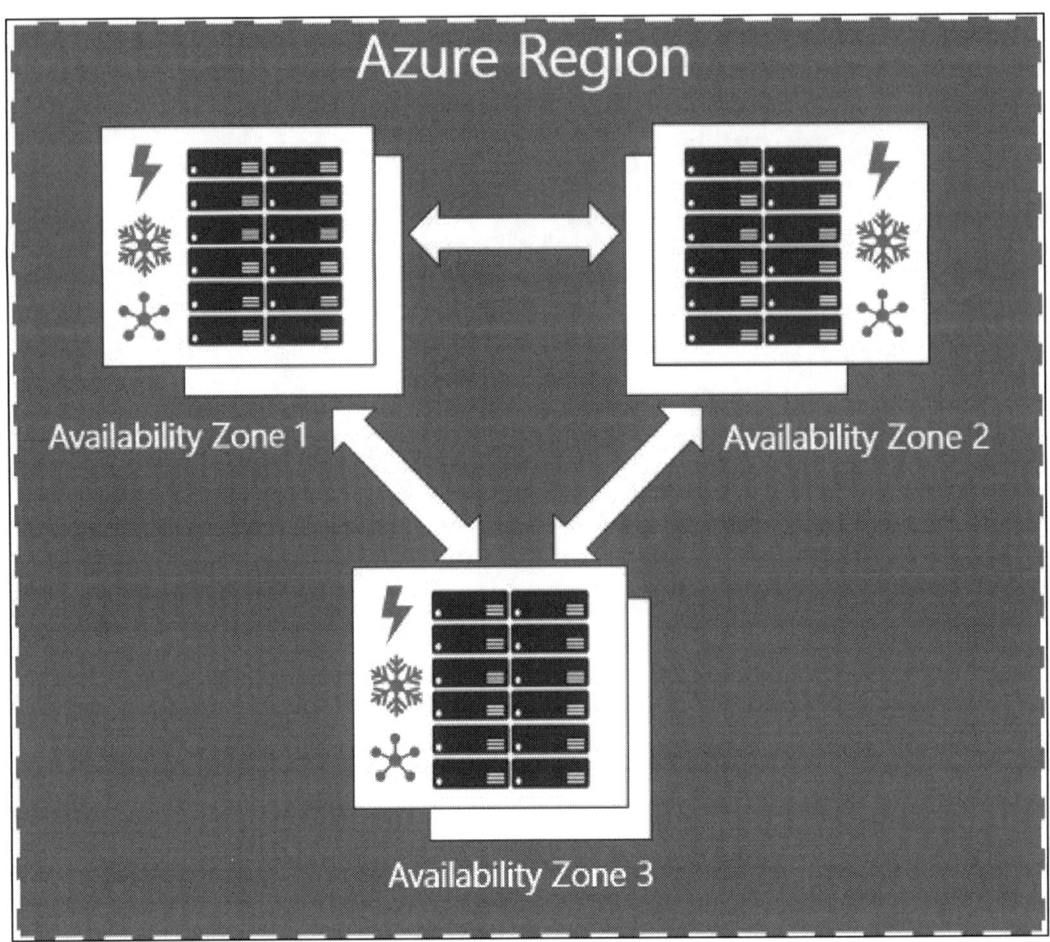

Figure 02-05: Azure Availability Zones

In the image above, you can see the availability zone configuration. When you deploy a VM into a region with an availability zone, you will be presented with an option to deploy in Zone 1, 2, and 3. These zones are logical representations of physical data centers, which means a deployment to Zone 1 in one subscription does not mean that Zone 1 represents the same datacenter in another subscription.

Availability Sets

Availability sets are related to Availability Zones, but instead of spreading workloads across datacenters in a region, they spread workloads across servers and racks in a datacenter. Since nearly all workloads in Azure are virtual, you can use availability sets to guarantee that the two VMs containing your Always On availability group members are not running on the same physical host. Availability sets can provide up to 99.95% availability and should be used when Availability Zones are unavailable in a region, or an application cannot tolerate intra-zone latency.

SQL Server High Availability Options

SQL Server provides two practical options for high availability: Always On availability groups and Failover Cluster Instances. In addition, using availability groups for your Virtual Machines also provides the option to allow for disaster recovery.

Always On availability groups (AG)

Always On availability groups can be implemented between two or more (up to a maximum of nine) SQL Server instances running on Azure virtual machines or across an on-premises data center and Azure. In an availability group, database transactions are committed to the primary replica, and then the transactions are sent either synchronously or asynchronously to all secondary replicas. The physical distance between the servers (whether or not they are in the same Azure region) dictates which availability mode you should choose. Generally, asynchronous availability mode is recommended if the workload requires the lowest possible latency or the secondary replicas are geographically spread apart. The synchronous mode will help ensure that each transaction is committed to one or more secondaries before allowing the application to continue. Always On availability groups provide high availability and disaster recovery because a single availability group can support synchronous and asynchronous availability modes. The failover unit for an availability group is a group of databases, not the entire instance.

SQL Server Failover Cluster Instances

If you want to protect the entire instance, you can use a SQL Server Failover Cluster Instance (FCI), which offers high availability for an entire instance in a single region. An FCI does not provide disaster recovery without combining other features like availability groups or log shipping. FCIs also require shared storage provided on Azure using shared file storage or Storage Spaces Direct on Windows Server.

For Azure workloads, availability groups are the preferred solution for newer deployments because the shared storage requirement of FCIs increases the complexity of deployments.

SQL Server Disaster Recovery Options

While the Azure platform offers 99.9% uptime by default, disasters can still affect the application uptime. You must have a proper disaster recovery plan in place when you are performing any type of migration. Azure offers us several methods to ensure that your SQL Server on a virtual machine is protected in the event of a disaster. There are two components to this protection. First, there are Azure platform options like geo-replicated storage for backups along with Azure Site Recovery, an all-encompassing disaster recovery solution for all of your workloads. Second, there are SQL Server-specific offerings like Availability Groups and backups.

Native SQL Server Backups

Backups are considered the lifeblood of any database administrator, and it is not any different when working with a cloud solution. With SQL Server on an Azure virtual machine, you have granular control of when backups occur and where they are stored. You can use SQL agent jobs to back up directly to a URL linked to Azure blob storage. Azure provides the option to use geo-redundant storage (GRS) or read-access geo-redundant storage (RA-GRS) to ensure that your backup files are stored safely across the geographic landscape.

Note: As part of the Azure SQL VM service provider, you can automatically manage your backups by the platform.

Azure Backup for SQL Server

The Azure Backup solution requires an agent to be installed on the virtual machine. Azure backup also provides a central location that you can use to manage and monitor the backups for meeting any specified RPO/RTO metrics.

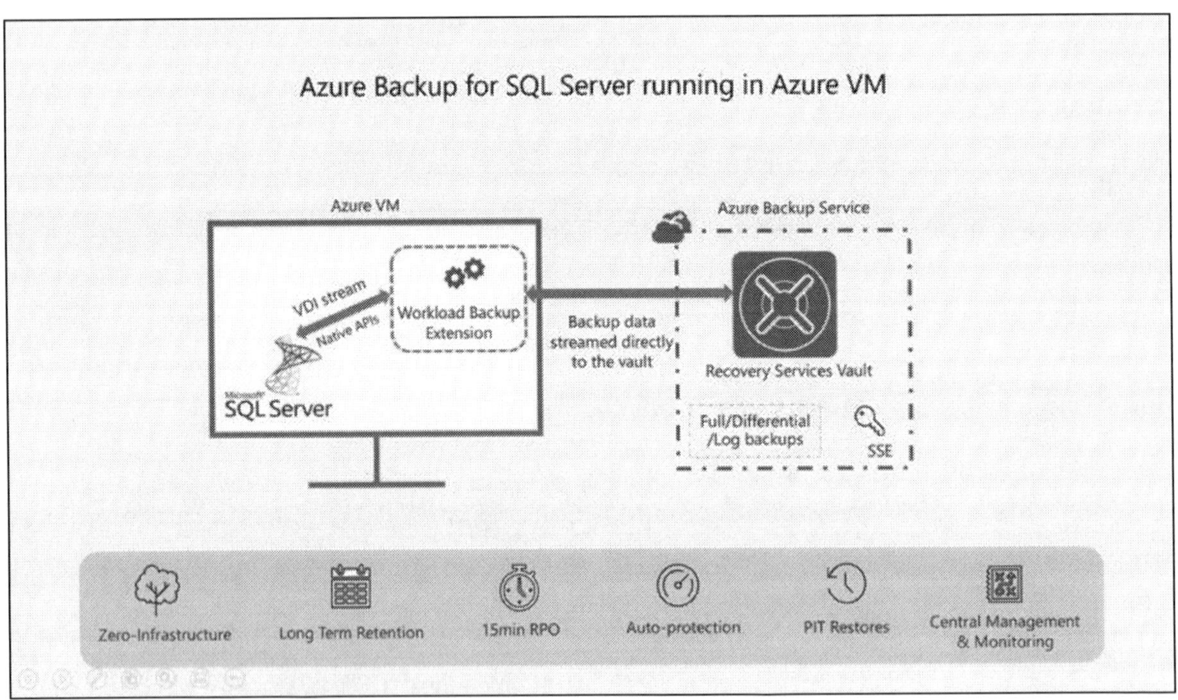

Figure 02-06: Azure Backup for SQL Server

As shown above, the Azure Backup solution is a comprehensive enterprise backup solution that provides long-term data retention, automated management, and additional data protection. This option costs more than simply performing your backups or using the Azure resource provider for SQL Server, but it does offer a complete backup feature set.

Availability Groups

In addition to the high availability scenarios described above, Always On availability groups can be used for disaster recovery. You can implement up to nine database replicas across Azure regions and stretch this architecture further using Distributed Availability Groups. Availability Groups ensure that a viable copy of your database(s) is in another location beyond the primary region. By doing so, you ensure that your data ecosystem is protected against natural disasters and some human-made ones.

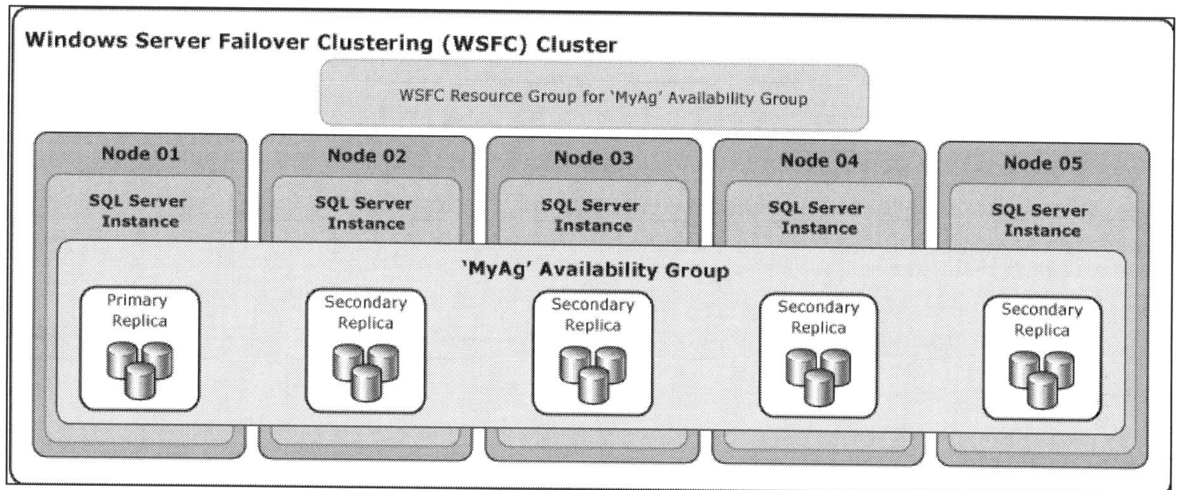

Figure 02-07: Availability Groups

The image above shows a logical diagram of an Always On availability group running on a Windows Server Failover Cluster. There are one primary and four secondary replicas. In this scenario, all five replicas could be synchronous or some combination of synchronous and asynchronous replicas. Keep in mind that the unit of failover is the group of databases and not the instance.

EXAM TIP: While a failover cluster instance provides HA at an instance level, it does not provide disaster recovery.

Azure Site Recovery

Azure Site Recovery is a low-cost solution that performs block-level replication of your Azure virtual machine. This service offers various options, including the ability to test and verify your disaster recovery strategy. This solution is best used for stateless environments (for example, web servers) versus transactional database virtual machines. Azure Site Recovery is supported for use with SQL Server, but you will need to set a higher recovery point that means potential loss. In this case, your RTO will essentially be your RPO.

Deploy SQL Server to Azure Virtual Machines

The Azure ecosystem offers several different methods for the provision of a new SQL Server instance on an Azure virtual machine. Each method provides different capabilities, such as having a repeatable process (via scripting languages like PowerShell) or accomplishing the goal without understanding programming constructs via the Azure portal.

Azure Marketplace

The Azure Marketplace is a centralized location that offers the ability to generate Azure resources based on a predesigned template. For example, you can quickly create a SQL Server 2019 instance on Windows Server 2019 with a couple of mouse clicks and some basic information like the virtual machine name and some SQL Server configuration information. Once provided, Azure Resource Manager will initiate the creation of the virtual machine, and it will be up and running within minutes.

The blade for SQL Server 2019 on Windows Server 2019 in the Azure Marketplace is shown below. This blade gives you the option of pre-set configurations that support OLTP or Data Warehouse workloads and allows you to specify storage, patching, and backup options.

Figure 02-08: Azure Marketplace

The disadvantage of using the portal to create Azure resources is that it is not easily repeatable. However, it is easy to get started with the portal, and a new administrator can quickly get up and running by using the portal.

Storage Considerations

SQL Server requires good storage performance to deliver robust application performance, whether an on-premises instance or installed in an Azure VM. Azure provides a wide variety of storage solutions to meet the needs of your workload. While

Azure offers various types of storage (blob, file, queue, table), in most cases, SQL Server workloads will use Azure managed disks. The exceptions are that a Failover Cluster Instance can be built on file storage, and backups will use blob storage. Azure-managed disks act as a block-level storage device that is presented to your Azure VM. Managed disks offer several benefits, including 99.999% availability, scalable deployment (you can have up to 50,000 VM disks per subscription per region), and integration with availability sets and zones for offering higher levels of resiliency in case of failure.

Azure-managed disks all offer two types of encryption, including Azure Server-side encryption and Azure Disk encryption. Azure Server-side encryption is provided by the storage service and acts as encryption-at-rest provided by the storage service. In comparison, Azure Disk encryption uses BitLocker on Windows and DM-Crypt on Linux to provide OS and Data disk encryption inside the VM. Both technologies integrate with Azure Key Vault and allow you to bring your encryption key.

> EXAM TIP: Each VM will have at least two disks associated with it: the operating system disk and the temporary disk.

Operating System disk – Each virtual machine will require an operating system disk that contains the boot volume. The operating system will be automatically installed on the operating system disk.

Temporary disk – Each virtual machine will include one disk used for temporary storage. This storage is intended to be used for data that does not need to be durable, such as page files or swap files. Because the disk is temporary, you should not use it to store any critical information like database or transaction log files, as they will be lost during maintenance or a virtual machine reboot. This drive will be mounted as D:\ on Windows and /dev/sdb1 on Linux.

Additionally, you can and should add additional data disks to your Azure VMs running SQL Server.

Data disks – The term data disk is used in the Azure portal, but in practice, these are just additional managed disks added to a VM. These disks can be pooled to increase the available IOPs and storage capacity using Storage Spaces on Windows or Logical Volume Management on Linux.

Furthermore, each disk can be one of several types:

- **Standard HDD** was the original storage offering on Azure that offered cost-effective storage for non-I/O intensive workloads. An everyday use case for standard disks is SQL Server backups.

- **Standard SSD** is a solid-state drive with similar latency and IOPS to the standard HDD drives at sizes up to 4 TB. However, this type offers significant performance gains at larger volumes. Standard SSDs do offer guaranteed performance levels, while Standard HDD disks do not.
- **Premium SSD** is the most commonly used type of disk for SQL Server workloads. It is presented in all regions, supporting a wide variety of VM types.
- **Ultra SSD** offers the lowest latency (submillisecond) and the maximum potential IOPs. Ultra SSD lets you configure IOPs, storage volume, and bandwidth independently for more granular cost control.

Data files should be stored in their pool with read-caching on the Azure disks. Transaction log files will not benefit from this caching, so they should go into their pool without caching. TempDB can optionally go into its pool or use the VM's temporary disk that offers low latency being physically attached to the physical server where the VMs are running. Properly configured Premium SSD will see latency in single-digit milliseconds. For mission-critical workloads that require latency lower than that, you should consider Ultra SSD.

Deploying via PowerShell/CLI

PowerShell is an object-orienting programming language that can quickly and efficiently create a virtual machine (and other resources) within the Azure ecosystem. PowerShell gives you granular control over various aspects of the virtual machine, such as size, name, IP address, and even storage.

```
# Variables for common values
$resourceGroup = "myResourceGroup"
$location = "westeurope"
$vmName = "myVM"

# Create user object
$cred = Get-Credential -Message "Enter a username and password for the virtual machine."

# Create a resource group
New-AzResourceGroup -Name $resourceGroup -Location $location

# Create a virtual machine
New-AzVM `
  -ResourceGroupName $resourceGroup `
  -Name $vmName `
  -Location $location `
  -ImageName "Win2016Datacenter" `
  -VirtualNetworkName "myVnet" `
  -SubnetName "mySubnet" `
  -SecurityGroupName "myNetworkSecurityGroup" `
  -PublicIpAddressName "myPublicIp" `
  -Credential $cred `
  -OpenPorts 3389
```

Figure 02-09: PowerShell Script That Defines Parameters and Creates an Azure Resource Group

The image above shows a PowerShell script that defines parameters and creates an Azure resource group along with a virtual machine with a predefined virtual network.

Azure Command Line Interface (CLI) uses scripting to create Azure resources, including virtual machines. Its simplistic nature allows you to accomplish the same goal as PowerShell in fewer actual code lines.

```
az group create --name myResourceGroup --location eastus

az vm create \
    --resource-group myResourceGroup \
    --name myVM \
    --image win2016datacenter \
    --admin-username azureuser
```

Figure 02-10: Azure CLI Script That Defines Parameters and Creates An Azure Resource Group

As the image shows, the CLI is less verbose in the code required to create new resources.

Deploying Using Azure Resource Manager Templates

Azure Resource Manager Templates benefit from deploying a complete set of resources in one single declarative template. This includes building dependencies into the templates and using parameters to change specific values at deployment time. Once you have a template, there are several ways with which you can deploy it, including an Azure

DevOps pipeline or through the custom deployments blade in the Azure portal. You can use the Azure portal to export a Resource Manager template to JSON for future deployment.

```
{
  "$schema": "https://schema.management.azure.com/schemas/2019-04-01/deploymentTemplate.json#",
  "contentVersion": "1.0.0.0",
  "parameters": {
    "adminUsername": {
      "type": "string",
      "metadata": {
        "description": "Username for the Virtual Machine."
      }
    },
    "adminPassword": {
      "type": "securestring",
      "metadata": {
        "description": "Password for the Virtual Machine."
      }
    },
    "dnsLabelPrefix": {
      "type": "string",
      "metadata": {
        "description": "Unique DNS Name for the Public IP used to access the Virtual Machine."
      }
    },
    "windowsOSVersion": {
      "type": "string",
      "defaultValue": "2016-Datacenter",
      "allowedValues": [
        "2008-R2-SP1",
        "2012-Datacenter",
        "2012-R2-Datacenter",
        "2016-Nano-Server",
        "2016-Datacenter-with-Containers",
        "2016-Datacenter",
        "2019-Datacenter"
      ],
      "metadata": {
        "description": "The Windows version for the VM. This will pick a fully patched image of this given Windows version."
      }
```

Figure 02-11: Deploying using Azure Resource Manager Templates

The image above is an example of an Azure Resource Manager template that can repeatedly deploy a group of Azure resources. Templates can be deployed directly from the Azure portal or via scripting languages that reference the templates, such as PowerShell, the Azure CLI, or through DevOps workflows like Azure DevOps.

The image above highlights the PowerShell and Azure CLI code to deploy an Azure Resource Group, prompting the user for the resource group name and the target Azure region.

SQL Server Migration Options

Azure Infrastructure as a Service (IaaS) solutions are frequently used when migrating your on-premises environment to the cloud. There are several tools available to help with the migration process. This next section looks at some of the tools and methods for migration.

Azure Migrate Tool

This migration tool offers a location to evaluate and migrate on-premises servers, infrastructure, applications, and data to Azure. It will provide discoverability and proper assessments of your servers regardless of whether they are physical or VMWare/Hyper-V virtual machines.

Azure Migrate will also help to ensure that you select the appropriate virtual machine size so that workloads will have enough resources available. In addition, the tool will provide a cost estimation so that you can budget accordingly.

To utilize the Azure Migrate tool, you must deploy a lightweight appliance deployed on a virtual or physical machine. Once the on-premises servers are discovered, the appliance will continually send metadata about each server (along with performance metrics) to Azure Migrate, which resides in the cloud.

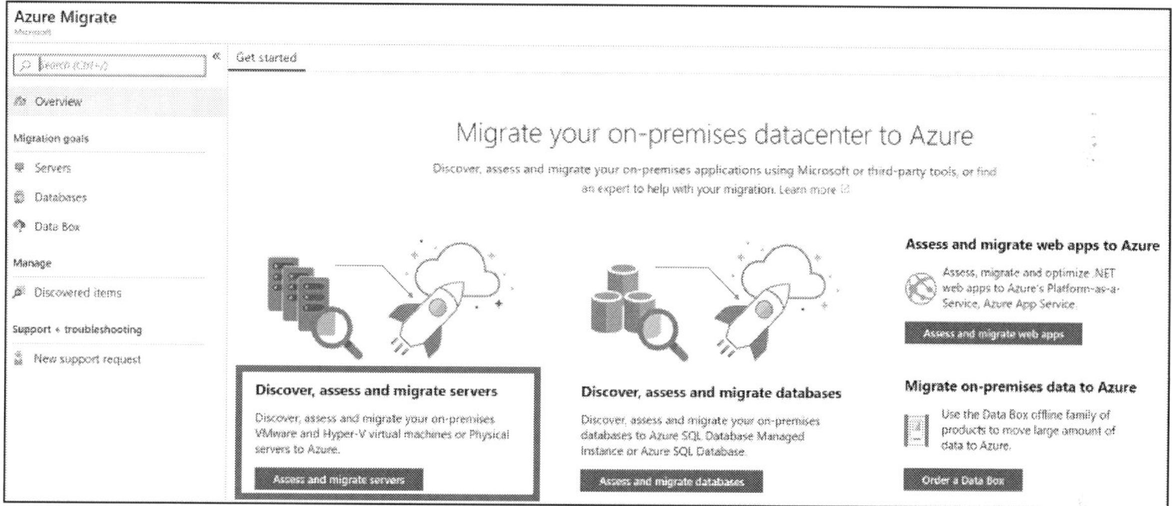

Figure 02-12: Azure Migrate Tool

As shown above, the Azure Migrate experience can be kicked off from the portal to begin the migration process. The service consists of a unified migration platform that provides a single portal to track your entire migration to Azure.

Several additional tools can be used to map your server estate and identify compatibility with your target Azure platform:

- MAP (MAP) Toolkit—The Microsoft Assessment and Planning Toolkit automatically gathers inventory of all SQL Servers in your network, gathers version and server information, and provides reports on the information gathered.
- Database Experimentation Assistant—This tool can evaluate version upgrades of SQL Server by checking syntax compatibility while providing a platform to evaluate query performance on the target version.

Data Migration Assistant

The MAP toolkit and Database Experimentation assistant can help you identify your databases and highlight any incompatibilities or potential performance issues in your database. Still, the Data Migration Assistant (DMA) is a comprehensive toolkit that assesses, identifies new features you can use to benefit your application, and ultimately performs the migration. This tool can be used to migrate between versions of SQL Server, from on-premises to an Azure VM or Azure SQL Database or Azure SQL Managed Instance.

One of the main benefits of the DMA is the ability to assess queries both from Extended Event trace files and SQL queries from an external application, for example, T-SQL queries in the C# application code for your application. You can generate a full report using a C# source and upload the migration assessment to the DMA. The DMA mitigates the risk of moving to a newer version of SQL Server or Azure SQL Database.

Azure Database Migration Service

The Azure Database Migration Service (DMS) is designed to support a broad mix of different migration scenarios with different source and target databases as well as both offline (one-time) and online (continuous data sync) migration scenarios. The DMS supports migrating to and from SQL Server to Azure SQL Database and Azure SQL Managed Instance. The offline source and target pairs are shown in Table 2 below:

AZURE DATABASE MIGRATION SERVICE	
Target	**Source**
Azure SQL DB	SQL Server
	RDS SQL
	Oracle
Azure SQL DB MI	SQL Server
	RDS SQL
	Oracle
Azure SQL VM	SQL Server
	Oracle
Azure Cosmos DB	MongoDB
Azure DB for MySQL	MySQL
	RDS MySQL
Azure DB for PostgreSQL	PostgreSQL

	RDS PostgreSQL

Table 02-02: Azure Database Migration Services

The source and target pairs for online migration are shown in Table 3 below:

AZURE DATABASE MIGRATION SERVICE	
Target	**Source**
Azure SQL DB	SQL Server
	RDS SQL
	Oracle
Azure SQL DB MI	SQL Server
	RDS SQL
	Oracle
Azure SQL VM	SQL Server
	Oracle
Azure Cosmos DB	MongoDB
Azure DB for MySQL	MySQL
	RDS MySQL
Azure DB for PostgreSQL	PostgreSQL
	RDS PostgreSQL
	Oracle

Table 02-03: Azure Database Migration Services

The Data Migration Service has a few prerequisites that are common across migration scenarios. It would help if you create a virtual network in Azure, so if your migration scenarios involve on-premises resources, you will need to create a VPN or ExpressRoute connection from your office to Azure. Several network ports are required for connectivity, and once the prerequisites are in place, the time to complete migration will depend on the volume of data and the rate of change in the databases.

Several traditional and more manual approaches for migrating databases to Azure include backup and restore, log shipping, replication, and adding an Availability group replica in Azure. These solutions were not designed primarily for performing migrations, but they can be used for this purpose. The technique you use for physically

migrating your data will depend on the amount of downtime you can sustain during the migration process.

Deploy Azure SQL Database

The platform as a Service (PaaS) offering for SQL Server can be an excellent solution for specific workloads. The PaaS offering provides less granular control over the infrastructure and relegates management of the underlying components (memory, CPU, storage, operating system, etc.) to the cloud provider, namely Microsoft.

This part will focus on ways to provision and deploy both Azure SQL Database. Azure SQL manages instances and provides clear and definitive guidance on various options when migrating to this platform.

Deploying SQL Server in Azure

Platform as a Service (PaaS) provides a complete development and deployment environment in the cloud, which is used for simple cloud-based applications and advanced enterprise applications.

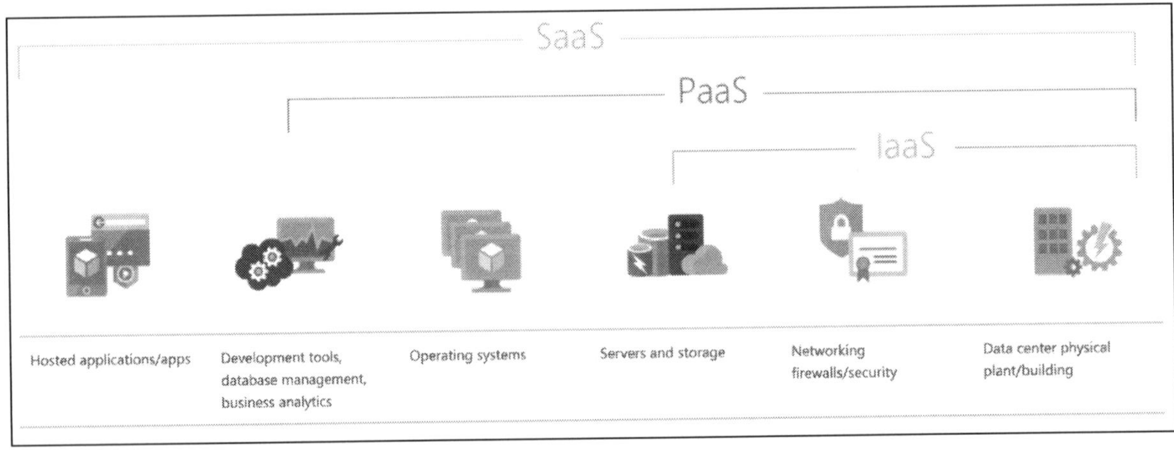

Figure 02-13: PaaS Options for Deploying SQL Server in Azure

As shown in the image above, PaaS includes cloud provides operating systems, and management of your solution. For example, in Azure SQL Database and Azure SQL Managed Instance, the high availability, OS and SQL Server features, and the Azure platform provides backups.

You will explore the Azure SQL database in the following section. Azure SQL Database is available in three different deployment options:

- A single database – A single database that is billed and managed on a per-database level
- Elastic Pools – A group of databases that are managed together and share a standard set of resources

- Hyperscale – a single database offering that allows databases to scale much beyond the 4-TB limit of an Azure SQL Database

Even in the cloud, all services are backed by physical hardware. The Azure SQL Database allows you to choose from two different purchasing models:

- Database Transaction Unit (DTU) – DTUs are calculated based on the formula combining compute, storage, and I/O resources
- vCore – The vCore model allows you to purchase a specified number of vCores based on your given workloads. vCore is the default purchasing model when purchasing Azure SQL Database resources. vCore databases have a specific relationship between the number of cores and the amount of memory and storage provided to the database

Azure SQL Database also includes:

- Automatic backups
- Automatic patching
- Built-in high availability
- SQL Server feature enhancements without the need to upgrade software

Service Tier Options

PaaS comes in several different service tiers. Each tier has varying capabilities, which provide a wide range of options when choosing this platform.

The DTU model is available in three different service tiers:

- Basic
- Standard
- Premium

You can purchase vCore databases in three different service tiers given below:

- General Purpose – This tier is for general-purpose workloads. It is backed by Azure premium storage and has higher latency than Business Critical
- Business Critical – This tier is for high-performing workloads offering the lowest latency of either service tier. This tier is backed by local SSDs instead of Azure blob storage. It also offers the highest resilience to failure as well as provides a built-in read-only database replica that can be used to off-load reporting workloads
- Hyperscale – Hyperscale databases can scale far beyond the 4 TB limit of the other Azure SQL Database offerings and have a unique architecture that supports databases of up to 100 TB

Backups

One of the essential features of the platform as a Service offering is backups. In this case, backups are performed automatically without any intervention. Backups are stored in Azure blob geo-redundant storage and are retained for between 7 and 35 days by default, based on the service tier of the database. Essential and vCore databases default to seven days of retention, and on the vCore databases, this value can be adjusted by the administrator. The retention time can be extended by configuring long-term retention (LTR), which would allow you to retain backups for up to 10 years. To provide redundancy, you are also able to use read-accessible geo-redundant blob storage. This storage would replicate your database backups to a secondary region. It would also allow you to read from that secondary region if needed. It is worth stating that manual backups of databases are not permitted, and the platform will deny any request to do so.

Database Backups are taken on a given schedule:

- Full – Once a week
- Differential – Every 12 hours
- Log – Every 5-10 minutes depending on transaction log activity

This backup schedule should meet the needs of most recovery point/time objectives (RPO/RTO). However, each customer should evaluate whether or not they meet his business requirements.

If the need to restore a database arises, there are several options available. Due to the nature of the platform as a Service, you cannot manually restore a database using conventional methods, such as issuing the T-SQL command RESTORE DATABASE.

Regardless of which restore method is implemented, it is not possible to restore over an existing database. If a database needs to be restored, the existing database must be dropped or renamed before initiating the restore. Furthermore, keep in mind that depending on the platform service tier, restoration timings could fluctuate. It is recommended that you test the restore process to obtain baseline metrics on how long a restore could take.

The available restore options are:

- Restore using the Azure portal – using the Azure portal, you have the option of restoring a database to the same Azure SQL Database server, or you can use the restore to create a new database on a new server in any Azure region
- Restore using scripting Languages – Both PowerShell and Azure CLI can be utilized to restore a database

Active Geo-replication

Geo-replication is a business continuity feature that asynchronously replicates a database of up to four secondary replicas. As transactions are committed to the primary (and its replicas within the same region), the transactions are sent to the secondaries to be replayed. Because this process asynchronous,the calling application does not have to wait for the secondary replica to commit the transaction before SQL Server returns control to the caller.

The secondary databases are readable and can be used to off-load read-only workloads, thus freeing up resources for transactional workloads on the primary or placing data closer to your end-users. Furthermore, the secondary databases can be in the same region as the primary or in another Azure region.

With geo-replication, you can initiate a failover either manually by the user or from the application. If a failover occurs, you potentially will need to update application connection strings to reflect the new endpoint of what is now the primary database.

Failover groups

Failover groups are built on top of the technology used in geo-replication but provide a single endpoint for connection. The primary reason for using failover groups is that the technology provides endpoints that can be utilized to route traffic to the appropriate replica. Your application can then connect after a failover without connection string changes.

Serverless

The name "Serverless" can be confusing as you still deploy your Azure SQL Database to a logical server to which you connect. Azure SQL Database serverless is a compute tier that will automatically scale up or down the resources for a given database based on demand. If the workload no longer requires to compute resources, the database will become "paused," and you will not be charged during the period when the database is in this state. When a connection attempt is made, the database will "resume" and become available. Moreover, resuming the database is not instantaneous.

Another difference between serverless and the average vCore model of Azure SQL Database is that you can specify a minimum and a maximum number of vCores. Memory and I/O limits are proportional to the range that is specified.

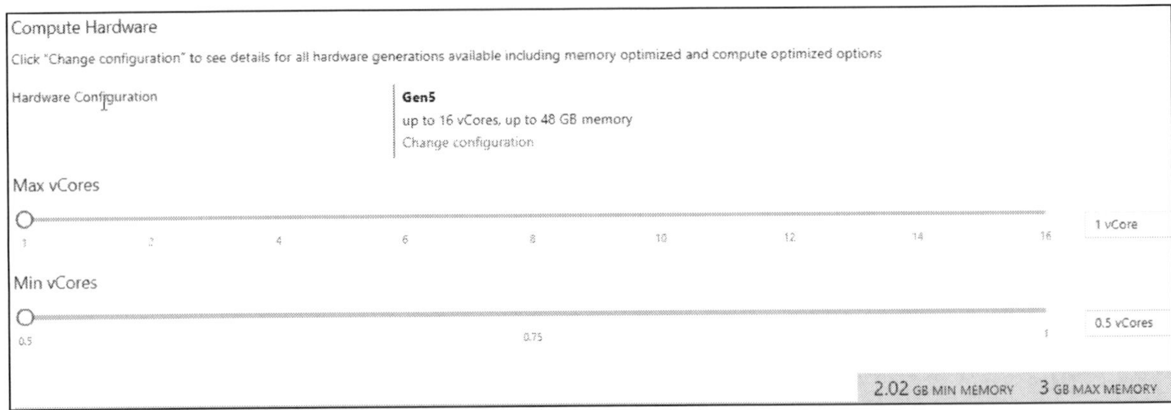

Figure 02-14: Azure SQL Database Serverless

The image above shows the configuration screen for a serverless database in the Azure portal. You have an option to select a minimum (as low as half of a vCore) and maximum (as high as 16 vCores). You should note that databases that are not deployed as serverless are referred to as "provisioned."

The setting to control pausing is known as autopause delay with a minimum value of 60 minutes and a maximum value of seven days. If the database has been idle for that period, it will then pause. Once the database has been inactive for a specified time, it will be paused until a subsequent connection is attempted. Any serverless applications should be configured to handle connection errors and include retry logic, as connecting to a paused database will generate a connection error.

Serverless is not fully compatible with all features in Azure SQL Database as some features are running background processes all the time. These features include:

- Geo-replication
- Long-term backup retention
- A job database in elastic jobs
- The sync database in SQL Data Sync (Data Sync is a service that replicates data between a group of databases)

Hyperscale

Azure SQL Database has been limited to 4 TB of storage per database for many years. This restriction is due to a physical limitation of the Azure infrastructure. Azure SQL Database Hyperscale changes the paradigm and allows for databases to be 100 TB or more. Hyperscale introduces new horizontal scaling techniques to add compute nodes as the data sizes grow. You must note that once an Azure SQL Database is converted to Hyperscale, you would not be able to change it back to a "regular" Azure SQL Database.

Deploy SQL Database Elastic Pool

Elastic pools are deployment option in which you purchase Azure compute resources (CPU, memory, and storage) that is then shared among multiple databases defined as

belonging to the same pool. An easy comparison with an on-premises SQL Server is that an elastic pool is like a SQL Server instance with multiple user databases. By using elastic pools, you can easily manage pool resources while at the same time potentially saving costs. Elastic pools also facilitate easy scalability up to the set limits. The resources are there if a single database within the pool needs resources due to an unpredictable workload.

Managing Pool Resources

The Azure portal delivers a wealth of information regarding the state and health of the elastic pool. You can view resource utilization and see which database is consuming the most resources. This information can help diagnose performance issues or identity a database that might not be a good fit for the pool, such as when one database is consuming the vast majority of pool resources. The image below shows an elastic pool with actual resource utilization.

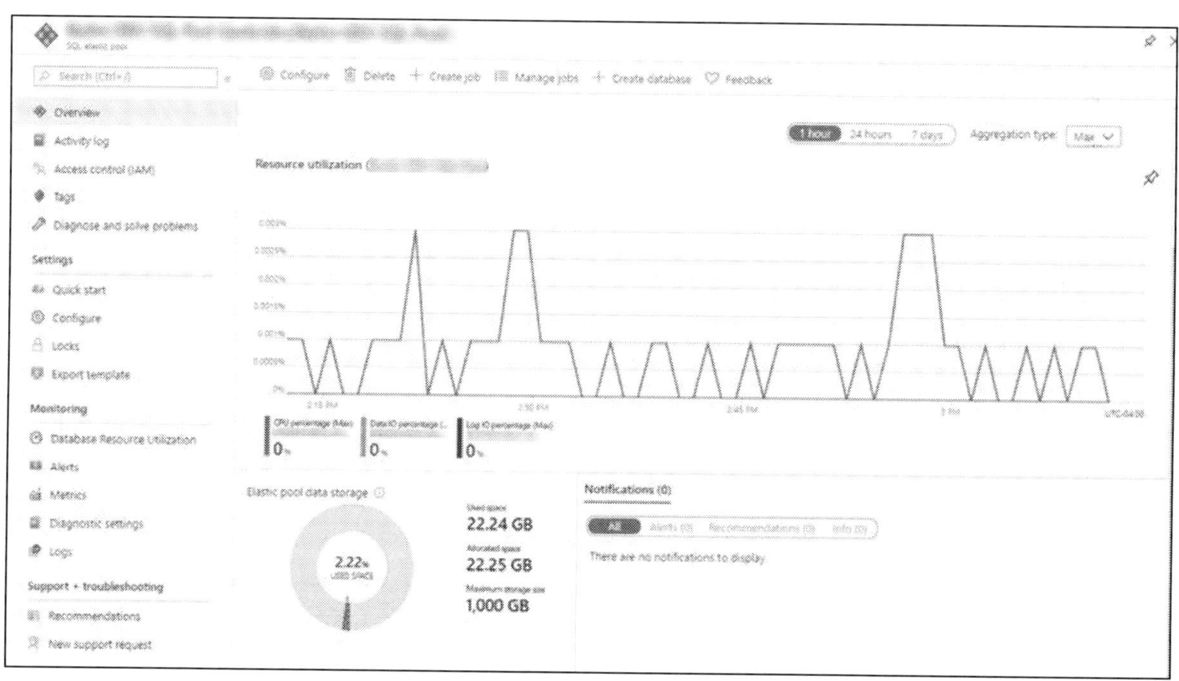

Figure 02-15: Managing Pool Resources

If you need to adjust the pool to decrease or increase resources allocated to the pool, you can make that change via the Configure option in the Settings section of the Elastic Pool management blade.

From that blade, you can quickly and easily adjust:

- Pool size, including DTUs, vCores, and storage size
- Service tier
- Resources per database
- Which databases are included in the pool by adding or removing them

As shown in the image below, you can adjust numerous settings in the Elastic Pool. You can change the total size of the pool and add or remove databases from the pool as needed. These changes can be made online, including the min and max DTUs or vCores per database. Active connections will be dropped as the resizing completes.

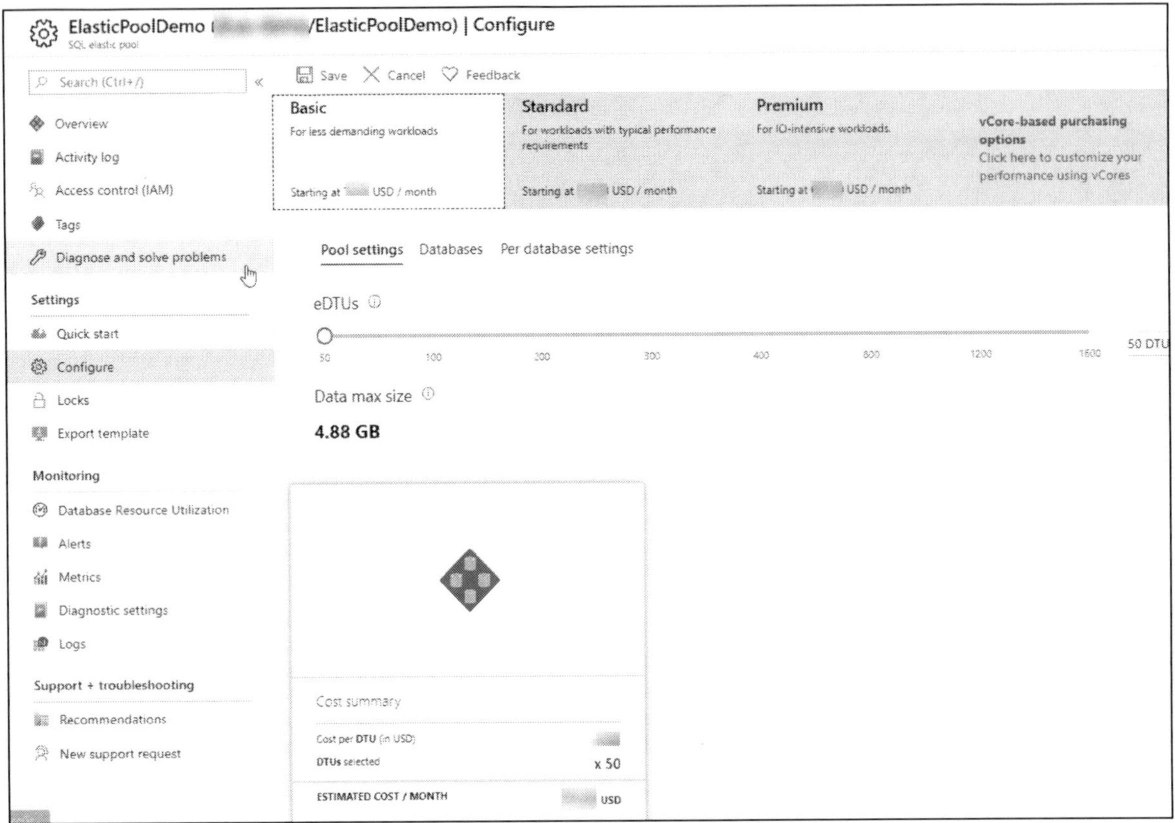

Figure 02-16: Elastic Pool

The most helpful feature is monitoring Database Resource Utilization, as shown in the image below. This feature allows you to see how databases are performing within the pool quickly.

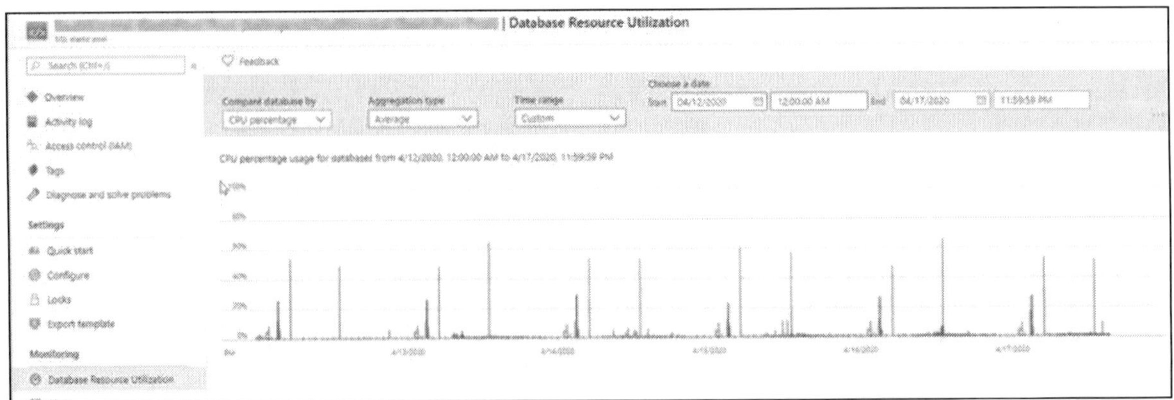

Figure 02-17: Database Resource Utilization

An elastic pool is a good fit for multi-tenant databases where each tenant copies the database. You can balance the workload across databases to not allow one database to monopolize all the pool's resources.

Deploy SQL Managed Instance

While many organizations initially migrate to Azure using IaaS offerings, the platform (PaaS) offers additional benefits. One key benefit is that you no longer have to install or patch SQL Server as the service performs this function. Additionally, consistency checking and backups are also part of the managed service, while additional security and performance tools are also included in the PaaS offerings.

Azure SQL Managed Instance is a fully functional SQL Server instance that is almost 100% compatible with your on-premises ecosystem, including features like SQL Agent, access to tempdb, cross-database query, and standard language runtime (CLR). The service uses the same infrastructure as Azure SQL Database. It includes all the benefits of the PaaS service, such as automatic backups, automatic patching, and built-in high availability, just to name a few.

Azure SQL Managed Instance Features

Azure SQL Managed Instance allows for easy migration paths for existing applications by allowing restores from on-premises backups. Unlike Azure SQL Database, which is designed around single database structures, Managed Instance provides an entire SQL Server instance, allowing up to 100 databases and accessing the system databases. Managed instance provides other features that are not available in Azure SQL Database, including cross-database queries, common language runtime (CLR). Along with the msdb system database, it allows the use of SQL Agent.

Options

There are two service tiers available when creating an Azure SQL Managed Instance, including Business Critical and General Purpose. They are the same as the Azure SQL Database vCore model (managed instance is purchased using the vCore model). However, there are minimal functionality differences between the two tiers. Business Critical includes In-Memory OLTP as well as offers a readable secondary, neither of which is available with the General Purpose tier. Both tiers offer the same levels of availability and allow for independent configuration of storage and compute.

High Availability

Because the PaaS Service backs Azure SQL Database Managed Instance, it has high availability backed into the product. A standalone Managed Instance offers a 99.99% Service Level Agreement (SLA), which guarantees 52.60 minutes of downtime per year. The architecture is the same as Azure SQL Database with General Purpose using storage replication for availability and Business critical using multiple replicas.

Backups

Automatic backups are also automatically configured for Azure SQL Managed Instance. One key difference between Azure SQL Managed Instance and Azure SQL Database is that you can manually make a copy-only backup of a database with MI. It would be best to back up to a URL since access to the local storage is not permissible. You can also configure long-term retention (LTR) for retaining automatic backups for up to 10 years in geo-redundant Azure blob storage.

Database backups occur on the same schedule as with Azure SQL Database. These schedules are not adjustable.

- Full – Once a week
- Differential – Every 12 hours
- Transaction Log – Every 5-10 minutes depending on transaction log usage

Restoring a database to an Azure SQL Managed Instance is similar to the Azure SQL Database process. You can use:

- Azure portal
- PowerShell
- Azure CLI

However, there are some limitations when restoring. Both instances must reside within the same Azure subscription and same Azure region to restore from one instance to another. You also cannot restore the entire managed instance but only individual databases within the Managed Instance itself.

However, since it is a PaaS service, there are some limitations. As with Azure SQL Database, you cannot restore over an existing database, you have to drop or rename the existing database before restoring it from backup. You can execute a RESTORE command since Managed Instance is a fully functional SQL Server instance, while it is impossible with Azure SQL Database.

- It would help if you restored it from a URL endpoint as you do not have access to local drives.
- You can use the following options (in addition to specifying the database):
    - FILELISTONLY
    - HEADERONLY
    - LABELONLY
    - VERIFYONLY
- Backup files having multiple log files cannot be restored
- Backup files having multiple backup sets cannot be restored
- Backups having In-Memory/FILESTREAM cannot be restored

By default, the databases in a managed instance are encrypted using Transparent Data Encryption (TDE) with a Microsoft managed key. To take a user-initiated copy-only backup, you must turn off TDE for the specific database. If a database is encrypted, you can restore it. However, you will need to ensure that you have access to either the certificate or asymmetric key used to encrypt the database. If you do not have either of those two items, you will not restore the database to a Managed Instance.

Disaster Recovery

Azure SQL Database Managed Instance offers auto-failover groups as a means to implement disaster recovery. This feature protects the entire managed instance and all of its databases, not just specific databases. This process asynchronously replicates data from the Azure SQL Managed Instance to a secondary. However, it is currently limited to the paired Azure region of the primary copy, and only one replica is allowed.

Like Azure SQL Database, auto-failover groups offer read-write and read-only listener endpoints, facilitating easy connection string management. In the event of a failover, application connection strings will be automatically routed to the appropriate instance. Fairly consistent with Azure SQL Database, these endpoints follow a slightly different format, <fog-name>.zone_id.database.windows.net, whereas Azure SQL Database is in the <fog-name>.secondary.database.windows.net format.

Each managed instance, primary and secondary, must be within the same DNS zone. This placement will ensure that the same multi-domain certificate can be used for client connection authentication between either of the two instances in the same failover group. You can specify a "DNS Zone Partner" through various methods such as the Azure portal, PowerShell, or Azure CLI.

Deploy MariaDB, MySQL, and PostgreSQL on Azure

When development speed is of the essence, open-source database platforms are usually unmatched when delivering a fully managed ready-to-roll database for applications. Many developers prefer open-source systems for this very reason. Microsoft has rounded out its relational database offerings by providing open-source database platforms such as MySQL, MariaDB, and PostgreSQL. These platforms are a great compliment to the existing Azure SQL offerings.

Open Source Offerings

The Azure ecosystem offers three different open-source database platforms. Each of these services comes with native high availability, automatic patching, automatic backups, and the highest level of security protection. Microsoft fully supports these offerings from the service through the database engine.

Azure Database for MySQL is a fully managed enterprise-grade database service that can easily lift and shift customer environments to the Azure cloud. Customers can use their existing frameworks and languages to ensure that migration does not disrupt any business activity. In addition, the service has built-in high availability and dynamic scaling, which helps to meet any fluctuation in performance demands.

Azure Database for MariaDB is similar to the MySQL offering. It also allows for the continued use of frameworks and languages of your choice. The service also provides high availability and dynamic scaling to ensure that customer demands are met within a moment's notice. The service allows for horizontal scaling and is available with Hyperscale, which allows for unparalleled performance. Azure Database for PostgreSQL Hyperscale is ideal for multi-tenant applications, with minor code changes allowing data sharing.

Service Tiers

There are three service tiers for each offering. Each tier has an ideal workload for which it is designed and allows you to choose various performance options.

- Basic – This tier is best for light workloads that need minimal compute and I/O performance.
- General Purpose – This tier is great for most workloads requiring scalable I/O throughput along with a healthy balance of computing and memory.
- Memory-Optimized – This tier is suitable for workloads that demand high performance and require in-memory speed for quick processing of transactions along with higher concurrency.

The service tiers offered by the open-source platforms provide a wide range of performance options and allow you to choose the best one for your given workload. The following versions shown in the table are available in the service for each database.

SERVICE TIERS	
Database	**Supported Versions**
MariaDB	10.2-10.3
MySQL	5.6-8.0
Postgres	9.5-11

Table 02-04: Service Tiers

> **Note:** While the Azure service will perform minor upgrades, you need to restore a backup into a new version to execute a significant upgrade.

How To Deploy Postgresql To Azure

Like the Azure SQL offerings, deployment for MariaDB, MySQL, and PostgreSQL is supported by using all standard Azure methods, including the Azure portal, PowerShell, Azure Resource Manager templates, and the Azure CLI. There is limited support for PowerShell cmdlets for these platforms.

Single Database

In the Azure portal, click on **Create a Resource** on the main portal blade, as shown below. Then look for Azure Database for PostgreSQL and select **Create**.

Select **Single Server** or **Hyperscale**. Hyperscale is typically used for large-scale databases that scale out across multiple nodes. Click the appropriate Create button.

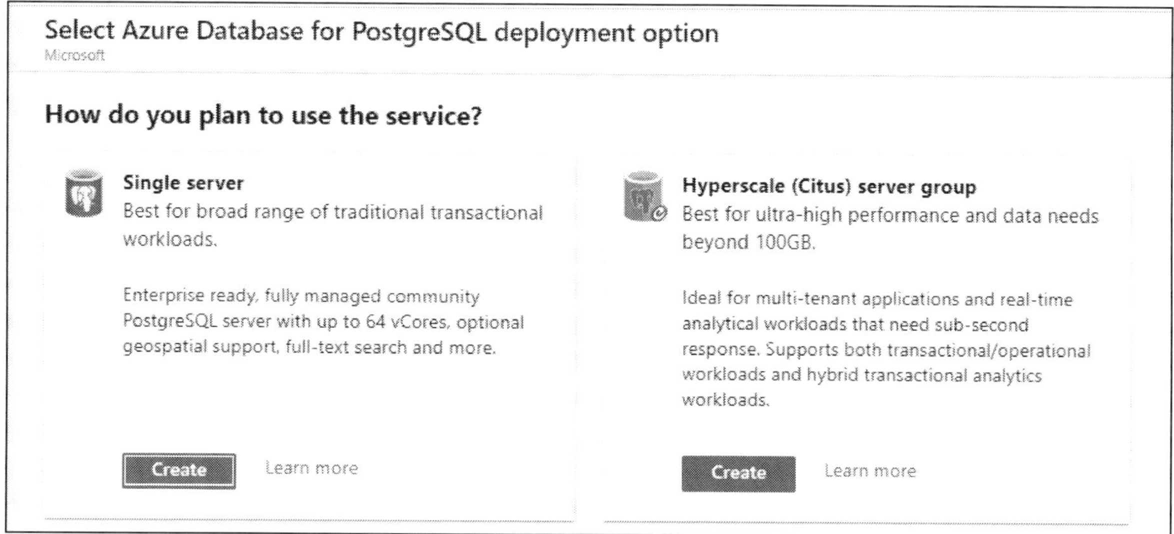

Figure 02-18: Azure Database for PostgreSQL

You will supply the Resource Group, Server Name, Region, Version, Username, and Password as shown in the image below.

Single server
Microsoft

Basics Tags Review + create

Create an Azure Database for PostgreSQL server. Learn more

Project details

Select the subscription to manage deployed resources and costs. Use resource groups like folders to organize and manage all your resources.

Subscription * : Dev-Test-Lab

Resource group * : (New) Demo
Create new

Server details

Enter required settings for this server, including picking a location and configuring the compute and storage resources.

Server name * : postgresqldemo

Data source * : None | Backup

Location * : (US) East US

Version * : 10

Compute + storage : **Basic**
2 vCores, 50 GB storage
Configure server

Administrator account

Admin username * : Enter server admin login name

Password * : Enter password

Confirm password * : Confirm the above password

Review + create | Next : Tags >

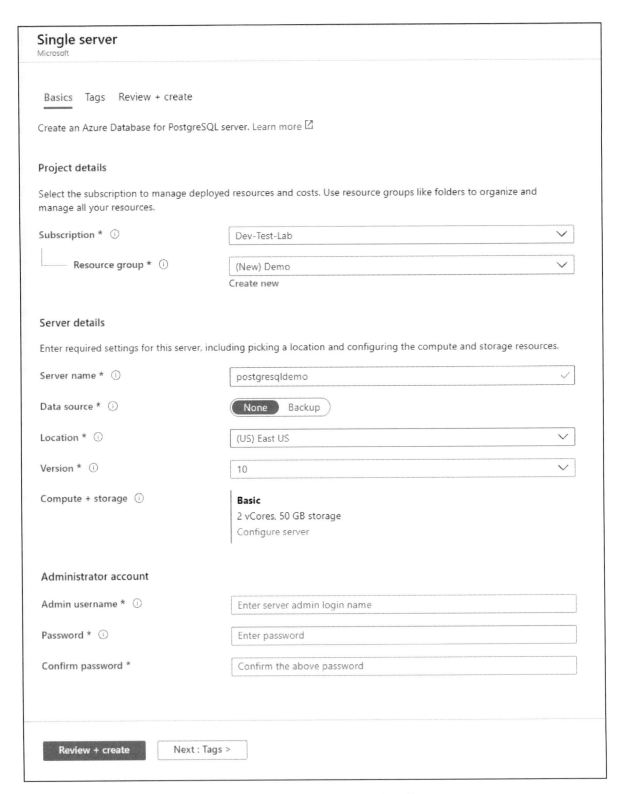

Figure 02-19: Resource Group Details

Click on **Configure Server**. Then select the appropriate service tier for your applications and workloads, as shown in the image below. Click **OK**.

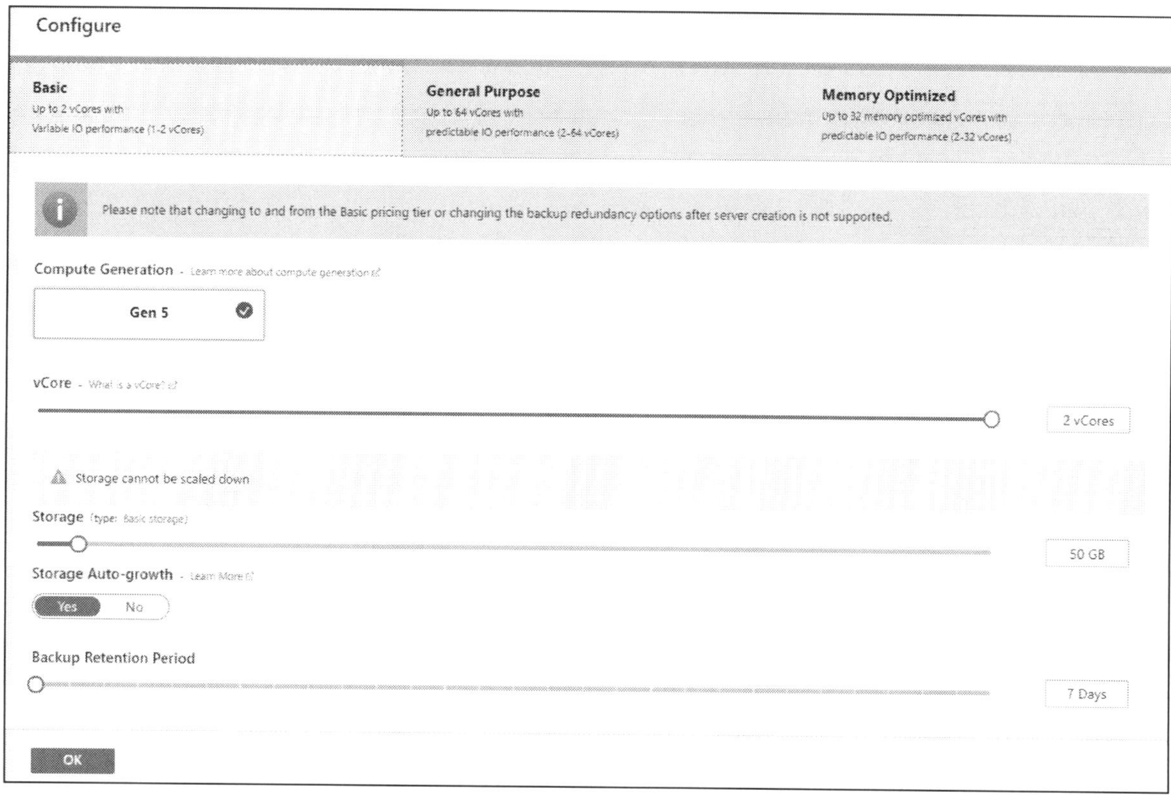

Figure 02-20: Storage and Properties Configuration

The image above also shows that you can configure the amount of storage and storage properties.

As mentioned above, you can use the Azure CLI to deploy Azure Database for PostgreSQL, as seen below.

```
az postgres server create --resource-group myresourcegroup --name mydemoserver `
--location westus --admin-user myadmin --admin-password <server_admin_password> `
--sku-name GP_Gen4_2 --version 9.6
```

Figure 02-21: Deploy Azure Database for PostgreSQL

Azure Database for PostgreSQL Hyperscale

While Hyperscale shares a name with Azure SQL Database and offers horizontal scalability to support substantial data volumes, the Hyperscale technology for PostgreSQL is implemented differently. Hyperscale allows the servers for Azure Database for PostgreSQL (called nodes) to work together in a "shared nothing" architecture design. Nodes are added to a server group where each server group has a coordinator node and multiple workers nodes. Applications send their queries to the coordinator node, which relays them to relevant worker nodes and gathers the results.

Creating a Hyperscale PostgreSQL deployment is different than deploying a single instance of the service. In this case, Hyperscale allows you to deploy additional worker nodes along with a coordinator node. You can deploy up to 20 worker nodes by default (this number is a soft limit; you can contact Microsoft support). You can also configure high availability for each node to ensure that any disruption has minimal impact on your applications.

Deploy MySQL and MariaDB to Azure

When deploying MySQL or MariaDB, you have similar options to PostgreSQL. You can deploy using the Azure portal, Azure CLI, or Azure Resource Manager templates. There are similar sizing and availability choices, as detailed below.

HA Configuration

High availability for Azure Database for MySQL and Azure Database for MariaDB comes packaged in with the service, so less administrative work needs to be done. The service provides a guaranteed high level of availability, offering an uptime of 99.99%. This percentage of uptime equates to a maximum of 52.60 minutes of downtime per year.

If a node interruption occurs, the database server will automatically create a new node and attach the storage to this new node. As mentioned with Azure SQL Database, it is essential to ensure that applications that connect to the database service include retry logic, also known as connection resiliency, in their database connections.

Scale-Out Reads Using Read Replicas

The Azure Service makes it easy to scale out read workloads using read replicas for MySQL and MariaDB. The example below illustrates the procedure for MySQL. However, MariaDB uses a similar process.

To enable replication, click on **Replication** in the **Settings** section of the **MySQL** blade in the Azure portal, as shown in the image below.

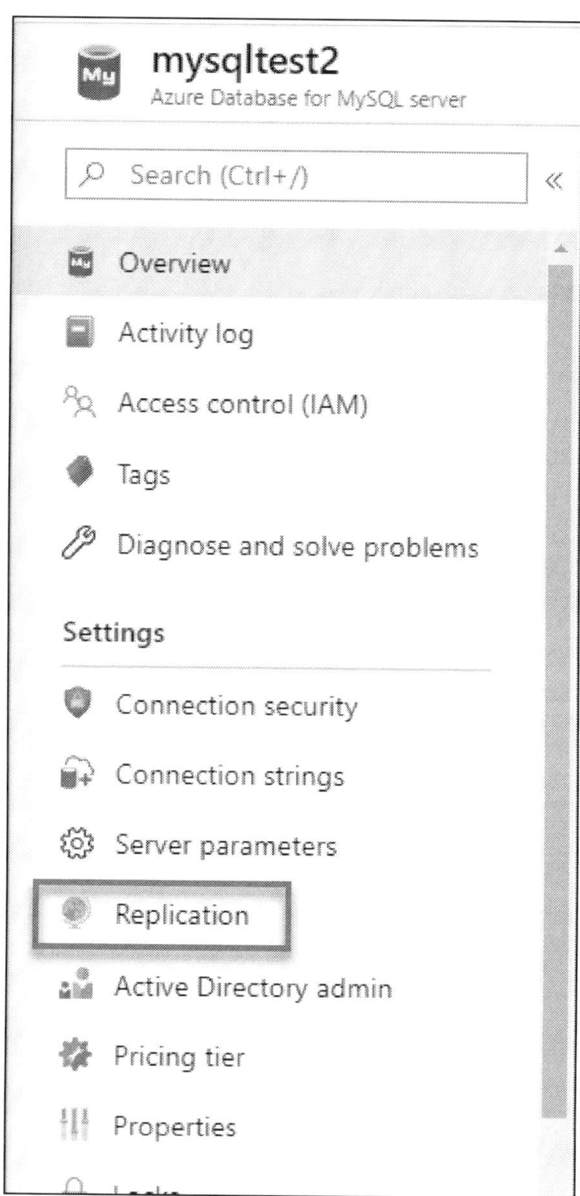

Figure 02-22: Scale-Out Reads Using Read Replicas

Click **Add Replica** as shown in the image below.

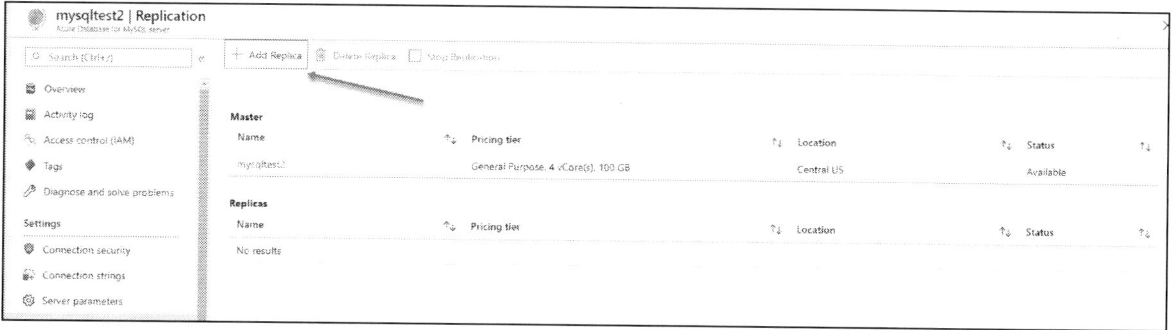

Figure 02-23: Scale-Out Reads Using Read Replicas

Provide a new server name and specify which Azure region it should reside in, as shown in the image below.

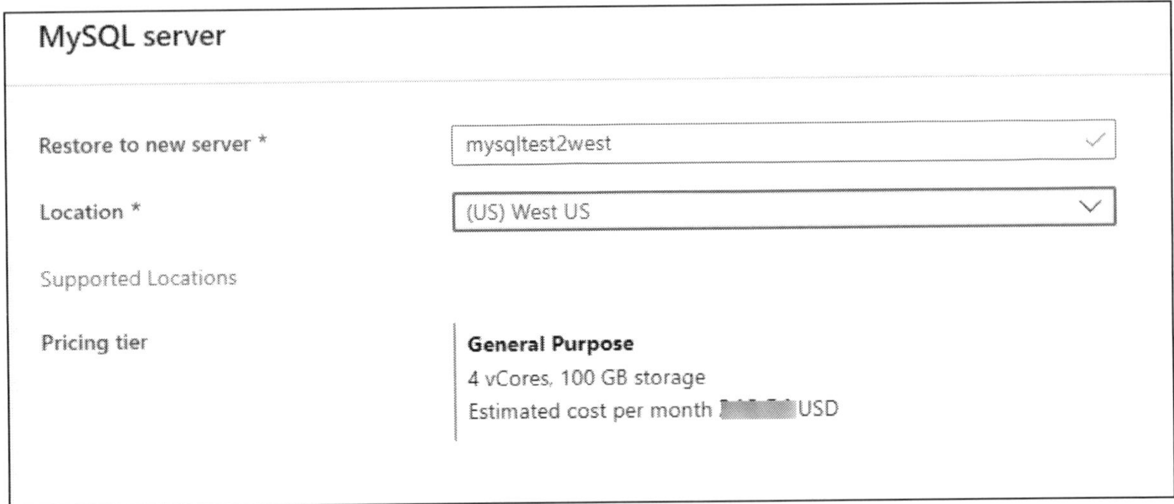

Figure 02-24: SQL Server Name

Click **OK**.

SSL Options for MySQL and MariaDB

Azure Database for MySQL and MariaDB both support the use of SSL to encrypt network traffic between the database and the client application. To implement this encryption, you must change the Enforce SSL Connection for your database, as shown in the image below.

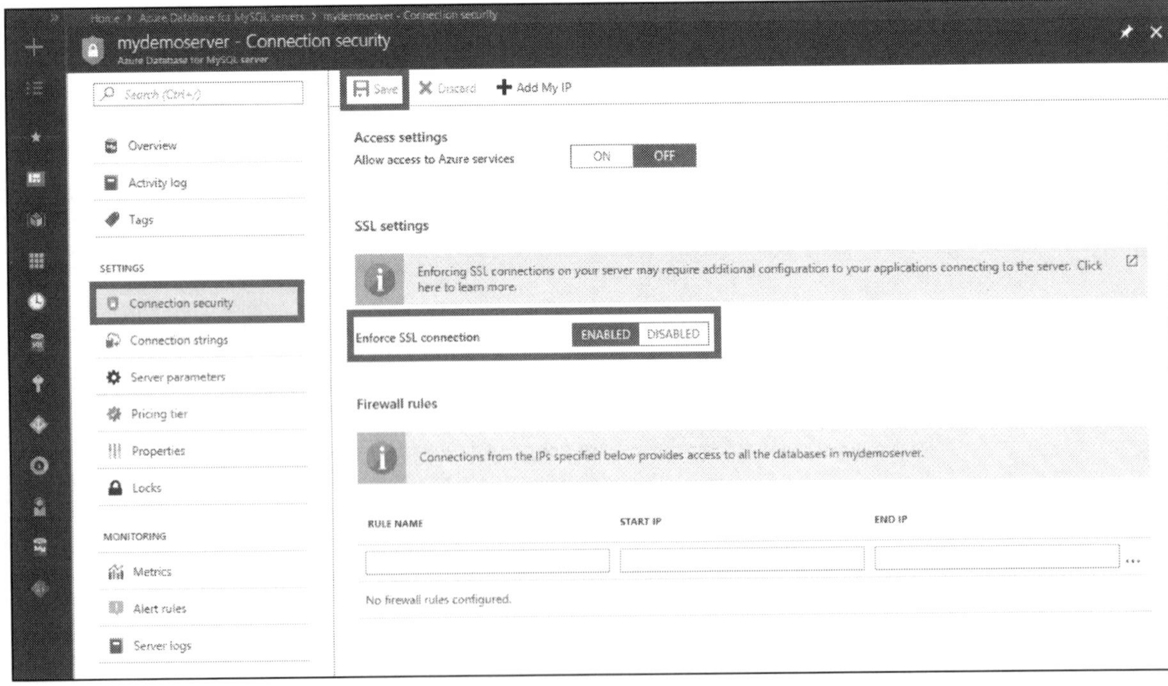

Figure 02-25: SSL Options for MySQL and MariaDB

You also need to download the public root certificate and include the path to the certificate in your client connection. After completing both of these tasks, your network traffic will be encrypted.

Database Migration Options

Many organizations are migrating their Oracle databases to Azure PostgreSQL to reduce licensing costs. Migrating to the Azure Database platform is made more accessible by the Azure Database Migration Service (DMS). The DMS supports homogenous migrations (for example, MySQL in a VM to Azure Database for MySQL) and heterogeneous migrations (for example, Oracle in a VM to Azure Database for PostgreSQL). DMS performs an initial load of your on-premises database or database running in an Azure VM to Azure Database. It then continuously syncs new database transactions to the Azure target. When you are ready to cut over to the target Azure service, you can stop the replication and switch the connection strings in your application to the Azure Database.

Lab 02-01: SQL Server On An Azure Virtual Machine

Introduction

SQL Server service is accessible on the Azure cloud. SQL Server on Azure VM operates in the same way that it operates for on-premises machines. That means you can install your SQL Server on VM, set your configurations, and even use your own existing SQL Server license. This lab will study what SQL Server on Azure VM is and when to select it.

Problem

You are a database administrator, and you have to make a test environment for use. The concept will use SQL Server on an Azure Virtual Machine.

Solution

As a database administrator, you will form a new SQL Database, including a Virtual Network Endpoint. Azure Data Studio will be used to assess the use of a SQL Notebook for data querying and reviewing the results. You will also set up a new Azure Database for PostgreSQL for testing.

SQL Server On An Azure Virtual Machine

1. Click on the **Search Result** for Azure SQL that appears in the results under Services.

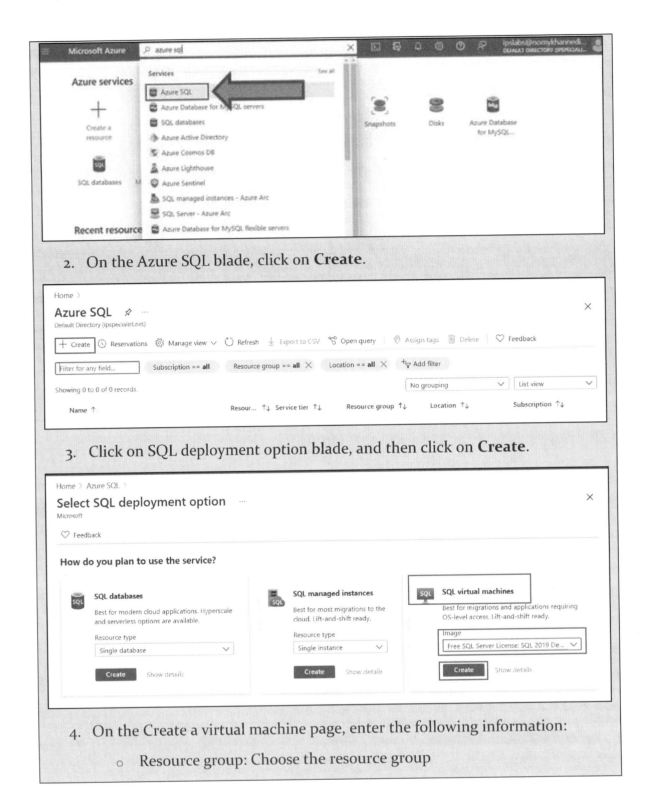

2. On the Azure SQL blade, click on **Create**.

3. Click on SQL deployment option blade, and then click on **Create**.

4. On the Create a virtual machine page, enter the following information:
   - Resource group: Choose the resource group

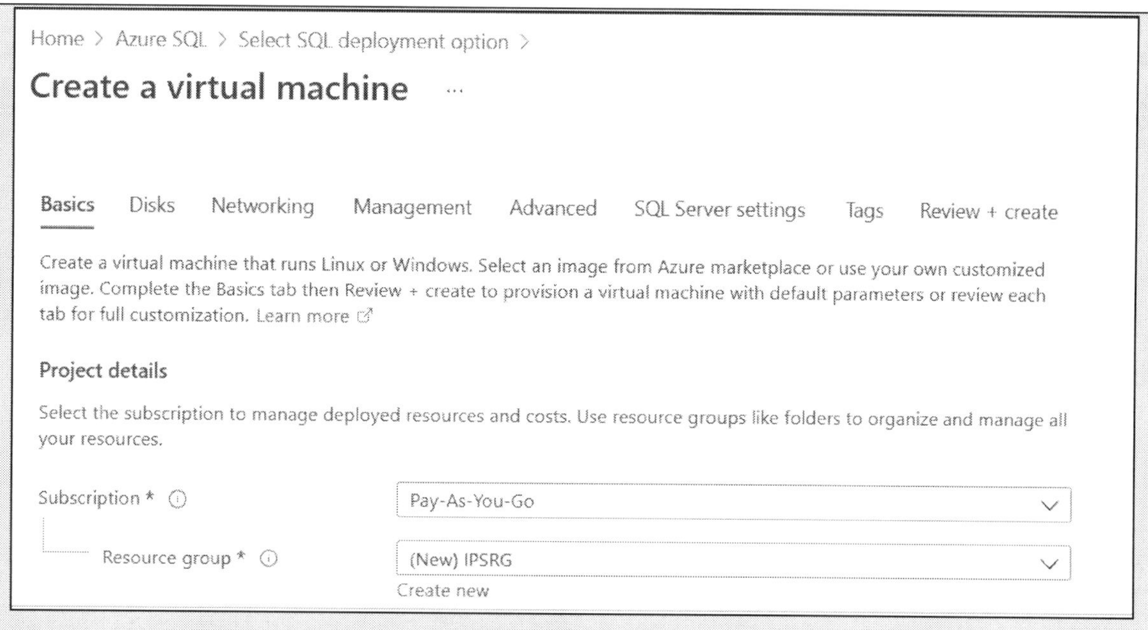

- Virtual machine name: **azureSQLserverVM**
- Region: Choose one of the **Recommended** US regions
- Availability Options: **No infrastructure redundancy is required**
- Azure spot instance: **No** (do not check the box)
- Size: Standard **DS2_v2** (You will need to select 'see all sizes' to find **DS2_v2** -- 2 vCPUs, 7 GiB memory)

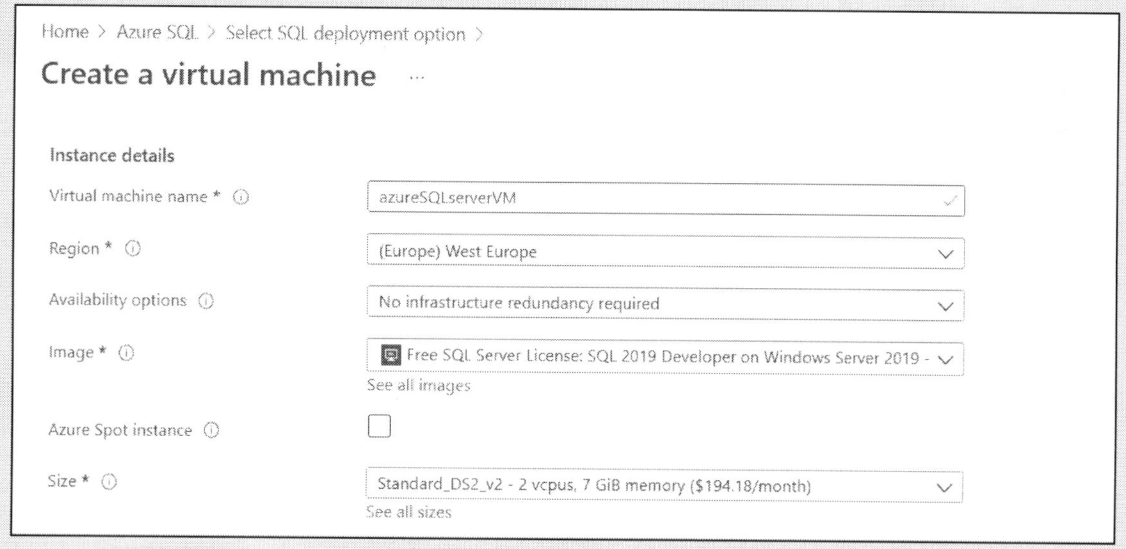

- Administrator account username: **ipsadmin**
- Administrator account password: **Azur3Pa$$2020**

Home > Azure SQL > Select SQL deployment option >

Create a virtual machine ...

Size * Standard_DS2_v2 - 2 vcpus, 7 GiB memory ($194.18/month)
See all sizes

Administrator account
Username * ipsadmin
Password * •••••••••••••
Confirm password * •••••••••••••

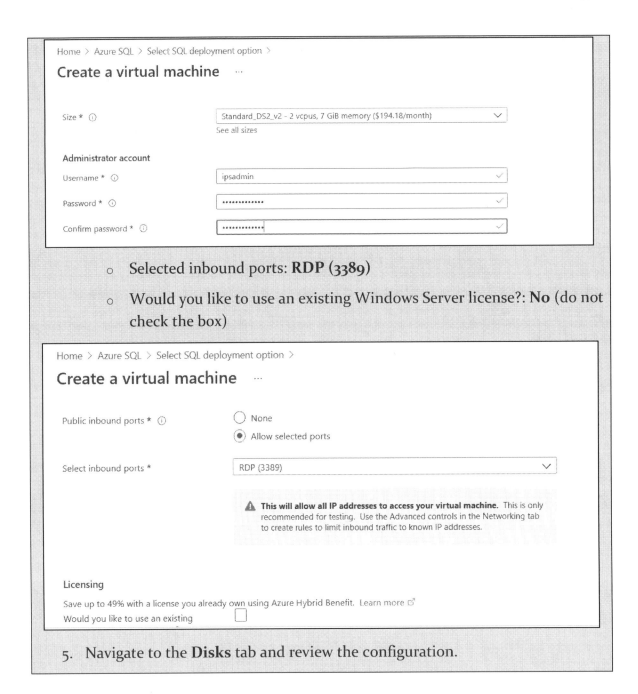

- Selected inbound ports: **RDP (3389)**
- Would you like to use an existing Windows Server license?: **No** (do not check the box)

Home > Azure SQL > Select SQL deployment option >

Create a virtual machine ...

Public inbound ports * None / Allow selected ports

Select inbound ports * RDP (3389)

This will allow all IP addresses to access your virtual machine. This is only recommended for testing. Use the Advanced controls in the Networking tab to create rules to limit inbound traffic to known IP addresses.

Licensing
Save up to 49% with a license you already own using Azure Hybrid Benefit. Learn more
Would you like to use an existing

5. Navigate to the **Disks** tab and review the configuration.

Home > Azure SQL > Select SQL deployment option >

Create a virtual machine ...

Public inbound ports * ⓘ — None / Allow selected ports

Select inbound ports * — RDP (3389)

⚠ **This will allow all IP addresses to access your virtual machine.** This is only recommended for testing. Use the Advanced controls in the Networking tab to create rules to limit inbound traffic to known IP addresses.

Licensing

Save up to 49% with a license you already own using Azure Hybrid Benefit. Learn more

Would you like to use an existing

Review + create | < Previous | Next : Disks >

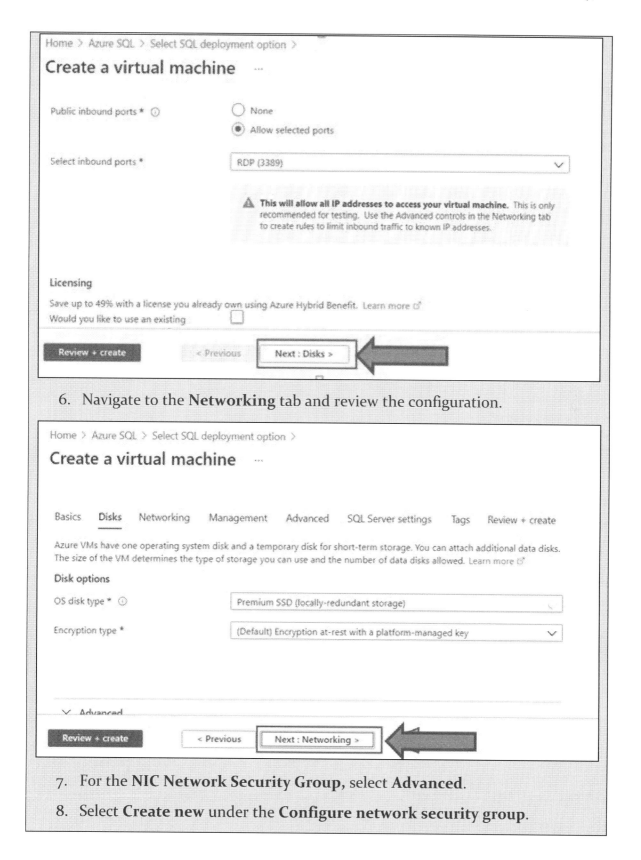

6. Navigate to the **Networking** tab and review the configuration.

Home > Azure SQL > Select SQL deployment option >

Create a virtual machine ...

Basics | Disks | Networking | Management | Advanced | SQL Server settings | Tags | Review + create

Azure VMs have one operating system disk and a temporary disk for short-term storage. You can attach additional data disks. The size of the VM determines the type of storage you can use and the number of data disks allowed. Learn more

Disk options

OS disk type * ⓘ — Premium SSD (locally-redundant storage)

Encryption type * — (Default) Encryption at-rest with a platform-managed key

Advanced

Review + create | < Previous | Next : Networking >

7. For the **NIC Network Security Group,** select **Advanced**.
8. Select **Create new** under the **Configure network security group**.

NIC network security group ⓘ	◯ None ◯ Basic ◉ Advanced
Configure network security group *	(new) azureSQLserverVM-nsg Create new
Accelerated networking ⓘ	☑

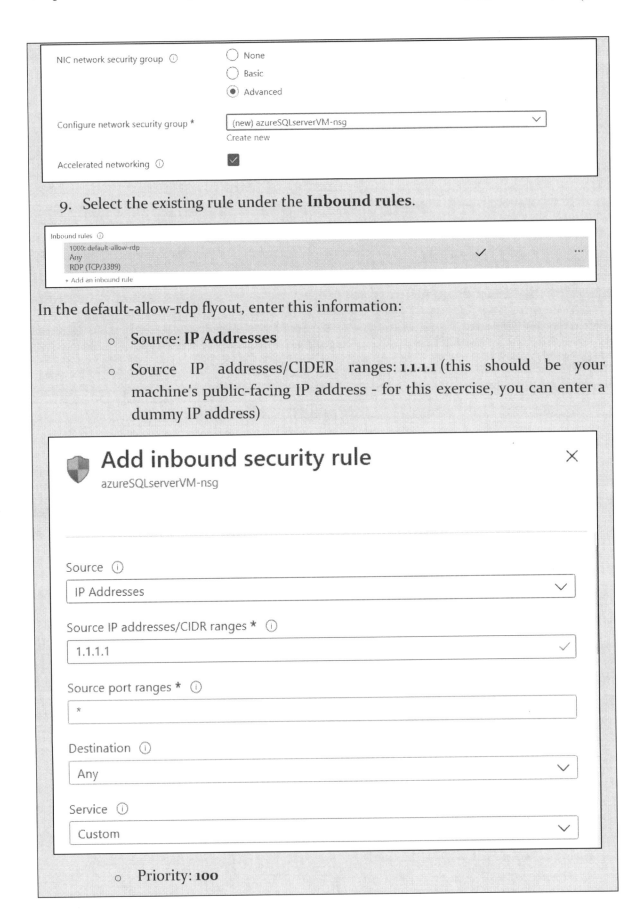

9. Select the existing rule under the **Inbound rules**.

Inbound rules ⓘ
1000: default-allow-rdp
Any
RDP (TCP/3389)
+ Add an inbound rule

In the default-allow-rdp flyout, enter this information:

- Source: **IP Addresses**
- Source IP addresses/CIDER ranges: **1.1.1.1** (this should be your machine's public-facing IP address - for this exercise, you can enter a dummy IP address)

Add inbound security rule
azureSQLserverVM-nsg

Source ⓘ
IP Addresses

Source IP addresses/CIDR ranges * ⓘ
1.1.1.1

Source port ranges * ⓘ
*

Destination ⓘ
Any

Service ⓘ
Custom

- Priority: **100**

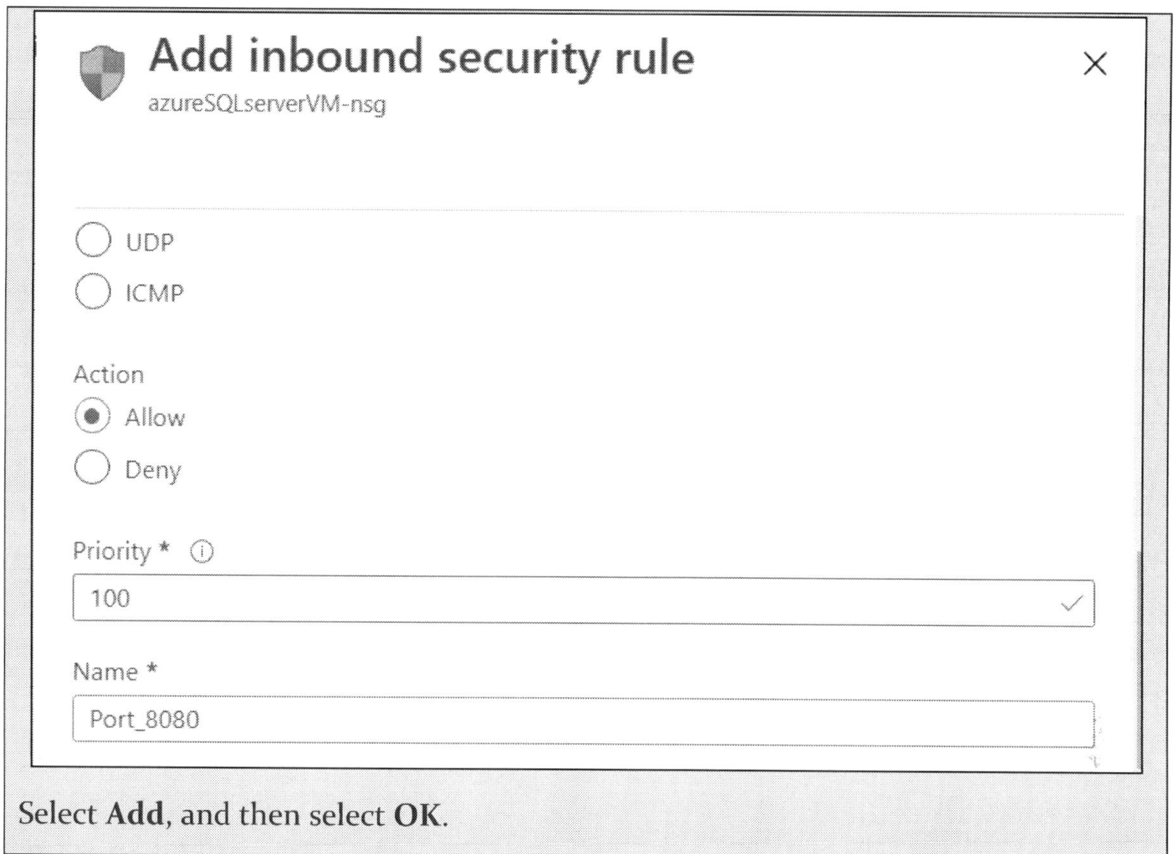

Select **Add**, and then select **OK**.

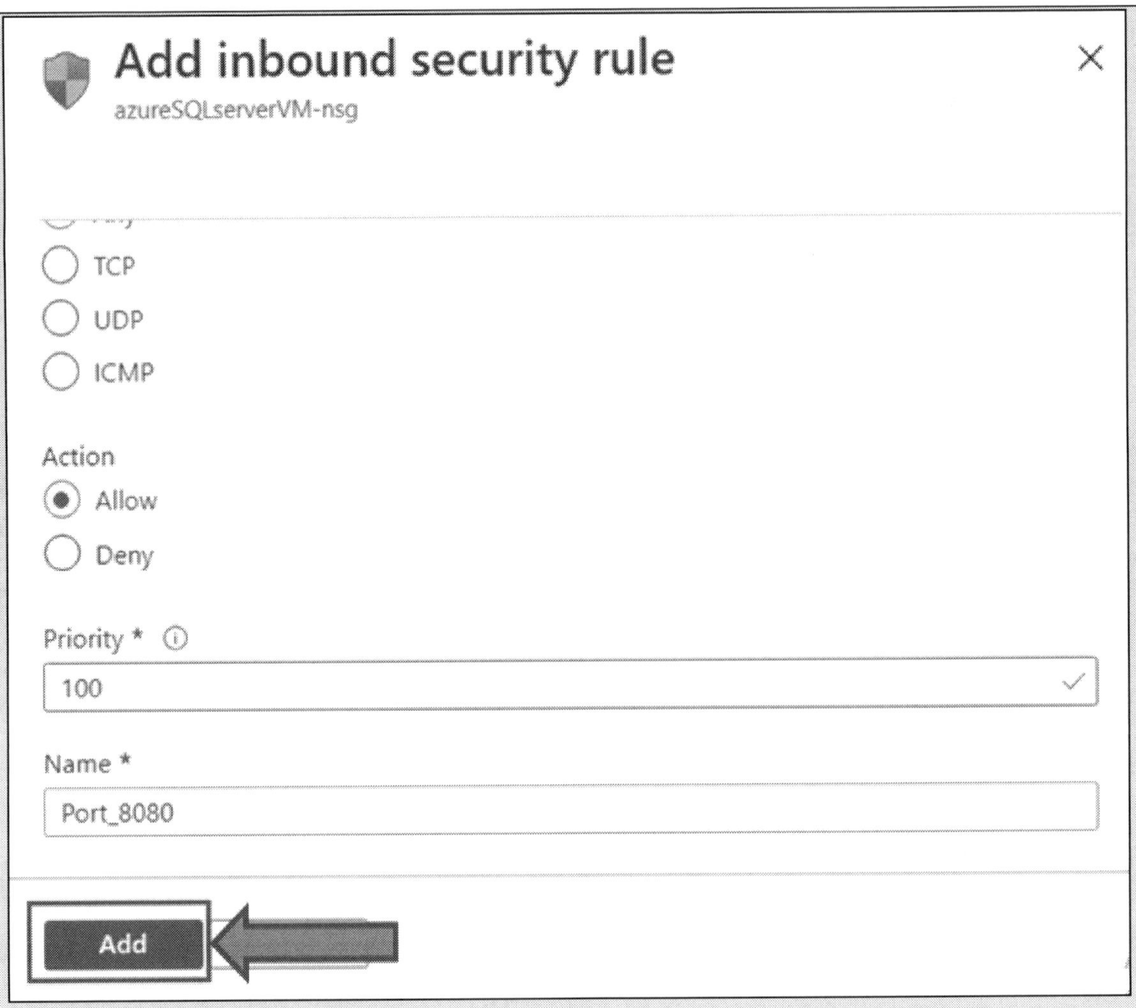

10. Navigate to the **Management** tab and review the configuration.

Home > Azure SQL > Select SQL deployment option >

Create a virtual machine ...

Create new

NIC network security group ⓘ ◯ None ◯ Basic ◉ Advanced

Configure network security group * (new) azureSQLserverVM-nsg

Create new

Accelerated networking ⓘ ☑

Load balancing

You can place this virtual machine in the backend pool of an existing Azure load balancing solution. Learn more

Review + create | < Previous | Next : Management >

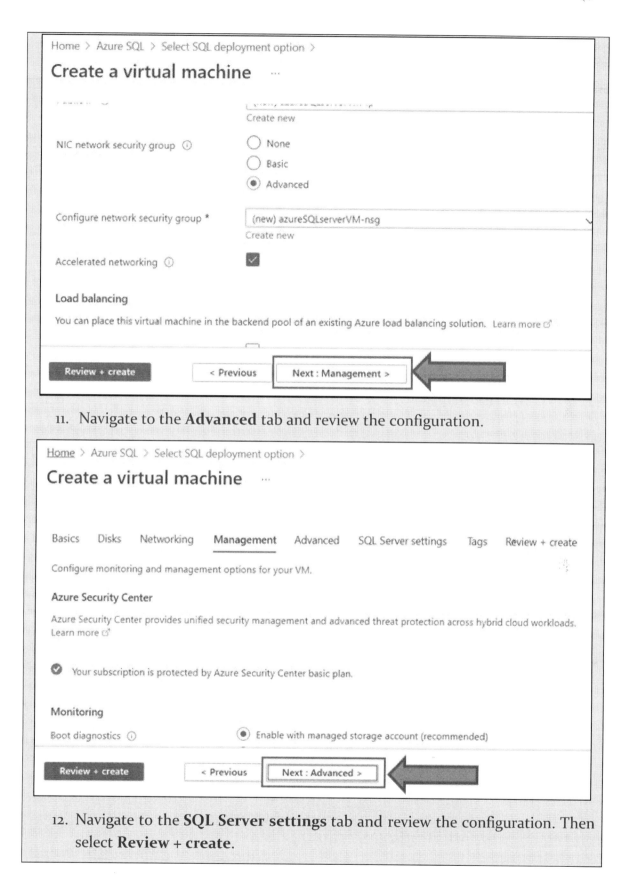

11. Navigate to the **Advanced** tab and review the configuration.

Home > Azure SQL > Select SQL deployment option >

Create a virtual machine ...

Basics Disks Networking Management Advanced SQL Server settings Tags Review + create

Configure monitoring and management options for your VM.

Azure Security Center

Azure Security Center provides unified security management and advanced threat protection across hybrid cloud workloads. Learn more

Your subscription is protected by Azure Security Center basic plan.

Monitoring

Boot diagnostics ⓘ ◉ Enable with managed storage account (recommended)

Review + create | < Previous | Next : Advanced >

12. Navigate to the **SQL Server settings** tab and review the configuration. Then select **Review + create**.

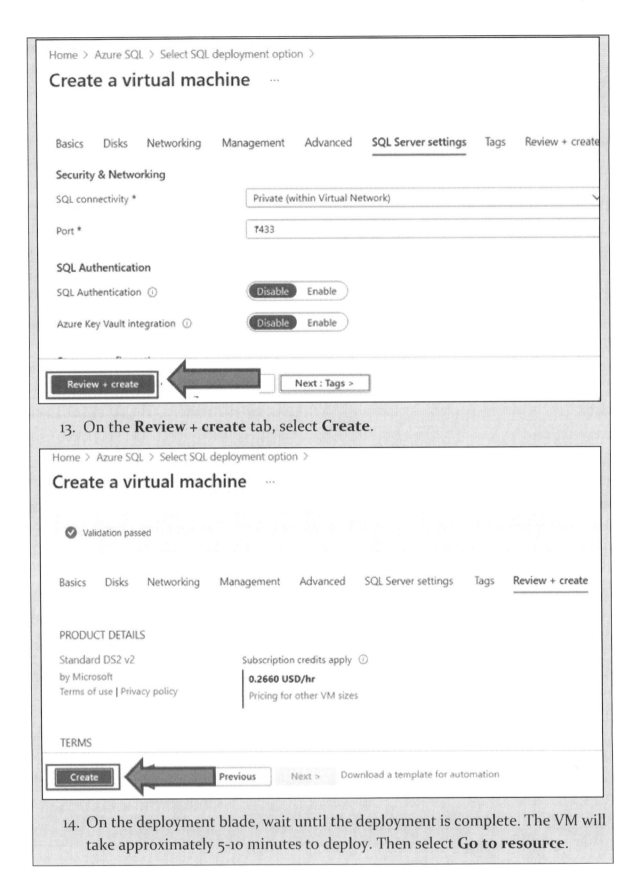

13. On the **Review + create** tab, select **Create**.

14. On the deployment blade, wait until the deployment is complete. The VM will take approximately 5-10 minutes to deploy. Then select **Go to resource**.

Notifications

More events in the activity log → Dismiss all

Deployment succeeded

Deployment 'CreateVm-microsoftsqlserver.sql2019-ws2019-sqldev-20210929215646' to resource group 'IPSRG' was successful.

Go to resource | Pin to dashboard

a minute ago

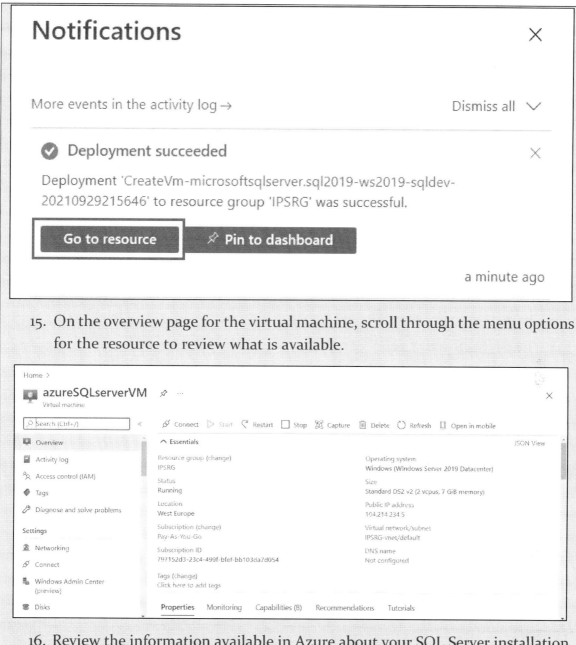

15. On the overview page for the virtual machine, scroll through the menu options for the resource to review what is available.

Home >

azureSQLserverVM

Virtual machine

Search (Ctrl+/)

Connect | Start | Restart | Stop | Capture | Delete | Refresh | Open in mobile

Overview
Activity log
Access control (IAM)
Tags
Diagnose and solve problems
Settings
Networking
Connect
Windows Admin Center (preview)
Disks

Essentials JSON View

Resource group (change): IPSRG
Status: Running
Location: West Europe
Subscription (change): Pay-As-You-Go
Subscription ID: 797152d3-23c4-499f-bfef-bb103da7d054
Tags (change): Click here to add tags
Operating system: Windows (Windows Server 2019 Datacenter)
Size: Standard DS2 v2 (2 vcpus, 7 GiB memory)
Public IP address: 104.214.234.5
Virtual network/subnet: IPSRG-vnet/default
DNS name: Not configured

Properties | Monitoring | Capabilities (8) | Recommendations | Tutorials

16. Review the information available in Azure about your SQL Server installation.

The Azure portal gives you powerful tools to manage a SQL Server hosted in a virtual machine. These tools include control over automated patching, automated backups, and giving you an easy way to set up high availability.

Deploy an Azure SQL Database

Create a Virtual Network

1. Open the left navigation pane, then select **Virtual networks**.

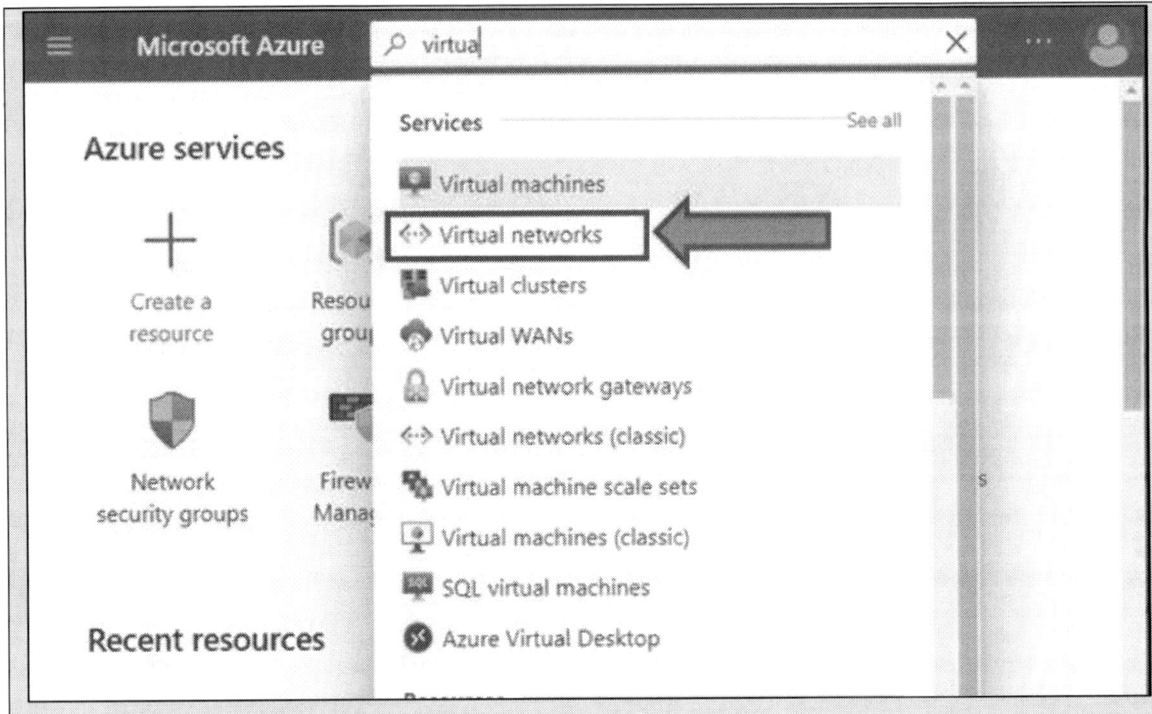

2. Select **Create** and then complete the Basics page with the following information:
   - Resource Group: **IPSRG**
   - Name: **AzureSQL-vnet**
   - Region: Select the same region when the Resource Group was created (the region nearest to your location)
   - Select **Next: IP Addresses**

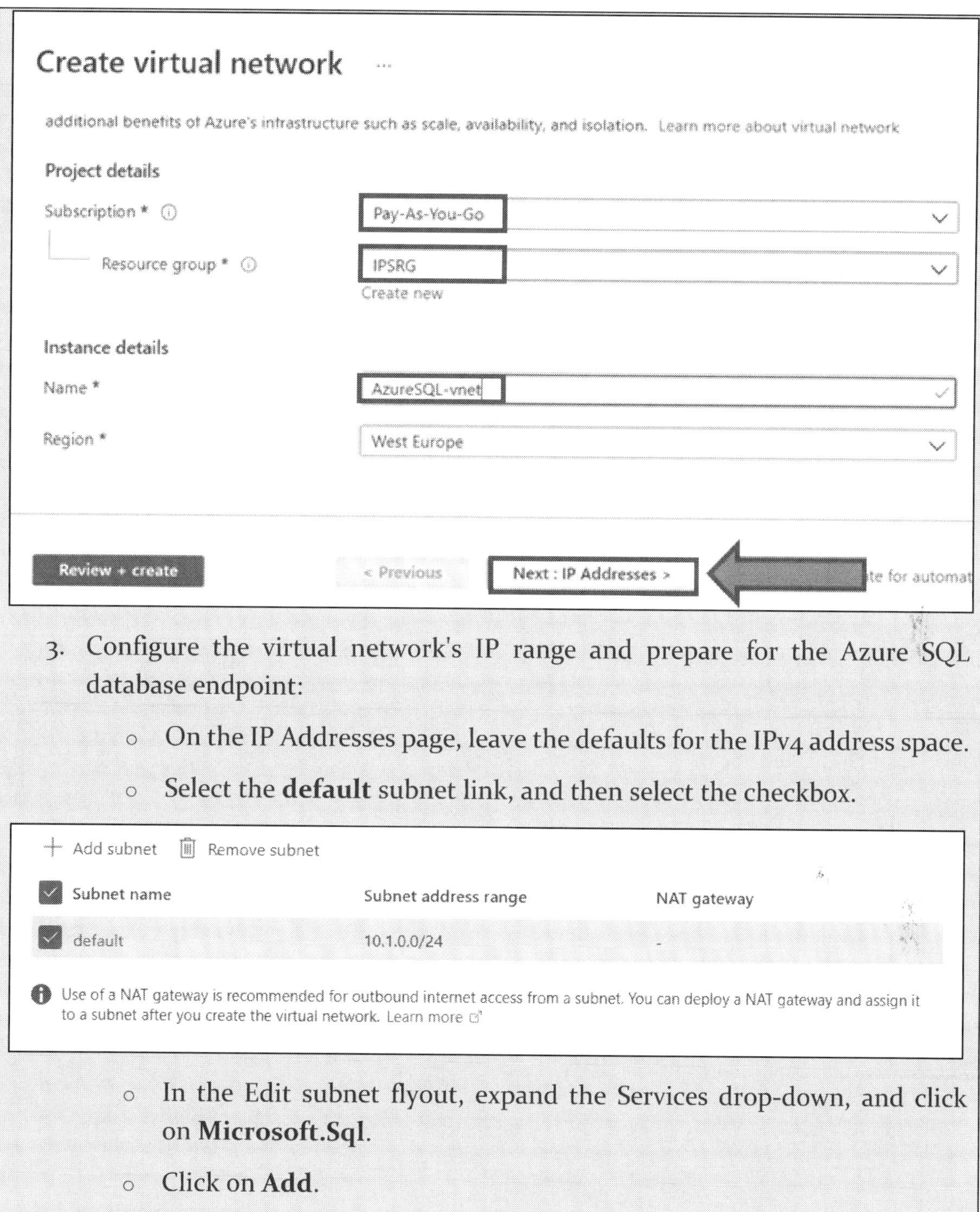

3. Configure the virtual network's IP range and prepare for the Azure SQL database endpoint:
    - On the IP Addresses page, leave the defaults for the IPv4 address space.
    - Select the **default** subnet link, and then select the checkbox.
    - In the Edit subnet flyout, expand the Services drop-down, and click on **Microsoft.Sql**.
    - Click on **Add**.

Add subnet

Select all

Microsoft.AzureActiveDirectory

Microsoft.AzureCosmosDB

Microsoft.CognitiveServices

Microsoft.ContainerRegistry

Microsoft.EventHub

Microsoft.KeyVault

Microsoft.ServiceBus

Microsoft.Sql

Filter services

Microsoft.Sql

Add

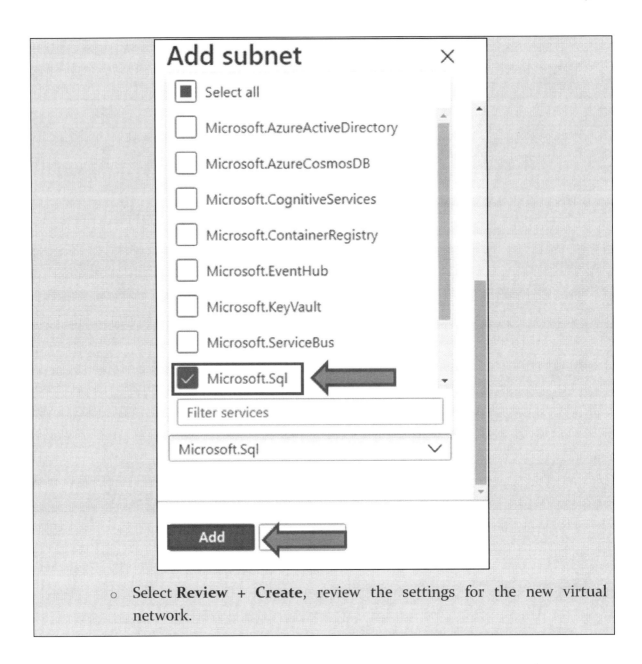

- Select **Review + Create**, review the settings for the new virtual network.

Create virtual network ...

Add IPv6 address space

The subnet's address range in CIDR notation (e.g. 192.168.1.0/24). It must be contained by the address space of the virtual network.

+ Add subnet   Remove subnet

Subnet name	Subnet address range	NAT gateway
default	10.1.0.0/24	-

Use of a NAT gateway is recommended for outbound internet access from a subnet. You can deploy a NAT gateway and assign it to a subnet after you create the virtual network. Learn more

Review + create   Previous   Next : Security >   Download a template for automation

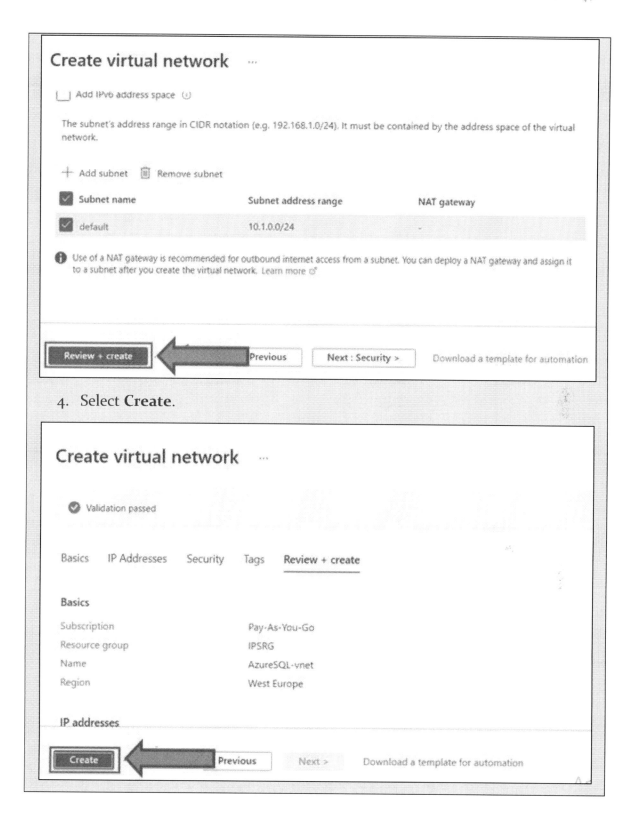

4. Select **Create**.

Create virtual network ...

Validation passed

Basics   IP Addresses   Security   Tags   Review + create

Basics

Subscription	Pay-As-You-Go
Resource group	IPSRG
Name	AzureSQL-vnet
Region	West Europe

IP addresses

Create   Previous   Next >   Download a template for automation

Deploy an Azure SQL Database

12. From the Azure portal, click on + **Create a Resource** in the left side navigation bar.

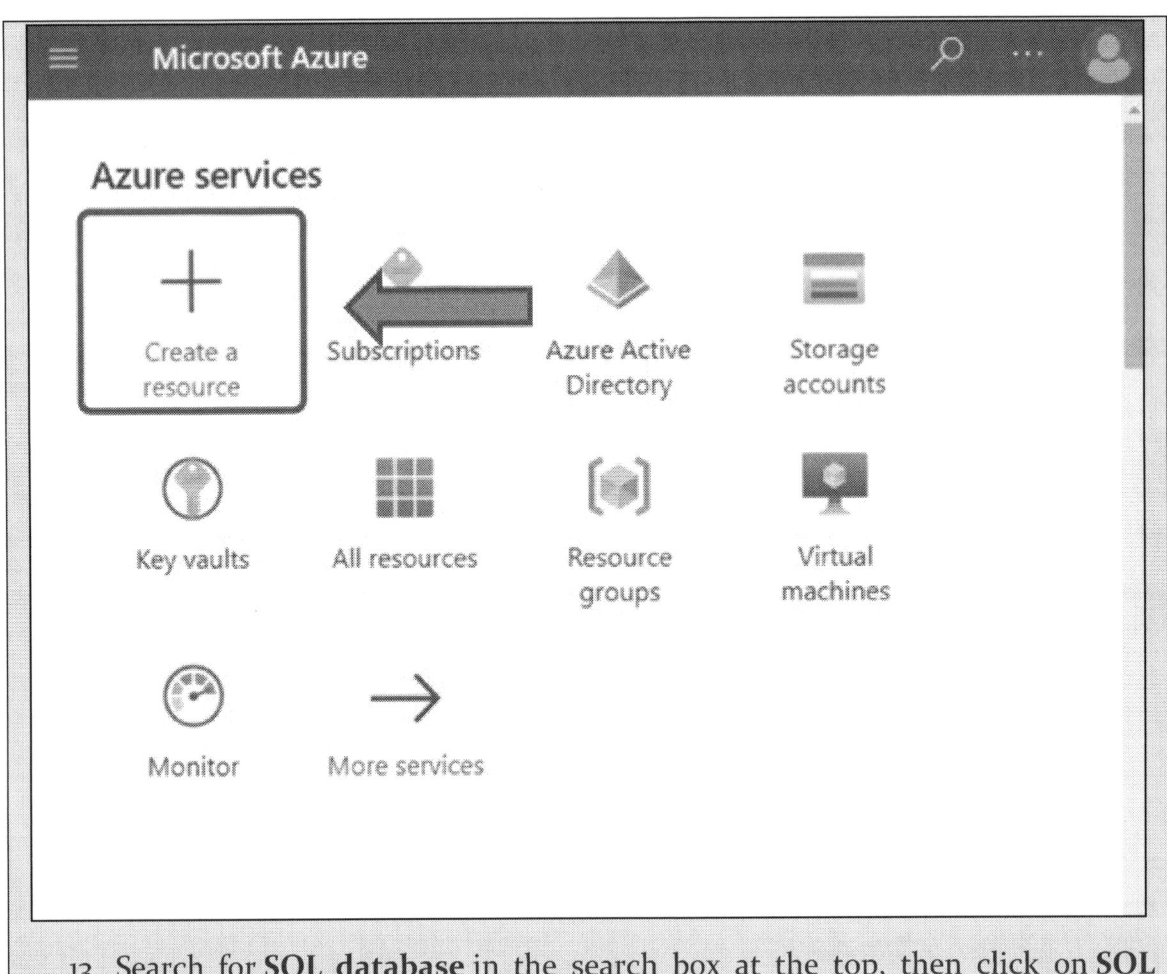

13. Search for **SQL database** in the search box at the top, then click on **SQL Database** from the list of options.

sql database

Services — See all

SQL databases

SQL Server stretch databases

Dedicated SQL pools (formerly SQL DW)

Azure Database for MySQL servers

Reservations

Azure SQL

Azure Database for MySQL flexible servers

Azure Database for PostgreSQL flexible servers

Azure Database for PostgreSQL server groups

Azure Database for PostgreSQL servers

Resources

No results were found.

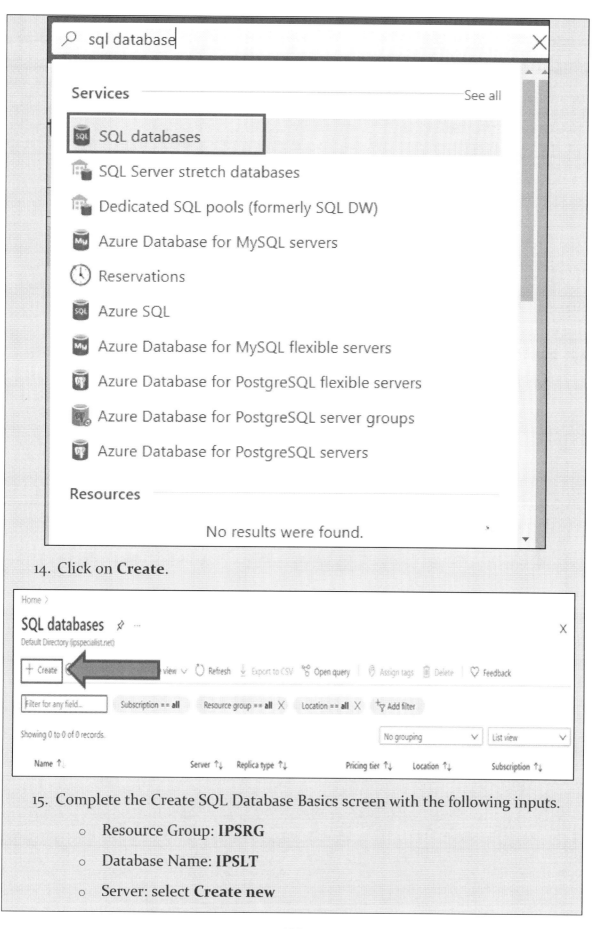

14. Click on **Create**.

Home >

SQL databases

Default Directory (ipspecialist.net)

+ Create | view | Refresh | Export to CSV | Open query | Assign tags | Delete | Feedback

Filter for any field... | Subscription == all | Resource group == all | Location == all | Add filter

Showing 0 to 0 of 0 records. | No grouping | List view

Name | Server | Replica type | Pricing tier | Location | Subscription

15. Complete the Create SQL Database Basics screen with the following inputs.
    - Resource Group: **IPSRG**
    - Database Name: **IPSLT**
    - Server: select **Create new**

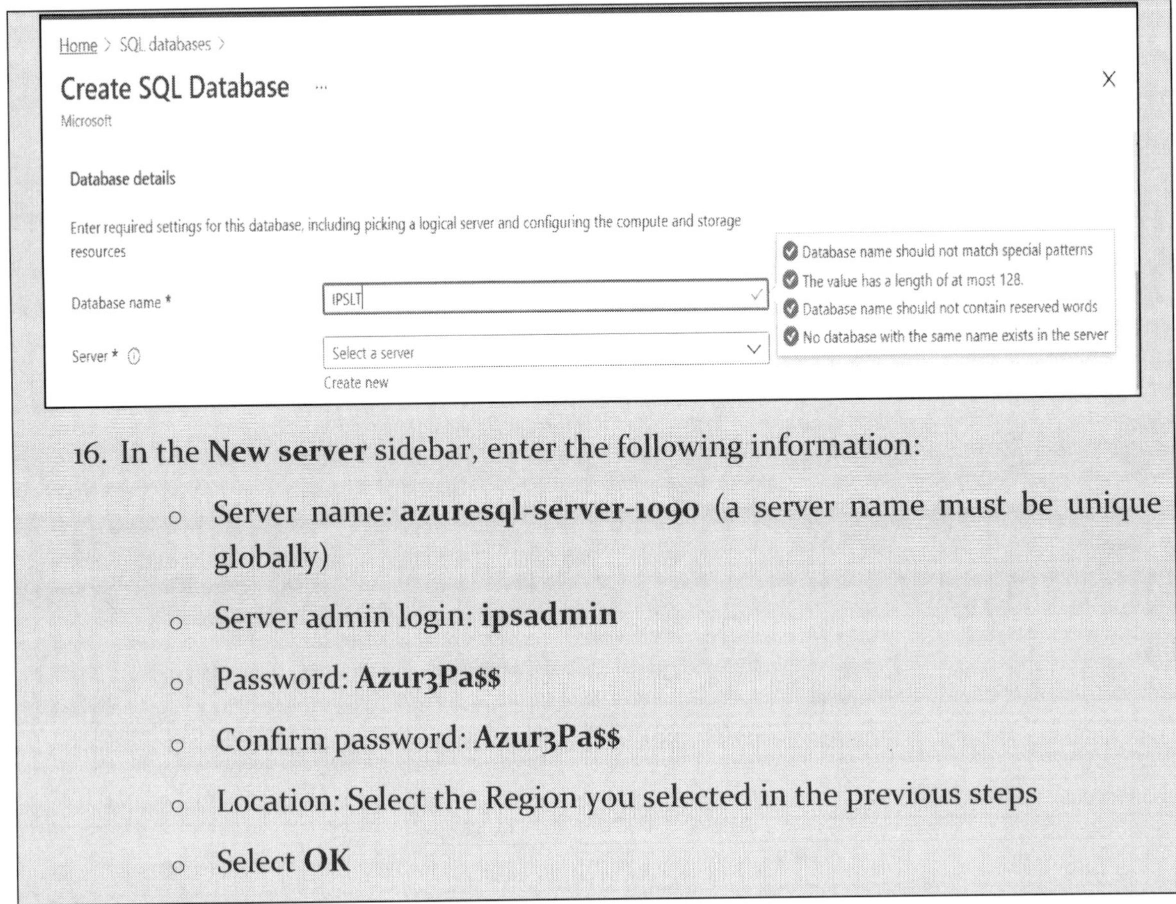

16. In the **New server** sidebar, enter the following information:
    - Server name: **azuresql-server-1090** (a server name must be unique globally)
    - Server admin login: **ipsadmin**
    - Password: **Azur3Pa$$**
    - Confirm password: **Azur3Pa$$**
    - Location: Select the Region you selected in the previous steps
    - Select **OK**

New server
Microsoft

Server name *
azuresql-server-1090
.database.windows.net
Server admin login *
ipsadmin
Password *
•••••••••
Confirm password *
•••••••••
Location *
(US) East US

OK

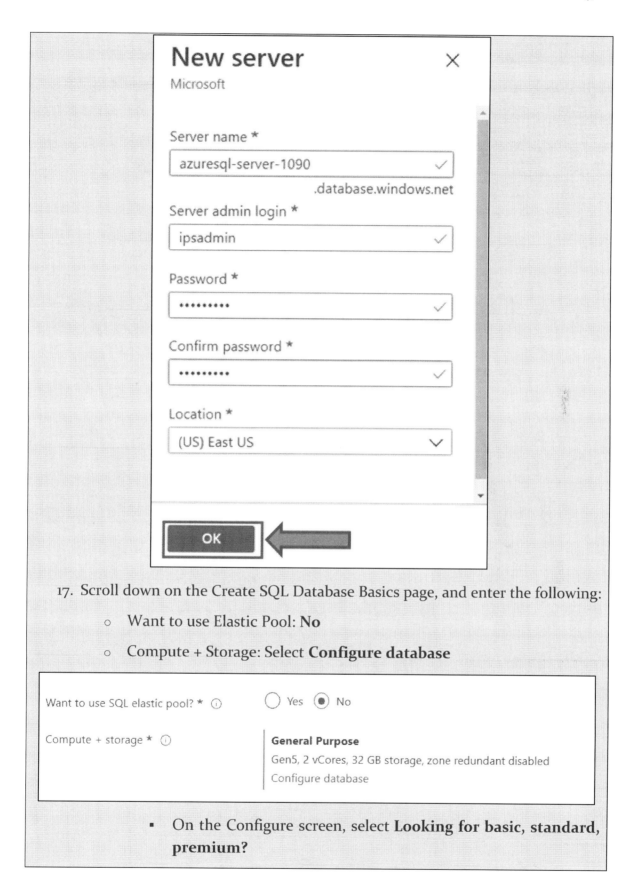

17. Scroll down on the Create SQL Database Basics page, and enter the following:
    - Want to use Elastic Pool: **No**
    - Compute + Storage: Select **Configure database**

Want to use SQL elastic pool? * Yes No
Compute + storage * General Purpose
Gen5, 2 vCores, 32 GB storage, zone redundant disabled
Configure database

- On the Configure screen, select **Looking for basic, standard, premium?**

Configure

Feedback

Looking for basic, standard, premium?

General Purpose

Scalable compute and storage options

500 - 20,000 IOPS
2-10 ms latency

Compute tier

Provisioned

Compute resources are pre-allocated

Billed per hour based on vCores configured

Serverle

Compute resources ar

Billed per second based

Compute Hardware

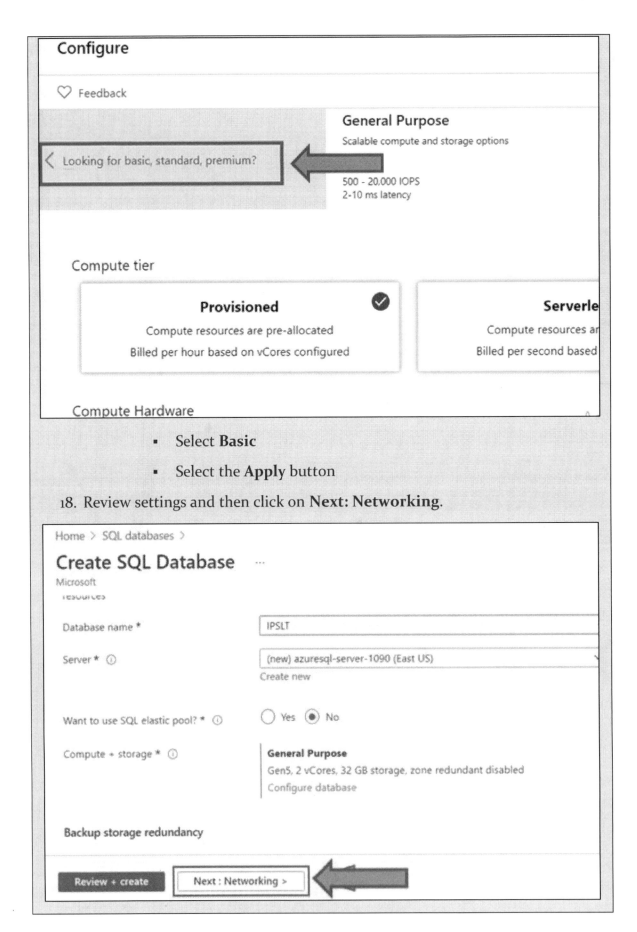

- Select **Basic**
- Select the **Apply** button

18. Review settings and then click on **Next: Networking**.

Home > SQL databases >

Create SQL Database ...

Microsoft

Database name * IPSLT

Server * (new) azuresql-server-1090 (East US)

Create new

Want to use SQL elastic pool? * Yes No

Compute + storage * General Purpose

Gen5, 2 vCores, 32 GB storage, zone redundant disabled

Configure database

Backup storage redundancy

Review + create Next : Networking >

19. On the Networking screen, for the Connectivity method, select the **Private endpoint** radio button.

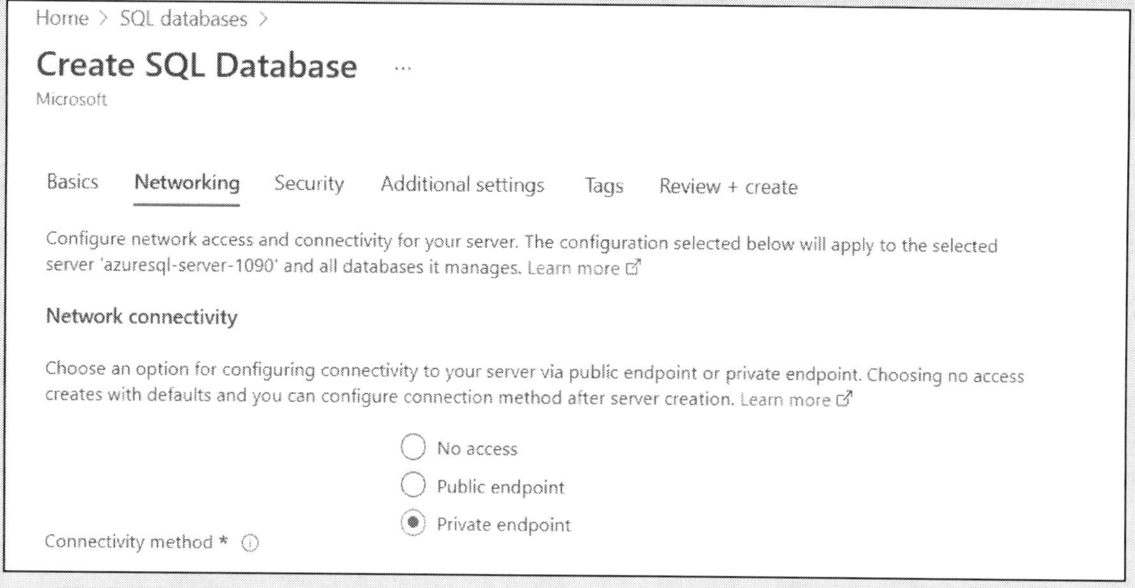

20. Then select the **Add private endpoint** link under Private endpoints

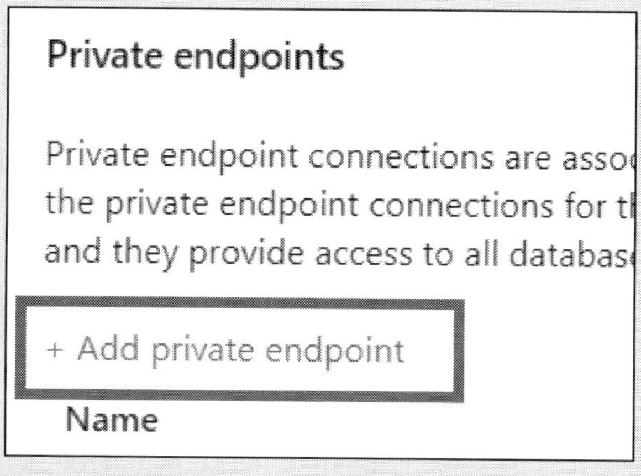

21. Complete the Create private endpoint flyout as follows:

    - Resource group: **IPSRG**
    - Location: The same Region that was selected for previous parts of this lab
    - Name: **AzureSQL-Endpoint**
    - Target sub-resource: **SqlServer**
    - Virtual network: **AzureSQL-vnet**
    - Subnet: **default (10.x.0.0/24)**
    - The Private DNS integration options can remain at the default

- Review settings before selecting **OK**

Create private endpoint

Subscription * ⓘ — Pay-As-You-Go

Resource group * ⓘ — IPSRG

Create new

Location * — East US

Name * ⓘ — AzureSQL-Endpoint

Target sub-resource * — SqlServer

Networking

To deploy the private endpoint, select a virtual network subnet. Learn more about private endpoint networking

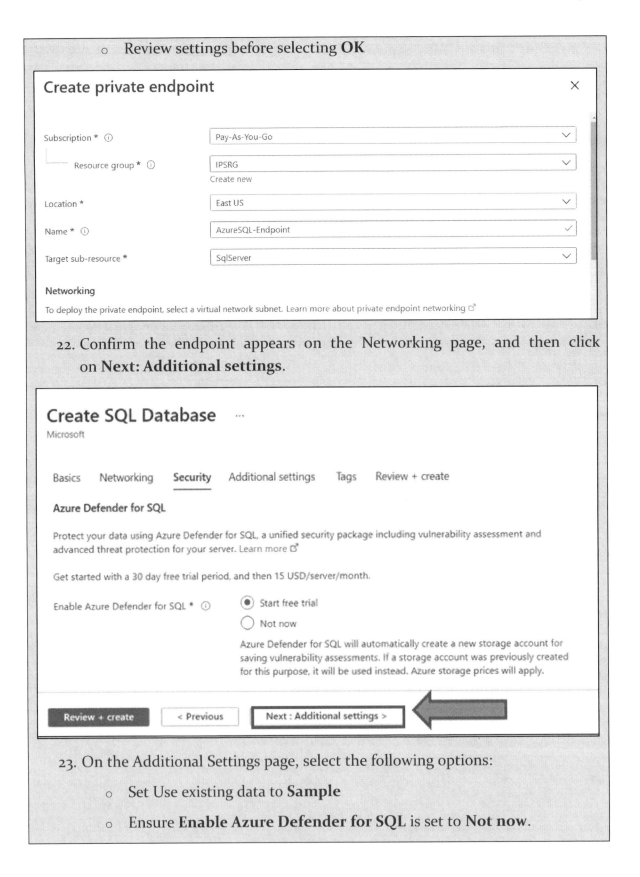

22. Confirm the endpoint appears on the Networking page, and then click on **Next: Additional settings**.

Create SQL Database ...

Microsoft

Basics Networking Security Additional settings Tags Review + create

Azure Defender for SQL

Protect your data using Azure Defender for SQL, a unified security package including vulnerability assessment and advanced threat protection for your server. Learn more

Get started with a 30 day free trial period, and then 15 USD/server/month.

Enable Azure Defender for SQL * ⓘ — (●) Start free trial ( ) Not now

Azure Defender for SQL will automatically create a new storage account for saving vulnerability assessments. If a storage account was previously created for this purpose, it will be used instead. Azure storage prices will apply.

Review + create | < Previous | Next : Additional settings >

23. On the Additional Settings page, select the following options:
    - Set Use existing data to **Sample**
    - Ensure **Enable Azure Defender for SQL** is set to **Not now**.

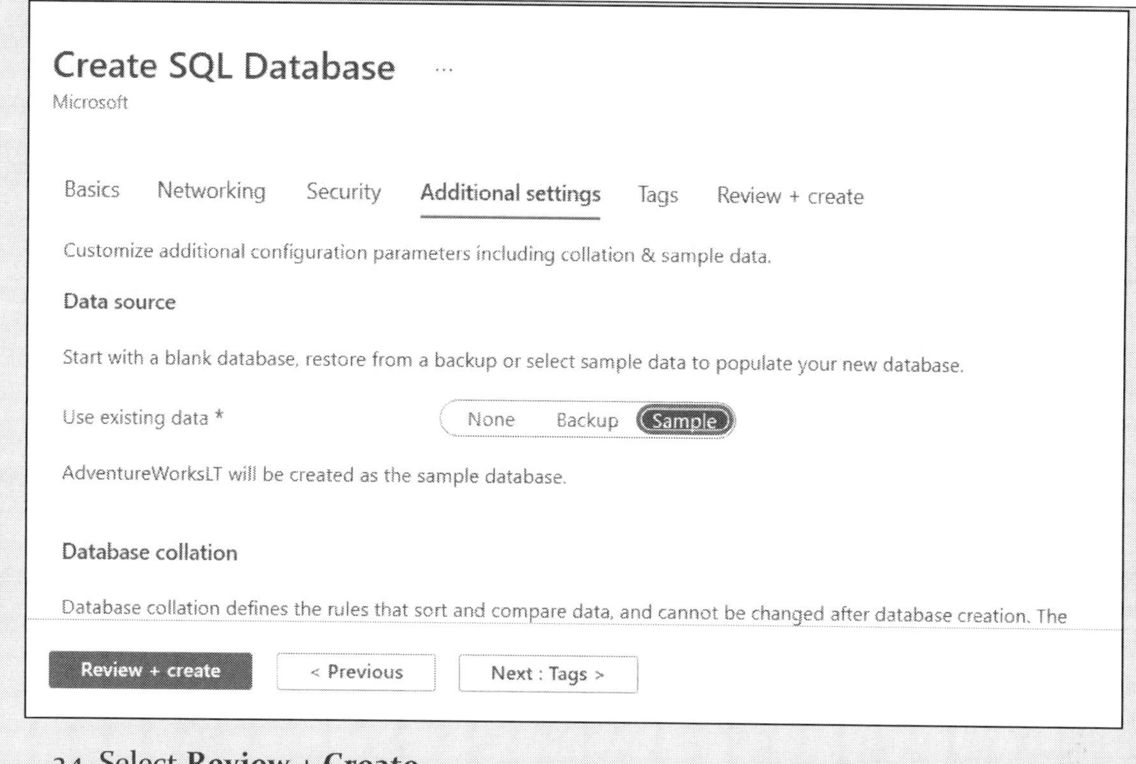

24. Select **Review + Create**.

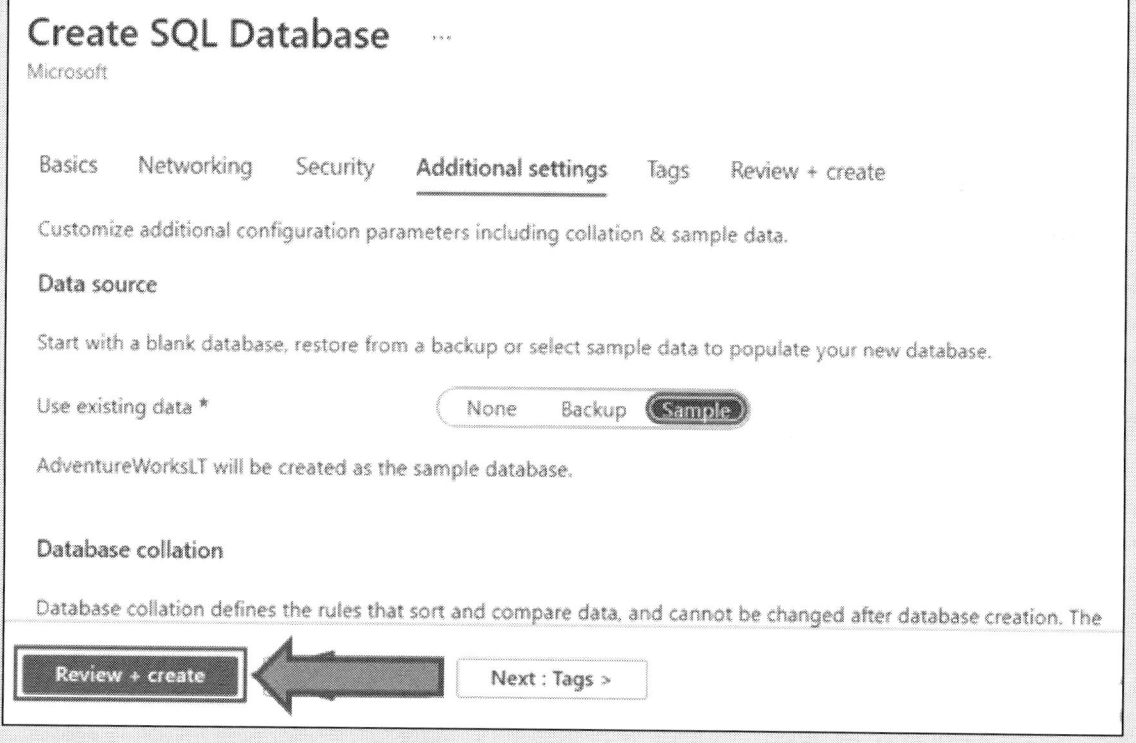

25. Review the settings before selecting **Create**.
26. Once the deployment is complete, select **Go to resource**.

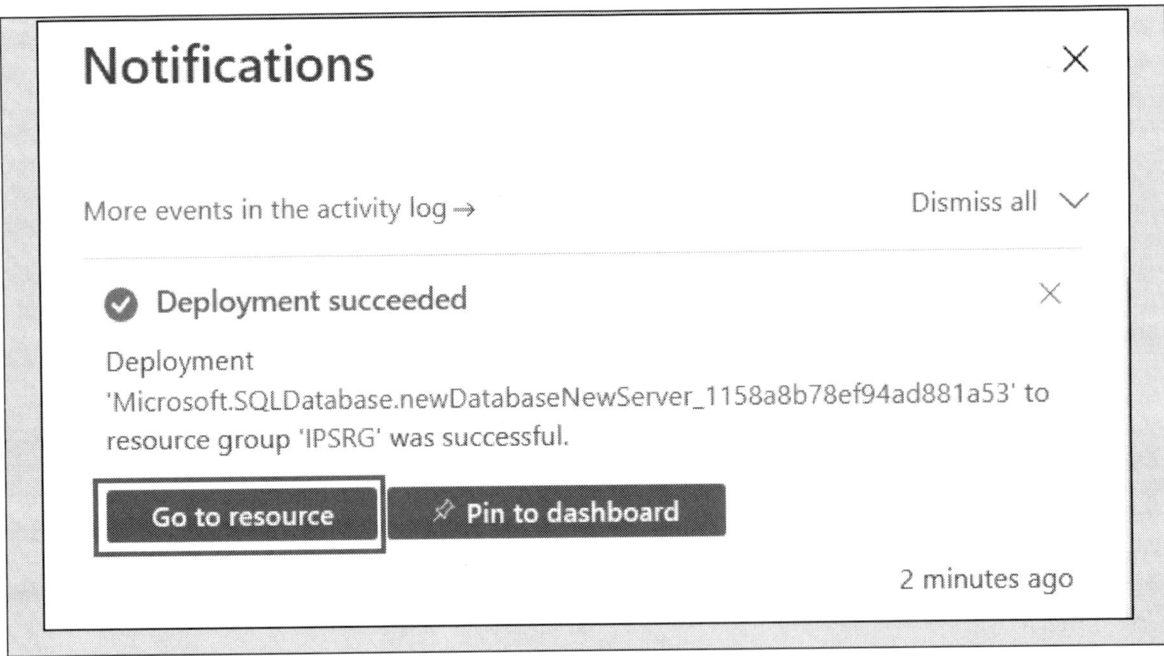

New SQL Server

1. On the IPSLT overview page, copy the link for the **Server name** in the top section.

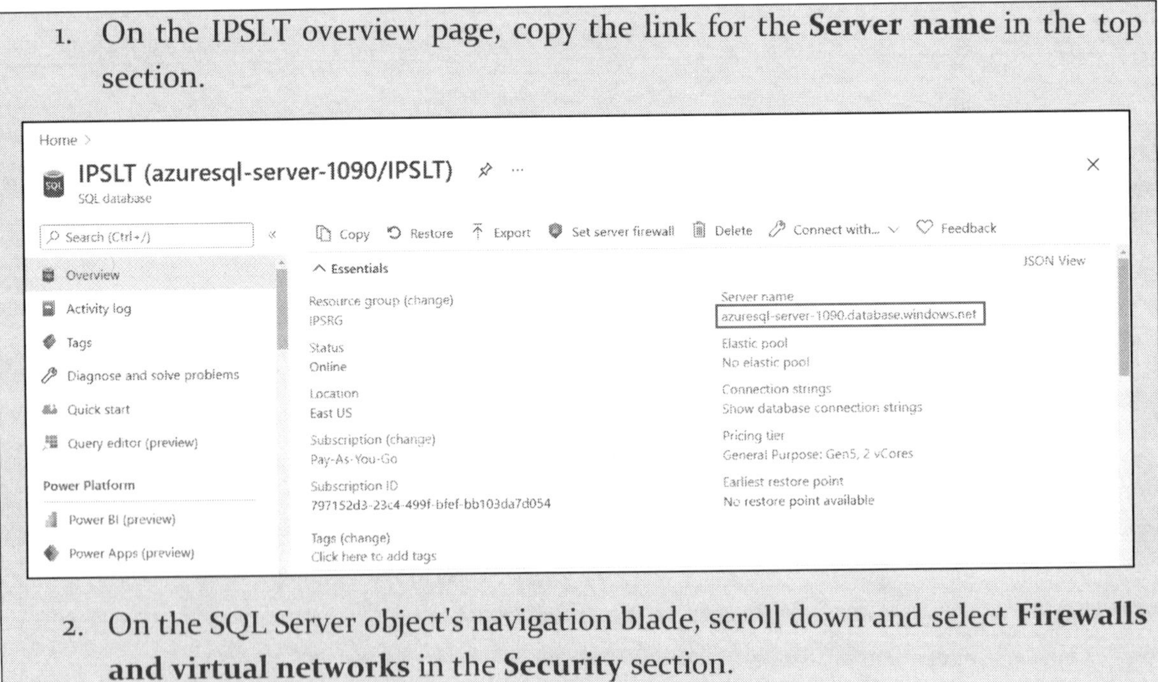

2. On the SQL Server object's navigation blade, scroll down and select **Firewalls and virtual networks** in the **Security** section.

Security

Advanced data security

Auditing

Firewalls and virtual networks

Private endpoint connections

Transparent data encryption

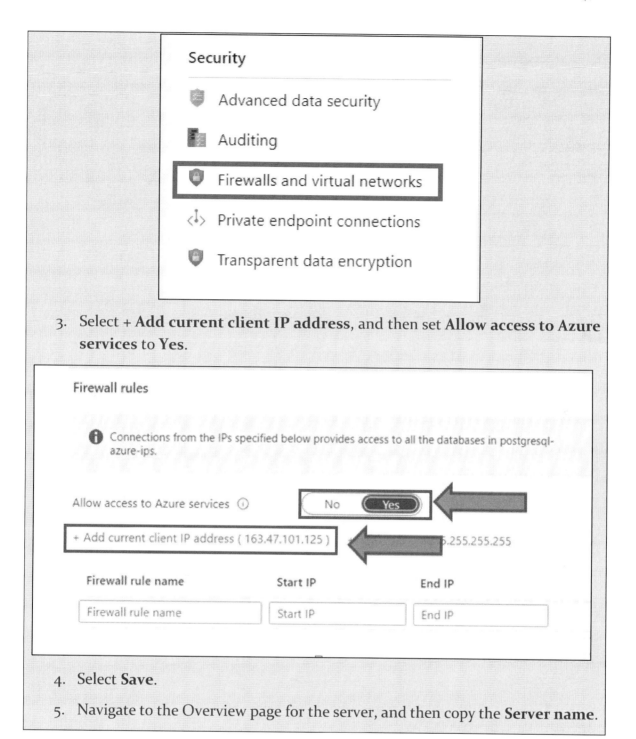

3. Select + **Add current client IP address**, and then set **Allow access to Azure services** to **Yes**.

Firewall rules

Connections from the IPs specified below provides access to all the databases in postgresql-azure-ips.

Allow access to Azure services No Yes

+ Add current client IP address (163.47.101.125)

Firewall rule name Start IP End IP

4. Select **Save**.
5. Navigate to the Overview page for the server, and then copy the **Server name**.

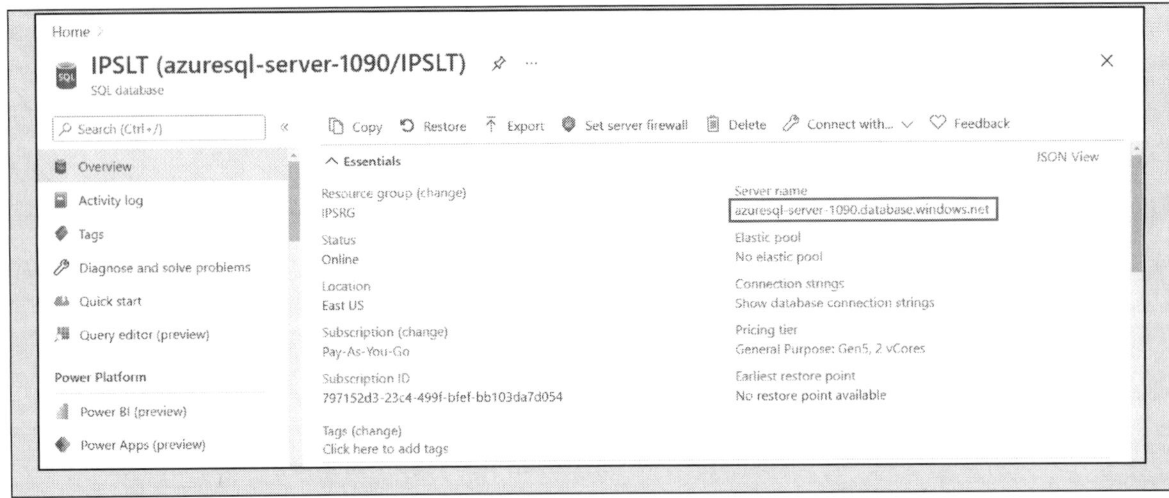

Register Azure SQL DB Instance in Azure Data Studio (ADS)

1. Launch Azure Data Studio from the windows toolbar.
2. Select **Connections** in ADS' left sidebar, then the **Add Connection** button.

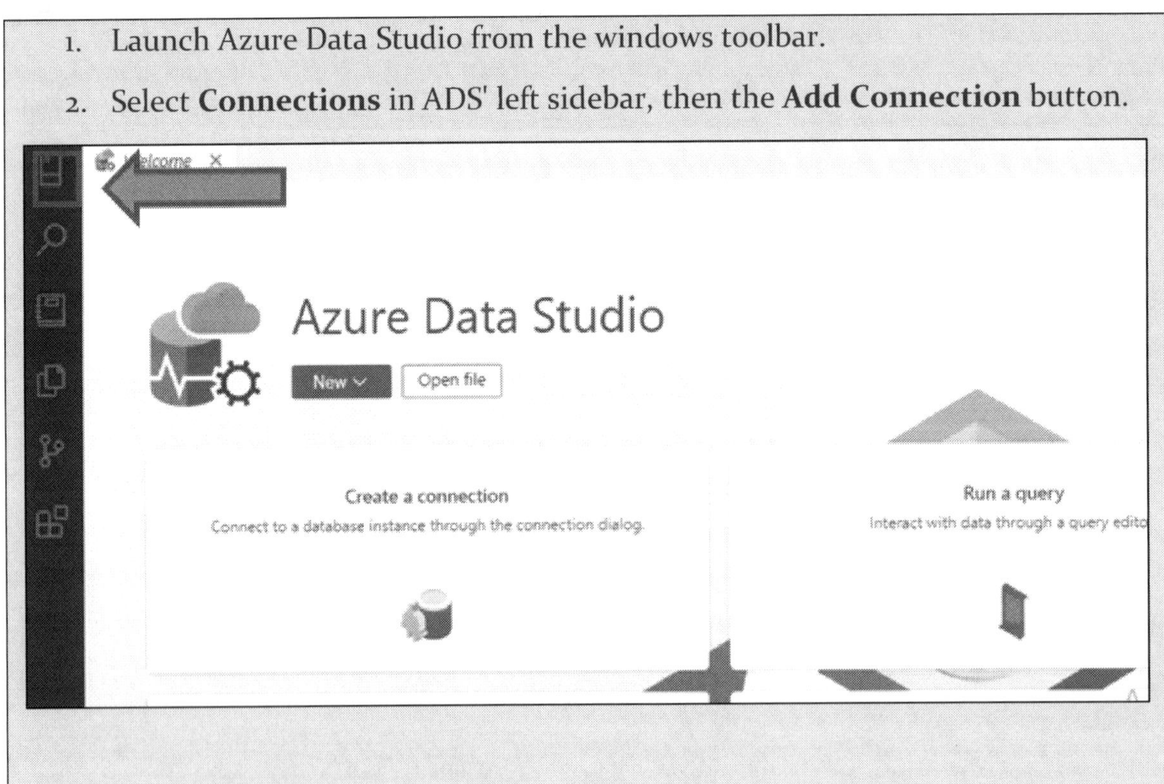

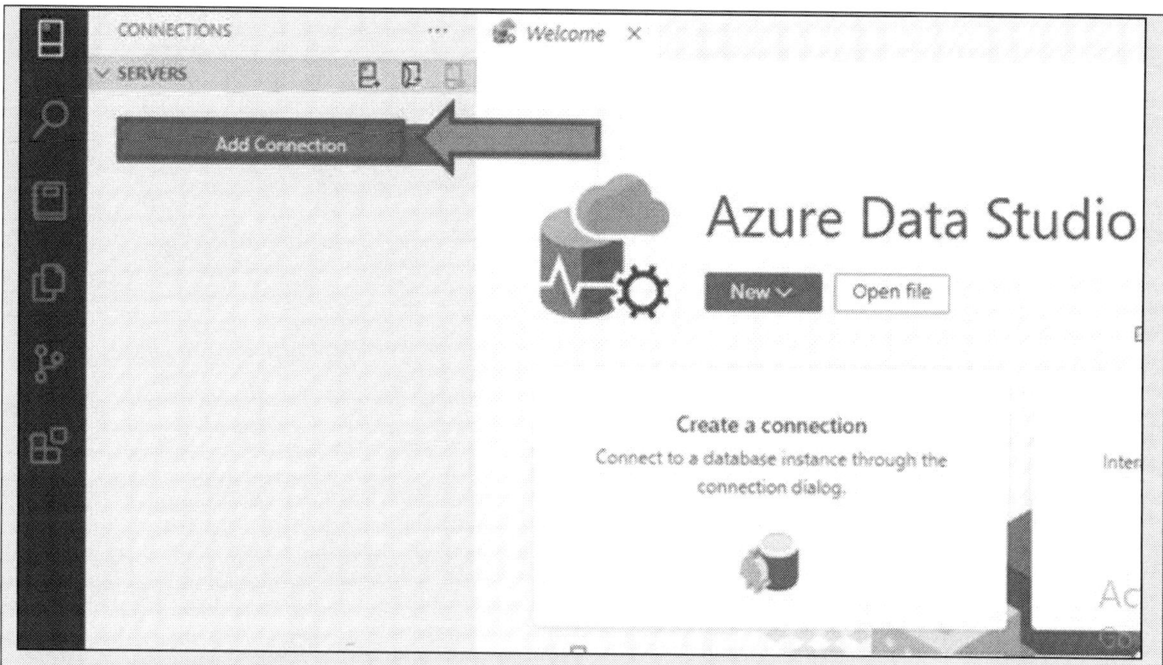

3. In the **Connection** sidebar, fill out the **Connection Details** section with connection information to connect to the AdventureWorksLT database created in the previous steps.
    - Connection Type: **Microsoft SQL Server**
    - Server: Paste the server name you copied earlier.
    - Authentication Type: **SQL Login**
    - User name: **ipsadmin**
    - Password: **Azur3Pa$$**
    - Expand the Database drop-down to select **IPSLT**
    - Server group will remain on **<default>**.
    - Name (optional) can be populated with a friendly name of the database if desired.
    - Review settings and select **Connect**.

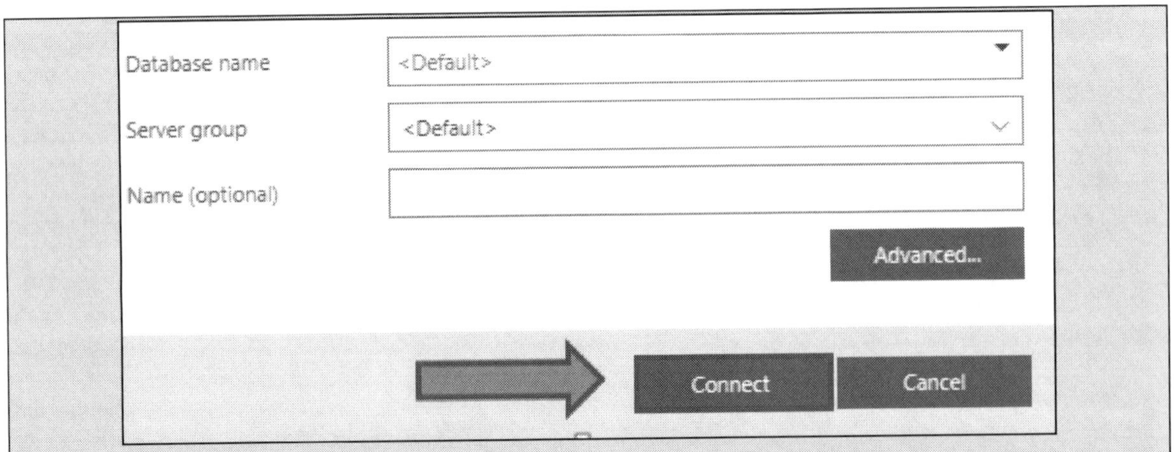

4. ADS will connect to the database and show some basic information, including a partial list of objects.

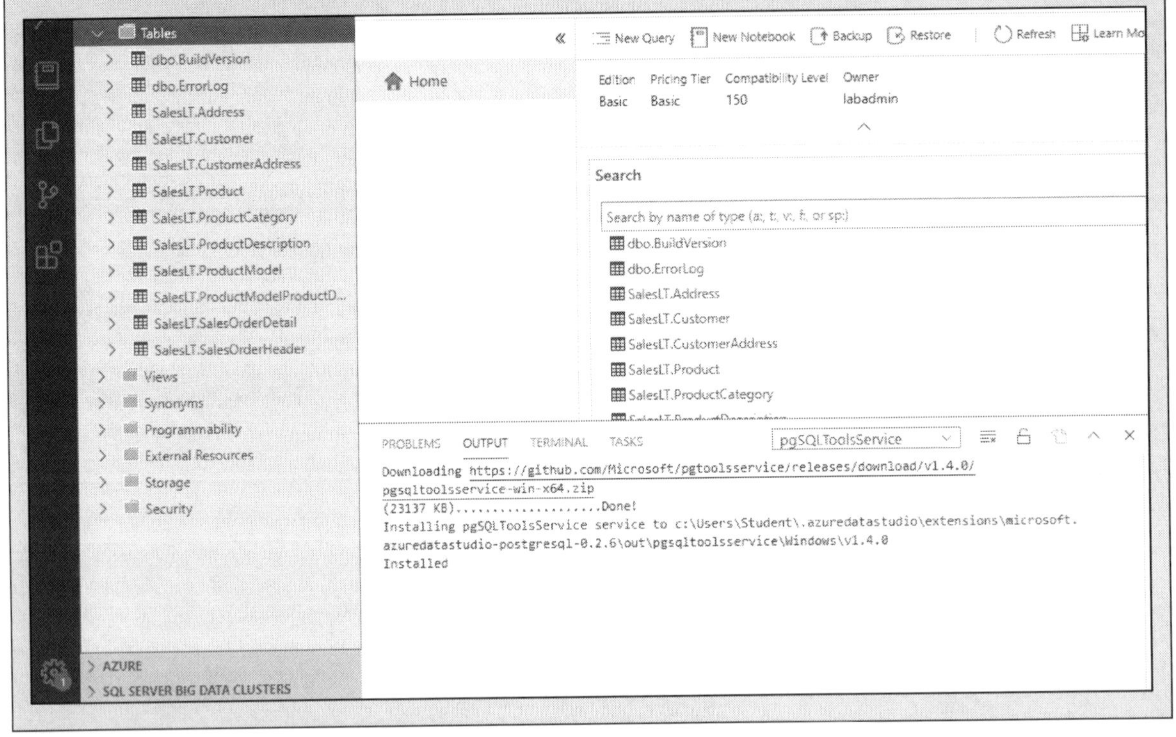

SQL Database with a SQL Notebook

1. In ADS, connected to this lab's IPSLT database, select **New Notebook**.

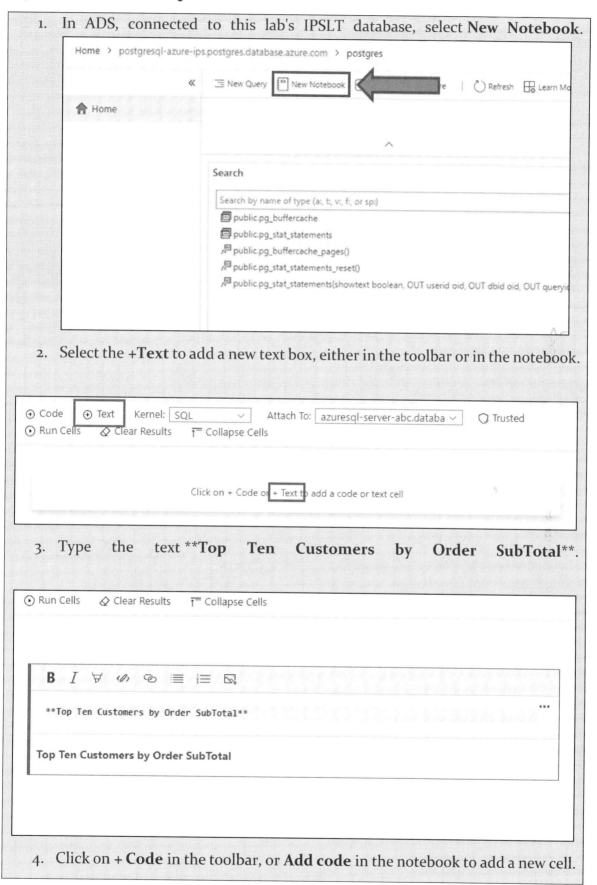

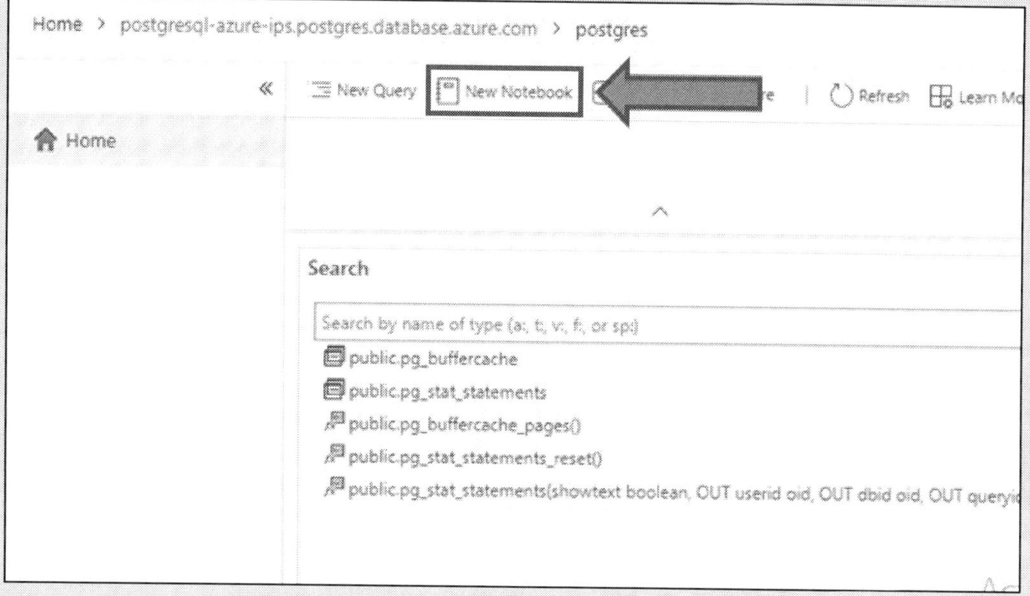

2. Select the +**Text** to add a new text box, either in the toolbar or in the notebook.

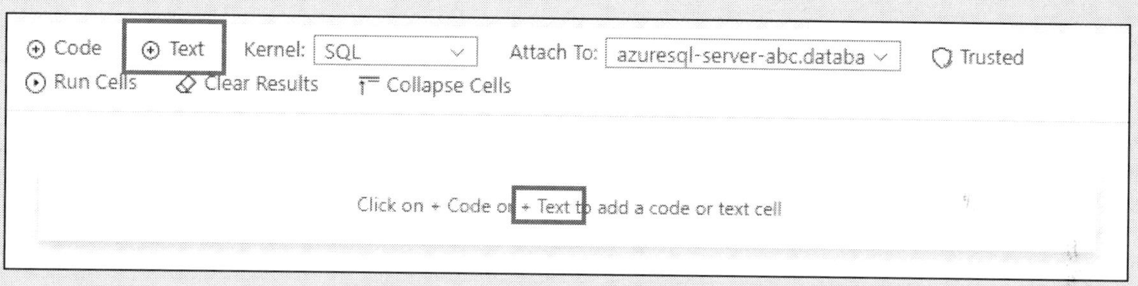

3. Type the text ****Top Ten Customers by Order SubTotal****.

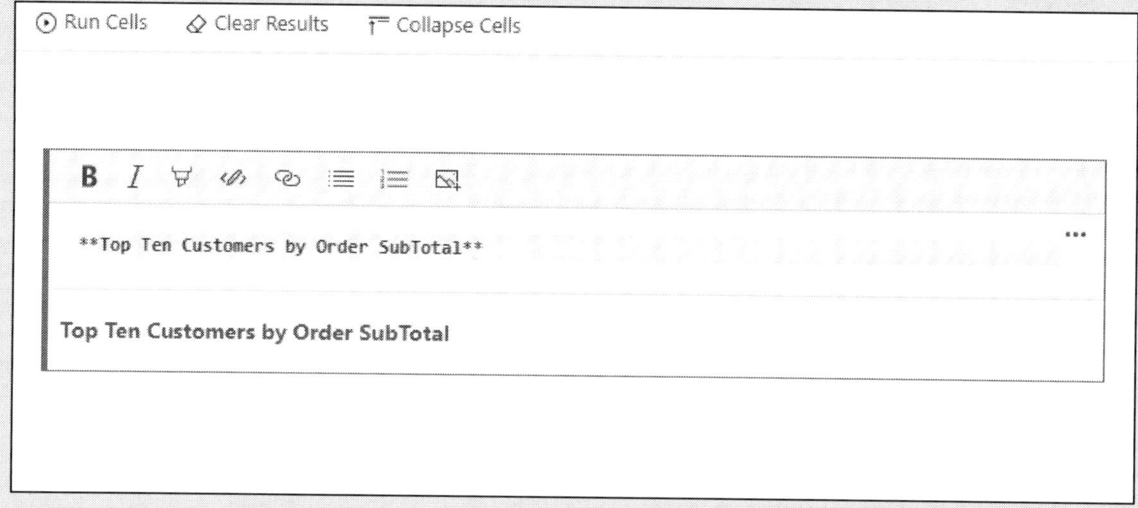

4. Click on + **Code** in the toolbar, or **Add code** in the notebook to add a new cell.

Code Text Kernel: SQL Attach To: azuresql-server-abc.databa Trusted
Run Cells Clear Results Collapse Cells

Top Ten Customers by Order SubTotal

Add code

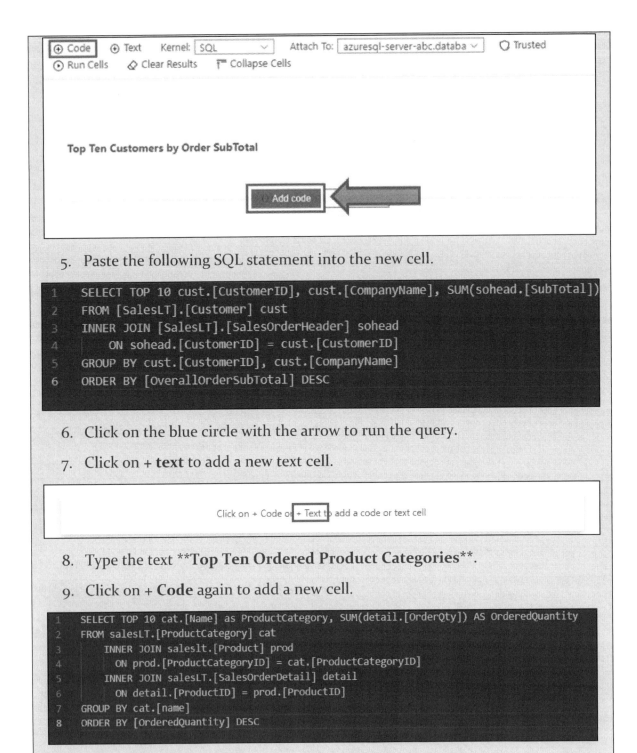

5. Paste the following SQL statement into the new cell.

```
SELECT TOP 10 cust.[CustomerID], cust.[CompanyName], SUM(sohead.[SubTotal])
FROM [SalesLT].[Customer] cust
INNER JOIN [SalesLT].[SalesOrderHeader] sohead
    ON sohead.[CustomerID] = cust.[CustomerID]
GROUP BY cust.[CustomerID], cust.[CompanyName]
ORDER BY [OverallOrderSubTotal] DESC
```

6. Click on the blue circle with the arrow to run the query.
7. Click on + **text** to add a new text cell.

Click on + Code or + Text to add a code or text cell

8. Type the text ****Top Ten Ordered Product Categories****.
9. Click on + **Code** again to add a new cell.

```
SELECT TOP 10 cat.[Name] as ProductCategory, SUM(detail.[OrderQty]) AS OrderedQuantity
FROM salesLT.[ProductCategory] cat
    INNER JOIN saleslt.[Product] prod
      ON prod.[ProductCategoryID] = cat.[ProductCategoryID]
    INNER JOIN salesLT.[SalesOrderDetail] detail
      ON detail.[ProductID] = prod.[ProductID]
GROUP BY cat.[name]
ORDER BY [OrderedQuantity] DESC
```

10. Select on the blue circle with the arrow to execute the query.
11. Select the Run Cells button in the toolbar to run all cells in the notebook and present results.

Run Cells Clear Results Collapse Cells

```
INNER JOIN [SalesLT].[SalesOrderHeader] sohead
    ON sohead.[CustomerID] = cust.[CustomerID]
GROUP BY cust.[CustomerID], cust.[CompanyName]
ORDER BY [OverallOrderSubTotal] DESC
```

Top Ten Ordered Product Categories

```
SELECT TOP 10 cat.[Name] as ProductCategory, SUM(detail.[OrderQty]) AS OrderedQuan
FROM salesLT.[ProductCategory] cat
    INNER JOIN saleslt.[Product] prod
          ON prod.[ProductCategoryID] = cat.[ProductCategoryID]
    INNER JOIN salesLT.[SalesOrderDetail] detail
           ON detail.[ProductID] = prod.[ProductID]
GROUP BY cat.[name]
ORDER BY [OrderedQuantity] DESC
```

12. Select **Save** and then close the tab for the notebook from inside of ADS.
13. From the **File** menu, select **Open File**, and open the notebook you just saved.

On completing this exercise, you have seen how to create a SQL database in Azure and connect to it securely from a client machine.

Deploy a PostgreSQL Database

1. From the Azure portal, select + **Create a Resource**.

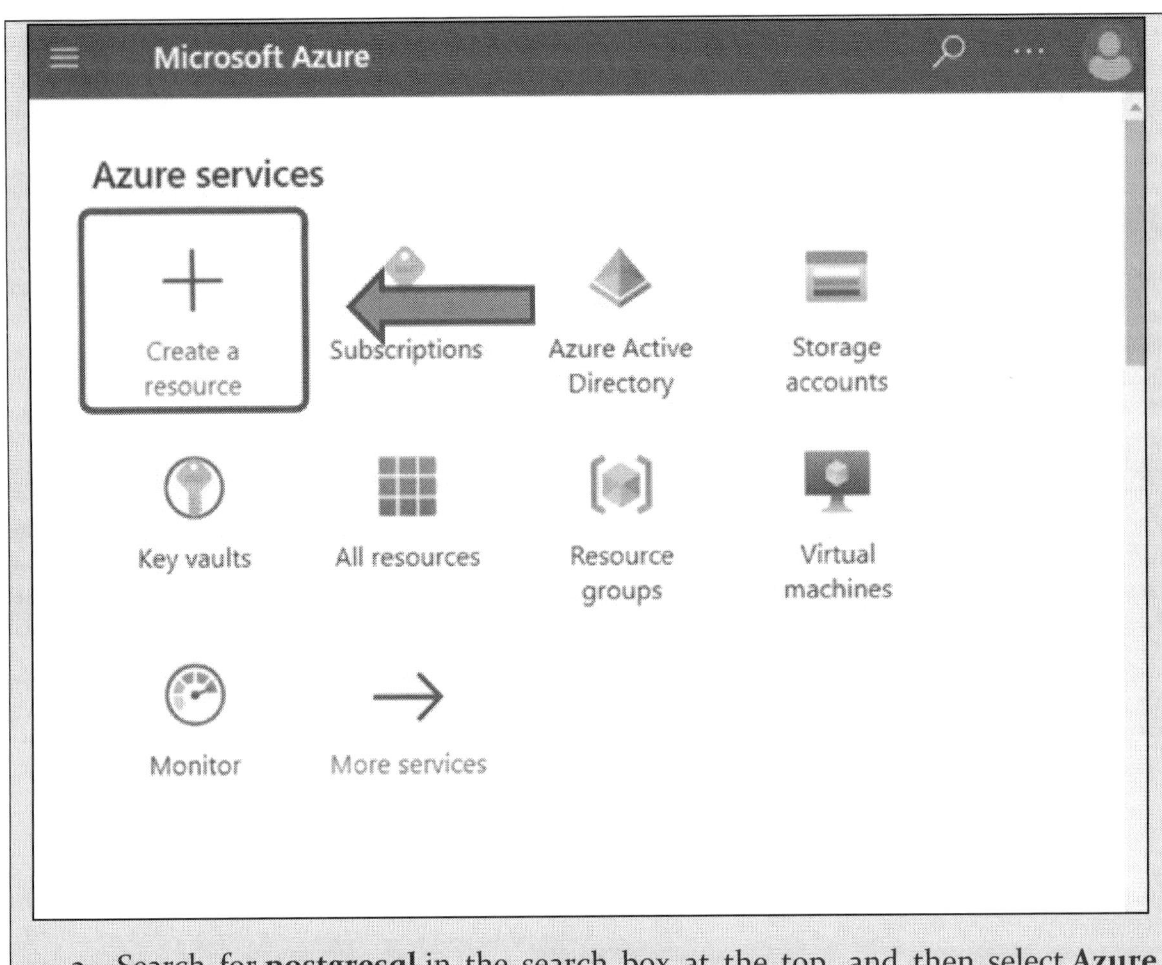

2. Search for **postgresql** in the search box at the top, and then select **Azure Database for PostgreSQL** in the results.

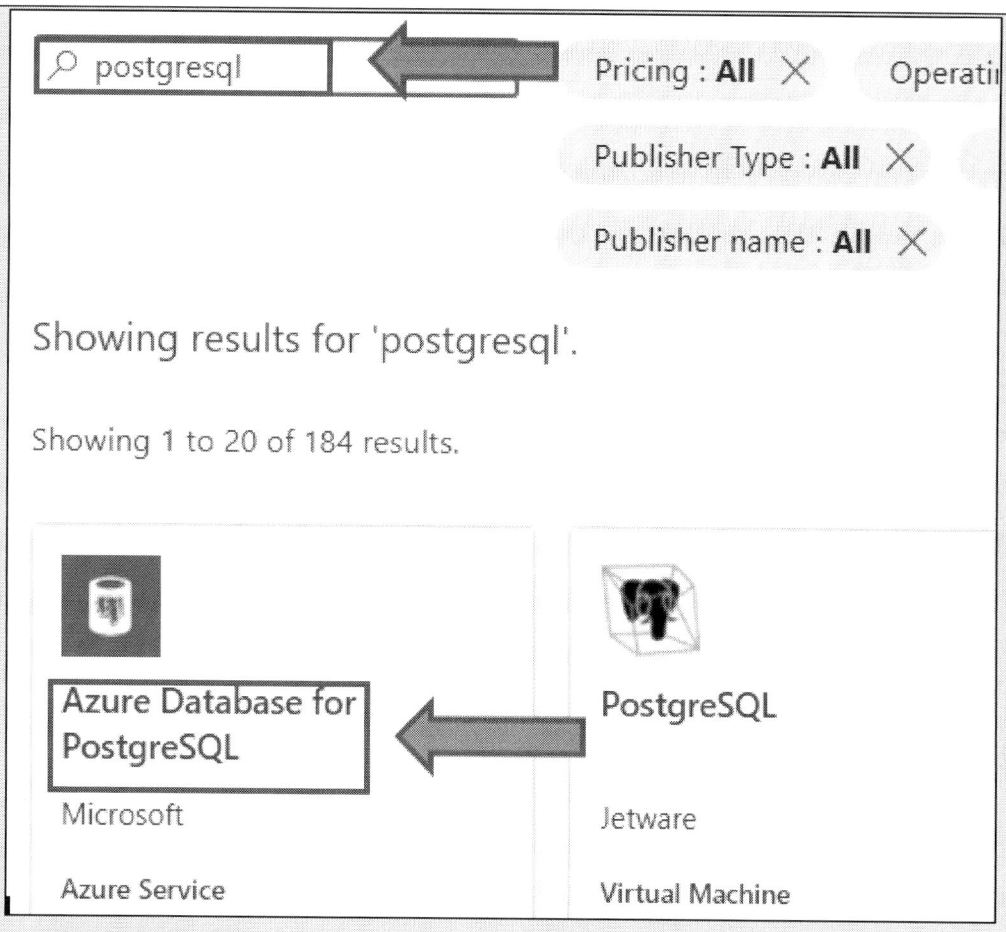

postgresql

Pricing : **All**

Operati

Publisher Type : **All**

Publisher name : **All**

Showing results for 'postgresql'.

Showing 1 to 20 of 184 results.

Azure Database for PostgreSQL
Microsoft
Azure Service

PostgreSQL
Jetware
Virtual Machine

3. Select **Create**.

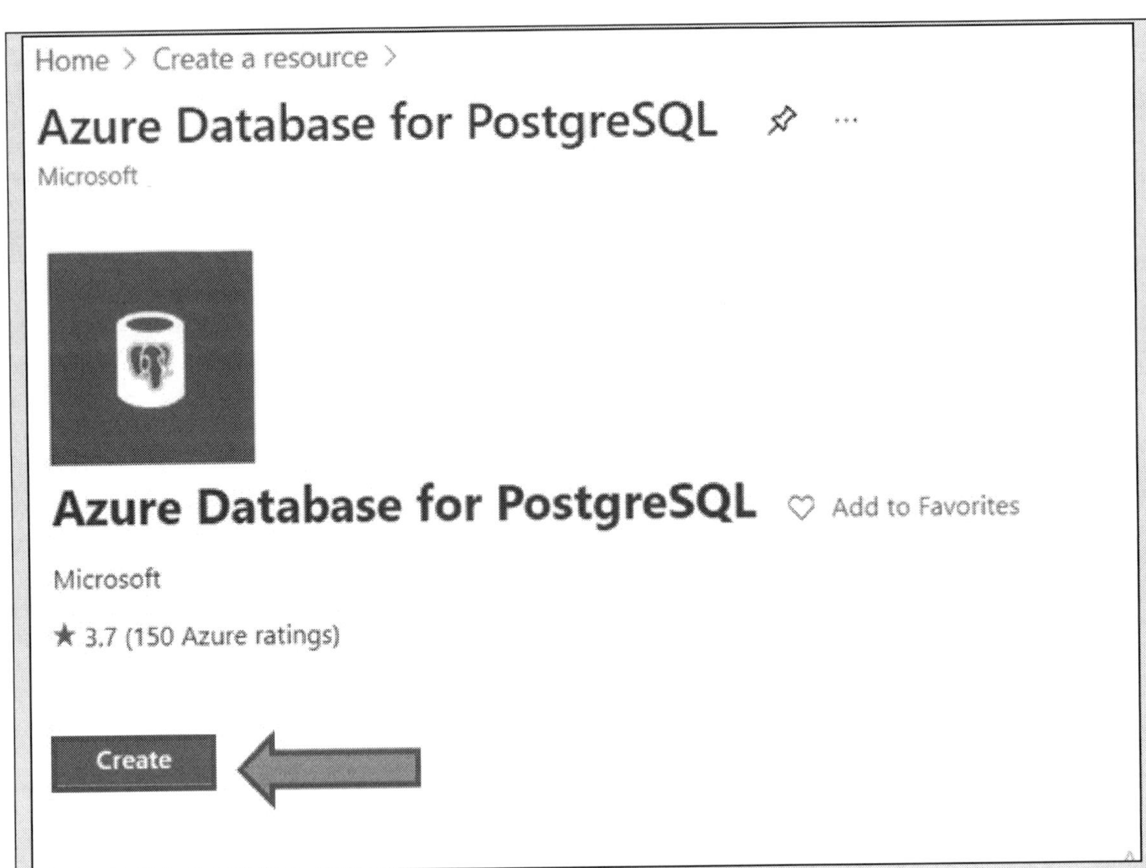

4. Select **Create** for the Single Server option.

How do you plan to use the service?

Single server

Best for broad range of traditional transactional workloads.

Enterprise ready, fully managed community PostgreSQL server with up to 64 vCores, optional geospatial support, full-text search and more.

5. Complete the Single Server Basics screen with the following information:

- Resource Group: **IPSRG**
- Server Name: **postgresql-azure-ips** (add additional characters as a server name must be unique)
- Data source: **None**
- Location: Select the Region closest to you, which has been used throughout this lab.
- Version: **10**

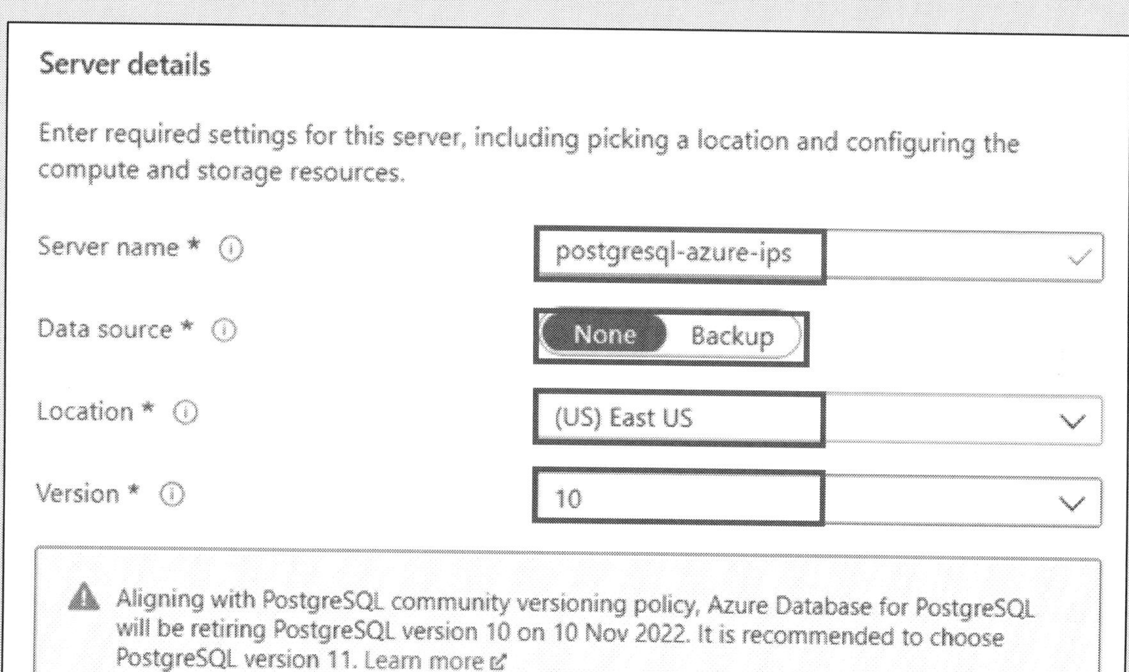

- Select **Configure Server** link under **Compute + storage**.

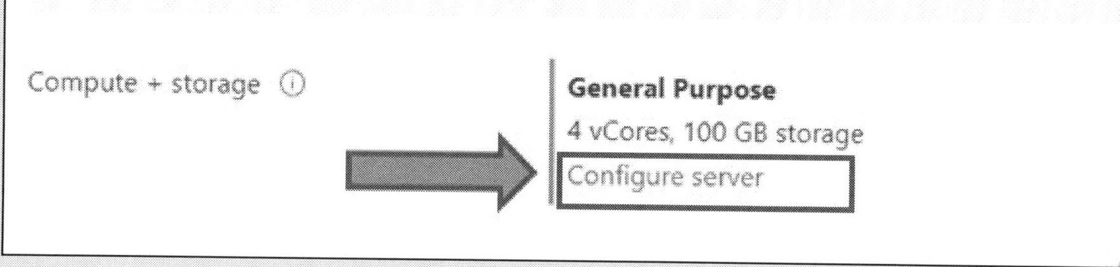

  - Select the **Basic** tab.
  - Slide the vCore slider to the left to select **1 vCore**.
  - Select **OK**.

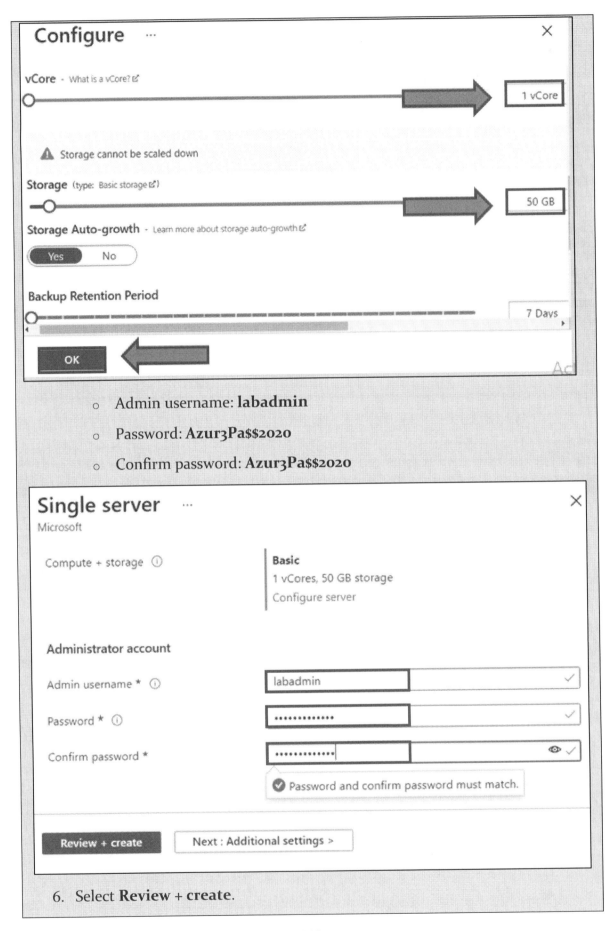

- Admin username: **labadmin**
- Password: **Azur3Pa$$2020**
- Confirm password: **Azur3Pa$$2020**

6. Select **Review + create**.

Single server ...
Microsoft

Compute + storage — Basic, 1 vCores, 50 GB storage, Configure server

Administrator account

Admin username * — labadmin

Password * — ••••••••••••••

Confirm password * — ••••••••••••••

Password and confirm password must match.

Review + create | ...ional settings >

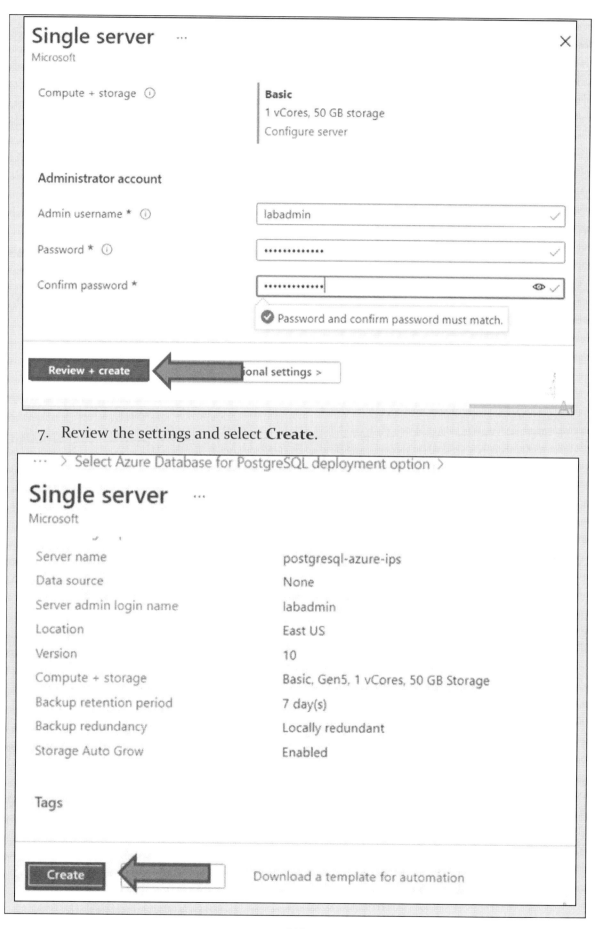

7. Review the settings and select **Create**.

... > Select Azure Database for PostgreSQL deployment option >

Single server ...
Microsoft

Server name	postgresql-azure-ips
Data source	None
Server admin login name	labadmin
Location	East US
Version	10
Compute + storage	Basic, Gen5, 1 vCores, 50 GB Storage
Backup retention period	7 day(s)
Backup redundancy	Locally redundant
Storage Auto Grow	Enabled

Tags

Create | Download a template for automation

8. When the deployment is complete, select **Go to resource**.

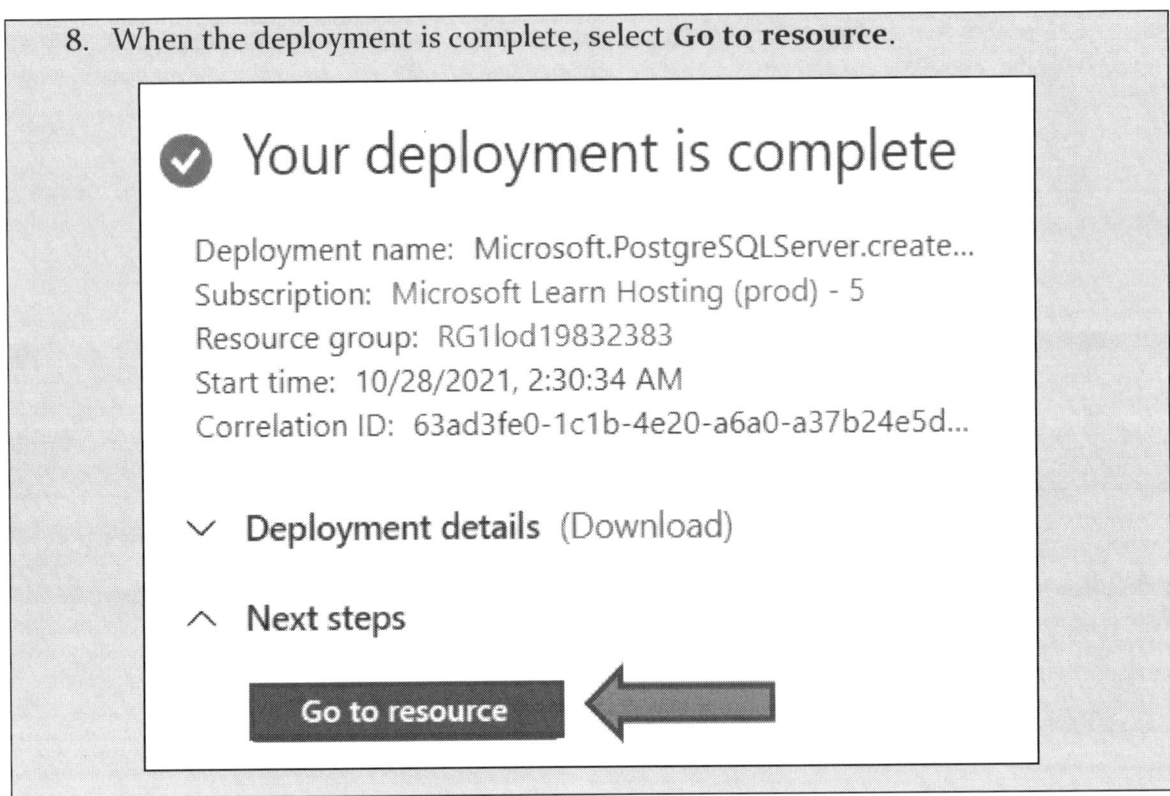

Enable All Azure Services Access to a PostgreSQL Database

1. Click on **Connection security** under Settings on the left navigation.

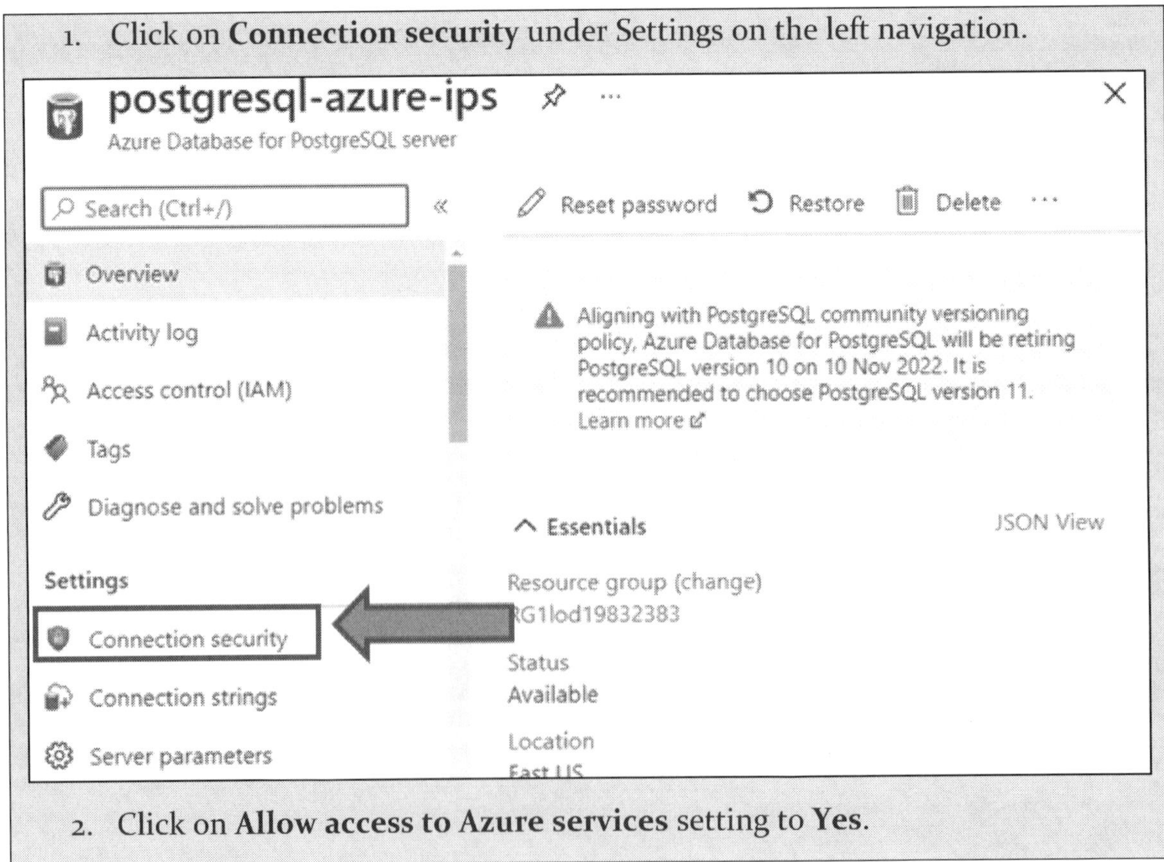

2. Click on **Allow access to Azure services** setting to **Yes**.

3. Click on **+ Add current client IP address**.

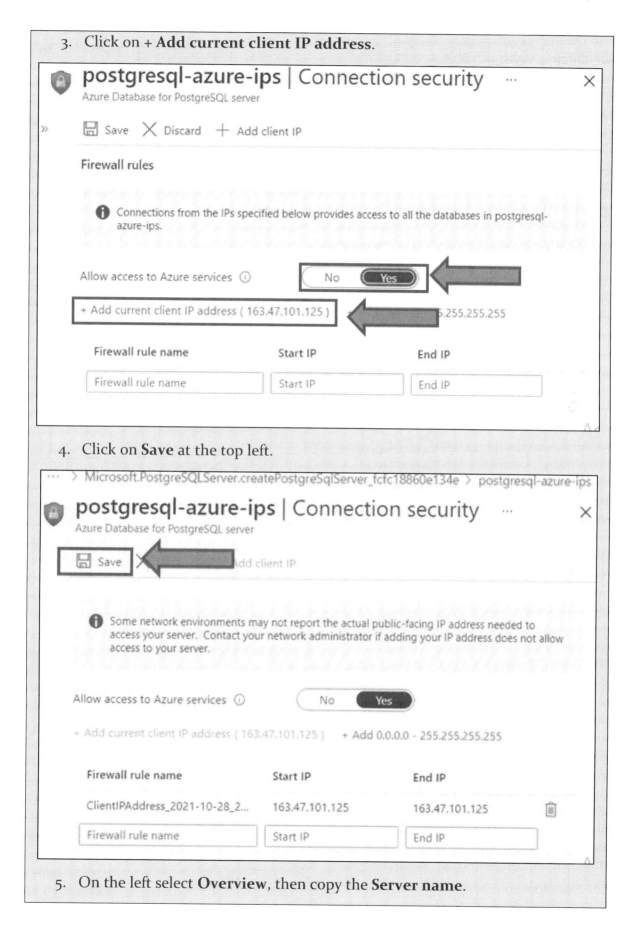

4. Click on **Save** at the top left.

5. On the left select **Overview**, then copy the **Server name**.

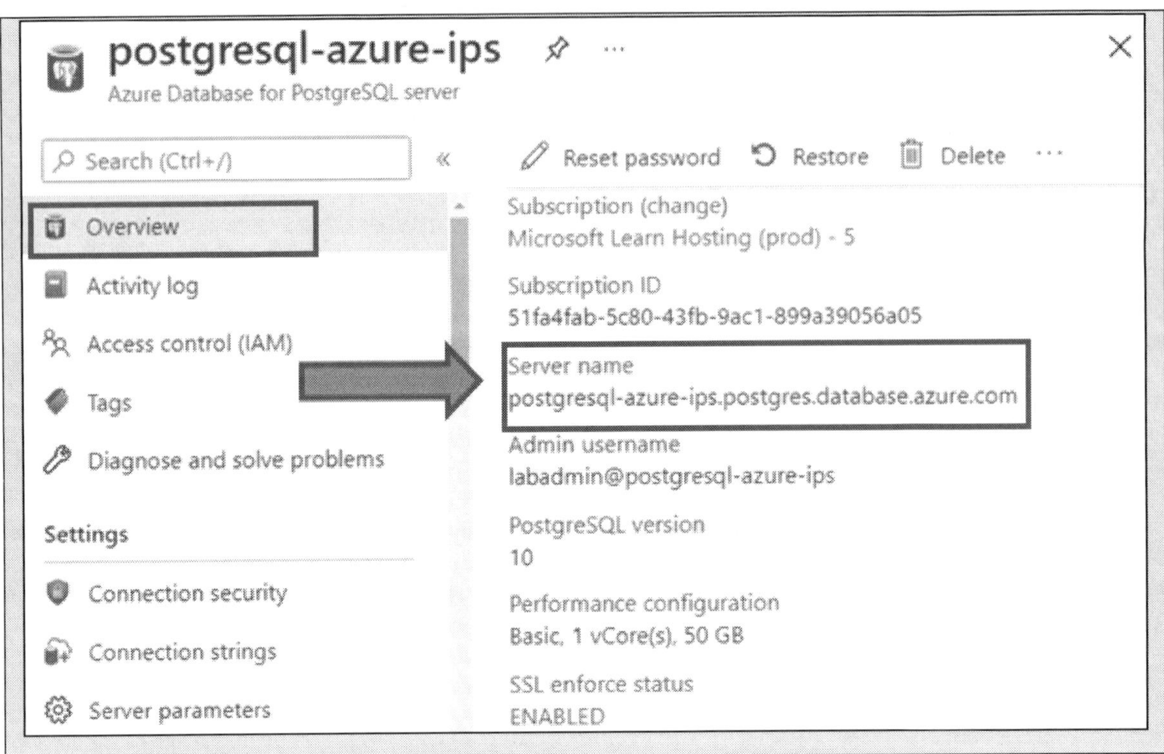

Connect to the PostgreSQL Database with Azure Data Studio (ADS)

1. In Azure Data Studio, make sure the Connections sidebar is expanded.
2. Click on the **Connections** button in the left navigation bar, if not.

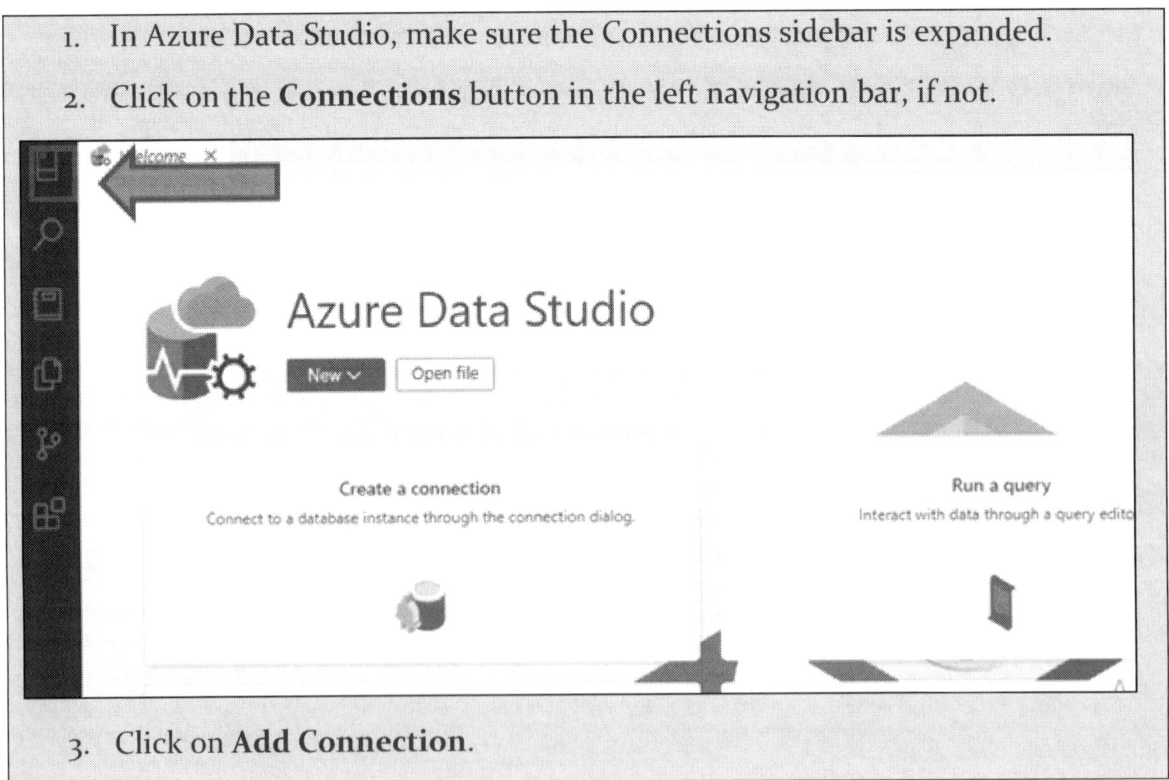

3. Click on **Add Connection**.

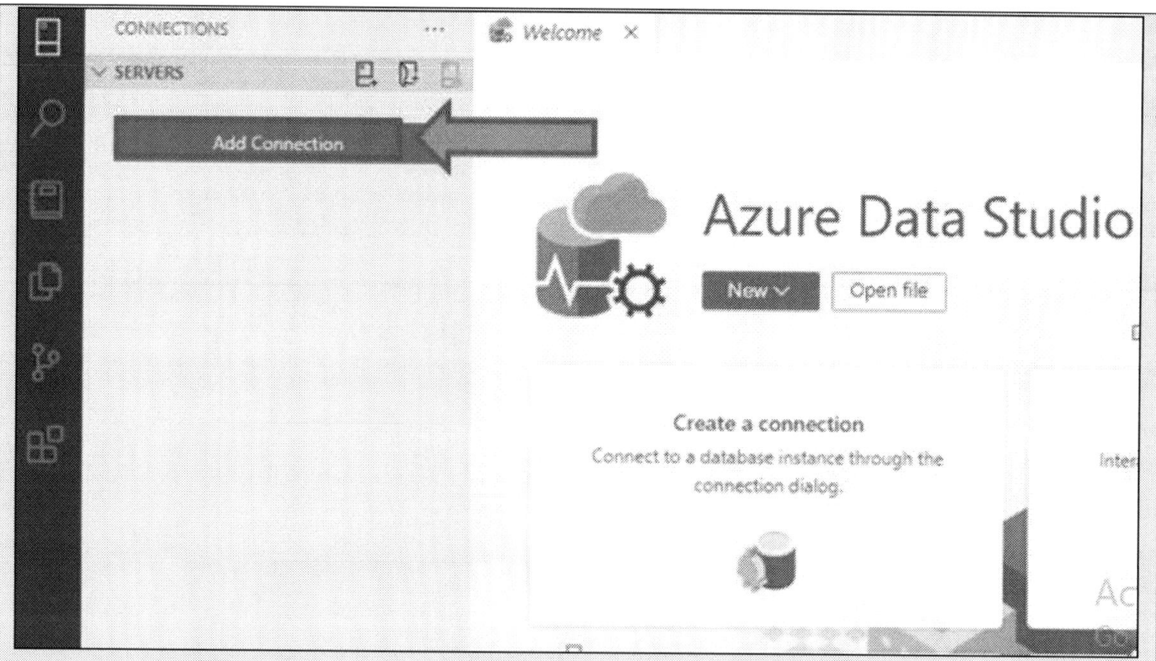

4. In the Connection Details sidebar, type the following information to link to the previous Task's PostgreSQL database:
    - Connection Type: **PostgreSQL**
    - Server: Paste the name you copied from the Azure portal.
    - Authentication Type: **Password**
    - User name: **labadmin@postgresql-azure-ips** (note that the user name must include the hostname. This is the first part up to the period in the server name.)
    - Password: **Azur3Pa$$2020**
    - Database name: **<default>**
    - Server group: **<default>**
    - Name (optional): You can add a friendly name for the database server if you like. It can be left blank.
5. Click on **Connect**.

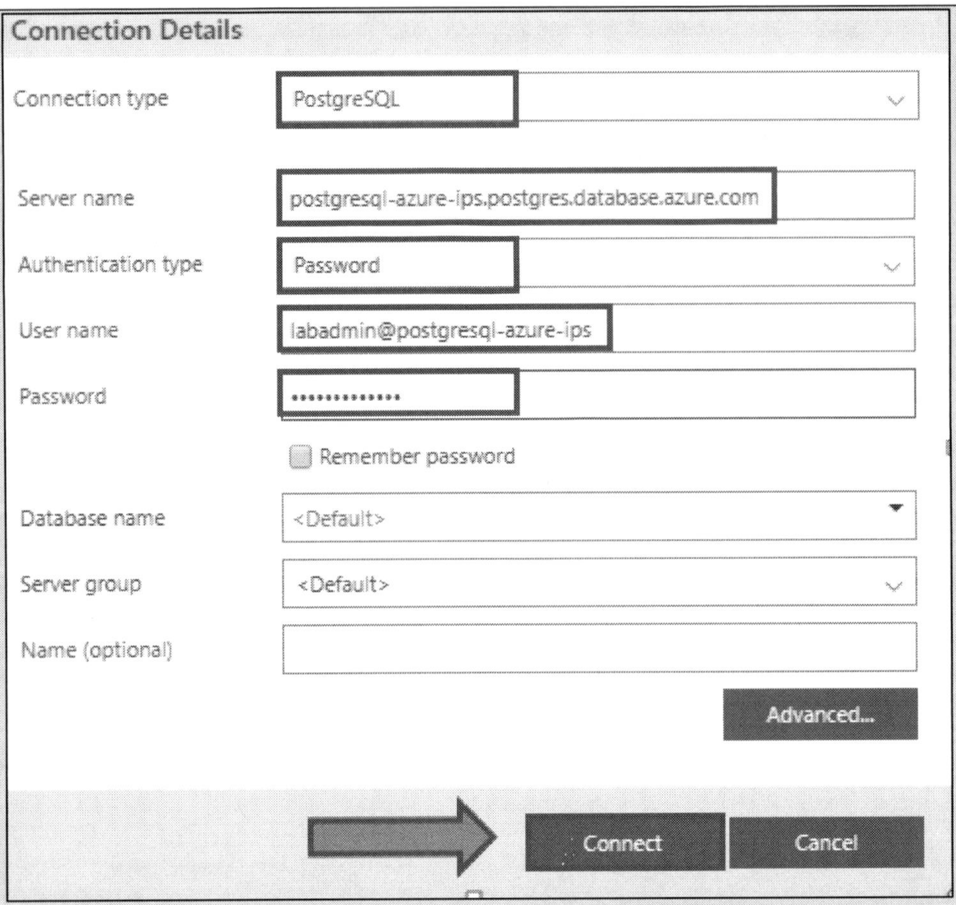

6. Azure Data Studio is now linked to your PostgreSQL database server.

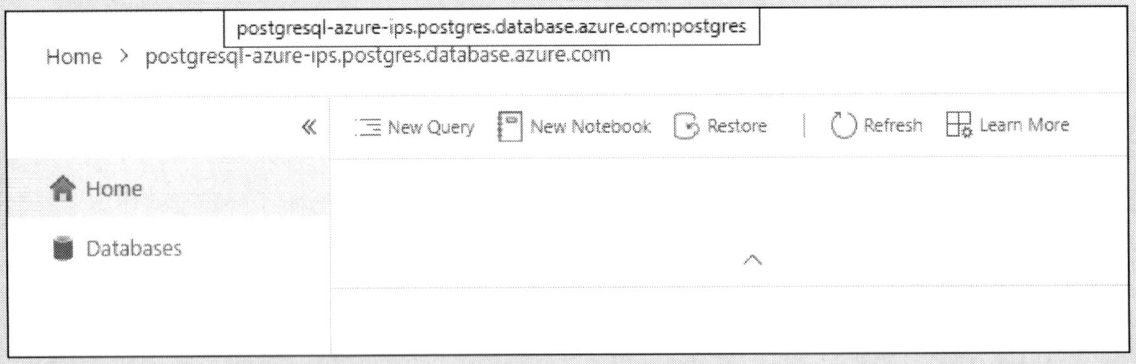

7. Click on **Databases**. Double-click on the **postgres** database.

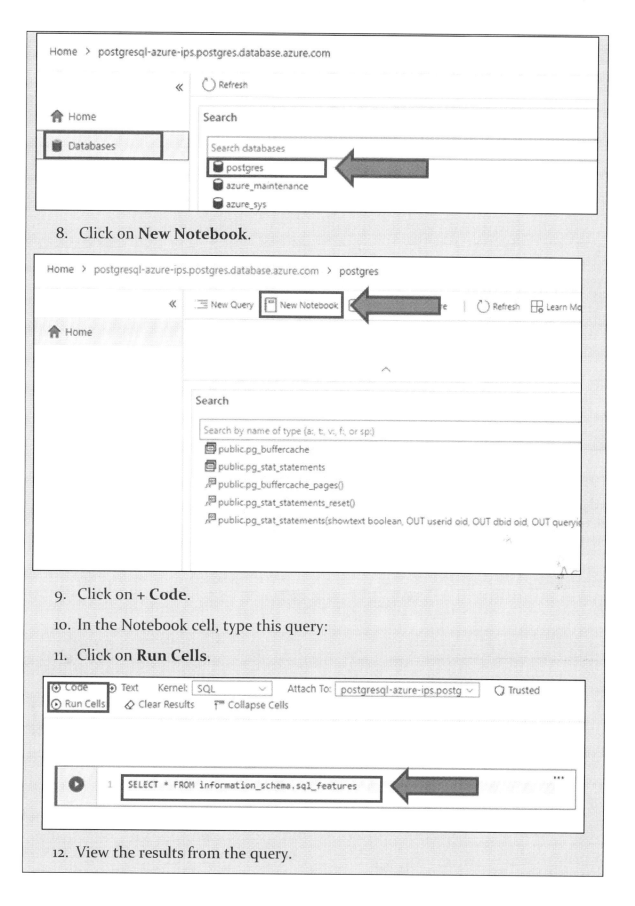

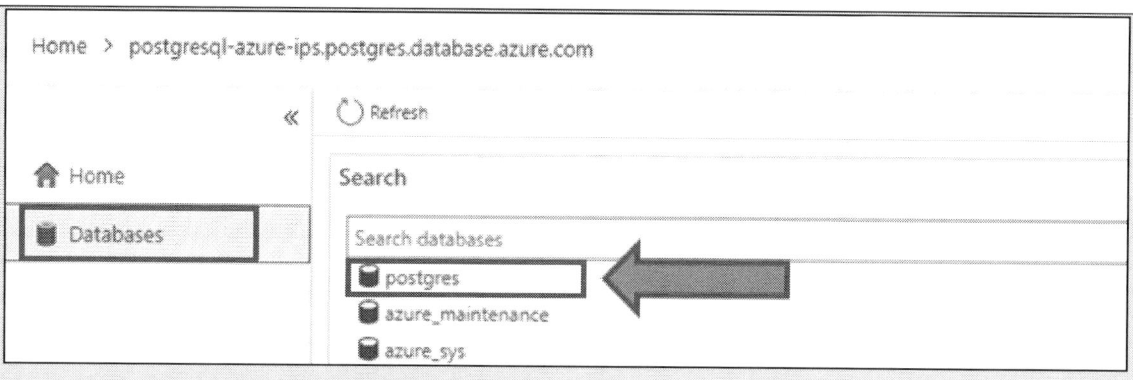

8. Click on **New Notebook**.

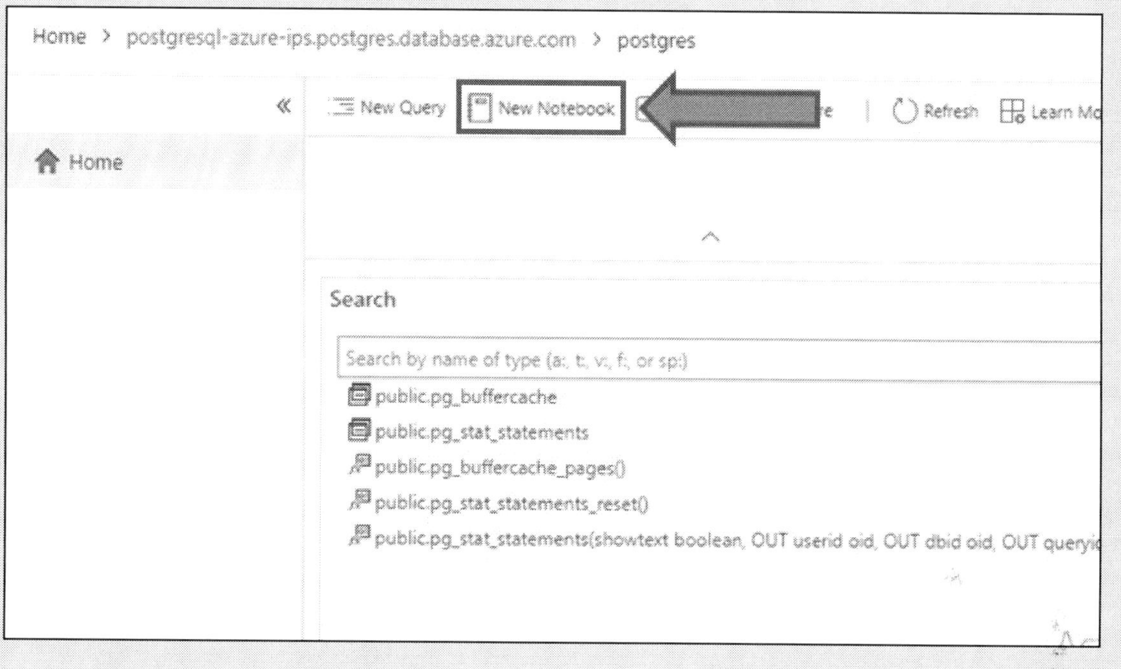

9. Click on + **Code**.

10. In the Notebook cell, type this query:

11. Click on **Run Cells**.

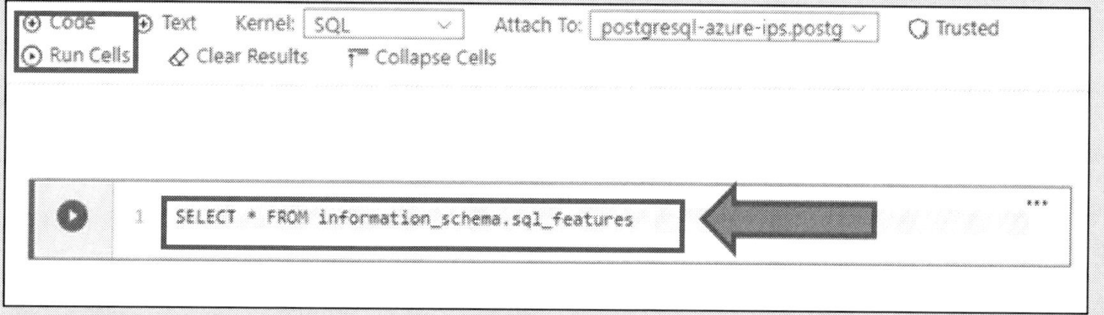

```
SELECT * FROM information_schema.sql_features
```

12. View the results from the query.

```
[1]    SELECT * FROM information_schema.sql_features
```

(671 row(s) affected)

Total execution time: 00:00:00.568

	feature_id	feature_name	sub_feature_id	sub_feature_name
1	B011	Embedded Ada	NULL	NULL
2	B012	Embedded C	NULL	NULL
3	B013	Embedded COBOL	NULL	NULL
4	B014	Embedded Fortran	NULL	NULL
5	B015	Embedded MUMPS	NULL	NULL
6	B016	Embedded Pascal	NULL	NULL
7	B017	Embedded PL/I	NULL	NULL

Mind Map

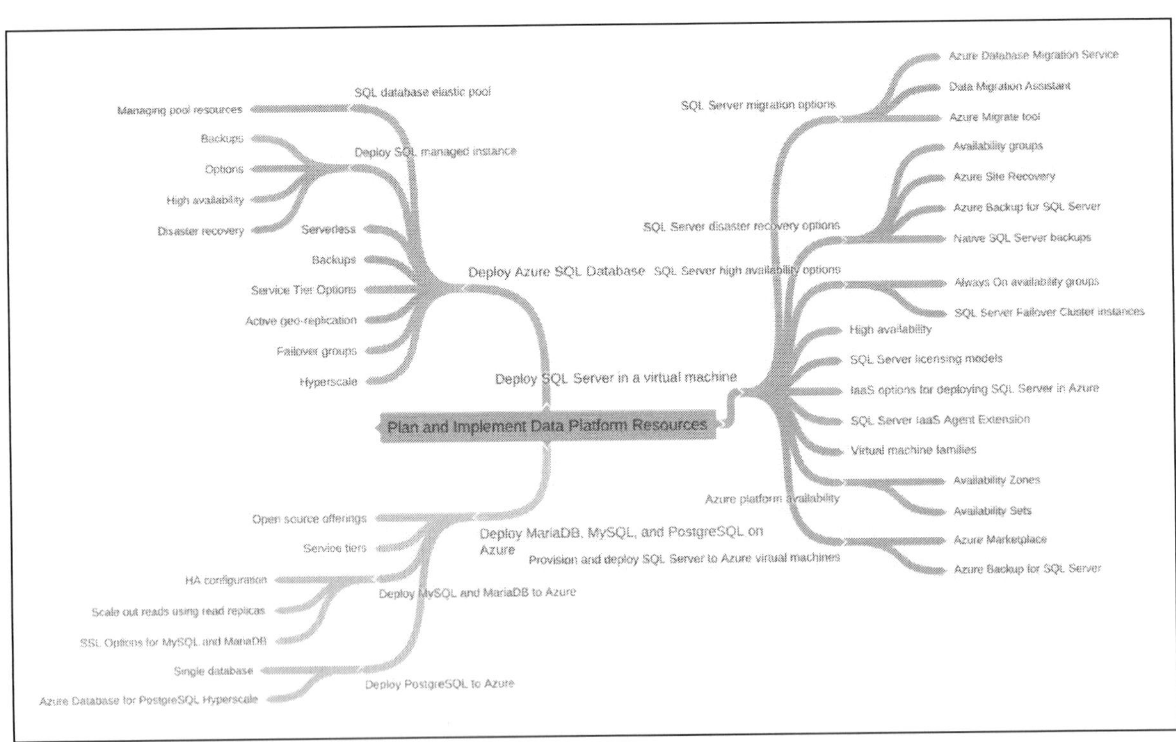

Figure 02-26: Mind Map

Practice Questions

1. Which SSD storage provides the lowest latency in Azure?

A. Ultra

B. Premium

C. Standard

D. None of the above

2. Each VM will have at least _____ disks associated with it.

A. Two

B. Three

C. Four

D. Five

3. There are _____ service tiers available when creating an Azure SQL Managed Instance.

A. Two

B. Three

C. Four

D. Five

4. Which option will you use to migrate your databases from an on-premises SQL Server to an Azure VM?

A. Microsoft Assessment and Planning Toolkit

B. Database Experimentation Assistant

C. Data Migration Assistant

D. None of the above

5. To reduce the cost of an Azure SQL Server VM, you intend to run full time for three years. Which option should you choose?

A. Availability set

B. Azure Reserved VM Instances

C. Pay as You Go Licensing

D. None of the above

6. When using a single Azure Virtual Machine in conjunction with Azure-managed storage, what guarantee of availability does the service provide?

A. 99%

B. 99.9%

C. 99.99%

D. None of the above

7. Which option should you choose to spread workloads across data centers in a region?

A. Availability sets

B. Availability zones

C. Availability units

D. None of the above

8. Which service performs block-level replication of your Azure virtual machine?

A. Azure Site Recovery

B. Azure Backup for SQL Server

C. Availability Groups

D. None of the above

9. You need to migrate a set of databases that use distributed transactions from an on-premises SQL Server. What will you choose?

A. Azure SQL Database

B. Azure SQL Database Hyperscale

C. Azure SQL managed instance

D. None of the above

10. You are building a new cloud database that you expect to grow to 50 TB. What will you choose?

A. Azure SQL Database managed instance

B. Azure SQL Database Serverless

C. Azure SQL Database Hyperscale

D. None of the above

11. You are building a database for testing purposes that will be used less than 8 hours a day and is likely to be 20 GB in size. What is your best cost-effective option?

A. Azure SQL Database Serverless

B. Azure SQL Database Elastic Pools

C. Azure SQL Database managed instance

D. None of the above

12. How often do differential backups occur with Azure SQL-managed instances?

A. Every 1 hour

B. Every 12 hours

C. Every 24 hours

D. None of the above

13. You are deploying a mission-critical MySQL database to support an e-commerce site that depends on low latency. What should you configure your application to do to handle transient errors?

A. Connection resiliency

B. Secure Socket Layer (SSL)

C. An Azure Virtual Network

D. None of the above

14. Which of the following is a benefit of Azure Database for PostgreSQL?

A. Managed automated backups

B. Automatic Query Tuning

C. Automated cross-region disaster recovery

D. None of the above

15. What is the process to upgrade a major version of Azure Database for MySQL?

A. The service performs the update for you

B. Create a dump and restore it to a server at the higher version

C. Change the version of the server in the portal

D. None of the above

Chapter 03: Implement a Secure Environment for a Database Service

Configure Database Authentication and Authorization

Describe Active Directory and Azure Active Directory

What is the difference between Azure Active Directory and Windows Server Active Directory that we refer to collectively as 'Active Directory'? Since Azure Active Directory interacts with Active Directory, it is especially perplexing for new administrators. Both technologies provide authentication and identity management services but in distinct ways. Active Directory employs a protocol called Kerberos to give authentication via tickets and is queried by the Lightweight Directory Access Protocol (LDAP). For authentication, Azure Active Directory employs HTTPS protocols, such as SAML and OpenID Connect. Whereas, for permission, Azure Active Directory employs OAuth.

In most businesses, you cannot join a Windows Server to an Azure Active Directory domain and work together to deliver a single set of user IDs because the two services have different use cases. Azure Active Directory Connect is a service that links your Active Directory identities to your Azure Active Directory.

Authentication and Identities

SQL Server installations on-premises and SQL Server installations within Azure Virtual Machines both offer two forms of authentication:

- SQL Server authentication
- Windows authentication

SQL Server-specific login name and password information are saved within SQL Server. It is saved either in the master database or, in the case of confined users, in the user database when utilizing SQL Server authentication. Users connect to the SQL Server using the same Active Directory account that they use to get into their PC when using Windows Authentication (as well as accessing file shares and applications).

Because SQL Server authentication permits login information to be seen in plain text while being transferred across the network, Active Directory authentication is thought to be more secure. Furthermore, Active Directory authentication simplifies the management of user turnover. If a user quits the company and you use Windows authentication, the administrator simply needs to lock that user's single Windows account rather than identifying each SQL login.

Similarly, Azure SQL Database provides two forms of authentication:

- SQL Server authentication
- Azure Active Directory authentication

SQL Server authentication is the same authentication technique that SQL Server has supported from its inception, where user credentials are kept in either the master database or the user database. Using Azure Active Directory authentication, the user can use the same username and password to access additional resources, such as the Azure portal or Microsoft 365.

As previously stated, Azure Active Directory may be set up to sync with on-premises Active Directory. This option allows users to use the same usernames and passwords to access both on-premises and Azure resources. Azure Active Directory enhances security by allowing administrators to establish multi-factor authentication (MFA).

When MFA is activated on an account, a second level of authentication is required after entering the proper login and password. MFA can be set to use the Windows Authenticator program by default, which will send a push notification to the phone. Other possibilities for the default MFA action include sending a text message with an access code to the recipient or having the user enter an access code generated with the Microsoft Authenticator application. If a user has MFA enabled, the Universal Authentication with MFA option in Azure Data Studio and SQL Server Management Studio must be used.

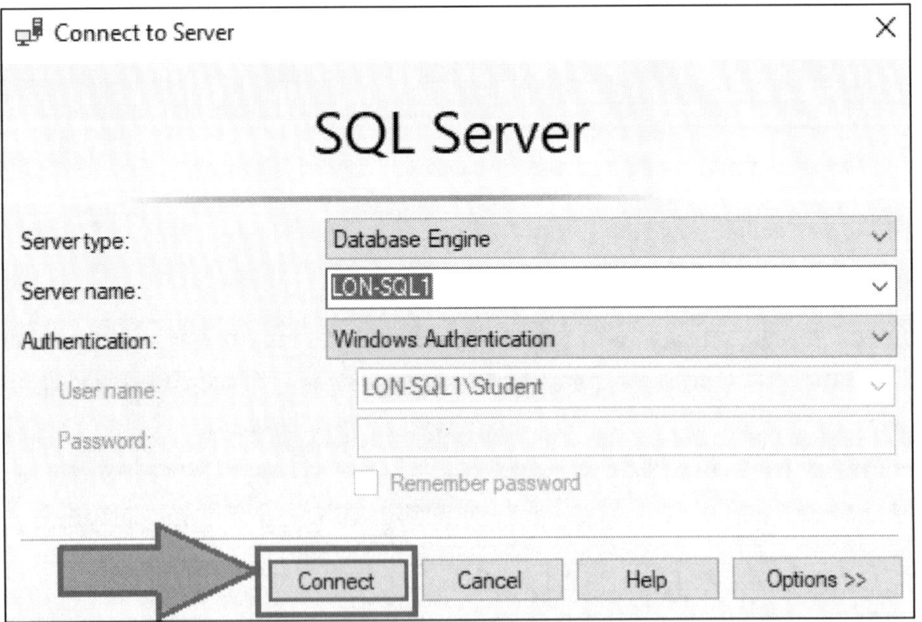

Figure 03- 01: SQL Server Management Studio

EXAM TIP: Azure SQL Database for SQL Server and Azure Database for PostgreSQL both support setting the database server to use Azure Active Directory Authentication.

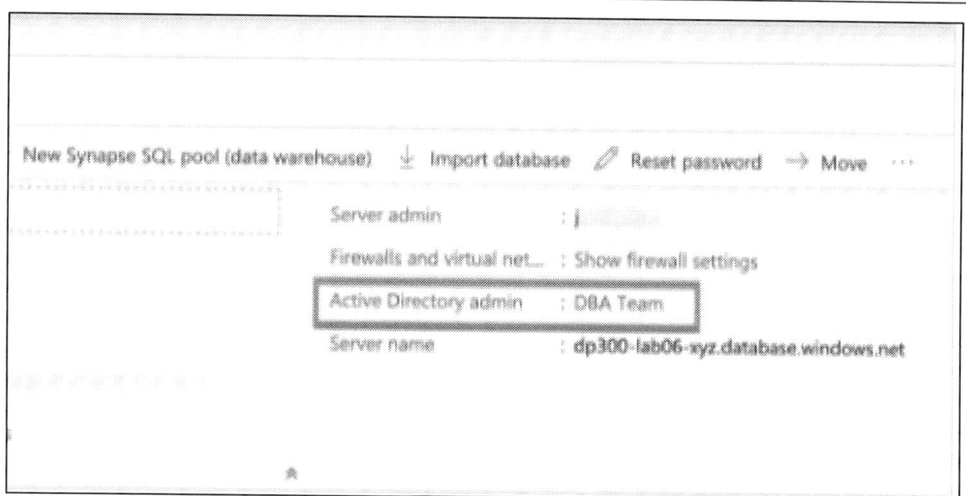

Figure 03-02: Azure Active Directory Authentication

This login grants the administrator access to all databases on the system. It is a good idea to add this account to an Azure Active Directory group so that access is not dependent on a single login. This group is referred to as the 'DBA team,' as shown in the figure above. The Azure Active Directory Admin account provides special permissions and grants the account or group that possesses that permission, sysadmin level access to the server and all of its databases. The admin account is only configured through Azure Resource Manager and not at the database level. You must use the Azure portal, PowerShell, or CLI to modify the account or group.

Security Principals

Security Principals are entities that can request SQL Server resources and to which permissions can (generally) be granted. SQL Server has various sets of security principles. Security principals can exist at the server or database level and might be individuals or collections. Some sets have a membership that is controlled by SQL Server administrators, while others have a fixed membership.

The server-level security principles we will be addressing are logins and server roles. Administrators can create new logins, but no new server roles can be created.

We will look at users, database roles, and application roles at the database level.

Schemas and Securables

Before delving into the specifics of security principles, we must first grasp the notions of securables and schemas. For securables, SQL Server and Azure SQL Database offer three scopes. Securables are database resources to which the authorization system controls access. A table, for example, is securable. SQL Server contains securables in nested hierarchies called scopes to simplify access control. The server, database, and schema are the three secure scopes. A schema is a collection of objects in your database that allow things to be organized into distinct namespaces.

Each user has a predefined schema. When a user attempts to access an object without supplying a schema name, as in SELECT name FROM customers, the item is presumed to be in the user's default schema. If no such object exists in the default schema, SQL Server will look to see if it exists in the predefined dbo schema. The user will receive an error notice if there is no object with the supplied name in either the user's default schema or the dbo schema. It is the best practice to always give the schema name when accessing objects. Thus, the above selection would be something like: SELECT name FROM SalesSchema.customers.

Note: If a user has not been assigned a default schema, it is set to dbo.

When a user creates an object without specifying a schema, SQL Server will attempt to construct it in the user's default schema. The object cannot be generated if the user has not been granted authorization to create objects in their default schema.

Logins and Users

A login name used to access your SQL database is set up as a login within the instance regardless of the kind of authentication used. These logins are configured at the SQL Server instance level and saved in the master database. However, contained users, which are introduced at the database level, can be configured. These users can be set up as SQL Server Authentication users, Windows Authentication users, or Azure Active Directory users (depending on which platform you are using). To create these users, the database must be set up for partial containment, which is enabled by default in Azure SQL Database and optionally in SQL Server.

These users can only access the database that the user has been assigned to. For the purposes of Azure SQL Database, it is recommended that users be created in the scope of the user database rather than the master database, as seen below:

```
SQL

CREATE USER [dba@contoso.com] FROM EXTERNAL PROVIDER;

GO
```

Figure 03-03: Sample Code

In the context of the user database, the create user statement is executed. The user in the above example is an Azure Active Directory user, as indicated by the FROM EXTERNAL PROVIDER expression.

If SQL Server logins are generated at the instance level, a user should be created within the database that maps the user to the server-based login, as demonstrated in the following example:

```
SQL

USE Master

GO

CREATE LOGIN demo WITH PASSWORD = 'Pa55.w.rd'

GO

USE WideWorldImporters

GO

CREATE USER demo FROM LOGIN demo

GO
```

Figure 03-04: Sample Code

Database Roles

As you can expect, database security may get challenging for applications with a large number of users. Most database applications utilize role-based security to make things easier for both administrators and auditors. Roles are essentially security groups with a shared set of rights. Combining permissions into a role enables the creation of a collection of roles for a certain application. Administrators with complete access to all databases and servers, reporting users who just read the database, and an application account with access to write data into the database are some examples of roles. When the program is designed, the roles may be established, and then users can be allocated to those roles when they require database access. Role-based Access Control (RBAC) is a computer system architecture that is used to manage authorization in Azure Resource Manager.

SQL Server and Azure SQL Database both have built-in Microsoft-defined roles as well as the ability to build custom roles. Custom roles can be generated on the server or in the database. However, server roles cannot be provided direct access to database

objects. Server roles are not accessible in Azure SQL Database but only in SQL Server and Azure SQL Managed Instance.

Permissions within a database can be granted to the users that reside within the database. If many users require the same access, you can establish a database role and assign the necessary permissions to this role. Users can be added as database role members, where members of the database role will inherit the database role's permissions.

```
SQL

CREATE USER [DP300User1] WITH PASSWORD = 'Pa55.w.rd'

GO

CREATE USER [DP300User2] WITH PASSWORD = 'Pa55.w.rd'

GO

CREATE ROLE [SalesReader]

GO

ALTER ROLE [SalesReader] ADD MEMBER [DP300User1]

GO

ALTER ROLE [SalesReader] ADD MEMBER [DP300User2]

GO

GRANT SELECT, EXECUTE ON SCHEMA::Sales TO [SalesReader]

GO
```

Figure 03-05: Sample Code

In the above example, two users are established, followed by the creation of a role called SalesReader. After adding the two new users to the newly created role, the role is granted SELECT and EXECUTE permissions on the Sales schema. Any user with that role can choose from any object in the Sales database and run any stored procedure in the schema.

Application Roles

Application roles can also be created in a SQL Server or Azure SQL Database database. Users, unlike database roles, are not added to an application role. The user activates an

application role by entering the application role's pre-configured password. Once the role is activated, the permissions assigned to the application role are assigned to the user until the role is deactivated.

Built-in Database Roles

Within each database, Microsoft SQL Server has multiple fixed database roles with predefined rights. These roles grant their members a set of predefined permissions. These roles function identically in Azure SQL Database and SQL Server.

Users who need to create additional users in the database can be assigned the role db_accessadmin. This role does not provide access to the schema of any of the tables, nor does it provide access to the database's data.

Members of the role db backup operator can be assigned to users who need to back up a database in a SQL Server or Managed Instance. In an Azure SQL Database, the role db_backupoperator grants no access.

Users that require the ability to read from every table and view in the database can be assigned the role db_datareader.

Users that require the ability to INSERT, UPDATE, and DELETE data from all tables and views in the database can be assigned the role db_datawriter.

Users that require the ability to create or change database objects can be assigned the role db_ddladmin. Members of this job have the ability to update the definition of any object of any type, but they do not have the ability to read or write data in the databases.

When users have been granted permissions through other roles or directly, the role, db_denydatareader can be used to block them from reading data from any object in the database.

When users have been granted permissions through other roles or directly, the role, db_denydatawriter can be used to block them from writing data to any object in the database.

Users that require administrative access to the database can be assigned the role db_owner. By default, members of the db_owner role can perform any activity within the database. Users in the db_owner role, unlike the true database owner with the user name dbo, can be prevented from reading data by placing them in other database roles, such as db_denydatareader, or by denying them access to objects. Only trusted people should be allowed to join this database role.

Users that need to grant access to other users within the database can join the role db_securityadmin. Users of this job are not explicitly provided access to the database's data. Nonetheless, members of this role can grant themselves access to the database's tables, and only trusted people should be allowed to join this database role.

All database users are automatically assigned the public role as this position has no permissions assigned to it by default. Permissions can be provided for the public role, but you should carefully evaluate whether this is something you truly want to undertake. If you grant permissions to the public role, these permissions will be granted to any user, including the guest account, if it is enabled.

Many applications can be met by the built-in database roles. However, for applications that require more granular security (for example, when you only want to provide access to a certain subset of tables), a custom role is typically a preferable solution.

Azure SQL Database features two extra roles that are defined in the Azure SQL server's master database.

Members of the master database with the role dbmanager can create other databases in the Azure SQL Database environment. In an on-premises Microsoft SQL Server, this position is similar to the dbcreator fixed server role.

The loginmanager role in the master database allows its members to generate additional server logins. In an on-premises Microsoft SQL Server, this role is equal to the securityadmin fixed server role.

Fixed Server Roles

SQL Server and Azure SQL Managed Instance both feature a number of fixed server roles in addition to database roles. These roles grant permissions across the entire server. SQL Server logins, Windows accounts, and Windows groups are examples of server-level principles that can be introduced to fixed server roles. Fixed server roles have predefined permissions, and no new server roles can be introduced. Given below are the fixed server roles:

Sysadmin—Members of the sysadmin role have complete control over the server.

Serveradmin—Serveradmins can change server-wide configuration settings (such as Max Server Memory) and shut down the server.

Securityadmin—Members of the securityadmin job have the ability to manage logins and associated properties (for example, changing the password of a login). Members can also give and withdraw rights at the server and database levels. This role should be considered equivalent to the sysadmin role.

Processadmin—Members of the processadmin position have the ability to terminate processes operating within SQL Server.

Setupadmin—Members of the setupadmin position can use T-SQL to add and remove associated servers.

Bulkadmin—Members of the bulkadmin role can execute the T-SQL query BULK INSERT.

Diskadmin—Members of the diskadmin position can manage SQL Server backup devices.

Dbcreator—Members of the dbcreator role can create, restore, change, and delete any database.

Public—Every SQL Server login is assigned to the public user role. Permissions can be granted, refused, or revoked from the public position, unlike the other set server roles.

Describe Database and Object Permissions

All Relational Database Management solutions have four fundamental permissions that govern data manipulation language (DML) operations. These are:

- SELECT
- INSERT
- UPDATE
- DELETE

All SQL Server platforms, as well as Azure SQL Database for MySQL and Azure SQL Database for PostgreSQL, are affected by these permissions. On tables and views, all of these permissions can be granted, revoked, or denied. When permission is granted using the GRANT statement, it is granted to the user or role specified in the GRANT statement. The DENY command can also be used to deny permissions to users.

> EXAM TIP: If a user is allowed one permission and then denied another, the DENY will always take precedence over the grant, and the user will be denied access to the specific item.

```
GRANT SELECT ON dbo.Company to Demo
GO
DENY SELECT ON dbo.Company to Demo
GO
EXECUTE AS USER =  'Demo'

SELECT Name, Address FROM dbo.Company

Messages
Msg 229, Level 14, State 5, Line 17
The SELECT permission was denied on the object 'Company', database 'WideWorldImporters', schema 'dbo'.

Completion time: 2020-05-13T14:42:28.8361616-07:00
```

Figure 03-06: Sample Code

In the preceding example, the user Demo is granted SELECT permissions on the dbo.Company table before being denied SELECT permissions. When the user attempts

to run a query that selects from the dbo.Company table, the user receives an error stating that the SELECT permission was denied.

Table and View Permissions

Tables and views are the objects in a database to which permissions can be granted. You can also limit the columns that a certain security principal can access within those tables and views (user or login). Row-level security is also available in SQL Server and Azure SQL Database, which can be leveraged to further restrict access.

When the SELECT permission is granted, the user will be able to view the data contained within the object (table or view). When denied, the user will be unable to view the data contained within the object.

When the INSERT permission is granted, the user will be able to insert data into the object. When rejected, the user is unable to insert data into the object.

When the UPDATE permission is given, the user will be able to update data within the object. When denied, the user is unable to update data in the object.

When the DELETE permission is given, the user will be able to delete data from the object. When denied, the user is unable to delete data from the object.

Additional rights for Azure SQL Database and Microsoft SQL Server can be granted, revoked, or denied as needed.

The CONTROL permission offers the objects complete control. This permits the person who has this permission to do whatever they want with the item, including deleting it.

The REFERENCES permission allows the user to inspect the object's foreign keys. This permission is also supported by Azure SQL Database for MySQL and Azure SQL Database for PostgreSQL.

The TAKE OWNERSHIP permission grants the user the power to take possession of an object.

The VIEW CHANGE TRACKING permission allows the user to view the object's change tracking settings.

The VIEW DEFINITION permission allows the user to view the object's definition.

Function and Stored Procedure Permissions

Functions and stored procedures, like tables and views, have a variety of permissions that can be granted or denied.

The ALTER permission allows the user to change the definition of an object.

The CONTROL permission offers the user complete control over the object.

The EXECUTE permission allows the user to execute the item. Azure SQL Database for MySQL and Azure SQL Database for PostgreSQL can both be granted this access.

The VIEW CHANGE TRACKING permission allows the user to view the object's change tracking settings.

The VIEW DEFINITION permission allows the user to view the object's definition.

Explain EXECUTE AS User

The EXECUTE AS [user] or EXECUTE AS [login] commands (available exclusively in SQL Server and Azure SQL Managed Instance) allow you to modify the user context. Following commands and statements will be run with the permissions granted to the new context

If a user has permission and no longer needs it, permissions can be deleted (either grants or denies) using the REVOKE command. The revoke command will remove any GRANT or DENY permissions for the specified right from the user.

Ownership Chains

Permissions are subject to a notion known as chaining, which allows users to inherit permissions from other objects. A function or stored procedure that accesses a table during execution is the most common example of chaining. If the stored procedure and the table share the same owner, the stored procedure can be executed and access the table even if the user does not have direct access to the table. This access is possible because the user inherits the stored procedure's access permissions to the table. However, it is possible only for the period of the stored procedure's execution and only within the context of the stored procedure's execution.

In the example below, a new user is created and added as a member of a new SalesReader role, which is then granted authority to choose from any object and execute any procedure in the Sales schema. The Sales schema is then used to create a stored procedure that accesses a table in the Production schema.

The sample then switches to the new user and tries to select directly from the table in the Production schema.

```
USE AdventureWorks2016;
GO
CREATE USER [DP300User1] WITH PASSWORD = 'Pa55.w.rd';
GO
CREATE ROLE [SalesReader];
GO
ALTER ROLE [SalesReader] ADD MEMBER [DP300User1];
GO
GRANT SELECT, EXECUTE ON SCHEMA::Sales TO [SalesReader];
GO
CREATE OR ALTER PROCEDURE Sales.DemoProc
as
SELECT P.Name, Sum(SOD.LineTotal) as TotalSales
,SOH.OrderDate
FROM Production.Product P
INNER JOIN Sales.SalesOrderDetail SOD on SOD.ProductID
= P.ProductID
INNER JOIN Sales.SalesOrderHeader SOH on
SOH.SalesOrderID = SOD.SalesOrderID
GROUP BY P.Name, SOH.OrderDate
ORDER BY TotalSales DESC;
GO
EXECUTE AS USER = 'DP300User1';
SELECT P.Name, Sum(SOD.LineTotal) as TotalSales
,SOH.OrderDate
FROM Production.Product P
INNER JOIN Sales.SalesOrderDetail SOD on SOD.ProductID
= P.ProductID
INNER JOIN Sales.SalesOrderHeader SOH on
SOH.SalesOrderID = SOD.SalesOrderID
GROUP BY P.Name, SOH.OrderDate
ORDER BY TotalSales DESC;
```

Figure 03-07: Sample Code

The above query returns an error indicating that the user DP300User1 lacks SELECT permission since the role to which the user belongs does not have any privileges in the Production schema. We may now try to run the stored procedure:

```
EXECUTE AS USER = 'DP300User1';

EXECUTE Sales.DemoProc;
```

Figure 03-08: Sample Code

Because the role to which the DP300User1 belongs has to EXECUTE access on the Sales schema, the user has EXECUTE permission on the stored procedure. We have an

unbroken ownership chain because the table is owned by the same person as the procedure. Thus, the execution will succeed, and the results will be returned.

When dynamic SQL is utilized within stored procedures, permission changes do not apply. The reason dynamic SQL breaks the permission chain is that it is executed outside of the context of the invoking stored procedure. This behavior can be seen by altering the above-stored procedure to use dynamic SQL, as shown below:

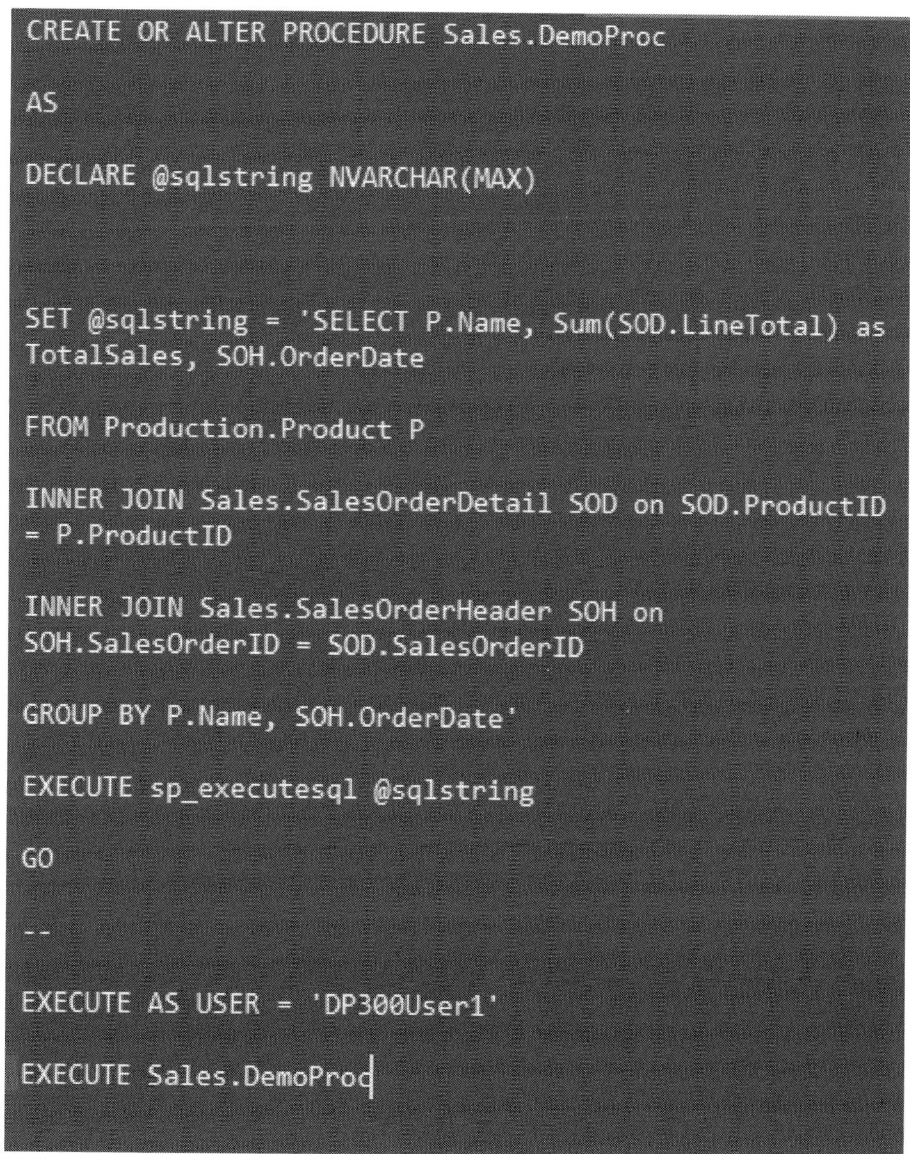

```
CREATE OR ALTER PROCEDURE Sales.DemoProc

AS

DECLARE @sqlstring NVARCHAR(MAX)



SET @sqlstring = 'SELECT P.Name, Sum(SOD.LineTotal) as
TotalSales, SOH.OrderDate

FROM Production.Product P

INNER JOIN Sales.SalesOrderDetail SOD on SOD.ProductID
= P.ProductID

INNER JOIN Sales.SalesOrderHeader SOH on
SOH.SalesOrderID = SOD.SalesOrderID

GROUP BY P.Name, SOH.OrderDate'

EXECUTE sp_executesql @sqlstring

GO

--

EXECUTE AS USER = 'DP300User1'

EXECUTE Sales.DemoProc
```

Figure 03-09: Sample Code

The DP300User1 will receive an error stating that the user lacks SELECT permission on the Production. Product table, just as if the user had attempted to run the query directly. Permission chains do not apply, and the user account running the dynamic SQL must have access to the tables and views utilized by the code in the dynamic SQL.

Policy of Least Privilege

The notion of least privilege is straightforward. The fundamental idea underlying the concept is that users and programs should only be granted the rights required to execute the task, while applications should only be granted permissions that are required to execute the task at hand.

For example, if an application accesses all data using stored procedures, the application should only have access to the stored procedures and not to the tables.

Dynamic SQL

Dynamic SQL is a notion in which a query is constructed programmatically. T-SQL statements can be generated within a stored procedure or a query using dynamic SQL. Below is a simple example:

```
SELECT 'BACKUP DATABASE ' + name + ' TO DISK
=''\\backup\sql1\' + name + '.bak'''
FROM sys.databases
```

Figure 03-10: Sample Code

The preceding query will generate a series of T-SQL statements to back up the server's whole database. This generated T-SQL is often run using sp_executesql or handed to another program to execute.

Protect Data In-transit and at Rest

Role of Firewalls

Firewalls are used to keep unauthorized users from gaining access to protected resources. Each Azure SQL Database corresponds to a public IP address provided by Microsoft. Each Azure region will have one or more public IP addresses through which you can connect to your database gateway, which will subsequently connect you to your database. Azure includes built-in firewalls to block access in order to secure your database and data. There are two types of firewall rules in Azure SQL Database:

- Server level firewall rules
- Database level firewall rules

Instead of SQL Server Logins, both server and database-level firewalls employ IP Address rules. This enables all users with the same public IP Address to connect to the SQL Server. In most cases, this will be the company's outbound IP address.

Server-level firewalls are set up to allow users to connect to the master database as well as all databases on the instance. Database-level firewalls are used to permit or deny access to certain databases based on IP addresses.

The Azure portal or the sp_set_firewall_rule stored procedure from the master database can be used to configure server-level firewall rules. Only the sp_set_database_firewall_rule stored procedure from the user database is used to configure database-level firewall rules. If the connection string specifies a database name, Azure SQL Database will seek for a server-level firewall rule in the master database first, followed by a database-level firewall rule. The connection will be completed if one of these exists. If neither exists and the user is connecting using SQL Server Management Studio or Azure Data Studio, the user will be prompted to add a firewall rule, as illustrated below:

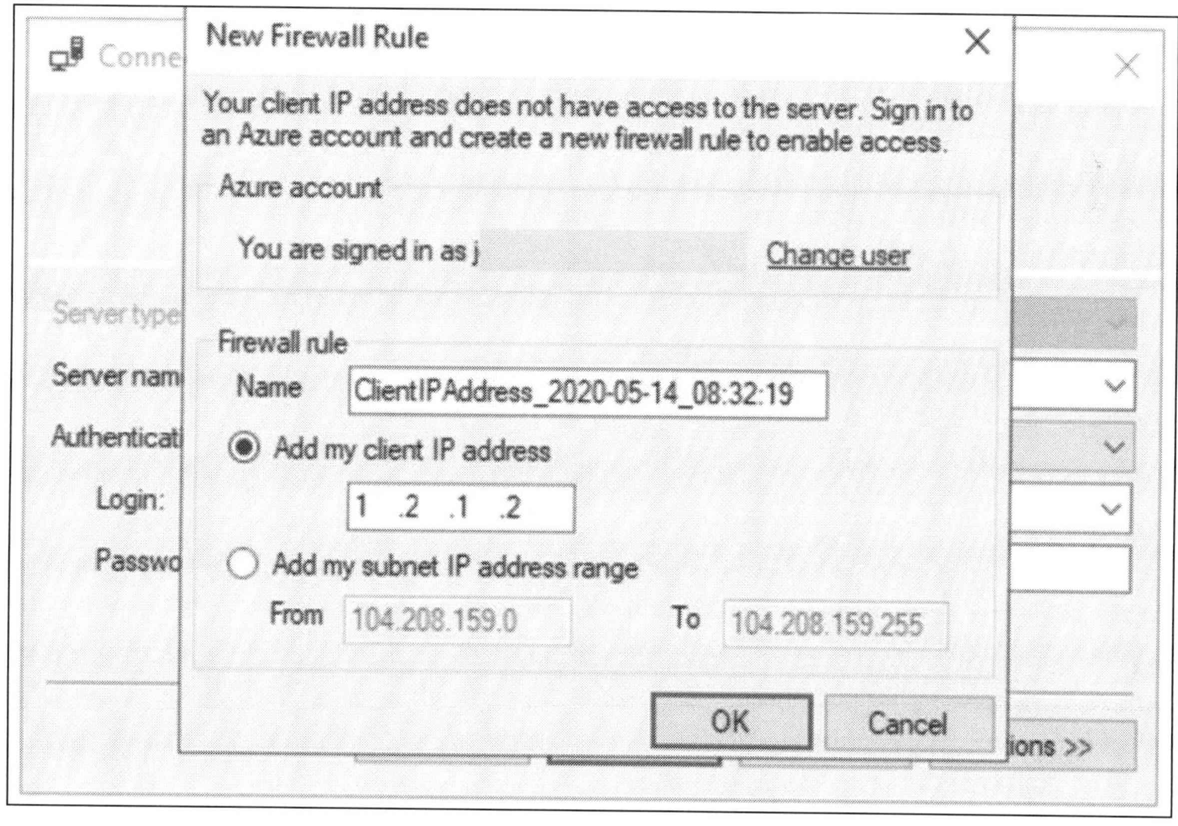

Figure 03-11: Firewall Rule

Virtual Network Endpoints

Endpoints of a virtual network accept traffic from a specific Azure Virtual Network. These rules apply to the server as well as the database. Furthermore, the service endpoint only applies to one region, which is the region of the underlying endpoint. Another consideration is that the virtual network connected to the Azure SQL Database must have outbound access to the public IP address for Azure SQL Database, which may be specified using Azure SQL Database service tags.

Private Link

You can use the Private Link functionality to connect to Azure SQL Database (and other PaaS products) via a private endpoint. A private endpoint enables a connection to your Azure SQL Database to be routed solely through the Azure backbone network rather than the public internet. This feature allows you to have a private IP address on your Virtual Network. Another advantage of a private link is that it allows Azure Express Route connections to be routed through it. Private links provide various additional benefits, including cross-region private connectivity and data leakage prevention by only permitting connections to certain resources.

Explain Encryption at Rest

It is critical to think about encryption for both data at rest and data in transit. This topic discusses data encryption at rest.

Encryption at Rest

It is critical to understand what encryption at rest means. At-rest encryption does not encrypt data at the table or column level. Anyone with the necessary permissions can read, copy, and even share the data. Encryption at rest prevents someone from restoring a backup to an unsecured server or copying all database and transaction log files and attaching them to another unsecured server.

Transparent Data Encryption

Transparent Data Encryption (TDE) in Microsoft SQL Server encrypts all data within a target database at the page level. Data is encrypted when it is written to a data page on disks, while it is decrypted when the data page is read into memory. As a result, all data pages on the disk are encrypted. A database file cannot be accessed by anyone who is not authorized. Because a backup procedure simply copies the data pages from the database file to the backup media, database backups will also be encrypted. During the backup process, no decryption is performed.

Enabling TDE in Azure SQL Database is straightforward. TDE is enabled by default in Azure SQL Database databases created after May 2017. TDE will be deactivated by default in databases created before May 2017, and TDE will need to be manually enabled in these databases. TDE is enabled in databases built after February 2019 when using Azure SQL Managed Instance. TDE will be deactivated in databases established before February 2019. Enabling TDE in an Azure SQL Database database is as simple as editing the database using the Azure portal. Enable data encryption from the "Transparent Data Encryption" pane.

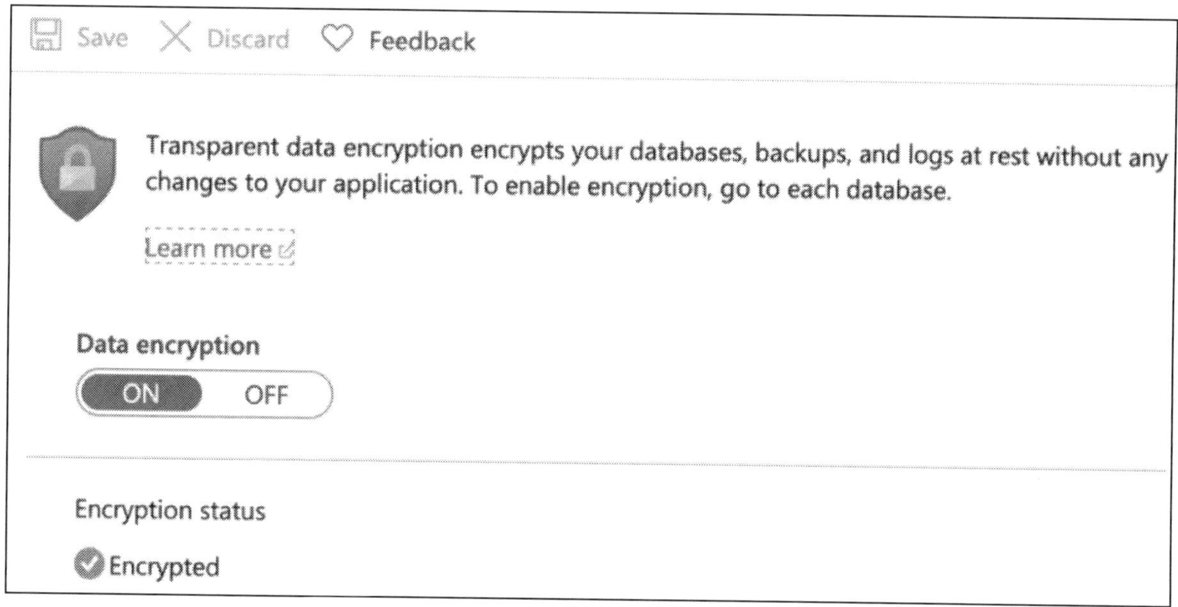

Figure 03-12: Transparent Data Encryption

By default, databases in Azure SQL Database are encrypted with a certificate given by Microsoft. Microsoft Azure does offer a Bring Your Own Key option, which allows you to use a certificate issued by your organization and uploaded to Azure. If your firm removes the certificate from Azure, the database connections will be blocked, and no access to the database will be available.

Enabling TDE in a Microsoft SQL Server database is a simple process that requires only a few T-SQL statements. The CREATE MASTER KEY ENCRYPTION command is used to create a master key within the master database. Then, using the CREATE CERTIFICATE command, a certificate is created in the master database that will be used for encryption. The database encryption key is subsequently created, allowing you to enable TDE using the CREATE DATABASE ENCRYPTION KEY command. Once the encryption key has been generated, it must be enabled with the ALTER DATABASE command. The whole list of commands is listed below:

```
SQL
USE master;
GO
CREATE MASTER KEY ENCRYPTION BY PASSWORD = 'Pa55.w.rd';
GO
CREATE CERTIFICATE MyServerCert
 WITH SUBJECT = 'TDEDemo_Certificate';
GO

USE TDE_Demo;
GO

CREATE DATABASE ENCRYPTION KEY
 WITH ALGORITHM = AES_256 ENCRYPTION BY SERVER CERTIFICATE MyServerCert;
GO

ALTER DATABASE TDE_Demo SET ENCRYPTION ON;
GO
```

Figure 03-13: Sample Code

Once TDE is enabled, encrypting the database will take some time since each database page must be read, encrypted, and written back to disk. The greater the size of the database, the longer this operation will take. This is a background process that runs at a low priority to avoid overloading the system's IO or CPU.

Once the TDE certificate has been created, it must be manually backed up and kept in a secure location. To handle encryption keys, SQL Server interfaces with Enterprise Key Managers (EKMs). Azure Key Vault is an example of an EKM. It is critical to manage the certificate because if the certificate is lost and the database needs to be restored from a backup, the restore will fail since the database cannot be read. To use TDE with databases in an Always On availability group, the certificate used to encrypt the database must be backed up and restored to the other servers in the availability group hosting copies of the database.

Encryption at Rest for MySQL and PostgreSQL

There is no TDE-like process in Azure SQL Database for MySQL or Azure SQL Database for PostgreSQL. The Azure environment in which they are run, on the other hand, supports disk encryption. This technique encrypts the databases that are stored on the disk, making the data on it illegible if the disk housing the database is compromised. This service, like TDE within Azure SQL Database, provides a Bring Your Own Key service. You can use this service to upload your own certificate and have it utilized for encryption.

Azure Disk Encryption

In addition to these SQL Server security features, Azure VMs contain an extra layer of protection in the form of Azure Disk Encryption, which helps protect and safeguard data while meeting organizational and regulatory requirements. When you use TDE, your data is protected by several layers of encryption, these include Azure Disk Encryption, as well as SQL Server database files encryption and backup.

The Role of Azure Key Vault in Transparent Data Encryption

Azure Key Vault is a method of storing and gaining access to secrets. Key Vault acts as a secure space for those secrets to be accessible in a secure manner, often programmatically, whether they are passwords, certificates, or keys. Key Vault data has its own RBAC policies that are independent of the Azure subscription. This means that unless specifically allowed, someone in the role of subscription admin will not have access to the Key Vault.

SQL Server, whether running in an Azure Virtual Machine or on-premises, supports storing certificates for features, such as Transparent Data Encryption, Backup Encryption, and Always Encrypted in Azure Key Vault. While this setting is difficult in an on-premises system, it is simple when utilizing the SQL VM Resource Provider, as seen in the figure below:

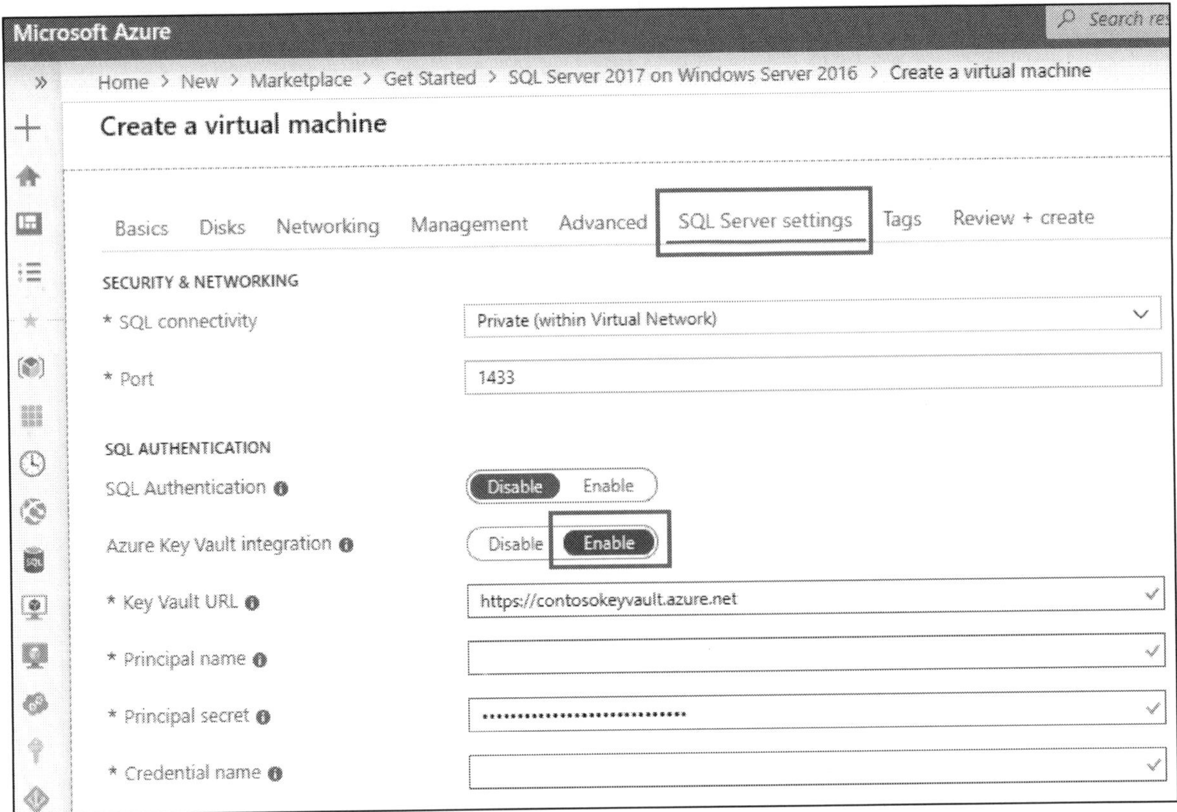

Figure 03-14: SQL VM Resource Provider

To configure the Azure Key Vault integration, you must specify the Key Vault URL, the Principal name, the Principal secret, and the credential name. This task can be performed during VM creation or on an existing VM.

To configure SQL Server to connect to Azure Key Vault, first, create a standard SQL Server login within the instance. Following that, a Credential must be created and linked to the login. The name of the key vault should be used to identify the credential. You need to use the application ID from Azure Key Vault as the credential's secret. After creating the credential, an asymmetric key can be generated in the Azure Key Vault. Within the SQL Server database, an asymmetric key can then be constructed. Using the CREATE ASYMMETRIC KEY command with the FROM PROVIDER syntax, the key in the database may be mapped to the Azure Key Vault asymmetric key.

EXAM TIP: Once an asymmetric key is generated in the database, it can be used for TDE, Backup Encryption, or Always Encrypted.

Object Encryption and Secure Enclaves

SQL Server, in addition to allowing encryption at rest via transparent data encryption, enables encrypting data inside columns with Always Encrypted. Once the data has been

encrypted, the application accessing the database must have the necessary certificate to view the plain text values of the data.

Always Encrypted enables data encryption within the client application. This encryption is performed automatically depending on the settings in the Microsoft SQL Server database, which inform the application of the encryption settings on the database column. Always Encrypted employs both a master encryption key and a column encryption key. With both keys, each column can be encrypted with a distinct encryption key for optimal data security. Always Encrypted includes a number of key stores for storing the encryption certificate. The figure below shows an example of enabling Always Encrypted. NationalIDNumber and BirthDate are both in plain text, as illustrated below:

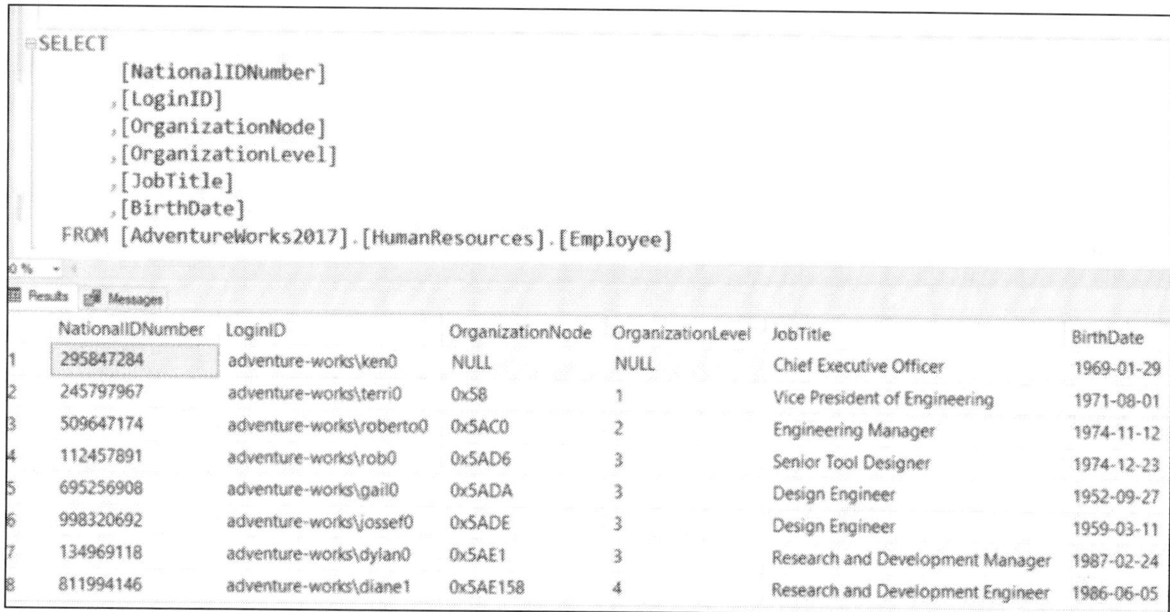

```
SELECT
      [NationalIDNumber]
      ,[LoginID]
      ,[OrganizationNode]
      ,[OrganizationLevel]
      ,[JobTitle]
      ,[BirthDate]
  FROM [AdventureWorks2017].[HumanResources].[Employee]
```

	NationalIDNumber	LoginID	OrganizationNode	OrganizationLevel	JobTitle	BirthDate
1	295847284	adventure-works\ken0	NULL	NULL	Chief Executive Officer	1969-01-29
2	245797967	adventure-works\terri0	0x58	1	Vice President of Engineering	1971-08-01
3	509647174	adventure-works\roberto0	0x5AC0	2	Engineering Manager	1974-11-12
4	112457891	adventure-works\rob0	0x5AD6	3	Senior Tool Designer	1974-12-23
5	695256908	adventure-works\gail0	0x5ADA	3	Design Engineer	1952-09-27
6	998320692	adventure-works\jossef0	0x5ADE	3	Design Engineer	1959-03-11
7	134969118	adventure-works\dylan0	0x5AE1	3	Research and Development Manager	1987-02-24
8	811994146	adventure-works\diane1	0x5AE158	4	Research and Development Engineer	1986-06-05

Figure 03- 15: Enabling Always Encrypted

The following images demonstrate how we can use Always Encrypted to encrypt both of these columns. The encryption might be done with T-SQL, but in this example, you will see the SQL Server Management Studio wizard. The wizard may be accessed by right-clicking on the table name in Object Explorer, as illustrated below:

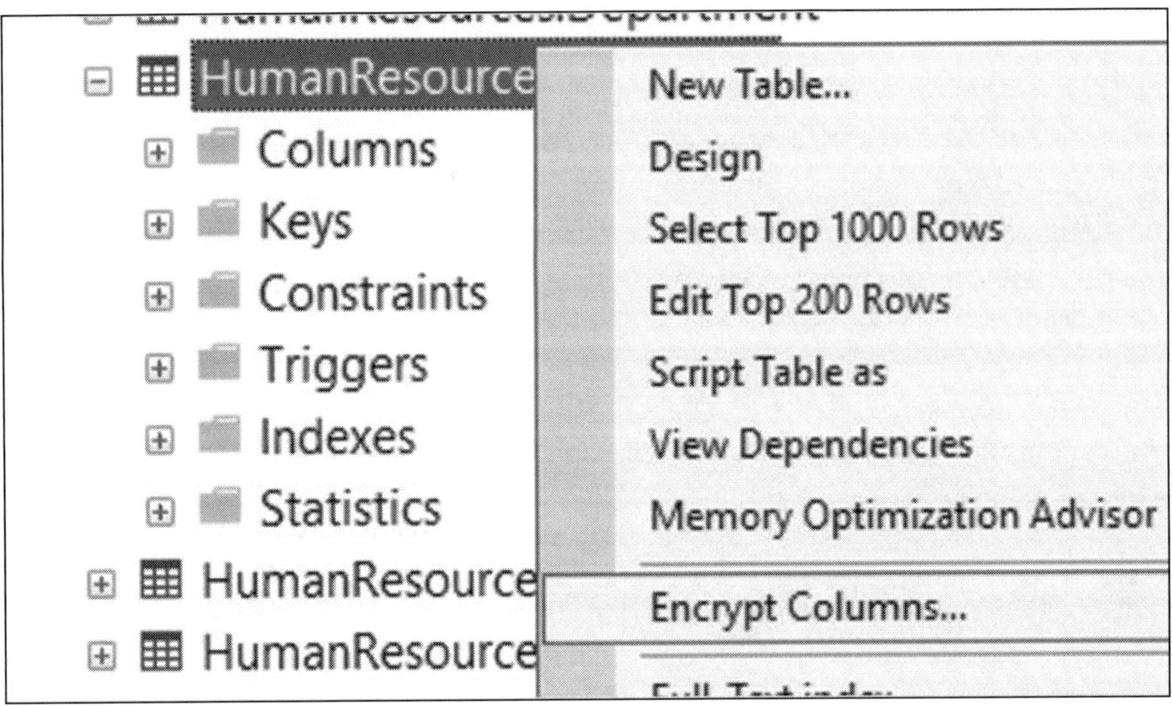

Figure 03-16: Accessing Wizard

The wizard will launch when you click on **Encrypt Columns**.

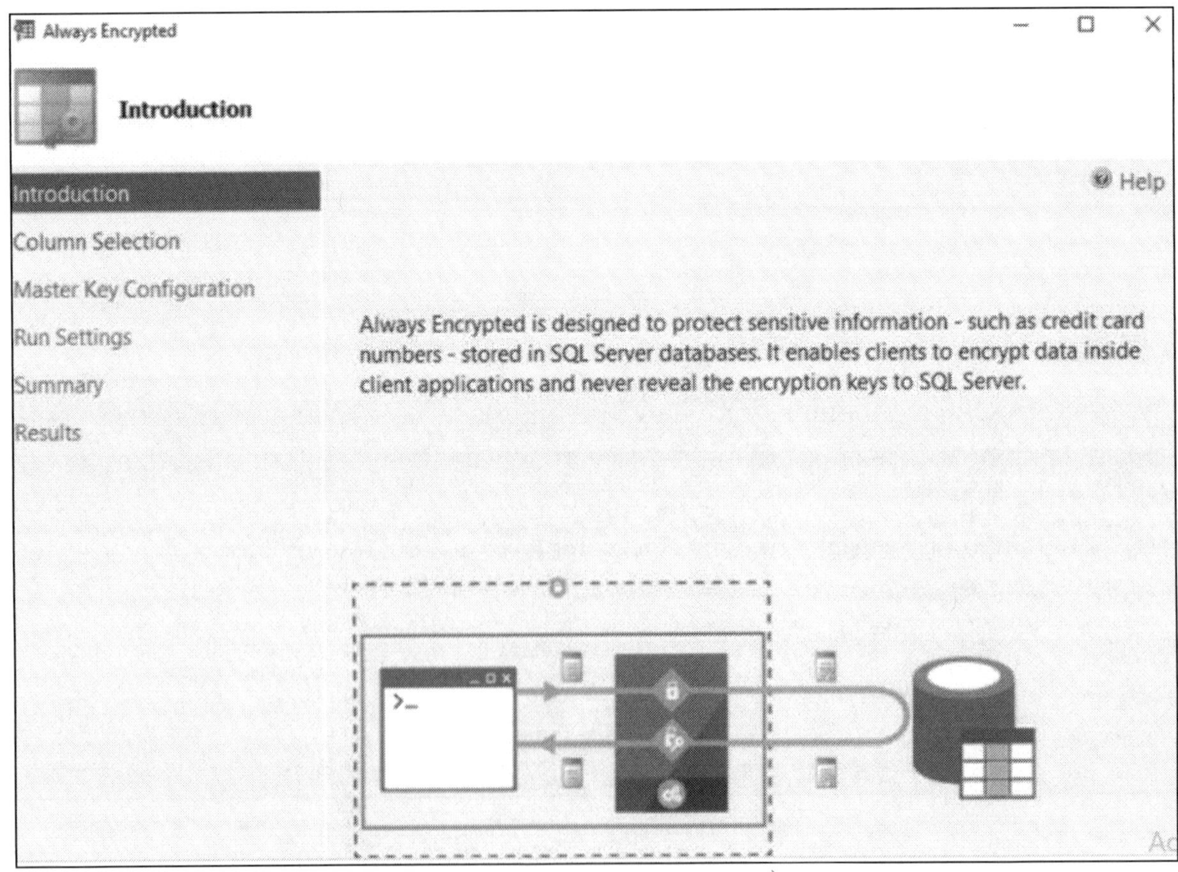

Figure 03- 17: Wizard from SQL Management Studio

The Always Encrypted launch screen can be seen in the image below. Next, you need to select the columns you want to encrypt.

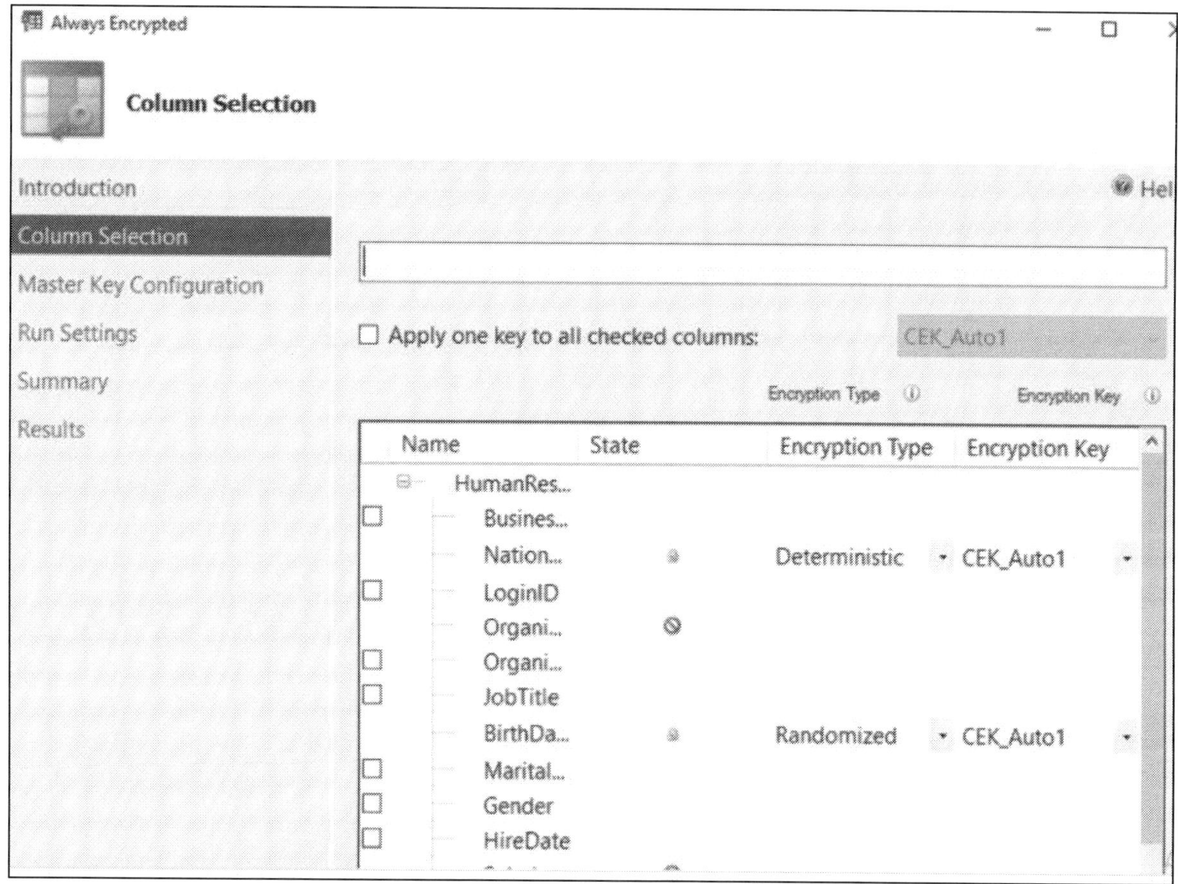

Figure 03-18: Always Encrypted Launch Screen

There are two forms of encryption specified in the image above. Deterministic encryption is used for the NationalIDNumber column, while Randomized encryption is used for the BirthDate field. Randomized encryption is safer than Deterministic encryption, although it has fewer applications. After the column is established, the kind of encryption cannot be modified. Randomized encryption would be used for columns with a small number of well-known different values that could be guessed by someone with access to the encrypted values.

EXAM TIP: A three-digit credit card verification number is an example of a possibly guessable column.

The use of Always Encrypted with Randomized encryption is more limited because randomization means that the same value is not always encrypted in the same way. The only thing you can do with columns encrypted with Randomized is to return them in your results. With Deterministic encryption, a given value is always encrypted to the same string, allowing us to compare columns to a constant and compare columns to other columns for joins, grouping, and indexing.

Always Encrypted with Secure Enclaves (available in SQL Server 2019) overcomes these constraints by enabling pattern matching, comparison operations, and column indexing utilizing Randomized encryption.

Another thing to keep in mind is that the wizard is producing a column encryption key, which is the key used to encrypt the data. Each encrypted column might have its own key, or, as demonstrated above, both columns can be encrypted using the same key.

After you have determined which columns to encrypt, click **Next** to access the Master Key Configuration screen:

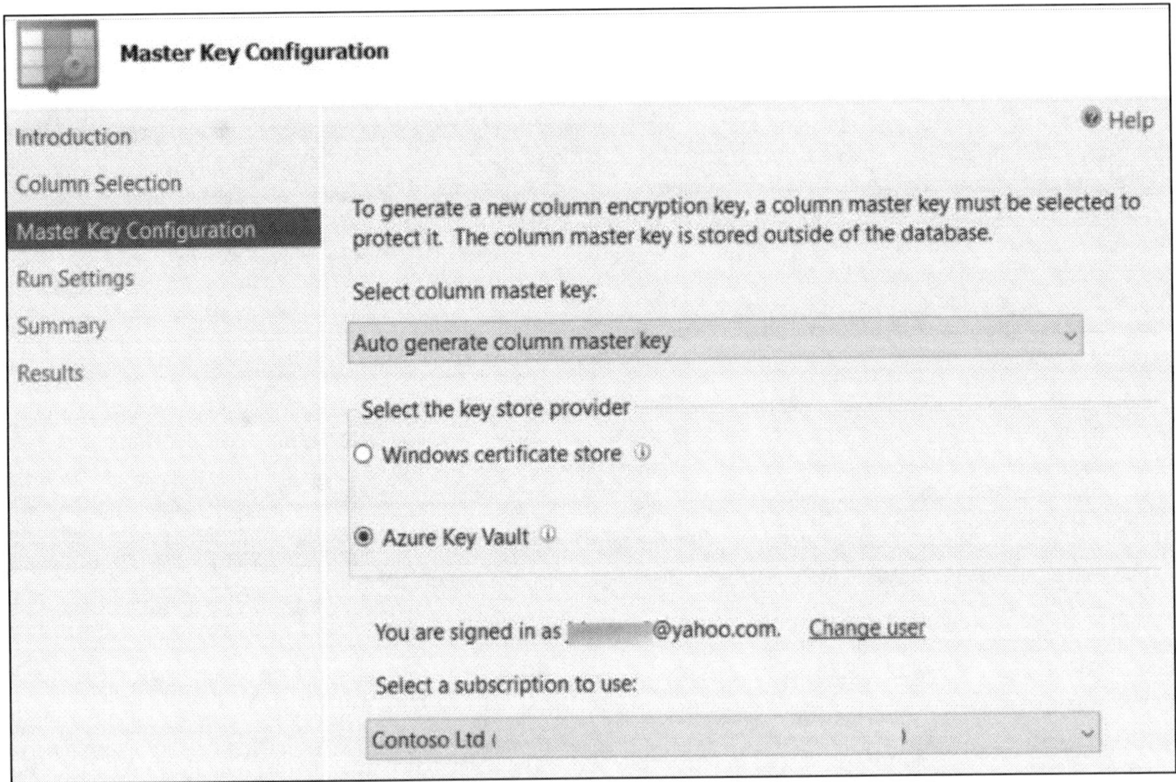

Figure 03-19: Master Key Configuration Screen

Create the column master key, which is used to encrypt the column encryption keys on this screen. If you're using T-SQL to encrypt the columns, you can supply your own key. This key must be kept in a key store like the Windows Certificate Store, Azure Key Vault, or a hardware security module. The database engine never stores the column master key and merely keeps track of where it is kept. By not storing the master key, data access is protected against users who have complete access to the database.

The key should be stored in a third-party key store, such as Azure Key Vault, for the utmost level of protection. Never generate keys on the server that hosts your database, as the key may be retrieved from memory on that server. After you click **Next**, the wizard gives you the option to either complete the encryption procedure immediately or produce a PowerShell script. After you finish the operation, anyone who queries the data without the key will see it as encrypted ciphertext.

To decrypt data from an Always Encrypted column, your application must connect to the database using an Always Encrypted driver. The application has access to the key store, which stores the Always Encrypted keys, then it can get the data. The driver encrypts data that is written back to the database at the client.

In addition to the driver, the application's connection string must have the parameter "Column Encryption Setting=enabled." This setting will cause the program to perform a metadata query for each column that it uses. To reduce the number of metadata lookups, modify the application by modifying the SqlCommandColumnEncryptionSetting on the SqlConnection objects within the.NET application. Disabled, Enabled, or ResultSet values are given. These options must be selected for each database query sent by the application.

The Disabled setting prevents the application from running any metadata queries against the database in response to that query.

The Enabled setting causes the application to run metadata queries for all columns in the T-SQL statement's SELECT clause as well as the WHERE clause.

The ResultSet option causes the metadata queries to be conducted just for the values specified in the SELECT statement.

To decide which setting of the SqlCommandColumnEncryptionSetting to employ, you must first know where the encrypted columns appear in the statement.

Secure Enclaves

Always Encrypted now supports a feature called secure enclaves, which enables for more robust querying of encrypted data starting with SQL Server 2019. A secure enclave is a protected memory section within the SQL Server process that serves as a trusted execution environment for processing encrypted data. This enclave appears to SQL Server as a black box, and no data or code can be viewed, even with a debugger. The architecture of this procedure is depicted in the figure below:

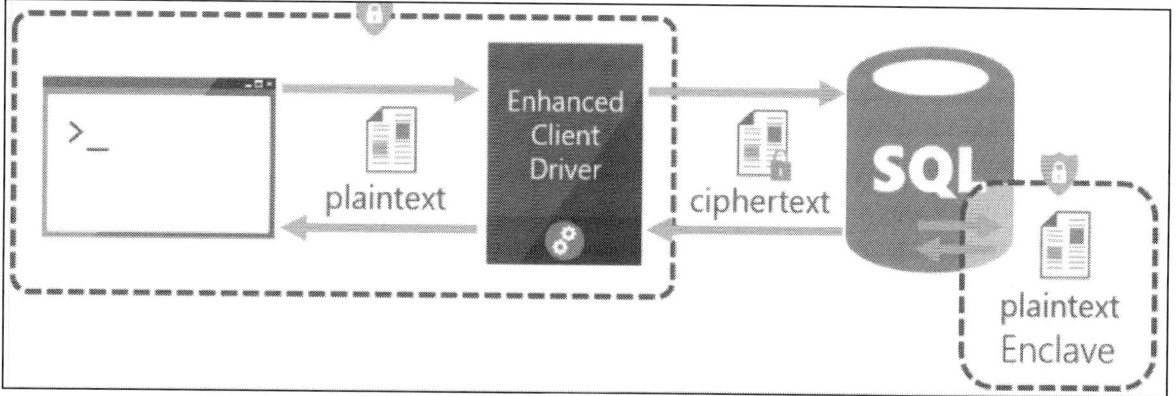

Figure 03- 20: Secure Enclaves

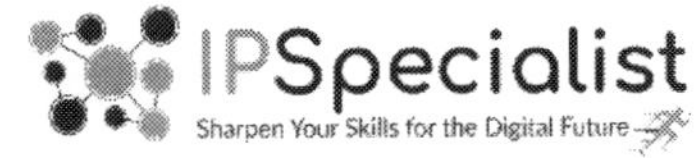

Using Randomized encryption, secure enclaves enable pattern matching and range comparison on data stored in columns.

Dynamic Data Masking

Users can access safe data without seeing the complete value, thanks to Dynamic Data Masking. This masking allows users who do not need to access sensitive data, such as credit card numbers, tax identification numbers, etc., to view the column containing the data but not the actual data stored in the table. It is important to note that Dynamic Data Masking is a presentation layer feature, making unmasked data always visible to administrators. The optimal use case for Dynamic Data Masking is to disguise data from application users who do not have direct database access.

Dynamic Data Masking can be done on the Azure portal or with T-SQL, as seen below:

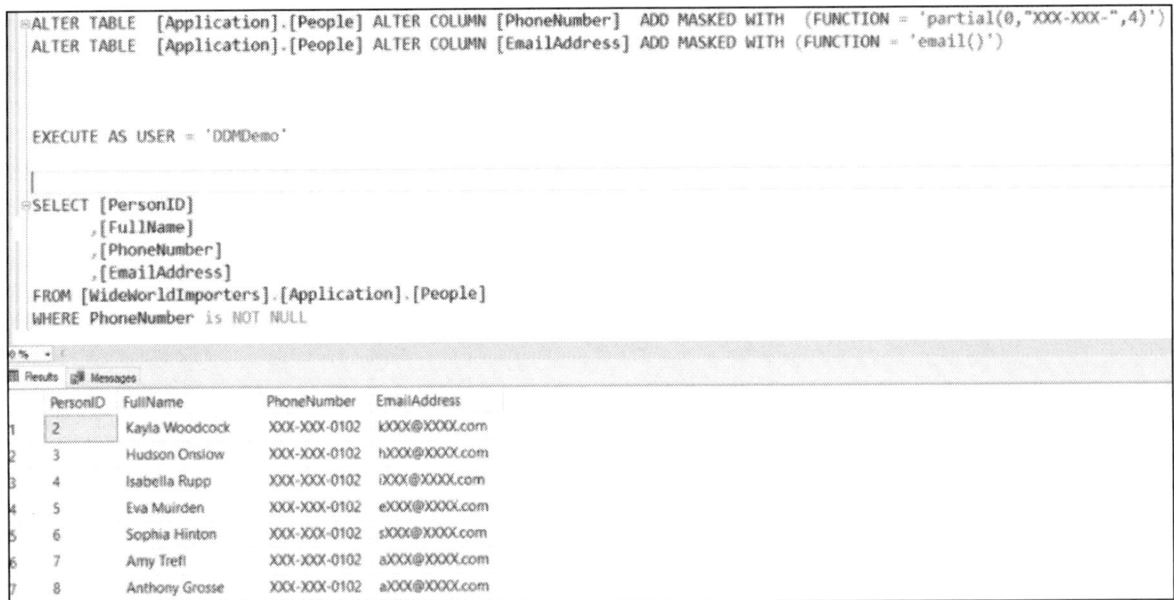

```
ALTER TABLE  [Application].[People] ALTER COLUMN [PhoneNumber]  ADD MASKED WITH  (FUNCTION = 'partial(0,"XXX-XXX-",4)')
ALTER TABLE  [Application].[People] ALTER COLUMN [EmailAddress] ADD MASKED WITH (FUNCTION = 'email()')


EXECUTE AS USER = 'DDMDemo'

SELECT [PersonID]
      ,[FullName]
      ,[PhoneNumber]
      ,[EmailAddress]
FROM [WideWorldImporters].[Application].[People]
WHERE PhoneNumber is NOT NULL
```

	PersonID	FullName	PhoneNumber	EmailAddress
1	2	Kayla Woodcock	XXX-XXX-0102	kXXX@XXXX.com
2	3	Hudson Onslow	XXX-XXX-0102	hXXX@XXXX.com
3	4	Isabella Rupp	XXX-XXX-0102	iXXX@XXXX.com
4	5	Eva Muirden	XXX-XXX-0102	eXXX@XXXX.com
5	6	Sophia Hinton	XXX-XXX-0102	sXXX@XXXX.com
6	7	Amy Trefl	XXX-XXX-0102	aXXX@XXXX.com
7	8	Anthony Grosse	XXX-XXX-0102	aXXX@XXXX.com

Figure 03-21: Dynamic Data Masking

In the preceding example, the phone number and email address are both hidden from a user named DDMDemo, who has only SELECT access to the table. The last four digits of the phone number are visible to the user because they are disguised using a 'partial' function that replaces all but the last four digits in the column. This masking is regarded as a custom function. In addition to T-SQL, you can build dynamic masking rules in the Azure portal if you use Azure SQL Database.

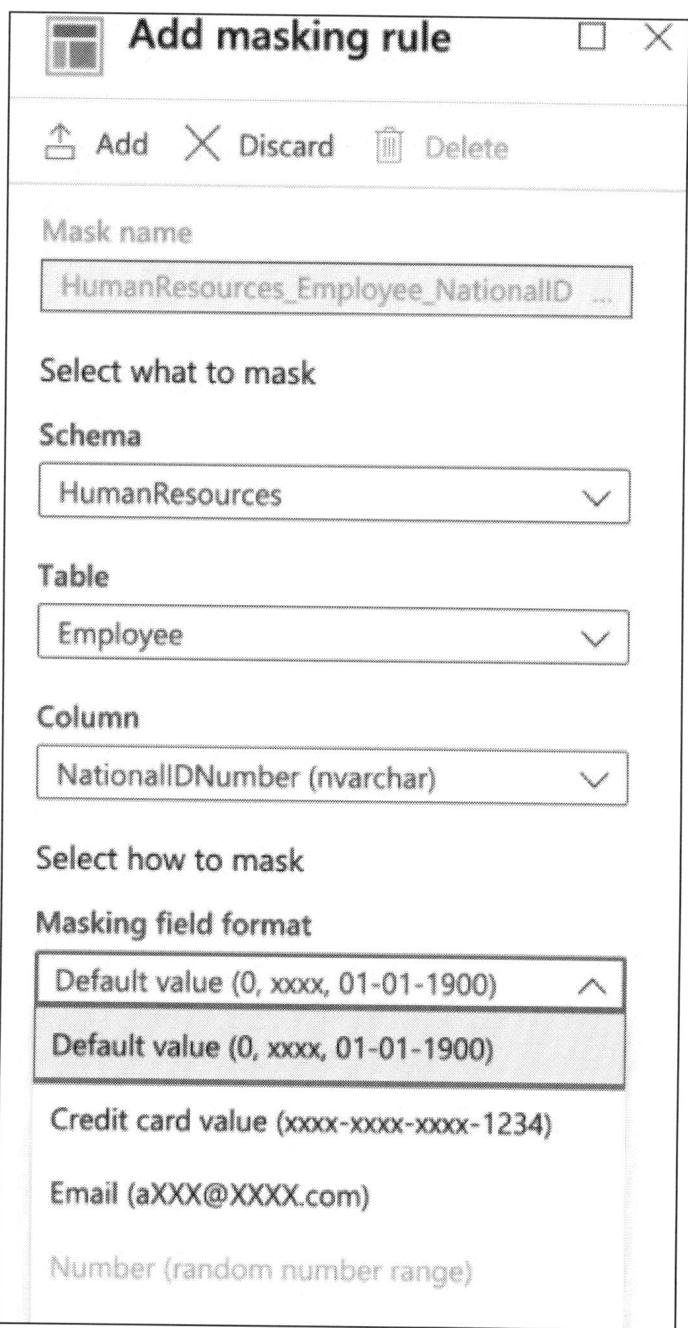

Figure 03- 22: Add Masking Rule

Navigate to your database in the Azure portal and select **Dynamic Data Masking** in the security section of the main blade to access the screen where you can add a masking rule.

Dynamic Data Masking enables a wide range of masking schemes, such as Default, Credit Card, Social Security Number, Random Number, and Custom Text.

The default masking option completely covers the data in the column, not revealing any of the values to the user. For string values, the user would see XXXX, 0 for numbers, and 01.01.1900 for date values.

The Credit Card masking option masks everything and save the last four characters, allowing consumers to see the last four digits. This masking can be handy for customer service representatives who need to see the final four digits of a credit card number but not the whole number. The information is displayed in the standard format of a credit card number, XXXX-XXXX-XXXX-1234.

The Social Security Number option covers all except the last four characters, revealing the United States Social Security Number in the format XXX-XX-1234.

On numeric columns, the Random Number masking option should be utilized. Instead of the true value, it displays a random number as the masked value. A distinct number is presented each time the record is queried.

Custom Text Masking allows you to specify any restrictions that are required. This option allows text to be masked with any value and a configurable amount of characters to be displayed at each end of the masked value. If the length of the masked value is equal to or less than the number of characters specified by the mask, only the masked characters are displayed.

Dynamic Data Masking is useful for exporting a replica of your production database to a lower environment for development purposes, which may have fewer security constraints. If you use the credentials of a lower-privileged user who does not have UNMASK permissions to run the export procedure, the data will be exported in its masked format.

Implement Compliance Controls for Sensitive Data

Data Classification

Confidential information contained in a Microsoft SQL Server or Azure SQL Database should be categorized. This categorization informs SQL Server users and other programs about the sensitivity of the data being stored. The database's data classification is done column by column. A single table can include some columns that are public, some columns that are confidential, and some columns that are highly confidential. Data classification was first introduced in SQL Server Management Studio, where it was stored via extended properties of objects. This metadata is now kept in a catalog view called sys.sensitivity_classifications in SQL Server 2019 (and Azure SQL Database).

EXAM TIP: The Azure portal includes a management pane for data classification in your Azure SQL Database. You can get to this page by clicking **Data Discovery and**

Classification in the Advanced Data Security screen, which is located in the Security section of your Azure SQL Database's main blade.

Data classification can be configured in both the Azure portal and SQL Server Management Studio. The classification engine analyzes your database for columns with names, suggesting they may contain sensitive information. As an example, a column named email would be classed as holding sensitive personal information by default. Because it is dependent on the column name, a column named column1 that contains email addresses would not be categorized as sensitive personal information.

Columns can be classified using the sensitivity wizard in SQL Server Management Studio, the Advanced Data Security panel in the Azure portal for Azure SQL Database, or the T-SQL command ADD SENSITIVITY CLASSIFICATION, as illustrated below:

```
SQL

ADD SENSITIVITY CLASSIFICATION TO

[Application].[People].[EmailAddress]

WITH (LABEL='PII', INFORMATION_TYPE='Email')

GO
```

Figure 03-23: Sample Code

Advanced Threat Protection

As part of the Advanced Threat Protection (ATP) feature, Microsoft provides a range of protections for Azure SQL Database databases. ATP monitors connections to Azure SQL Database databases as well as queries conducted against them. The Azure portal is where you can configure ATP. This screen can be accessed via the Security section of your database's main blade.

ADVANCED DATA SECURITY

ON OFF

Advanced Data Security costs USD/server/month. It includes Data Discovery & Classification, Vulnerability Assessment and Advanced Threat Protection. We invite you to a trial period for the first 30 days, without charge.

VULNERABILITY ASSESSMENT SETTINGS

Subscription
Contoso Ltd

Storage account
sqldbdiag198

Periodic recurring scans
ON OFF

Send scan reports to
demo@contoso.com

Also send email notification to admins and subscription owners

ADVANCED THREAT PROTECTION SETTINGS

Send alerts to
demo@contoso.com

Also send email notification to admins and subscription owners

Advanced Threat Protection types
All

All
SQL injection
SQL injection vulnerability
Data exfiltration
Unsafe action
Brute Force
Anomalous client login

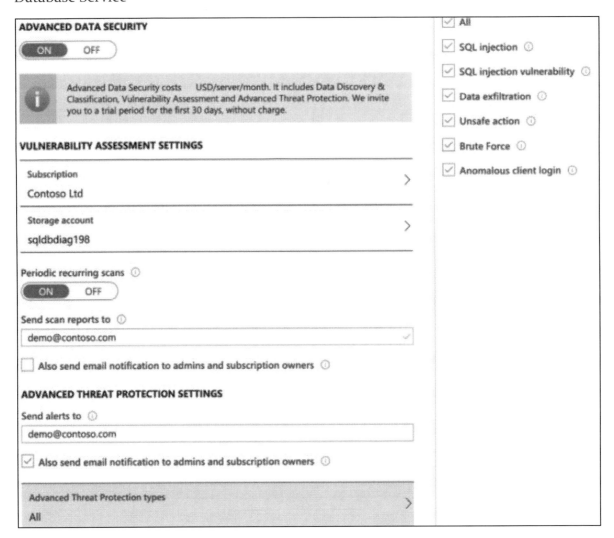

Figure 03-24: Advanced Data Security

To get the most out of Advanced Threat Protection, you need to enable auditing on your databases. If ATP finds an abnormality, auditing will allow for a more in-depth inquiry into the cause of the problem. Alerts for the following threats are supported by ATP:

Vulnerability to SQL Injection

This warning looks for T-SQL code entering your database that may be vulnerable to SQL injection attacks. A stored procedure call that did not sanitize user inputs is an example.

Potential SQL Injection

This alert is raised when an attacker actively attempts to carry out a SQL injection attack.

Access From an Unusual Location

When a user logs in from an odd geographic location, this alert is generated.

Access From an Unusual Azure Data Center

This alert is searching for attacks from an uncommon Azure data center.

Access From an Unfamiliar Principal

This alert is triggered when a person or application logs in to a database that they have never used before.

Access From a Potentially Harmful Application

This alert detects popular database attack tools.

Brute Force SQL Credentials

This warning is issued when a large number of login attempts with various credentials fail.

SQL Injection

SQL injection is one of the most widely utilized ways for data breaches. The essence of the attack is that a SQL command is attached to the backend of a form field in the web or application frontend (often via a website) to break the original SQL Script and execute the SQL script that was injected into the form field. This SQL injection most commonly occurs when your client application has dynamically produced SQL. The root cause of a SQL Injection attack is poor coding practices in both the client application and the database stored procedures. Many developers have learned better development methods, but SQL injection remains a significant problem. It is due to the number of legacy apps that are still in a log with newer applications constructed by developers that did not consider SQL injection seriously while developing the application.

Assume, for example, that the frontend web application generates the following dynamic SQL statement:

```sql
SQL

SELECT * FROM Orders WHERE OrderId=25
```

Figure 03- 25: Sample Code

This T-SQL is generated when a user navigates to the company's website's sales order history section and inputs 25 into the form field for the order ID number. Assume, however, that the user enters more than simply an ID number, such as "25; DELETE FROM Orders;."

In that situation, the query submitted to your database might look like this:

```
SQL

SELECT * FROM Orders WHERE OrderID=25; DELETE FROM Orders;
```

Figure 03- 26: Sample Code

The query in the preceding example works by informing the SQL database via the semicolon ";" that the statement has concluded and that another statement should be run. The database then executes the next command, resulting in the deletion of all rows from the Orders table.

The initial SELECT query is executed normally with no errors generated. However, when you look at the Orders table, you will notice that there are no rows, and the batch's second query that deletes all records was also run.

One method for preventing SQL injection attacks is to search for keywords in the text of the parameters or values provided in the form fields. However, this technique only gives a bare minimum of security because there are numerous ways to force these attacks to function. Passing in binary data, having the database engine transform the binary data back to a text string, and then executing the string are some of these injection tactics. Run the T-SQL code below to see a simplified example of this problem.

```
SQL

DECLARE @v varchar(255)

SELECT @v = cast(0x73705F68656C706462 as varchar(255))

EXEC (@v)
```

Figure 03-27: Sample Code

When accepting data from a user, whether a customer or an employee, one excellent technique to verify that the value will not be utilized in a SQL injection attack is to validate that the data entered is of the desired data type. If a number is expected, the client program should ensure that a number is indeed returned. If a text string is expected, ensure that it is the correct length and does not contain any binary data. The client application should be able to validate all user-supplied data. Validation can be accomplished by either telling the user of the problem and allowing the user to remedy the problem or by gracefully exiting with an error and no commands sent to the database or file system.

While repairing your application code should always be a priority, it may not always be achievable in some instances. Therefore, having Advanced Threat Protection can offer an additional layer of protection for your important data.

Lab 3-01: Ensuring the Security of the Database Environment

Introduction

In most businesses, you cannot join a Windows Server to an Azure Active Directory domain and work together to deliver a single set of user IDs because the two services have different use cases. Azure Active Directory Connect is a service that links your Active Directory identities to your Azure Active Directory.

Firewalls are used to keep unauthorized users from gaining access to protected resources. Each Azure SQL Database corresponds to a public IP address provided by Microsoft. Azure includes built-in firewalls to block access in order to secure your database and data.

Problem

You have been employed as a Senior Database Administrator to help assure the database environment's security of your company. These tasks will be centered on the Azure SQL Database. You will discover how to set up authentication and authorization for the Azure SQL database.

Solution

You will ensure the database's security through the following different steps:

- Authorize access to Azure SQL Database with Azure Active Directory
- Configure a server-based firewall rule using the Azure portal
- Enable Advanced Data Security and Data Classification

Pre-requisites:

To perform this lab, you must have the following:

- Azure SQL Server
- Azure SQL Database
- SQL Server Management Studio

Step 1: Authorize access to Azure SQL Database with Azure Active Directory

1. Select All resources from the Azure portal's home page.

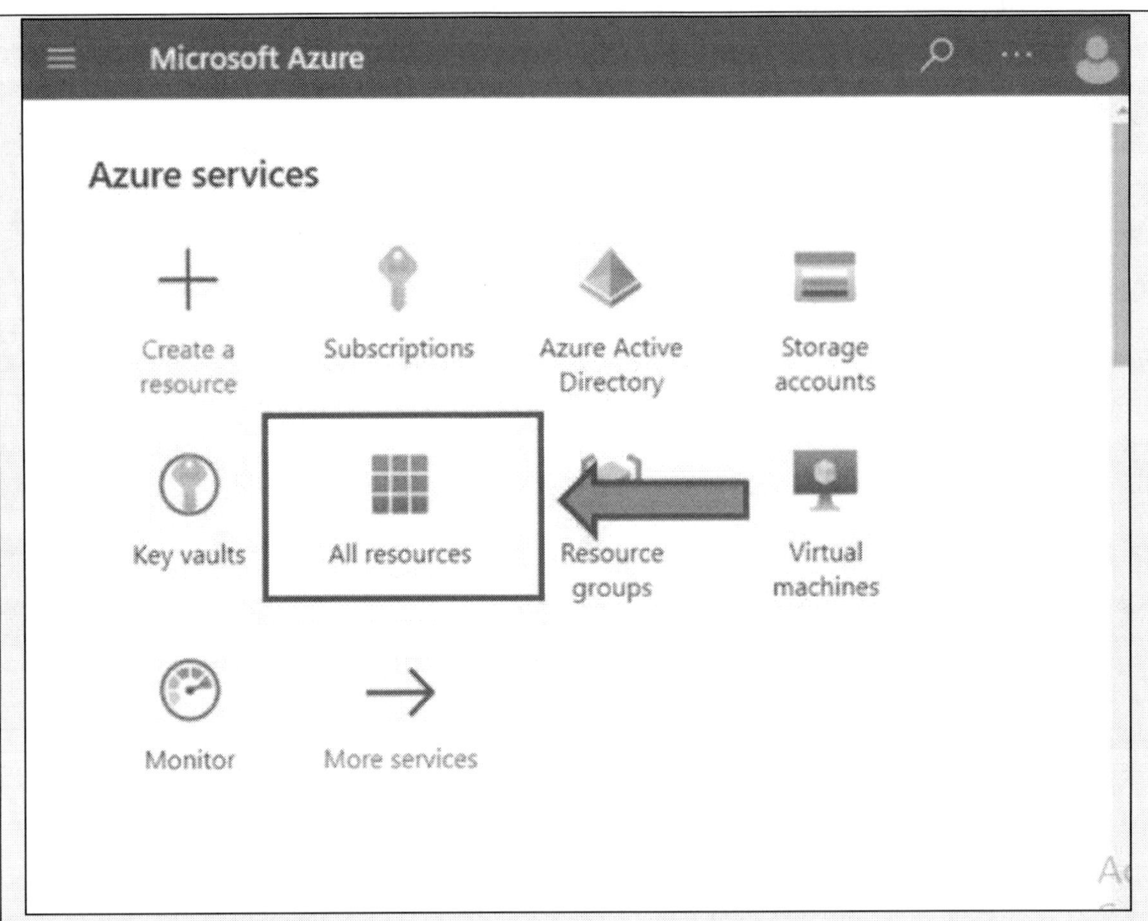

2. Select your Azure SQL Database server, and then click the **Not Configured** next to Active Directory Admin.

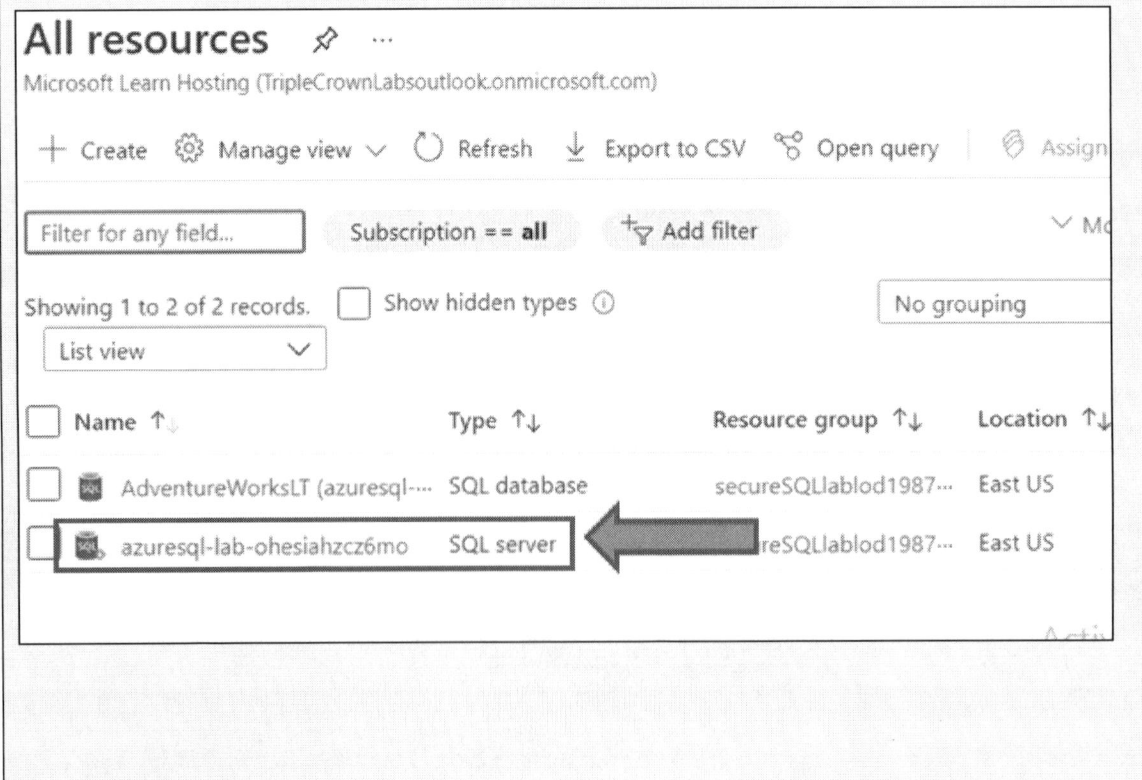

3. Select **Set admin** on the following screen:

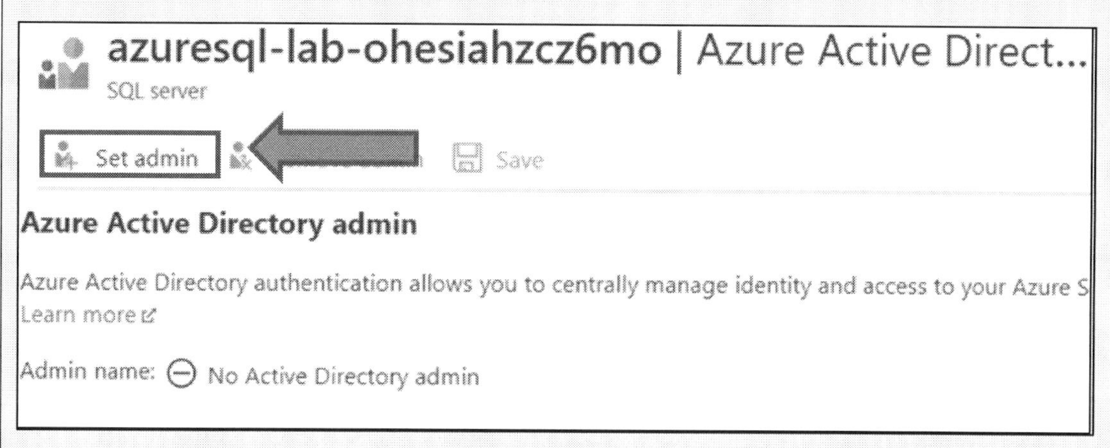

4. Look for the Azure username you used to log into the Azure portal in the Set admin screen.

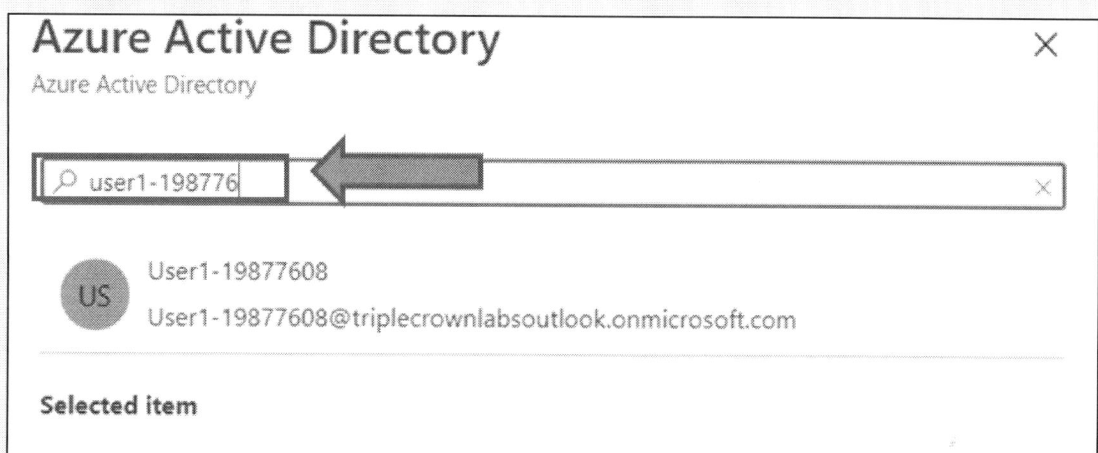

When you have discovered it, click the **Select** button and then the **username**. You will be taken back to the previous Active Directory Admin screen.

Azure Active Directory

Azure Active Directory

user1-198776

User1-19877608
User1-19877608@triplecrownlabsoutlook.onmicrosoft.com
Selected

Selected item

User1-19877608
User1-19877608@triplecrownlabsoutlook.onmicrosoft.com

Remove

Select

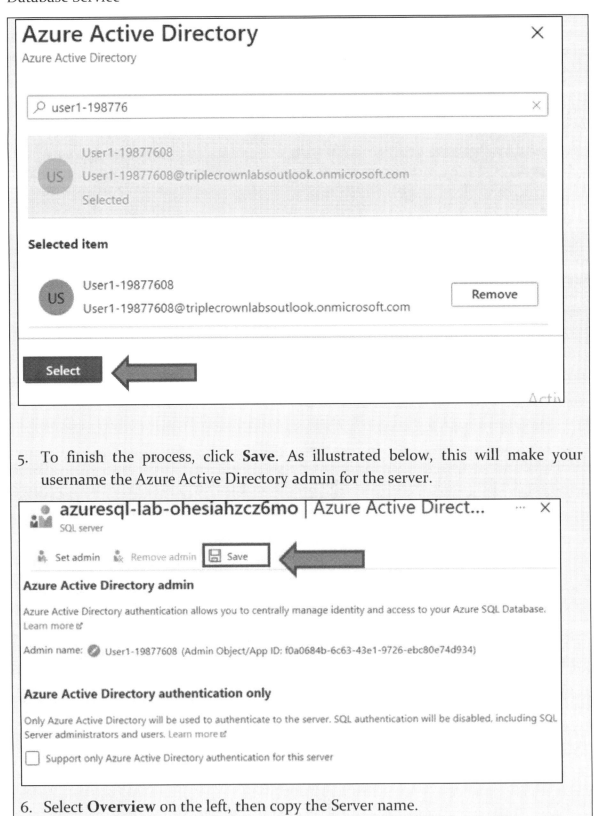

5. To finish the process, click **Save**. As illustrated below, this will make your username the Azure Active Directory admin for the server.

azuresql-lab-ohesiahzcz6mo | Azure Active Direct...

SQL server

Set admin   Remove admin   Save

Azure Active Directory admin

Azure Active Directory authentication allows you to centrally manage identity and access to your Azure SQL Database. Learn more

Admin name: User1-19877608 (Admin Object/App ID: f0a0684b-6c63-43e1-9726-ebc80e74d934)

Azure Active Directory authentication only

Only Azure Active Directory will be used to authenticate to the server. SQL authentication will be disabled, including SQL Server administrators and users. Learn more

Support only Azure Active Directory authentication for this server

6. Select **Overview** on the left, then copy the Server name.

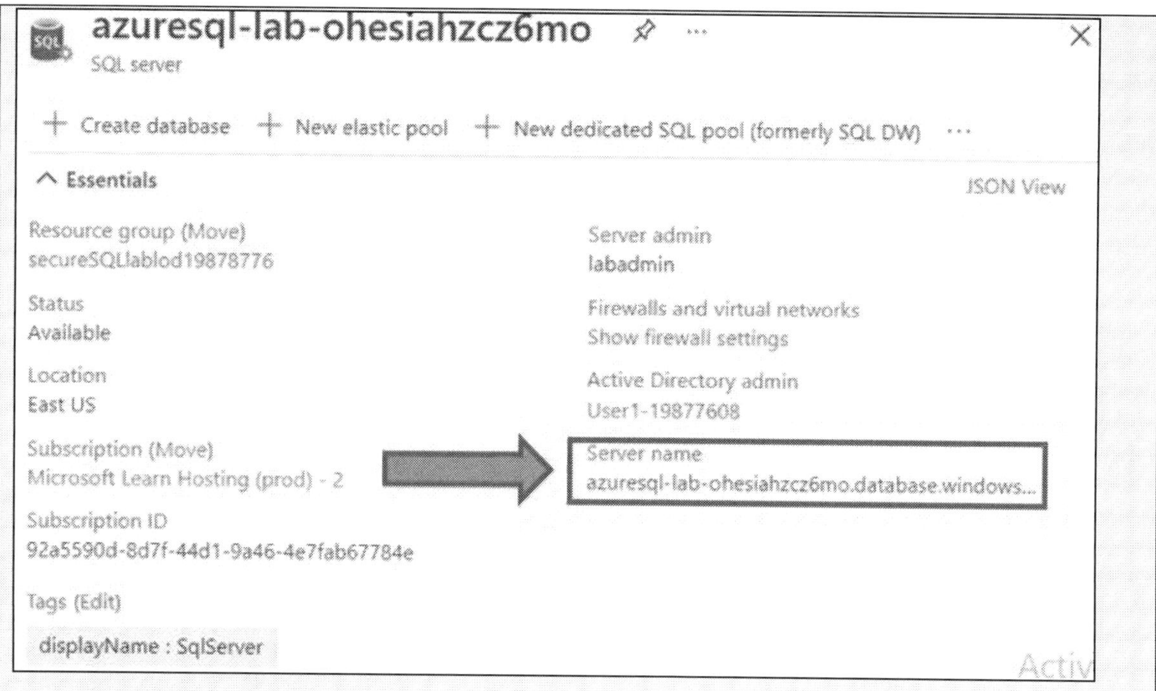

7. Select **Connect** > **Database Engine** in SQL Server Management Studio. Fill up the Server name field with the name of your server. Change the authentication type to Azure Active Directory Universal with Multi-Factor Authentication (MFA).
8. Select **Connect**.

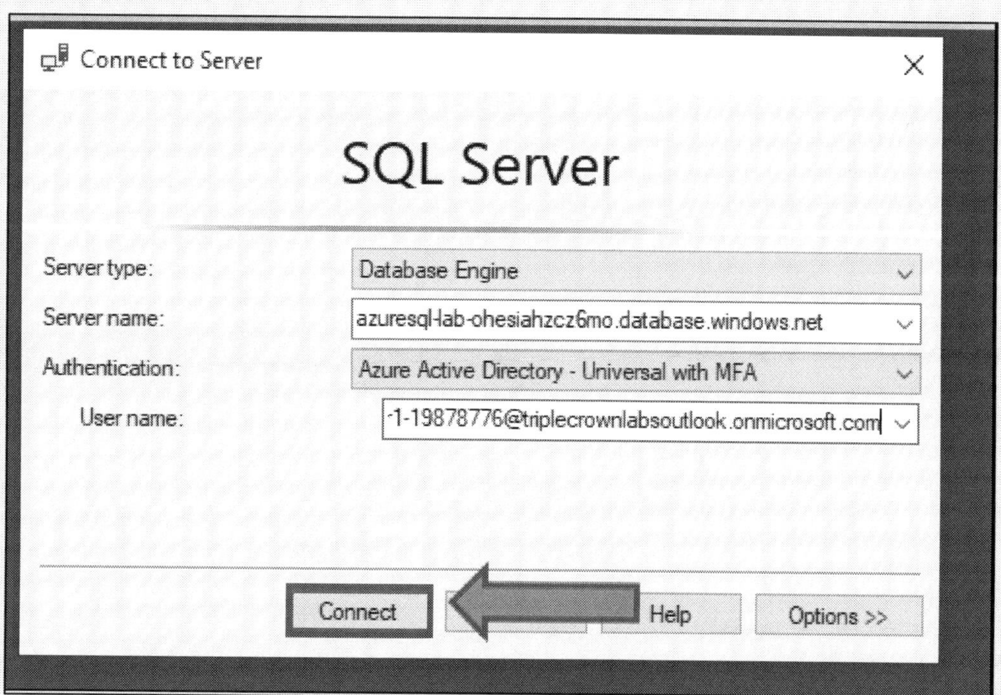

Manage Access to Database Objects

In this section, you will handle database and object access. The first step is to create two users in your database.

1. Expand Databases using the Object Explorer.
2. Select **New Query** from the menu that appears when you right-click on AdventureWorksLT.

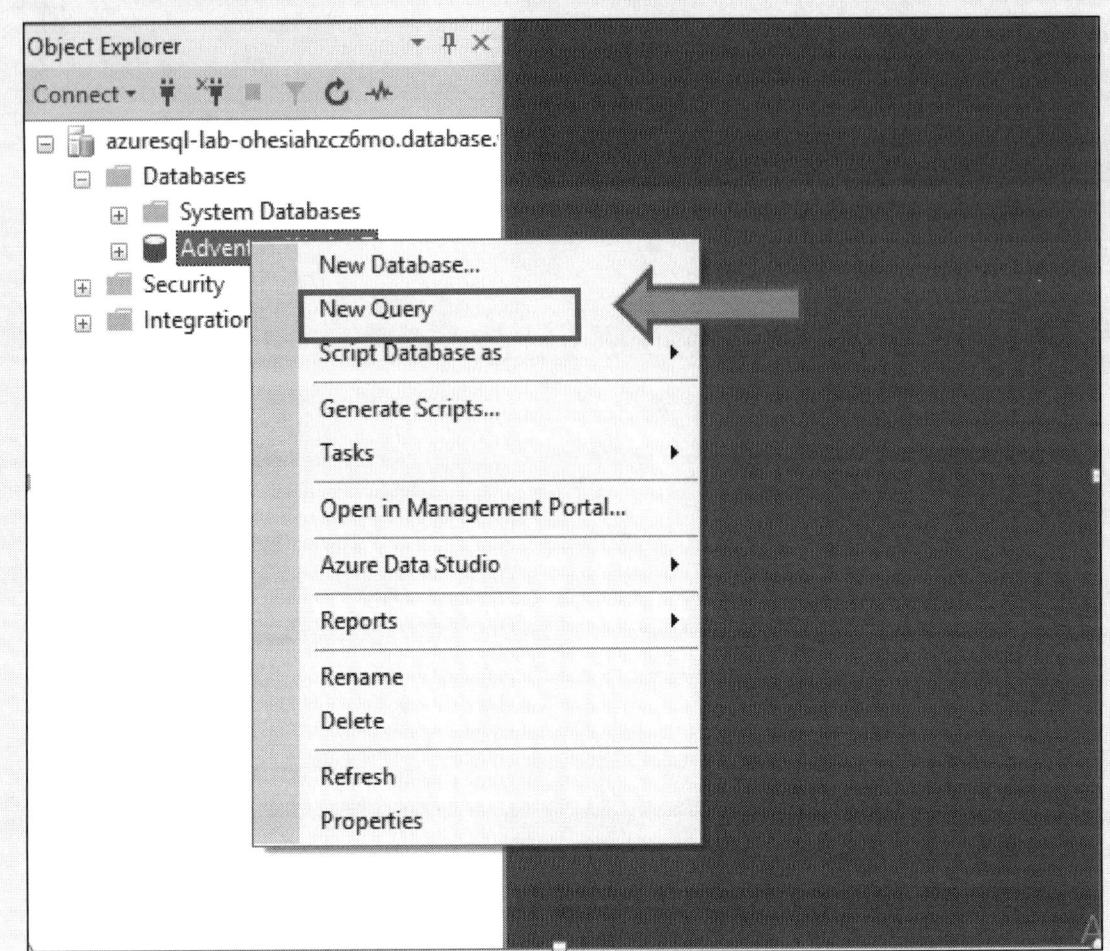

3. Copy and paste the following T-SQL into the new query box. To create the two users, run the query.

```
CREATE USER [DP300User1] WITH PASSWORD = 'Azur3Pa$$';
GO

CREATE USER [DP300User2] WITH PASSWORD = 'Azur3Pa$$';
GO
```

It should be noted that these users are created inside the scope of the AdventureWorksLT database. You will next construct a custom role and assign it to the users.

4. In the same query window as in step 1, run the following T-SQL.

```
CREATE ROLE [SalesReader];
GO

ALTER ROLE [SalesReader] ADD MEMBER [DP300User1];
GO

ALTER ROLE [SalesReader] ADD MEMBER [DP300User2];
GO
```

Next, in the SalesLT schema, add a new stored procedure.

5. In your query window, run the T-SQL.

```
CREATE OR ALTER PROCEDURE SalesLT.DemoProc
AS
SELECT P.Name, Sum(SOD.LineTotal) as TotalSales ,SOH.OrderDate
FROM SalesLT.Product P
INNER JOIN SalesLT.SalesOrderDetail SOD on SOD.ProductID = P.ProductID
INNER JOIN SalesLT.SalesOrderHeader SOH on SOH.SalesOrderID = SOD.SalesOrder
GROUP BY P.Name, SOH.OrderDate
ORDER BY TotalSales DESC
GO
```

Then, to test the security, use the EXECUTE AS USER syntax. This enables the database engine to run a query in your user's context.

6. Run the following T-SQL.

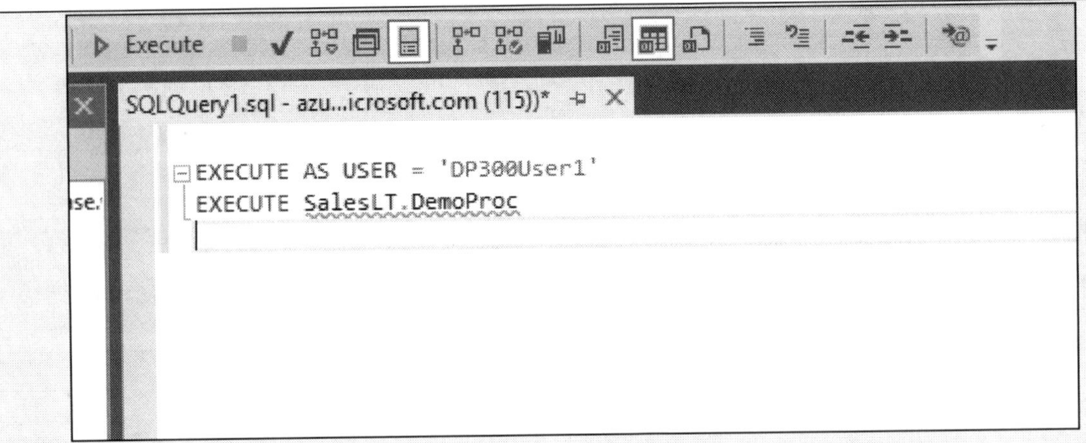

The T-SQLy will fail, and the following message will be a result of this.

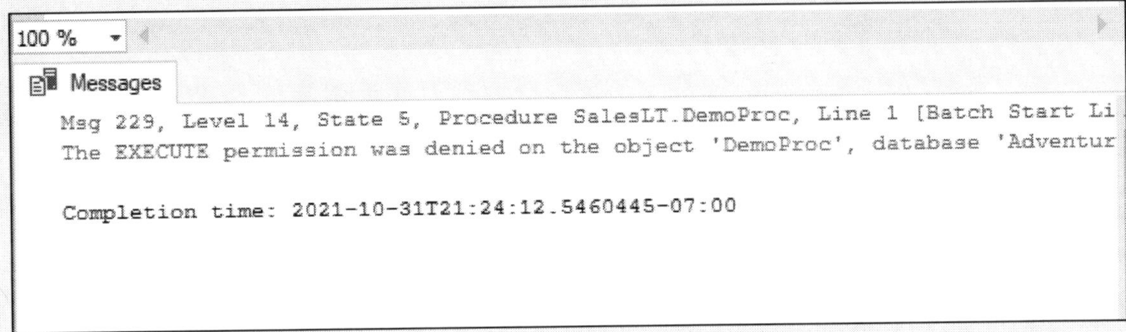

7. Next, grant the role permission to conduct the store procedure. Run the T-SQL code below:

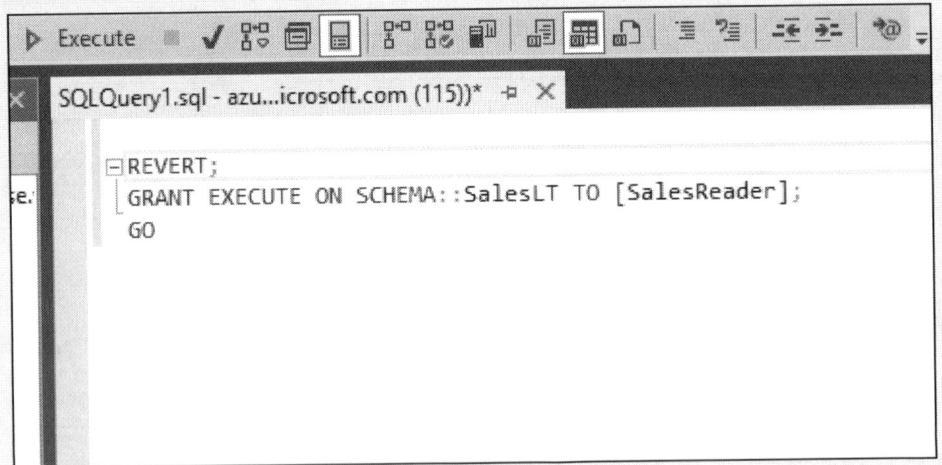

The first command returns control of the execution context to the database owner.

8. Run the previous T-SQL again.

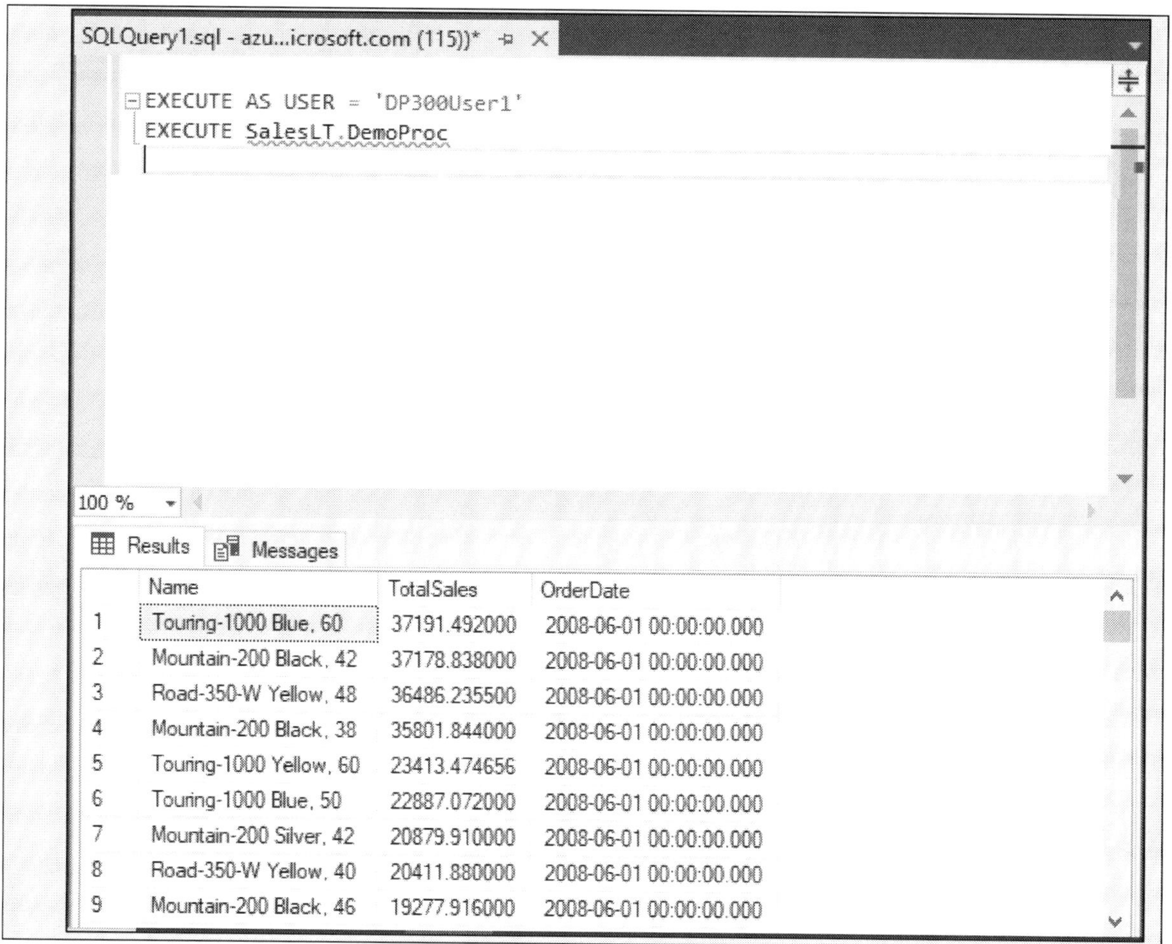

Step 2: Configure a server-based firewall rule using the Azure portal

1. Type **SQL servers** into the search bar at the top of the Azure portal.

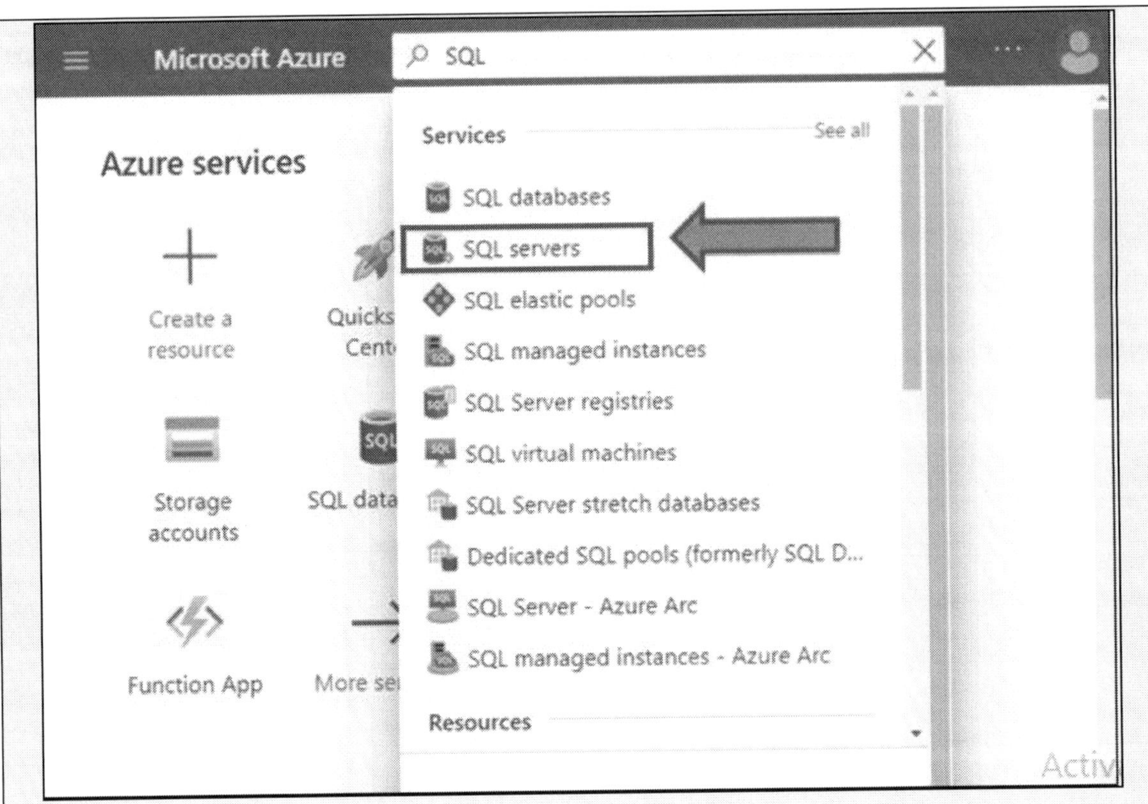

2. The SQL servers icon will be displayed. Select **SQL servers**, followed by the name of your SQL server.

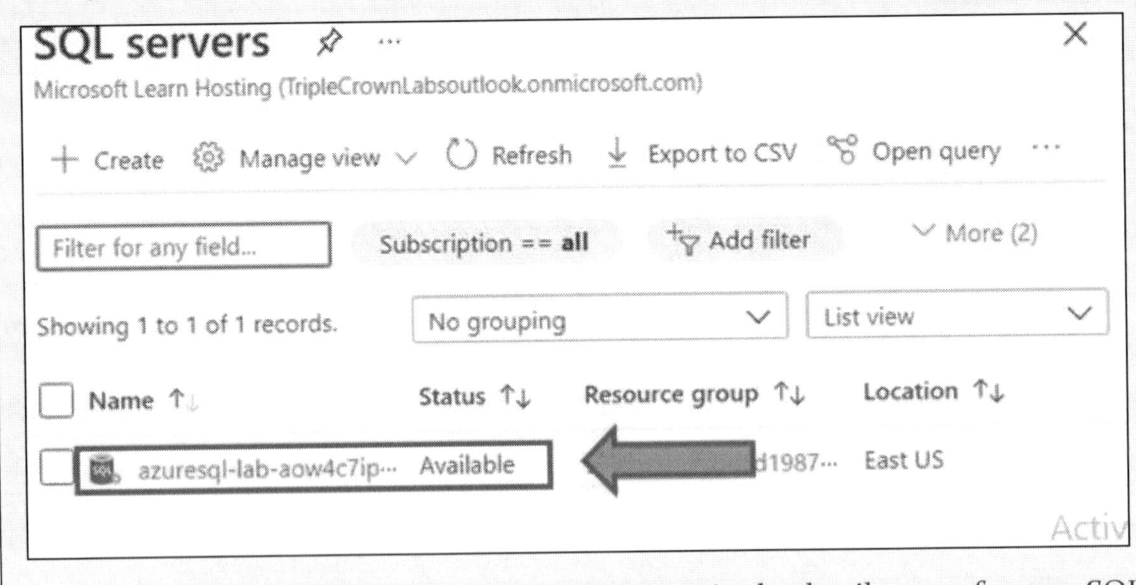

3. Move your mouse to the right of the server name in the detail screen for your SQL server and click **Copy to clipboard** button as shown below:

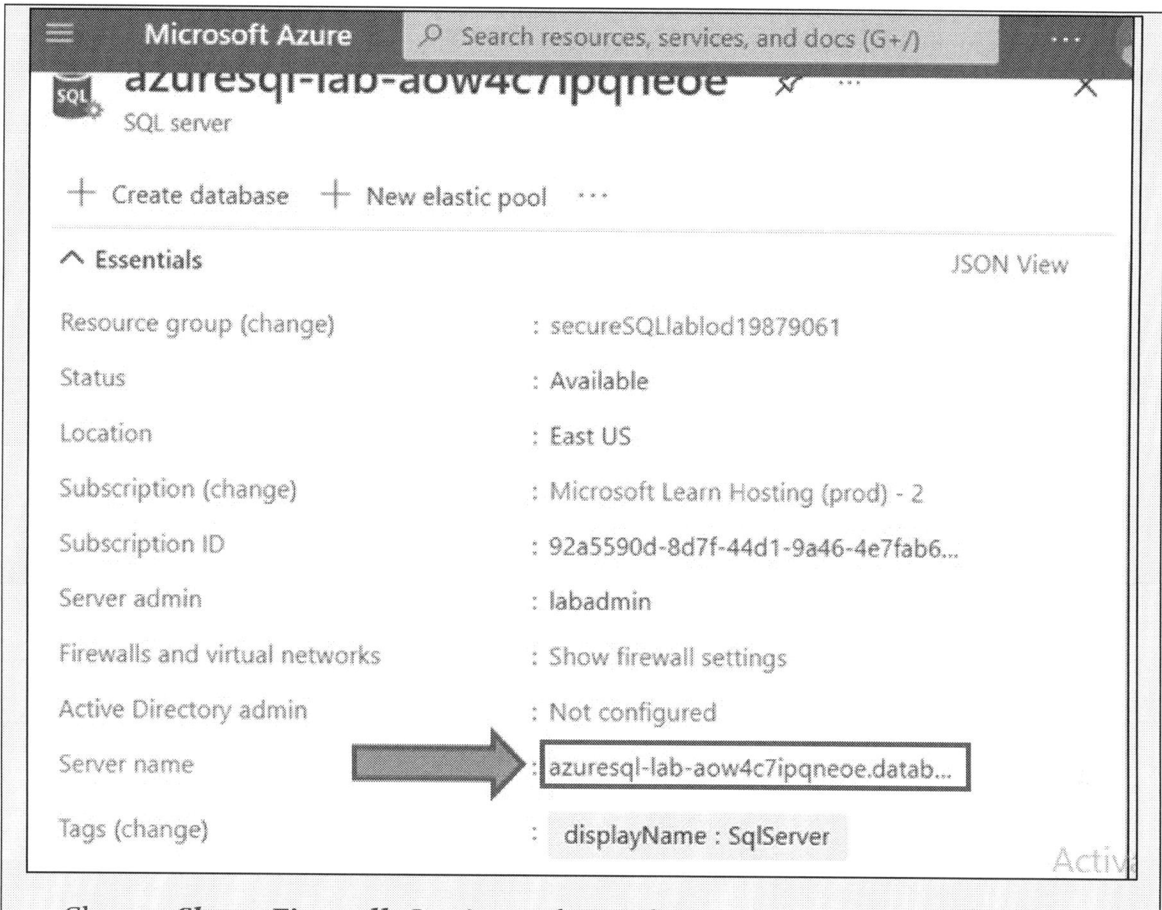

4. Choose **Show Firewall Settings** above the server name you copied to the clipboard. Select + **Add client IP** as shown below, and then **Save**.

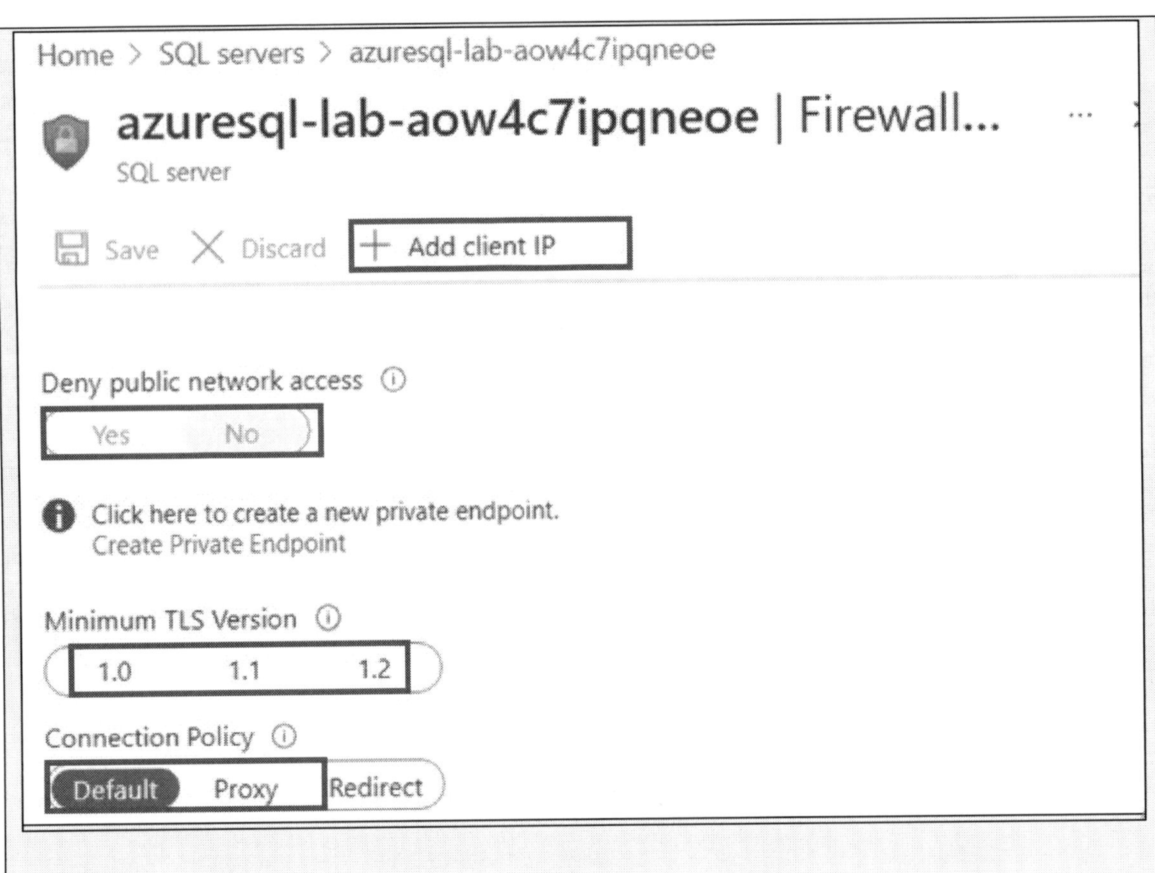

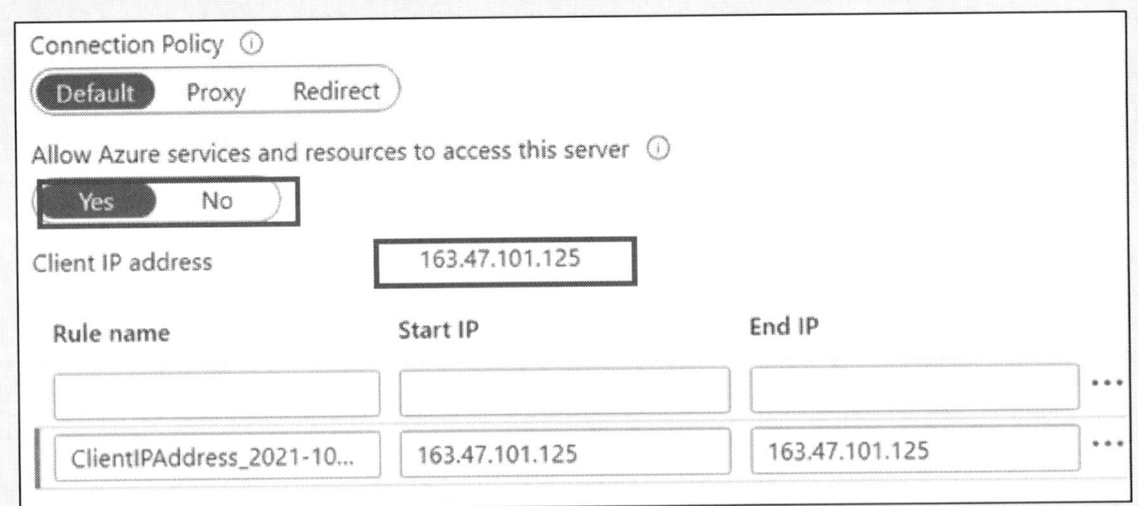

These configurations will allow you to connect to your Azure SQL Database server using SQL Server Management Studio or any other client tools. Make a note of your client's IP address because you will need it later in this exercise.

Connect to a SQL Server and create a database in Azure

1. Open SQL Server Management Studio by going to the Start menu and selecting **Microsoft SQL Server Tools 18 > SQL Server Management Studio**. Copy and paste the name of your Azure SQL database server, then login in with your credentials.

Select **Connect**.

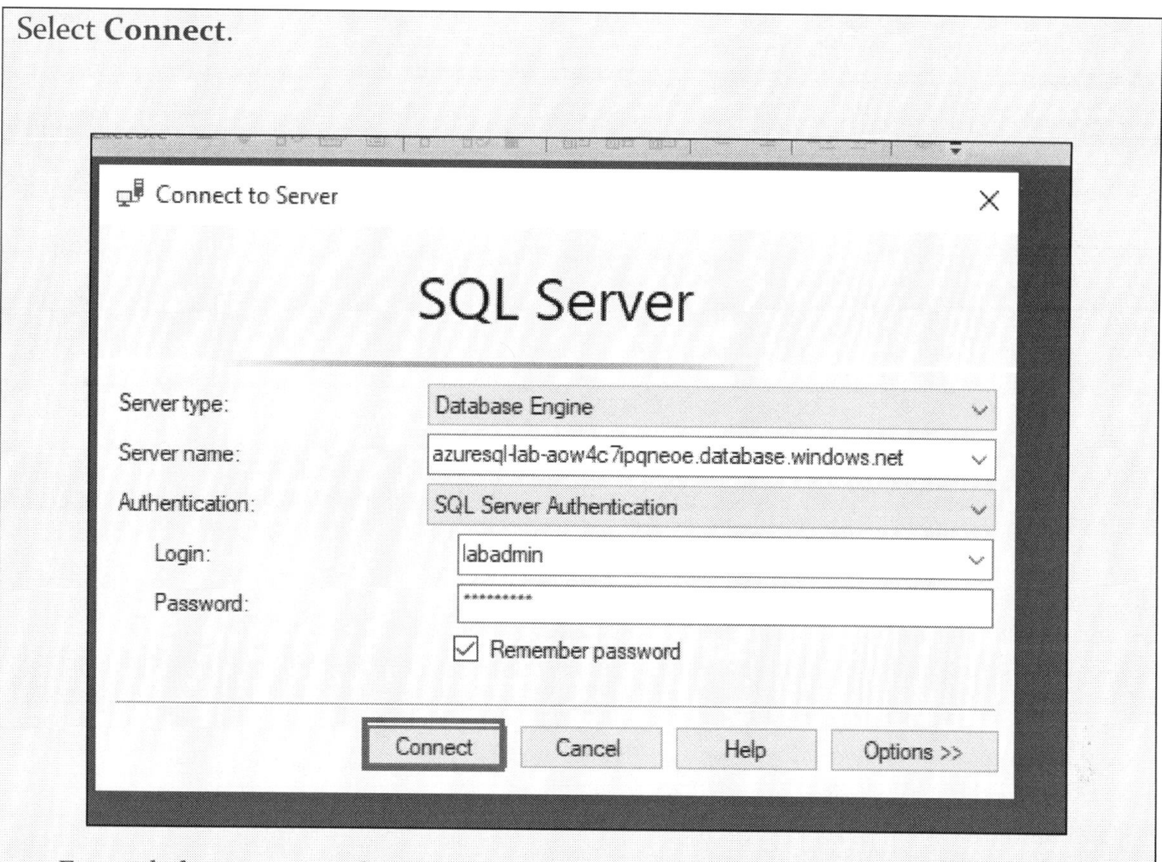

2. Expand the server node in Object Explorer, then right-click on **Databases** and select **Import Data-tier Application**.

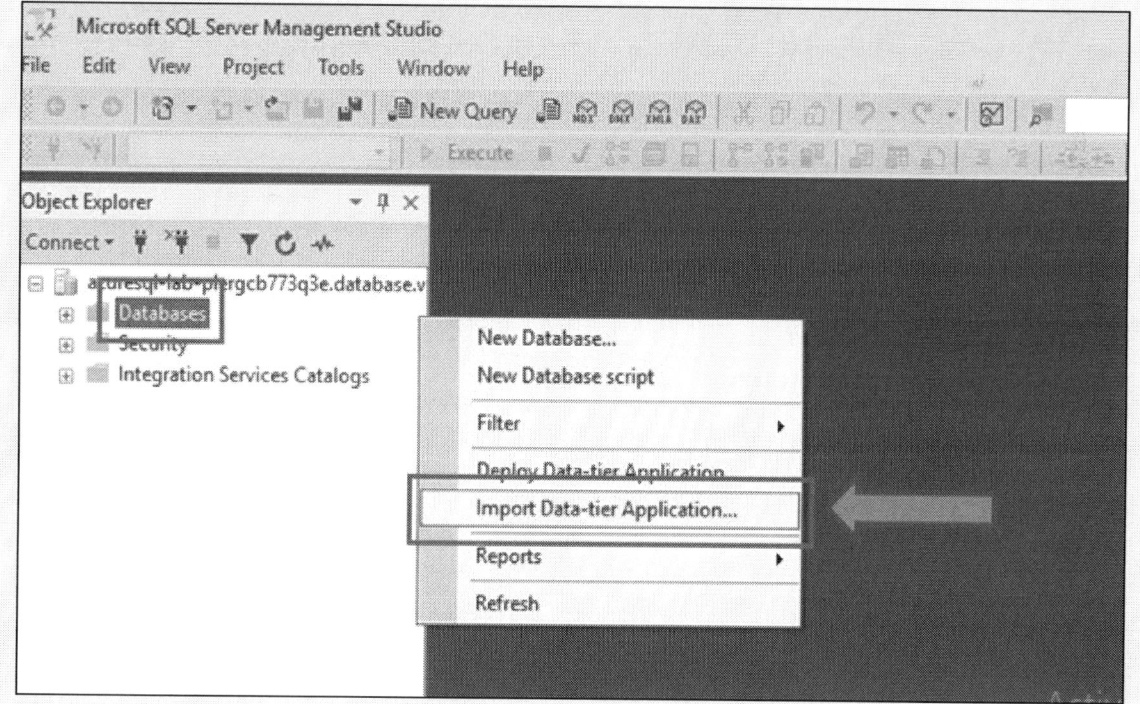

3. Select **Next** on the first screen of the Import Data Tier Application dialogue.

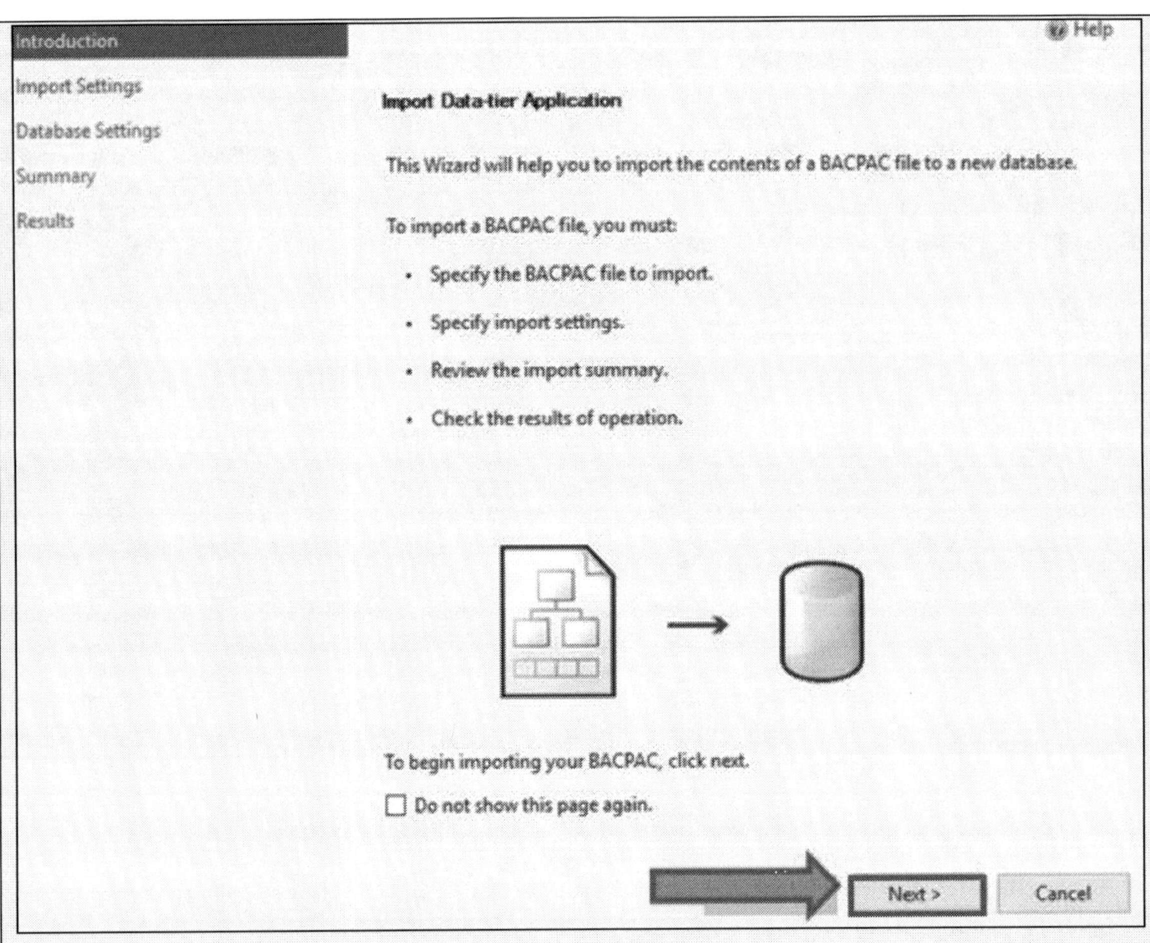

4. Select **Browse** in the Import Settings page, navigate to the folder containing your database, select the file, and then click **Open**. Then, on the Import Data-tier application screen, press the **Next** button.

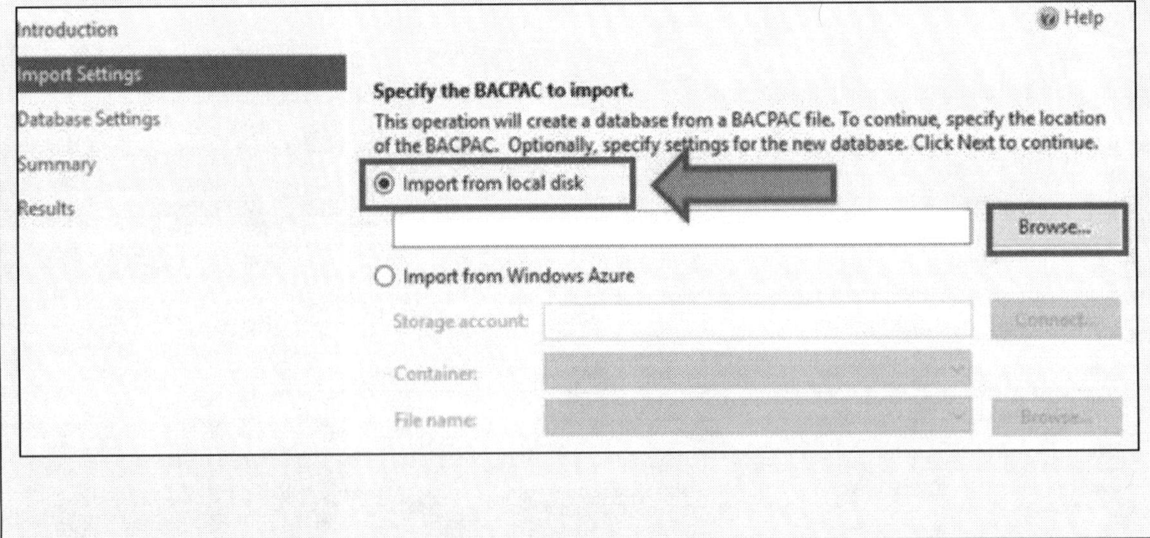

Specify the BACPAC to import.

This operation will create a database from a BACPAC file. To continue, specify the location of the BACPAC. Optionally, specify settings for the new database. Click Next to continue.

Import from local disk

D:\LabFiles\Secure Environment\AdventureWorks.bacpac

Import from Windows Azure

Storage account: Connect...

Container:

File name: Browse...

Temporary file name:

C:\Users\Student\AppData\Local\Temp\temp_bacpac-2021103118490 Browse...

Next > Cancel

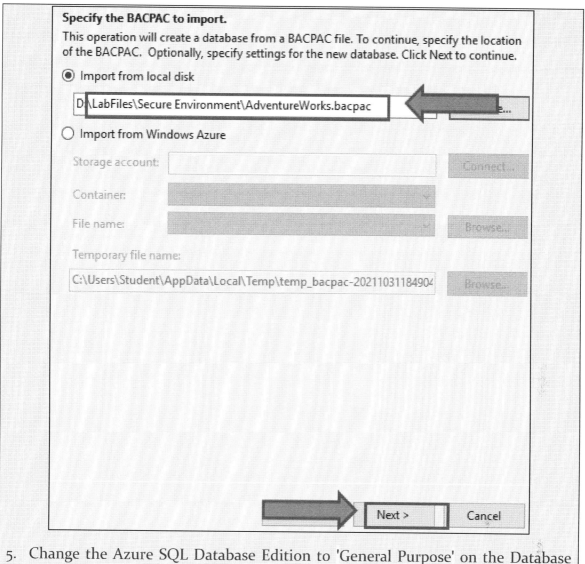

5. Change the Azure SQL Database Edition to 'General Purpose' on the Database Settings screen. Select **Next** after changing the Service Objective to GP_Gen5_2.

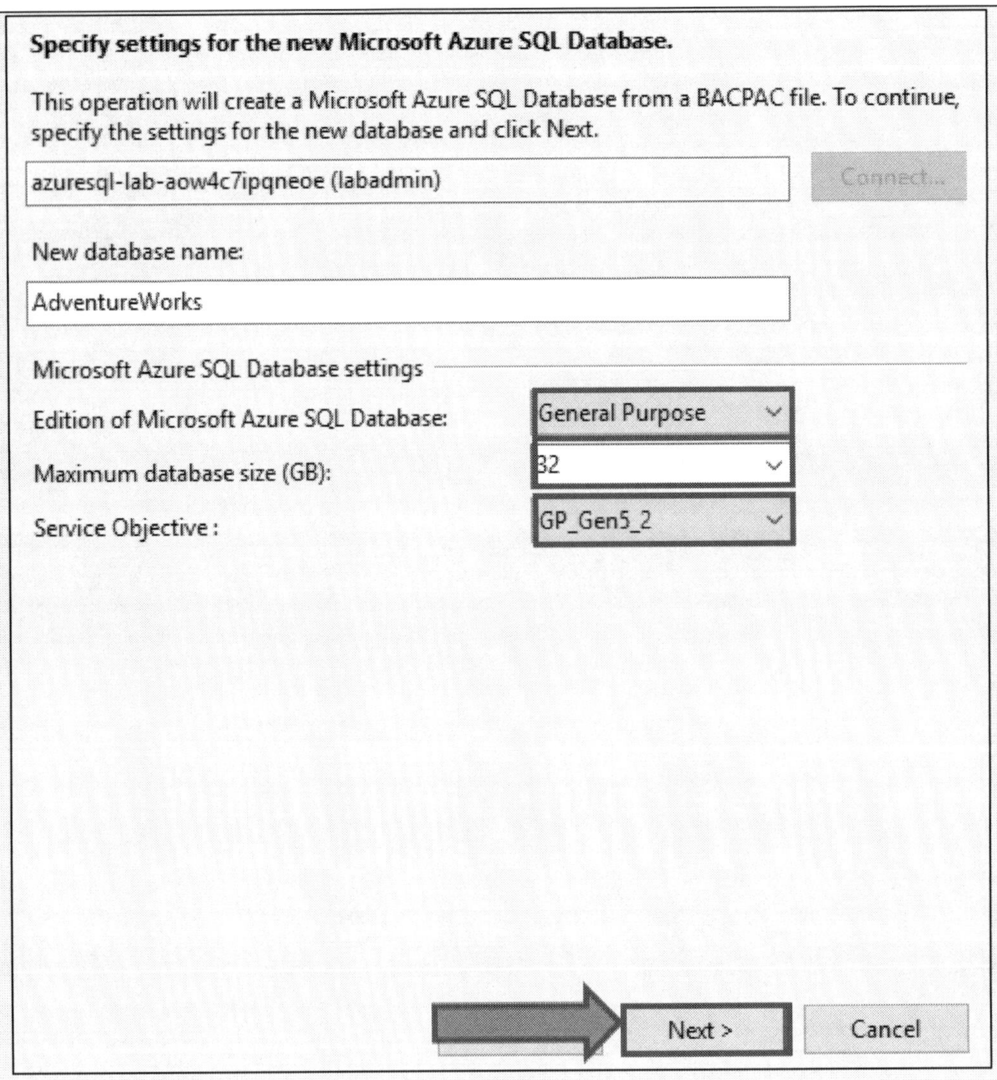

Specify settings for the new Microsoft Azure SQL Database.

This operation will create a Microsoft Azure SQL Database from a BACPAC file. To continue, specify the settings for the new database and click Next.

azuresql-lab-aow4c7ipqneoe (labadmin) Connect...

New database name:

AdventureWorks

Microsoft Azure SQL Database settings

Edition of Microsoft Azure SQL Database: General Purpose

Maximum database size (GB): 32

Service Objective : GP_Gen5_2

Next > Cancel

6. Select **Finish** from the Summary screen. When your import is finished, the results will be displayed below.

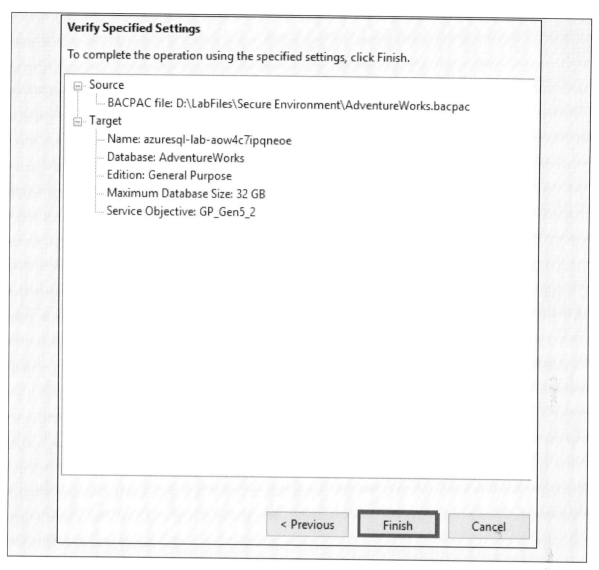

Verify Specified Settings

To complete the operation using the specified settings, click Finish.

- Source
  - BACPAC file: D:\LabFiles\Secure Environment\AdventureWorks.bacpac
- Target
  - Name: azuresql-lab-aow4c7ipqneoe
  - Database: AdventureWorks
  - Edition: General Purpose
  - Maximum Database Size: 32 GB
  - Service Objective: GP_Gen5_2

< Previous | Finish | Cancel

Operation Complete

Summary:

Name	Result
Importing database	Success
Creating deployment plan	Success
Initializing deployment	Success
Verifying deployment plan	Success
Analyzing deployment plan	Success
Importing package schema and data into database	Success
Updating database	Success
Importing data	Success
Processing Import.	Success
Disabling indexes.	Success
Disabling index 'PK_DatabaseLog_DatabaseLogID'.	Success
Disabling index 'AK_Department_Name'.	Success
Disabling index 'AK_Employee_LoginID'.	Success
Disabling index 'AK_Employee_NationalIDNumber'.	Success
Disabling index 'AK_Employee_rowguid'.	Success
Disabling index 'IX_Employee_OrganizationLevel_OrganizationNode'.	Success
Disabling index 'IX_Employee_OrganizationNode'.	Success

< Previous   Next >   Close

Create a firewall rule using SQL statements

1. Right-click the **AdventureWorks** database that you just imported in the Object Explorer.
2. Choose **New Query**.

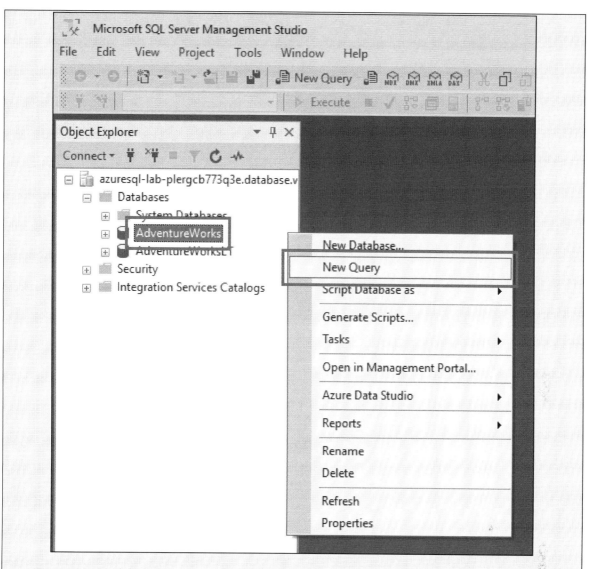

3. By pasting the following T-SQL query into your query window and selecting 'Execute' or pressing F5, you may run it.

Replace both occurrences of n.n.n.n with your previously copied client IP address. If necessary, return to the firewall settings in the Azure portal to copy your client IP address again.

```
EXECUTE sp_set_database_firewall_rule @name = N'ContosoFirewallRule',
@start_ip_address = '163.47.101.125', @end_ip_address = ' 163.47.101.125'
```

4. Following that, you will create a user in the AdventureWorks database. Choose **New Query** and run the following T-SQL.

Use this command to create a user in the AdventureWorks database. In the following step, you will sign in with your username and password.

5. To perform this command, click the **Execute** button.

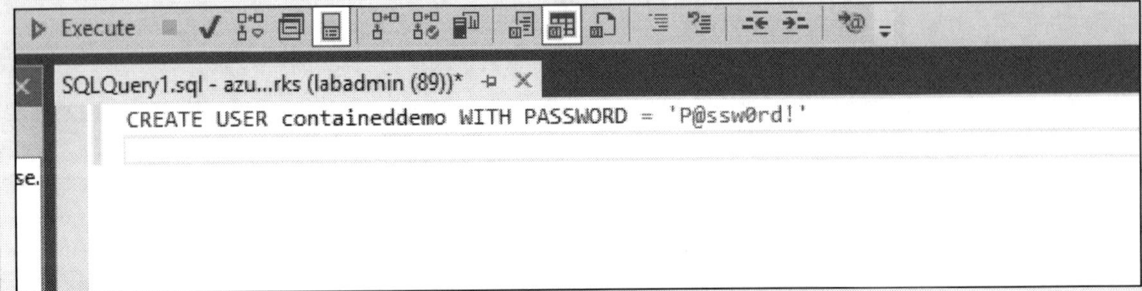

6. In SSMS, go to Object Explorer and click **Connect**, then **Database Engine**.

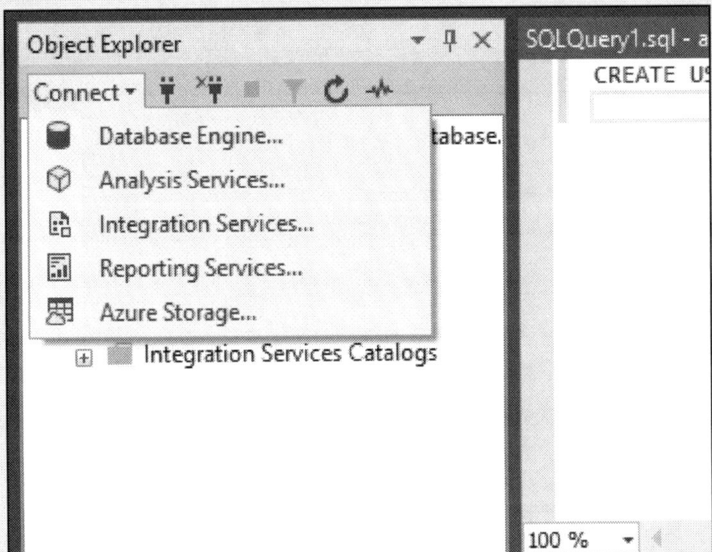

7. Connect using the credentials you created in step 4.
   - Login: containeddemo
   - Password: P@ssword!

It attempted to sign in to the master database rather than AdventureWorks where the user was established; hence the connection failed.

8. To change the connection context, click **OK** to exit the error notice and then **Options** in the 'Connect to Server' dialogue box, as shown below:
9. On the Connection Options page, type **AdventureWorks** in the Connect to database area and then click **Connect**. Do not Use the auto-populated dropdown list.

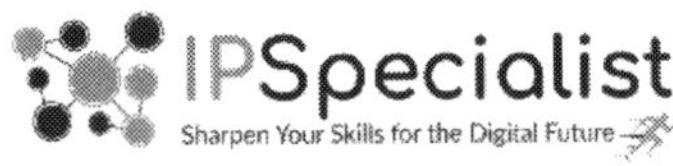

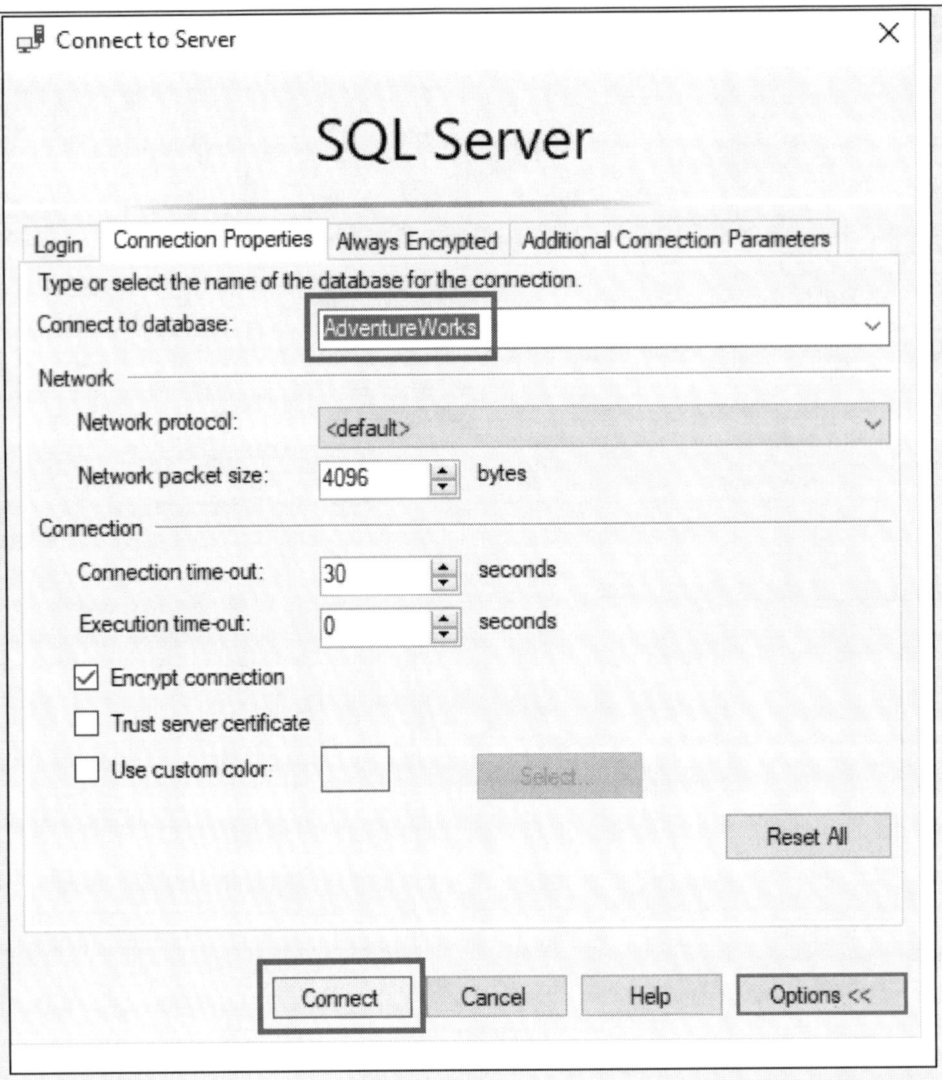

Connect to Server
SQL Server
Login
Connection Properties
Always Encrypted
Additional Connection Parameters
Type or select the name of the database for the connection.
Connect to database:
AdventureWorks
Network
Network protocol:
<default>
Network packet size:
4096
bytes
Connection
Connection time-out:
30
seconds
Execution time-out:
0
seconds
Encrypt connection
Trust server certificate
Use custom color:
Select...
Reset All
Connect
Cancel
Help
Options <<

This connection bypasses the master database and directs you to AdventureWorks, the only database to which the newly formed user has access.

Object Explorer
Connect
azuresql-lab-plergcb773q3e.database.windows.net (SQL Server 12.0.2000.8 - labadmin)
Databases
System Databases
AdventureWorks
AdventureWorksLT
Security
Integration Services Catalogs
azuresql-lab-plergcb773q3e.database.windows.net (SQL Server 12.0.2000.8 - containeddemo)
Databases
Integration Services Catalogs

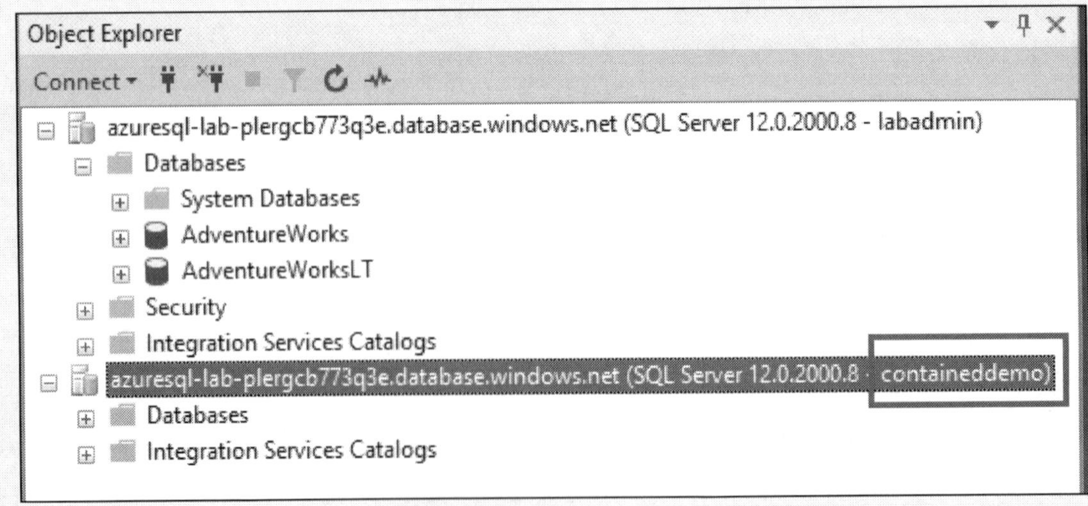

10. Expand the Databases section for the containeddemo connection, then right-click **AdventureWorks** and choose **New Query**.

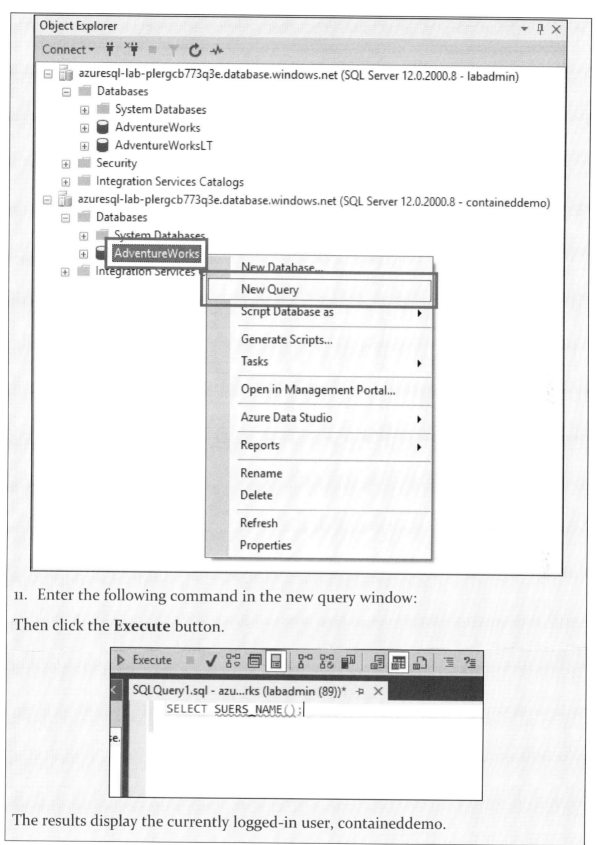

11. Enter the following command in the new query window:

Then click the **Execute** button.

```
SELECT SUERS_NAME();
```

The results display the currently logged-in user, containeddemo.

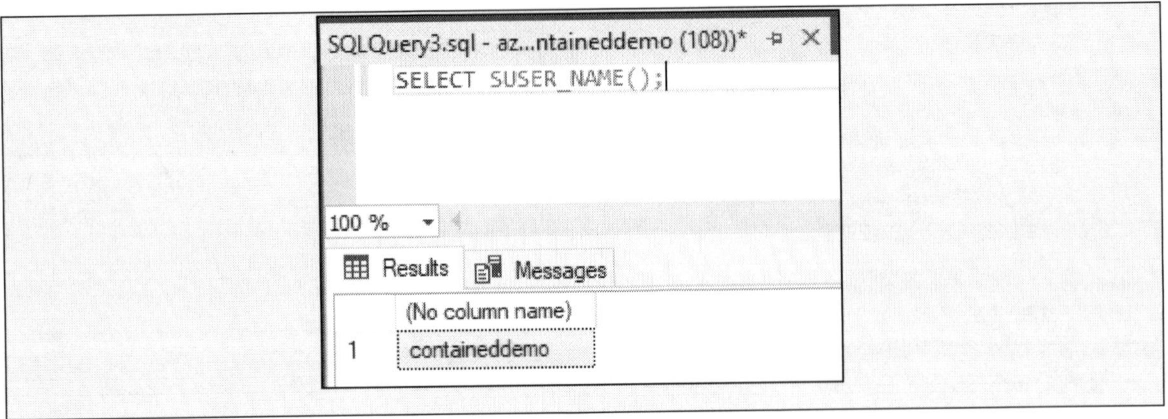

Step 3: Enable Advanced Data Security and Data Classification

1. Select **All resources** from the Azure portal's home page.

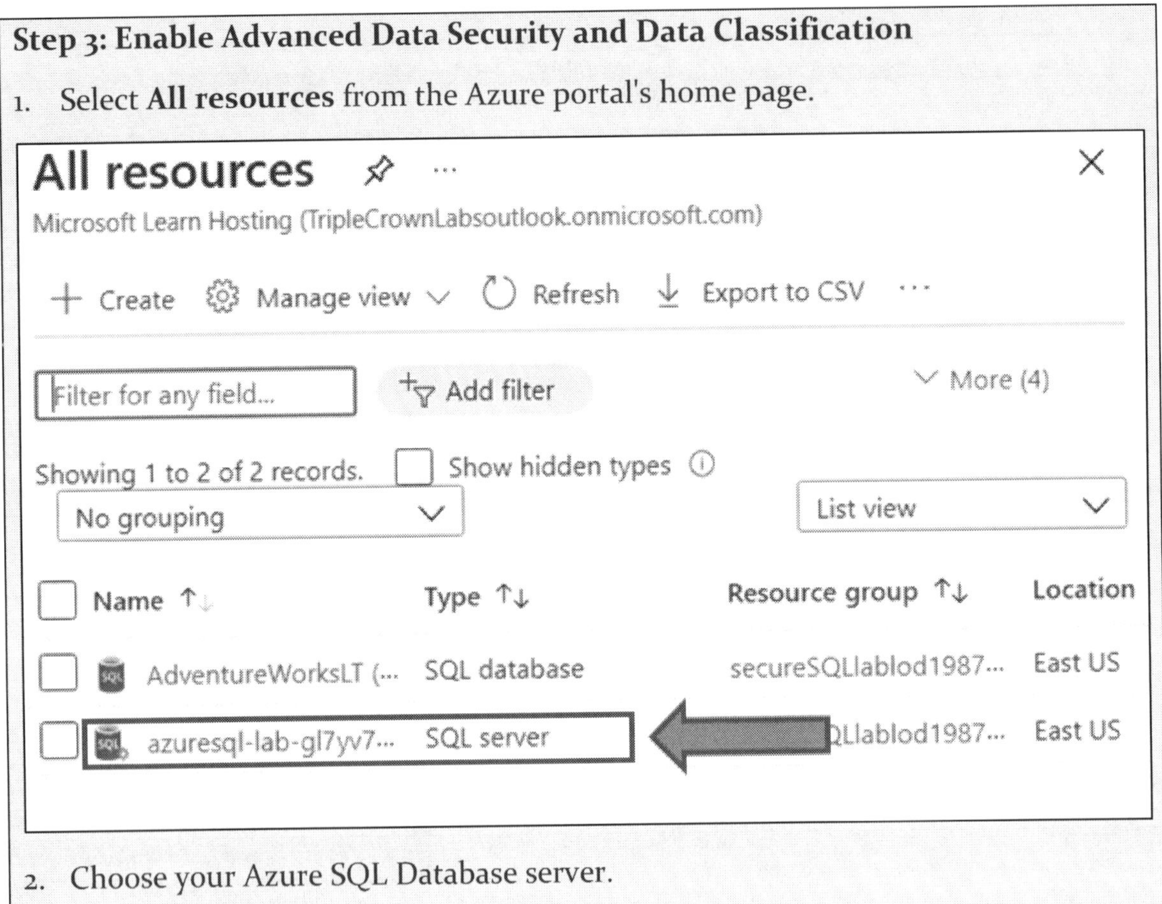

2. Choose your Azure SQL Database server.

All resources

Microsoft Learn Hosting (TripleCrownLabsoutlook.onmicrosoft.com)

+ Create | Manage view | Refresh | Export to CSV

Filter for any field... | Add filter | More (4)

Showing 1 to 2 of 2 records. Show hidden types

No grouping | List view

Name	Type	Resource group	Location
AdventureWorksLT (...	SQL database	secureSQLlablod1987...	East US
azuresql-lab-gl7yv7...	SQL server	secureSQLlablod1987...	East US

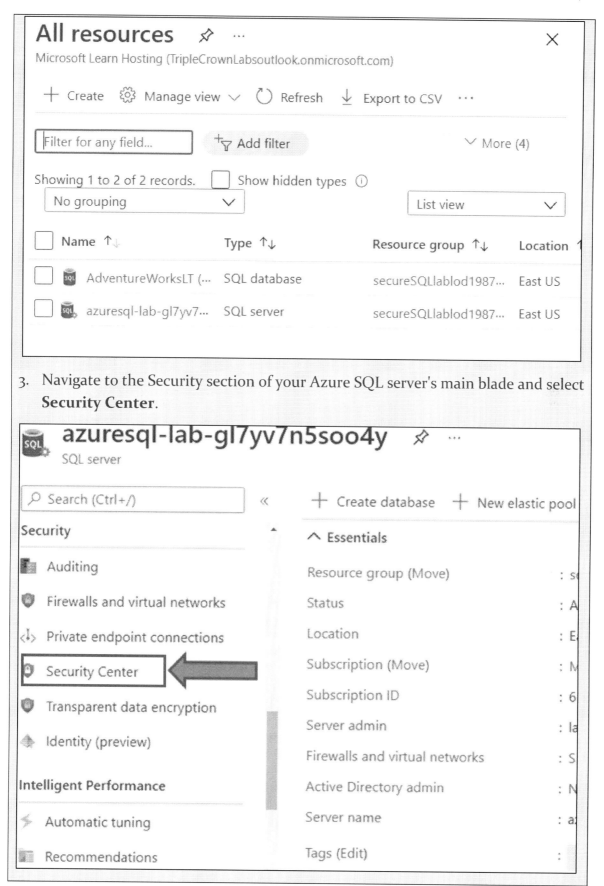

3. Navigate to the Security section of your Azure SQL server's main blade and select **Security Center**.

azuresql-lab-gl7yv7n5soo4y

SQL server

Search (Ctrl+/) | + Create database | + New elastic pool

Security
- Auditing
- Firewalls and virtual networks
- Private endpoint connections
- Security Center
- Transparent data encryption
- Identity (preview)

Intelligent Performance
- Automatic tuning
- Recommendations

Essentials

Resource group (Move)
Status
Location
Subscription (Move)
Subscription ID
Server admin
Firewalls and virtual networks
Active Directory admin
Server name
Tags (Edit)

4. Toggle the AZURE DEFENDER FOR SQL toggle switch to **ON**, and then choose **Storage account**.

AZURE DEFENDER FOR SQL

ON OFF

Azure Defender for SQL costs 15 USD/server/month. It includes Vulnerability Assessment and Advanced Threat Protection. We invite you to a trial period for the first 30 days, without charge.

VULNERABILITY ASSESSMENT SETTINGS

Subscription
Microsoft Learn Hosting (prod) - 4
Select Subscription

Storage account
sqlvauwfmjtbfkrqws
Select Storage account

Periodic recurring scans
ON OFF

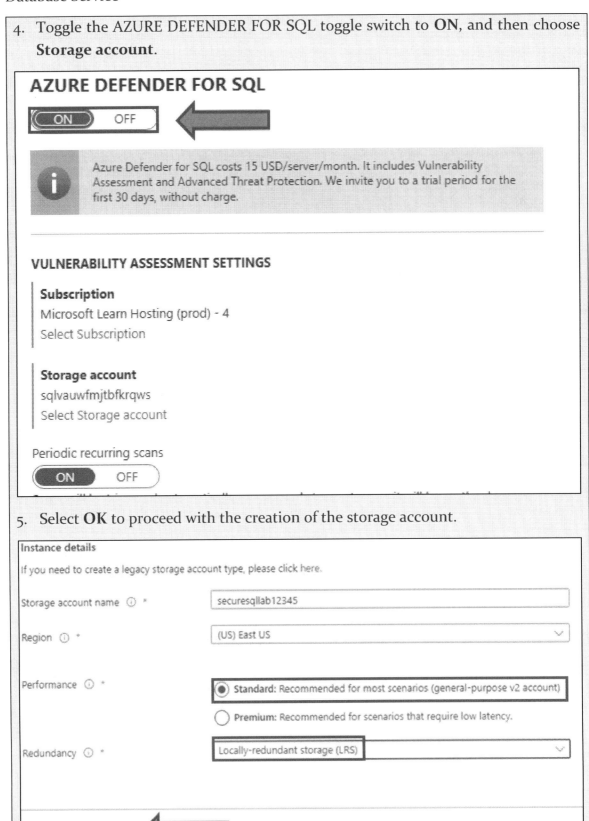

5. Select **OK** to proceed with the creation of the storage account.

Instance details
If you need to create a legacy storage account type, please click here.

Storage account name ⓘ * securesqllab12345

Region ⓘ * (US) East US

Performance ⓘ * Standard: Recommended for most scenarios (general-purpose v2 account)
Premium: Recommended for scenarios that require low latency.

Redundancy ⓘ * Locally-redundant storage (LRS)

Review + create < Previous Next : Advanced >

6. Toggle the Periodic recurring scans switch to **ON**. In the 'Send scan reports to' and 'Send alerts to' dialogue boxes, enter the email address associated with your

Azure account. Find the box that says "Send email notifications to admins and subscription owners" and uncheck it.

7. Select **Advanced Threat Detection** kinds and go through the options. Select **OK** after checking all of the boxes.

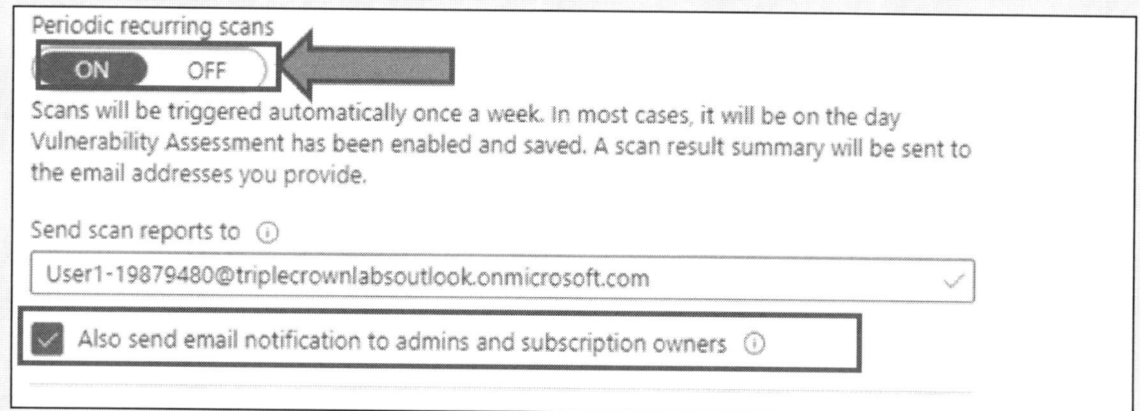

8. Choose **Save**.

Enable data classification on an Azure SQL database

1. Select **Overview** from the left navigation.
2. Make a note of the Server name for later use in this lab.

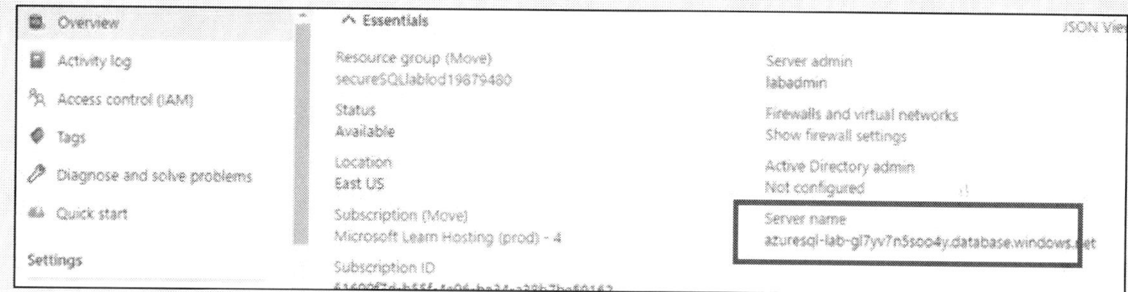

3. In the Azure portal, navigate to the AdventureWorksLT database by scrolling down in the overview screen for the Azure SQL server and selecting the database name.

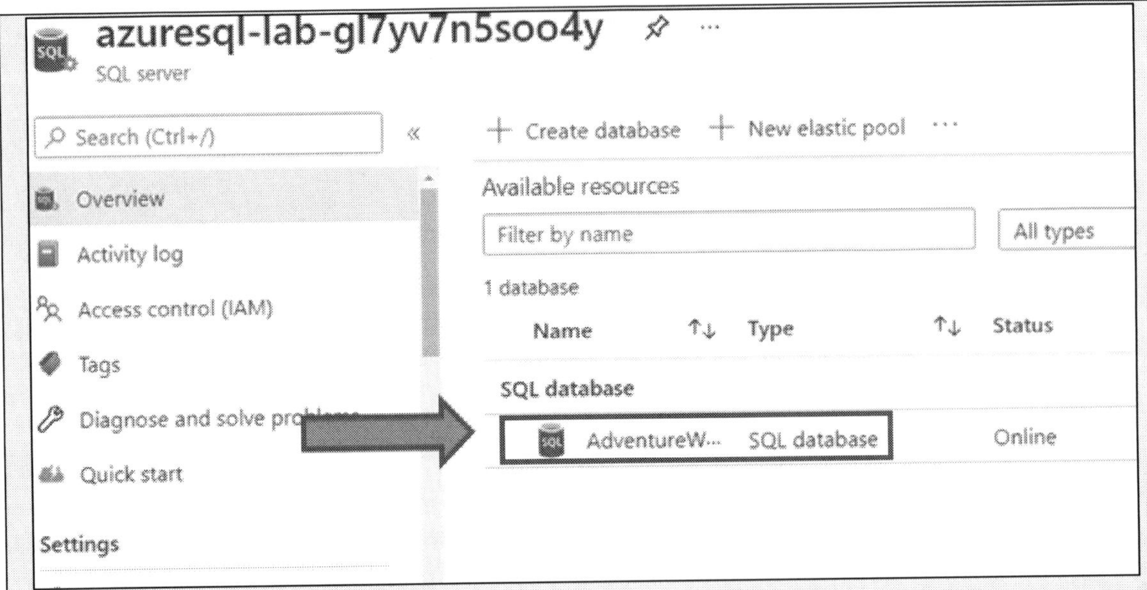

4. Select **Data Discovery & Classification** from the Security section of your Azure SQL Database's main blade.

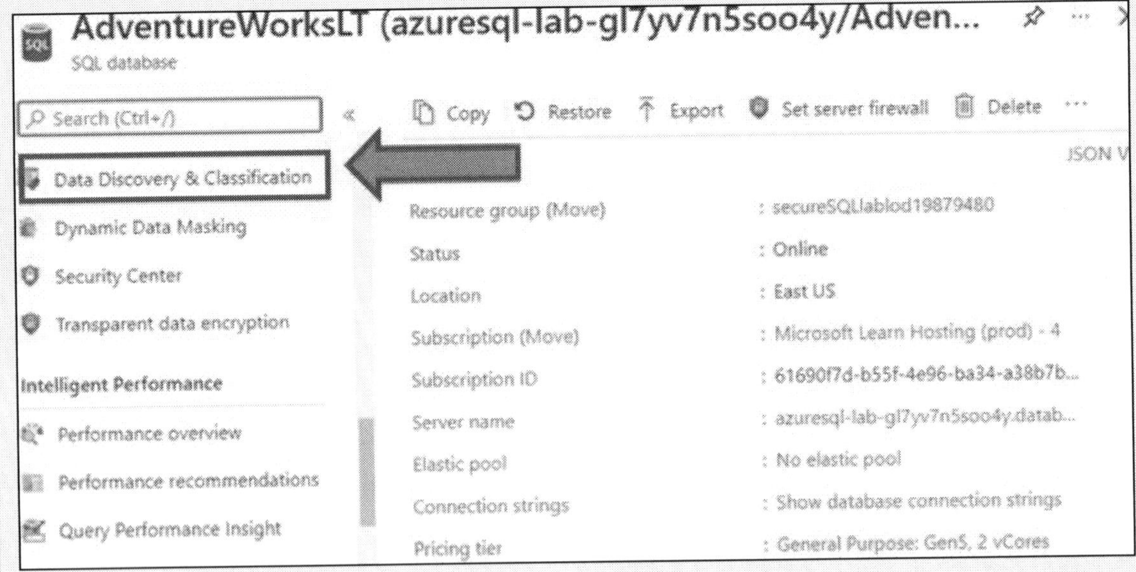

5. On the Data Discovery & Classification screen, you will notice an informational message that says, 'We have found 15 columns with classification recommendations'. Choose that link.

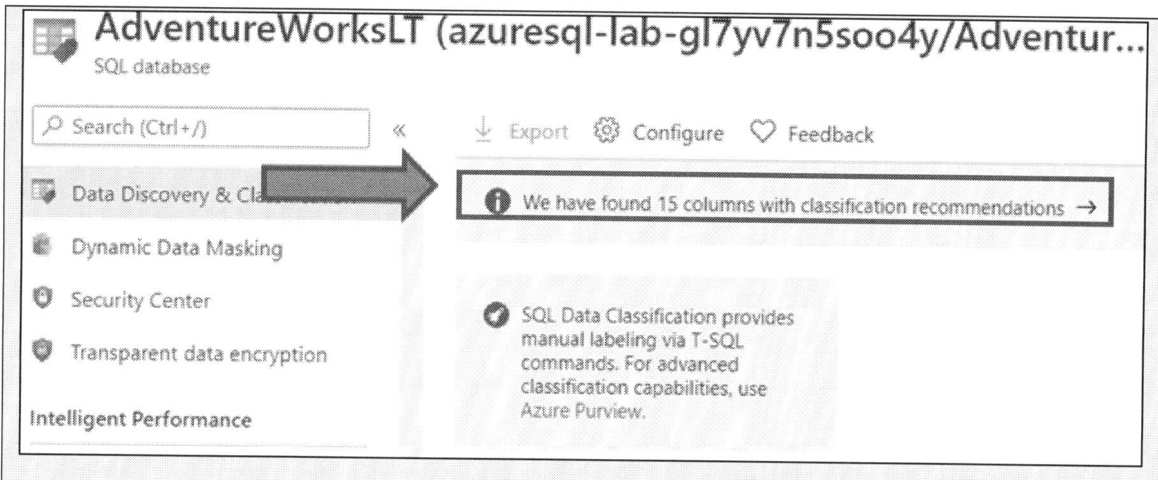

6. On the next 'Data Discovery & Classification screen,' check the box next to 'Select All,' then select **Accept selected recommendations**, and finally **Save** to save the classifications into the database.

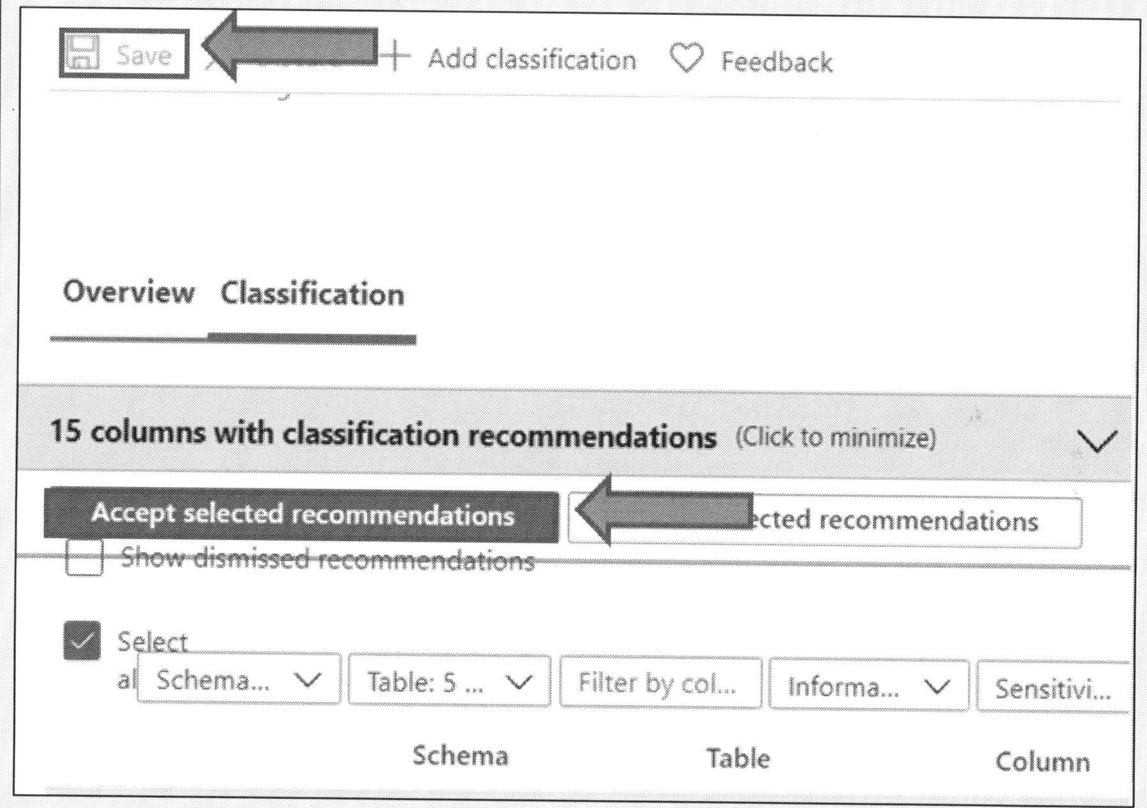

View data classification in SQL Server Management Studio

1. Open SQL Server Management Studio by going to the Start menu and selecting **Microsoft SQL Server Tools 18 > SQL Server Management Studio**. Enter the name of your Azure SQL database server and your credentials.

Select **Connect**.

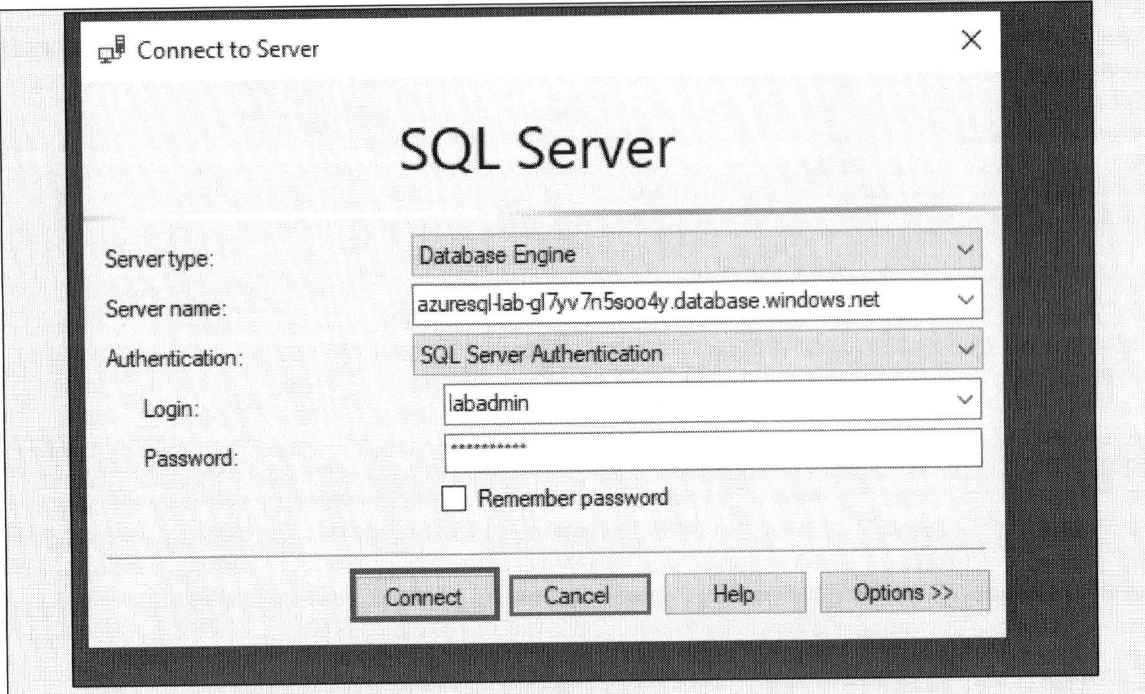

2. You will be requested to create a new firewall rule with your client's IP address. Sign in using your Azure credentials. Then click **OK**.

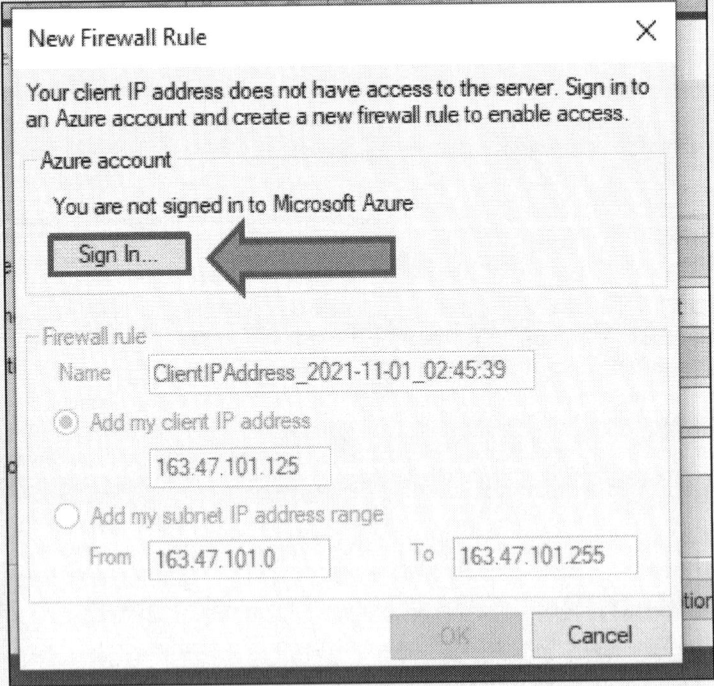

3. Expand the server node and then the Databases node in the Object Explorer.
4. Select **New Query** from the dropdown menu when you right-click on the **AdventureWorksLT** database.

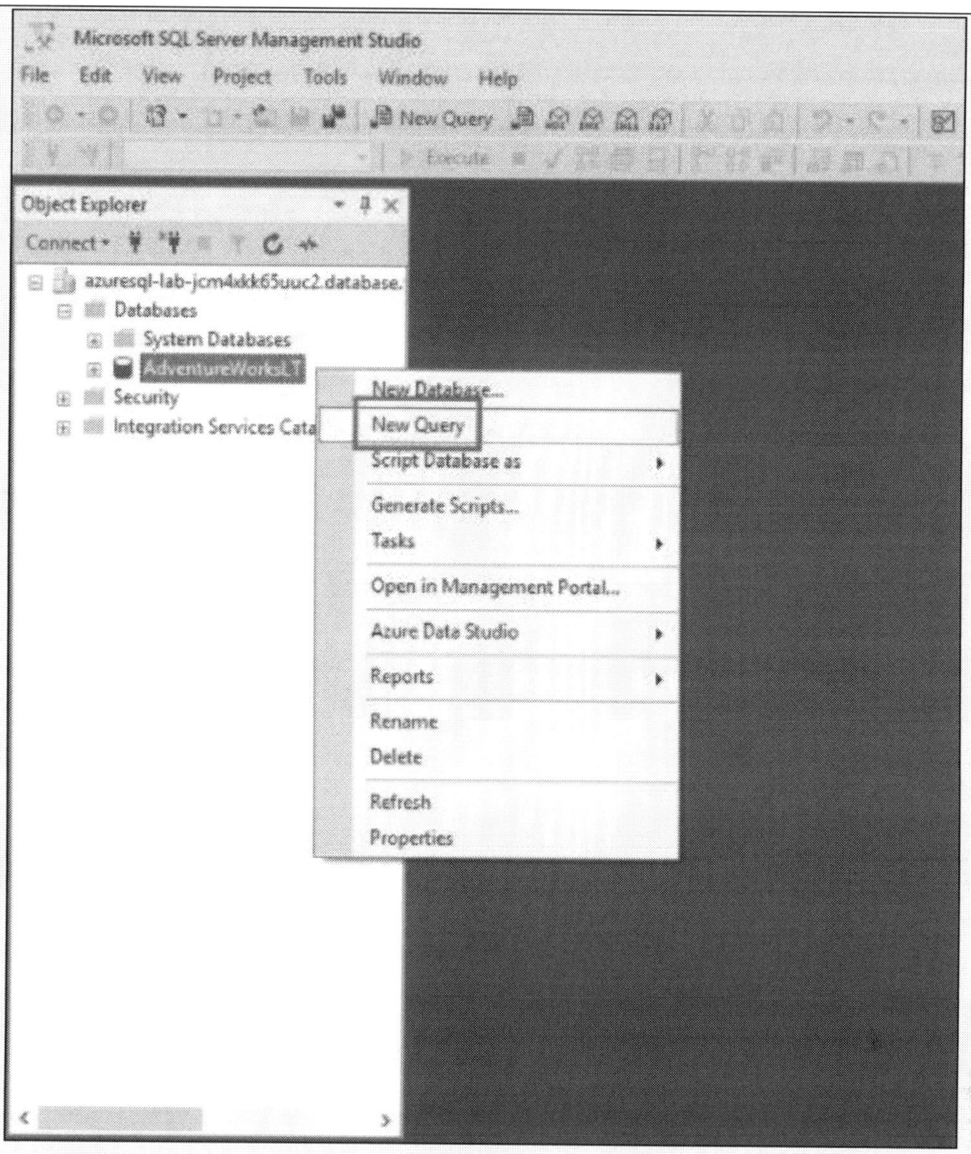

5. In the new query box, run the following query.

As illustrated below, this query will return the results of your classed columns.

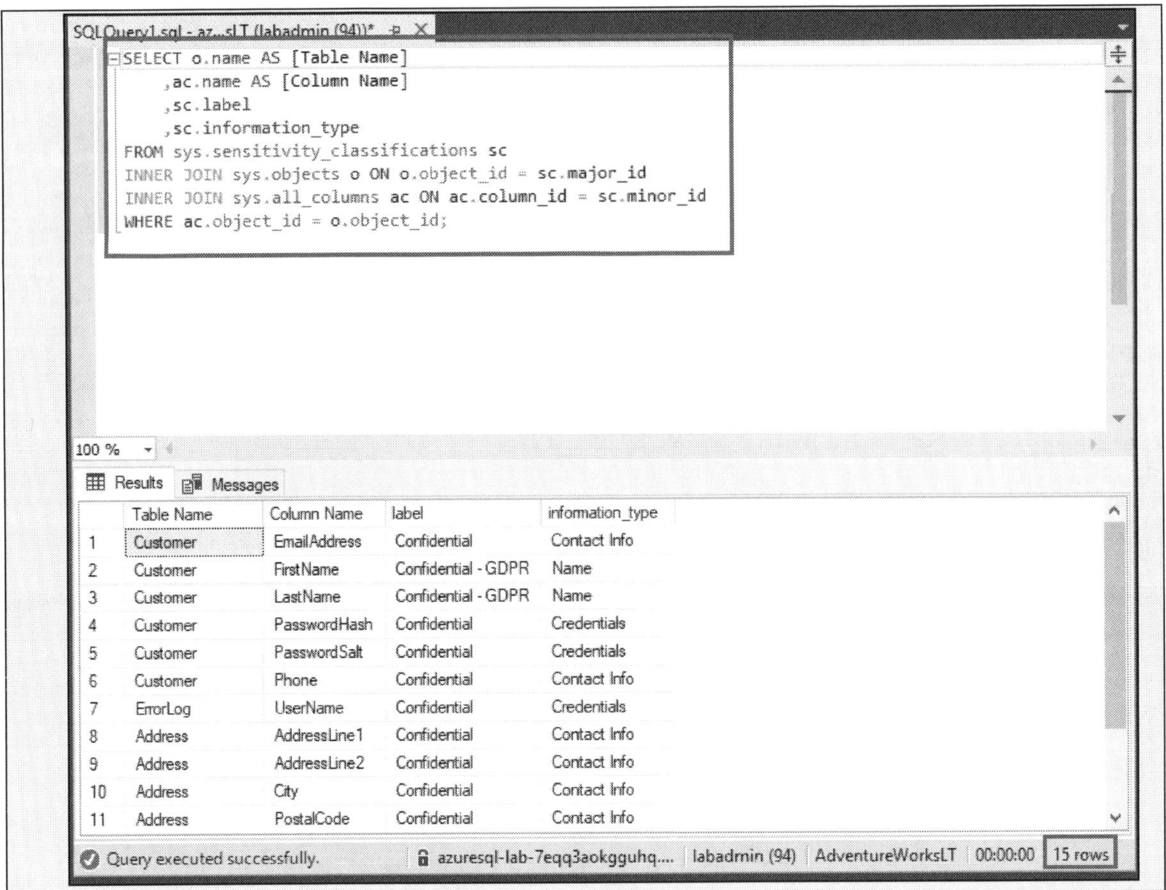

Mind Map

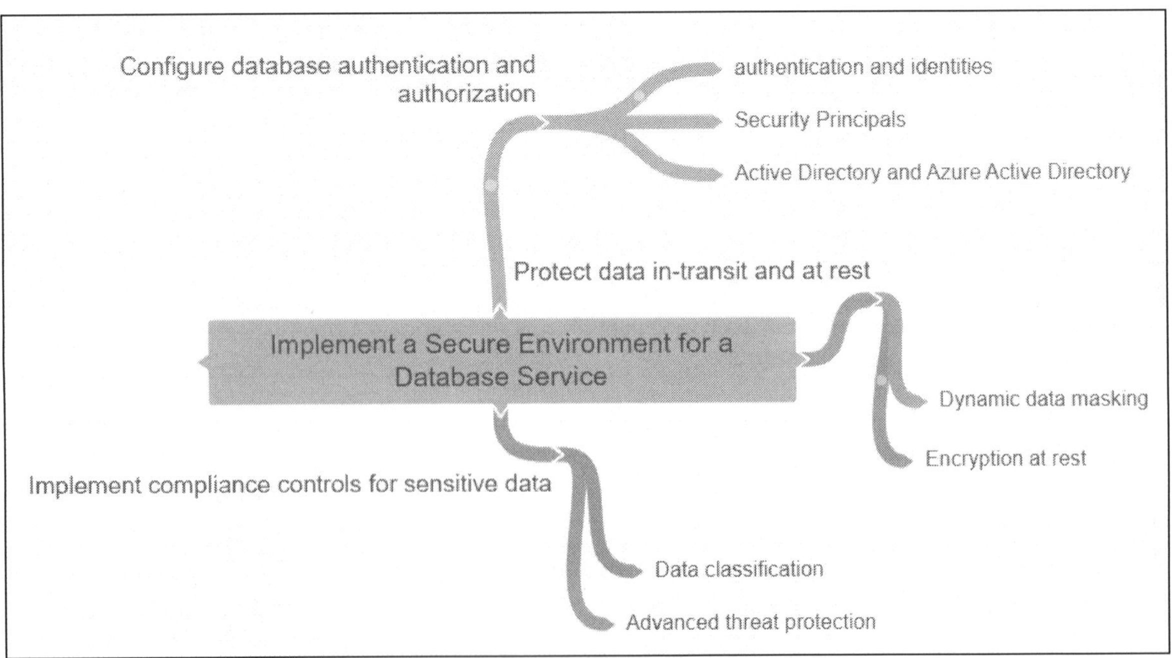

Figure 03- 28: Mind Map

Practice Questions

1. In SQL Server 2019, where the data from data classification is stored?

A. In each object's extended properties

B. In the catalog view sys.sensitivity classifications

C. In the catalog view sys.all columns

2. Which of the following threats is Advanced Threat Protection analyzes?

A. Weak passwords

B. Open Firewall rules

C. SQL Injection

3. Which form of attack is most typically connected with dynamic SQL?

A. SQL Injection

B. Brute Force

C. Data Exfiltration

4. For authorization, Azure Active Directory uses which of the following protocol?

A. Kerberos

B. LDAP

C. OAuth

5. In SQL Server, which database contains information about logins?

A. master

B. model

C. msdb

6. Which of the following role enables users to add new users to a database?

A. db_datareader

B. db_accessadmin

C. db_securityadmin

7. Which permission grants the user the ability to perform any action on a database object?

A. Control

B. Delete

C. View Definition

8. Which database objects are authorized for insert access?

A. Functions

B. Tables

C. Procedures

9. Which feature enables a user to run a stored procedure even if they do not have access to the tables mentioned in the stored procedure?

A. Ownership chaining

B. Principle of least privilege

C. Granular security

10. What type of security object is necessary to enable transparent data encryption?

A. Credential

B. Master Key

C. Login

11. Which feature stops members of the sysadmin role from seeing data values in a table?

A. Always Encrypted

B. Dynamic Data Masking

C. Transparent Data Encryption

12 Which of the following is a valid location for Always Encrypted keys?

A. Azure Key Vault

B. Azure Automation

C. Azure Blob Storage

13. Which feature provides an Azure SQL Database with a private IP address?

A. Network Endpoints

B. Private Link

C. Database Firewall

14. Which Azure service acts as a resource firewall?

A. Network Security Group

B. Virtual Network

C. Virtual Machine

D. Azure Resource Manager

15. In Azure SQL Database, which strategy can be used to implement database firewall rules?

A. Running a PowerShell script

B. Running an Azure CLI script

C. Executing a T-SQL statement

Chapter 04: Monitor and Optimize Operational Resources in SQL Server

Introduction

Having a solid understanding of the baseline workload of your server and database is critical to understanding performance anomalies. The Azure platform lets you use the Azure Monitor to gather baseline performance data about both PaaS and IaaS resources. Within Windows, the Performance Monitor lets you gather detailed performance information about your SQL Server. Azure SQL Database contains additional detailed query performance information through Query Performance Insight.

The Query Store helps you quickly recognize your most expensive queries and find any changes in performance. It offers a powerful and complete data collection by automating the query plan and execution runtime. SQL Server and Azure SQL offer locking and blocking to manage concurrency and ensure data consistency. You can regulate the isolation levels in SQL Server to help manage concurrency. Finally, fragmentation can arise in indexes over time as inserts and deletes happen.

Proper storage configuration is important to the performance of your Azure Virtual Machines. SQL Server must run on premium disk storage or ultra-disk for optimal performance. You can use the Resource Provider for SQL Server to automate the creation of your storage for your SQL Servers on Azure Virtual Machines. You can use Resource Governor to accomplish differing workloads in the same SQL Server.

Describe Performance Monitoring

A major part of the job of a database administrator is proper performance monitoring. This task does not change when moving to a cloud platform. While Azure provides tools for monitoring, you may lack some particular controls around hardware that you would have in an on-premises environment, which makes understanding how to find and resolve performance bottlenecks, while in Azure SQL, much more critical.

Describe Performance Monitoring Tools

Azure provides various methods to monitor the performance of your resources and create a baseline. Each method can be tailored for a specific metric. The metrics that you can monitor will vary depending on the type of Azure resource you are monitoring. For example, Azure SQL Database and SQL Server on an Azure Virtual Machine will have different metrics available in the Azure portal.

The following examples are focused on an Azure Virtual Machine:

When you deploy an Azure Virtual Machine from the Azure Marketplace, an agent is installed in the virtual machine that offers a basic set of operating system metrics offered to you in the Azure portal. This agent supplies metrics to Azure Monitor, a comprehensive platform monitoring solution that gathers and displays a standard set of metrics from Azure resources. In the case of a virtual machine, the default metrics captured are CPU, network utilization, and disk read and write operations. You can capture additional metrics beyond the Azure monitor by allowing Monitoring Insights for your virtual machine, as shown in the following image:

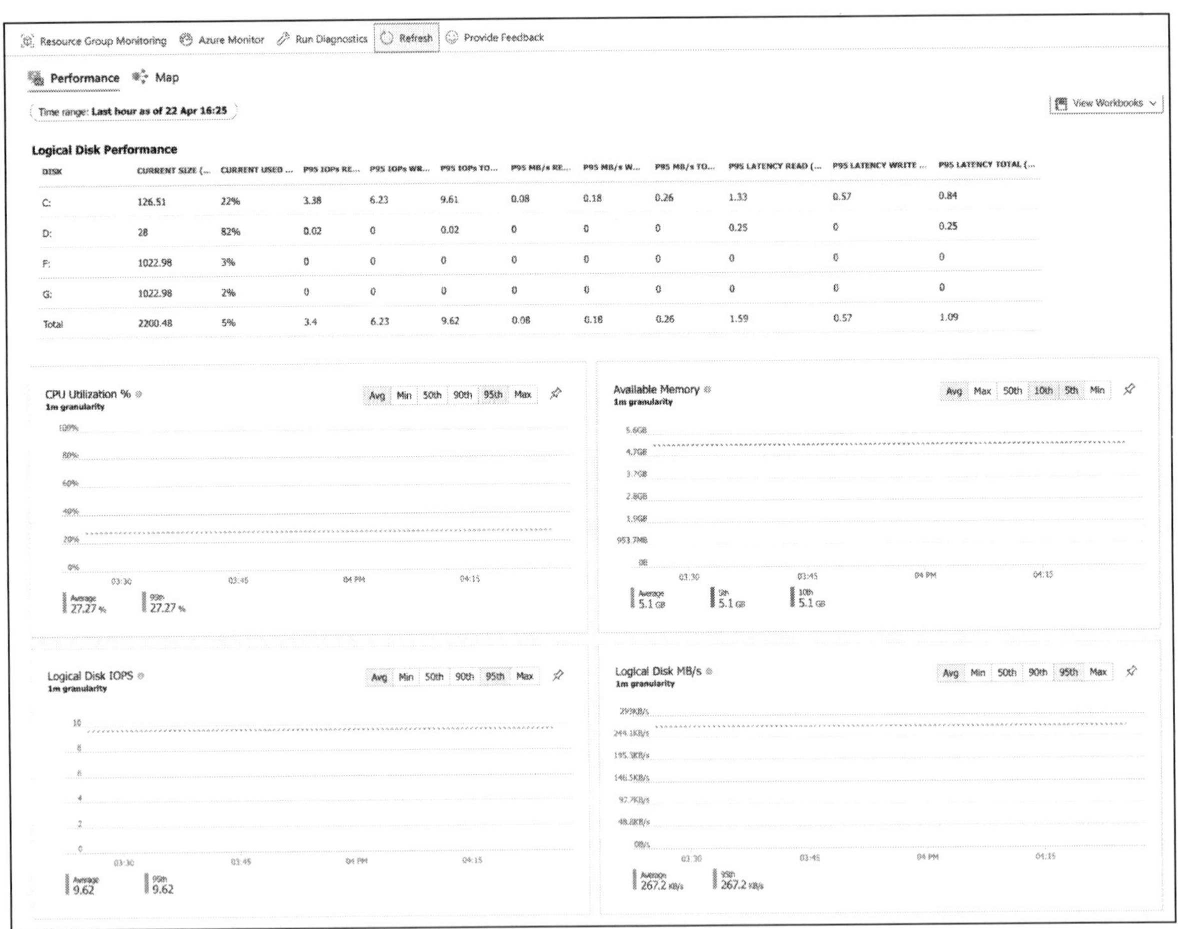

Figure 04-01: Performance Monitoring Tools

These metrics pertain to the operating system, not SQL Server. You will observe that the namespace for each metric is the virtual machine host, not SQL Server.

Azure Monitoring Insights lets you gather additional data points like storage latency, available memory, and disk capacity. These Azure Monitor Insights can be one way of viewing a performance baseline for your Azure Virtual Machine, including I/O performance, memory, and CPU utilization. This data is kept in an Azure Log Analytics workspace. Azure Log Analytics is the main tool in Azure for keeping and querying log files of all types.

If you create a virtual machine with one of the pre-configured SQL Server images in the Azure Marketplace, you can also get the SQL virtual machine resource provider as shown in the following image:

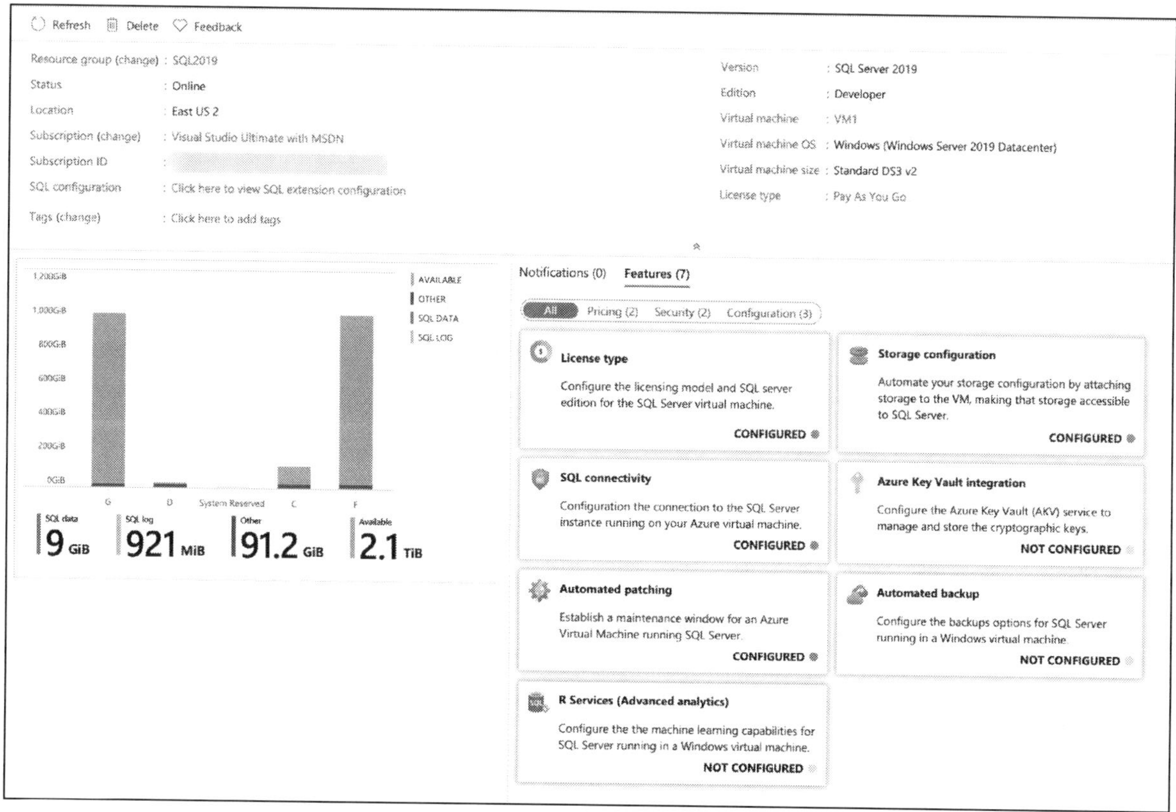

Figure 04-02: Virtual Machine with One of the Pre-configured SQL Server Images

You can launch this screen in the Azure portal by moving to the **Settings** section of the main blade for an Azure Virtual Machine, then clicking on the **SQL Server configuration** option. To get the view from the screen above, click on **Manage SQL Virtual Machine**.

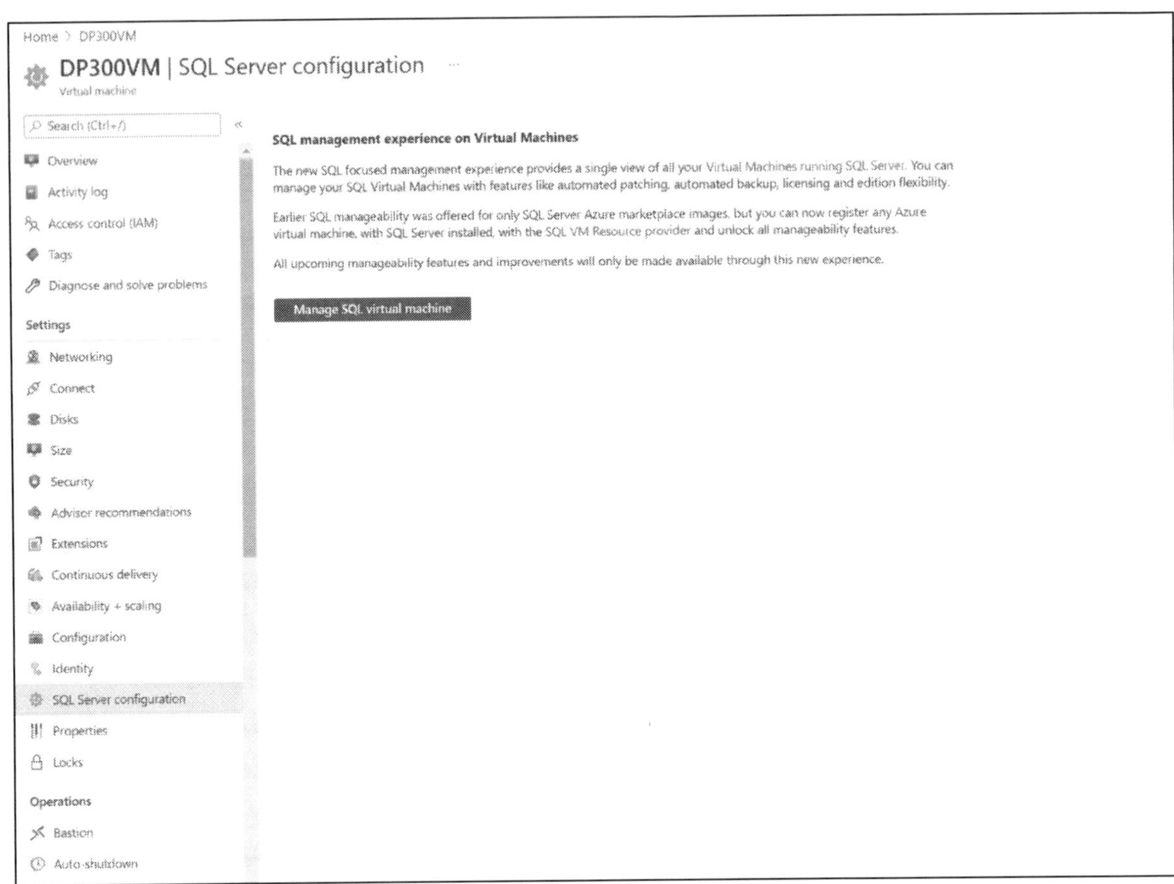

Figure 04-03: SQL Server Configuration

This dashboard lets you see how much space your database files and transaction log file are consuming and lets you manage the features provided by the resource provider like automated patching and storage configuration. You can manually install the SQL Resource Provider for other installations of SQL Server on Azure Virtual Machine if that was not initially defined as part of the virtual machine.

SQL Server on an Azure Virtual Machine

Whether using an on-premises server or an Azure Virtual Machine, the Windows Server platform has a native Performance Monitor tool that lets you easily and routinely monitor performance metrics. Perfmon works with counters for both the operating systems and installed programs. When SQL Server is installed on the operating system, the database engine forms its group of specific counters.

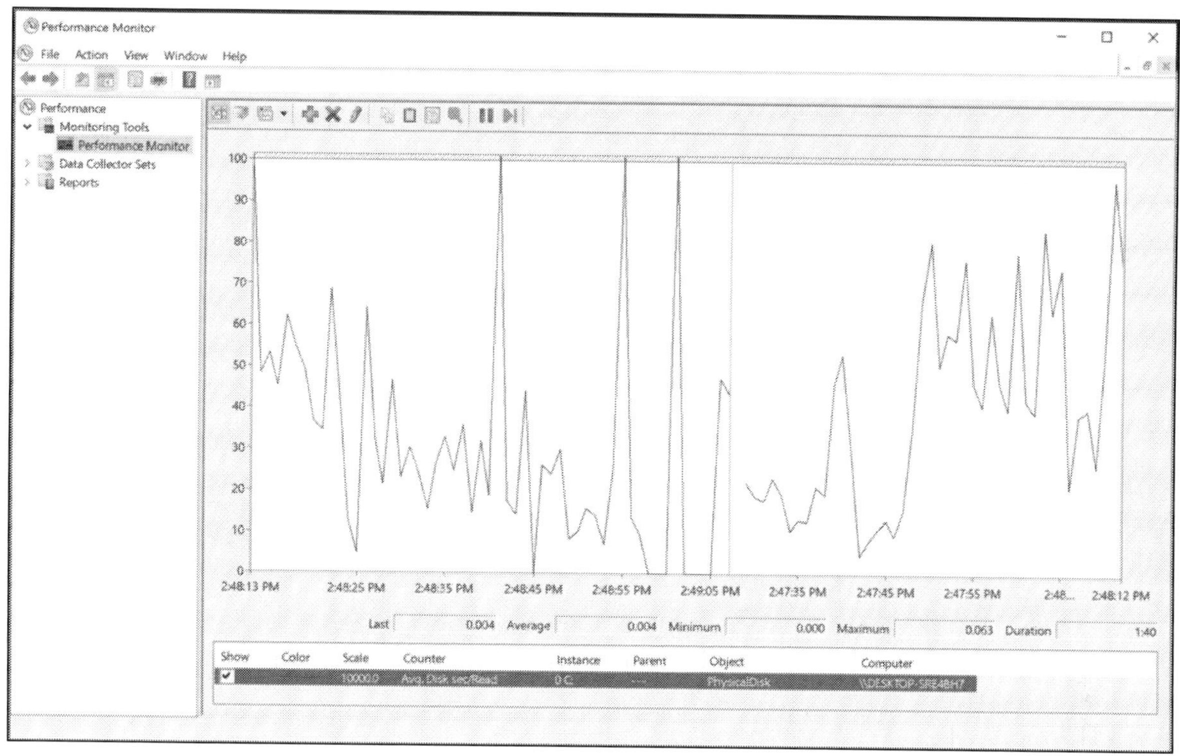

Figure 04-04: Performance Monitor with SQL Server on an Azure Virtual Machine

The above image displays the reporting interface of Performance Monitor, with a single counter being collected. This screen is reached from launching Performance Monitor in Windows and displays a live tracker of a specific performance counter. In many cases, you will detect multiple counters in the same session. Data can be kept locally and analyzed, but in larger environments, you can forward performance monitor results into Azure Monitor, where you can have a single view across many servers.

Describe Critical Performance Metrics

You have observed how to collect data in both Azure Monitor and Windows Performance Monitor. You will now study how to create metrics in Azure Monitor, which lets you trigger alerts or execute automated error responses.

Azure Metrics

The Azure Monitor service contains the ability to track various metrics about the overall health of a given resource. Azure Monitor Metrics is a powerful subsystem that lets you analyze and visualize your performance data and trigger alerts that notify administrators or automated actions that can activate an Azure Automation runbook or a webhook. You also have the option to archive your Azure Metrics data to Azure Storage since operational data is only stored for 93 days. Metrics are collected at regular intervals and are the gateway for alerting processes that help resolve issues rapidly and efficiently.

Metric Alerts

Azure Monitor Alerts can be scoped in three ways. For example, using Azure Virtual Machines as an example, you can specify the scope as:

- A list of virtual machines in one Azure region within a subscription
- All virtual machines (in one Azure region) in one or more resource groups in a subscription
- All virtual machines (in one Azure region) in one subscription

In this manner, you can generate an alert rule based on resources contained within resource groups, as shown:

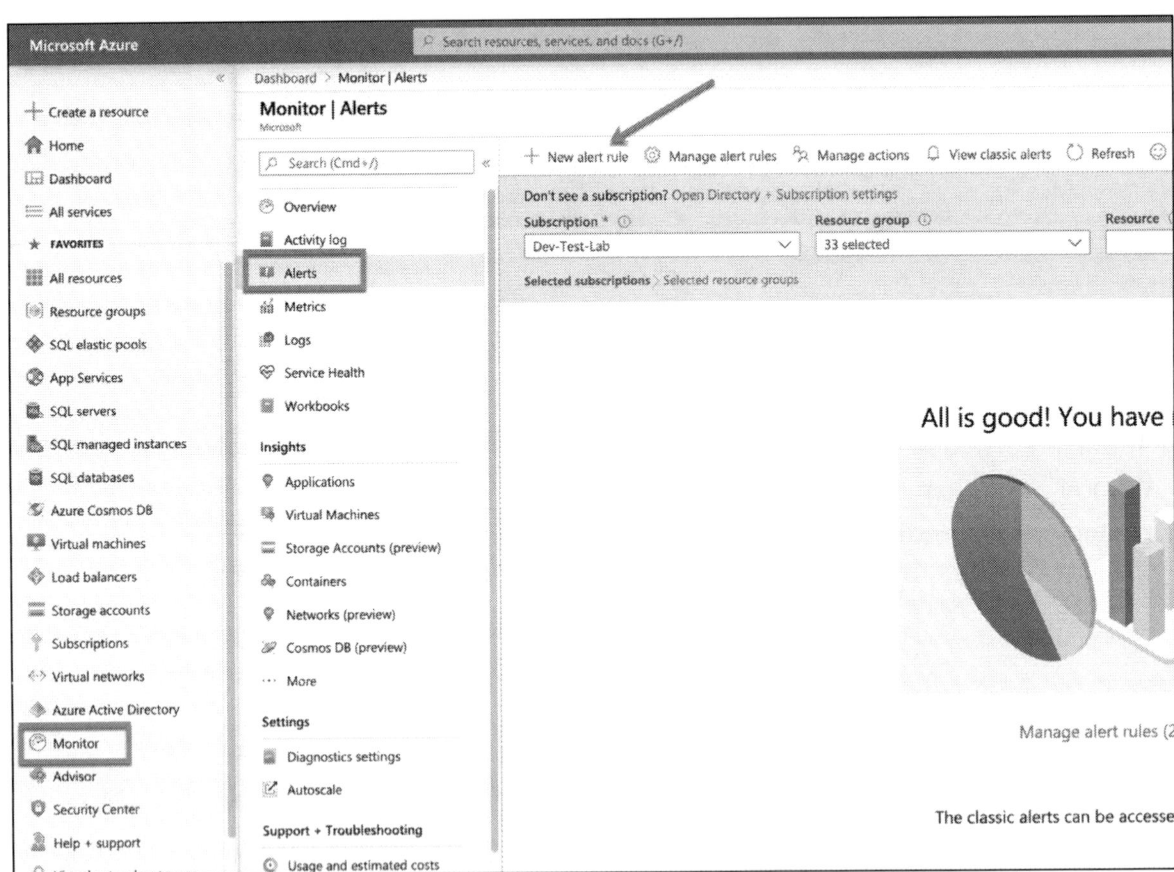

Figure 04-05: Create Metric Alerts

The example shown below reveals a virtual machine named SQL2019, on which you are generating an alert that is at the scope of the individual virtual machine.

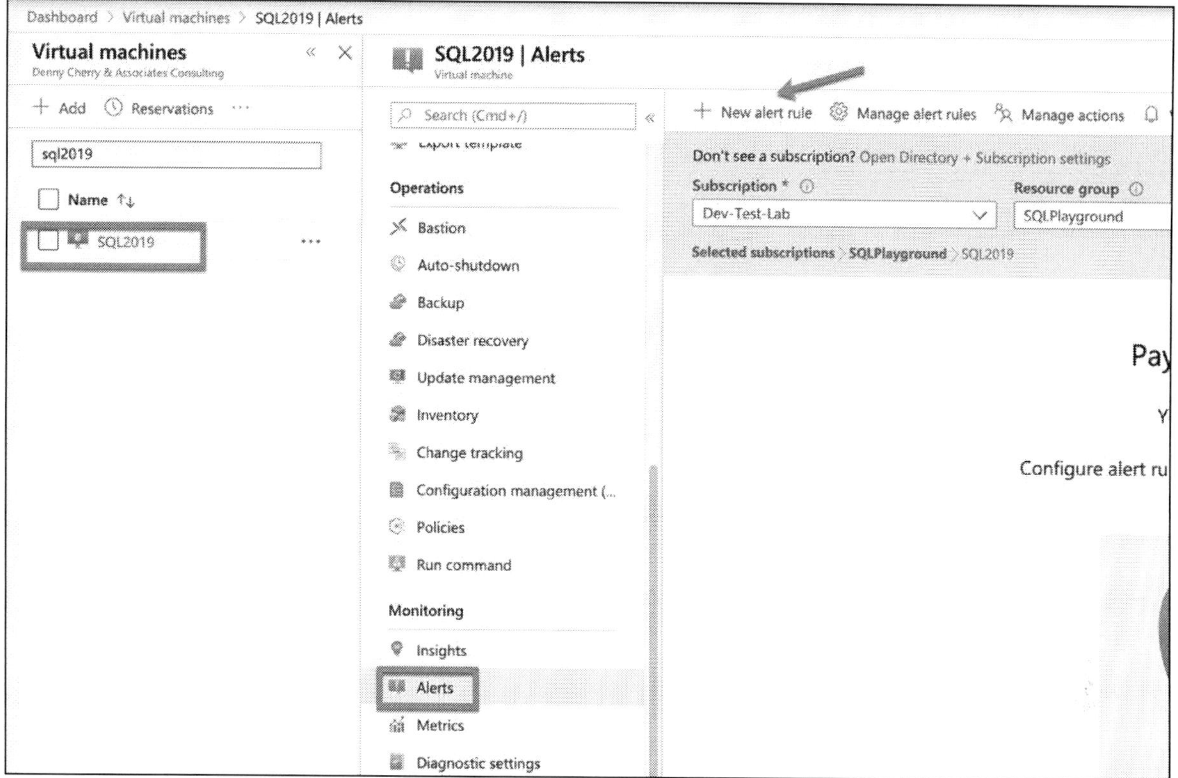

Figure 04-06: New Alert Rule

From the alerts screen, click on New Alert Rule. If an alert is generated from within the scope of a resource, the resource values must be populated for you. You can see that the resource is the SQL2019 virtual machine, the subscription is Dev-Test-Lab, and the resource group in which it resides is SQLPlayground.

Under the Condition section, click **Add**.

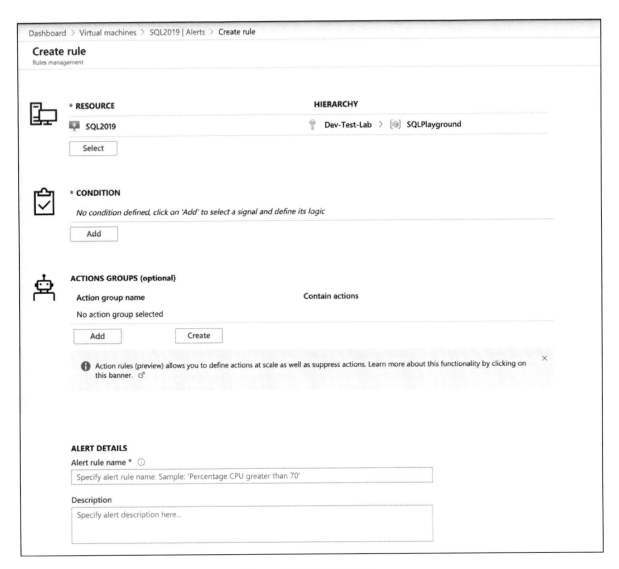

Figure 04-07: Add Rule

Choose the metric that you wish to receive an alert on. The following image displays the metric Percentage CPU, which will be selected later on in the example.

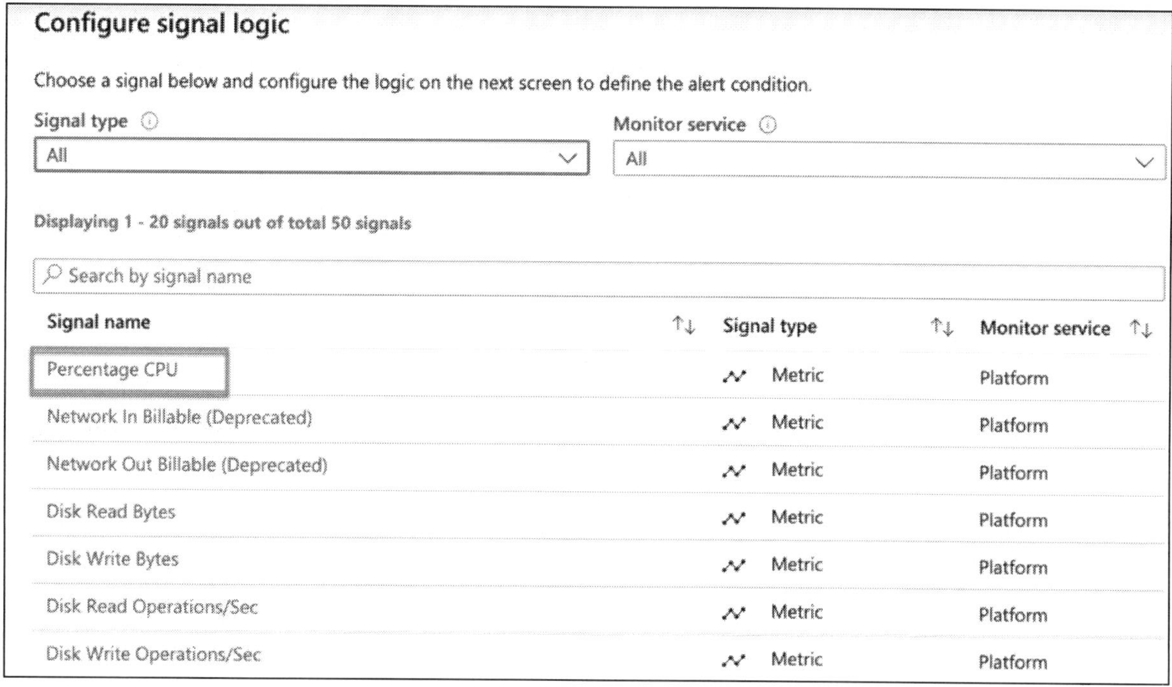

Figure 04-08: Metric Alert

The alerts can be configured in a static manner (for example, raise an alert when CPU goes over 95%) or in a dynamic fashion using Dynamic Thresholds. Dynamic Thresholds study the historical behavior of the metric and generate an alert when the resources are operating abnormally. These Dynamic Thresholds can sense seasonality in your workloads and adjust the alerting accordingly.

If Static alerts are used, you should offer a threshold for the selected metric. This threshold means that if the CPU utilization surpasses 80 percent over a given period, an alert will be fired and react as you have specified. In this example, 80 percent was specified.

Both types of alerts provide Booleans operators such as the 'greater than' or 'less than' operators. There are aggregate measurements to select from Boolean operators, such as average, minimum, maximum, count, average, and total. It is easy to construct a flexible alert with these options available, that will suit just about any enterprise-level alerting.

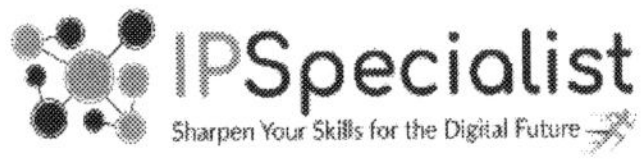

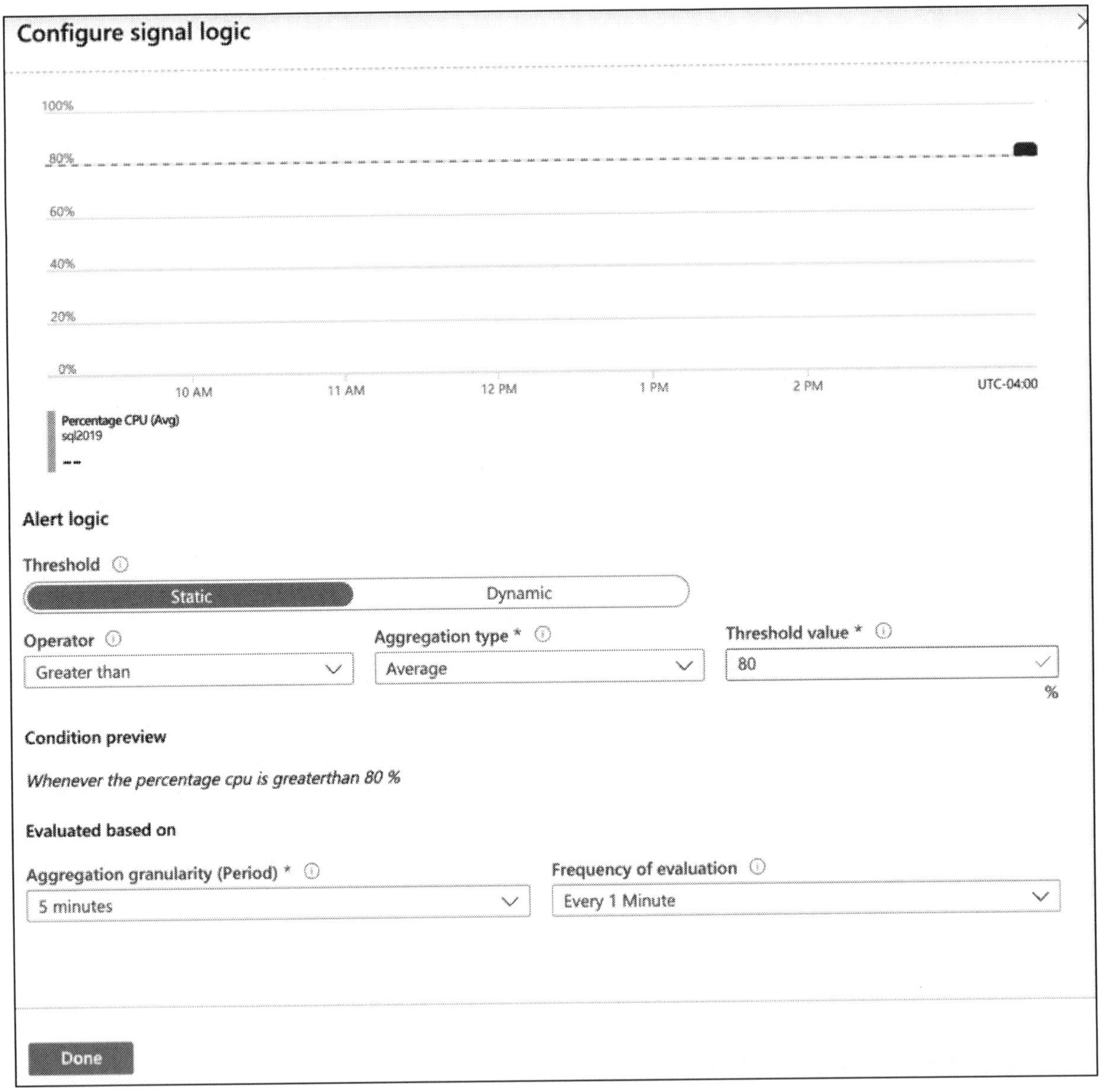

Configure signal logic
100%
80%
60%
40%
20%
0%
10 AM
11 AM
12 PM
1 PM
2 PM
UTC-04:00
Percentage CPU (Avg)
sql2019
Alert logic
Threshold
Static
Dynamic
Operator
Greater than
Aggregation type *
Average
Threshold value *
80
%
Condition preview
Whenever the percentage cpu is greaterthan 80 %
Evaluated based on
Aggregation granularity (Period) *
5 minutes
Frequency of evaluation
Every 1 Minute
Done

Figure 04-09: Alert Logic

After generating the alert, an action group should be configured to notify administrators or launch an automation process.

You can configure the email or SMS details, as can be observed below. You can reach this screen by clicking **Edit Details** under **Configure** or adding a new action, bringing up the configuration screen.

With an action group, there are numerous ways in which you can respond to the alert. The following options are available for defining the action to take:

- Automation Runbook
- Azure Function
- Email Azure Resource Manager Role

- Email/SMS/Push/Voice
- ITSM
- Azure Logic App
- Secure Webhook
- Webhook

There are two categories to these actions—notification, which means notifying an administrator or group of administrators of an event, and automation, which is taking a defined action to respond to a performance condition.

Review Older Performance Data

One of the advantages of utilizing the Azure Monitor is to easily and quickly review past gathered metrics. If you observe a resource, you will note a date-time selector in the upper right-hand corner. Azure Monitor Metrics will be reserved for 93 days, after which they are purged. However, you do have the choice to archive them to Azure Storage.

You can also choose a smaller window of time such as the last 30 minutes, last hour, last 4 hours, or last 12 hours as an example. The flexibility of Azure monitor lets administrators identify issues quickly and diagnose past issues potentially.

SQL Server Metrics that Matter

Microsoft SQL Server is a well-instrumented part of the software that gathers a great deal of performance metadata. The database engine has metrics that can be monitored to help identify and increase performance-related issues. Some operating system metrics are only viewable from within performance monitor, while others can be opened through T-SQL queries, particularly by selecting from the dynamic management views (DMVs). Some metrics are exposed in both locations, so knowing where to find specific metrics is important. An example of an OS metric not available directly through SQL Server is the seconds per disk read and write for the disk volume. Combining these two metrics can help you better understand if a performance issue relates to database structure or a physical storage bottleneck.

Establish Baseline Metrics

Having the data collected over time lets you identify changes from the normal state. Baselines can be as simple as a chart of CPU utilization over time or complex metrics aggregations to provide granular level performance data from specific application calls. The granularity of your baseline will depend on the criticality of the performance of your database and application.

With any type of application workload, it is imperative to establish a working baseline. A baseline will help you recognize if an ongoing issue must be considered within normal parameters or has exceeded given thresholds. Without a baseline, every issue

encountered might be considered normal and therefore not require any additional intervention.

Correlating SQL Server and Operating System Performance

When deploying SQL Server on an Azure virtual machine, it is essential to correlate the performance of SQL Server with the performance of the underlying operating system. If you are using Linux as the operating system, you will have to install InfluxDB, Collectd, and Grafana to capture data similar to Windows Performance Monitor. These services gather data from SQL Server and offer a graphical interface to review the data. Utilizing these tools on Linux or Performance Monitor on Windows can be used in conjunction with looking at SQL Server-specific data such as SQL Server wait for statistics. Using these tools together will let you identify bottlenecks in hardware or code. The following Performance Monitor counters are a sampling of useful Windows metrics and can allow you to capture a good baseline for a SQL Server workload:

Processor(_Total)% Processor Time - This counter measures the CPU utilization of all of the processors on the server. It is a good indication of the overall workload, and when used in conjunction with other counters, this counter can identify problems with query performance.

Paging File(_Total)% Usage - In a properly configured SQL Server, memory would not page to the paging file on disk. However, in some configurations, you may have other services running, which consume system memory and lead to the operating system paging memory to disk resulting in performance degradation.

PhysicalDisk(_Total)\Avg. Disk sec/Read and Avg. Disk sec/Write - This counter offers a good metric for how the storage subsystem is working. Your latency values in most cases must not be above 20 ms, and with Premium Storage, you should see values less than 10 ms.

System\Processor Queue Length - This number specifies the number of threads waiting for the processor's time. If it is higher than zero, it specifies CPU pressure, representing your workload could benefit from more CPUs.

SQLServer: Buffer Manager\Page Life Expectancy - Page life expectancy specifies how long SQL Server expects a page to live in memory. You have to monitor this value over time and calculate sudden drops.

SQLServer: SQL Statistics\Batch Requests/sec - This counter is good for evaluating how consistently busy a SQL Server is over time. There is no right or wrong value, but you can use this value in conjunction with % Processor time to better understand your workload and baselines.

SQLServer: SQL Statistics\SQL Compilations/sec and SQL Re-Compilations/sec - These counters will be updated when SQL Server has to compile or recompile an execution plan for a query because there is no remaining plan in the plan cache, or because a plan was canceled because of a change. Recompiles can indicate T-SQL with recompile query hints or indicate memory pressure on the plan cache caused by many ad-hoc queries or simple memory pressure.

These counters are just a sample of the available performance monitor counters that are available to you. While the above counters provide a good performance baseline, you may need to examine more counters to identify specific performance problems.

Wait Statistics

Wait statistics are available across the Azure SQL platform. SQL Server has a track of these metrics when a thread is being executed and is forced to wait on an unavailable resource. This information is easily identifiable via the dynamic management view (DMV) sys.dm_os_wait_stats. This information is helpful to understand the baseline performance of your database and can classify specific performance issues both with query execution and hardware limitations. Identifying the appropriate wait type and corresponding resolution will be critical for resolving performance issues.

Describe Azure Intelligent Insights

One of the advantages of using the Azure SQL Database is the baseline performance collection built into the Azure platform. Beyond the simple Azure Monitor data collection, Azure SQL Database Intelligent Insights is a part of Azure SQL Database that lets you analyze the performance of your queries. This feature is built using data from the Query Store, which is allowed in your Azure SQL Database at creation time. The Query Store automatically collects query performance metrics, including runtime statistics and execution plan history. It also retains this set of metrics over time (the duration depends on the storage option you choose), letting you investigate performance issues you may have encountered in the past. Azure SQL Database Intelligent Insights uses Query Store data that was exposed to the Azure portal for viewing. You can access this dashboard by clicking Query Performance Insight in the Intelligent Performance section of the main blade of your Azure SQL Database.

To enable Intelligent Insights, you have to add diagnostic settings to your database.

Home > | Diagnostic settings > Diagnostics settings

Diagnostics settings

Save Discard Delete Provide feedback

A diagnostic setting specifies a list of categories of platform logs and/or metrics that you want to collect from a resource, and one or more destinations that you would stream them to. Normal usage charges for the destination will occur. Learn more about the different log categories and contents of those logs

Diagnostic settings name *

Category details

log

- [x] SQLInsights
- [x] AutomaticTuning
- [x] QueryStoreRuntimeStatistics
- [x] QueryStoreWaitStatistics
- [x] Errors
- [x] DatabaseWaitStatistics
- [x] Timeouts
- [x] Blocks
- [x] Deadlocks

metric

- [x] Basic
- [x] InstanceAndAppAdvanced
- [x] WorkloadManagement

Destination details

- [x] Send to Log Analytics

Subscription: Visual Studio Ultimate with MSDN

Log Analytics workspace: DefaultWorkspace-424d0f78-5980-4d31-98ec-...

- [ ] Archive to a storage account
- [ ] Stream to an event hub

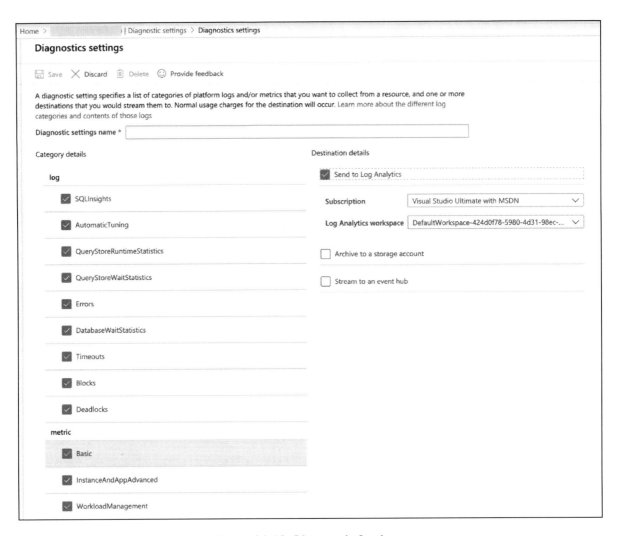

Figure 04-10: Diagnostic Settings

Intelligent Insights Storage Options

You have three options for where to store the Intelligent Insights data, and the data is stored in a different format in each one. If you choose Azure storage, your data is stored in extended events format with an XEL extension. Those files can only be viewed on the Azure SQL server where they were created. If you choose an Event Hub, the data is stored in Avro format, a binary JSON format used for event reporting. Finally, if you use Log Analytics as a destination, your data is stored in Log Analytics and can be queried using the Kusto Query Language.

SQL Insights in Azure Log Analytics

The other benefit of storing your data in Azure Log Analytics is the Azure SQL Analytics dashboard.

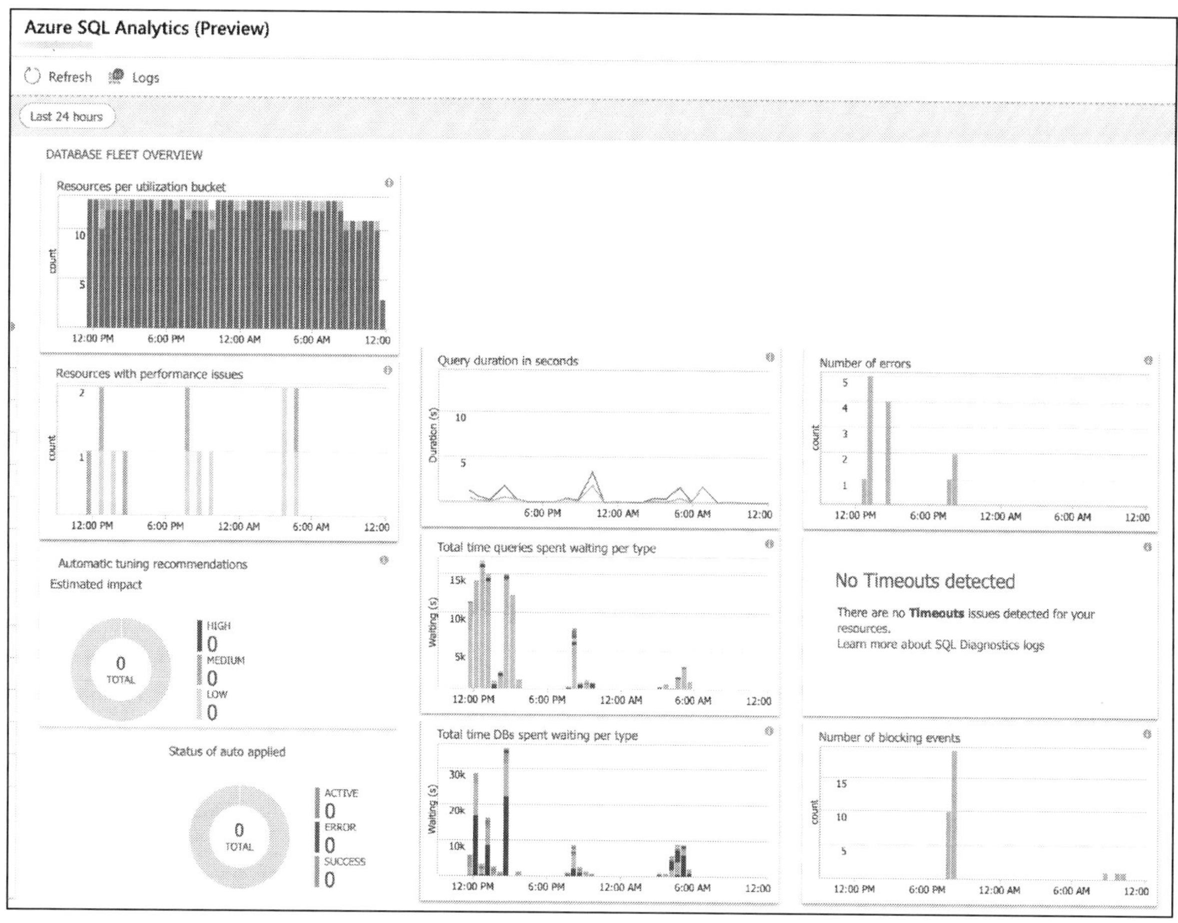

Figure 04-11: SQL Insights in Azure Log Analytics

The dashboard can be reached by navigating to your Log Analytics workspace and then clicking Workspace summary in the general section of the Overview blade. You can then click through to Azure SQL Analytics. Azure SQL Analytics is a cloud monitoring solution that brings together performance metrics at scale and across multiple subscriptions in a single view. In addition to visualization and data collection, it has built-in intelligence for troubleshooting activities. It also allows for custom monitoring alerts and rules that enable flexibility to identify issues and resolve them quickly. It supports Azure SQL Database, single instance, elastic pools, and Azure SQL Managed Instances.

Identify problematic queries

Identifying which queries are consuming the most resources is the first step in any database performance tuning endeavor. In older versions of SQL Server, this required extensive tracing and a series of complex SQL scripts, making data gathering cumbersome.

Azure SQL Database offers Query Performance Insight, which allows the administrator to quickly identity expensive queries. In the Intelligent Performance section, you can navigate to Query Performance Insight in the main blade for your Azure SQL Database.

When you launch Query Performance Insight, you will discover three buttons to allow you to filter for long-running queries, top resource-consuming queries, or a custom filter. The default value is Resource Consuming Queries. This tab will show you the top five queries sorted by the particular resource that you select on the left. In this case, it was sorted by CPU. You also have the additional options of sorting by Data IO and Log IO metrics.

You can drill into individual queries by clicking on the row within the lower grid. Each row will be identified with a unique color that correlates to the color within the bar graph above it.

Switching to Long Running Queries, you can see a similar layout as before. In this case, the metrics are limited to the top five queries sorted by duration from the previous 24 hours and are a sum aggregation. As with top resource-consuming queries, you can examine specific queries by clicking on the row within the grid below the graph.

Switching to the custom tab, there is a little more flexibility compared to the other two options.

Within this tab, you can further define how you wish to examine performance data. It offers you several drop-down menus that will drive the visual representation of the data. The key metrics are CPU, Log IO, Data IO, and memory. These metrics are the aspects of database performance, the upper limits determined by the service tier, and compute resources of your Azure SQL Database.

If you drill into an individual query, you will be able to see the query ID and the query itself, as well as the query aggregation type and associated period. Furthermore, the query ID also correlates to the query ID located within the Query Store. Metrics gleaned from Query Performance Insights can be easily located within the Query Store for deeper analysis or possibly problem resolution if needed.

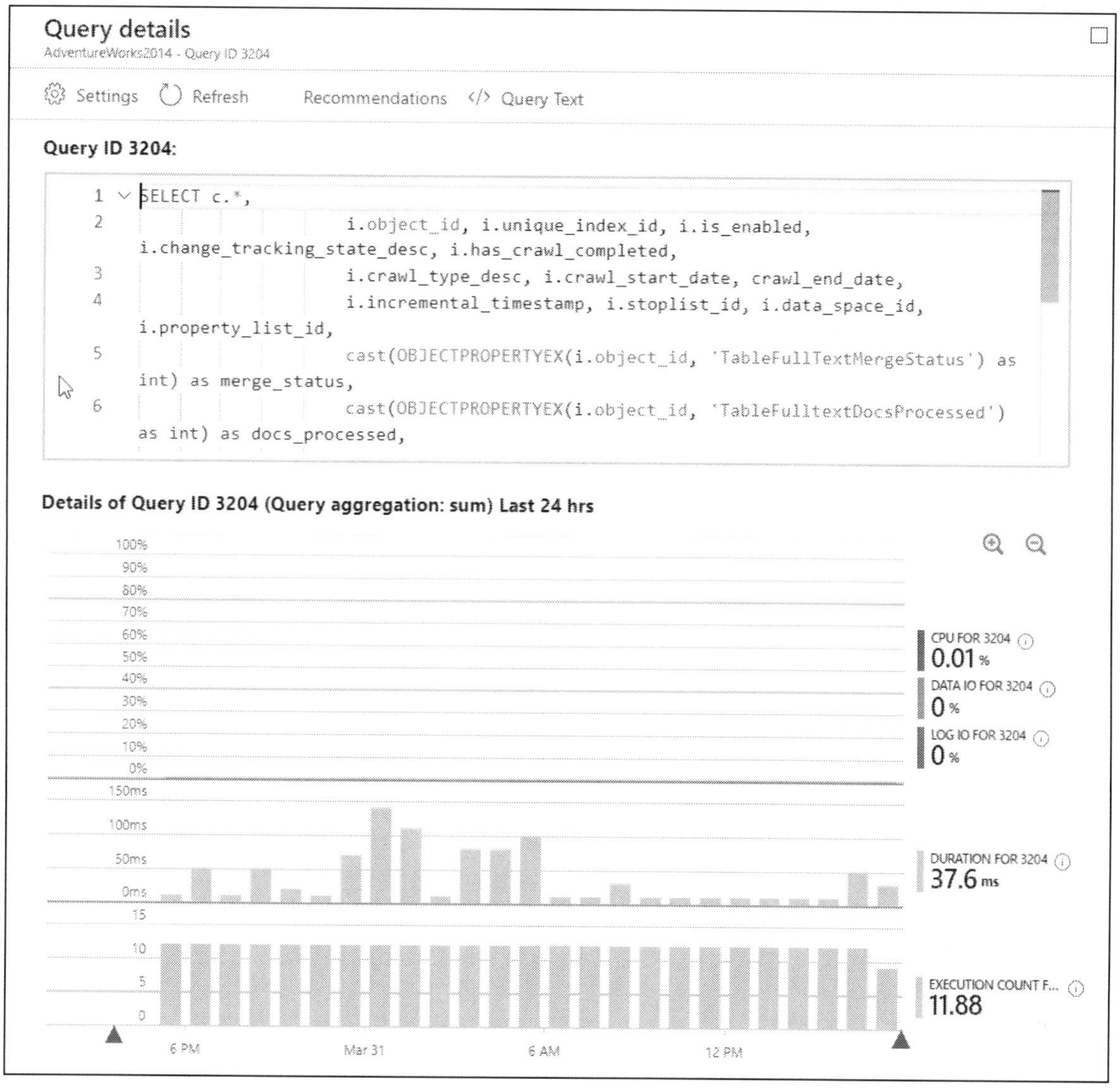

Query details
AdventureWorks2014 - Query ID 3204

Settings Refresh Recommendations </> Query Text

Query ID 3204:

```
SELECT c.*,
                    i.object_id, i.unique_index_id, i.is_enabled,
i.change_tracking_state_desc, i.has_crawl_completed,
                    i.crawl_type_desc, i.crawl_start_date, crawl_end_date,
                    i.incremental_timestamp, i.stoplist_id, i.data_space_id,
i.property_list_id,
                    cast(OBJECTPROPERTYEX(i.object_id, 'TableFullTextMergeStatus') as
int) as merge_status,
                    cast(OBJECTPROPERTYEX(i.object_id, 'TableFulltextDocsProcessed')
as int) as docs_processed,
```

Details of Query ID 3204 (Query aggregation: sum) Last 24 hrs

100%
90%
80%
70%
60%
50%
40%
30%
20%
10%
0%
150ms
100ms
50ms
0ms
15
10
5
0
6 PM
Mar 31
6 AM
12 PM
CPU FOR 3204
0.01 %
DATA IO FOR 3204
0 %
LOG IO FOR 3204
0 %
DURATION FOR 3204
37.6 ms
EXECUTION COUNT F...
11.88

Figure 04-12: Query Performance Insights

While Query Performance Insight does not show the query's execution plan, you can quickly identify that query and use the information to extract the plan from the Query Store in your database.

Explore Causes of Performance Issues

A common scenario that the DBA faces is when a user notifies the DBA about problems with the performance of a report or operation. Typically, this notification happens well after the problem occurs. In the past, it was difficult or impossible to retrieve data related to query execution because the data was stored in memory caches and was very transient.

To gather this data with SQL Server, you needed to have a third-party tool or build a custom monitoring solution. This tool would actively collect and maintain performance information. Third-party or custom solutions are no longer necessary. In SQL Server 2016, Microsoft introduced the Query Store, which acts as a data recorder for the database engine. The Query Store is focused on query performance and changes in execution plans.

Describe SQL Server Query Store

The Query Store can be thought of as a flight data recorder for SQL Server. It collects and permanently stores and aggregates performance information. In older versions of SQL Server, this information was either transient or not collected. The Query Store captures run time information such as duration, logical I/O, CPU usage, and other metrics for query executions in a specific user database. It also captures the estimated execution plan for each execution, allowing you to detect an execution plan that has regressed in performance quickly. The catalog views that make up the Query Store are stored in the user database and are shown in this image:

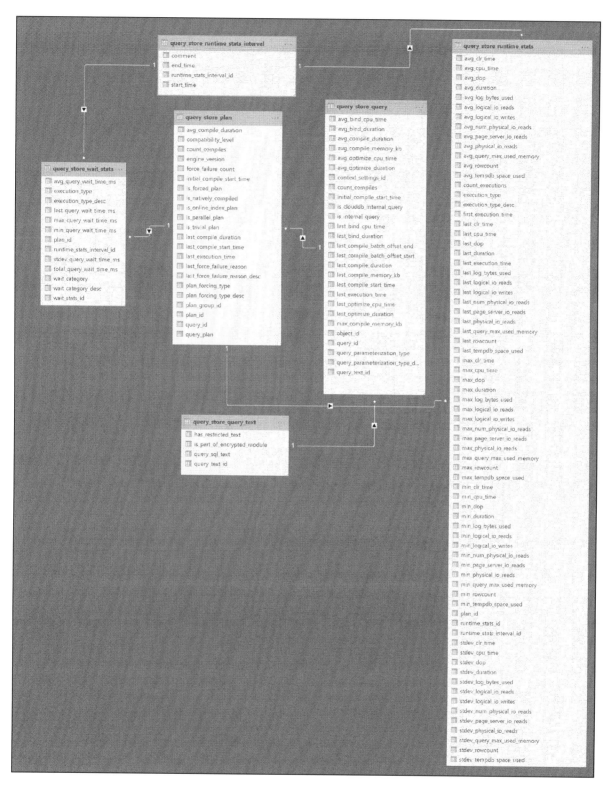

Figure 04-13: SQL Server Query Store

There are two types of data being captured. One is the data about the query itself, it includes number of executions, the plan is used in the execution, the query text, and the other is the performance information, which collects runtime statistics for each

execution of the query. Each query execution has a large number of runtime metrics captured for each execution of the query.

Query Store Reports

SQL Server Management Studio offers several out-of-the-box reports that allow you to quickly gather information from the Query Store. The current list of built-in reports is shown in the image below. You can reach this menu by using SQL Server Management Studio, clicking on a user database in Object Explorer, and expanding the Query Store folder.

Query Store
Regressed Queries
Overall Resource Consumption
Top Resource Consuming Queries
Queries With Forced Plans
Queries With High Variation
Query Wait Statistics
Tracked Queries

Figure 04-14: Query Store Reports

Most of these reports can be filtered by the following execution metrics:

- CPU Milliseconds
- Duration
- Logical Reads
- Logical Writes
- Physical Reads
- CLR Time
- Degree of Parallelism
- Memory Consumption
- Row Count
- Log Memory Used
- TempDB Memory Use

- Wait Time

In addition to these metrics, you can choose a statistic to refine your data further.

- Average
- Maximum
- Minimum
- Standard Deviation
- Total

You can further filter based on a time interval, which allows you to retroactively troubleshoot a performance problem that may have happened several days ago. The built-in reports include:

Regressed Queries - This report shows any queries where execution metrics have degraded in the period of interest (last hour, day, and week). This report is useful for evaluating the impact of minor or major changes in server configuration or database schema.

Overall Resource Consumption - This report allows you to observe the most impactful queries in your database quickly. This report allows clicking through to the "Top Resource Consuming Queries" report, which enables you to gather execution plan information.

Top Resource Consuming Queries - This report shows the query and query plan for the most impactful queries in a database for some time. This data allows you to observe if a query has multiple execution plans and whether or not those plans have high variability in performance.

Queries with Forced Plans — This report contains information about plan forcing and any plan that is forcing failures (a situation where a forced execution plan was not honored).

Queries with High Variation - This report showcases queries that have a high degree of variance between executions and can be sorted by any of the above execution metrics.

Query Wait Statistics - This report allows you to see waits statistics aggregated and drill-through to get further information on queries that spent the most time waiting. Note that this wait information is aggregated and not as detailed as you might observe in the *sys.dm_os_wait_stats* DMV.

Tracked Queries - This report is filtered by query_Id and allows you to view the performance of a specific query and its execution plans. You can manually enter a query_id or add queries from the regressed or top resource-consuming query reports. The query_id can be captured from the catalog *view sys.query_store_query*.

The performance overhead of the Query Store

Collecting data in any system has an execution cost of CPU cycles, memory, and disk utilization known as observer overhead. The Query Store is designed to minimize the impact of its data collection. Data for the Query Store is written to memory for each new query and execution of an existing query. If this information were written to disk for each execution, the performance overhead would be significant, so SQL Server uses a setting called **DATA_FLUSH_INTERVAL_SECONDS** to control the frequency of flushing the Query Store data to disk. The data is flushed every 15 minutes by default, but this value is a user-configurable setting per database. This process of collecting the query and runtime information and writing it to disk is shown in the image below:

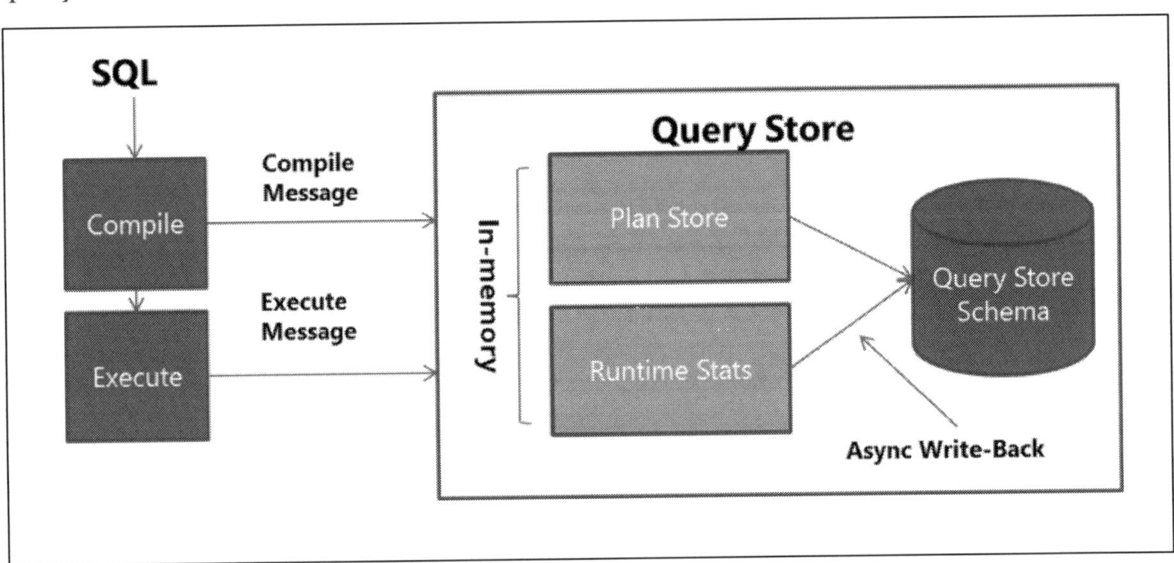

Figure 04-15: Performance Overhead of the Query Store

The other important setting to note in the Query Store options is **Max Size (MB)**, which sets the amount of storage for the data collected. The default value is 100 MB and is commonly increased to around 1-2 GB depending on the volume of queries executed against a database. Some workloads with a high number of unique ad-hoc queries, characteristic of applications written in Entity Framework, may see high data volume. If the size of the data stored on disk exceeds the **Max Size (MB),** the Query Store will go into read-only mode until more space is added or cleanup happens. The default value for time-based cleanup is 30 days; however, the **size-based cleanup mode** option will remove older queries as the Query Store approaches its max size. You will want to balance the amount of data you keep and the amount of space consumed on a disk.

The other setting you should note is **Query_Capture_Mode** which defaults to Auto. This value means queries with little compilation time and duration are ignored, along with infrequent queries. This default was changed in SQL Server 2019 and Azure SQL. The older default was All, which captures all queries executed. There are also options of

none (collect no queries) and Custom, which was introduced in SQL Server 2019, which allows you to use metrics such as execution count, compile CPU time, and execution time to limit which queries are captured. This setting is useful for a database where most of the queries are unique, as these unique queries can cause the Query Store to grow rapidly in size.

Plan Forcing in the Query Store

Another benefit of the Query Store is the ability to force a given execution plan for a query. Since the query can store multiple execution plans for a given query, you can have the database engine force a known good plan for a given query. Plan forcing in the Query Store also drives the automatic tuning feature introduced in SQL Server 2017, which uses the last known good execution plan for a given query after a performance regression occurs. Plan forcing should be used for queries that have suddenly changed execution plans and experienced significant execution time regression. Plan forcing offers quick mitigation for a performance problem, but you should always investigate what caused the performance regression and look to resolve the cause of the execution plan variability. Those fixes could be adding an index or looking to rewrite part of a query.

Describe Blocking and Locking in SQL Server

One feature of relational databases is locking, which is essential to maintain the ACID model's atomicity, consistency, and isolation properties. All RDBMSs will block actions that would violate the consistency and isolation of rights to a database. When programming in SQL, programmers are accountable for starting and ending transactions at the correct point to ensure the logical consistency of their data. In turn, the database engine provides locking mechanisms that also protect the logical consistency of the tables affected by those queries. These actions are a foundational part of the relational model.

On SQL Server, blocking occurs when one process holds a lock on a specific resource (row, page, table, database), and a second process attempts to acquire a lock with an incompatible lock type on the same resource. Typically, locks are held for a very short period, and when the process holding the lock releases it, the blocked process can then acquire the lock and complete its transaction.

SQL Server locks the smallest amount of data needed to complete the transaction successfully. This behavior allows maximum concurrency. For example, if SQL Server is locking a single row, all other rows in the table are available for other processes to use so that work can go on. However, each lock requires memory resources, so it is not cost-effective for one process to have thousands of individual locks on a single table. SQL Server tries to balance concurrency with cost. One of the techniques used is called lock

escalation. If SQL Server needs to lock more than 5000 rows on a single object in a single statement, it will escalate the multiple row locks to a single table lock.

Locking is normal behavior and happens many times during a normal day. Locking only becomes a problem when it causes blocking that is not quickly resolved. There are two types of performance issues that can be caused by blocking:

- A process holds locks on a set of resources for an extended period before releasing them. These locks cause other processes to block, which can degrade query performance and concurrency
- A process gets locked on a set of resources and never releases them. This problem requires administrator intervention to resolve.

Another blocking scenario is deadlocking, which occurs when one transaction has a lock on a resource, and another transaction has a lock on a second resource. Each transaction then attempts to lock on the resource that is currently locked by the other transaction. Theoretically, this scenario would lead to an infinite wait, as neither transaction could complete. However, the SQL Server engine has a mechanism for detecting these scenarios. It will kill one of the transactions to alleviate the deadlock, based on which transaction has performed the least amount of work that would need to be rolled back. The transaction that is killed is known as the deadlock victim. Deadlocks are recorded in the *system_health* extended event session, which is enabled by default.

It is important to understand the concept of a transaction. By default, SQL Server and Azure SQL Database are in auto-commit mode, which means the changes made by the statement below would automatically be written to the database's transaction log upon completion.

```
INSERT INTO DemoTable (A) VALUES (1);
```

To allow developers to have more granular control over their application code, SQL Server also allows you to control your transactions explicitly. The query below would take a lock on a row in the DemoTable table that would not be released until a subsequent command to commit the transaction was added.

```
BEGIN TRANSACTION
INSERT INTO DemoTable (A) VALUES (1);
```

The proper way to write the above query is as follows:

```
BEGIN TRANSACTION
INSERT INTO DemoTable (A) VALUES (1);
```

COMMIT TRANSACTION

The COMMIT TRANSACTION command explicitly commits a record of the changes to the transaction log. The changed data will eventually make its way into the data file asynchronously. These transactions represent a unit of work to the database engine. If the developer forgets to issue the COMMIT TRANSACTION command, the transaction will stay open, and the locks will not be released. This is one of the main reasons for long-running transactions. They are not long-running, but they have just not been handled properly.

The other mechanism the database engine uses to help the concurrency of the database is row versioning. When a row versioning isolation level is enabled in the database, the engine maintains versions of each modified row in TempDB. This is typically used in mixed-use workloads to prevent reading queries from blocking queries writing to the database.

Isolation Levels

SQL Server offers several isolation levels to allow you to define the level of consistency and correctness you need to be guaranteed for your data. Isolation levels let you find a balance between concurrency and consistency. The isolation level does not affect the locks taken to prevent data modification; a transaction will always get an exclusive lock on the modifying data. However, your isolation level can affect the length of time that your locks are held. Lower isolation levels increase the ability of multiple user processes to access data simultaneously; however, it also increases the data consistency risks that can occur. The isolation levels in SQL Server are as follows:

Read Uncommitted - This is the lowest isolation level available. Dirty reads are allowed, which means one transaction may see changes made by another transaction that has not yet been committed.

Read Committed - This level allows a transaction to read data previously read but not modified by another transaction without waiting for the first transaction to finish. This level also releases read locks as soon as the select operation is performed. This is the default SQL Server level.

Repeatable Read - This level has read and write locks attained on selected data till the end of the transaction.

Serializable - This is the highest level of isolation where transactions are completely isolated. Read and write locks are acquired on selected data and not released until the end of the transaction.

SQL Server also includes two isolation levels that include row-versioning.

Read Committed Snapshot - In this level, read operations take no row or page locks. The engine presents each operation with a transactionally consistent snapshot of the data as it existed at the start of the query. This level is typically used when users run frequent reporting queries against an OLTP database to prevent the read operations from blocking the write operations.

Snapshot - This level provides transaction-level read consistency through row versioning. This level is vulnerable to update conflicts. If a transaction running under this level reads data modified by another transaction, an update by the snapshot transaction will be terminated and rollback. This is not an issue with reading committed snapshot isolation.

There is no way to set a global isolation level for all queries running in a database or for all queries run by a particular user. It is a session-level setting.

Monitoring for Blocking Problems

Identifying blocking problems can be troublesome as they can be sporadic. A better way to monitor blocking problems is to do so on an ongoing basis using the Extended Events engine. A DMV called sys.dm_tran_locks can be joined with sys.dm_exec_requests to provide further information on the locks that each session holds.

Blocking problems typically fall into two categories:

- **Poor Transactional Design**: As shown above, a transaction that has no COMMIT TRANSACTION will never end. While that is a simple example, doing too much work in a single transaction or having a distributed transaction that uses a linked server connection can lead to unpredictable performance.
- **Long-running Transactions**: They are caused by schema design. Frequently this can be an update on a column with a missing index or poorly designed update query.

> EXAM TIP: Monitoring for locking-related performance problems allows you to identify performance degradation related to locking quickly.

Describe Data File Fragmentation

Fragmentation on storage happens when a group of data that must be stored together is fragmented into many pieces that are not contiguous on disk. Historically, non-contiguous data was problematic on systems with hard disk drives, which performed much better when executing sequential reads and writes (reading or writing a set of data in contiguous sectors on the disk). Modern solid-state devices (SSDs) reduce the impact

of fragmentation, at least at the operating system level, but they can still be impactful within the data files used by SQL Server.

Fragmentation occurs when indexes (both clustered and nonclustered) have pages in which the logical ordering of the index, which is based on the data value of the index key, does not match the physical ordering of the pages. Fragmentation occurs when the engine modifies pages when performing insert or update operations. If there is no longer space on an existing page for the new value, the page will split. Split pages can degrade performance, particularly for scan operations, because additional I/O is required to retrieve the data. Fragmentation can be reduced by using the fill factor setting when creating an index. A low fill factor value leaves free space on the pages for inserted and updated rows.

Configure SQL Server resources for Optimal Performance

One of the challenges administrators face in the cloud is balancing costs and performance. Both Azure and SQL Server provide many options for configuration to meet the needs of small and large workloads. Choosing the right storage and sizing your virtual machine are critical steps in meeting the performance needs of your applications and balancing cloud costs. Proper configuration of SQL Server resources like TempDB, which can easily become a performance bottleneck, and Resource Governor, which can be used to manage multi-tenant workloads, are also important for properly maintaining your server performance.

Azure Storage for SQL Server Virtual Machines

Storage performance is a critical component of an I/O heavy application like a database engine. Azure offers a broad array of storage options and can even build your storage solution to meet your workload requirements.

Azure Storage is a highly scalable, secure storage platform that offers a range of solutions to meet the needs of many applications. This course focuses on databases; thus, you will learn about the aspects of blob storage that apply to SQL Server workloads, which are disk, file, and blob storage. Note that all the above types of storage support encryption at rest with either a Microsoft managed or a user-defined encryption key.

Blob Storage - Blob storage is object-based storage and includes cold, hot, and archive storage tiers. In a SQL Server environment, blob storage will typically be used for database backups, using SQL Server's backup to URL functionality.

File Storage - File storage is effectively a file share that can be mounted inside a virtual machine without setting up any hardware. SQL Server can use File storage as a storage target for a failover cluster instance.

Disk Storage - Azure-managed disks provide block storage that is offered to a virtual machine. These disks are managed just like a physical disk in an on-premises server, except that they are virtualized. There are several performance tiers within managed disks, depending on your workload. This type of storage is the most commonly used type for SQL Server data and transaction log files.

Azure Managed Disks

Azure-managed disks are block-level storage volumes that are presented to Azure Virtual Machines. Block-level storage refers to raw volumes of storage created and treated as an individual hard drive. These block devices can be managed within the operating system, and the storage tier is not aware of the disk's contents. An alternate to block storage is object storage, where files and metadata are stored on the underlying storage system. Azure Blob Storage is an example of an object storage model. While object storage works well for many modern development solutions, most workloads running in virtual machines will use block storage.

The configuration of your managed disks is important to the performance of your SQL Server workloads. Suppose you are moving from an on-premises environment. In that case, it is important to capture metrics like **average disk seconds/read** and **average disk seconds/write** from Performance Monitor, as explained earlier. Another metric to capture is the I/O Operations per Second, which can be captured using the **SQL Server: Resource Pool Stats Disk Read and Write IO/sec** counters, which show how many IOPs SQL Servers are serving at its peak. It is important to understand your workloads. You will want to design your storage and virtual machine to meet the needs of those workload peaks without incurring significant latency. Note that each Azure Virtual Machine type has a limit on IOPs.

Azure managed disks come in four types:

Ultra Disk - Ultra disks support high-IO workloads for mission-critical databases with low latency.

Premium SSD - Premium SSD disks are high-throughput and low latency and can meet the needs of most database workloads running in the cloud.

Standard SSD - Standard SSDs are designed for lightly used dev/test workloads or web servers that do a small IO and require predictable latency.

Standard HDD - Standard HDDs are suitable for backups and file storage that is infrequently accessed.

Typically, production SQL Server workloads will use either Ultra disk or Premium SSD or a combination of the two. Ultra disks are typically used where you are looking for submillisecond latency in response time. Premium SSDs typically have single-digit millisecond response time but have lower costs and more flexibility in design. Premium SSDs also support read-caching, which can benefit read-heavy database workloads by reducing the number of trips to the disk. The read cache is stored on the local SSD (the D:\ drive on Windows or /dev/sdb1/ on Linux), which can help reduce the number of round trips to the actual disk.

Striping Disks for Maximum Throughput

One of the ways to get higher performance and volume out of Azure disks is to stripe your data across multiple disks. This technique does not apply to Ultra disk, as you can scale IOPs, throughput, and maximum size independently on a single disk. However, with Premium SSDs, it can be beneficial to scale both IOPs and storage volume. To stripe disks in Windows, you add the number of disks you would like to the VM and create a pool using Storage Spaces. Do not configure any redundancy for your pool (which would limit your performance). The redundancy is provided by the Azure framework, which keeps three copies of all disks in synchronous replication to protect against a disk failure. When you create a pool, your pool has the sum of the IOPs and the sum of the volume of all the disks in your pool. For example, if you used 10 P30 disks for each TB and had 5000 IOPs per disk, you would have a 10-TB volume with 50,000 IOPs available.

SQL Server Storage Configuration Best Practices

There are a few recommendations for best practices for SQL Server on Azure VMs and their storage configuration:

- Make a separate volume for data and transaction log files
- Allow read caching on the data file volume
- Do not allow any caching on the log file volume
- Plan for an additional 20% of IOPs and throughput when building your storage for your VM to handle workload peaks
- Use the D: drive (the locally attached SSD) for TempDB files because TempDB is restored upon server restart, so there is no risk of data loss
- Allow instant file initialization to reduce the impact of file-growth activities
- Move trace file and error log directories to data disks
- For workloads needing storage latency under one millisecond, consider using Ultra disk over Premium SSD

Azure Virtual Machine Resource Provider

One way to reduce the complexity of building storage for your SQL Server on an Azure Virtual Machine is to use the SQL Server templates in the Azure Marketplace, which allows you to configure your storage as part of your deployment, as shown below. You can configure the IOPs as needed, and the template will perform the work of creating your storage spaces pools within Windows.

Configure storage

Storage optimization: General | Transactional processing | Data warehousing

Data storage

These disks will be attached to your virtual machine as data disks and will be stored in storage as page blobs.

Data drive location *: F:\data
Disk type *: Premium SSD

Disk type	Size (GiB)	Max IOPS	Max throughput	Number of disks
1024 GiB, Premium SSD (...	1024	5000	200	1

1024 GiB, 5000 IOPS, 200 MB/s

Log storage

Transaction logs are a critical component of the database as they record all transactions and database modifications made by each transaction.

Shared drive space *: Use a separate drive for lo...
Log drive location *: G:\log
Disk type *: Premium SSD

Disk type	Size (GiB)	Max IOPS	Max throughput	Number of disks
1024 GiB, Premium SSD (...	1024	5000	200	1

1024 GiB, 5000 IOPS, 200 MB/s

TempDb storage

The tempDb system database is a global resource that is available to all users connected to the instance of SQL Server. It is used to store temporary user objects and internal objects created by the database engine.

Shared drive space *: Use local SSD drive
TempDb drive location *: D:\tempDb

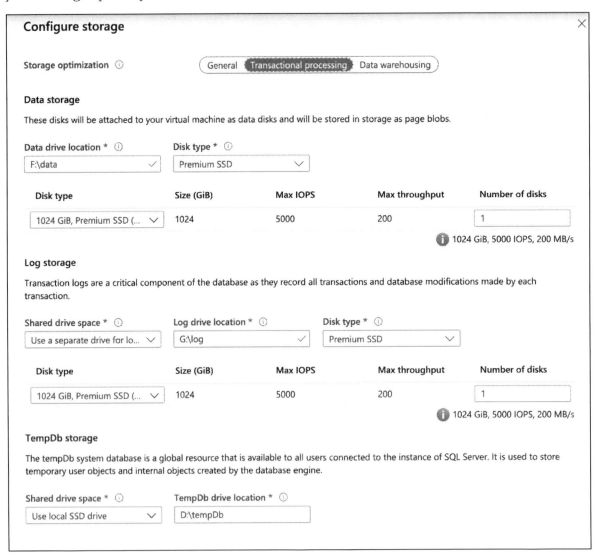

Figure 04-16: Azure Virtual Machine Resource Provider

This resource provider also supports adding TempDB to the local SSD drive and produces a scheduled task to create the folder on startup.

Describe Virtual Machine Resizing

There are many size options for Azure Virtual Machines. For SQL Server workloads, the main characteristics are the amount of memory available and the number of input and output operations (IOPs) the virtual machine can perform.

Using Constrained Cores

Typically, SQL Server is licensed by the core, and Azure will use a fixed CPU core to memory ratio. However, you may have workloads that require large amounts of memory but do not need the default amount of allocated CPUs to get that amount of memory. In these cases, it may be useful to use Azure's constrained cores.

You can reduce software licensing costs with constrained cores while getting the full amount of memory, storage, and I/O bandwidth. This is good for database workloads that are not CPU-intensive and can benefit from high memory, storage, and I/O bandwidth while using a constrained vCPU count.

Using General-purpose Virtual Machines

Most SQL Server production workloads will run on the general-purpose or memory-optimized families of Azure Virtual Machines. Larger workloads requiring more memory and CPU resources will land in memory-optimized virtual machines, but many production applications can run comfortably on general-purpose virtual machines.

Resizing Virtual Machines

Azure supports resizing your virtual machine. This operation does require a restart; however, restarting a virtual machine is typically a fast process. In some cases, depending on what virtual machine type you are switching to and from, you may need to deallocate your virtual machine and then resize. This operation does extend the duration of the outage but should not take more than a few minutes.

Optimize Database Storage

To optimize database storage, you should consider proportional fill and tempdb configuration.

What is Proportional Fill

If you are inserting one gigabyte of data into a SQL Server database with two data files, you would expect the size of each of your data files to increase by roughly 512 megabytes. However, this equal growth is not necessarily the case, as SQL Server will insert data into data files in different volumes based on the size of the data file. If your data files were two gigabytes in size in the above example, you would expect an even distribution of data. However, if one of your data files was 10 gigabytes, and the other was one gigabyte, roughly 900 MB would go into the ten-gigabyte file and 100 MB into the one-gigabyte file. While this behavior occurs in any database, with the write-intensive nature of tempdb, an uneven write pattern could cause a bottleneck in the largest file, as more of the writes would happen there.

Tempdb Configuration in SQL Server

SQL Server 2016 changed this behavior by detecting the number of CPUs available at setup, configuring the correct number of files, up to 8, and sorting the data files evenly. Additionally, the behavior of trace flags 1117 and 1118 are built into the database engine, but only for tempdb. For tempdb heavy workloads, there may be benefits to increasing the number of tempdb files beyond eight to the number of CPUs on your machine.

> **Note:** SQL Server uses tempdb for much more than storing user-defined temporary tables.

Work tables used to store intermediate query results, sorting operations, and the version store for row versioning are among just a few of the uses for tempdb. Due to this utilization, it is important to place tempdb on the lowest latency storage possible and properly configure its data files.

Another common best-practice recommendation was to create multiple tempdb data files. Before SQL Server 2016, tempdb defaulted to having only one data file. This single file meant that there could be contention for multiple processes trying to access system pages of the tempdb database. One common solution to this contention problem was to enable trace flag 1118, which changed the way extents were allocated. As SQL Server uses a proportional fill algorithm for databases with multiple data files, it was also important to ensure that those files were of the same size and grew at the same rate. To support this, many DBAs used trace flag 1117, which forced all databases with multiple data files to grow them at the same rate.

Control SQL Server Resources

While some SQL Servers or Azure SQL managed instances support only one applications' database (this configuration is commonly seen in mission-critical applications), many other servers support databases for multiple applications with different performance requirements and different peak workload cycles. Balancing these differing requirements can be challenging to the administrator. One of the ways to balance server resources is to use Resource Governor, which was introduced to SQL Server 2008.

Resource Governor is a feature in SQL Server and Azure SQL managed instance that allows you to granularly control how much CPU, physical IO, and memory resources can be used by an incoming request from an application. Resource Governor is enabled at the instance level and allows you to define how connections are treated using a classifier function, which subdivides sessions into workload groups. Each workload group is configured to use a specific pool of system resources.

Resource Pools

A resource pool represents physical resources available on the server. SQL Server always has two pools, default and internal, even when Resource Governor is not enabled. The internal pool is used by critical SQL Server functions and cannot be restricted. The default pool, and any resource pools you explicitly define, can be configured with limits on the resources it can use. You can specify the following limits for each non-internal pool:

- Min/Max CPU percent
- Cap of CPU percent
- Min/Max memory percent
- NUMA node affinity
- Min/Max IOPs per volume

Except for min/max CPU percent, all other resource pool settings represent hard limits and cannot be exceeded. Min/Max CPU percentage will only apply when there is CPU contention. For example, if you have a maximum of 70%, the workload may use up to 100% available CPU cycles. If other workloads are running, the workload will be restricted to 70%.

Workload Group

A workload group is a container for session requests based on their classification by the classifier function. There are two built-in groups, default and internal, like resource pools, and each workload group can only belong to one resource pool. However, a resource pool can host multiple workload groups. All connections would go into the default workload group unless passed into another user-defined group by the classifier function.

> EXAM TIP: By default, the default workload group uses the resources assigned to the default resource pool.

Classifier Function

The classifier function is run when a connection is established to the SQL Server instance and classifies each connection into a given workload group. If the function gives back a NULL, default, or the name of the non-existent workload group, the session is moved into the default workload group. Since the classifier is run at every connection, it must be tested for efficiency.

Resource Governor Use Cases

Resource Governor is used primarily in multi-tenant scenarios where a group of databases shares a single SQL Server instance. Performance needs to be kept consistent for all server users. You can also use Resource Governor to limit the resources used by maintenance operations like consistency checks and index rebuilds, to try to guarantee sufficient resources for user queries during your maintenance windows.

Configure Databases for Performance

In recent versions of SQL Server, Microsoft has moved more configuration options to the database level, giving you more granularity in how your databases behave. Along with those options, they have introduced features as part of intelligent query processing, which allows the query optimizer to make better choices. The Azure Database offerings for PostgreSQL and MySQL also offer intelligent options to help you better understand the performance of your databases.

Describe Database Scoped Configuration Options

SQL Server has always had configuration options that were set at the database level. For example, the recovery model has always been a database setting, but as more complex features have been introduced to the database, more options have been added. Many of these options are tied to the databases' compatibility level, a database-level configuration option. Database configuration options break down into two groups, with a minor difference:

- Options configured by the ALTER DATABASE SCOPED CONFIGURATION syntax in T-SQL
- Options configured by the ALTER DATABASE syntax in T-SQL

There is no significance to the different ways to set these options. Options that are set using ALTER DATABASE include:

- **Database Recovery Model** - Whether the database is in the full or simple recovery model
- **Automatic Tuning Option** - Whether to enable the force last good plan
- **Auto Create and Update Statistics** - Allows the database to create and update statistics and allows for the option of asynchronous statistics updates
- **Query Store Options** - The Query Store options are configured here
- **SnapshotIsolation** - You can configure snapshot isolation and read committed snapshot isolation

The above settings are a subset of the configurable options.

Database scoped options were introduced in SQL Server 2016 and allow several formerly configured options at the server level. Some of the options include:

- **Maximum Degree of Parallelism** - This setting allows a database to configure its MaxDOP setting and override the server's setting.
- **Legacy Cardinality Estimation** - This setting allows for the database to use the older cardinality estimator. Some queries may have degraded performance under the newer cardinality estimator, introduced in SQL Server 2014, and may benefit from this setting. You should note that if you use this option in conjunction with a newer compatibility level, you can still get the benefits of Intelligent Query Processing in compatibility level 140 or 150.
- **Last Query Plan Stats** - This allows you to capture the values of the last actual execution plan for a query. This feature is only active in compatibility level 150.
- **Optimize for Ad Hoc Workloads** - This option uses the optimizer to store a stub query plan in the plan cache. This can help reduce the size of the plan cache for workloads with many single-use queries.

Database Compatibility Level

Each database has its compatibility level, which controls the behavior of the query optimizer for that database. You can manage this setting when upgrading SQL Server to ensure that your queries have similar execution plans to the older version. Microsoft will support running on an older compatibility level for an extended period. You should attempt to move towards newer compatibility levels, as many of the new performance features in Intelligent Query Processing are only available under compatibility level 140 or 150.

Describe Intelligent Query Processing

In SQL Server 2017 and 2019, and with Azure SQL, Microsoft has introduced many new features into compatibility levels 140 and 150. Many of these features correct what were formerly anti-patterns, like using user-defined scalar value functions and using table variables. These features break down into a few families of features:

- Adaptive Query Processing
- Table Variable Deferred Compilation
- Batch Mode on Rowstore
- Scalar UDF Inlining
- Approximate Query Processing

Adaptive Query Processing

Adaptive query processing includes several options that make query processing more dynamic, based on the execution context. These options include several features that enhance the processing of queries.

- **Adaptive Joins** - the database engine defers the choice of the join between hash and nested loops based on the number of rows going into the join. Adaptive joins currently only work in batch execution mode
- **Interleaved Execution** - Currently, this feature supports multi-statement table-valued functions (MSTVF). Before SQL Server 2017, MSTVFs used a fixed row estimate of either one or 100 rows, depending on the version of SQL Server. This estimate could lead to suboptimal query plans if the function returned many more rows. With interleaved execution, an actual row count is generated from the MSTVF before the rest of the plan is compiled
- **Memory Grant Feedback** - SQL Server generates a memory grant in the initial plan of the query, based on row count estimates from statistics. Severe data could lead to either over-or under-estimates of row counts, which can cause over-grants of memory that decrease concurrency, or under-grants, which can cause the query to spill data to tempdb. With Memory Grant Feedback, SQL Server detects these conditions and decreases or increases the amount of memory granted to the query to avoid the spill or overallocation

These features are all automatically enabled under compatibility mode 150 and require no other changes to enable.

Table Variable Deferred Compilation

Like MSTVFs, table variables in SQL Server execution plans carried a fixed row count estimate of one row. Like MSTVFs, this fixed estimate led to poor performance when the variable had a much larger row count than expected. With SQL Server 2019, table variables are now analyzed and have an actual row count. The deferred compilation is similar to interleaved execution for MSTVFs, except it is performed at the first query compilation rather than dynamically within the execution plan.

Batch Mode on a Row Store

Batch execution mode was introduced to SQL Server 2012 in conjunction with column store indexes. Batch execution mode allows data to be processed in batches instead of row by row. Queries that incur high CPU costs for calculations and aggregations will see the largest benefit from this processing model.

EXAM TIP: More workloads can benefit from batch mode processing by separating batch processing and column store indexes.

Scalar User-defined Function Inlining

In older versions of SQL Server, scalar functions performed poorly for several reasons. Scalar functions were executed iteratively, effectively processing one row at a time. They did not have proper cost estimation in an execution plan and did not allow parallelism in a query plan. With user-defined function inlining, these functions are transformed into scalar subqueries in place of the user-defined function operator in the execution plan. This transformation can lead to significant gains in performance for queries that involve scalar function calls.

Approximate Count Distinct

A common data warehouse query pattern is to execute a distinct count of orders or users. This query pattern can be expensive against a large table. Approximate count distinct introduces a much faster approach to gathering a distinct count by grouping rows. This function guarantees a 2% error rate with a 97% confidence interval.

Describe Query Store in Azure Database for MySQL and PostgreSQL

One of the value-added features in Azure Database for MySQL and PostgreSQL is an implementation of the Query Store in each database. While a slightly different implementation of the feature than in Azure SQL, the Query Store offers the DBA insightful, actionable performance information.

Query Store in Azure Database for MySQL

The Query Store in MySQL allows you to track query performance over time and quickly identify the longest-running and most expensive queries in your databases. The data for all users, databases, and queries are stored in your instance's MySQL schema database. Like Azure SQL Database, the Azure portal includes a Query Performance Insight dashboard, highlighting expensive queries and waiting statistics for your instance.

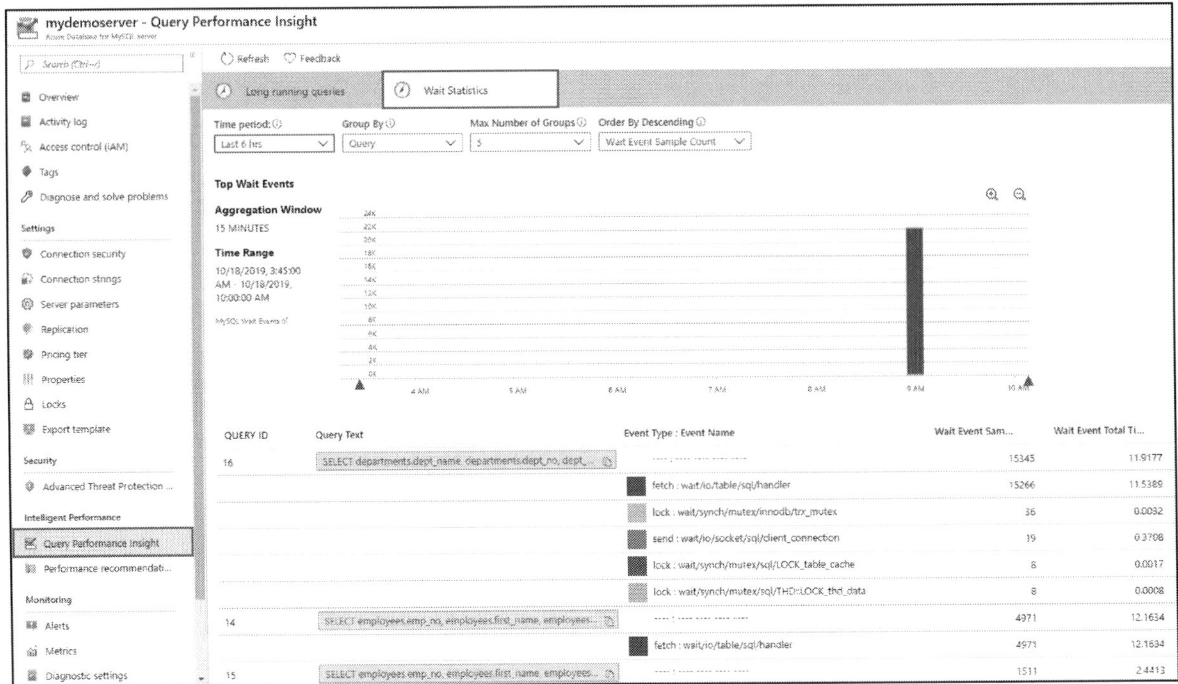

Figure 04-17: Query Store in Azure Database for MySQL

The Azure portal also includes a performance recommendations section based on the data in the Query Store.

Query Store in Azure Database for PostgreSQL

In a similar implementation to Azure Database for MySQL, PostgreSQL stores its Query Store information in a database named **azure_sys** in your instance. You can also capture wait-for statistics. The feature is not enabled by default and should be enabled by the DBA in the server parameter settings for your instance. Like the Query Store in Azure SQL, you can change the capture mode from all queries to top queries or no queries. You can also adjust the data retention period and frequency of wait stats sampling. Just like Azure SQL and Azure Database for MySQL, when you enable the Query Store, you can access Query Performance Insights and performance recommendations in the Azure portal.

Describe Performance-related Maintenance Tasks in SQL Server

Even when your database is in the cloud, ongoing performance-related maintenance tasks are critical to the overall success of your applications. Whether a SQL Server instance is in an Azure Virtual Machine or Azure SQL Database, you need to ensure your statistics are current and your indexes are well organized.

Maintain Indexes

Beyond proper indexing, index maintenance is an important part of a performance, especially for queries that scan tables or indexes. The query optimizer utilizes statistical information from the indexes to attempt to build the most optimal execution plan. While this execution plan is usually "good enough," having healthy indexes and statistics will ensure that any given plan will perform at optimal efficiency. Index maintenance should be performed regularly as data in your databases changes over time.

> **Note:** You could change your index maintenance strategy based on the frequency of modifications to your data.

Rebuild and Reorganize

Index fragmentation occurs when logical ordering within index pages does not match the physical ordering. Pages can be out of order during routine data modification statements such as UPDATE, DELETE, and INSERT. Fragmentation can introduce performance issues because of the additional I/O required to locate the data referenced by the pointers within the index pages.

An index reorganization is an online operation that will defragment the index's leaf level (both clustered and nonclustered). This defragmentation process will physically reorder the leaf-level pages to match the logical order of the nodes from left to right. During this process, the index pages are also compacted based on the configured fill-factor value.

A rebuild can be online or offline depending on the command executed or the edition of SQL Server utilized. An offline rebuild process will drop and re-create the index itself. If you can do so online, a new index will be built parallel to the existing index. Once the new index has been built, the existing one will be dropped, and then the new one will be renamed to match the old index name. Remember that the online version will require additional space as the new index is built parallel to the existing index.

The common guidance for index maintenance is:

- >5% but <30% Reorganize the index
- >30% Rebuild the index

Use these numbers as general recommendations, but not as hard and fast rules. Depending on your workload and data, you may need to be more aggressive. In some cases, you may be able to defer index maintenance for databases that mostly perform queries seeking specific pages.

Starting with SQL Server 2017, Microsoft introduced the ability to have resumable rebuild operations. This option provides more flexibility in controlling how much

impact a rebuild operation might impose on a given instance. With SQL Server 2019, the ability to control an associated maximum degree of parallelism further provides more granular control to database administrators.

SQL Server on an Azure Virtual Machine

With SQL Server being installed within an Azure virtual machine, you have access to scheduling services such as the SQL Agent or the Windows Task Scheduler. These automation tools can assist in keeping the amount of fragmentation within indexes to a minimum. A balance between a rebuild and a reorganization of indexes must be found with larger databases to ensure optimal performance. The flexibility provided by SQL Agent or Task Scheduler allows you to run custom jobs.

Azure SQL Database

Due to the nature of the Azure SQL Database, you do not have access to SQL Server Agent nor to the Windows Task Scheduler. Without these services, index maintenance must be controlled from outside of the database. There are three ways to manage maintenance operations:

- Azure Automation Runbooks
- SQL Agent Job from SQL Server in an Azure Virtual Machine
- Azure SQL elastic jobs

Azure SQL Managed Instance

With SQL Server on an Azure Virtual Machine, you can schedule jobs on an Azure SQL Managed Instance via the SQL Server Agent. Using the SQL Server Agent provides flexibility to execute code specifically designed to reduce fragmentation within the indexes in the database.

Maintain Statistics

When doing performance tuning in Azure SQL, understanding the importance of statistics is critical.

Statistics are stored in the user database as large binary objects (blobs). These blobs contain statistical information about the distribution of data values in one or more columns of a table or indexed view.

The query optimizer uses column and index statistics to determine cardinality, the number of rows a query is expected to return. Statistics contain information about the distribution of data values within a column. The query optimizer then uses cardinality estimates to generate the execution plan. Cardinality estimates also help the optimizer determine what type of operation is required (for example, index seek or scan) to retrieve the requested data.

Describe Automatic Tuning

The Query Store provides database administrators with in-depth insights on query plans and performance metrics. By default, execution plans evolve due to schema changes, index modifications, or changes to the data that cause updates to the statistics. This evolution can cause queries to perform poorly as the execution plan no longer meets the demands of the given query.

Automatic Tuning Features

SQL Server 2017 introduced a feature called automatic tuning. Automatic tuning allows gathering and applying machine learning against performance metrics to provide suggested improvements or even allow self-correction. Automatic tuning, whether on-premises or in the cloud, allows you to identify issues caused by query execution plan regression. Additionally, in Azure SQL Database, you have the option to further improve query performance by index tuning. Azure SQL Database automatic tuning can identify indexes that should be added or removed from the database to enhance query performance.

Automatic Plan Correction

Using Query Store, the database engine can identify when query execution plans have regressed in their performance. While you can manually identify a regressed plan through the user interface, the Query Store also provides the option to notify you automatically.

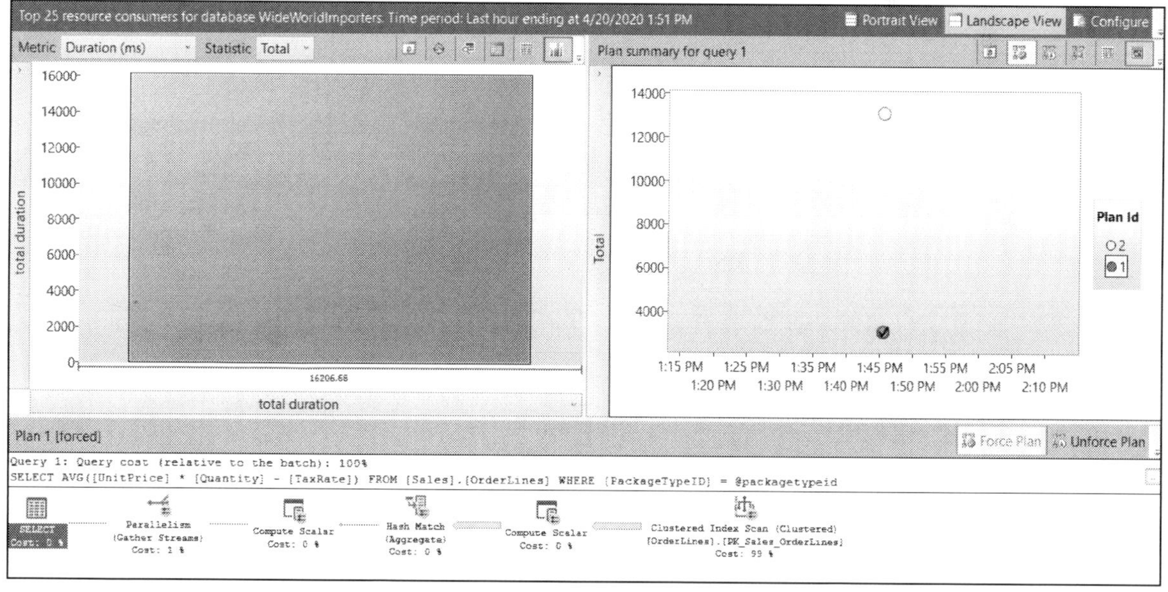

Figure 04-18: Automatic Plan Correction

In the example above, you can see a checkmark on Plan ID 1, which means that the plan has been forced. Once the feature has been enabled, the database engine will

automatically force any recommended query execution plan where the number of errors in the previous plan is higher than the recommended plan, the estimated CPU gain is greater than 10 seconds, or a plan was forced and continues to be better than the previous one. The plan will revert to the last known good plan after 15 executions of the query.

When plan forcing occurs automatically, the database engine will apply the last known good plan and continue to monitor query execution plan performance. If the forced plan does not perform better than the previous plan, it will be enforced and force a new plan to be compiled. If the forced plan continues to outperform the previously bad plan, it will remain forced until a recompile occurs.

Automatic Index Management

Azure SQL Database can perform automatic index tuning. Over time, the database will learn about existing workloads and recommend adding or removing indexes to provide better performance. Like forcing improved query plans, the database can be configured to allow for automatic index creation or removal depending on existing index performance, as shown below:

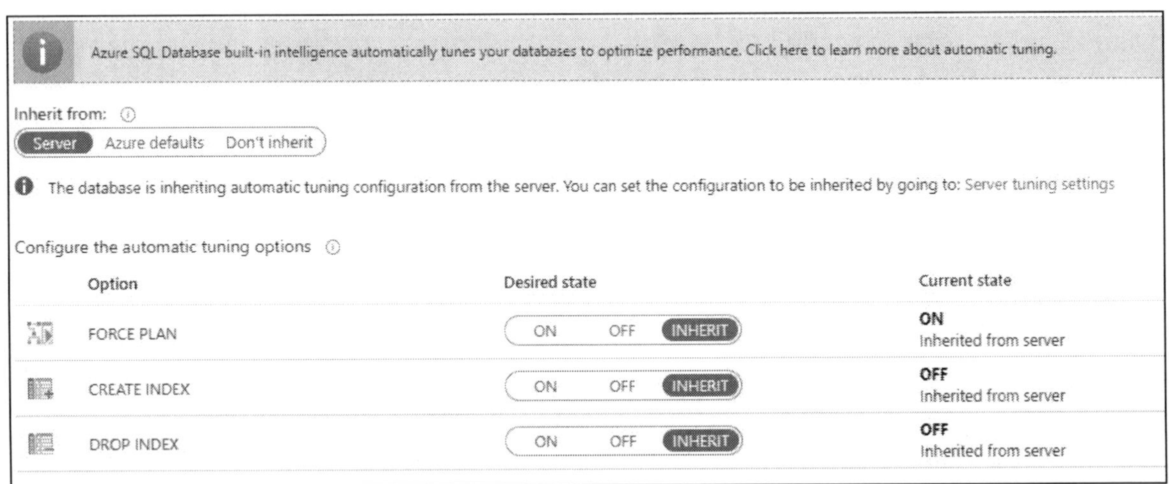

Figure 04-19: Automatic Index Management

When enabled, the Performance Recommendations blade will identify indexes created or dropped depending on query performance. Remember, this feature is not available for on-premises databases and only available for Azure SQL Database.

Creating new indexes can consume resources, and the timing of the index creations is critical to ensure no negative impact is felt on your workloads. Azure SQL Database will monitor windows of time to implement new indexes to avoid causing performance issues. If resources are needed for existing workloads and potentially unavailable to create an index, the tuning action is postponed until resources are available. If a newly created index does not increase query performance, it will be dropped quickly. This

monitoring process will validate that any actions are taken only help performance and do not degrade it. If an index is dropped and query performance noticeably degrades, the recently dropped index will be recreated automatically.

Lab 04-01: Monitor and Optimize Operational Resources in SQL Server

Introduction

A database performance monitor for several databases, including SQL Server, works for many servers and links across an entire IT infrastructure. It lets you manage your relational database management system (RDBMS). It allows the discovery and simple display of SQL Server database performance metrics, which you can then reference to understand your SQL Server's needs and capabilities better, and make changes for improvements in the future.

Problem

You have been appointed as a database administrator to find performance-related issues and provide practical solutions to resolve any issues found. It would help if you used the Azure portal to find the performance issues and propose methods to resolve them.

Solution

SQL Server and Azure SQL have added many features in current releases to improve performance. Many of these features can be enabled at the individual database level and may also be controlled using the database's compatibility level. The Azure Database for MariaDB/MySQL/PostgreSQL includes the Query Store, which helps you identify problematic queries.

Maintaining indexes and statistics can help offer consistent performance for your queries. SQL Server and Azure SQL Databases automatically update statistics based on the percentage of rows modified. Additionally, Azure SQL Database automates the creation of new indexes and the removal of unused indexes.

Step 01: Isolate Problems with Monitoring

Connect to the Lab Environment

1. Click on the Microsoft Edge browser from the toolbar and navigate to https://portal.azure.com.

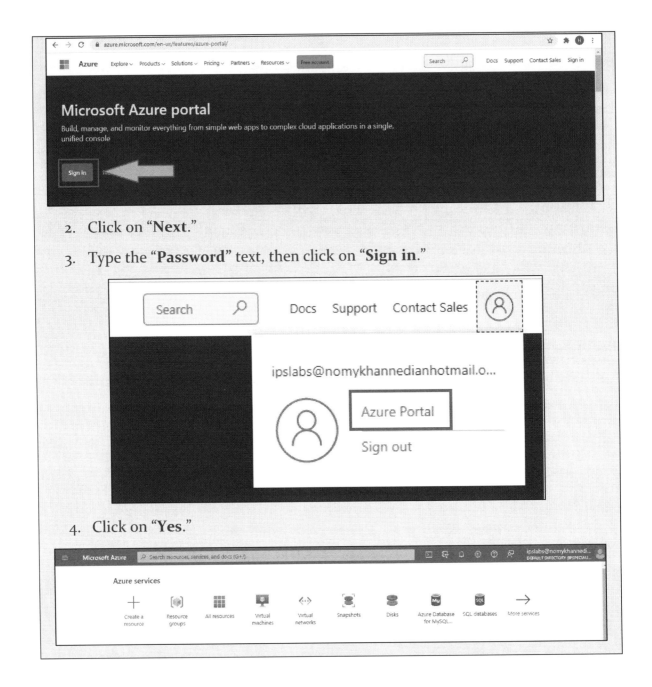

2. Click on "**Next**."
3. Type the "**Password**" text, then click on "**Sign in**."
4. Click on "**Yes**."

Review CPU Utilization in Azure portal

6. From the Home screen, select the menu, and select "**SQL Databases**."

sql database

Services See all

SQL databases

SQL Server stretch databases

Dedicated SQL pools (formerly SQL DW)

Azure Database for MySQL servers

Reservations

Azure SQL

Azure Database for MySQL flexible servers

Azure Database for PostgreSQL flexible servers

Azure Database for PostgreSQL server groups

Azure Database for PostgreSQL servers

Resources

No results were found.

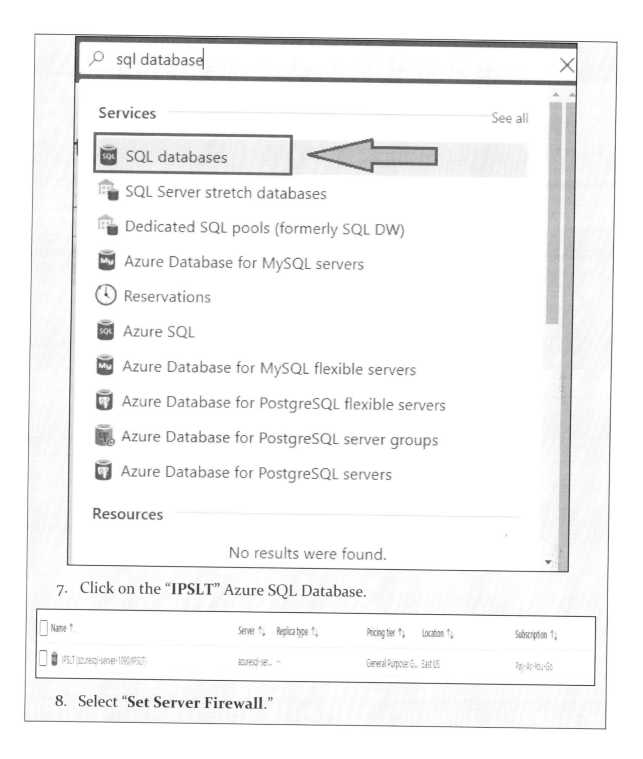

7. Click on the "**IPSLT**" Azure SQL Database.

Name ↑	Server ↑↓	Replica type ↑↓	Pricing tier ↑↓	Location ↑↓	Subscription ↑↓
IPSLT (azuresql-server-1090/IPSLT)	azuresql-ser...	--	General Purpose: G...	East US	Pay-As-You-Go

8. Select "**Set Server Firewall**."

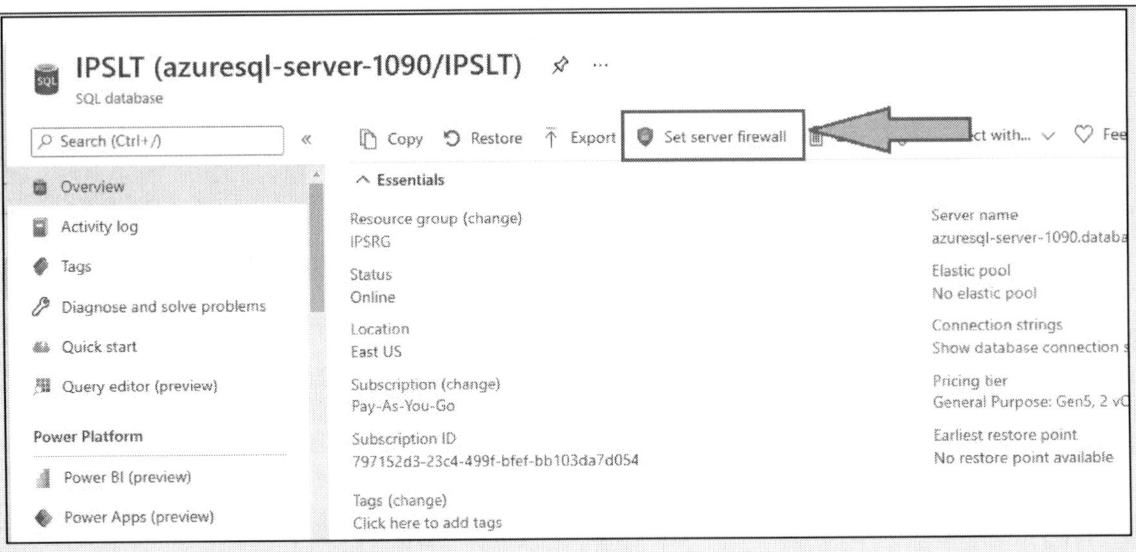

9. Select "**Add Client IP**" and click "**Save**."

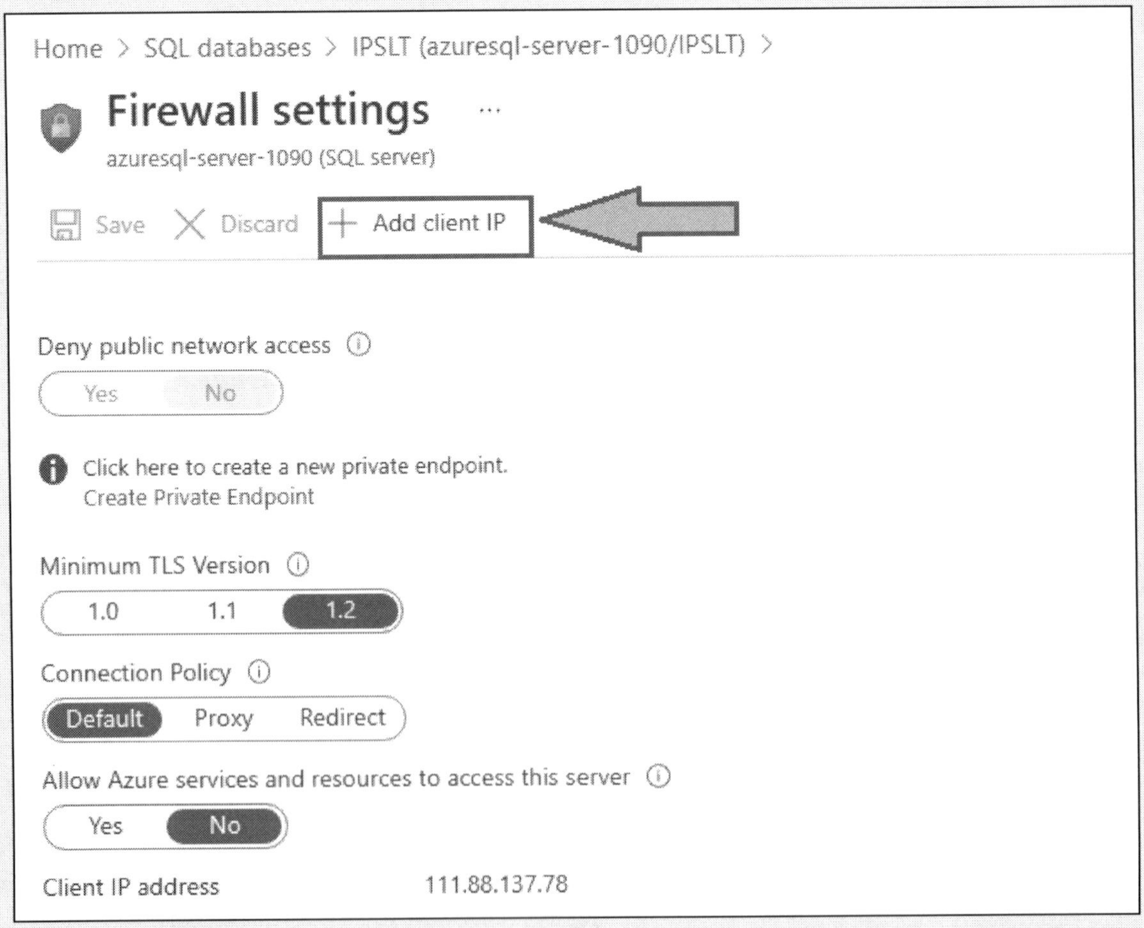

10. Click "**OK**."

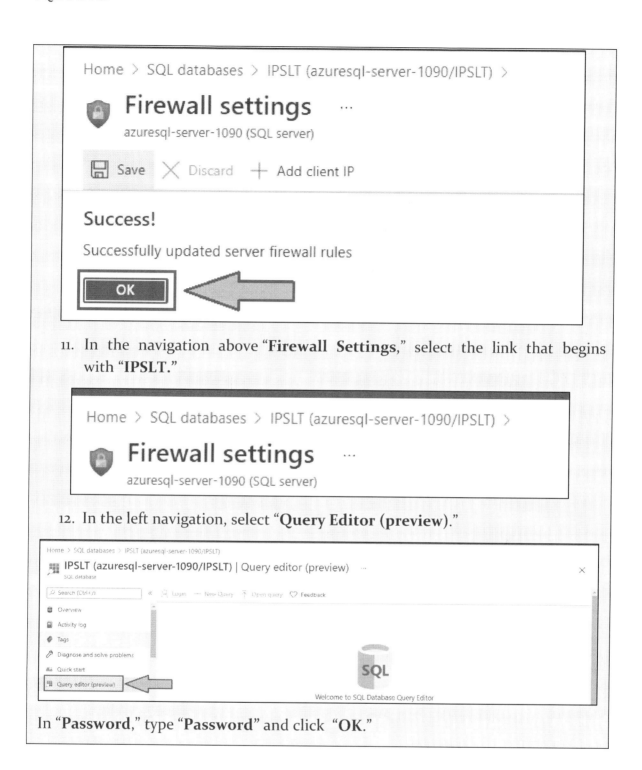

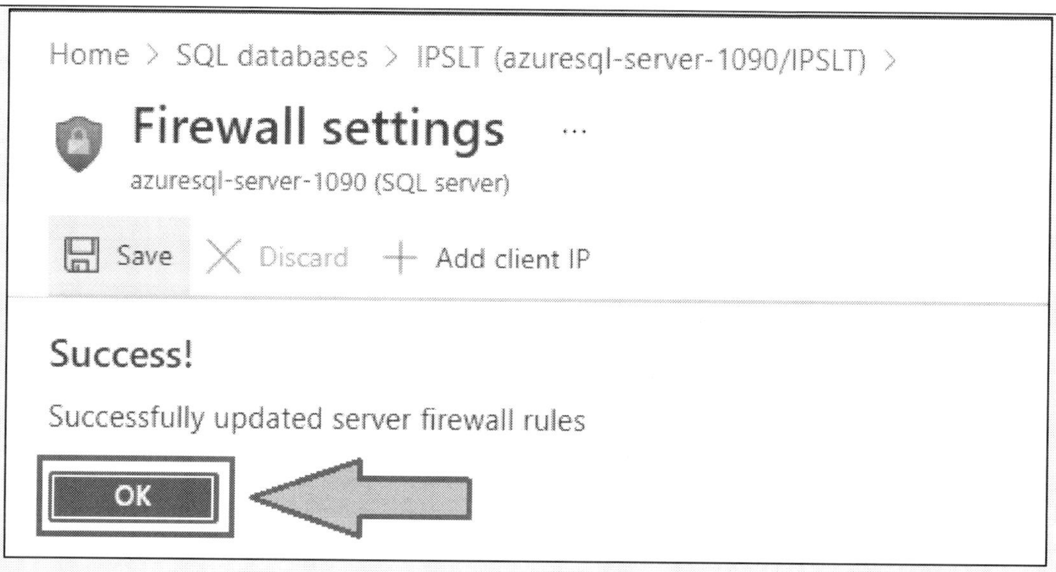

11. In the navigation above "**Firewall Settings**," select the link that begins with "**IPSLT.**"

12. In the left navigation, select "**Query Editor (preview)**."

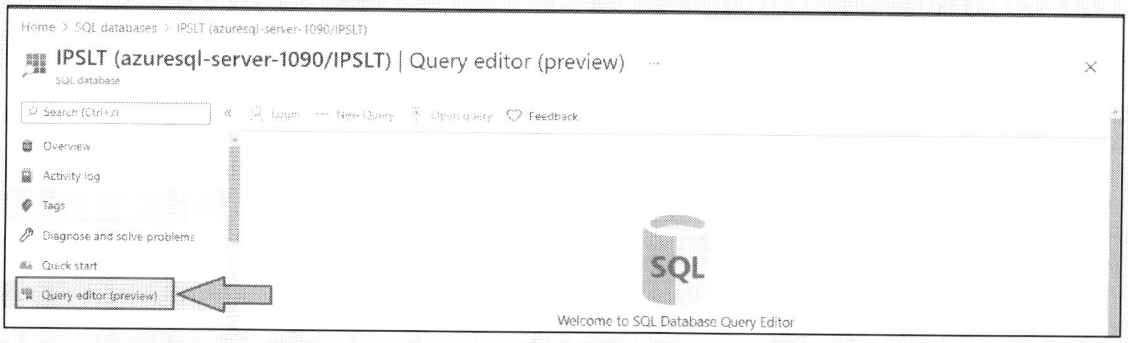

In "**Password**," type "**Password**" and click "**OK**."

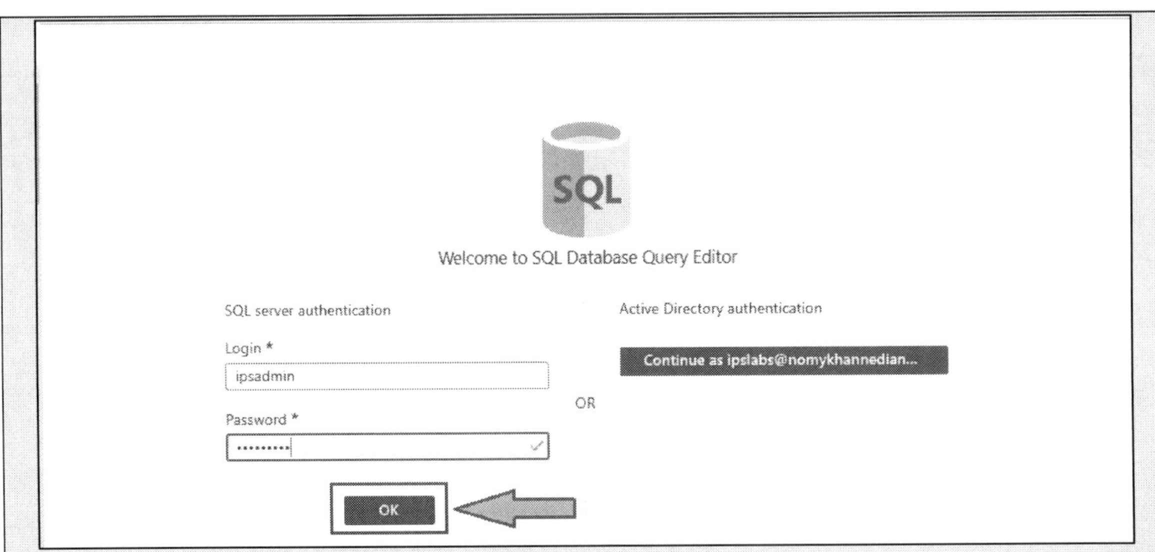

13. In "**Query 1**," type the following query and select "**Run**."

```
DECLARE @Counter INT
SET @Counter=1
WHILE ( @Counter <= 10000)
BEGIN
    SELECT AVG(UnitPrice)
    FROM SalesLT.SalesOrderDetail
    GROUP BY ModifiedDate
    SET @Counter  = @Counter  + 1
END
```

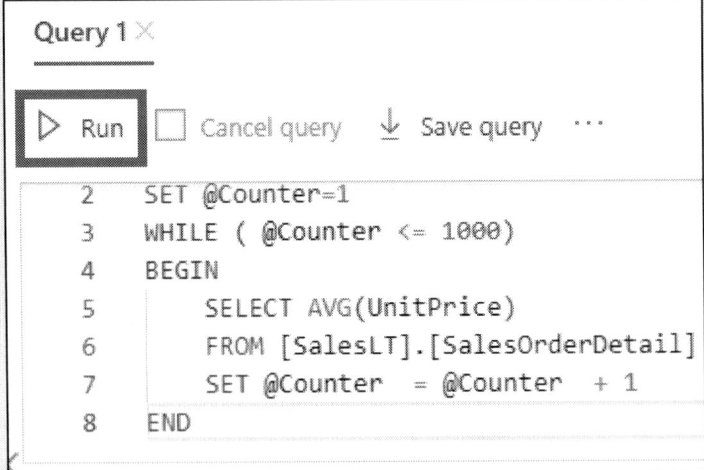

14. Wait for the query to complete.
15. Locate the "**Metrics**" icon on the "**Monitoring**" section of the blade for the database.

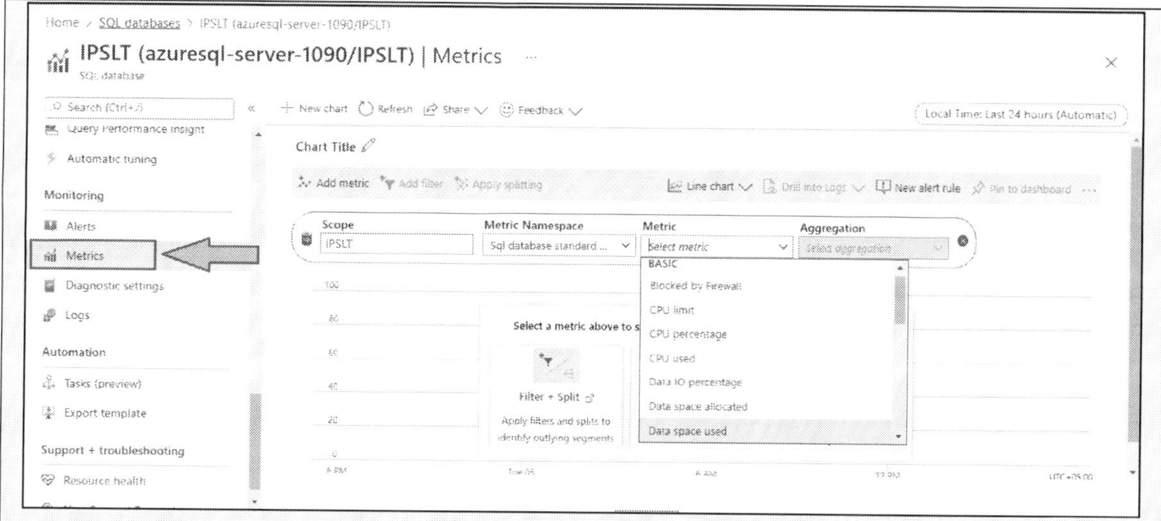

16. Change the "**Metric**" menu option to reflect "**CPU Percentage**."

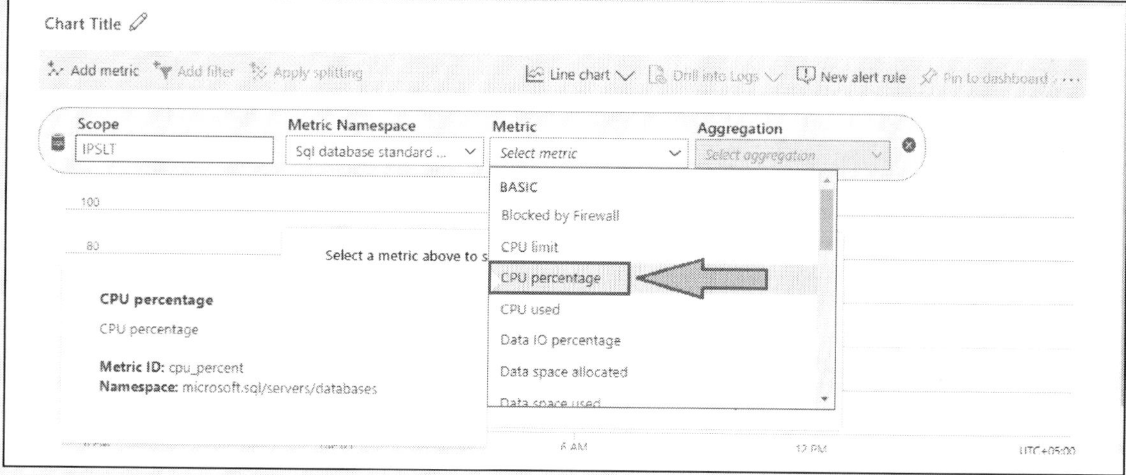

17. Select an "**Aggregation** of **Avg**."

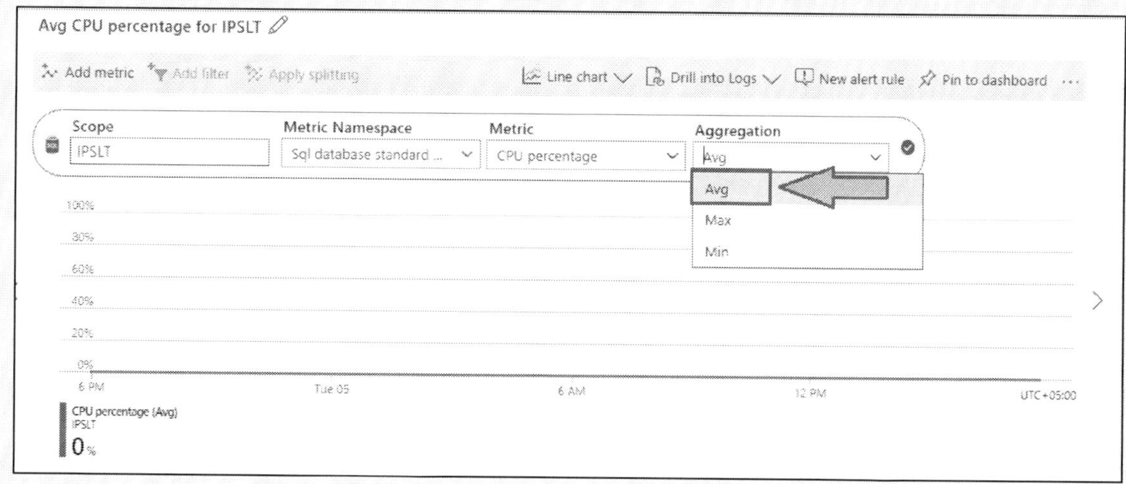

Identify High CPU Consuming Queries

1. Locate the "**QueryPerformanceInsight**" icon on the "**Intelligent Performance**" section of the blade for the IPSLT database.

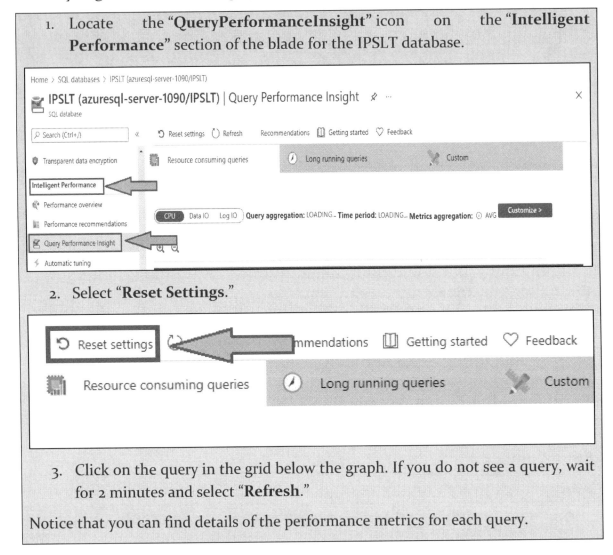

2. Select "**Reset Settings.**"

3. Click on the query in the grid below the graph. If you do not see a query, wait for 2 minutes and select "**Refresh.**"

Notice that you can find details of the performance metrics for each query.

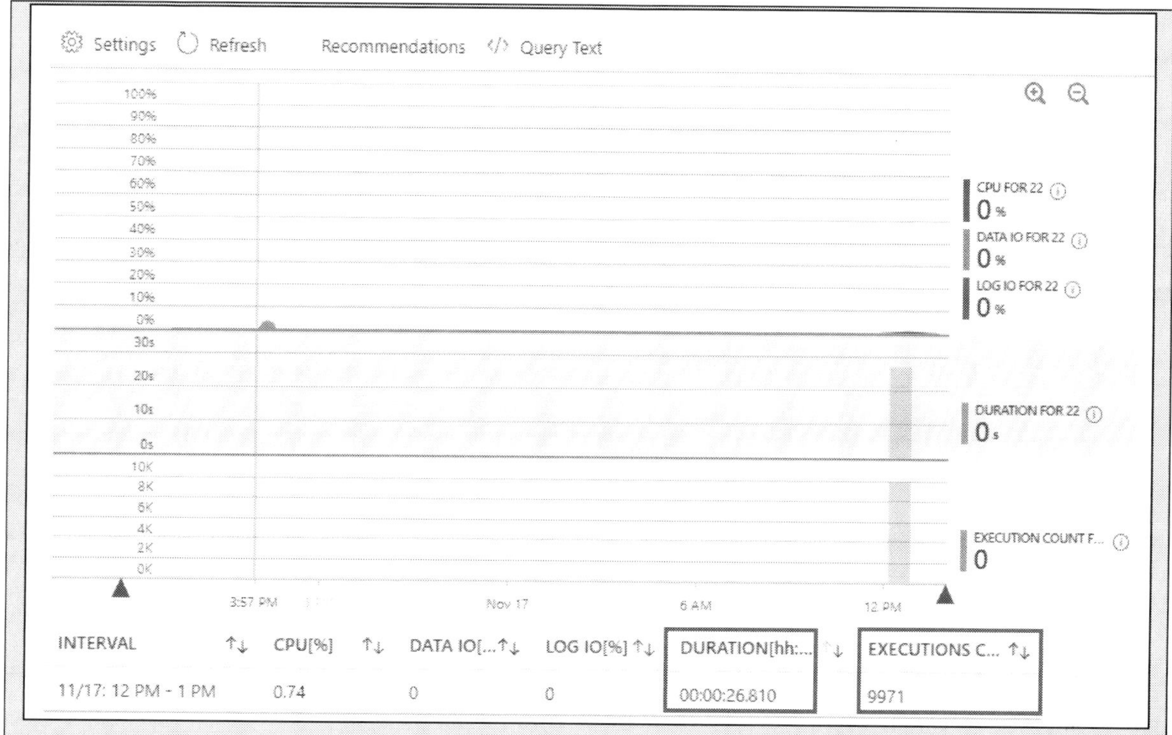

For this query, you can see that the total duration was over 20 seconds and that it ran approximately 10,000 times.

Step 02: Identify and Resolve Blocking Issues

Run Blocked Queries Report

Pre-Requisite

In this lab, you will be using a database that has been previously created in chapter 02: Lab 02-01.

1. Start "**SQL Server Management Studio.**"

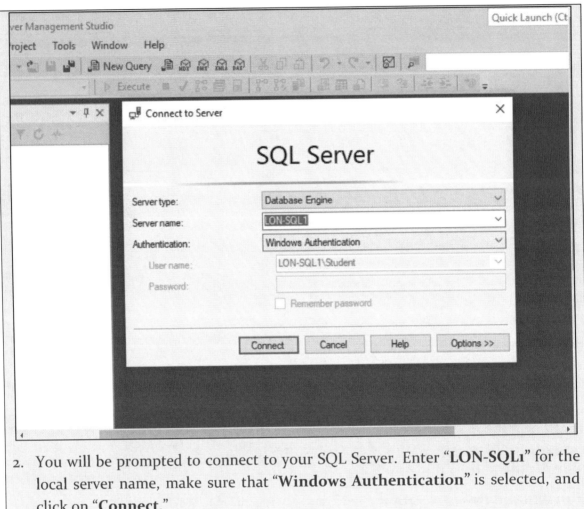

2. You will be prompted to connect to your SQL Server. Enter "**LON-SQL1**" for the local server name, make sure that "**Windows Authentication**" is selected, and click on "**Connect**."

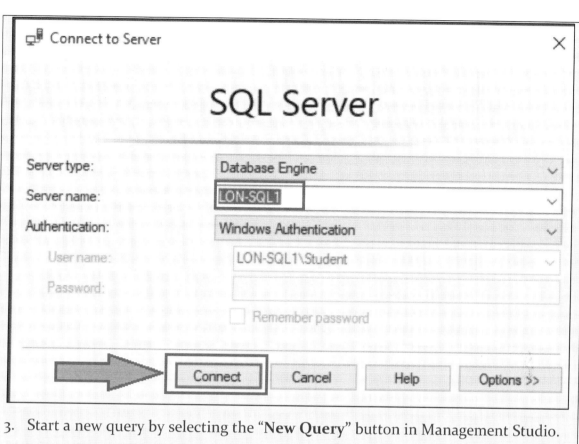

3. Start a new query by selecting the "**New Query**" button in Management Studio.

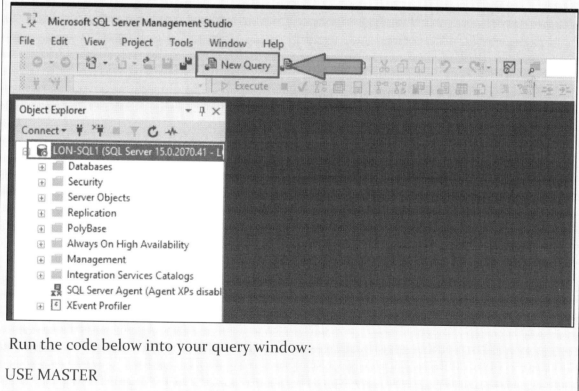

Run the code below into your query window:

```
USE MASTER
GO
```

```
CREATE EVENT SESSION [Blocking] ON SERVER
ADD EVENT sqlserver.blocked_process_report(
ACTION(sqlserver.client_app_name,sqlserver.client_hostname,sqlserver.database_id,sqlserver.database_name,sqlserver.nt_username,sqlserver.session_id,sqlserver.sql_text,sqlserver.username))
ADD TARGET package0.ring_buffer
WITH (MAX_MEMORY=4096 KB, EVENT_RETENTION_MODE=ALLOW_SINGLE_EVENT_LOSS, MAX_DISPATCH_LATENCY=30 SECONDS, MAX_EVENT_SIZE=0 KB,MEMORY_PARTITION_MODE=NONE, TRACK_CAUSALITY=OFF,STARTUP_STATE=ON)
GO
-- Start the event session
ALTER EVENT SESSION [Blocking] ON SERVER
STATE = start;
GO
```

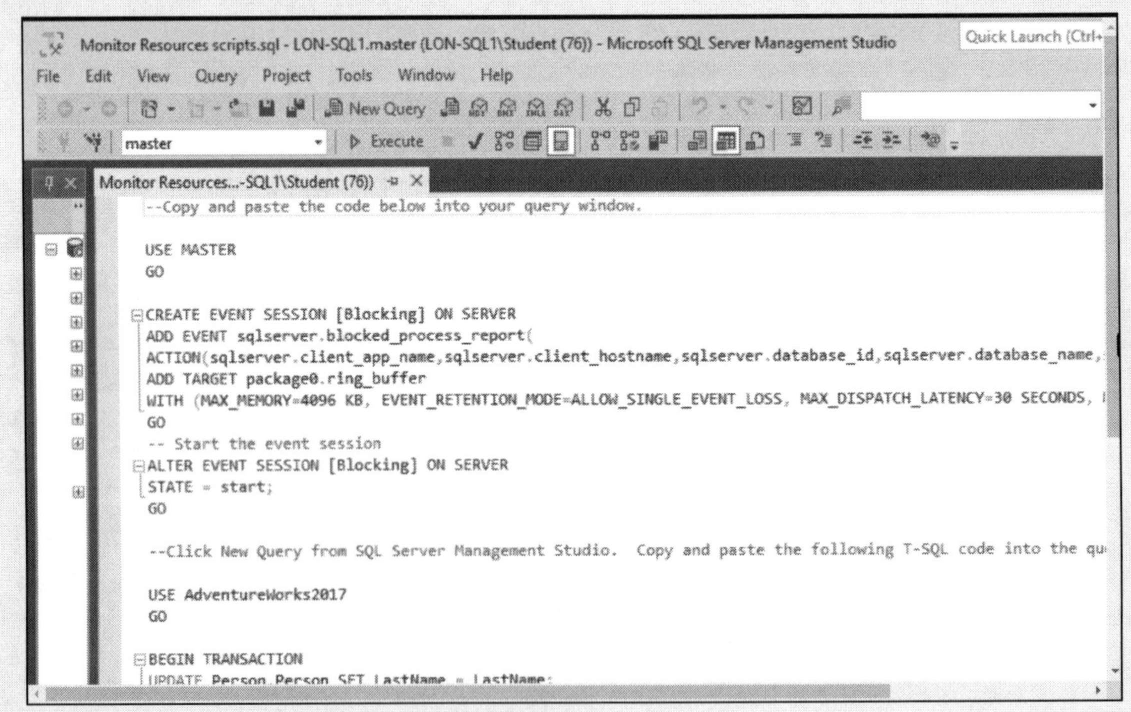

4. Select "**Execute**" to execute this query.

Monitor Resources scripts.sql - LON-SQL1.master (LON-SQL1\Student (76)) - Microsoft SQ

File Edit View Query Project Tools Window Help

New Query | master | Execute

Monitor Resources...-SQL1\Student (76))

```
--Copy and paste the code below into your query window.

USE MASTER
GO

CREATE EVENT SESSION [Blocking] ON SERVER
ADD EVENT sqlserver.blocked_process_report(
ACTION(sqlserver.client_app_name,sqlserver.client_hostname,sq
ADD TARGET package0.ring_buffer
WITH (MAX_MEMORY=4096 KB, EVENT_RETENTION_MODE=ALLOW_SINGLE_E
GO
-- Start the event session
ALTER EVENT SESSION [Blocking] ON SERVER
STATE = start;
```

```
--Click New Query from SQL Server Management Studio. Copy an
```

100 %

Results | Messages

	LastName	FirstName	Title
1	White	David	NULL
2	Williams	David	NULL
3	Wilson	David	NULL
4	Wright	David	NULL
5	Wruck	David	NULL
6	Yalovsky	David	NULL
7	Yang	David	NULL
8	Alexander	David	NULL

	LastName	FirstName	Title
1	White	David	NULL
2	Williams	David	NULL

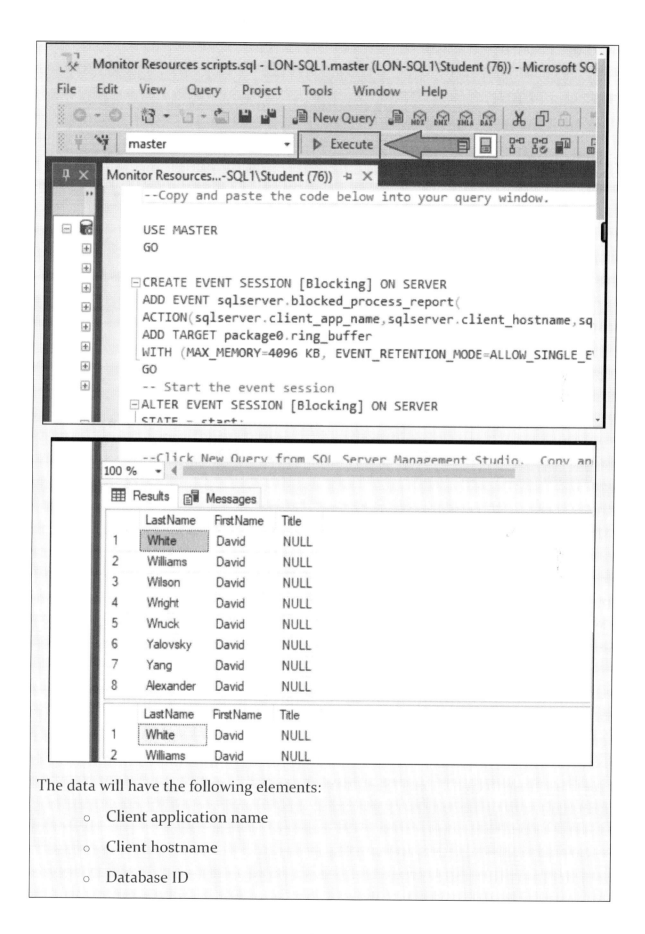

The data will have the following elements:

- Client application name
- Client hostname
- Database ID

- Database name
- NT Username
- Session ID
- T-SQL Text
- Username

5. Select "**NewQuery**" from SQL Server Management Studio. Select the Execute button to execute this query. Run the following T-SQL code into the query window:

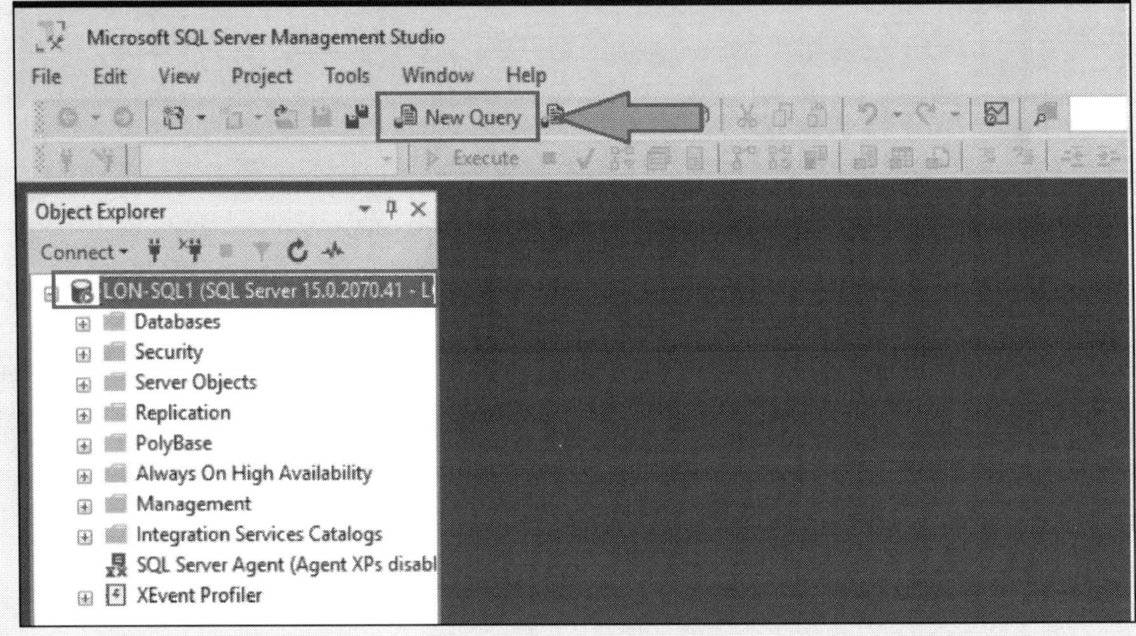


```
USE AdventureWorks2017
GO
BEGIN TRANSACTION
UPDATE Person.Person SET LastName = LastName;
GO
```

SQLQuery1.sql - LON-SQL1.AdventureWorks2017 (LON-SQL1\Student (69))* - Microsoft SC

File Edit View Query Project Tools Window Help

New Query

AdventureWorks2017 ▶ Execute

SQLQuery1.sql - LO...SQL1\Student (69))*

```
USE AdventureWorks2017
GO
BEGIN TRANSACTION
UPDATE Person.Person SET LastName = LastName;
GO
```

100 %

Messages

```
(19972 rows affected)

Completion time: 2021-10-21T22:55:28.9231372-07:00
```

100 %

Query executed successfully.

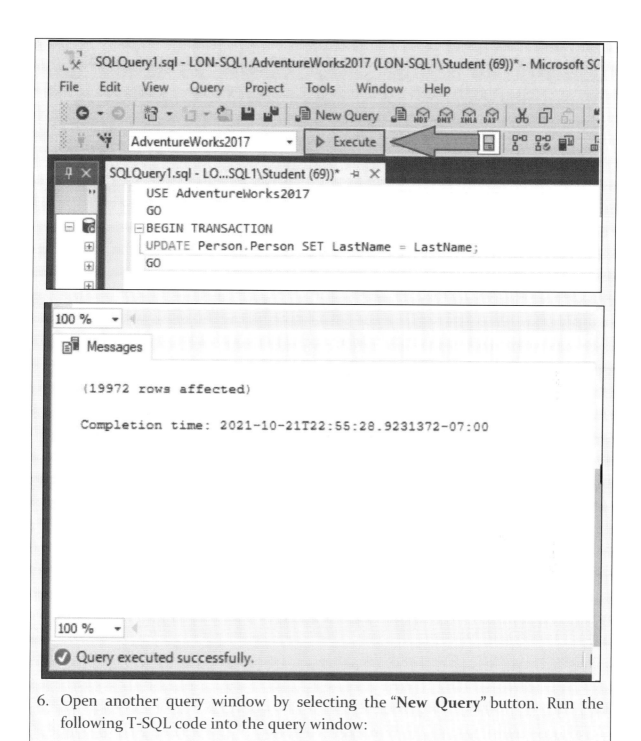

6. Open another query window by selecting the "**New Query**" button. Run the following T-SQL code into the query window:

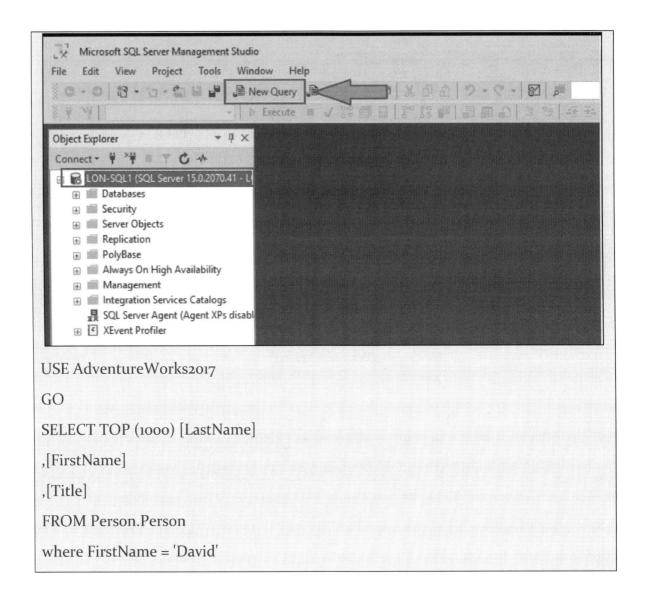


```
USE AdventureWorks2017
GO
SELECT TOP (1000) [LastName]
,[FirstName]
,[Title]
FROM Person.Person
where FirstName = 'David'
```

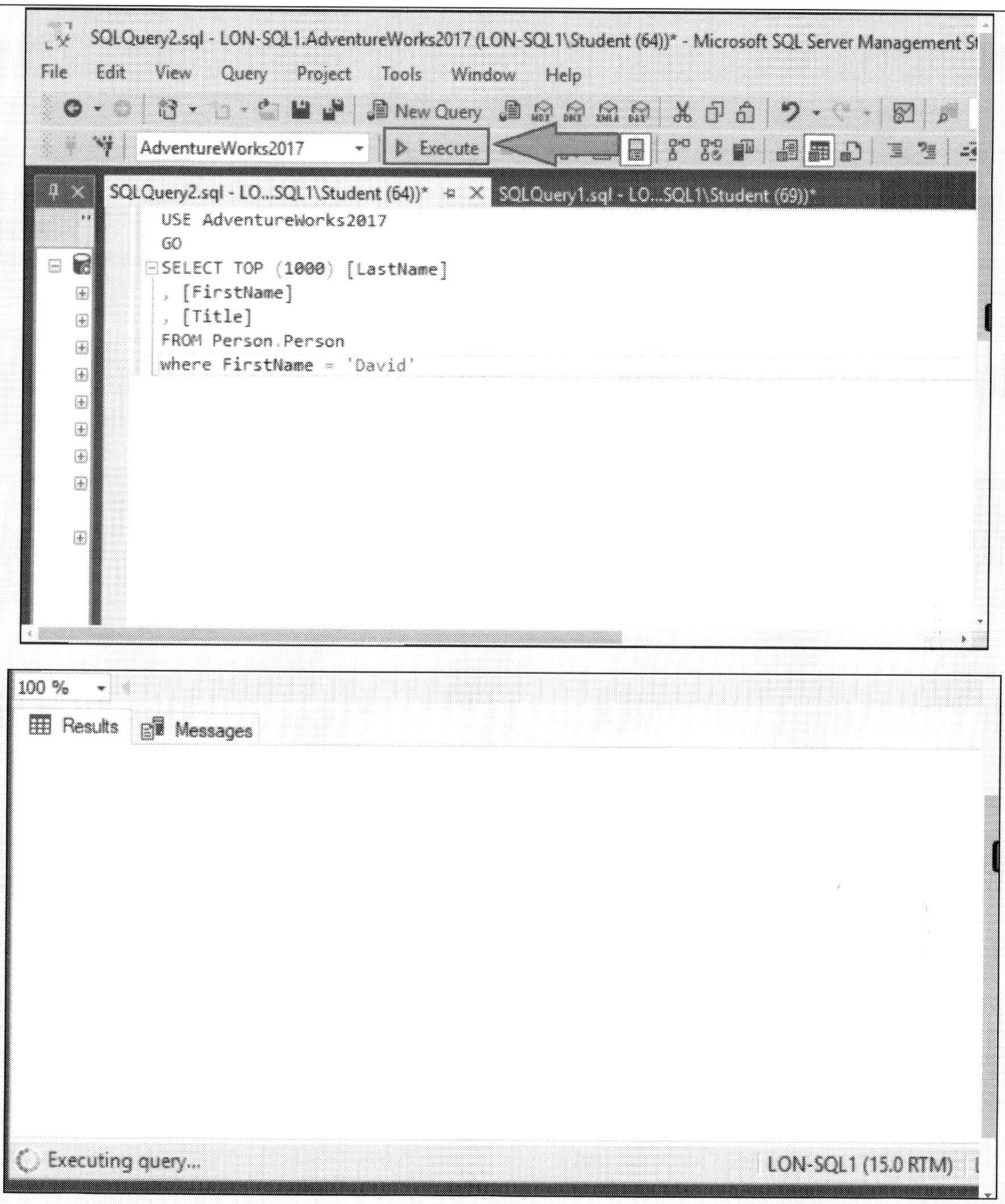

```
USE AdventureWorks2017
GO
SELECT TOP (1000) [LastName]
, [FirstName]
, [Title]
FROM Person.Person
where FirstName = 'David'
```

7. In Object Explorer, navigate to Management, and expand the hive by clicking the plus sign.

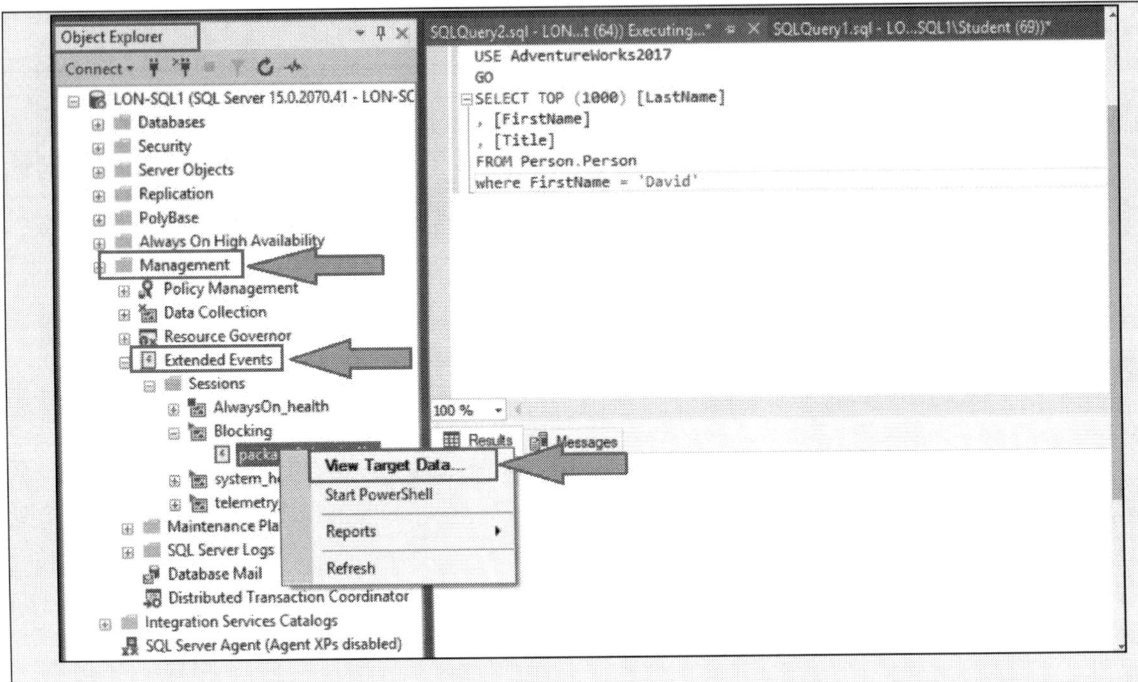

8. Select the hyperlink.

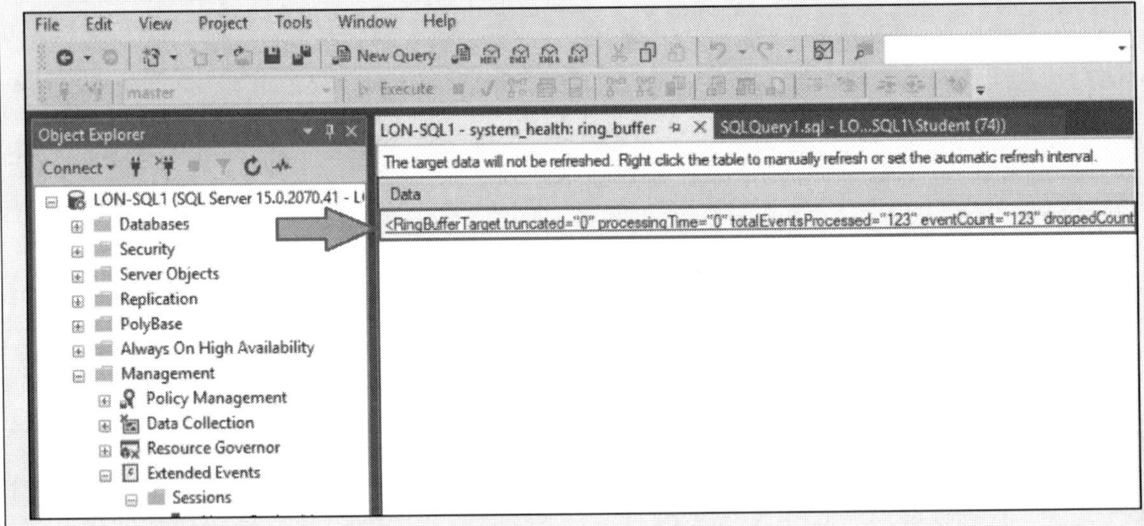

9. The XML will show you which processes are being blocked and which processes are causing the blocking. You can see the queries that ran in this process as well as system information.

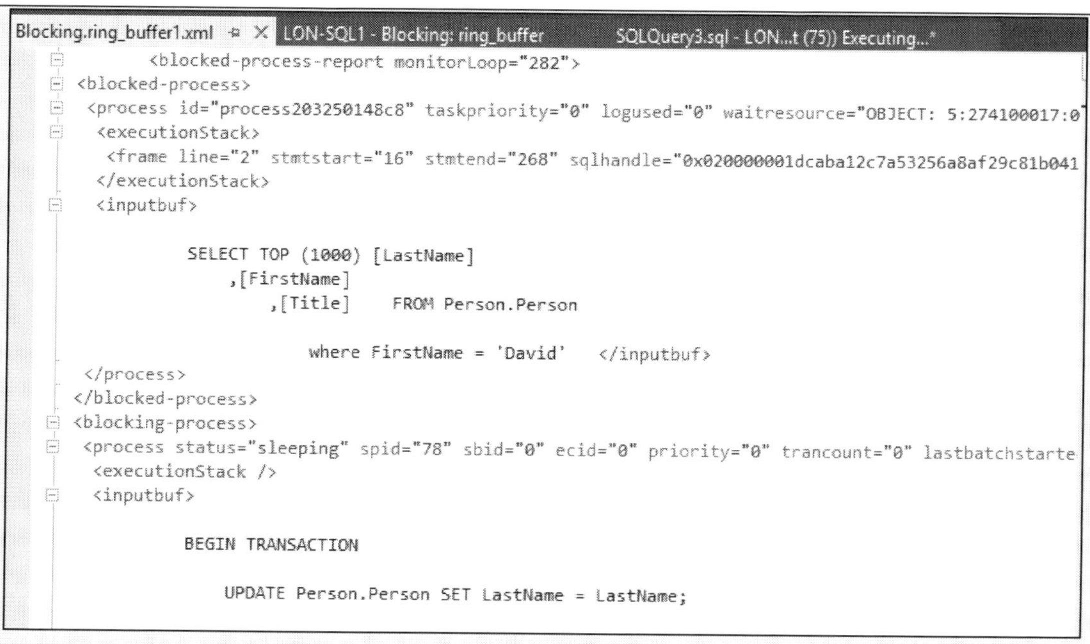

```
Blocking.ring_buffer1.xml   LON-SQL1 - Blocking: ring_buffer   SQLQuery3.sql - LON...t (75)) Executing...*
        <blocked-process-report monitorLoop="282">
 <blocked-process>
  <process id="process203250148c8" taskpriority="0" logused="0" waitresource="OBJECT: 5:274100017:0
   <executionStack>
    <frame line="2" stmtstart="16" stmtend="268" sqlhandle="0x020000001dcaba12c7a53256a8af29c81b041
   </executionStack>
   <inputbuf>

            SELECT TOP (1000) [LastName]
                ,[FirstName]
                    ,[Title]    FROM Person.Person

                        where FirstName = 'David'   </inputbuf>
  </process>
 </blocked-process>
 <blocking-process>
  <process status="sleeping" spid="78" sbid="0" ecid="0" priority="0" trancount="0" lastbatchstarte
   <executionStack />
   <inputbuf>

            BEGIN TRANSACTION

                UPDATE Person.Person SET LastName = LastName;
```


10. Right-click "**Blocking**" and select "**Stop Session**."

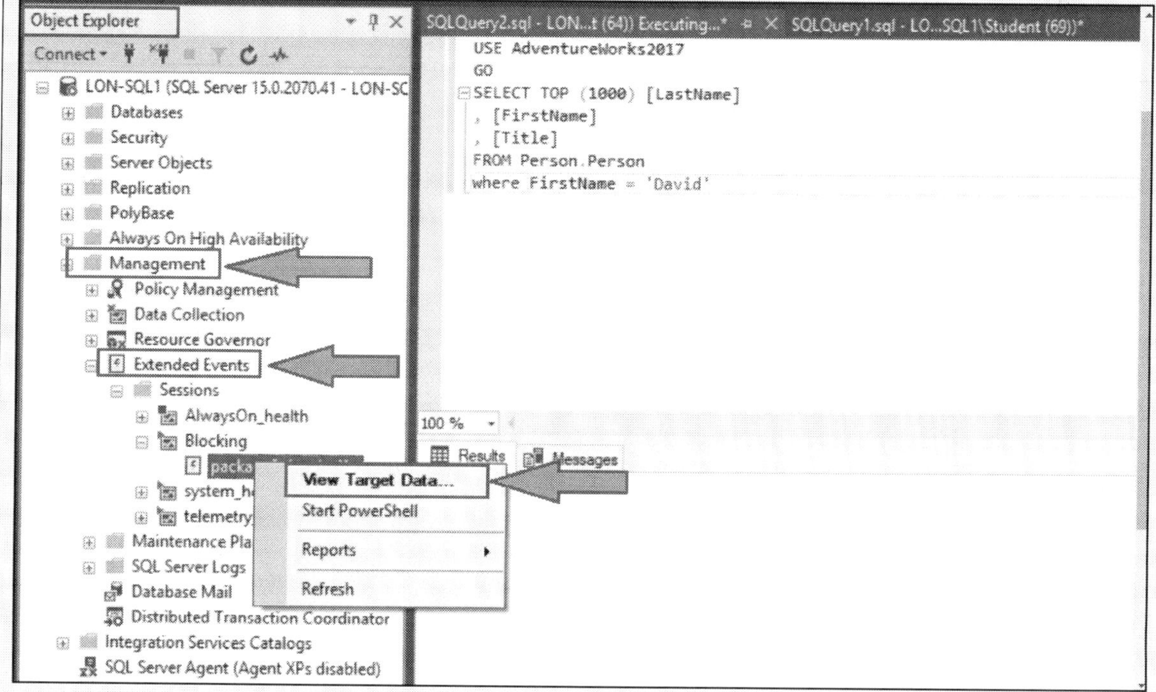

11. Return to the query tab you opened in step 6, and write "**ROLLBACK TRANSACTION**" on the line below the query.

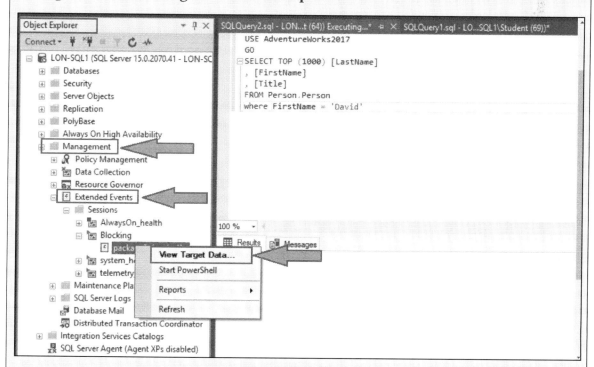

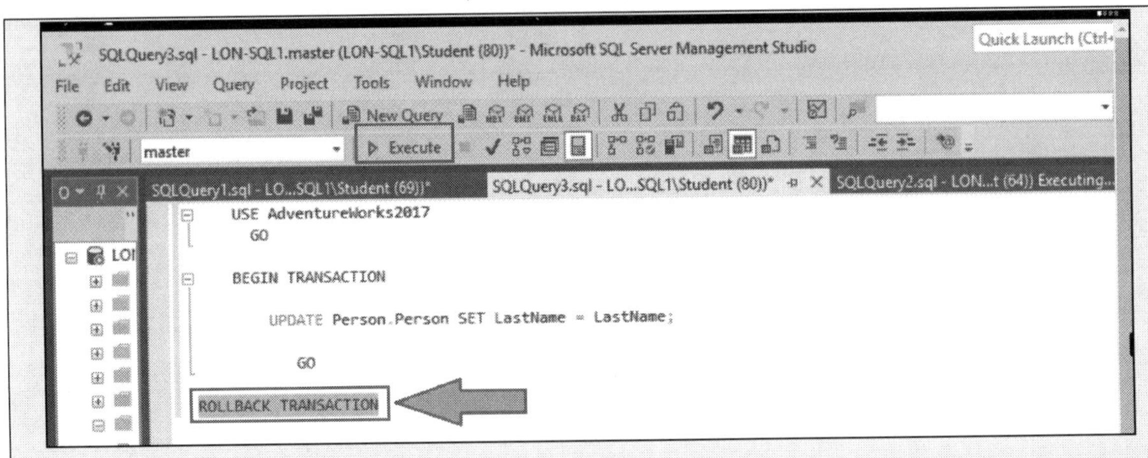

12. Navigate back to the query tab you opened in Step 7. You will notice that the query has now been completed.

Enable Read Commit Snapshot Isolation

1. Select "**NewQuery**" from SQL Server Management Studio. Select the Execute button to execute this query. Run the following T-SQL code into the query window:

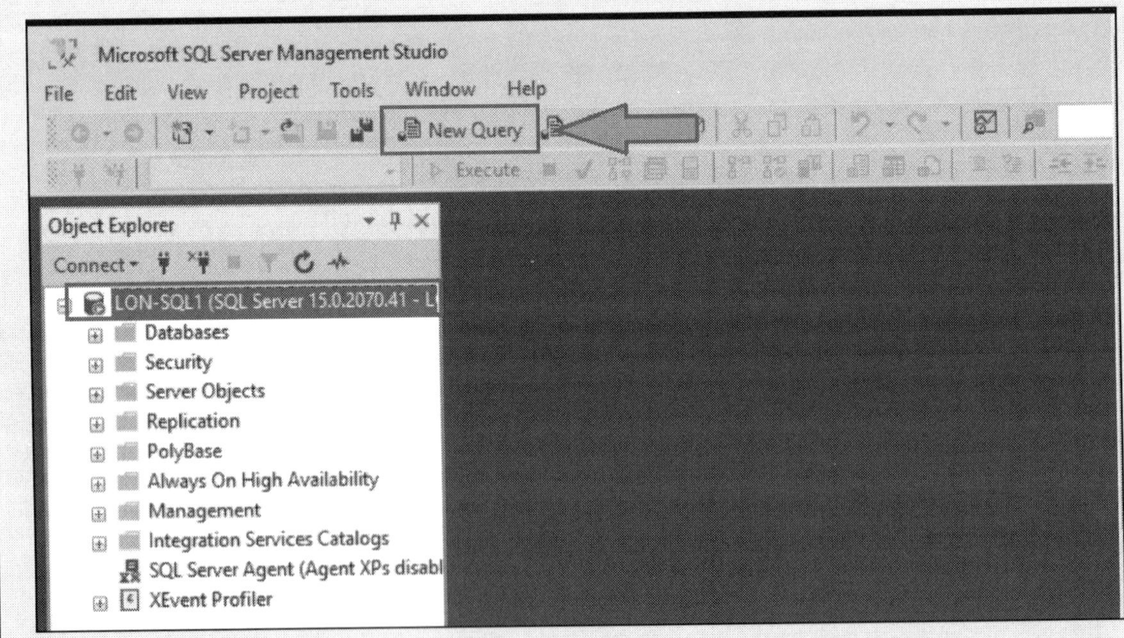


```
USE master
GO
ALTER DATABASE AdventureWorks2017 SET READ_COMMITTED_SNAPSHOT ON WITH ROLLBACK IMMEDIATE;
GO
```

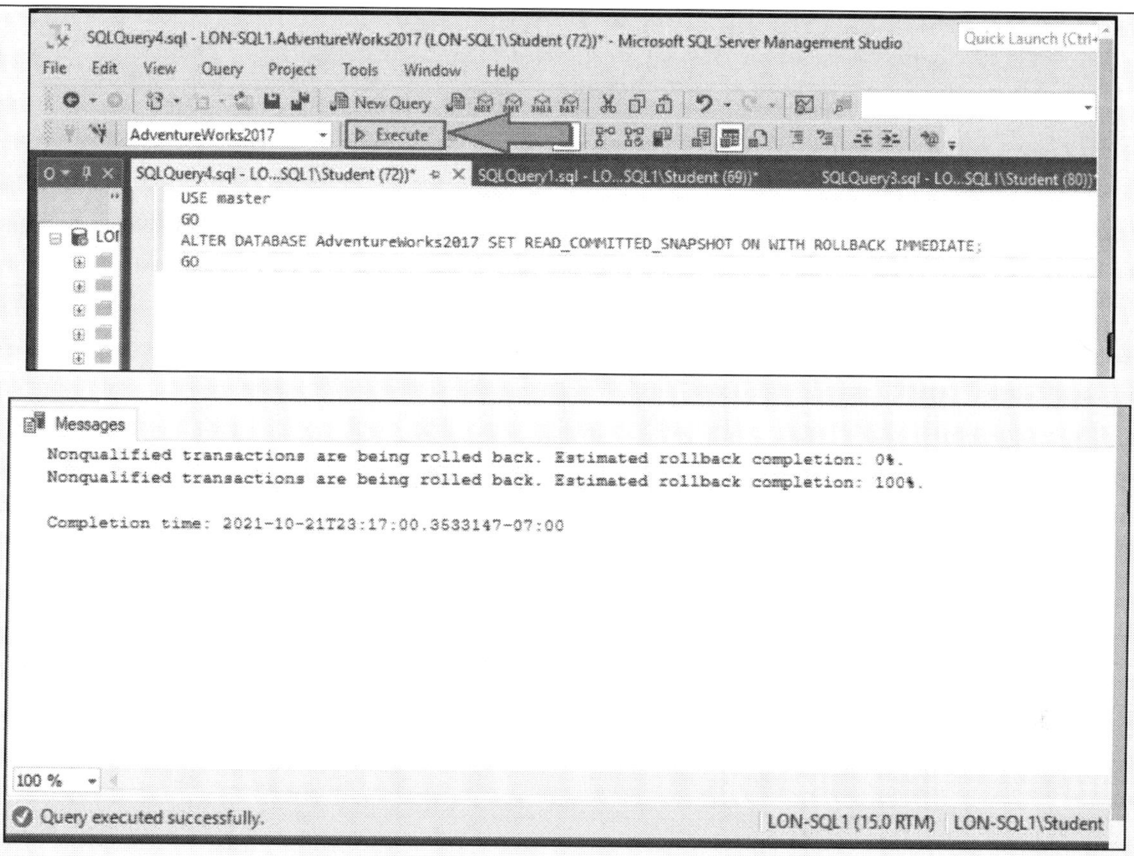

```
USE master
GO
ALTER DATABASE AdventureWorks2017 SET READ_COMMITTED_SNAPSHOT ON WITH ROLLBACK IMMEDIATE;
GO
```

```
Nonqualified transactions are being rolled back. Estimated rollback completion: 0%.
Nonqualified transactions are being rolled back. Estimated rollback completion: 100%.

Completion time: 2021-10-21T23:17:00.3533147-07:00
```

Query executed successfully.

2. Run the query.

```
USE AdventureWorks2017
GO
BEGIN TRANSACTION
UPDATE Person.Person SET LastName = LastName;
GO
```

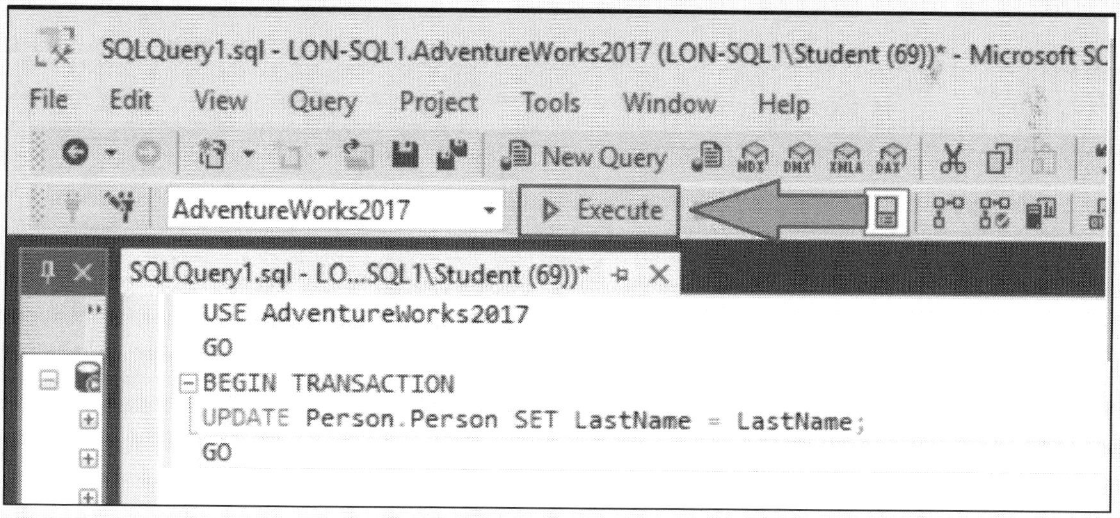

Messages

```
(19972 rows affected)

Completion time: 2021-10-21T23:18:16.3569359-07:00
```

100 %

Query executed successfully. | LON-SQL1 (15.0 RTM) | LON-SQL1\Student (64) | Adventu

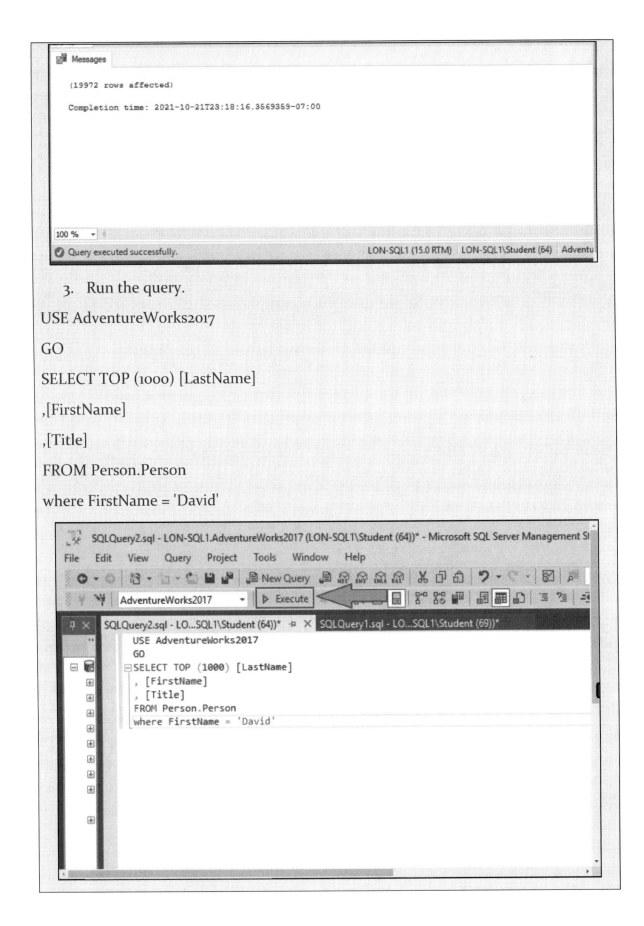

3. Run the query.

USE AdventureWorks2017

GO

SELECT TOP (1000) [LastName]

,[FirstName]

,[Title]

FROM Person.Person

where FirstName = 'David'

SQLQuery2.sql - LON-SQL1.AdventureWorks2017 (LON-SQL1\Student (64))* - Microsoft SQL Server Management St

File Edit View Query Project Tools Window Help

New Query

AdventureWorks2017 | Execute

SQLQuery2.sql - LO...SQL1\Student (64))* | SQLQuery1.sql - LO...SQL1\Student (69))*

```
USE AdventureWorks2017
GO
SELECT TOP (1000) [LastName]
, [FirstName]
, [Title]
FROM Person.Person
where FirstName = 'David'
```

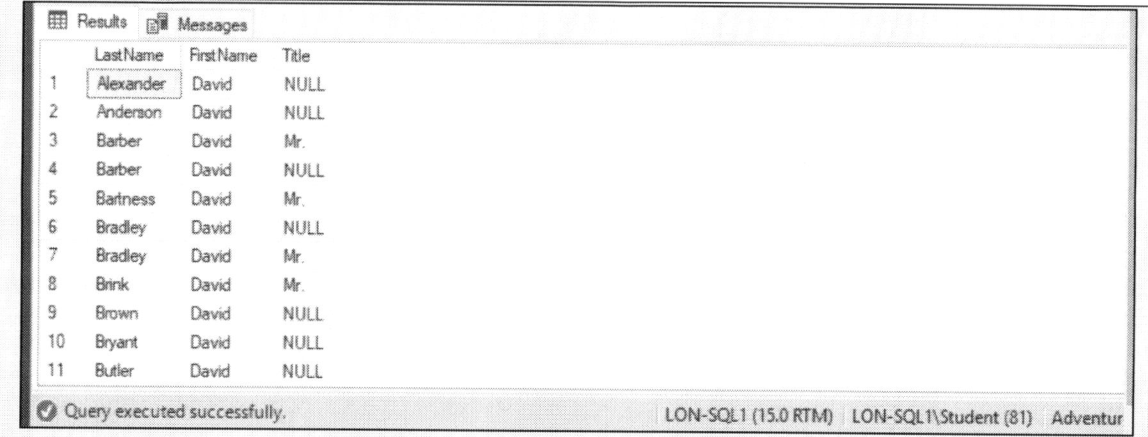

	LastName	FirstName	Title
1	Alexander	David	NULL
2	Anderson	David	NULL
3	Barber	David	Mr.
4	Barber	David	NULL
5	Bartness	David	Mr.
6	Bradley	David	NULL
7	Bradley	David	Mr.
8	Brink	David	Mr.
9	Brown	David	NULL
10	Bryant	David	NULL
11	Butler	David	NULL

4. Consider why the query in step 3 now completes whereas the UPDATE blocked it in the previous task.

Read Commit Snapshot Isolation is an optimistic form of transaction isolation, and the last query will show the latest committed version of the data rather than being blocked.

Step 03: Detect and Correct Fragmentation Issues

Pre-Requisite

In this lab, you will be using a database that has been previously created in chapter 02: Lab 02-01.

Identify Fragmentation

1. Start "**SQL Server Management Studio.**"

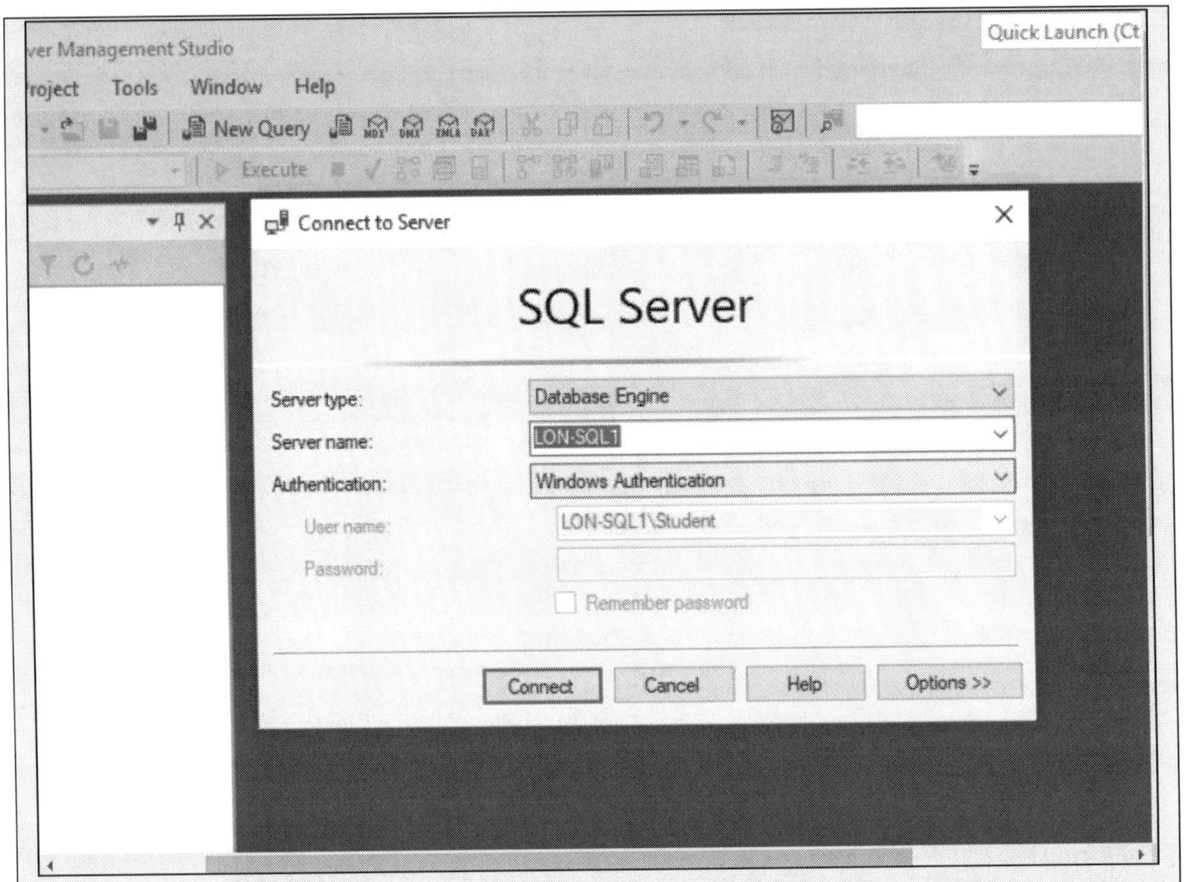

2. You will be prompted to link to your SQL Server. Enter "**LON-SQL1**" for the local server name, make sure that "**Windows Authentication**" is selected, and click on "**Connect**."

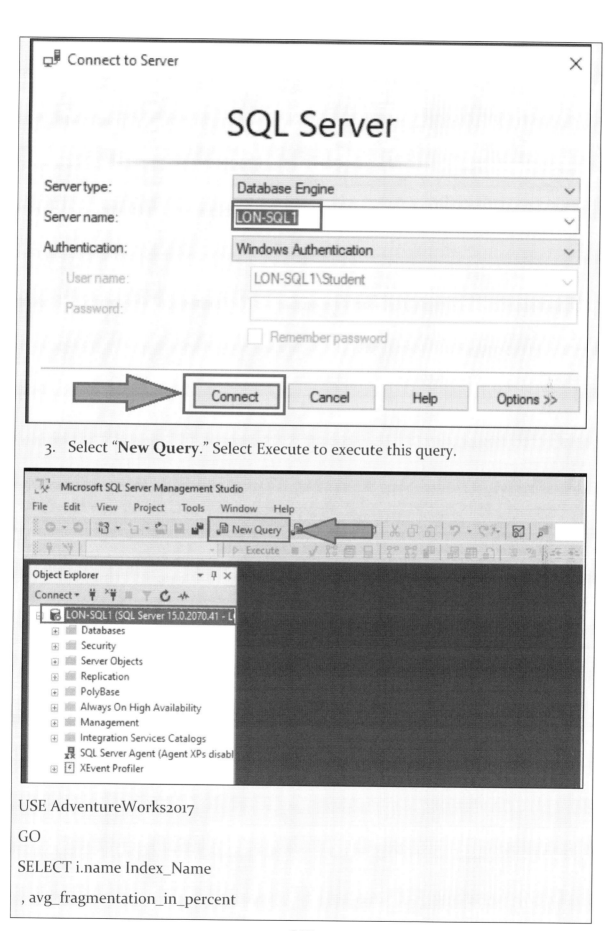

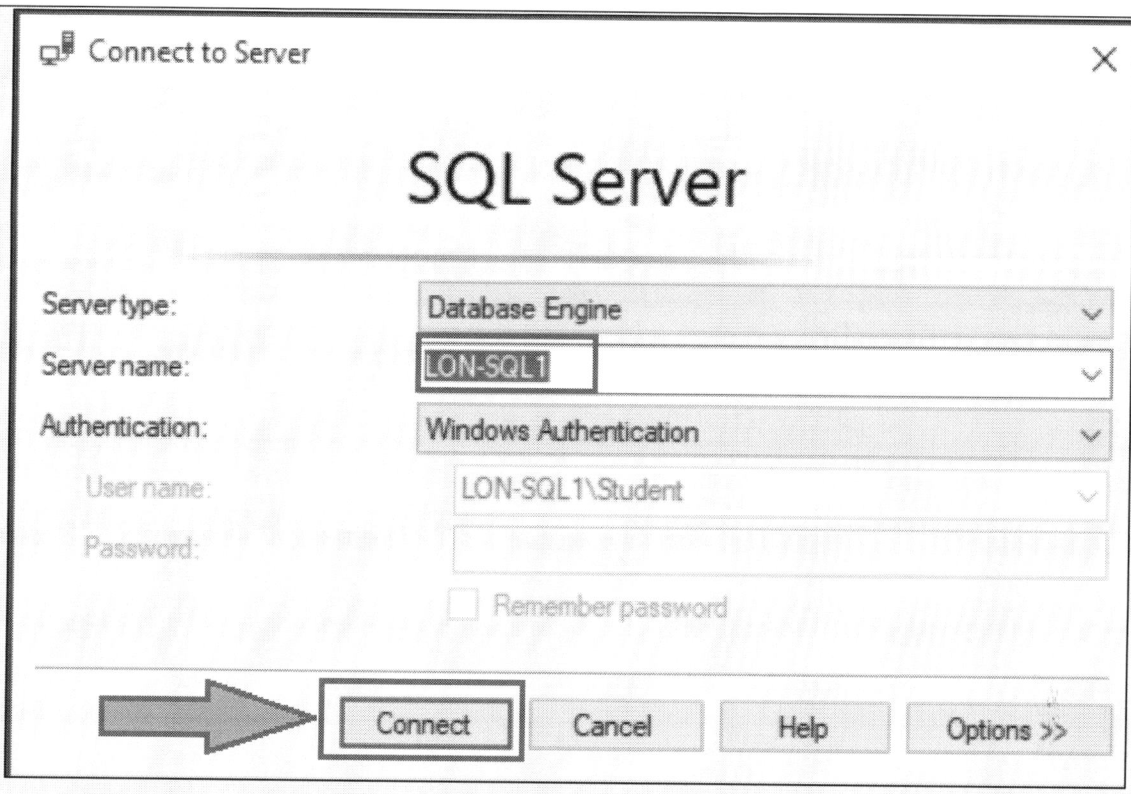

3. Select "**New Query**." Select Execute to execute this query.

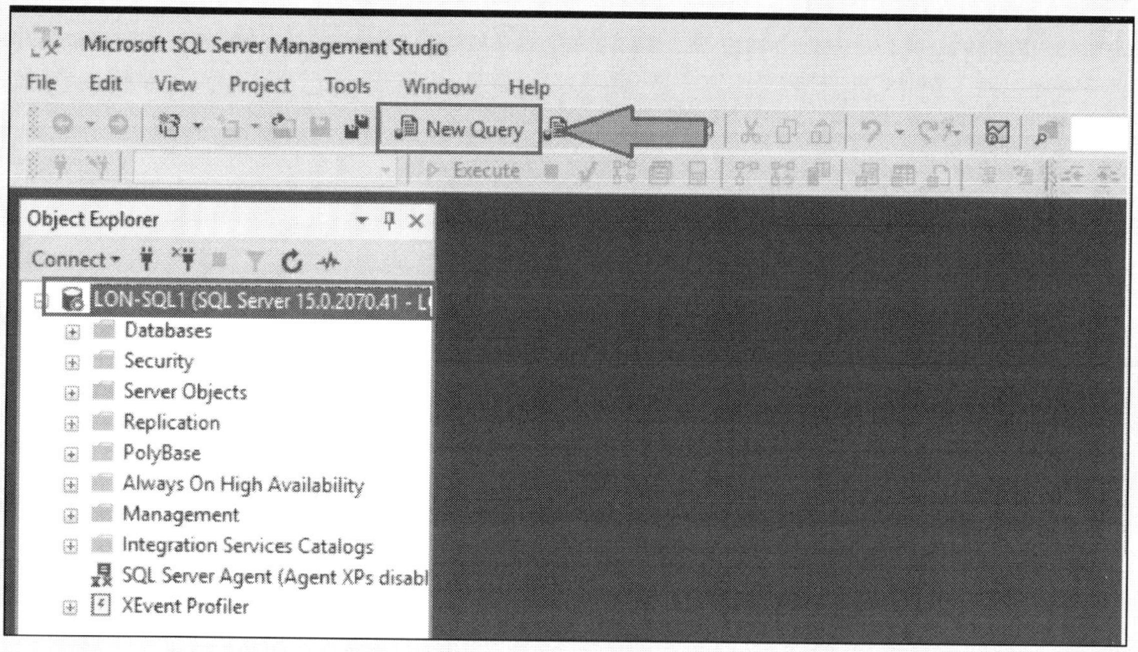

USE AdventureWorks2017

GO

SELECT i.name Index_Name

, avg_fragmentation_in_percent

```
, db_name(database_id)
, i.object_id
, i.index_id
, index_type_desc
FROM
sys.dm_db_index_physical_stats(db_id('AdventureWorks2017'),object_id('person.address'),NULL,NULL,'DETAILED') ps
INNER JOIN sys.indexes i ON ps.object_id = i.object_id
AND ps.index_id = i.index_id
WHERE avg_fragmentation_in_percent > 50 -- find indexes where fragmentation is greater than 50%
```

```
exercise_steps.sql - LON-SQL1.master (LON-SQL1\Student (71)) - Microsoft SQL Server Management Studio
File Edit View Query Project Tools Window Help
New Query
master    Execute
exercise_steps.sql...N-SQL1\Student (71))
-- Step 4

USE AdventureWorks2017
GO

SELECT i.name Index_Name
 , avg_fragmentation_in_percent
 , db_name(database_id)
 , i.object_id
 , i.index_id
 , index_type_desc
FROM sys.dm_db_index_physical_stats(db_id('AdventureWorks2017'),object_id('person
 INNER JOIN sys.indexes i ON ps.object_id = i.object_id
 AND ps.index_id = i.index_id
WHERE avg_fragmentation_in_percent > 50 -- find indexes where fragmentation is gr

-- Step 5
```

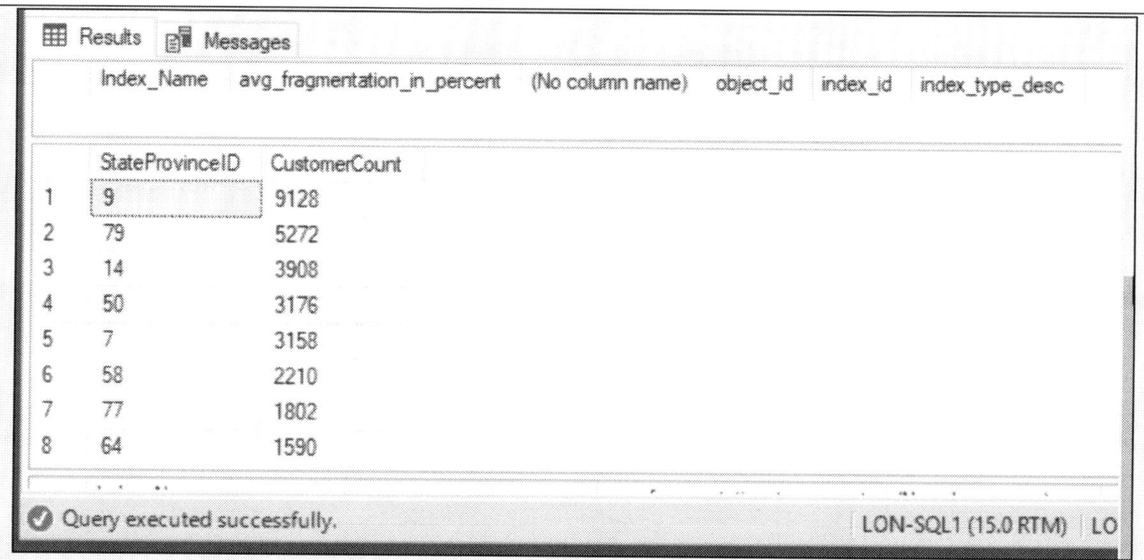

	StateProvinceID	CustomerCount
1	9	9128
2	79	5272
3	14	3908
4	50	3176
5	7	3158
6	58	2210
7	77	1802
8	64	1590

This query will report any indexes that have a fragmentation of above 50%.

4. Select "**New Query**." Select Execute to execute this query.

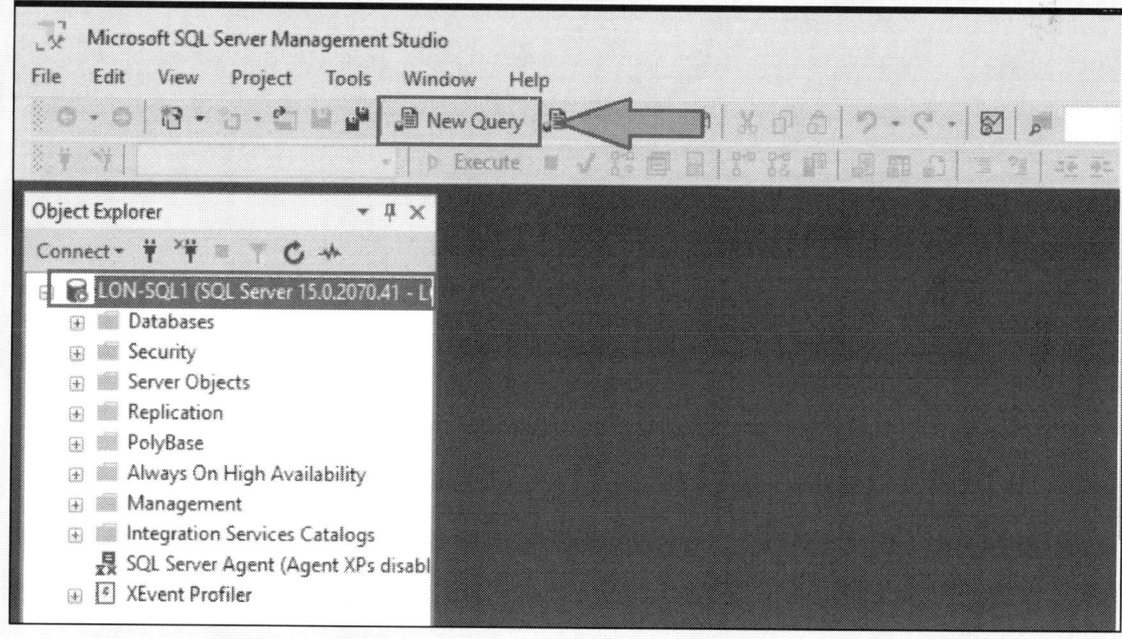


```
USE AdventureWorks2017
GO
INSERT INTO [Person].[Address]
([AddressLine1]
,[AddressLine2]
,[City]
```

```
,[StateProvinceID]
,[PostalCode]
,[SpatialLocation]
,[rowguid]
,[ModifiedDate])
SELECT AddressLine1,
AddressLine2,
'Amsterdam',
StateProvinceID,
PostalCode,
SpatialLocation,
newid(),
getdate()
from Person.Address;
GO
```

```
--Copy and paste the code below into your query window.

USE MASTER
GO

CREATE EVENT SESSION [Blocking] ON SERVER
ADD EVENT sqlserver.blocked_process_report(
ACTION(sqlserver.client_app_name,sqlserver.client_hostname,sqlserver.database_id,
ADD TARGET package0.ring_buffer
WITH (MAX_MEMORY=4096 KB, EVENT_RETENTION_MODE=ALLOW_SINGLE_EVENT_LOSS, MAX_DISPA
GO
-- Start the event session
ALTER EVENT SESSION [Blocking] ON SERVER
STATE = start;
GO

--Click New Query from SQL Server Management Studio. Copy and paste the followin
```

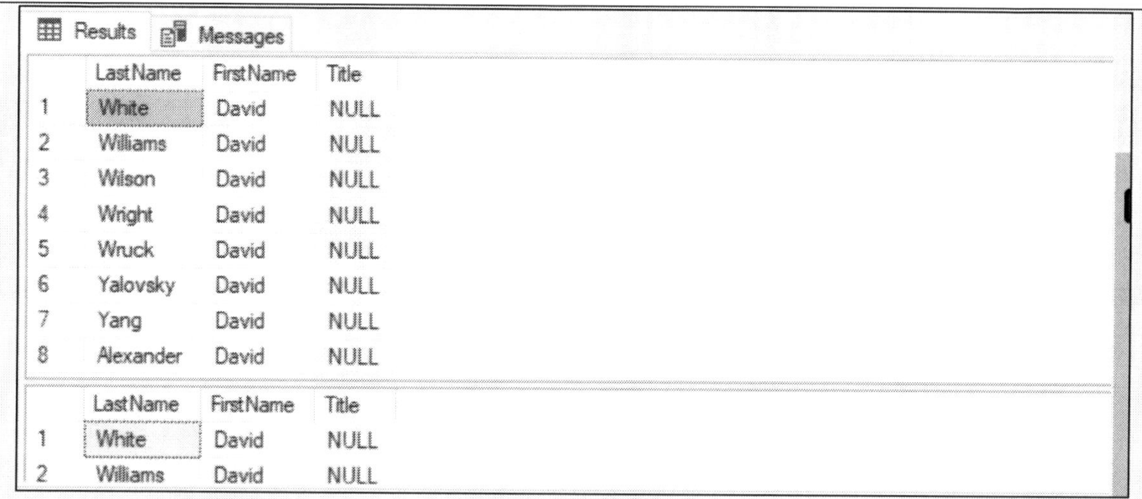

This query will enhance the fragmentation level of the Person, Address table, and its indexes by adding a large number of new records.

5. Execute the first query again.

```
USE AdventureWorks2017
GO
SELECT i.name Index_Name
, avg_fragmentation_in_percent
, db_name(database_id)
, i.object_id
, i.index_id
, index_type_desc
FROM
sys.dm_db_index_physical_stats(db_id('AdventureWorks2017'),object_id('person.address'),NULL,NULL,'DETAILED') ps
INNER JOIN sys.indexes i ON ps.object_id = i.object_id
AND ps.index_id = i.index_id
WHERE avg_fragmentation_in_percent > 50 -- find indexes where fragmentation is greater than 50%
```

exercise_steps.sql - LON-SQL1.master (LON-SQL1\Student (71)) - Microsoft SQL Server Management Studio

File Edit View Query Project Tools Window Help

New Query

master

Execute

exercise_steps.sql...N-SQL1\Student (71))

```
-- Step 4

USE AdventureWorks2017
GO

SELECT i.name Index_Name
 , avg_fragmentation_in_percent
 , db_name(database_id)
 , i.object_id
 , i.index_id
 , index_type_desc
FROM sys.dm_db_index_physical_stats(db_id('AdventureWorks2017'),object_id('person
 INNER JOIN sys.indexes i ON ps.object_id = i.object_id
 AND ps.index_id = i.index_id
WHERE avg_fragmentation_in_percent > 50 -- find indexes where fragmentation is gr

-- Step 5
```

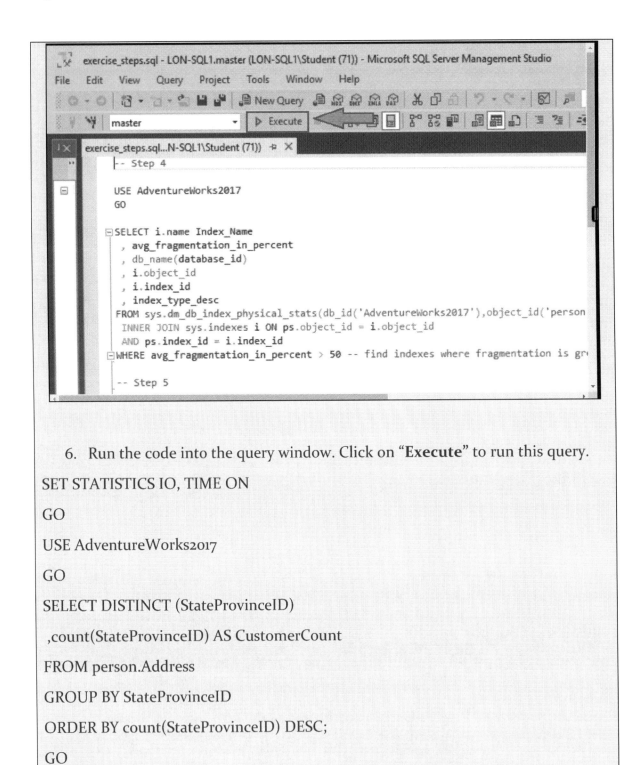

6. Run the code into the query window. Click on "**Execute**" to run this query.

```
SET STATISTICS IO, TIME ON
GO
USE AdventureWorks2017
GO
SELECT DISTINCT (StateProvinceID)
,count(StateProvinceID) AS CustomerCount
FROM person.Address
GROUP BY StateProvinceID
ORDER BY count(StateProvinceID) DESC;
GO
```

```
SET STATISTICS IO, TIME ON
GO
USE AdventureWorks2017
GO
SELECT DISTINCT (StateProvinceID)
, count(StateProvinceID) AS CustomerCount
From person.Address
GROUP BY StateProvinceID
ORDER BY count(StateProvinceID) DESC;
GO
```

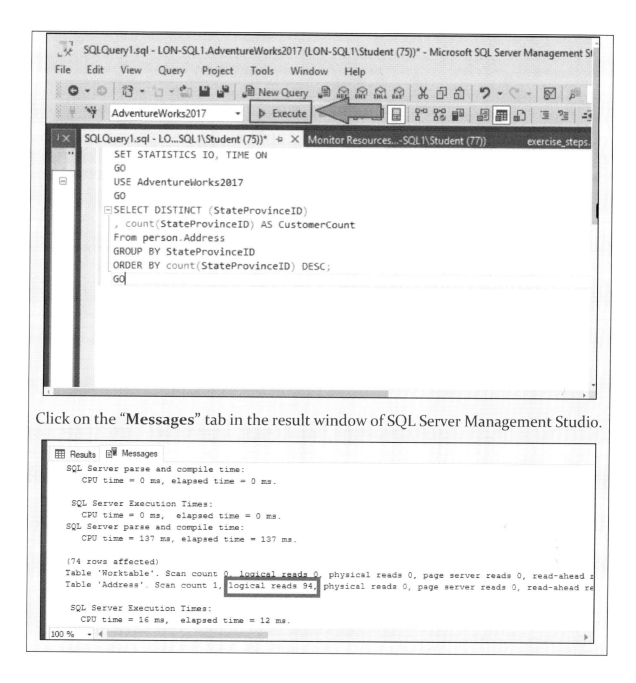

Click on the "**Messages**" tab in the result window of SQL Server Management Studio.

```
SQL Server parse and compile time:
   CPU time = 0 ms, elapsed time = 0 ms.

 SQL Server Execution Times:
   CPU time = 0 ms,  elapsed time = 0 ms.
SQL Server parse and compile time:
   CPU time = 137 ms, elapsed time = 137 ms.

(74 rows affected)
Table 'Worktable'. Scan count 0, logical reads 0, physical reads 0, page server reads 0, read-ahead r
Table 'Address'. Scan count 1, logical reads 94, physical reads 0, page server reads 0, read-ahead re

 SQL Server Execution Times:
   CPU time = 16 ms,  elapsed time = 12 ms.
```

Rebuild Indexes

1. Select "**New Query**." Run the code into the query window.

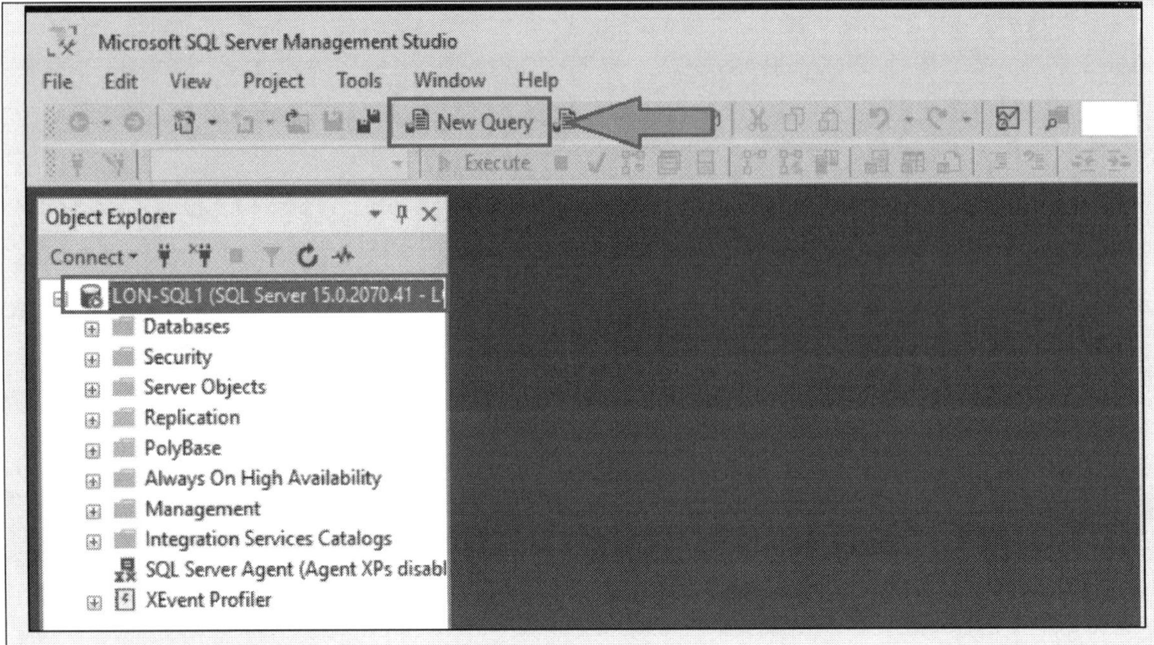

2. Run the code into the query window.

```
USE AdventureWorks2017
GO
ALTER INDEX [IX_Address_StateProvinceID] ON [Person].[Address] REBUILD PARTITION = ALL WITH (PAD_INDEX = OFF, STATISTICS_NORECOMPUTE = OFF, SORT_IN_TEMPDB = OFF, IGNORE_DUP_KEY = OFF, ONLINE = OFF, ALLOW_ROW_LOCKS = ON, ALLOW_PAGE_LOCKS = ON)
```

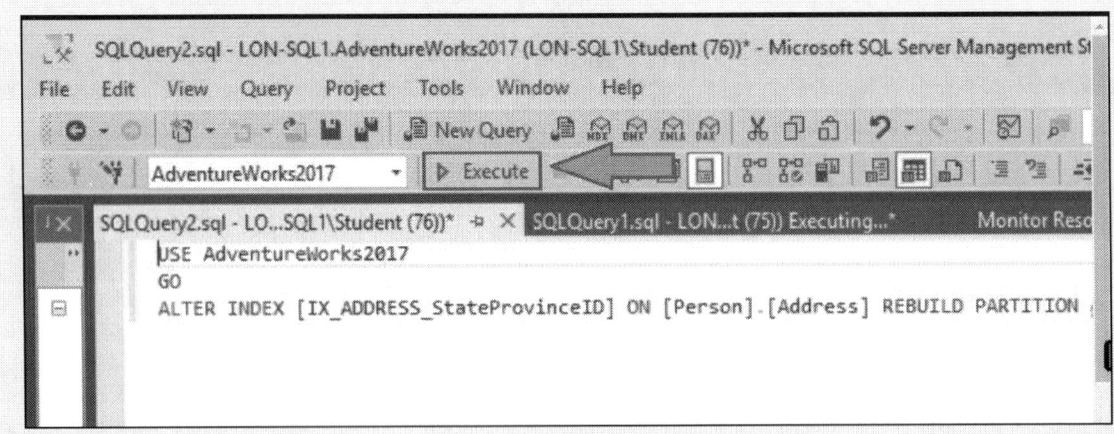

3. Re-run the query from step 4 in the first task.

```
USE AdventureWorks2017
GO
```

```
SELECT i.name Index_Name
 , avg_fragmentation_in_percent
 , db_name(database_id)
 , i.object_id
 , i.index_id
 , index_type_desc
FROM
sys.dm_db_index_physical_stats(db_id('AdventureWorks2017'),object_id('person.address'),NULL,NULL,'DETAILED') ps
 INNER JOIN sys.indexes i ON ps.object_id = i.object_id
 AND ps.index_id = i.index_id
WHERE avg_fragmentation_in_percent > 50 -- find indexes where fragmentation is greater than 50%
```

exercise_steps.sql - LON-SQL1.master (LON-SQL1\Student (71)) - Microsoft SQL Server Management Studio

File Edit View Query Project Tools Window Help

New Query | master | Execute

exercise_steps.sql...N-SQL1\Student (71))

```
-- Step 4

USE AdventureWorks2017
GO

SELECT i.name Index_Name
  , avg_fragmentation_in_percent
  , db_name(database_id)
  , i.object_id
  , i.index_id
  , index_type_desc
FROM sys.dm_db_index_physical_stats(db_id('AdventureWorks2017'),object_id('person
 INNER JOIN sys.indexes i ON ps.object_id = i.object_id
 AND ps.index_id = i.index_id
WHERE avg_fragmentation_in_percent > 50 -- find indexes where fragmentation is gr

-- Step 5
```

Results | Messages

	Index_Name	avg_fragmentation_in_percent	(No column name)	c
1	AK_Address_rowguid	98.6263736263736	AdventureWorks2017	
2	IX_Address_AddressLine1_AddressLine2_City_StateP...	98.671096345515	AdventureWorks2017	
3	IX_Address_AddressLine1_AddressLine2_City_StateP...	90	AdventureWorks2017	

	StateProvinceID	CustomerCount
1	9	9128
2	79	5272
3	14	3908
4	50	3176
5	7	3158
6	58	2210
7	77	1802

```
WHERE avg_fragmentation_in_percent > 50 -- find indexes where fragmentation is greater than 50%
```

4. Re-run the query from step 6 in the first task.

```
GO
USE AdventureWorks2017
GO
SELECT DISTINCT (StateProvinceID)
 ,count(StateProvinceID) AS CustomerCount
FROM person.Address
GROUP BY StateProvinceID
ORDER BY count(StateProvinceID) DESC;
GO
```

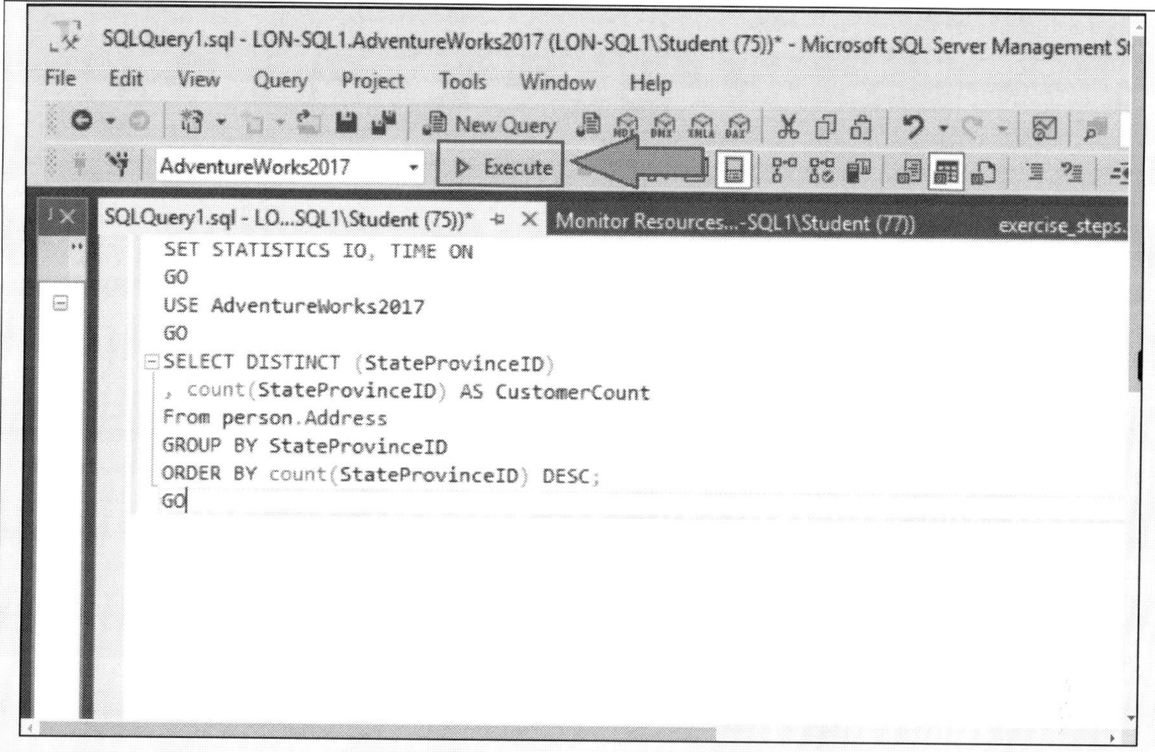

Results | Messages

	StateProvinceID	CustomerCount
1	9	4564
2	79	2636
3	14	1954
4	50	1588
5	7	1579
6	58	1105
7	77	901
8	64	795
9	70	453
10	53	412
11	161	398

Query executed successfully. | LON-SQL1 (15.0 RTM) | LON-SQL1\Student (63)

Because the index has been rebuilt, it will now be as efficient as possible, and the logical reads should decrease.

Mind Map

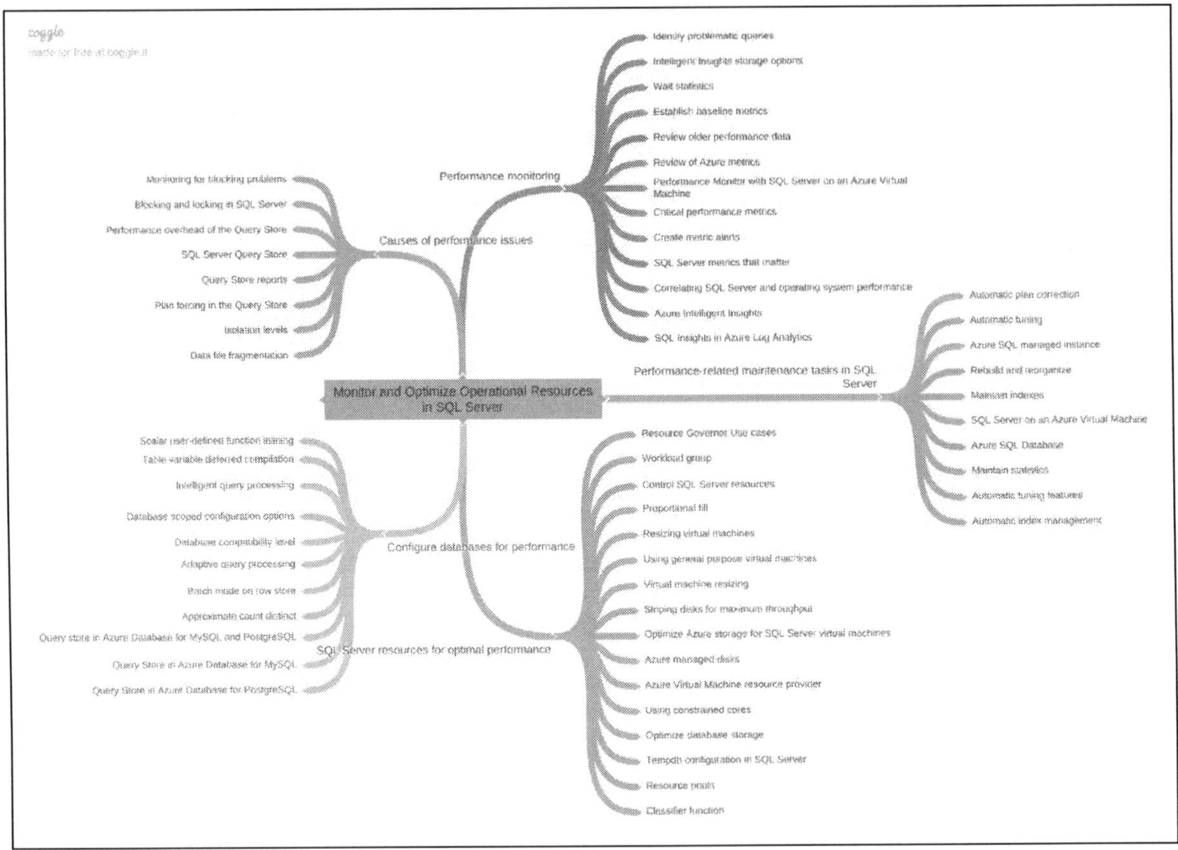

Figure 04-20: Mind Map

Practice Questions

1. Which Intelligent Insights options provide SQL Insights?

A. Log Analytics

B. Azure Storage

C. Event Hub

D. None of the above

2. Which Performance Monitor counter reflects how long SQL Server expects to retain data in memory?

A. Page Life Expectancy

B. Processor Queue Length

C. Paging File Usage

D. None of the above

3. If you want to see the sizes of your SQL Server Databases running in an Azure VM, which tool should you use?
A. The SQL VM Resource Provider

B. Azure Monitor

C. Intelligent Insights

D. None of the above

4. Which isolation level should you choose if you want to prevent users reading data from blocking users writing data?

A. Serializable

B. Read Committed Snapshot Isolation

C. Repeatable Read

D. None of the above

5. Which DMV shows sessions holding locks?
A. Sys.query_store_queries

B. Sys.dm_tran_locks

C. Sys.databases

D. None of the above

6. Which Query Store catalog view provides the Query ID to allow for query tracking?
A. Sys.query_store_plan

B. Sys.query_store_runtime_statistics

C. Sys.query_store_queries

D. None of the above

7. Which type of storage should be used in conjunction with Azure VMs for SQL Server data files?
A. Table storage

B. Blob storage

C. Disk storage

D. None of the above

8. Which of the following can be limited using Resource Governor?

A. Buffer pool allocation

B. Write IOPs

C. Recompilation

D. None of the above

9. Which is an option from the SQL Server Resource Provider for Azure VMs?

A. Storage configuration

B. Changing the max degree of parallelism

C. Maintenance plan

D. None of the above

10. Which intelligent query processing feature allows for faster calculations of a large number of rows?

A. Batch mode on a row store

B. Approximate count distinct

C. Interleaved execution

D. None of the above

11. Which component of resource governor allows you to configure limits on system resources?

A. Workload groups

B. Classifier functions

C. Resource pools

D. None of the above

12. Which database setting affects the way the query optimizer generates execution plans?

A. Recovery model

B. Optimize for ad hoc workloads

C. Compatibility level

D. None of the above

13. Which platform supports automatic index management?

A. Azure SQL Managed Instance

B. Azure SQL Database

C. SQL Server in an Azure VM

D. None of the above

14. Which statistics option allows statistics to be updated while a query executes against the object the statistics are based on?

A. Auto Create Incremental Statistics

B. Auto Create Statistics

C. Auto Update Statistics Asynchronously

D. None of the above

15. Which DMV shows the status of a plan updated by automatic tuning?

A. sys.dm_db_tuning_recommendations

B. sys.dm_db_automatic_tuning_options

C. sys.query_store_query

D. None of the above

Chapter 05: Optimize Query Performance in SQL Server

Introduction

Database design is an important component of overall performance. Using the proper data types and storage mechanisms can also benefit the performance of your applications. The SQL Server platform provides several options for building indexes and compressing data for improved performance.

Understanding execution plans and using indexes are the basics of database performance. At the same time, you have to understand patterns and anti-patterns for relational databases and target for good query choices and proper indexing.

One of the DBA's challenges is to assess the impact of changes they make to code or data structures on a busy production system. While tuning a single query in isolation provides easy metrics such as elapsed time or logical reads, making minor tweaks on an active system may require deeper evaluation. SQL Server and Azure SQL are instrumented software and monitored at several levels.

Describe SQL Server Query Plans

The essential skill you must acquire in database performance tuning is reading and understanding query execution plans. The plan brief the behavior of the database engine as it executes queries and recovers the results.

Describe types of query plans

It is useful to understand how database optimizers work before diving into execution plan details. SQL Server uses what is known as a cost-based query optimizer. The query optimizer computes a cost for multiple possible plans based on the statistics on the columns being utilized and the possible indexes used for each operation in each query strategy. Based on this information, it calculates the total cost for each idea. Some difficult queries can have thousands of possible execution tactics. The optimizer does not assess every possible plan but uses heuristics to determine plans likely to have good performance. The optimizer will then pick the lowest cost plan of all the plans evaluated for a given query.

Because the query optimizer is cost-based, it should have good inputs for decision-making. The statistics SQL Server uses to monitor the distribution of data in columns and indexes should be kept up to date or cause suboptimal execution plans to be generated. SQL Server automatically updates its statistics as data modifies in a table; however, it may require regular updates for rapidly changing data. The engine uses

numerous factors when building a plan, including the database's compatibility level, row estimations based on statistics, and available indexes.

When a user submits a query to the database engine, the following points arise:

1. The query is analyzed for proper syntax, and a search of database objects is generated if the syntax is accurate.
2. The parse tree from Step 1 is taken as input to a database engine component called the Algebrizer for binding. This step authorizes that columns and objects in the query exist and identifies the data types being processed for a given question. This step outputs a query processor tree in the input for step 3.
3. Because query optimization is a comparatively expensive process in terms of CPU consumption, the database engine caches execution plans in a special area of memory called the plan cache. If a plan for an assigned question already exists, that plan is recovered from the cache. The queries whose plans are stored in the cache will each have a hash value generated based on the T-SQL in the query. This value is denoted as the query hash. When looking for a plan in cache, the engine will create an inquiry hash for the current question and see if it matches any remaining queries in the plan case.
4. If the plan does not exist, the Query Optimizer then uses its cost-based optimizer to generate some execution plan options based on the statistics about the columns, tables, and indexes used in the inquiry, as defined above. The output of this step is a query execution plan.
5. The query is then executed using an execution plan pulled from the plan cache or a new program generated in step 4. The output of this step is the results of your query.

Let us look at an example. Consider the following query:

```
SELECT orderdate

 ,avg(salesAmount)

FROM FactResellerSales

WHERE ShipDate = '2013-07-07'

GROUP BY orderdate;
```

Figure 05-01: Query Data

In this example, SQL Server will see the Order-Date, Ship-Date, and Sales-Amount columns in the table Fact-Reseller-Sales. If those columns occur, it will generate a hash

value for the question and observe the plan cache for a matching hash value. If there is a plan for a query with a matching hash, the engine will reprocess that plan. If there is no plan with a matching hash, it will observe the available statistics on the Order-Date and Ship-Date columns. The WHERE clause referencing the Ship-Date column is known as the predicate in this query. If a non-clustered index contains the Ship-Date column, SQL Server will most likely include that in the plan if the costs are lesser than retrieving data from the clustered index. The optimizer will then pick the lowest cost plan of the available plans and execute the query.

Query plans combine relational operators to recover the data and capture information, such as estimated row counts. Another element of the execution plan is the memory needed to perform operations such as joining or sorting data. The memory required by the query is called the memory grant. The memory grant is a good example of the importance of statistics. If SQL Server considers an operator that will return 10,000,000 rows when it is only 100, a much higher amount of memory is granted to the query. A memory grant that is higher than necessary can cause a twofold problem. First, the question may encounter a RESOURCE_SEMAPHORE wait, which specifies that the request is waiting for SQL Server to assign a large amount of memory. SQL Server defaults to waiting for 25 times the cost of the inquiry (in seconds) before executing, up to 24 hours. Second, when the query is run, if there is not enough memory available, the query will fall to temp DB, which is much slower than operating in memory.

The execution plan also stores other metadata about the query, including, but not limited to, the database compatibility level, the degree of parallelism of the query, and the parameters that are supplied if the query is parameterized.

You can observe query plans in either a graphical representation or text-based format. You can follow text-based plans anywhere you can execute TSQL queries. The text-based options are invoked with SET commands and apply only to the current connection.

Most DBAs desire to look at plans graphically because a graphical plan lets you see the plan as a whole, including what is called the 'shape' of the plan, much more easily. There are numerous ways you can view and save graphical query plans. The most collaborative tool used is SQL Server Management Studio, but the Azure Data Studio's estimated plans could also be observed. There are also third-party tools that support viewing graphical execution plans.

There are three different types of execution plans that can be seen.

Estimated Execution Plan: - This type is the execution plan produced by the query optimizer. The metadata and size of query memory grants are created on estimates from the statistics in the database at query compilation. To see a text-based estimated plan execute the command SET SHOWPLAN_ALL ON before running the question. The SET

option will stay in effect until you set it OFF. When you execute the query, you will look at the steps of the execution plan, but the query will NOT be executed, and you will not see any results.

Actual Execution Plan: - This type is the same plan as the estimated plan; however, this plan also has the execution context for the query, which contains the estimated and actual row counts, any execution warnings, the actual degree of parallelism (number of processors used) and elapsed and CPU times used during the execution. To see an actual text-based plan execute the command SET STATISTICS PROFILE ON before running the query. The query will publish, and you get the program and the results.

Live Query Statistics: - This plan observing option combines the estimated and actual plans into an animated plan that shows execution progress through the operators in the plan. It refreshes every second and displays the exact number of rows flowing through the operators. The other benefit to Live Query Statistics is that it shows the handoff from operator to operator, which may help troubleshoot various performance issues. Because the type of plan is animated, it is only accessible as a graphical plan.

Explain Estimated and Actual Query Plans

The operators who used an executive order will be the same as the estimated plan in nearly all cases. The difference is that the actual plan contains runtime statistics not taken in the estimated plan.

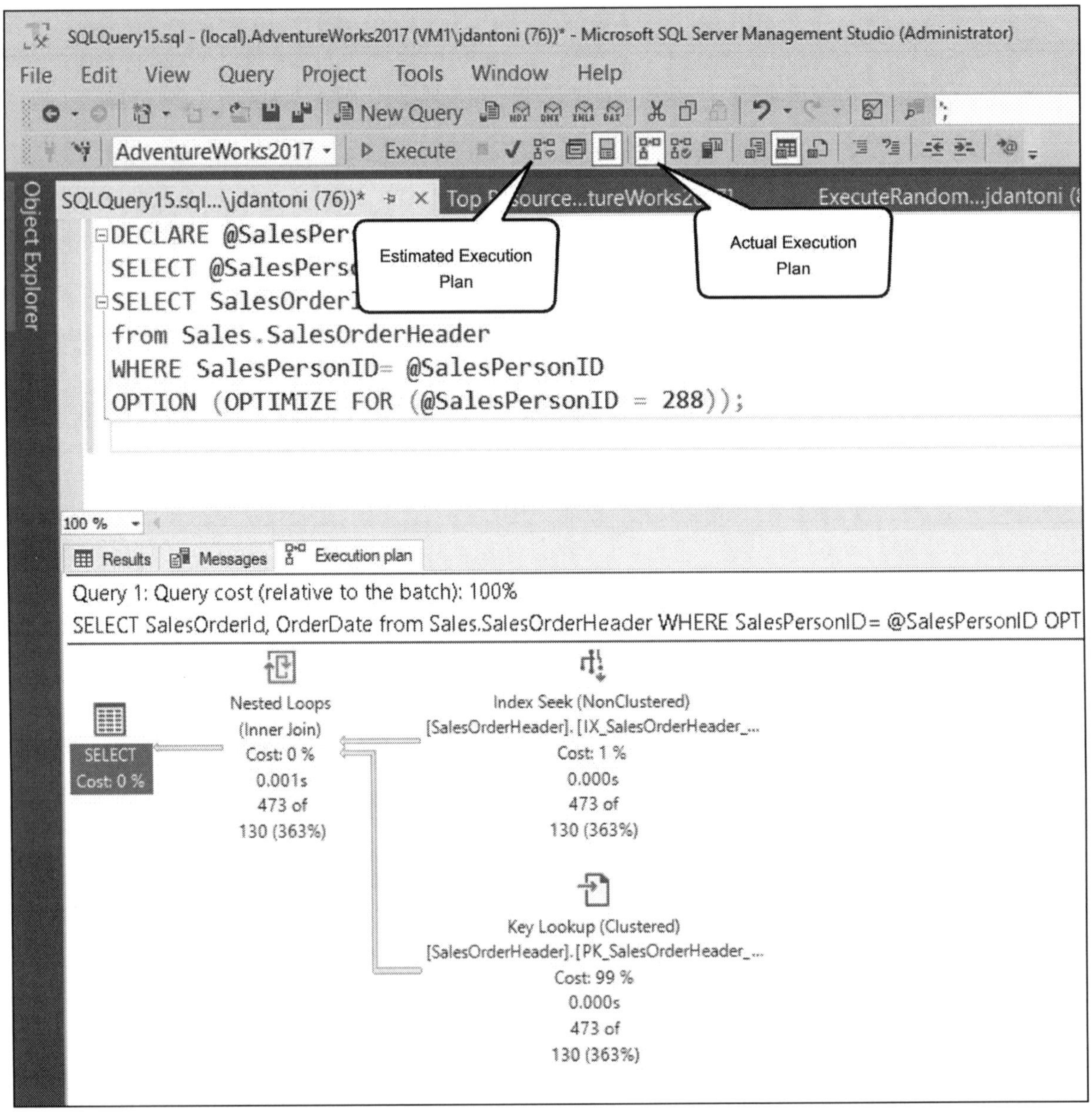

Figure 05-02: Estimated Plan in SSMS

As shown above, you can make an estimated plan in SSMS by selecting the button pointed to by the estimated query plan box (or using the keyboard command Control +L). You can create the actual plan by either selecting the icon shown or using the keyboard command Control +M and publishing the query. It is different from an estimated query plan, which does not need the query to be executed. The two option buttons work a bit differently. The Estimated Query Plan button immediately answers whatever query is highlighted (or the entire workspace, if nothing is highlighted). The Actual Execution plan button is a toggle. Once you select it, it says on and displays the Actual plan for all queries. To stop showing plans, you can select the button again, which will turn it off.

There is an overhead to publishing a query and creating an estimated execution plan, so observing execution plans must be done carefully in a production environment.

For the most part, you can use the estimated execution plan while writing your query to recognize its performance characteristics, find missing indexes, or notice query anomalies. The actual execution plan is best used to understand the query's runtime performance and the essential gaps in statistical data that cause the query optimizer to make suboptimal choices based on the available information.

Read a query plan

Execution plans display what tasks the database engine does while retrieving the data required to satisfy a query. Let us dive into the plan.

First, the query itself is shown below:

```
SELECT [stockItemName]
 ,[UnitPrice] * [QuantityPerOuter] AS CostPerOuterBox
 ,[QuantityonHand]
FROM [Warehouse].[StockItems] s
 JOIN [Warehouse].[StockItemHoldings] sh ON s.StockItemID = sh.StockItemID
ORDER BY CostPerOuterBox;
```

Figure 05-03: Query Data

This query links the Stock-Items table to the Stock-Item-Holdings table, where the column Stock-Item-ID is equal. Therefore, the database engine should reveal the first identity of those rows before it can process the rest of the query.

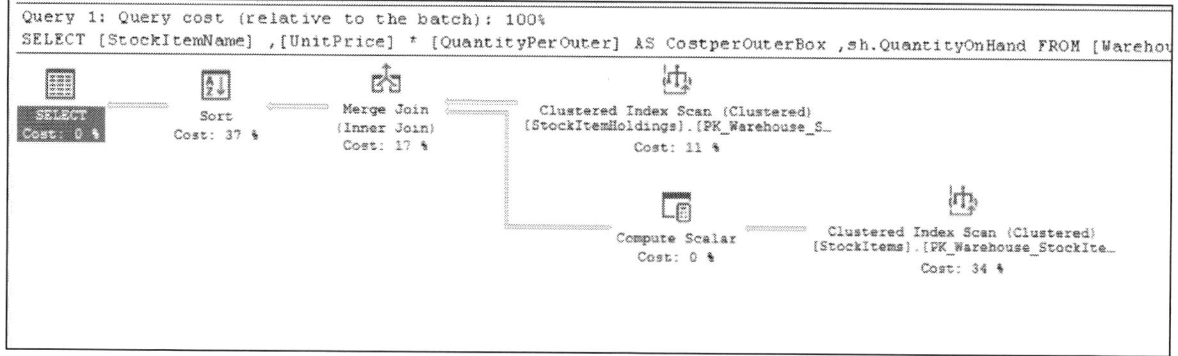

Figure 05-04: Query Cost

The SQL Server database engine has over 100 query operators that can make up for an execution plan. Each icon in the plan displays a specific operation, demonstrating the various actions and decisions that make up an execution plan. You will see that there is a cost percentage under each operator icon comparative to the total cost of the query. Even an operation that displays a cost of 0% still signifies some cost. 0% is generally due to rounding because the graphical plan costs are always presented as whole numbers, and the real percentage is something less than 0.5%.

PKWarehouseStock-Item-Holdings clustered index is the first operation in the query. The flow of execution in an execution plan is from right to left and top to bottom, so in the plan above, the Clustered Index Scan operation on the Stock-Item-Holdings. The widths of the lines that connect the operators are based on the estimated number of rows of data that flow onward to the next operator. A thick arrow indicates the large operator-to-operator transfer and may mean an opportunity to tune a query. You can also hold your mouse over an operator and see additional information in a ToolTip, as shown below.

```
Clustered Index Scan (Clustered)
[StockItems].[PK_Warehouse_StockIte…
Cost: 34 %
```

Clustered Index Scan (Clustered)
Scanning a clustered index, entirely or only a range.

Physical Operation	Clustered Index Scan
Logical Operation	Clustered Index Scan
Estimated Execution Mode	Row
Storage	RowStore
Estimated Operator Cost	0.0131613 (34%)
Estimated I/O Cost	0.0127546
Estimated Subtree Cost	0.0131613
Estimated CPU Cost	0.0004067
Estimated Number of Executions	1
Estimated Number of Rows	227
Estimated Number of Rows to be Read	227
Estimated Row Size	128 B
Ordered	True
Node ID	4

Object
[WideWorldImporters].[Warehouse].[StockItems].[PK_Warehouse_StockItems] [s]

Output List
[WideWorldImporters].[Warehouse].[StockItems].StockItemID, [WideWorldImporters].[Warehouse].[StockItems].StockItemName, [WideWorldImporters].[Warehouse].[StockItems].QuantityPerOuter, [WideWorldImporters].[Warehouse].[StockItems].UnitPrice

Figure 05-05: Clustered Index Scan

The tooltip highlights the cost and estimates for the estimated plan, and an actual plan will include the comparisons to the existing rows and expenses. Each operator also has properties that show you more than the tooltip does. If you right-click on a specific operator, you can select the Properties option from the context menu to see the full property list. This option will open up a separate Properties pane in SQL Server Management Studio, defaulting on the right side. Once the Properties pane is open, clicking on any operator will populate the Properties list with properties for that operator. Alternatively, you can open the Properties pane by clicking on view in the main SQL Server Management Studio menu and choosing Properties.

Properties

Clustered Index Scan (Clustered)

Misc	
Defined Values	[WideWorldImporters].[Warehouse].[StockItems].St(...
Description	Scanning a clustered index, entirely or only a range.
Estimated CPU Cost	0.0004067
Estimated Execution Mode	Row
Estimated I/O Cost	0.0127546
Estimated Number of Executions	1
Estimated Number of Rows	227
Estimated Number of Rows to be Read	227
Estimated Operator Cost	0.0131613 (34%)
Estimated Rebinds	0
Estimated Rewinds	0
Estimated Row Size	128 B
Estimated Subtree Cost	0.0131613
Forced Index	False
ForceScan	False
ForceSeek	False
Logical Operation	Clustered Index Scan
Node ID	4
NoExpandHint	False
Object	[WideWorldImporters].[Warehouse].[StockItems].[PK_V
Alias	[s]
Database	[WideWorldImporters]
Index	[PK_Warehouse_StockItems]
Index Kind	Clustered
Schema	[Warehouse]
Storage	RowStore
Table	[StockItems]
Ordered	True
Output List	[WideWorldImporters].[Warehouse].[StockItems].Stock
[1]	[WideWorldImporters].[Warehouse].[StockItems].Stock
[2]	[WideWorldImporters].[Warehouse].[StockItems].Stock
[3]	[WideWorldImporters].[Warehouse].[StockItems].Quan
[4]	[WideWorldImporters].[Warehouse].[StockItems].UnitP
Parallel	False
Physical Operation	Clustered Index Scan
Scan Direction	FORWARD
Storage	RowStore
TableCardinality	227

Figure 05-06: Clustered Index Scan

The Properties pane includes some additional information and shows the output list, which details the columns being passed to the next operator. Examining these columns in conjunction with a clustered index scan operator can indicate that an additional non-clustered index might be needed to improve the performance of the query. Since a clustered index scan operation is reading the entire table, in this scenario, a non-clustered index on the Stock-Item-ID column in each table could be more efficient.

Lightweight query profiling

As mentioned above, capturing actual execution plans, whether using SSMS or the Extended Events monitoring infrastructure, can have a large overhead and is typically only done in live site troubleshooting efforts. Observer overhead, as it is known, is the cost of monitoring a running application., This cost can be just a few percentage points of CPU utilization in some scenarios. Still, in other cases like capturing actual execution plans, it can significantly slow down individual query performance. The legacy profiling infrastructure in SQL Server's engine could produce up to 75% overhead for capturing query information, whereas the lightweight profiling infrastructure has a maximum overhead of around 2%.

Starting with SQL Server 2014 SP2 and SQL Server 2016, Microsoft introduced lightweight profiling and enhanced it with SQL Server 2016 SP1 and all later versions. In the first version of this feature, lightweight profiling collected row count and I/O utilization information (the number of logical and physical reads and writes performed by the database engine to satisfy a given query). In addition, It introduced a new extended event called query_thread_profile to allow data from each operator in a query plan to be inspected. In the initial version of lightweight profiling, using the feature requires trace flag 7412 to be enabled globally.

In newer releases (SQL Server 2016 SP2 CU3, SQL Server 2017 CU11, and SQL Server 2019), if lightweight profiling is not enabled globally, you can use the USE HINT query hint with QUERY_PLAN_PROFILE to help lightweight profiling at the query level. When a query with this hint completes execution, a query_plan_profile extended event generates an actual execution plan. You can see an example of a question with this hint:

```
SELECT [stockItemName]

 ,[UnitPrice] * [QuantityPerOuter] AS CostPerOuterBox

 ,[ QuantityonHand]

FROM [Warehouse].[StockItems] s

JOIN [Warehouse].[StockItems] sh ON s.StockItemID = sh.StockItemID

ORDER BY CostPerOuterBox

OPTION(USE HINT ('QUERY_PLAN_PROFILE');
```

Figure 05-07: Query Data

The last query plans stats.

SQL Server 2019 and Azure SQL Database support two further enhancements to the query-profiling infrastructure. First, default, lightweight profiling is enabled in SQL Server 2019 and Azure SQL Database and managed instances. Lightweight profiling is also a database scoped configuration option, called LIGHTWEIGHT_QUERY_PROFILING. With the database scoped option, you can disable the feature for any user databases independent of each other.

Second, a new dynamic management function called sys.dm_exec_query_plan_stats can show you the last known actual query execution plan for a given plan handle. To see the previous known exact query plan through the function, you can promote trace flag 2451 server-wide. Alternatively, you can enable this functionality using a database scoped configuration option called LAST_QUERY_PLAN_STATS.

You can combine this function with other objects to get the final execution plan for all cached queries as shown below:

```
SELECT *

FROM sys.dm_exec_cached_plans AS cp

CROSS APPLY sys.dm_exec_sql_text(plan_handle) AS st

CROSS APPLY sys.dm_exec_query_plan_stats(plan_handle) AS qps;

GO
```

Figure 05-08: Query Data

This functionality lets you quickly identify the runtime stats for the last execution of any query in your system, with minimal overhead. The image below shows how to retrieve the plan. If you click on the execution plan, XML, the first column of results, will display the execution plan offered in the second image below.

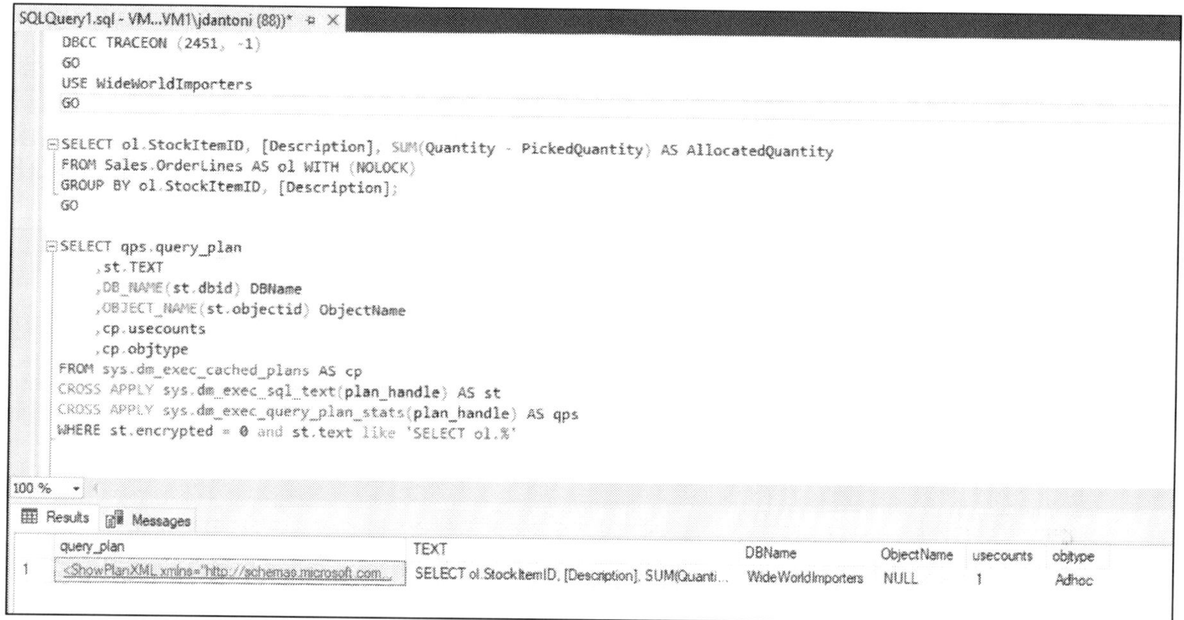

Figure 05-09: SQL Query

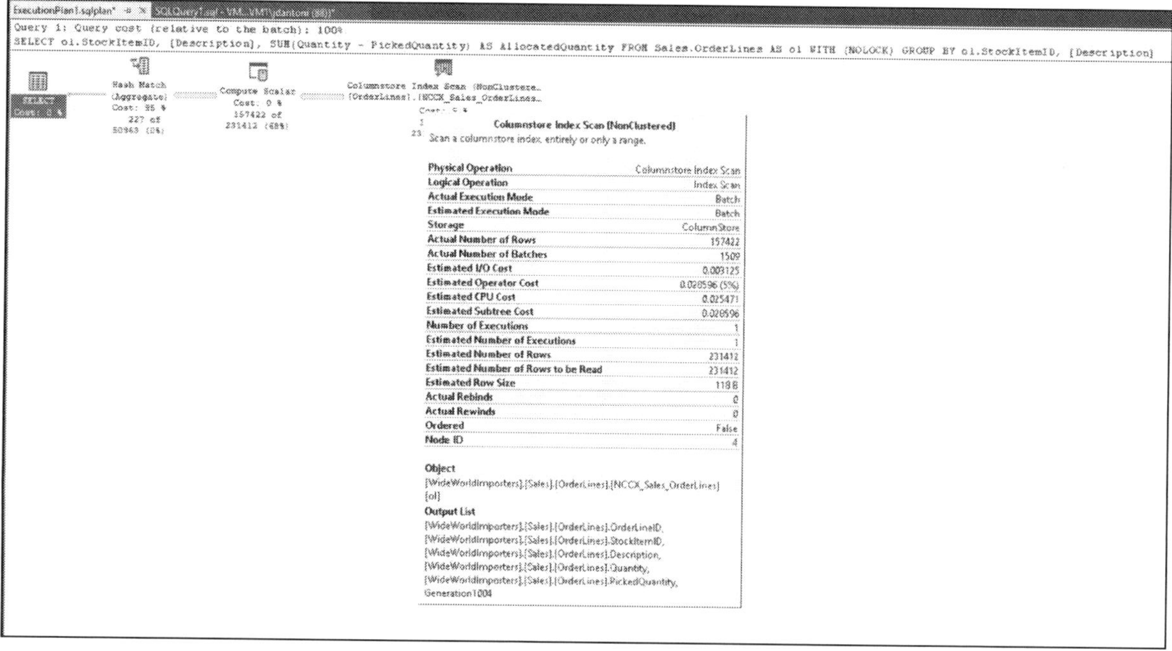

Figure 05-10: Execution Plan

As you can see from the properties of the Column-store Index Scan, the plan retrieved from the cache has an actual number of rows retrieved in the query.

Identify Problematic Query Plans

Most DBAs take the path to troubleshoot query performance to identify the problematic query (typically the query consuming the highest amount of system resources) and then retrieve that query's execution plan. There are two scenarios. One is that the query consistently performs poorly. Consistent poor performance can be caused by a few problems, including hardware resource constraints (though this situation typically will not affect a single query running in isolation), a suboptimal query structure, database compatibility settings, missing indexes, or poor choice of the plan by the query optimizer. The second scenario is that the query performs well for some executions but not others. A few other factors can cause this problem. The most common is data skew in a parameterized query with an efficient plan for some executions and a poor one for others. The other common factor in inconsistent query performance is blocking, where a query is waiting on another query to complete to gain access to a table or hardware contention.

Let us look at each of these potential problems in more detail.

Hardware constraints

For the most part, hardware constraints will not manifest themselves with single query executions. Still, they will be evident when production load is applied, and there is a limited number of CPU threads and a limited amount of memory to be shared among the queries. When you have CPU contention, it will usually be detectable by observing the performance monitor counter '% Processor Time,' which measures the CPU usage of the server. Looking deeper into SQL Server, you may see SOS_SCHEDULER_YIELD and CXPACKET wait for types when the server is under CPU pressure. However, with poor storage system performance, even single executions of an otherwise optimized query can be slow. Storage system performance is best tracked at the operating system level using the performance monitor counters 'Disk Seconds/Read' and 'Disk Seconds/Write,' which measure how long an I/O operation takes to complete. SQL Server will write to its error log if it detects poor storage performance (if an I/O takes longer than 15 seconds to top). If you look at wait statistics and see a high percentage of PAGEIOLATCH_SH waits in your SQL Server, you might have a storage system performance issue. Typically, hardware performance is examined at a high level early in the performance troubleshooting process because it is relatively easy to evaluate.

Most database performance issues can be attributed to suboptimal query patterns, but in many cases, running inefficient queries will put undue pressure on your hardware. For example, missing indexes could lead to CPU, storage, and memory pressure by retrieving more data than is required to process the query. It is recommended that you address suboptimal queries and tune them before handling the hardware issues. You will start looking at query tuning next.

Suboptimal query constructs

Relational databases perform best when executing set-based operations. Set-based operations perform data manipulation (INSERT, UPDATE, DELETE, and SELECT) in sets. Work is done on a set of values and produces either a single value or a result set. The alternative to set-based operations is to perform row-based work using a cursor or a while loop. This type of processing is known as row-based processing, and its cost increases linearly with the number of rows impacted. That linear scale is problematic as data volumes grow for an application.

While detecting suboptimal use of row-based operations with cursors or WHILE loops are important, there are other SQL Server anti-patterns that you should be able to recognize. Table-valued functions (TVF), particularly multi-statement table-valued roles, caused problematic execution plan patterns before SQL Server 2017. Many developers like to use multi-statement table-valued functions because they can execute multiple queries within a single task and aggregate the results into a single table. However, anyone writing T-SQL code needs to know the possible performance penalties for using TVs.

SQL Server has two types of table-valued functions, inline and multi-statement. If you use an inline TVF, the database engine treats it like a view. Multi-statement TVFs are treated like another table when processing a query. Because TVs are dynamic and SQL Server does not have statistics on them, it used a fixed row count when estimating the query plan cost. A static count can be fine if the number of rows is small; however, the execution plan could be inefficient if the TVF returns thousands or millions of rows.

Another anti-pattern has been scalar functions, which have similar estimation and execution problems. Microsoft has made a lot of headway on improving the performance of the patterns above with the introduction of Intelligent Query Processing in SQL Server 2017 and Azure SQL Database, under compatibility levels 140 and 150.

SARGArbility

The term SARGable in relational databases denotes a predicate (WHERE clause) in a detailed format that can leverage an index to speed up the query. Predicates in the correct format are called 'Search Arguments' or SARGs. In SQL Server, using a SARG means that the optimizer will evaluate using a non-clustered index on the column referenced in the SARG for a SEEK operation, instead of scanning the entire index (or the entire table) to retrieve a value.

The presence of a SARG does not guarantee the use of an index for a SEEK. The optimizer's costing algorithms could still determine that the index was too expensive. It could be the case if a SARG refers to a large percentage of rows in a table. The absence

of a SARG does mean that the optimizer will not even evaluate a SEEK on a non-clustered index.

Some examples of expressions that are not SARGs (sometimes said to be non-sargable) are those that include a LIKE clause with a wildcard at the beginning of the string to be matched, for example, WHERE Last Name LIKE '%SMITH%.' Other predicates that are not SARGs occur when using functions on a column, for example, WHERE CONVERT(CHAR(10), CreateDate,121) = '2020-03-22'. These queries with non-sargable expressions are usually identified by examining execution plans for index or table scans, where seeks should otherwise occur.

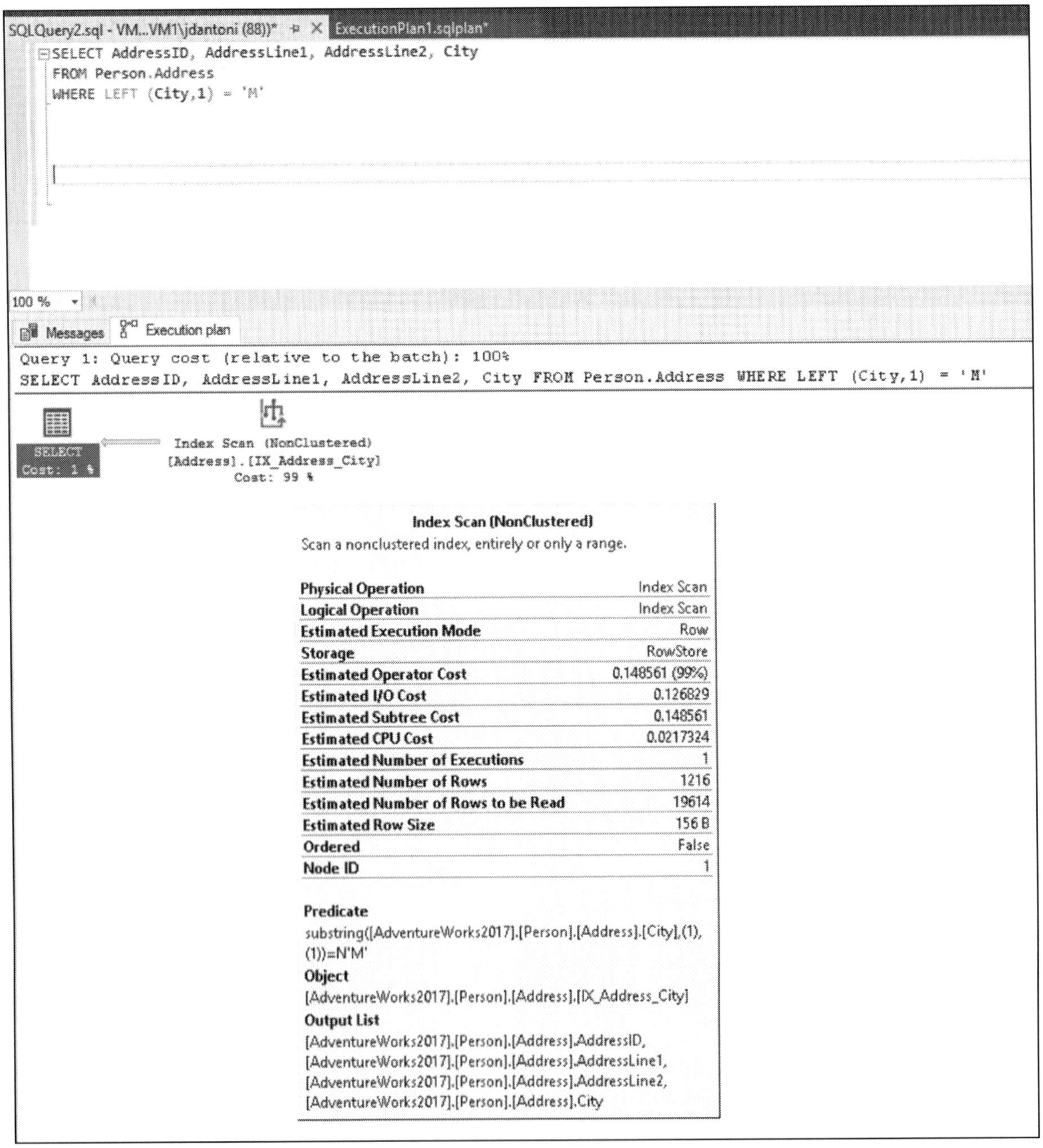

SQLQuery2.sql - VM...VM1\jdantoni (88))* ExecutionPlan1.sqlplan*

```
SELECT AddressID, AddressLine1, AddressLine2, City
FROM Person.Address
WHERE LEFT (City,1) = 'M'
```

100 %

Messages | Execution plan

Query 1: Query cost (relative to the batch): 100%
SELECT AddressID, AddressLine1, AddressLine2, City FROM Person.Address WHERE LEFT (City,1) = 'M'

SELECT Cost: 1 % ← Index Scan (NonClustered) [Address].[IX_Address_City] Cost: 99 %

Index Scan (NonClustered)
Scan a nonclustered index, entirely or only a range.

Physical Operation	Index Scan
Logical Operation	Index Scan
Estimated Execution Mode	Row
Storage	RowStore
Estimated Operator Cost	0.148561 (99%)
Estimated I/O Cost	0.126829
Estimated Subtree Cost	0.148561
Estimated CPU Cost	0.0217324
Estimated Number of Executions	1
Estimated Number of Rows	1216
Estimated Number of Rows to be Read	19614
Estimated Row Size	156 B
Ordered	False
Node ID	1

Predicate
substring([AdventureWorks2017].[Person].[Address].[City],(1),(1))=N'M'
Object
[AdventureWorks2017].[Person].[Address].[IX_Address_City]
Output List
[AdventureWorks2017].[Person].[Address].AddressID, [AdventureWorks2017].[Person].[Address].AddressLine1, [AdventureWorks2017].[Person].[Address].AddressLine2, [AdventureWorks2017].[Person].[Address].City

Figure 05-11: Execution Plan

There is an index on the City column used in the WHERE clause of the query, and while it is being used in this execution plan above, you can see the index is being scanned, which means the entire index is being read. The LEFT function in the predicate makes this expression non-SARGable. The optimizer will not evaluate using an index seek on the index on the City column.

You can write this query to use a predicate that is SARGable. The optimizer would then evaluate a SEEK on the index on the City column. An index SEEK, in this case, would read a much smaller set of rows, as shown below.

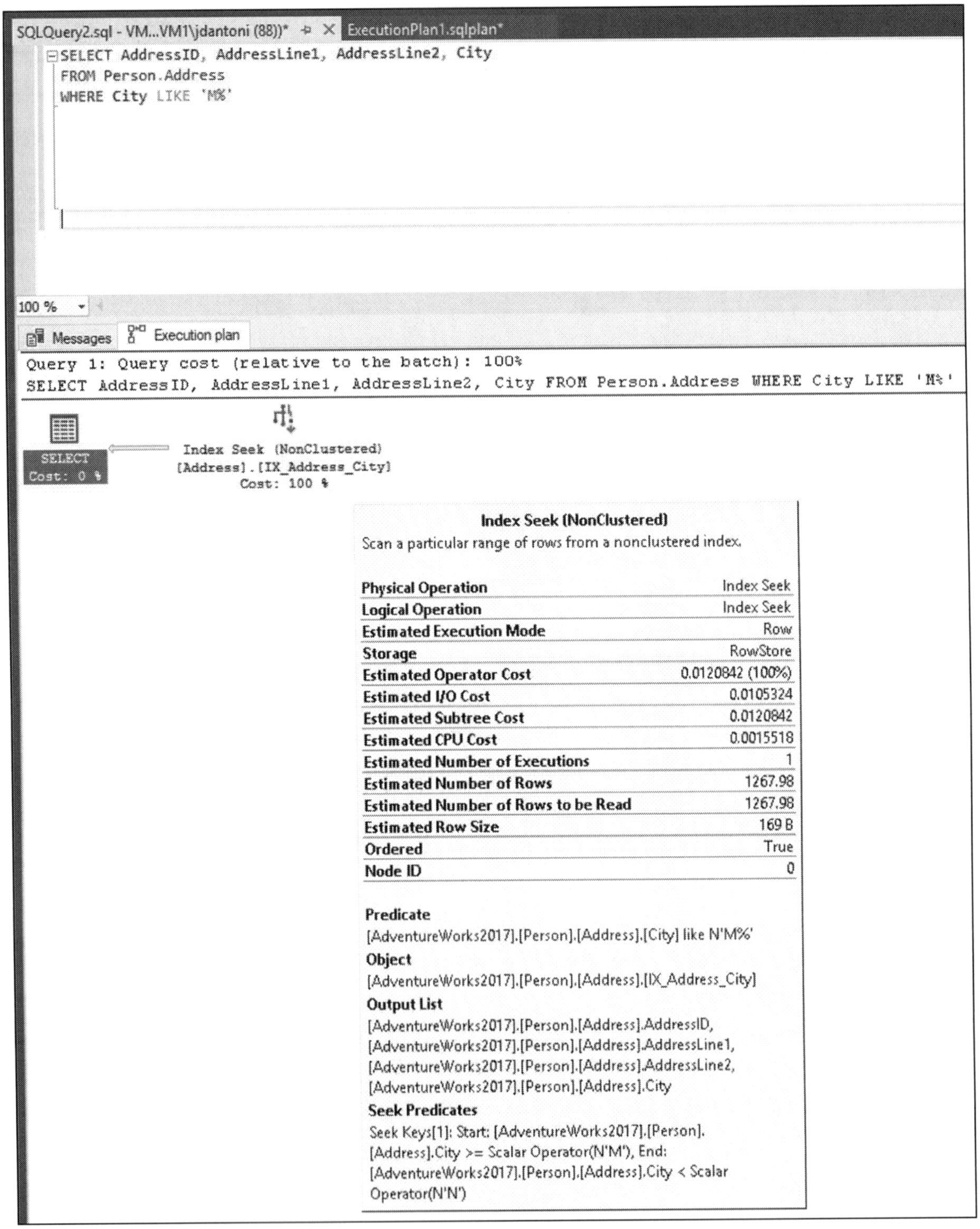

SQLQuery2.sql - VM...VM1\jdantoni (88))* ExecutionPlan1.sqlplan*

```
SELECT AddressID, AddressLine1, AddressLine2, City
FROM Person.Address
WHERE City LIKE 'M%'
```

100 %

Messages | Execution plan

```
Query 1: Query cost (relative to the batch): 100%
SELECT AddressID, AddressLine1, AddressLine2, City FROM Person.Address WHERE City LIKE 'M%'
```

SELECT
Cost: 0 %

Index Seek (NonClustered)
[Address].[IX_Address_City]
Cost: 100 %

Index Seek (NonClustered)

Scan a particular range of rows from a nonclustered index.

Physical Operation	Index Seek
Logical Operation	Index Seek
Estimated Execution Mode	Row
Storage	RowStore
Estimated Operator Cost	0.0120842 (100%)
Estimated I/O Cost	0.0105324
Estimated Subtree Cost	0.0120842
Estimated CPU Cost	0.0015518
Estimated Number of Executions	1
Estimated Number of Rows	1267.98
Estimated Number of Rows to be Read	1267.98
Estimated Row Size	169 B
Ordered	True
Node ID	0

Predicate

[AdventureWorks2017].[Person].[Address].[City] like N'M%'

Object

[AdventureWorks2017].[Person].[Address].[IX_Address_City]

Output List

[AdventureWorks2017].[Person].[Address].AddressID, [AdventureWorks2017].[Person].[Address].AddressLine1, [AdventureWorks2017].[Person].[Address].AddressLine2, [AdventureWorks2017].[Person].[Address].City

Seek Predicates

Seek Keys[1]: Start: [AdventureWorks2017].[Person].[Address].City >= Scalar Operator(N'M'), End: [AdventureWorks2017].[Person].[Address].City < Scalar Operator(N'N')

Figure 05-12: Execution Plan

An index SEEK is used by changing the LEFT function into a LIKE.

Some other database development anti-patterns are treating the database as a service rather than a data store. Using a database to convert data to JSON, manipulate strings, or perform complex calculations can lead to excessive CPU use and increased latency. Queries that try to retrieve all records and then perform computations in the database

can lead to excessive IO and CPU usage. Ideally, you should use the database for data access operations and optimized database constructs like aggregation.

Missing indexes

The most common performance problems you see as database administrators are due to a lack of useful indexes causing the engine to read far more pages than necessary to return the results of a query. While indexes are not free in terms of resources (adding additional indexes to a table can impact write performance and consume space), the performance gains they offer can offset the additional resource costs many times over. Frequently execution plans with these performance issues can be identified by the query operator "Clustered Index Scan" or the combination of the "Non-clustered index seek" and "Key Lookup" (which is more indicative of missing columns in an existing index). The database engine attempts to help with this problem by reporting on missing indexes in execution plans. The names and details of the indexes that have been deemed potentially useful are available through a dynamic management view called sys-.dm-db.-_missing-_index-_details. There are also other DMVs in SQL Server like sys.dm-_db.-_index-_usage-_statsandsys.dm, _db.-_index-_operational-_stats, highlighting the utilization of existing indexes. It may make sense to drop an index that is not used by any queries in the database. The missing index DMVs and plan warnings should only be a starting point for tuning your queries. It is important to understand your key queries and build indexes to support those queries. Creating all missing indexes without evaluating indexes in the context of each other is not recommended.

Missing and out-of-date statistics

You have learned about the importance of column and index statistics to the query optimizer. It is also important to understand conditions that can lead to out-of-date statistics and how this problem can manifest itself in SQL Server. SQL Server and Azure SQL Database and Managed Instance default to having auto-update statistics set to ON. Before SQL Server 2016, the default behavior of auto-update statistics was not to update statistics until the number of modifications to columns in the index was equal to about 20% of the number of rows in a table. Because of this behavior, you could have data modifications that were significant enough to change query performance but not update the statistics. Any plan that used the table with the changed data would be based on out-of-date statistics and frequently suboptimal. Before SQL Server 2016, you had the option of using trace flag 2371, which changed the needed number of modifications to be a dynamic value. As your table grew in size, the percentage of row modifications required to trigger a statistics update got smaller. Newer versions of SQL Server and Azure SQL Database and Managed Instance support this behavior by default. There is also a dynamic management function called sys.dm._ db.-_stats-properties, which shows you the last time statistics were updated and the number of modifications that

have been made since the previous update allowing you to quickly identity statistics that might need to be manually updated.

Poor optimizer choices

While the query optimizer does a good job of optimizing most queries, there are some edge cases where the cost-based optimizer may make impactful decisions that are not fully understood. There are many ways to address this, including query hints, trace flags, execution plan forcing, and other adjustments to reach a stable and optimal query plan. Microsoft has a support team that can help troubleshoot these scenarios.

In the below example from the database, a query hint is being used to tell the database optimizer always to use a city name of Seattle. This hint will not guarantee the best execution plan for all city values, but it will be predictable. The value of 'Seattle' for @city_name will only be used during optimization. The actual supplied value ('Ascheim') will be used during execution.

```
DECLARE @city_name nvarchar(30);

DECLARE @postal_code nvarchar(15);

SELECT @city_name = 'Ascheim';

SELECT @postal_code = 86171;

SELECT * FROM Person.Address

WHERE City = @city_name AND PostalCode = @postal_code

OPTION (OPTIMIZE FOR (@city_name = 'Seattle');
```

Figure 05-13: Query Data

The example shows that the query uses a hint (the OPTION clause) to tell the optimizer to use a specific variable value to build its execution plan.

Parameter sniffing

SQL Server caches query execution plans for future use. Since the execution plan retrieval process is based on the hash value, the query text has to be identical for every execution of the query for the cached plan to be used. To support multiple values in the same query, many developers use parameters passed in through stored procedures, as seen in the example below:

```
CREATE PROC GetAccountID (@Param INT)

AS

<other statements in procedure>

SELECT accountid FROM CustomerSales WHERE sales > @Param;

<other statements in procedure>

RETURN;


-- Call the procedure:

EXEC GetAccountID 42;
```

Figure 05-14: Query Data

Queries can also be explicitly parameterized using the procedure sp-executsql. However, explicit parameterization of individual queries is usually done through the application with some form (depending on the API) of PREPARE and EXECUTE. When the database engine executes that query for the first time, it will optimize the query based on the parameter's initial value, in this case, 42. This behavior, called parameter sniffing, allows the overall workload of compiling queries to be reduced on the server. However, if there is a data skew, query performance could vary widely. For example, in a table with 10 million records, 99% have an ID of 1, and the other 1% are unique numbers; performance will be based on which ID was initially used to optimize the query. This wildly fluctuating performance is indicative of data skew and is not an inherent problem with parameter sniffing. This behavior is a fairly common performance problem that you should know. It would help if you understood the options for alleviating the issue. There are a few ways to address this problem, but they each come with tradeoffs:

- Use the RECOMPILE hint in your query or the WITH RECOMPILE execution option in your stored procedures. This hint will cause the query or process to be recompiled every time it is executed, increasing CPU utilization on the server but always using the current parameter value.
- You can use the OPTIMIZE FOR UNKNOWN query hint. This hint will cause the optimizer to choose not to sniff parameters and compare the value with column data histogram. This option will not get you the best possible plan but will allow for a consistent execution plan.

➤ Rewrite your procedure or queries by adding logic around parameter values to only RECOMPILE for known troublesome parameters. In the example below, if the Sales-Person-ID parameter is NULL, the query will be executed with the OPTION (RECOMPILE).

```
CREATE OR ALTER PROCEDURE GetSalesInfo (@SalesPersonID INT = NULL)

AS

DECLARE @Recompile BIT = 1

 ,@SQLString NVARCHAR(500)


IF @SalesPersonID IS NULL

 SET @Recompile = 1


SELECT @SQLString = N'SELECT SalesOrderId, OrderDate FROM Sales.SalesOrderHeader WHERE SalesPersonID = @SalesPersonID'

IF @Recompile = 1

BEGIN

 SET @SQLString = @SQLString + N' OPTION(RECOMPILE)'

END


EXEC sp_executesql @SQLString

 ,N'@SalesPersonID INT'

 ,@SalesPersonID = @SalesPersonID

GO
```

Figure 05-15: Query Data

The example above is a good solution, but it does require a fairly large development effort and a firm understanding of your data distribution. It also may require maintenance as the data changes.

Evaluate Performance Improvements

SQL Server and Azure SQL are deeply instrumented software and monitored at several levels. One of the DBA's challenges is to evaluate the impact of changes they make to code or data structures on a busy production system. While tuning a single query in isolation offers easy metrics such as elapsed time or logical reads, making minor tweaks on a dynamic system may require deeper evaluation.

Describe Dynamic Management Views and Functions

SQL Server provides several hundred dynamic management objects. These objects contain system information that can use to monitor the health of a server instance, diagnose problems, and tune performance. Dynamic management views and functions

return internal data about the state of the database or the example. Dynamic Management Objects can be either viewed (DMVs) or processed (DMFs), but most people use the acronym DMV to refer to both types of object. There are two levels of DMVs: server scoped and database scoped. Server scoped objects require VIEW SERVER STATE permission on the server, and database scoped objects need the VIEW DATABASE STATE permission within the database. The names of the DMVs are all prefixed with sys. dm_ followed by the functional area and then the specific function of the object. SQL Server supports three categories of DMVs:

- Database-related dynamic management objects
- Query execution-related dynamic management objects
- Transaction related dynamic management objects

Note: For older versions of SQL Server (2012 and 2014) where the query store is unavailable, you can use the view sys.dm-exec-cached-plans in conjunction with the functions sys dm-exec-sql-text and sys.dm-exec-query-plan to return information about execution plans. However, unlike Query Store, you will not see changes in plans for a given query.

Azure SQL Database has a slightly different set of DMVs available than SQL Server; some objects are available only in Azure SQL Database, while others are only available in SQL Server. Some are scoped at the server level and are not applicable in the Azure model (the waits stats DMV below is an example of a server-scoped DMV). In contrast, others are specific to Azure SQL Database, like sys.dm-db.-resource stats, and provide Azure-specific information not available in (or relevant to) SQL Server.

Describe Wait Statistics

One holistic way of monitoring server performance is to evaluate what the server is waiting on. SQL Server is instrumented with a wait tracking system, which monitors each running thread and logs what resources the line is waiting on. Wait statistics are broken down into three types: resource waits, queue waits, and external waits.

- Resource waits occur when a worker thread in SQL Server requests access to a resource used by a thread. Examples of resources waits are locks, latches, and disk I/O waits.
- Queue waits occur when a worker thread is idle and waiting for work to be assigned. Example queue waits are deadlock monitoring and deleted record cleanup.
- External waits occur when SQL Server is waiting on an external process like a linked server query to complete. An example of an external delay is a network wait related to returning a large result set to a client application.

This data is aggregated in the DMV sys.dm_os_wait_stats (and in sys.dm_db_wait_stats in Azure SQL Database) and is also tracked for active sessions in sys.dm_exec_session_wait_stats. These statistics (SQL Server tracks over 900 wait types) allow the DBA to overview the server's performance and readily identify configuration or hardware issues. This data is persisted from the time of instance startup, but the data can be cleared as needed to observe changes.

Wait statistics are evaluated as a percentage of the total waits on the server.

	WaitType	Wait Percentage	AvgWait_Sec
1	REDO_THREAD_PENDING_WORK	24.75	0.1016
2	CXPACKET	17.19	0.0021
3	CXCONSUMER	12.24	0.0090
4	PARALLEL_REDO_TRAN_TURN	10.60	0.0029
5	SOS_SCHEDULER_YIELD	10.06	0.0022
6	BPSORT	3.80	0.0126
7	PAGEIOLATCH_SH	3.60	0.0029
8	BACKUPIO	2.01	0.0110
9	HTDELETE	1.83	0.1573
10	LATCH_EX	1.81	0.0047

Figure 05-16: Wait Statistics

The results of this query from sys.dm.-os-wait-stats show the wait type, the aggregation of Percent of time waiting (Wait Percentage), and the average wait time in seconds for each wait type. In this case, the server always has On Availability Groups in place, as indicated by the REDO_THREAD_PENDING_WORK and PARALLEL_REDO_TRAN_TURN wait for types. The relatively high percentage of CXPACKET and SOS_SCHEDULER_YIELD waits suggests that this server is under CPU pressure.

Many wait types relate to specific and common SQL Server performance issues:

- RESOURCE_SEMAPHORE waits—this wait type specifies queries waiting on memory to become available and may specify excessive memory grants to some queries. These wait types can be caused by out-of-date statistics, missing indexes, and extreme query concurrency. This problem is typically observed by long query runtimes or even time outs.
- LCK_M_X waits—frequent occurrences of this wait type can indicate a blocking problem that can be solved by either changing to the READ COMMITTED SNAPSHOT isolation level or making changes in indexing to reduce transaction times, or possibly better transaction management within T-SQL code.

- PAGEIOLATCH_SH waits—this wait type can indicate a problem with indexes (or a lack of useful indexes), where SQL Server is scanning too much data. Alternatively, if the wait count is low but the wait time is high, it can indicate storage performance problems. You can observe this behavior by analyzing the waiting _tasks _count and the wait _time _MS in the sys.dm-so _wait _stats DMV to calculate an average wait time for a given wait type.
- SOS_SCHEDULER_YIELD waits-- this wait type can indicate high CPU utilization, which is correlated with an increased number of large scans, or missing indexes, often in conjunction with high numbers CXPACKET waits.
- CXPACKET waits—if this wait type is high, it can indicate improper configuration. Before SQL Server 2019, the Max Degree of Parallelism (MaxDOP) default setting used all available CPUs for queries. Moreover, the cost threshold for parallelism (CTfP) setting defaults to 5, leading to small queries being published in parallel, limiting throughput. Reducing MaxDOP and increasing CTfP can decrease this wait type, but the CXPACKET wait type can also indicate high CPU utilization, typically fixed through index tuning.
- PAGEIOLATCH_UP—this wait type on data pages 2:1:1 can indicate Temp-DB contention on Page Free Space (PFS) data pages. Each data file has one PFS page per approximately 64MB of data. This wait is typically caused by only having one Temp-DB file, as before SQL Server 2016, the default behavior was to use one data file for Temp-DB. The best practice is to use one file per CPU core up to eight files. It is also important to ensure your Temp-DB data files are the same size and have the same auto-growth settings to ensure they are used evenly. SQL Server 2016 and higher control the growth of Temp-DB data files to ensure they grow in a consistent, simultaneous fashion.

In addition to the DMVs above, the Query Store tracks wait associated with a given query. This data is not tracked at the same granularity as the data in the DMVs but can provide a nice overview of what a query is waiting on.

Tune Indexes

The most common (and most effective) method for tuning T-SQL queries is to evaluate and adjust your indexing strategy. Properly indexed databases perform fewer IOs to return query results, and with fewer IOs, there is reduced pressure on both the IO and storage systems. Reducing IO even allows for better memory utilization. Keep in mind the read/write ratio of your queries. A heavy write workload may indicate that the cost of writing rows to additional indexes is not of many benefits. An exception will be if the workload performs mainly updates that also need to do lookup operations. Update operations that do lookups can benefit from additional indexes or columns added to an existing index. Your goal should always be to get the most benefit from the smallest number of indexes on your tables.

A common performance tuning approach is as follows:

- Evaluate existing index usage using sys.dm-db.-index _operational _stats and sys.dm-db._ index _usage _stats.
- Consider eliminating unused and duplicate indexes, but you should do this carefully. Some indexes may only be used during monthly/quarterly/annual operations and may be important for those processes. You may also consider creating indexes to support those operations just before the operations are scheduled to reduce the overhead of having otherwise unused indexes on a table.
- Review and evaluate expensive queries from the Query Store or Extended Events capture, and manually craft indexes to better serve those queries.
- Create the index(s) in a non-production environment, test query execution and performance, and observe performance changes. It is important to note any hardware differences between your production and non-production environments, as the amount of memory and the number of CPUs could impact your execution plan.
- After testing carefully, implement the changes to your production system.

Consider using a change control process for tracking changes that could impact application performance. Verify the column order of your indexes—the leading column drives column statistics and usually determines whether the optimizer will choose the index. Ideally, the top column will be selective and used in the WHERE clause of many of your queries. Finally, save the code in your source control before dropping an index, so the index can be quickly recreated if an infrequently run query requires the index to perform well.

Maintain Indexes

As data is inserted, updated, and deleted from indexes, the logical arrangement in the index will no longer match the physical ordering inside of the pages and between the pages, making up the indexes. Also, the data modifications can cause the data to become scattered or fragmented in the database over time. This fragmentation can degrade query performance when the database engine reads additional pages to locate needed data.

The SQL Server and Azure SQL platforms offer DMVs that allow you to detect fragmentation in your objects using the following DMVs. The most commonly used DMVs for this purpose are: sys.dm. Db. index-physical-stats, for b-tree indexes, and sys.dm._db._column _store _row _group _physical _stats, for column store indexes.

There are two options for index maintenance: reorganization and rebuilding. Reorganization defragments an index by physically reordering the leaf-level index pages to match the logical sorted order of the leaf nodes and compacting the index pages based on the index's fill factor setting. Rebuilding an index drops and recreates the pages

of the index. The specific guidelines for deciding to rebuild versus reorganize an index are that the index should be rebuilt when fragmentation is greater than 30%. However, the actual values vary from case to case. If an index is used heavily for scan operations, removing excess pages may help significantly. However, there will be limited benefits for seeking procedures. The reorganization has the advantage of being an online activity, whereas rebuilding requires a special ONLINE option. Indexes with less than 5% fragmentation do not need to be defragmented because the cost of defragmentation is greater than the performance benefits gained. Whenever you consider either rebuilding or reorganizing, you should verify that doing so provides performance improvements.

SQL Server 2017 introduced reusable index maintenance operations. This option allows index maintenance operations to be paused or take place in a time window and be resumed later. You can perform rebuild operations during a specific maintenance window giving you more control over the process. A good example of where to use reusable index operations is to reduce the impact of index maintenance in a busy production environment.

> EXAM TIP: Index rebuilds cause the statistics on the index to be updated, which can further help performance. Index reorganization does not update statistics.

Column-store maintenance

Column-store index fragmentation is not reported similarly to b-tree index fragmentation. A good metric to measure fragmentation in a column store index is based on the deleted rows in the index. Examine the sys.dm_db._column _store _row _group _physical _stats for deleted rows—, which will be caused by both updates and delete operations. If 20% or more of the rows are deleted, you should consider reorganizing your index. In a test environment, verify whether a reorganization improves the performance of the workloads using the column store index.

Explore Performance-Based Design

Database design is an important aspect of database performance, even though it is not always under the control of the database administrator. Many design decisions, such as choosing the right data types, can make large differences in the performance of your databases. You may be working with third-party vendor applications that you did not build. Whenever possible, it is important to design your database properly for the workload, whether online transaction processing (OLTP) or data warehouse workload.

Describe Normalization

Database normalization is a design process used to organize a given set of data into tables and columns in a database. Each table should contain data relating to a specific 'thing' and only have data supporting that same 'thing' included. This process aims to reduce duplicate data contained within your database to reduce the performance impact of database inserts and updates. For example, a customer address change is much easier to implement if the customer address is stored in the Customers table. The most common normalization forms are the first, second, and third normal forms described below.

First Normal Form

The first normal form has the following specifications:

- Create a separate table for each set of related data
- Eliminate repeating groups in individual tables
- Identify each collection of associated data with a primary key

, It would help if you did not use multiple columns in a single table to store similar data in this model. For example, if the product can come in various colors, you should not have multiple columns in a single row containing the different color values. The first table, below (Product Colors), is not in first normal form as there are repeating values for color. For products with only one color, there is wasted space. In addition, if a product came in more than three colors? Rather than setting a maximum number of colors, you can recreate the table as shown in the second table, Product Color. You also require the first normal form of a unique key for the table, which is a column (or columns) whose value uniquely identifies the row. Neither of the columns in the second table is unique, but the combination of Product ID and Color is amazing. When multiple columns are needed, you call that a composite key.

FIRST NORMAL FORM			
Product ID	**Color1**	**Color2**	**Color3**
1	Red	Green	Yellow
2	Yellow		
3	Blue	Red	
4	Blue		
5	Red		

Table 05-01: First Normal Form

Product ID	Color
1	Red

1	Green
1	Yellow
2	Yellow
3	Blue
3	Red
4	Blue
5	Red

Table 05-02: Product ID and Color

The third table, Product Info, is in first normal form because each row refers to a particular product, there are no repeating groups, and you have the column Product ID to use as a Primary Key.

TABLE 3				
Product ID	**Product Name**	**Price**	**Production Country**	**Short Location**
1	Widget	15.95	United States	US
2	Foop	41.95	United Kingdom	UK
3	Glombit	49.95	United Kingdom	UK
4	Sorfin	99.99	Republic of the Philippines	RepPhil
5	Stem Bolt	29.95	United States	US

Table 05-03: Product Description

Second Normal Form

The second normal form has the following specification, in addition to those required by the first normal form:

- If the table has a composite key, all attributes must depend on the complete key and not just part of it.

The second normal form is only relevant to tables with composite keys, like in the table Product Color, which is the second table above. This table has a composite key on Product ID and Color because only using both column values can you uniquely identify a row. Consider the case where the Product Color table also includes the product's price. If a product's price does not change with the color, you might see data as shown in this table:

SECOND NORMAL FORM		
ProductID	Color	Price
1	Red	15.95
1	Green	15.95
1	Yellow	15.95
2	Yellow	41.95
3	Blue	49.95
3	Red	49.95
4	Blue	99.95
5	Red	29.95

Table 05-04: Second Normal Form

The price value is dependent on the Product ID but not on the color. There are three rows for Product ID 1, so the price for that product is repeated three times. The problem with violating the second normal form is that you must update it everywhere to update the price. If you update the price in the first row, but not the second or third, you would have an 'update anomaly.' After the update, you would not tell the actual price for Product ID 1. The solution is to move the Price column to a table with Product ID as a single column key because that is the only column on which price depends. For example, you could use Table 3 to store the price.

If the price for a product was different based on the color of the product, then the fourth table would be in second normal form because the cost would depend on both parts of the key: Product ID and Color.

Third Normal Form

The third normal form is typically the aim for most OLTP databases. The third normal form has the following specification, in addition to those required by the second normal form:

- All non-key columns are non-transitively dependent on the primary key.

The transitive relationship implies that one column in a table is related to other columns through a second column. In the case of dependence, when you show that a column is dependent on another column, it means that it may derive the value from the other. For example, your age can be determined from your date of birth, making your age depends on your date of birth. Refer back to the third table, Product Info. This table is in second normal form, but not in the third. The Short Location column is dependent on the

Production Country column, which is not the key. Like the second normal form, violating the third normal form can update anomalies. If you updated the Short Location in one row, you would have inconsistent data without editing it in all the rows where that location occurred., You could create a separate table to store country names and their shortened forms to prevent this.

DE Normalization

While the third normal form is theoretically desirable, it is not possible for all data. A normalized database does not always offer you the best performance. Normalized data needs multiple join operations to acquire all the required data returned in a single query. There is a tradeoff between normalizing data when the number of joins needed to return query results have high CPU utilization and de-normalized data with lesser joins and less CPU required but opens up the possibility of update anomalies.

De-normalized data is not the same as un-normalized. For de-normalization, you start by designing tables that are normalized. Then you can add additional columns to some tables to reduce the number of joins needed, but as you do so, you are aware of the possible update anomalies. You then make sure you have triggers or other kinds of processing to ensure that all the duplicate data is updated when you perform an update.

> **Note:** De-normalized data can be more effective to query, especially for heavy reading workloads like a data warehouse. In those cases, additional columns may offer better query patterns and more simplistic queries.

Star Schema

While most normalization is aimed at OLTP workloads, data warehouses have their modeling structure, usually **de-normalized** models. This design uses fact tables, which record measurements or metrics for specific events like a sale, and joins them to dimension tables, smaller in row count but may have many columns to describe the fact data. Some example dimensions would include inventory, time, and geography. This design pattern makes the database easier to query and offers performance gains for reading workloads.

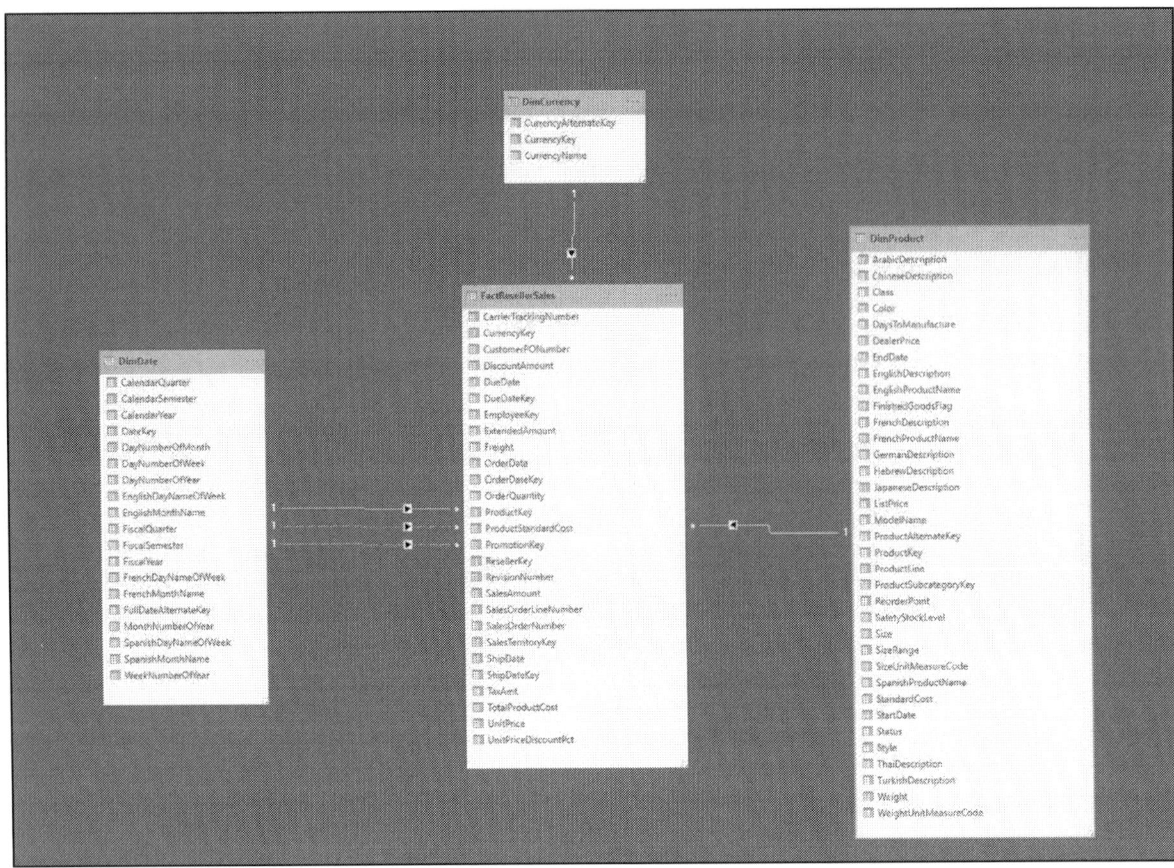

Figure 05-17: Star Schema

The above image displays an example of a star schema, including a *Fact Reseller Sales* fact table and dimensions for date, currency, and products. The fact table comprises data linked to the sales transactions, and the dimensions only contain data related to a particular element of the sales data. For example, the *Fact Reseller Sales* table comprises only a *Product Key* to show which product was sold. All details about each product are stored in the *Dim Product* table and linked to the fact table with the *Product Key* column.

A snowflake schema is associated with a star schema design, which uses a set of more normalized tables for a particular business entity. The following image displays an example of a single dimension for a snowflake schema. The Products dimension is normalized and kept in three tables called *Dim Product Category*, *Dim Product Subcategory*, and *Dim Product*.

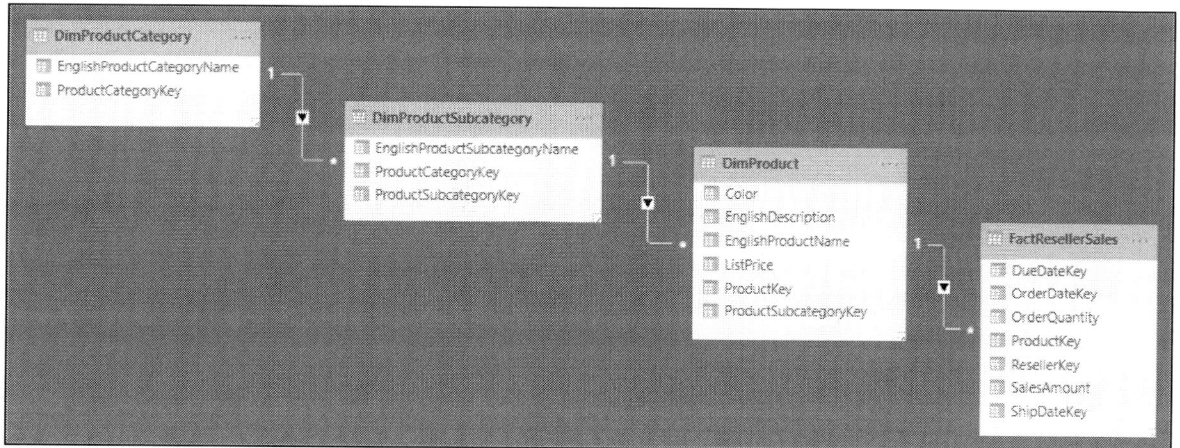

Figure 05-18: Snowflake Schema

The main difference between star and snowflake schemas is that the dimensions in a snowflake schema are normalized to reduce redundancy, saving storage space. The tradeoff is that your queries need more joins, which increases your complexity and reduces performance.

Choose Appropriate Data Types

SQL Server offers a wide variety of data types to choose from, and your choice can affect performance in several ways. Choosing the right data types for a given set of data is important, which will reduce the total storage required for the database and improve the performance of queries executed. Additionally, choosing data types that are much larger than needed can origin wasted space and require more pages than is necessary to be read. At the same time, SQL Server can convert some data types automatically (you call this an 'implicit conversion'; conversion can be costly and can also negatively impact query plans. The alternative is an explicit conversion, where you use the CAST or CONVERT function in your code to force a data type conversion. The image below indicates in which cases SQL Server can do an implicit conversion and in which cases you must explicitly convert data types in your code.

EXAM TIP: In some cases, conversions are not possible at all. For example, it cannot convert data. Conversions can negatively impact query performance by causing index scans where seeks would have been possible and additional CPU overhead from the transformation itself.

From \ To	binary	varbinary	char	varchar	nchar	nvarchar	datetime	smalldatetime	date	time	datetimeoffset	datetime2	decimal	numeric	float	real	bigint	int(INT4)	smallint(INT2)	tinyint(INT1)	money	smallmoney	bit	timestamp	uniqueidentifier	image	ntext	text	sql_variant	xml	CLR UDT	hierarchyid
binary		●	●	●	●	●	●	●	■	■	■	■	●	●	✕	✕	●	●	●	●	●	●	●	●	●	●	✕	✕	●	●	●	●
varbinary	●		●	●	●	●	●	●	■	■	■	■	●	●	✕	✕	●	●	●	●	●	●	●	●	●	●	✕	✕	●	●	●	●
char	■	■		●	●	●	●	●	●	●	●	●	●	●	●	●	●	●	●	●	●	●	●	■	●	●	●	●	●	●	●	●
varchar	■	■	●		●	●	●	●	●	●	●	●	●	●	●	●	●	●	●	●	●	●	●	■	●	●	●	●	●	●	●	●
nchar	■	■	●	●		●	●	●	●	●	●	●	●	●	●	●	●	●	●	●	●	●	●	■	●	✕	●	●	●	●	●	●
nvarchar	■	■	●	●	●		●	●	●	●	●	●	●	●	●	●	●	●	●	●	●	●	●	■	●	✕	●	●	●	●	●	●
datetime	■	■	●	●	●	●		●	●	●	●	●	■	■	■	■	■	■	■	■	■	■	■	■	✕	✕	✕	✕	●	✕	✕	✕
smalldatetime	■	■	●	●	●	●	●		●	●	●	●	■	■	■	■	■	■	■	■	■	■	■	■	✕	✕	✕	✕	●	✕	✕	✕
date	■	■	●	●	●	●	●	●		✕	●	●	✕	✕	✕	✕	✕	✕	✕	✕	✕	✕	✕	✕	✕	✕	✕	✕	●	✕	✕	✕
time	■	■	●	●	●	●	●	●	✕		●	●	✕	✕	✕	✕	✕	✕	✕	✕	✕	✕	✕	✕	✕	✕	✕	✕	●	✕	✕	✕
datetimeoffset	■	■	●	●	●	●	●	●	●	●		●	✕	✕	✕	✕	✕	✕	✕	✕	✕	✕	✕	✕	✕	✕	✕	✕	●	✕	✕	✕
datetime2	■	■	●	●	●	●	●	●	●	●	●		✕	✕	✕	✕	✕	✕	✕	✕	✕	✕	✕	✕	✕	✕	✕	✕	●	✕	✕	✕
decimal	●	●	●	●	●	●	●	●	✕	✕	✕	✕	◆	◆	●	●	●	●	●	●	●	●	●	●	✕	✕	✕	✕	●	✕	✕	✕
numeric	●	●	●	●	●	●	●	●	✕	✕	✕	✕	◆	◆	●	●	●	●	●	●	●	●	●	●	✕	✕	✕	✕	●	✕	✕	✕
float	●	●	●	●	●	●	●	●	✕	✕	✕	✕	●	●		●	●	●	●	●	●	●	●	✕	✕	✕	✕	✕	●	✕	✕	✕
real	●	●	●	●	●	●	●	●	✕	✕	✕	✕	●	●	●		●	●	●	●	●	●	●	✕	✕	✕	✕	✕	●	✕	✕	✕
bigint	●	●	●	●	●	●	●	●	✕	✕	✕	✕	●	●	●	●		●	●	●	●	●	●	●	✕	✕	✕	✕	●	✕	✕	✕
int(INT4)	●	●	●	●	●	●	●	●	✕	✕	✕	✕	●	●	●	●	●		●	●	●	●	●	●	✕	✕	✕	✕	●	✕	✕	✕
smallint(INT2)	●	●	●	●	●	●	●	●	✕	✕	✕	✕	●	●	●	●	●	●		●	●	●	●	●	✕	✕	✕	✕	●	✕	✕	✕
tinyint(INT1)	●	●	●	●	●	●	●	●	✕	✕	✕	✕	●	●	●	●	●	●	●		●	●	●	●	✕	✕	✕	✕	●	✕	✕	✕
money	●	●	●	●	●	●	●	●	✕	✕	✕	✕	●	●	●	●	●	●	●	●		●	●	●	✕	✕	✕	✕	●	✕	✕	✕
smallmoney	●	●	●	●	●	●	●	●	✕	✕	✕	✕	●	●	●	●	●	●	●	●	●		●	●	✕	✕	✕	✕	●	✕	✕	✕
bit	●	●	●	●	●	●	●	●	✕	✕	✕	✕	●	●	●	●	●	●	●	●	●	●		●	✕	✕	✕	✕	●	✕	✕	✕
timestamp	●	●	●	●	✕	✕	●	●	✕	✕	✕	✕	●	●	✕	✕	●	●	●	●	●	●	●		✕	●	✕	✕	✕	✕	✕	✕
uniqueidentifier	●	●	●	●	●	●	✕	✕	✕	✕	✕	✕	✕	✕	✕	✕	✕	✕	✕	✕	✕	✕	✕	✕		✕	✕	✕	●	✕	✕	✕
image	●	●	✕	✕	✕	✕	✕	✕	✕	✕	✕	✕	✕	✕	✕	✕	✕	✕	✕	✕	✕	✕	✕	●	✕		✕	✕	✕	✕	✕	✕
ntext	✕	✕	●	●	●	●	✕	✕	✕	✕	✕	✕	✕	✕	✕	✕	✕	✕	✕	✕	✕	✕	✕	✕	✕	✕		●	✕	●	✕	✕
text	✕	✕	●	●	●	●	✕	✕	✕	✕	✕	✕	✕	✕	✕	✕	✕	✕	✕	✕	✕	✕	✕	✕	✕	✕	●		✕	●	✕	✕
sql_variant	■	■	■	■	■	■	■	■	■	■	■	■	■	■	■	■	■	■	■	■	■	■	■	✕	■	✕	✕	✕		✕	✕	✕
xml	■	■	■	■	■	■	✕	✕	✕	✕	✕	✕	✕	✕	✕	✕	✕	✕	✕	✕	✕	✕	✕	✕	✕	✕	✕	✕	✕	○	●	✕
CLR UDT	■	■	■	■	■	■	✕	✕	✕	✕	✕	✕	✕	✕	✕	✕	✕	✕	✕	✕	✕	✕	✕	✕	✕	✕	✕	✕	✕	●	✕	✕
hierarchyid	■	■	■	■	■	■	✕	✕	✕	✕	✕	✕	✕	✕	✕	✕	✕	✕	✕	✕	✕	✕	✕	✕	✕	✕	✕	✕	✕	✕	✕	✕

■ Explicit conversion

● Implicit conversion

✕ Conversion not allowed

◆ Requires explicit CAST to prevent the loss of precision or scale that might occur in an implicit conversion.

○ Implicit conversions between xml data types are supported only if the source or target is untyped xml. Otherwise, the conversion must be explicit.

Figure 05-19: Data Types

SQL Server offers a set of system-supplied data types for all data that can be used in your tables and queries. SQL Server allows the creation of user-defined data types in either T-SQL or the .NET framework.

Design Indexes

SQL Server has several index types supporting different types of workloads. At a high level, an index can be thought of as an on-disk structure that is associated with a table or a view that enables SQL Server to more easily find the row or rows associated with

the index key (which consists of one or more columns in the table or view), compared to scanning the entire table.

Clustered Indexes

A common DBA job interview question asks the candidate the difference between a clustered and non-clustered index, as indexes are a fundamental data storage technology in SQL Server. A clustered index is the underlying table, stored in sorted order based on the key value. There can only be one clustered index on a given table because the rows can be stored in one order. A table without a clustered index is called a heap, and heaps are typically only used as staging tables. An important performance design principle is to keep your clustered index key as narrow as possible. When considering the key column(s) for your clustered index, you should consider unique or containing many distinct values. Another property of a good clustered index key is for records accessed sequentially and frequently used to sort the data retrieved from the table. The clustered index on the column used for sorting can prevent the cost of sorting every time that query executes because you can store data in the desired order.

When you say that the table is 'stored' in a particular order, you refer to the logical order, not necessarily the physical, on-disk order. Indexes have pointers between pages, and the pointers help create the logical order. When scanning an index 'in order, SQL Server follows the cursors from page to page. Immediately after creating an index, it is most likely also stored in physical order on the disk. Still, the arrows will give us the correct logical ordering after modifying the data and adding new pages to the index. Still, the new pages will probably not be in physical disk order.

Non-Clustered Indexes

Non-clustered indexes are a separate structure from the data rows. A non-clustered index has the key values defined for the index and a pointer to the data row that contains the key value. You can add additional non-key columns to the leaf level of the non-clustered index to cover more columns using the included columns feature in SQL Server. You can create multiple non-clustered indexes on a table.

An example of when you need to add an index or add columns to an existing non-clustered index is shown below:

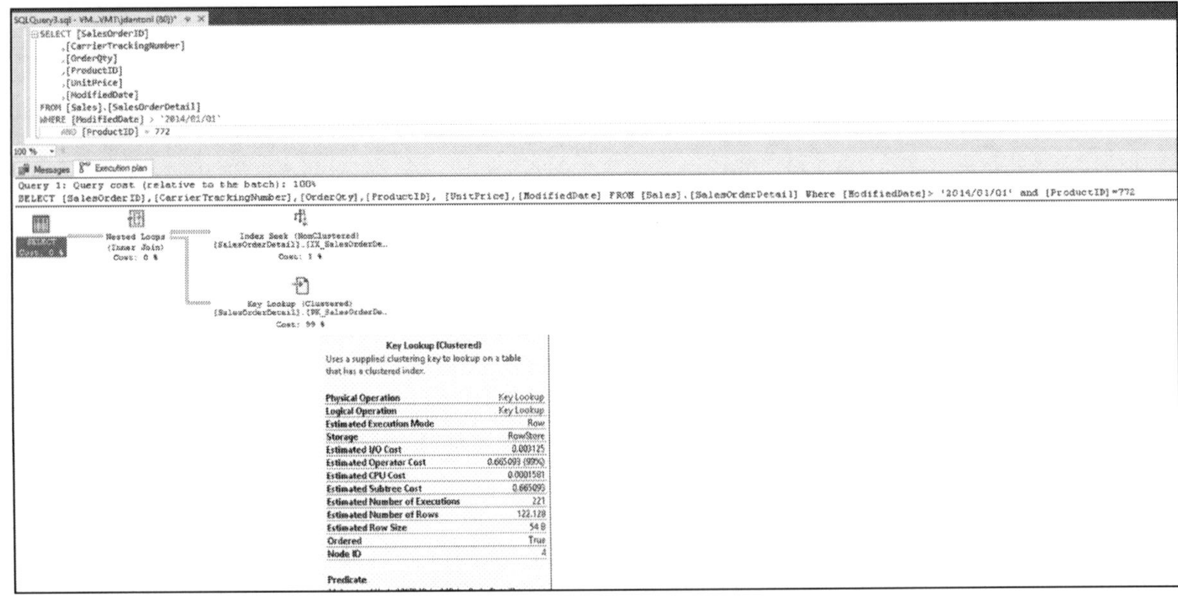

Figure 05-20: SQL Query

The query plan indicates that additional data will need to be retrieved from the clustered index (the table itself). There is a non-clustered index, but it only includes the product column. If you add the other columns in the query to a non-clustered index, as shown below, you can see the execution plan change to eliminate the key lookup.

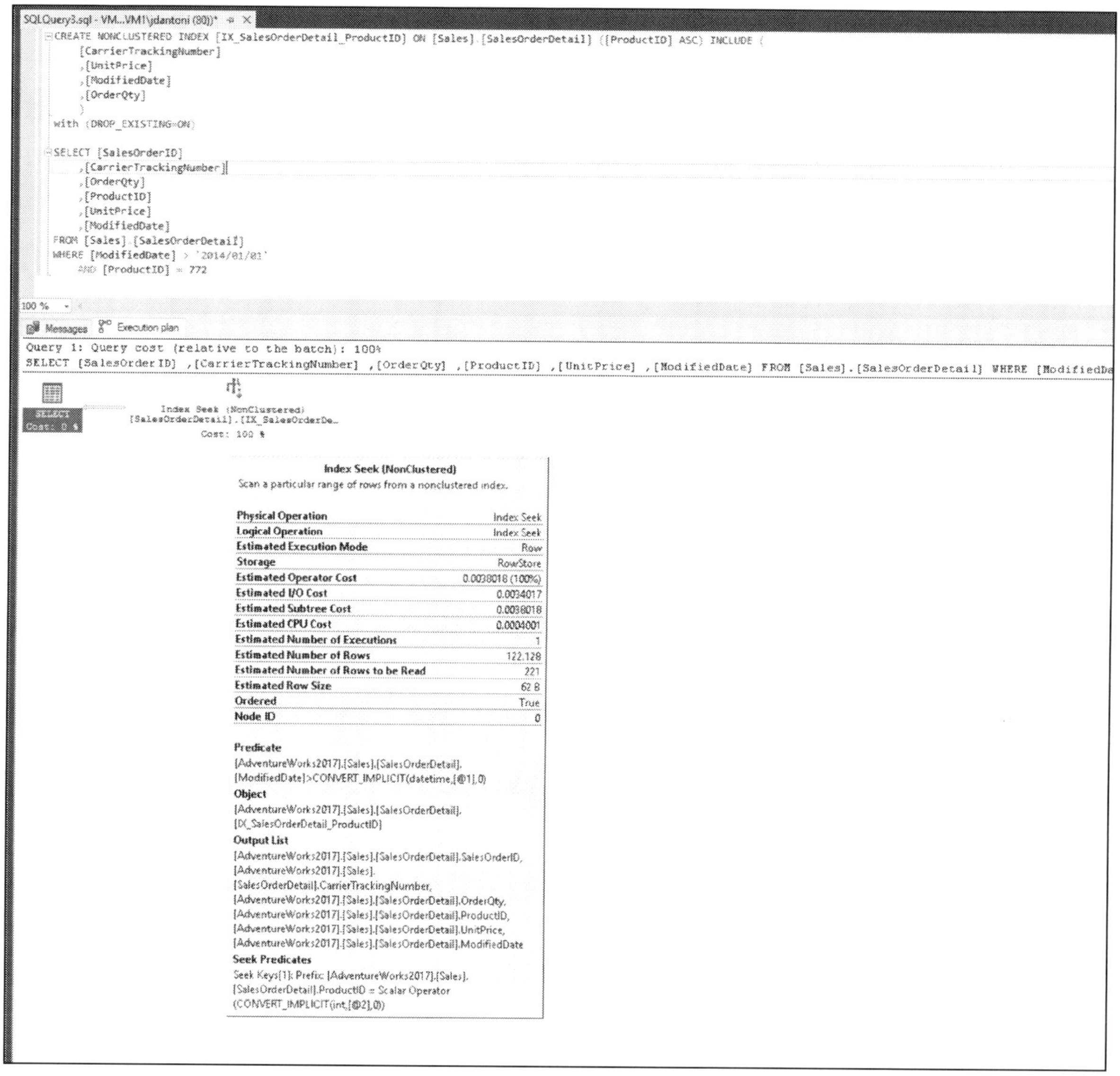

```
SQLQuery3.sql - VM...VM1\jdantoni (80))*
CREATE NONCLUSTERED INDEX [IX_SalesOrderDetail_ProductID] ON [Sales].[SalesOrderDetail] ([ProductID] ASC) INCLUDE (
    [CarrierTrackingNumber]
    ,[UnitPrice]
    ,[ModifiedDate]
    ,[OrderQty]
    )
with (DROP_EXISTING=ON)

SELECT [SalesOrderID]
    ,[CarrierTrackingNumber]
    ,[OrderQty]
    ,[ProductID]
    ,[UnitPrice]
    ,[ModifiedDate]
FROM [Sales].[SalesOrderDetail]
WHERE [ModifiedDate] > '2014/01/01'
    AND [ProductID] = 772
```

```
Query 1: Query cost (relative to the batch): 100%
SELECT [SalesOrderID] ,[CarrierTrackingNumber] ,[OrderQty] ,[ProductID] ,[UnitPrice] ,[ModifiedDate] FROM [Sales].[SalesOrderDetail] WHERE [ModifiedDa
SELECT Cost: 0 %    Index Seek (NonClustered) [SalesOrderDetail].[IX_SalesOrderDe... Cost: 100 %
```

Index Seek (NonClustered)
Scan a particular range of rows from a nonclustered index.

Physical Operation	Index Seek
Logical Operation	Index Seek
Estimated Execution Mode	Row
Storage	RowStore
Estimated Operator Cost	0.0038018 (100%)
Estimated I/O Cost	0.0034017
Estimated Subtree Cost	0.0038018
Estimated CPU Cost	0.0004001
Estimated Number of Executions	1
Estimated Number of Rows	122.128
Estimated Number of Rows to be Read	221
Estimated Row Size	62 B
Ordered	True
Node ID	0

Predicate
[AdventureWorks2017].[Sales].[SalesOrderDetail].[ModifiedDate]>CONVERT_IMPLICIT(datetime,[@1],0)
Object
[AdventureWorks2017].[Sales].[SalesOrderDetail].[IX_SalesOrderDetail_ProductID]
Output List
[AdventureWorks2017].[Sales].[SalesOrderDetail].SalesOrderID, [AdventureWorks2017].[Sales].[SalesOrderDetail].CarrierTrackingNumber, [AdventureWorks2017].[Sales].[SalesOrderDetail].OrderQty, [AdventureWorks2017].[Sales].[SalesOrderDetail].ProductID, [AdventureWorks2017].[Sales].[SalesOrderDetail].UnitPrice, [AdventureWorks2017].[Sales].[SalesOrderDetail].ModifiedDate
Seek Predicates
Seek Keys[1]: Prefix: [AdventureWorks2017].[Sales].[SalesOrderDetail].ProductID = Scalar Operator (CONVERT_IMPLICIT(int,[@2],0))

Figure 05-21: SQL Query

The index created above is an example of a covering index. In addition to the key column, you include additional columns to cover the query and eliminate the need to access the table itself.

Both non-clustered and clustered indexes can be defined as unique, meaning there can be no duplication of the key values. Individual indexes are automatically created when you create a PRIMARY KEY or UNIQUE constraint on a table.

This section focuses on b-tree indexes in SQL Server, also known as row store indexes. The general structure of a b-tree is shown below:

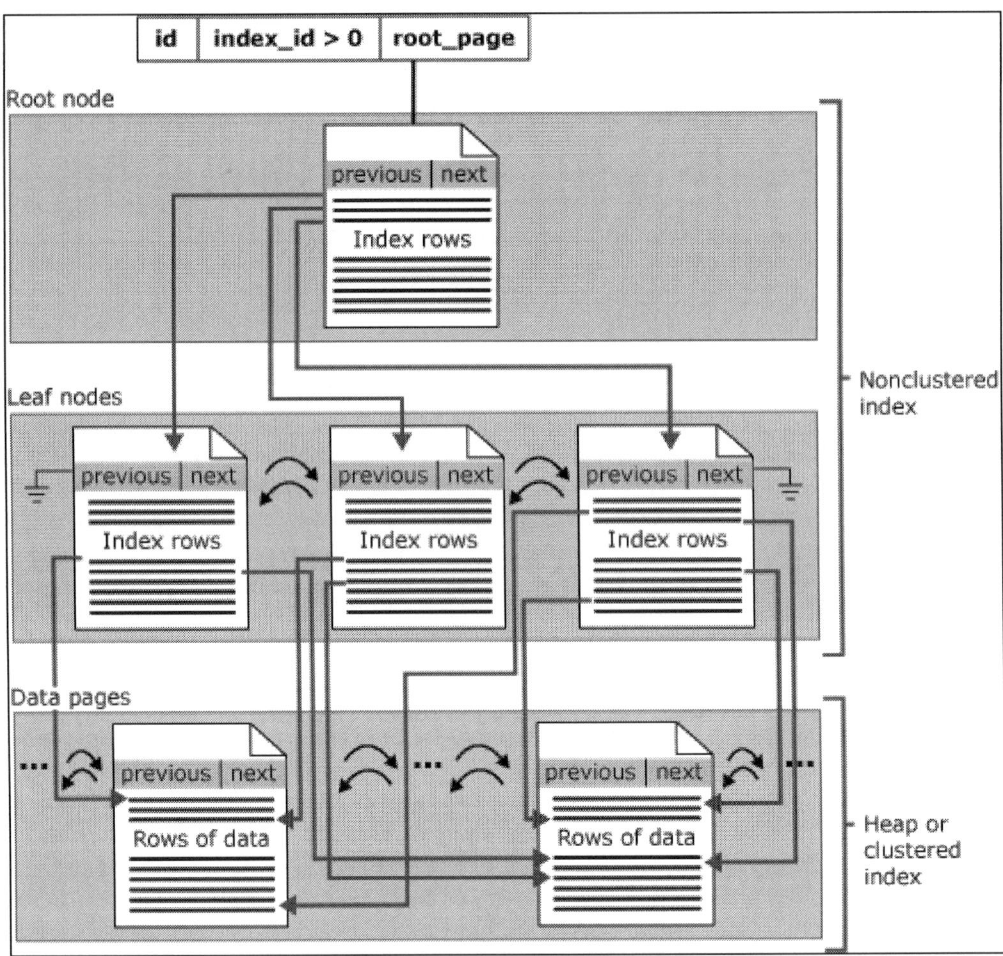

Figure 05-22: Index Page

Each page in an index b-tree is designated an index node, and the top node of the b-tree is named as the root node. The bottom nodes in an index are called leaf nodes and the collection of leaf nodes in the leaf level.

Index design is a little bit art and a little bit science. A narrow index with few columns in its key requires less time to update and has lower maintenance overhead; however, it may not be useful for as many queries as a wider index that includes more columns. You may need to experiment with several indexing approaches based on the columns selected by your application's queries. The query optimizer will generally choose the best existing index for a query; however, that does not mean that it is not possible to build a better index.

Properly indexing a database is a complex task. When planning your indexes for a table, you should keep a few basic principles in:

- Understand the workloads of the system. A table used mainly for insert operations will benefit far less from additional indexes than a table used for data warehouse operations with 90% read activity.

- Understand what queries are run most frequently, and optimize your indexes around those queries
- Understand the data types of the columns used in your queries. Indexes are ideal for integer data types or unique or non-null columns.
- Create non-clustered indexes on columns frequently used in predicates and join clauses, and keep those indexes as narrow as possible to avoid overhead.
- Understand your data size/volume – A table scan on a small table will be a relatively cheap operation, and SQL may decide to do a table scan simply because it is easy (trivial) to do. A table scan on a very large table would be very costly.

Another option, SQL Server, provides the creation of filtered indexes. Filtered indexes are best suited to columns in large tables where a large percentage of the rows have the same value in that column. A practical example would be an employee table shown below that stored the records of all employees, including ones who had left or retired.

```
CREATE TABLE [HumanResources].[Employee](
 [BusinessEntityID] [int] NOT NULL,
 [NationalIDNumber] [nvarchar](15) NOT NULL,
 [LoginID] [nvarchar](256) NOT NULL,
 [OrganizationNode] [hierarchyid] NULL,
 [OrganizationLevel] AS ([OrganizationNode].[GetLevel]()),
 [JobTitle] [nvarchar](50) NOT NULL,
 [BirthDate] [date] NOT NULL,
 [MaritalStatus] [nchar](1) NOT NULL,
 [Gender] [nchar](1) NOT NULL,
 [HireDate] [date] NOT NULL,
 [SalariedFlag] [bit] NOT NULL,
 [VacationHours] [smallint] NOT NULL,
 [SickLeaveHours] [smallint] NOT NULL,
 [CurrentFlag] [bit] NOT NULL,
 [rowguid] [uniqueidentifier] ROWGUIDCOL NOT NULL,
 [ModifiedDate] [datetime] NOT NULL)
```

Figure 05-23: Query Data

In this table, a column called Current Flag indicates if an employee is currently employed. A filtered index with a WHERE Current Flag = one on the Current Flag column would allow for efficient queries of current employees. This example uses the bit datatype, meaning only two values, 1 for the currently employed and 0 for those who are not presently employed.

Note: You can also create indexes on views that provide significant performance gains when statements contain query elements like aggregations and table joins.

Column Store Indexes

Column store indexes were introduced in SQL Server 2012 and offer improved performance for queries that run large aggregation workloads. This type of index was originally targeted at data warehouses. Still, over time column store indexes have been used in several other workloads to help solve query performance issues on large tables. As of SQL Server 2014, there are both non-clustered and clustered column store indexes. Like b-tree indexes, a clustered column store index is the table itself stored especially, and non-clustered column store indexes are stored independently of the table. Clustered column store indexes inherently include all the columns in a given table. However, unlike row store clustered indexes, clustered column store indexes are NOT sorted.

Non-clustered column store indexes are typically used in two scenarios; the first is when a column in the table has a data type not supported in a column store index. Most data types are supported, but XML, CLR, sql _variant, text, text, and image are not supported in a column store index. Since a clustered column store always contains all the table columns (because it IS the table), a non-clustered one is the only option. The second scenario is a filtered index—this scenario is used in an architecture called hybrid transactional analytic processing (HTAP), where data is loaded into the underlying table. At the same time, reports are being run on the table. By filtering the index (typically on a date field), this design allows for both good insert and reporting performance.

Column store indexes are unique in their storage mechanism in that each column in the index is stored independently. It allows for greater compression since data in the same column is likely similar. It offers a two-fold benefit — a query using a column store index only needs to scan the columns required to satisfy the query, reducing the total IO performed.

Column store indexes perform best on analytic queries that scan large amounts of data, like fact tables in a data warehouse. Starting with SQL Server 2016, you can augment a column store index with an additional b-tree non-clustered index, which can be helpful if some of your queries do lookups against singleton values.

Column store indexes also benefit from batch execution mode, which refers to processing a set of rows (typically around 900) versus the database engine processing those rows one at a time. Instead of loading each record independently and processing them, the query engine computes the calculation in that group of 900documants. This processing model reduces the number of CPU instructions dramatically. It works best for a query like the following:

SELECT SUM(Sales) FROM Sales Amount;

SQL Server 2019 also includes a batch mode for row store data. Batch mode can provide up to a 10x performance increase over traditional row processing. While batch mode for row store does not have the same level of reading performance as a column-store index, analytical queries may see up to a 5x performance improvement.

The other benefit column-store indexes offer to data warehouse workloads is an optimized load path for 102,400 rows or more bulk insert operations. While 102,400 is the minimum value to load directly into the column store, each collection of rows, called a row group, can be up to approximately 1,024,000 rows. Having fewer but fuller row groups makes your SELECT queries more efficient because fewer row groups need to be scanned to retrieve the requested records. These loads take place in memory and are directly loaded to the index. Data is written to a b-tree structure called a delta store for smaller volumes and asynchronously loaded into the index.

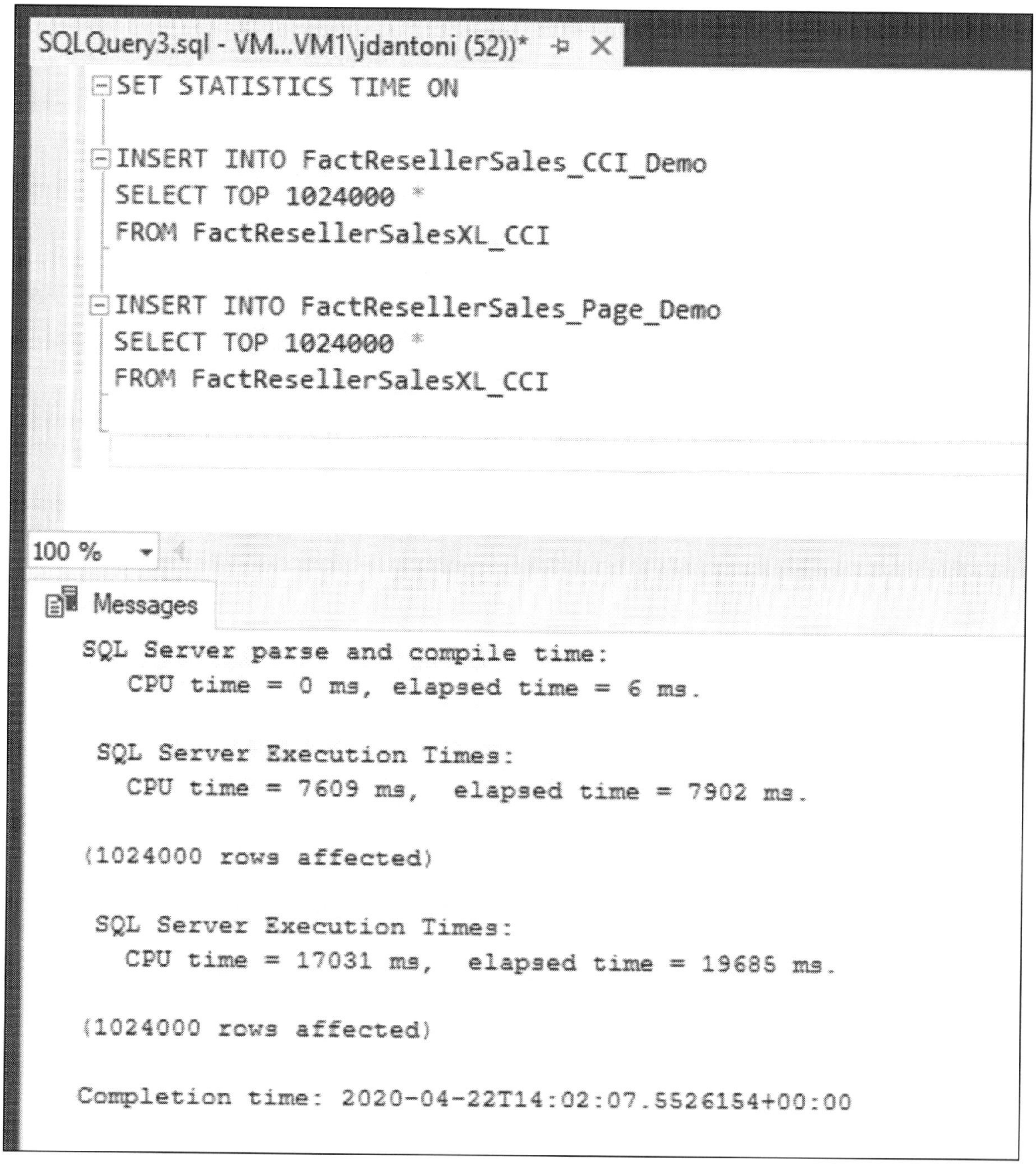

SQLQuery3.sql - VM...VM1\jdantoni (52))*

```
SET STATISTICS TIME ON

INSERT INTO FactResellerSales_CCI_Demo
SELECT TOP 1024000 *
FROM FactResellerSalesXL_CCI

INSERT INTO FactResellerSales_Page_Demo
SELECT TOP 1024000 *
FROM FactResellerSalesXL_CCI
```

100 %

Messages

```
SQL Server parse and compile time:
   CPU time = 0 ms, elapsed time = 6 ms.

 SQL Server Execution Times:
   CPU time = 7609 ms,  elapsed time = 7902 ms.

(1024000 rows affected)

 SQL Server Execution Times:
   CPU time = 17031 ms,  elapsed time = 19685 ms.

(1024000 rows affected)

Completion time: 2020-04-22T14:02:07.5526154+00:00
```

Figure 05-24: SQL Query

In this example, the same data is loaded into two tables; Fact Reseller Sales _CCI _Demo and Fact Reseller Sales _Page _Demo. The Fact Reseller Sales _CCI _Demo has a clustered column-store index, and the Fact Reseller Sales _Page _Demo has a clustered b-tree index with two columns and is page compressed. As you can see, each table is loading 1,024,000 rows from the Face Reseller Sales XL_CCI table. By using the SET STATISTICS TIME ON option, SQL Server keeps track of the elapsed time of the query execution. Loading the data into the column-store table took roughly 8 seconds, whereas loading into the compressed table took nearly 20 seconds. In this example, all the rows going into the column-store index are loaded into a single row group.

Loading less than 102,400 rows of data into a column-store index in a single operation is packed in a b-tree structure known as a delta store. The database engine moves this data into the column-store index using an asynchronous process called the tuple mover. You can also reorganize the index with the COMPRESS_ALL_ROW_GROUPS option to force the delta stores to be added and compressed into the column-store indexes. Having open delta stores can affect the performance of your queries performance because reading those records is less efficient than reading from the column store.

Describe Data Compression

As mentioned above, one of the key benefits of column-store indexes is the ability to compress your data. In addition to column-store compression, SQL Server offers a few other options for compressing data. While SQL Server still stores compressed data on 8 KB pages, when the data is compressed, more rows of data can be stored on a given page, which allows the query to read fewer pages. Reading fewer pages has a twofold benefit: it reduces the amount of physical IO performed, and it will enable more rows to be stored in the buffer pool, making efficient use of memory. The tradeoffs to compression are that it does require a small amount of CPU overhead; however, in most cases, the storage IO benefits far outweigh any additional processor usage.

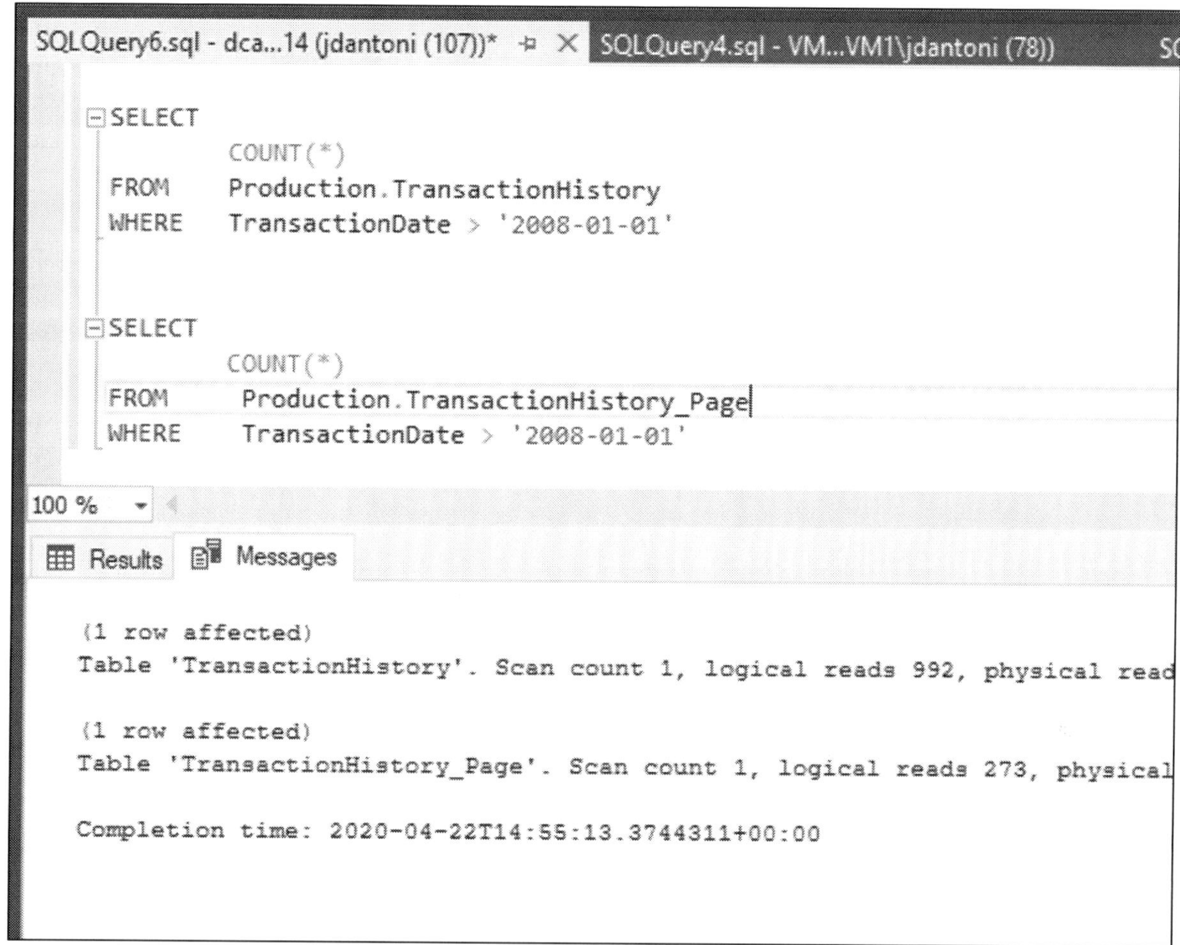

Figure 05-25: SQL Query

The image above shows this performance benefit. These tables have the same underlying indexes; the only difference is the clustered and non-clustered indexes on the production. Transaction History Page table is page compressed. The query against the page compressed object performs 72% fewer logical reads than those using uncompressed objects.

Compression is implemented in SQL Server at the object level. Each index or table can be compressed individually, and you have the option of compressing partitions within a partitioned table or index. You can evaluate the space you will save by using the sp_ estimate _data_ compression _savings system stored procedure. Before SQL Server 2019, this procedure did not support column-store indexes or column-store archival compression.

Row Compression

Row compression is fairly basic and does not incur much overhead; however, it does not offer the same amount of compression (measured by the percentage reduction in storage space required) that page compression may offer. Row compression stores every value of each column in a row, it is ensured that the the minimum amount of space is

needed to store that value. It uses a variable-length storage format for numeric data types like integer, float, and decimal, and it keeps fixed-length character strings using the variable-length form.

Page Compression

Page compression is a superset of row compression, as all pages will initially be row compressed before applying the page compression. Then a combination of techniques called prefix and dictionary compression is used to the data. Prefix compression eliminates redundant data in a single column, storing pointers back to the page header. After that step, dictionary compression searches for repeated values on a page and replaces them with tips, further reducing storage. The more redundancy in your data, the greater the space savings when you compress your data.

Column Store Archival Compression

Column store objects are always compressed. However, they can be further compressed using archival compression, which uses the Microsoft XPRESS compression algorithm on the data. This compression type is best used for infrequently read data but must be retained for regulatory or business reasons. While this data is further compressed, the CPU cost of decompression tends to outweigh any performance gains from IO reduction.

Lab 05-01: Identify Issues With A Database Design

Introduction

The database design process helps you simplify your corporate data management system's design, development, execution, and maintenance.

A database scheme can support saving disk storage space by decreasing data redundancy. Along with keeping data precise and reliable, it lets you access data in many ways.

Problem

You have been appointed as a Senior Database Administrator to help with performance issues when users query the database. Your goal is to recognize the problems in query performance and reduce them using techniques learned in this module.

Solution

You will execute queries with suboptimal performance, observe the query plans, and improve the database.

In this exercise, you will run a query to generate an actual execution plan and evaluate given execution plans (such as a key lookup).

Step 01: Examine the query and identify the problem.

Pre-Requisite

In this lab, you will be using a database that has been previously created in chapter 02: Lab 02-01.

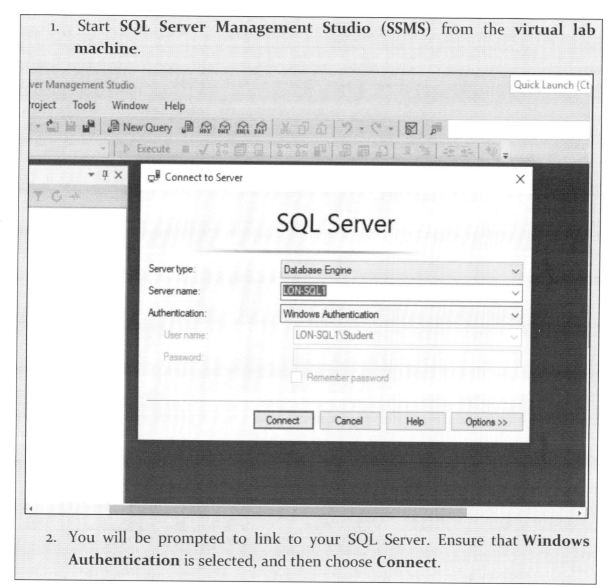

1. Start **SQL Server Management Studio (SSMS)** from the **virtual lab machine**.

2. You will be prompted to link to your SQL Server. Ensure that **Windows Authentication** is selected, and then choose **Connect**.

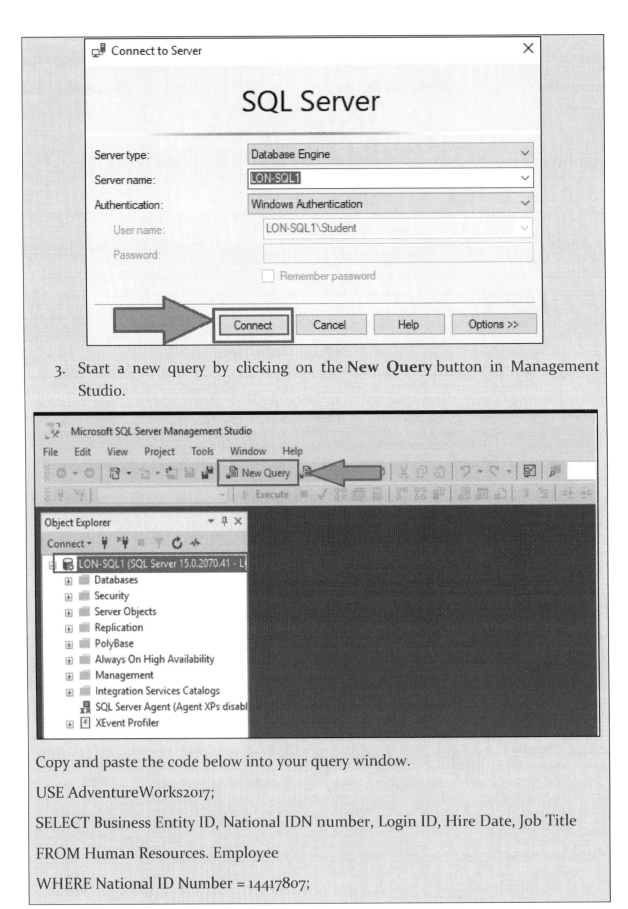

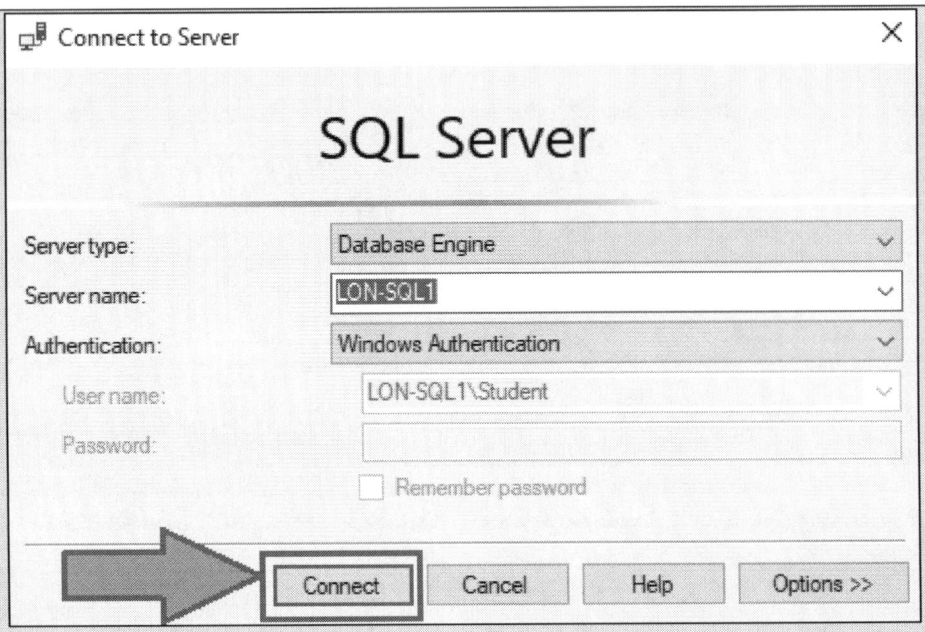

3. Start a new query by clicking on the **New Query** button in Management Studio.

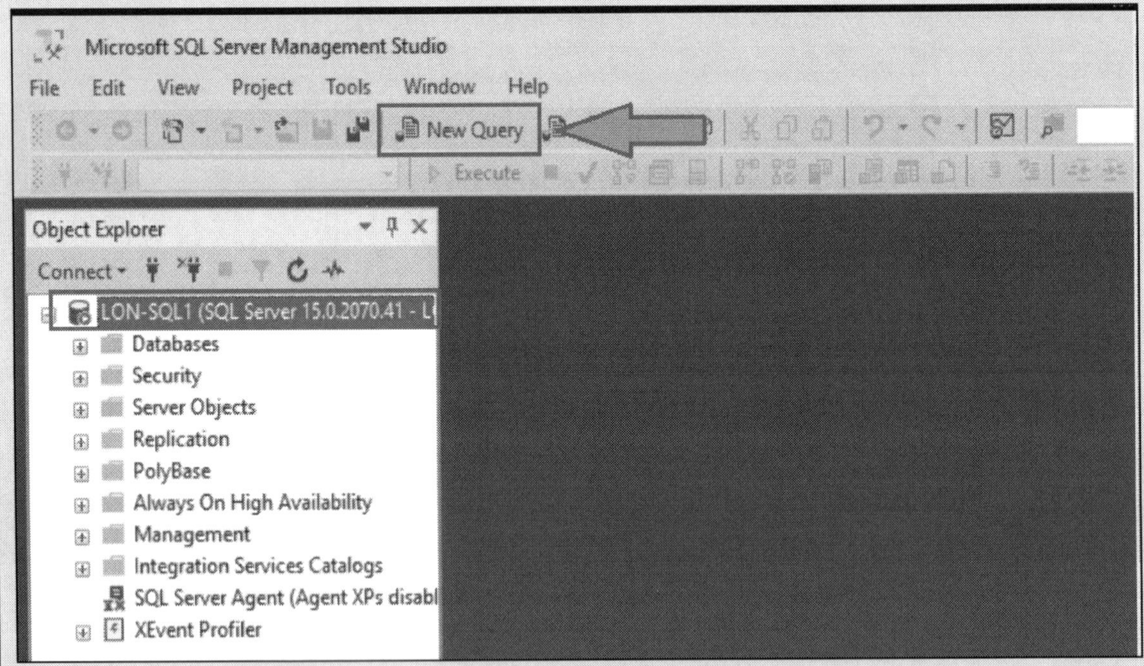

Copy and paste the code below into your query window.

USE AdventureWorks2017;

SELECT Business Entity ID, National IDN number, Login ID, Hire Date, Job Title

FROM Human Resources. Employee

WHERE National ID Number = 14417807;

exercise_steps.sql - LON-SQL1.master (LON-SQL1\Student (74)) - Microsoft SQL Server Management Studio

```
-- Examine the query and identify the problem - Step 5
-- ======

USE AdventureWorks2017;
SELECT BusinessEntityID, NationalIDNumber, LoginID, HireDate, JobTitle
FROM HumanResources.Employee
WHERE NationalIDNumber = 14417807;
```

Results | Messages

	BusinessEntityID	NationalIDNumber	LoginID	HireDate	JobTitle
1	28	14417807	adventure-works\guy1	2006-06-30	Production Technician - WC6

	BusinessEntityID	NationalIDNumber	LoginID	HireDate	JobTitle
1	28	14417807	adventure-works\guy1	2006-06-30	Production Technician - WC6

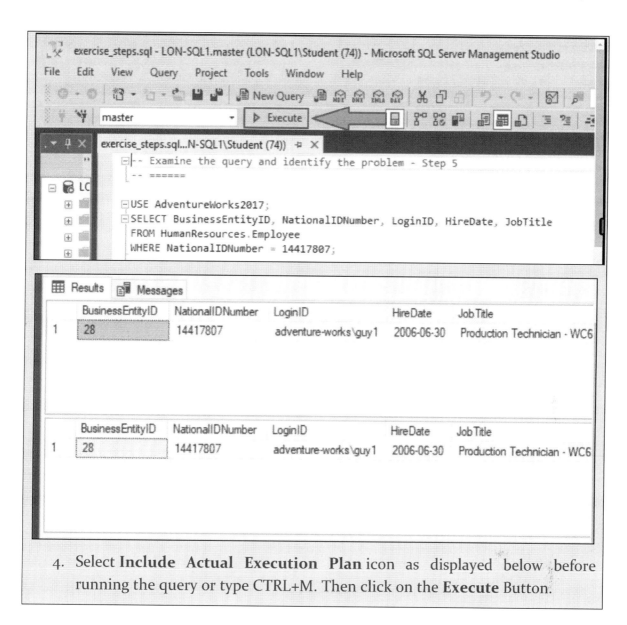

4. Select **Include Actual Execution Plan** icon as displayed below before running the query or type CTRL+M. Then click on the **Execute** Button.

exercise_steps.sql - LON-SQL1.AdventureWorks2017 (LON-SQL1\Student (74)) - Microsoft SQL Server Management

File Edit View Query Project Tools Window Help

New Query

AdventureWorks2017 Execute

exercise_steps.sql...N-SQL1\Student (74))

```
-- Examine the query and identify the problem - Step 5
-- ======

USE AdventureWorks2017;
SELECT BusinessEntityID, NationalIDNumber, LoginID, HireDate, JobTitle
FROM HumanResources.Employee
WHERE NationalIDNumber = 14417807;

-- Identify two ways to fix the warning issue - Step 3
-- ======

ALTER TABLE [HumanResources].[Employee] ALTER COLUMN [NationalIDNumber] INT N

-- Step 4
-- ======
```

100 %

Results Messages Execution plan

	BusinessEntityID	NationalIDNumber	LoginID	HireDate	JobTitle
1	28	14417807	adventure-works\guy1	2006-06-30	Production Technician - WC6

	BusinessEntityID	NationalIDNumber	LoginID	HireDate	JobTitle
1	28	14417807	adventure-works\guy1	2006-06-30	Production Technician - WC6

Query executed successfully. LON-SQL1 (15.0 RTM)

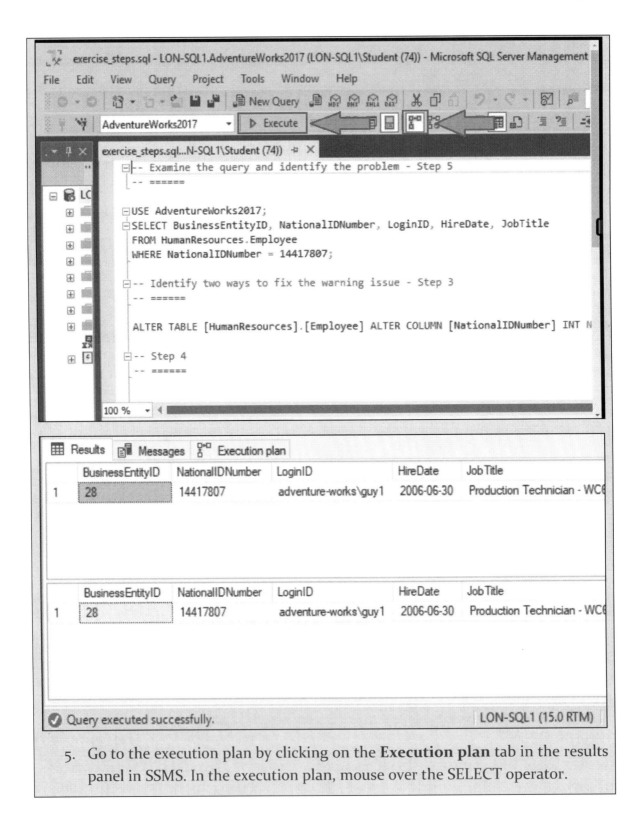

5. Go to the execution plan by clicking on the **Execution plan** tab in the results panel in SSMS. In the execution plan, mouse over the SELECT operator.

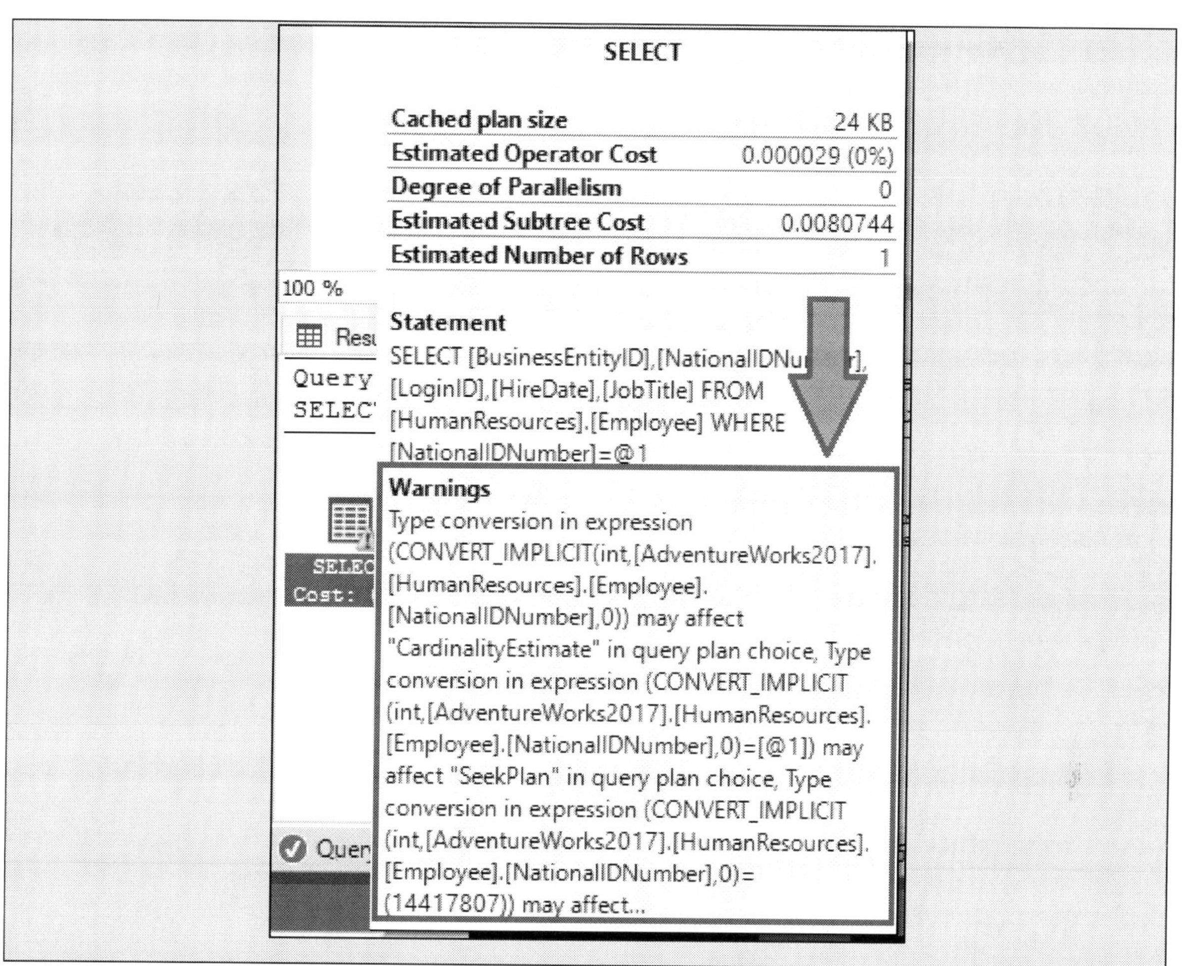

Identify Two Ways to Fix the Warning Issue

1. Fix the query using code as a solution.

Identify what field is causing the implicit conversion and why. If you review the query:

USE AdventureWorks2017;

SELECT Business Entity ID, National ID Number, Login ID, Hire Date, Job Title

FROM Human Resources. Employee

WHERE National ID Number = 14417807;

exercise_steps.sql - LON-SQL1.AdventureWorks2017 (LON-SQL1\Student (74)) - Microsoft SQL Server Management

File Edit View Query Project Tools Window Help

New Query

AdventureWorks2017 | Execute

exercise_steps.sql...N-SQL1\Student (74))

```
-- Examine the query and identify the problem - Step 5
-- ======

USE AdventureWorks2017;
SELECT BusinessEntityID, NationalIDNumber, LoginID, HireDate, JobTitle
FROM HumanResources.Employee
WHERE NationalIDNumber = 14417807;

-- Identify two ways to fix the warning issue - Step 3
-- ======

ALTER TABLE [HumanResources].[Employee] ALTER COLUMN [NationalIDNumber] INT N

-- Step 4
-- ======
```

100 %

Results | Messages | Execution plan

	BusinessEntityID	NationalIDNumber	LoginID	HireDate	JobTitle
1	28	14417807	adventure-works\guy1	2006-06-30	Production Technician - WC6

	BusinessEntityID	NationalIDNumber	LoginID	HireDate	JobTitle
1	28	14417807	adventure-works\guy1	2006-06-30	Production Technician - WC6

Query executed successfully. | LON-SQL1 (15.0 RTM)

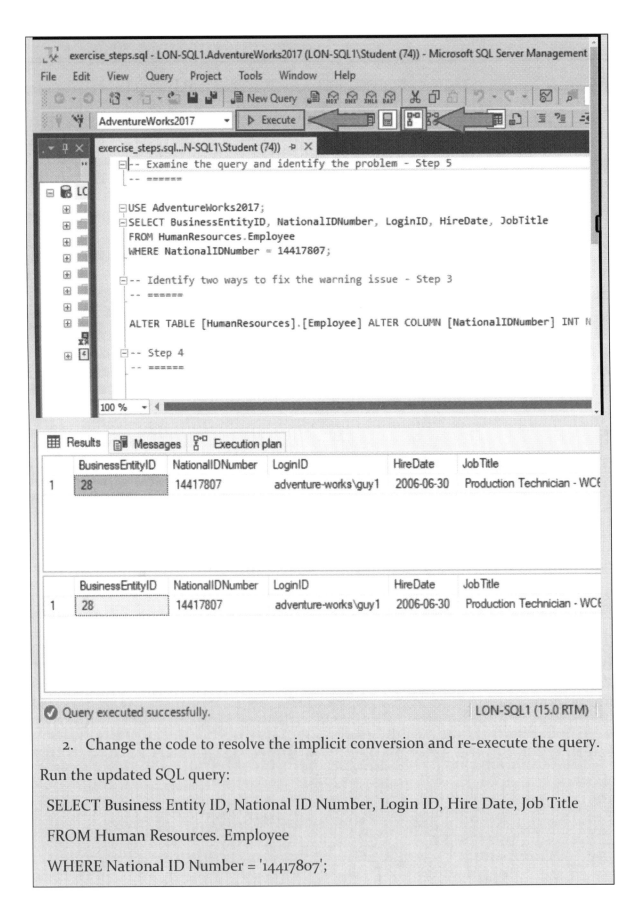

2. Change the code to resolve the implicit conversion and re-execute the query.

Run the updated SQL query:

SELECT Business Entity ID, National ID Number, Login ID, Hire Date, Job Title

FROM Human Resources. Employee

WHERE National ID Number = '14417807';

SQLQuery1.sql - LON-SQL1.AdventureWorks2017 (LON-SQL1\Student (51))* - Microsoft SQL Server Management St

File Edit View Query Project Tools Window Help

New Query

AdventureWorks2017 Execute

SQLQuery1.sql - LO...SQL1\Student (51))* exercise_steps.sql...N-SQL1\Student (74))

```
SELECT BusinessEntityID, NationalIDNumber, LoginID, HireDate, JobTitle
FROM HumanResources.Employee
WHERE NationalIDNumber = 14417807;
```

Results | Messages | Execution plan

	BusinessEntityID	NationalIDNumber	LoginID	HireDate	JobTitle
1	28	14417807	adventure-works\guy1	2006-06-30	Production Technician - WC6

Query executed successfully. LON-SQL1 (15.0 RTM)

Results | Messages | Execution plan

```
Query 1: Query cost (relative to the batch): 100%
SELECT [BusinessEntityID],[NationalIDNumber],[LoginID],[HireDate],[JobTitle] FROM [Hu...
```

SELECT Cost: 0 %

Nested Loops (Inner Join) Cost: 0 % 0.011s 1 of 1 (100%)

Index Seek (NonClustered) [Employee].[AK_Employee_NationalIDN... Cost: 50 % 0.011s 1 of 1 (100%)

Key Lookup (Clustered) [Employee].[PK_Employee_BusinessEnt...

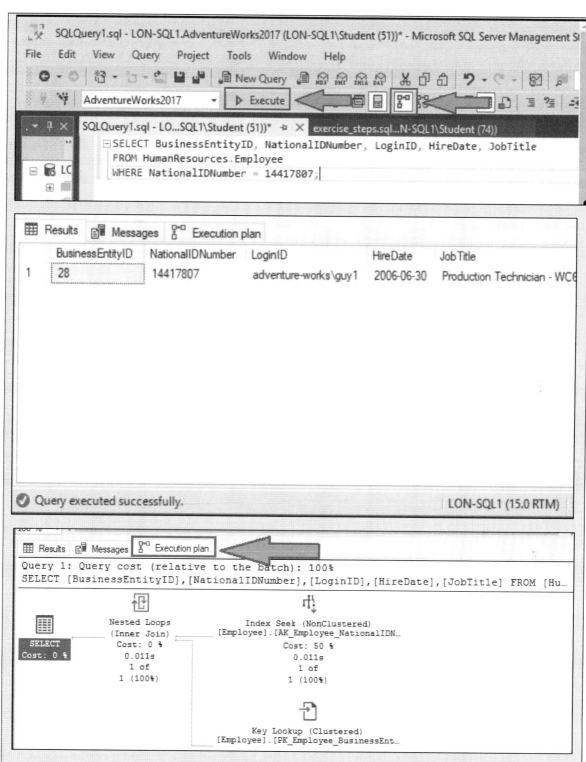

3. Fix the query using database changes.

Copy and paste the query into a new query window to modify the column's data type to fix the index. Attempt to run the query by clicking on **Execute** or pressing F5.

ALTER TABLE [Human Resources].[Employee] ALTER COLUMN [National ID Number] INT NOT NULL;

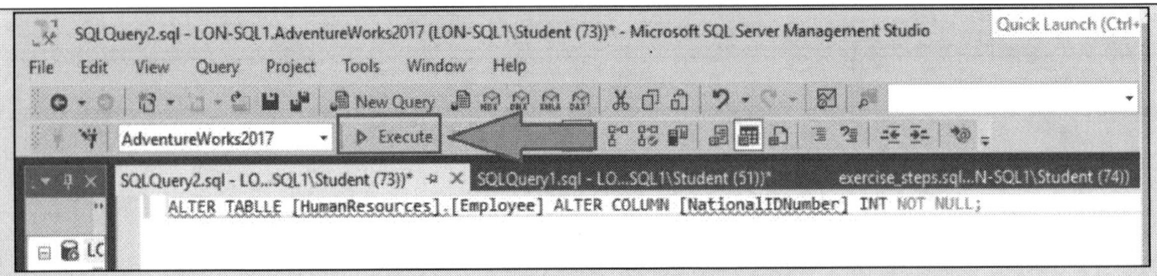

The changes to the table will resolve the conversion issue. However, this change leads to another case that you need to solve as a database administrator.

Msg 5074, Level 16, State 1, Line 1The index 'AK_ Employee _National ID Number' is dependent on column 'National ID Number.'

Msg 4922, Level 16, State 9, Line 1

ALTER TABLE ALTER COLUMN National ID Number failed because more objects access this column.

4. Please copy and paste the code into your query window and run it by clicking on Execute to resolve this issue.

```
USE AdventureWorks2017

GO

DROP INDEX [AK Employee _National ID Number] ON [Human
Resources].[Employee]

GO

ALTER TABLE [Human Resources].[Employee] ALTER COLUMN [National ID
Number] INT NOT NULL;

GO

CREATE UNIQUE NONCLUSTERED INDEX [AK_ Employee_ National IDN
umber] ON [Human Resources].[Employee]( [National ID Number] ASC );

GO
```

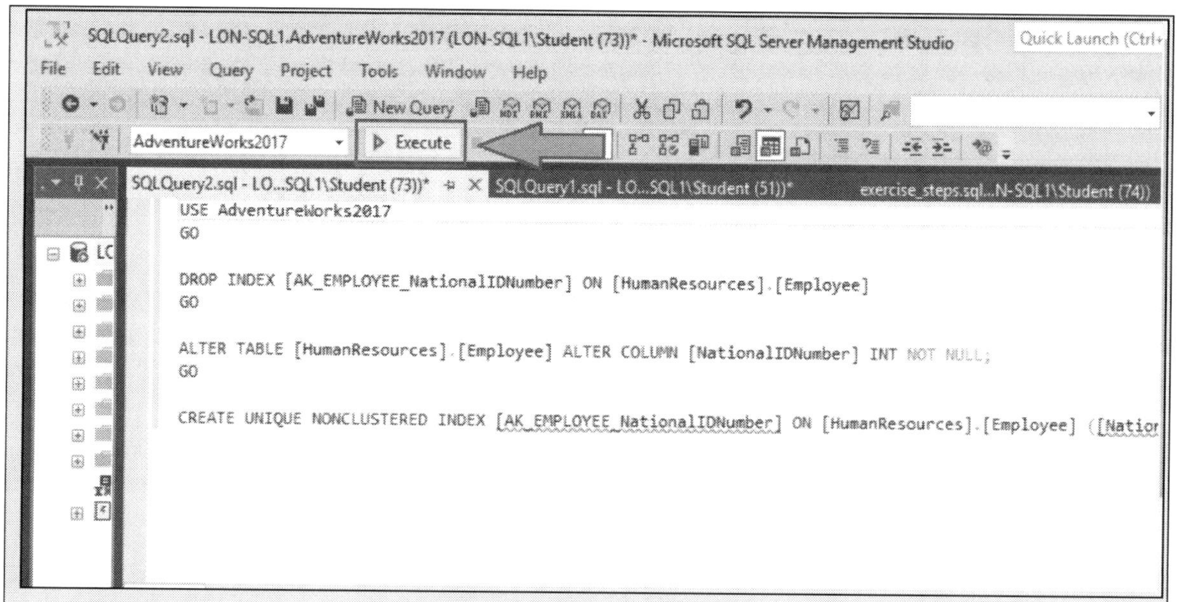

5. Re-execute the original query without the quotes.

USE AdventureWorks2017;

SELECT Business Entity ID, National ID Number, Login ID, Hire Date, Job Title

FROM Human Resources. Employee

WHERE National ID Number = 14417807;

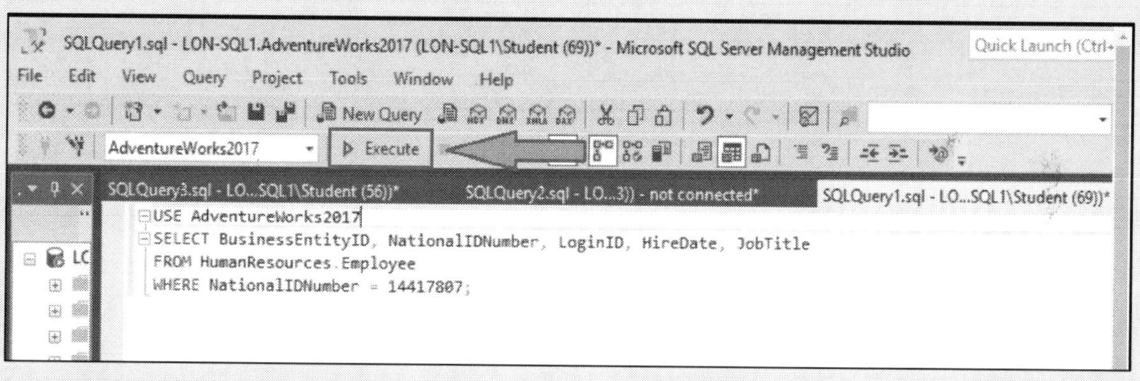

Examine the query plan and note that you can now use a number for the **National ID Number**.

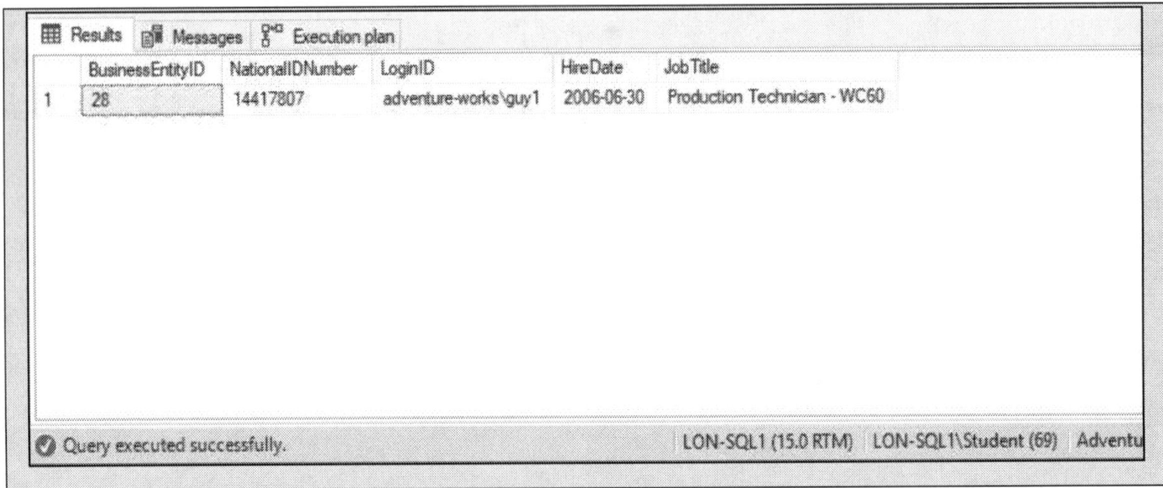

Step 02: Isolate Problem Areas In Poorly Performing Queries In A SQL Database

Pre-Requisite

In this lab, you will be using a database that you have previously created in chapter 02: Lab 02-01.

Run a Query to Generate an Actual Execution Plan

There are numerous ways to form an execution plan in SQL Server Management Studio.

1. Start **SQL Server Management Studio (SSMS) from the virtual lab machine.**

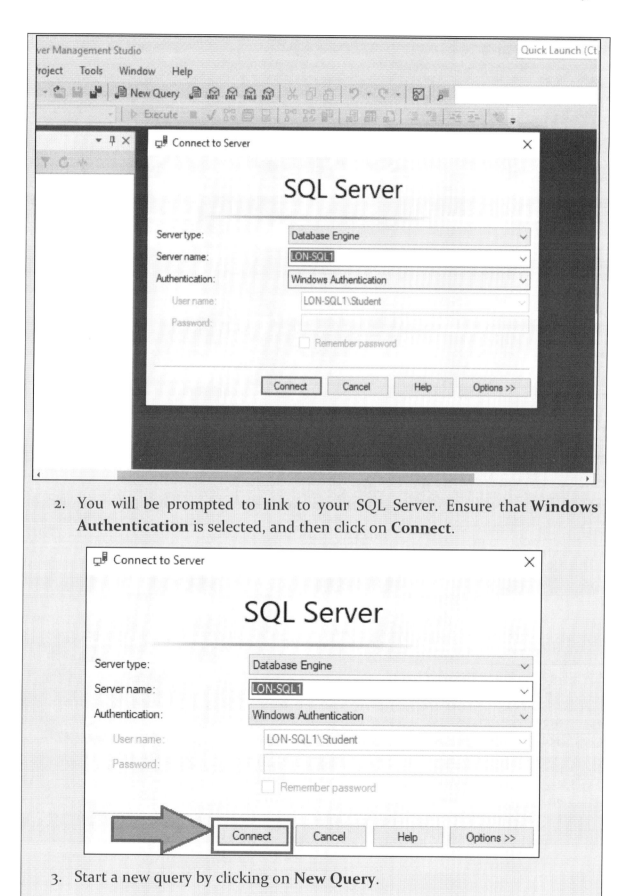

2. You will be prompted to link to your SQL Server. Ensure that **Windows Authentication** is selected, and then click on **Connect**.

3. Start a new query by clicking on **New Query**.

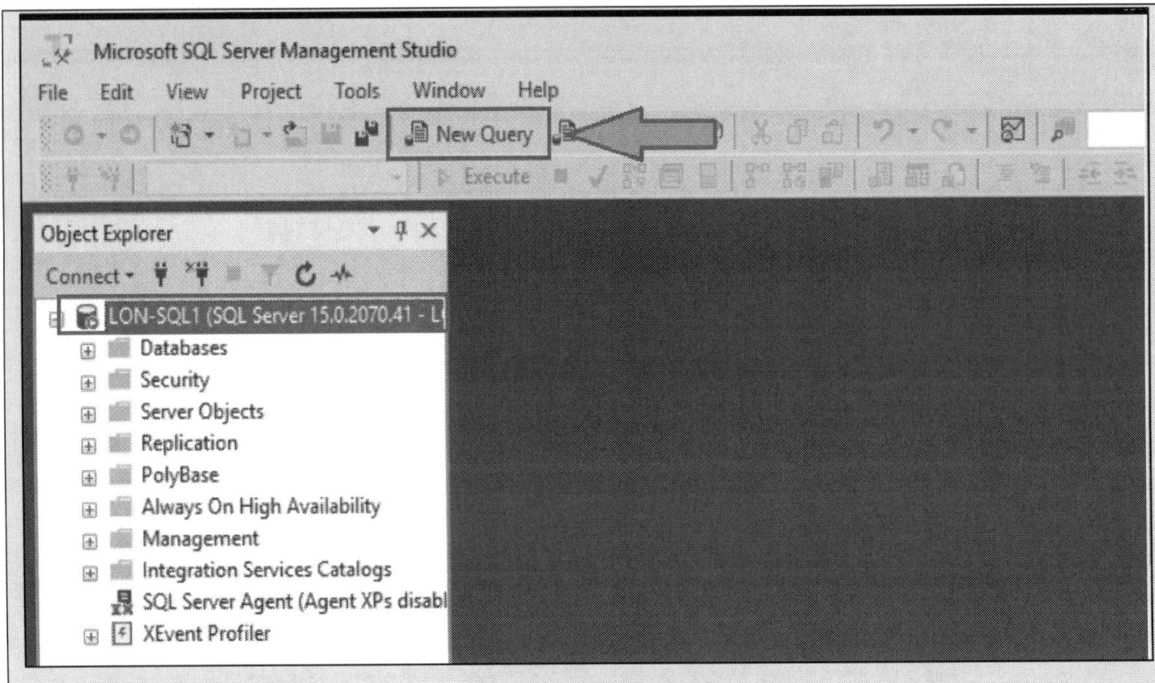

4. Copy and paste the code below into a new query window and run it by selecting **Execute** or pressing F5.

Use the **SHOWPLAN_ALL** setting to see a text version of a query's execution plan in the results pane instead of graphically in a separate tab.

```
USE AdventureWorks2017;
GO
SET SHOWPLAN_ALL ON;
GO
SELECT Business Entity ID
FROM Human Resources. Employee
WHERE National ID Number = '14417807';
GO
SET SHOWPLAN_ALL OFF;
GO
```

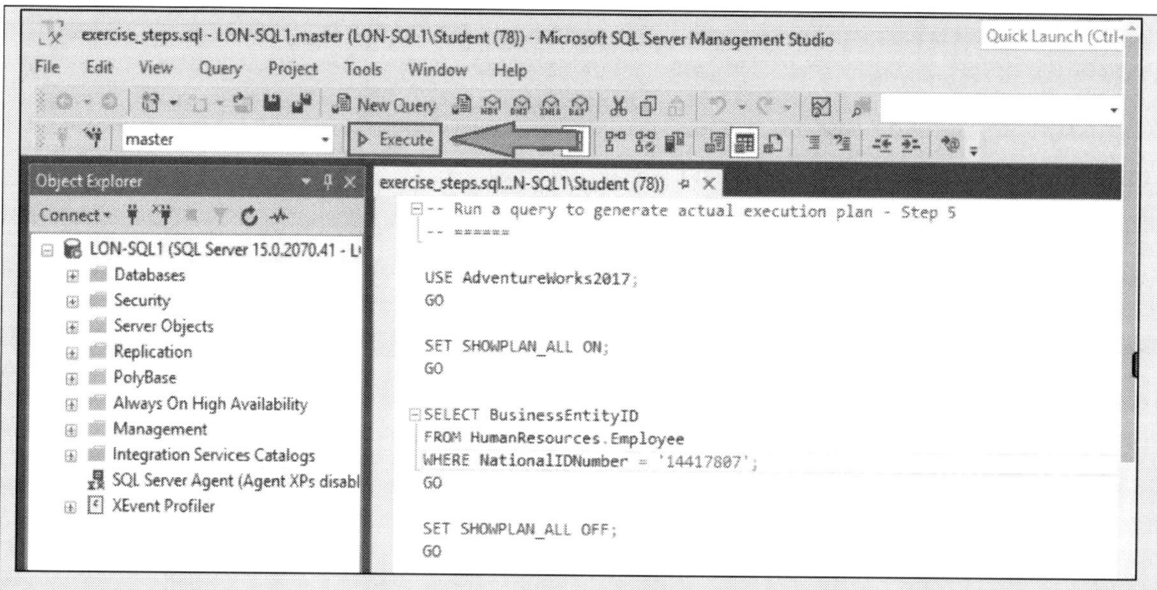

In your results, you will see a text version of the execution plan, instead of the effects of executing the **SELECT** statement,

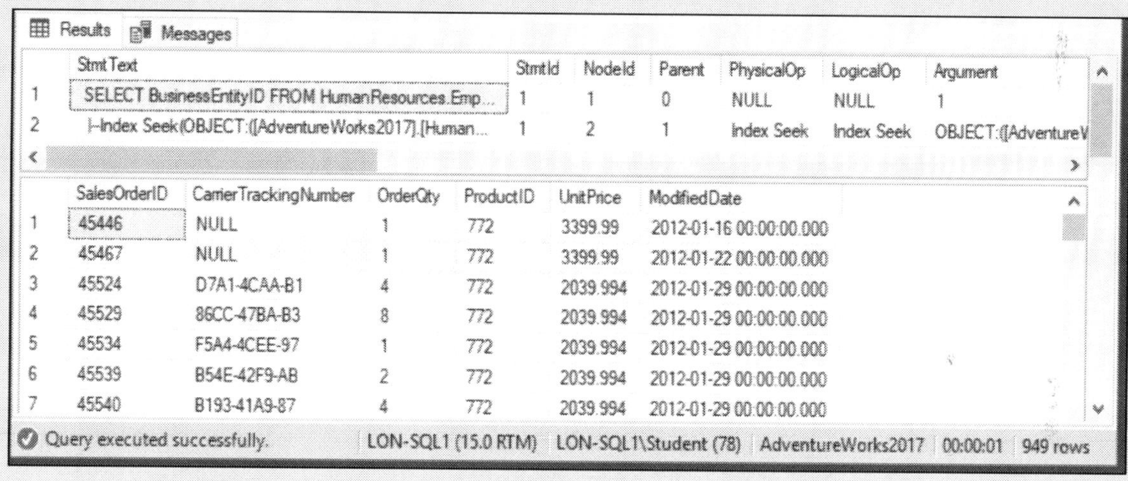

5. Examine the text in the second row's Stmt Text field:

|--Index Seek(OBJECT:([AdventureWorks2017].[HumanResources].[Employee].[AK_Employee_NationalIDNumber]), SEEK:([AdventureWorks2017].[HumanResources].[Employee].[NationalIDNumber]=CONVERT_IMPLICIT(nvarchar(4000),[@1],0)) ORDERED FORWARD)

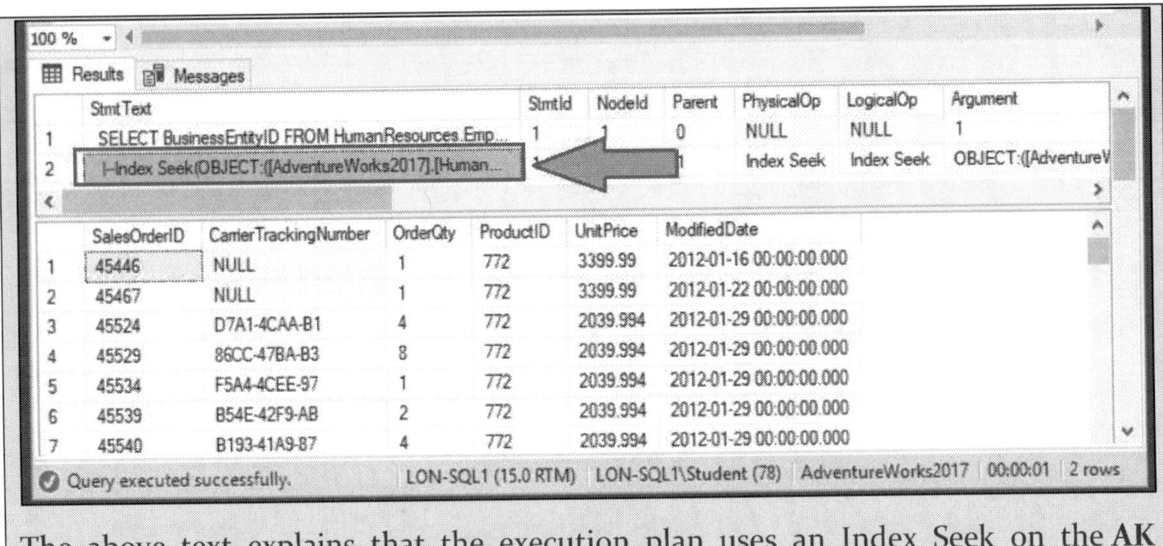

The above text explains that the execution plan uses an Index Seek on the **AK _Employee _National ID Number** key.

Resolve a Performance Problem from an Execution Plan

1. Copy and paste the code below into a new query window.

Select the **Include Actual Execution Plan** icon as displayed below before running the query or press CTRL+M. Execute the query by selecting **Execute** or press F5.

SET STATISTICS IO, TIME ON;

SELECT [Sales Order ID] ,[Carrier Tracking Number] ,[Order Qty] ,[Product ID], [Unit Price] ,[Modified Date]

FROM [AdventureWorks2017].[Sales].[Sales Order Detail]

WHERE [Modified Date] > '2012/01/01' AND [Product ID] = 772;

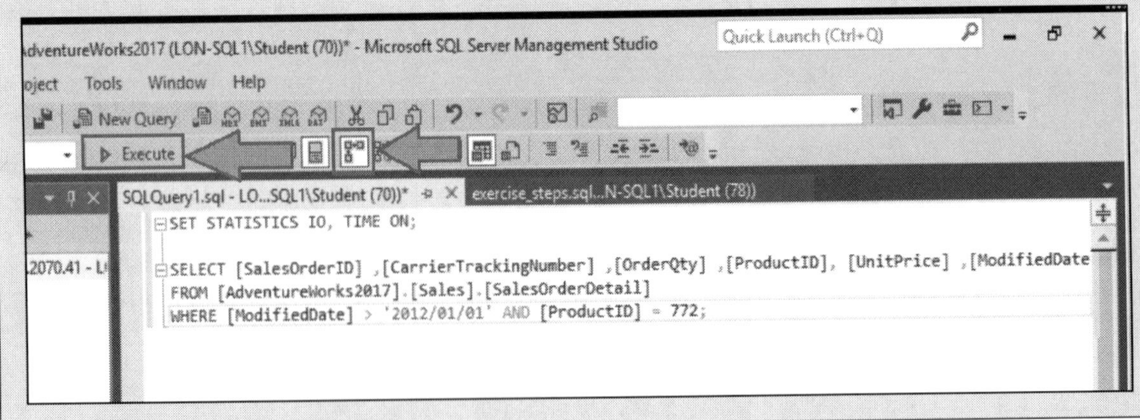

Results | Messages | Execution plan

	SalesOrderID	CarrierTrackingNumber	OrderQty	ProductID	UnitPrice	ModifiedDate
1	45446	NULL	1	772	3399.99	2012-01-16 00:00:00.000
2	45467	NULL	1	772	3399.99	2012-01-22 00:00:00.000
3	45524	D7A1-4CAA-B1	4	772	2039.994	2012-01-29 00:00:00.000
4	45529	86CC-47BA-B3	8	772	2039.994	2012-01-29 00:00:00.000
5	45534	F5A4-4CEE-97	1	772	2039.994	2012-01-29 00:00:00.000
6	45539	B54E-42F9-AB	2	772	2039.994	2012-01-29 00:00:00.000
7	45540	B193-41A9-87	4	772	2039.994	2012-01-29 00:00:00.000
8	45542	A757-4830-AE	3	772	2039.994	2012-01-29 00:00:00.000
9	45547	BE3F-40B0-95	3	772	2039.994	2012-01-29 00:00:00.000
10	45553	87C3-40D7-80	8	772	2039.994	2012-01-29 00:00:00.000
11	45554	24D3-4CD4-AB	2	772	2039.994	2012-01-29 00:00:00.000

Query executed successfully. | LON-SQL1 (15.0 RTM) | LON-SQL1\Student (70) | AdventureWorks2017 | 00:00:01 | 84 rows

SELECT
Cost: 0 %

Nested Loops
(Inner Join)
Cost: 0 %
0.011s
84 of
221 (38%)

Index Seek (NonClustered)
[SalesOrderDetail].[IX_SalesOrderDe...
Cost: 1 %
0.006s
221 of
221 (100%)

Key Lookup (Clustered)
[SalesOrderDetail].[PK_SalesOrderDe...
Cost: 99 %
0.004s
84 of
47520 (0%)

Query executed successfully. | LON-SQL1 (15.0 RTM) | LON-SQL1\Student (70) | AdventureWorks2017 | 00:00:01 | 84 rows

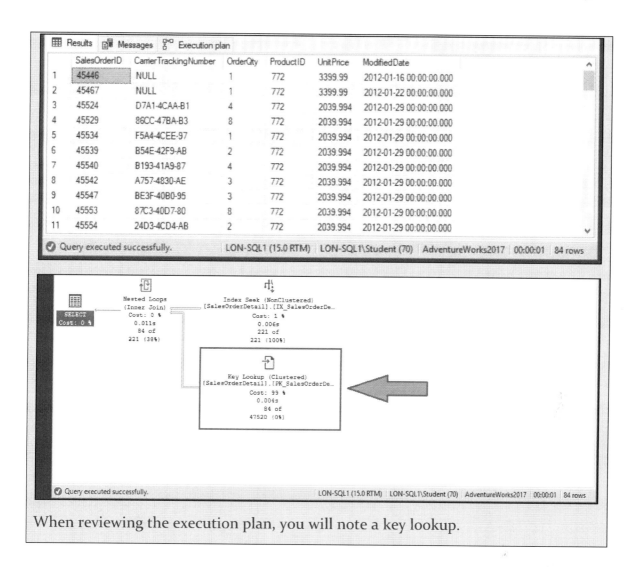

When reviewing the execution plan, you will note a key lookup.

Key Lookup (Clustered)

Uses a supplied clustering key to lookup on a table that has a clustered index.

Physical Operation	Key Lookup
Logical Operation	Key Lookup
Actual Execution Mode	Row
Estimated Execution Mode	Row
Storage	RowStore
Number of Rows Read	221
Actual Number of Rows	84
Actual Number of Batches	0
Estimated Operator Cost	0.665093 (99%)
Estimated I/O Cost	0.003125
Estimated CPU Cost	0.0001581
Estimated Subtree Cost	0.665093
Number of Executions	221
Estimated Number of Executions	221
Estimated Number of Rows	215.024
Estimated Row Size	54 B
Actual Rebinds	0
Actual Rewinds	0
Ordered	True
Node ID	4

Note the columns in the Output list, as these fields must be added to a covering index.

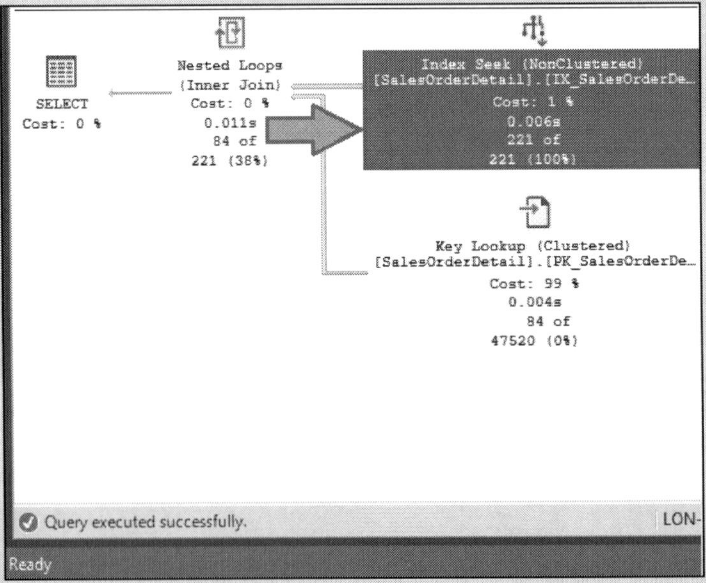

2. Fix the Key Lookup and rerun the query to see the new plan.

Key Lookups can be removed by adding a COVERING index that INCLUDES all fields being returned or searched in the query. In this example, the index only uses the Product ID.

CREATE NONCLUSTERED INDEX [IX_SalesOrderDetail_ProductID] ON [Sales].[SalesOrderDetail]

(

[Product ID] ASC

)

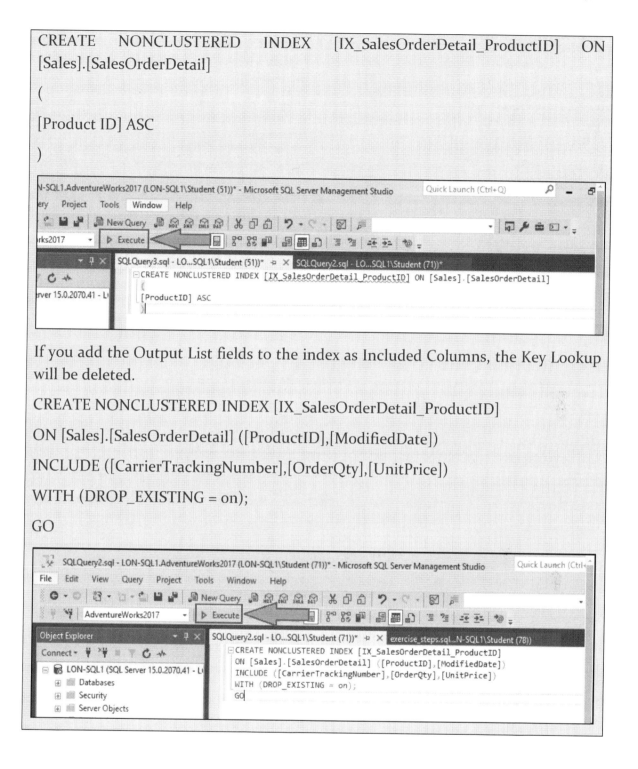

If you add the Output List fields to the index as Included Columns, the Key Lookup will be deleted.

CREATE NONCLUSTERED INDEX [IX_SalesOrderDetail_ProductID]

ON [Sales].[SalesOrderDetail] ([ProductID],[ModifiedDate])

INCLUDE ([CarrierTrackingNumber],[OrderQty],[UnitPrice])

WITH (DROP_EXISTING = on);

GO

Messages

Commands completed successfully.

Completion time: 2021-10-22T01:10:03.0859872-07:00

100 %

Query executed successfully. | LON-SQL1 (15.0 RTM) | LON-SQL1\Student (71) | Adventu

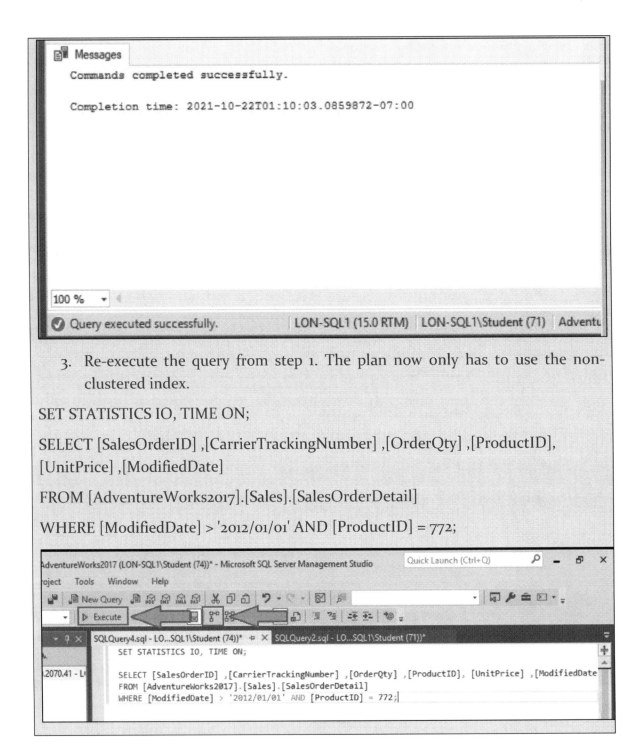

3. Re-execute the query from step 1. The plan now only has to use the non-clustered index.

SET STATISTICS IO, TIME ON;

SELECT [SalesOrderID] ,[CarrierTrackingNumber] ,[OrderQty] ,[ProductID], [UnitPrice] ,[ModifiedDate]

FROM [AdventureWorks2017].[Sales].[SalesOrderDetail]

WHERE [ModifiedDate] > '2012/01/01' AND [ProductID] = 772;

AdventureWorks2017 (LON-SQL1\Student (74))* - Microsoft SQL Server Management Studio

SQLQuery4.sql - LO...SQL1\Student (74))* | SQLQuery2.sql - LO...SQL1\Student (71))*

```
SET STATISTICS IO, TIME ON;

SELECT [SalesOrderID] ,[CarrierTrackingNumber] ,[OrderQty] ,[ProductID], [UnitPrice] ,[ModifiedDate
FROM [AdventureWorks2017].[Sales].[SalesOrderDetail]
WHERE [ModifiedDate] > '2012/01/01' AND [ProductID] = 772;
```

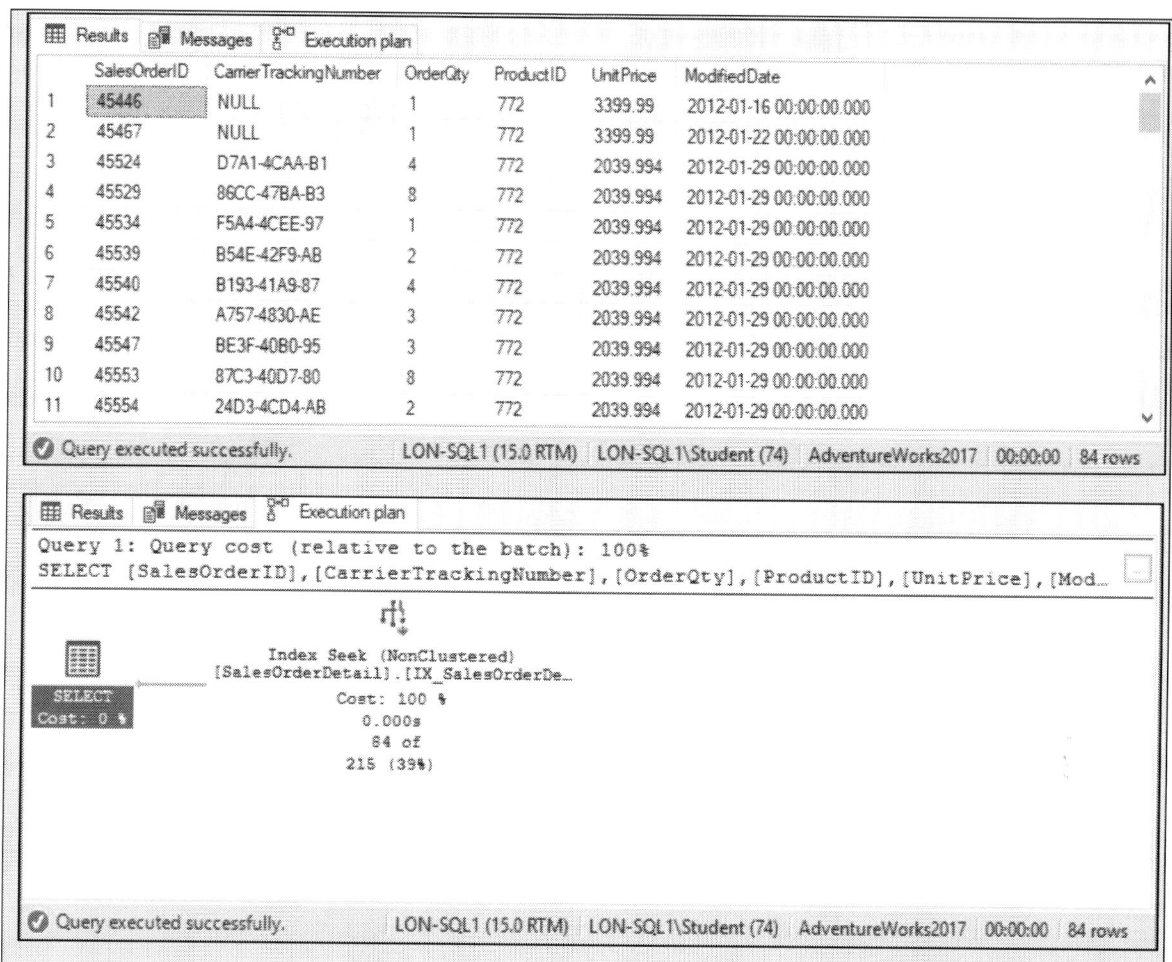

Use Query Store (QS) to detect and handle regression.

Next, you will run a workload to create query statistics for QS, examine Top Resource Consuming Queries to recognize poor performance, and see how to force a better execution plan.

Run a Workload to Generate Query Stats for Query Store

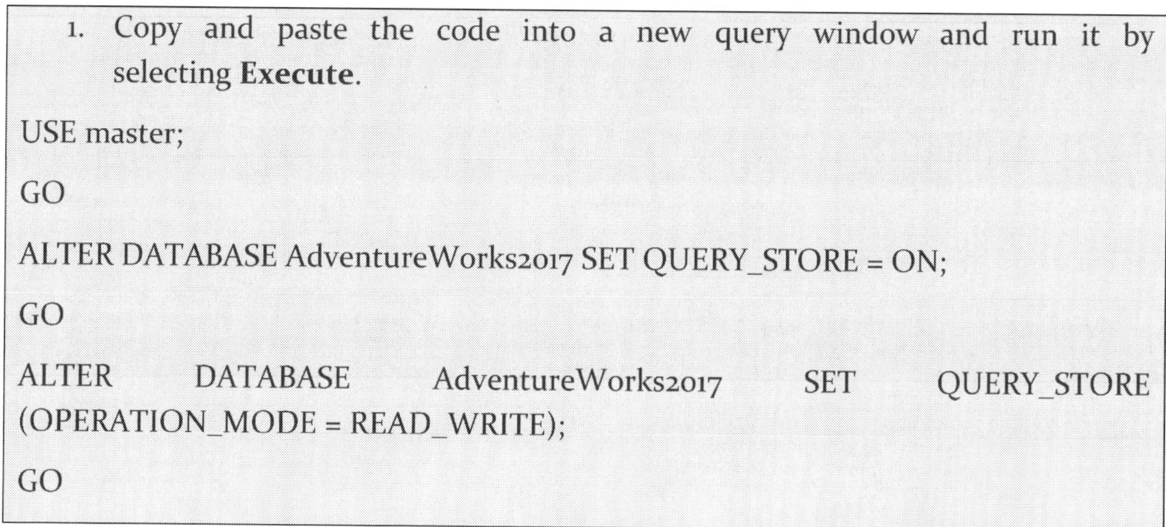

1. Copy and paste the code into a new query window and run it by selecting **Execute**.

USE master;

GO

ALTER DATABASE AdventureWorks2017 SET QUERY_STORE = ON;

GO

ALTER DATABASE AdventureWorks2017 SET QUERY_STORE (OPERATION_MODE = READ_WRITE);

GO

ALTER DATABASE AdventureWorks2017 SET COMPATIBILITY_LEVEL = 100;

GO

```
USE master;
GO

ALTER DATABASE AdventureWorks2017 SET QUERY_STORE = ON;
GO

ALTER DATABASE AdventureWorks2017 SET QUERY_STORE (OPERATION_MODE = READ_WRITE);
GO

ALTER DATABASE AdventureWorks2017 SET COMPATIBILITY_LEVEL = 100;
GO
```

```
Messages
Commands completed successfully.

Completion time: 2021-10-22T01:20:47.2657766-07:00
```

Query executed successfully.

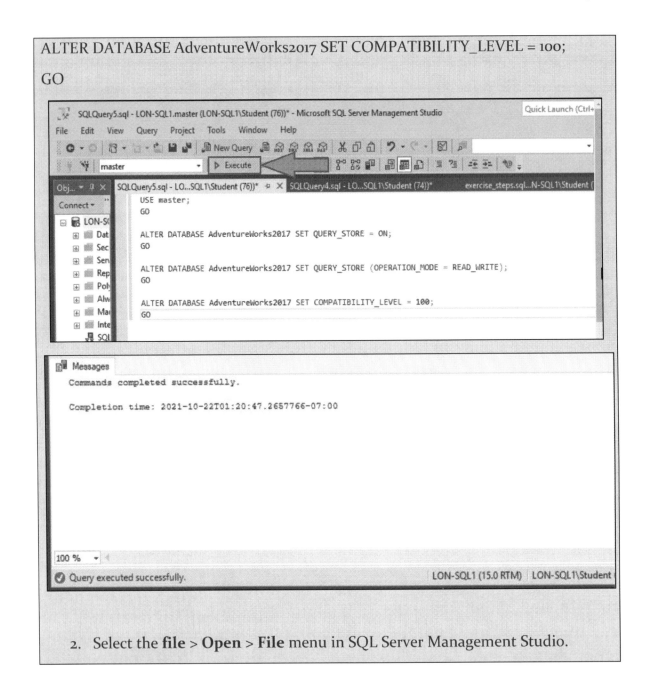

2. Select the **file** > **Open** > **File** menu in SQL Server Management Studio.

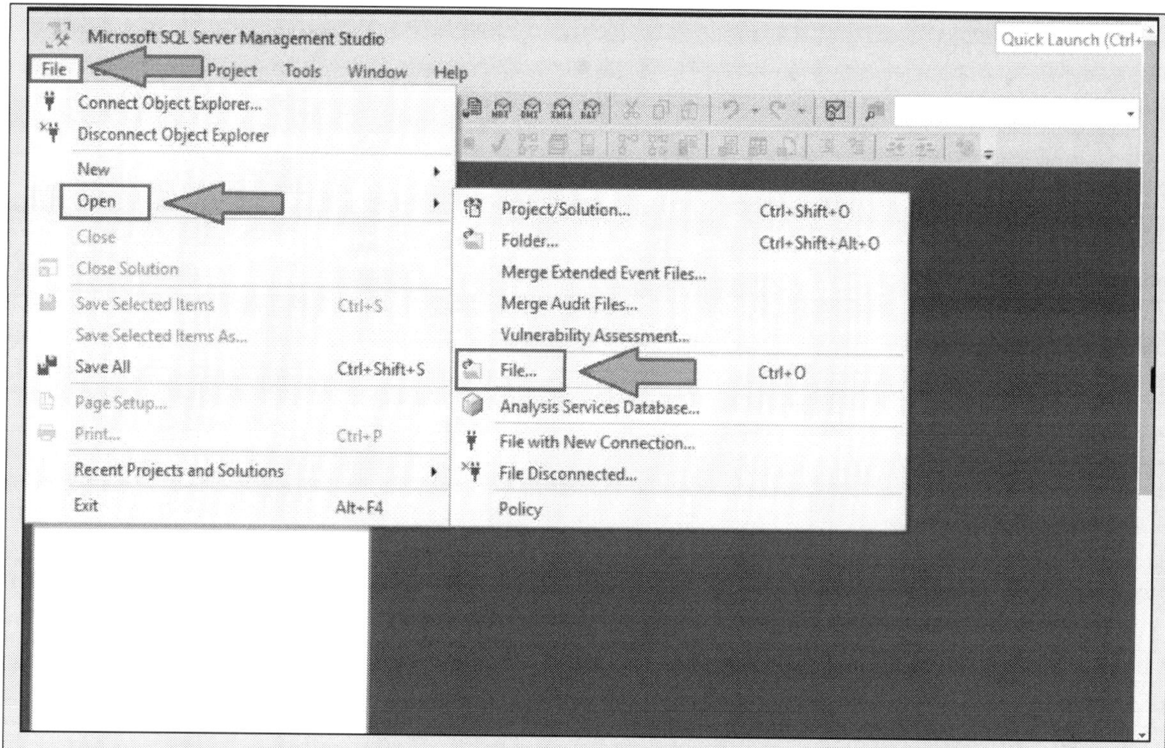

3. Go to the **D:\Labfiles\Query Performance\Create Random Workload Generator.SQL** file.

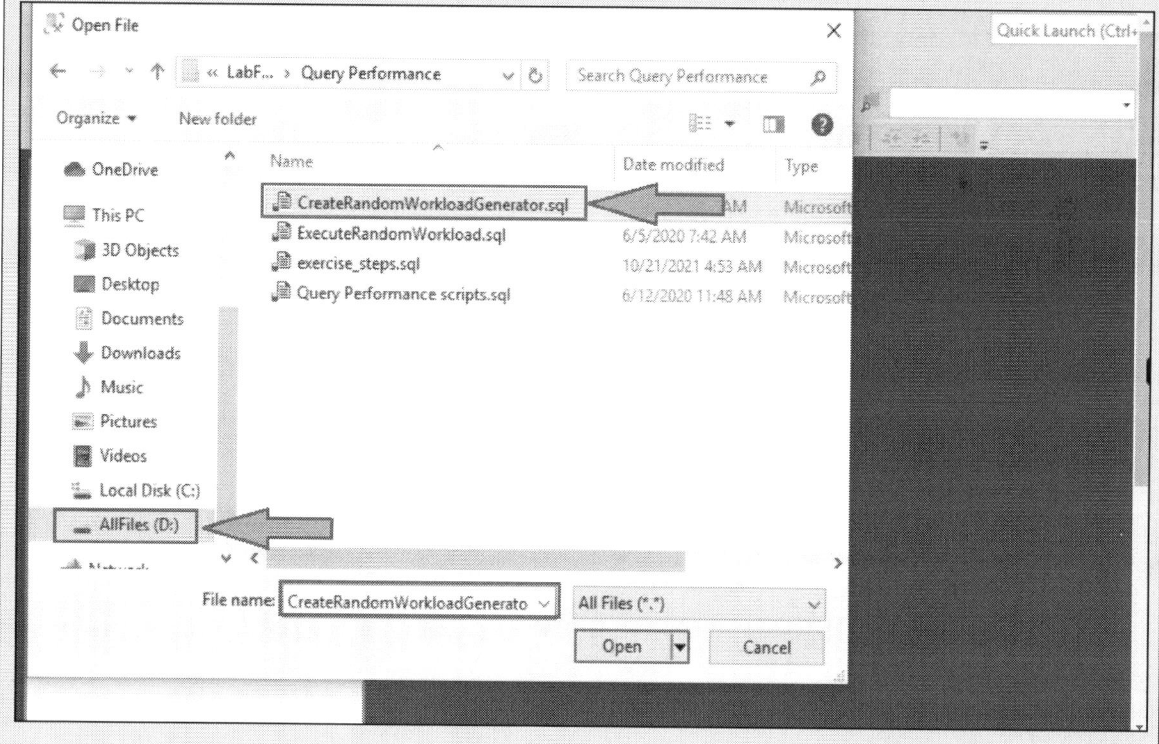

```
Use AdventureWorks2017
go
if exists(select name from sys.procedures where name='p_sel_SalesQuota')
begin
    drop procedure p_sel_SalesQuota
end
go
create procedure p_sel_SalesQuota
as
begin
    SELECT SalesQuota, SUM(SalesYTD) 'TotalSalesYTD', GROUPING(SalesQuota) AS 'Grouping'
    FROM Sales.SalesPerson
    GROUP BY SalesQuota WITH ROLLUP;
end
go

if exists(select name from sys.procedures where name='p_sel_Dept_Employee_Count')
begin
    drop procedure p_sel_Dept_Employee_Count
end
go
create procedure p_sel_Dept_Employee_Count(@i int, @x int)
as
begin
```

```
    SELECT D.Name
        ,CASE
        WHEN GROUPING_ID(D.Name, E.JobTitle) = 0 THEN E.JobTitle
        WHEN GROUPING_ID(D.Name, E.JobTitle) = 1 THEN N'Total: ' + D.Name
        WHEN GROUPING_ID(D.Name, E.JobTitle) = 3 THEN N'Company Total:'
            ELSE N'Unknown'
        END AS N'Job Title'
        ,COUNT(E.BusinessEntityID) AS N'Employee Count'
    FROM HumanResources.Employee E
        INNER JOIN HumanResources.EmployeeDepartmentHistory DH
            ON E.BusinessEntityID = DH.BusinessEntityID
        INNER JOIN HumanResources.Department D
            ON D.DepartmentID = DH.DepartmentID
    WHERE DH.EndDate IS NULL
        AND D.DepartmentID IN (@i,@x)
    GROUP BY ROLLUP(D.Name, E.JobTitle);
end
go
if exists(select name from sys.procedures where name='p_sel_Dept_Employees_by_Job_Titles')
begin
    drop procedure p_sel_Dept_Employees_by_Job_Titles
end
go
create procedure p_sel_Dept_Employees_by_Job_Titles(@i int, @x int)
```

```
as
begin
    SELECT D.Name
        ,E.JobTitle
        ,GROUPING_ID(D.Name, E.JobTitle) AS 'Grouping Level'
        ,COUNT(E.BusinessEntityID) AS N'Employee Count'
    FROM HumanResources.Employee AS E
        INNER JOIN HumanResources.EmployeeDepartmentHistory AS DH
            ON E.BusinessEntityID = DH.BusinessEntityID
        INNER JOIN HumanResources.Department AS D
            ON D.DepartmentID = DH.DepartmentID
    WHERE DH.EndDate IS NULL
        AND D.DepartmentID IN (@i,@x)
    GROUP BY ROLLUP(D.Name, E.JobTitle)
    HAVING GROUPING_ID(D.Name, E.JobTitle) = 0; --All titles
end
go
if exists(select name from sys.procedures where name='p_sel_Dept_Employees_Count_By_Title')
begin
    drop procedure p_sel_Dept_Employees_Count_By_Title
end
go
create procedure p_sel_Dept_Employees_Count_By_Title(@i int, @x int)
as
begin
```

```
    SELECT D.Name
        ,E.JobTitle
        ,GROUPING_ID(D.Name, E.JobTitle) AS 'Grouping Level'
        ,COUNT(E.BusinessEntityID) AS N'Employee Count'
    FROM HumanResources.Employee AS E
        INNER JOIN HumanResources.EmployeeDepartmentHistory AS DH
            ON E.BusinessEntityID = DH.BusinessEntityID
        INNER JOIN HumanResources.Department AS D
            ON D.DepartmentID = DH.DepartmentID
    WHERE DH.EndDate IS NULL
        AND D.DepartmentID IN (@i,@x)
    GROUP BY ROLLUP(D.Name, E.JobTitle)
    HAVING GROUPING_ID(D.Name, E.JobTitle) = 1; --Group by Name;
end
go




if exists(select name from sys.procedures where name='p_sel_get_originization_by_employee')
begin
    drop procedure p_sel_get_originization_by_employee
end
go
create procedure p_sel_get_originization_by_employee(@i int)
as
begin

    DECLARE @CurrentEmployee hierarchyid
```

```
    SELECT
        @CurrentEmployee=OrganizationNode
    from
        HumanResources.Employee
    where
        BusinessEntityID=@i



    SELECT OrganizationNode.ToString() AS Text_OrganizationNode, *
    FROM HumanResources.Employee
    WHERE OrganizationNode.GetAncestor(1) = @CurrentEmployee ;
end
go


if exists(select name from sys.procedures where name='p_sel_get_sales_per_sales_person')
begin
    drop procedure p_sel_get_sales_per_sales_person
end
go
Create Procedure p_sel_get_sales_per_sales_person(@i int)
as
Begin
SELECT CustomerID, OrderDate, SubTotal, TotalDue
FROM Sales.SalesOrderHeader
WHERE SalesPersonID = @i
ORDER BY OrderDate

select sum(subtotal), sum(totaldue)
```

```
FROM Sales.SalesOrderHeader
WHERE SalesPersonID = @i

end
go
if exists(select name from sys.procedures where name='p_sel_get_sales_per_by_sales_person')
begin
    drop procedure p_sel_get_sales_per_by_sales_person
end
go
Create Procedure p_sel_get_sales_per_by_sales_person
as
Begin
SELECT SalesPersonID, CustomerID, OrderDate, SubTotal, TotalDue
FROM Sales.SalesOrderHeader
group by grouping sets(SalesPersonID), CustomerID, OrderDate, SubTotal, TotalDue
ORDER BY SalesPersonID, OrderDate

select salespersonid, sum(subtotal), sum(totaldue)
FROM Sales.SalesOrderHeader
group by SalesPersonID
ORDER BY SalesPersonID

end

go
if exists(select name from sys.procedures where name='p_sel_aliased_select')
begin
    drop procedure p_sel_aliased_select
end
```

```
end
go
Create Procedure p_sel_product_info
as
Begin

SELECT Name, ProductNumber, ListPrice AS Price
FROM Production.Product
ORDER BY Name ASC

end
go
if exists(select name from sys.procedures where name='p_sel_products_withDTM_NULL')
begin
    drop procedure p_sel_products_withDTM_NULL
end
go
Create Procedure p_sel_products_withDTM_NULL(@i as int)
as
Begin

SELECT Name, ProductNumber, ListPrice AS Price
FROM Production.Product
WHERE ProductLine = NULL
AND DaysToManufacture < @i
ORDER BY Name ASC;

end
go
```

```
if exists(select name from sys.procedures where name='p_sel_products_withDTM_M')
begin
    drop procedure p_sel_products_withDTM_M
end
go
Create Procedure p_sel_products_withDTM_M(@i as int)
as
Begin

SELECT Name, ProductNumber, ListPrice AS Price
FROM Production.Product
WHERE ProductLine = 'M'
AND DaysToManufacture < @i
ORDER BY Name ASC;

end
go
if exists(select name from sys.procedures where name='p_sel_products_withDTM_R')
begin
    drop procedure p_sel_products_withDTM_R
end
go
Create Procedure p_sel_products_withDTM_R(@i as int)
as
Begin

SELECT Name, ProductNumber, ListPrice AS Price
FROM Production.Product
```

```
WHERE ProductLine = 'R'
AND DaysToManufacture < @i
ORDER BY Name ASC;

end
go
if exists(select name from sys.procedures where name='p_sel_products_withDTM_S')
begin
    drop procedure p_sel_products_withDTM_S
end
go
Create Procedure p_sel_products_withDTM_S(@i as int)
as
Begin

SELECT Name, ProductNumber, ListPrice AS Price
FROM Production.Product
WHERE ProductLine = 'S'
AND DaysToManufacture < @i
ORDER BY Name ASC;

end
go
if exists(select name from sys.procedures where name='p_sel_products_withDTM_T')
begin
    drop procedure p_sel_products_withDTM_T
end
go
Create Procedure p_sel_products_withDTM_T(@i as int)
```

```
as
Begin

SELECT Name, ProductNumber, ListPrice AS Price
FROM Production.Product
WHERE ProductLine = 'T'
AND DaysToManufacture < @i
ORDER BY Name ASC;

end

go
if exists(select name from sys.procedures where name='p_sel_discount_sales')
begin
    drop procedure p_sel_discount_sales
end
go
Create Procedure p_sel_discount_sales
as
Begin

SELECT p.Name AS ProductName,
NonDiscountSales = (OrderQty * UnitPrice),
Discounts = ((OrderQty * UnitPrice) * UnitPriceDiscount)
FROM Production.Product AS p
INNER JOIN Sales.SalesOrderDetail AS sod
ON p.ProductID = sod.ProductID
ORDER BY ProductName DESC;
```

```
end
go
if exists(select name from sys.procedures where name='p_calc_revenue_for_each_product')
begin
    drop procedure p_calc_revenue_for_each_product
end
go
Create Procedure p_calc_revenue_for_each_product
as
Begin

SELECT 'Total income is', ((OrderQty * UnitPrice) * (1.0 - UnitPriceDiscount)), ' for ',
p.Name AS ProductName
FROM Production.Product AS p
INNER JOIN Sales.SalesOrderDetail AS sod
ON p.ProductID = sod.ProductID
ORDER BY ProductName ASC;

end
go
if exists(select name from sys.procedures where name='p_sel_Employee_Jobtitles')
begin
    drop procedure p_sel_Employee_Jobtitles
end
go
Create Procedure p_sel_Employee_Jobtitles
as
Begin
```

```
SELECT DISTINCT JobTitle
FROM HumanResources.Employee
ORDER BY JobTitle;

end

go
if exists(select name from sys.procedures where name='p_ins_NewProducts')
begin
    drop procedure p_ins_NewProducts
end
go
Create Procedure p_ins_NewProducts
as
Begin
if exists(select name from sys.tables where name = 'NewProducts')
begin
    drop table dbo.NewProducts
end

SELECT * INTO dbo.NewProducts
FROM Production.Product
WHERE ListPrice > $25
AND ListPrice < $100;

end
go
if exists(select name from sys.procedures where name='p_sel_all_products_like')
begin
```

```
    drop procedure p_sel_all_products_like
end
go
Create Procedure p_sel_all_products_like(@i int)
as
begin
declare @pName char(5), @sqltext nvarchar(4000)

set @pname=(select left(name, 5) from Production.ProductModel where ProductModelID=@i)


set @sqltext='SELECT DISTINCT Name
FROM Production.Product AS p
WHERE EXISTS
    (SELECT *
     FROM Production.ProductModel AS pm
     WHERE p.ProductModelID = pm.ProductModelID
           AND pm.Name LIKE ' + ''''+ @pname + '%' + ''''+');'
exec sp_executesql @sqltext

end
go
if exists(select name from sys.procedures where name='p_sel_salesperson_by_bonus')
begin
    drop procedure p_sel_salesperson_by_bonus
end
go
Create Procedure p_sel_salesperson_by_bonus(@i int)
as
```

```
begin
declare @pmoney money, @sqltext nvarchar(4000)

set @pmoney=(select bonus from sales.SalesPerson where BusinessEntityID=@i)
set @sqltext='SELECT DISTINCT p.LastName, p.FirstName
FROM Person.Person AS p
JOIN HumanResources.Employee AS e
    ON e.BusinessEntityID = p.BusinessEntityID WHERE ' + cast(@pmoney as varchar(20)) +'IN
    (SELECT Bonus
     FROM Sales.SalesPerson AS sp
     WHERE e.BusinessEntityID = sp.BusinessEntityID);'

exec sp_executesql @sqltext

end
go
if exists(select name from sys.procedures where name='p_sel_max_price_double_average_model')
begin
    drop procedure p_sel_max_price_double_average_model
end
go
Create Procedure p_sel_max_price_double_average_model
as
Begin
SELECT p1.ProductModelID
FROM Production.Product AS p1
GROUP BY p1.ProductModelID
HAVING MAX(p1.ListPrice) >= ALL
```

```
    (SELECT AVG(p2.ListPrice)
     FROM Production.Product AS p2
     WHERE p1.ProductModelID = p2.ProductModelID);
end
go
if exists(select name from sys.procedures where name='p_sel_total_by_sales_order')
begin
    drop procedure p_sel_total_by_sales_order
end
go
Create Procedure p_sel_total_by_sales_order
as
Begin
SELECT SalesOrderID, SUM(LineTotal) AS SubTotal
FROM Sales.SalesOrderDetail
GROUP BY SalesOrderID
ORDER BY SalesOrderID;
end
go
if exists(select name from sys.procedures where name='p_sel_employee_name_by_product_sales')
begin
    drop procedure p_sel_employee_name_by_product_sales
end
go
Create Procedure p_sel_employee_name_by_product_sales(@i int)
as
Begin
declare @productNumber varchar(200)
set @productNumber=(select ProductNumber from production.Product where productid=@i)
```

```
    SELECT DISTINCT pp.LastName, pp.FirstName
    FROM Person.Person pp JOIN HumanResources.Employee e
    ON e.BusinessEntityID = pp.BusinessEntityID WHERE pp.BusinessEntityID IN
    (SELECT SalesPersonID
    FROM Sales.SalesOrderHeader
    WHERE SalesOrderID IN
    (SELECT SalesOrderID
    FROM Sales.SalesOrderDetail
    WHERE ProductID IN
    (SELECT ProductID
    FROM Production.Product p
    WHERE ProductNumber = @productNumber)));
end
go
if exists(select name from sys.procedures where name='p_sel_group_by_clause')
begin
    drop procedure p_sel_group_by_clause
end
go
Create Procedure p_sel_group_by_clause
as
Begin
    SELECT ProductID, SpecialOfferID, AVG(UnitPrice) AS 'Average Price',
        SUM(LineTotal) AS SubTotal
    FROM Sales.SalesOrderDetail
    GROUP BY ProductID, SpecialOfferID
    ORDER BY ProductID;
end
go
```

```
if exists(select name from sys.procedures where name='p_sel_results_by_price')
begin
    drop procedure p_sel_results_by_price
end
go
Create Procedure p_sel_results_by_price(@i int)
as
Begin
    declare @pmoney money
    set @pmoney=(select listprice from production.product where productid=@i)

    SELECT ProductModelID, AVG(ListPrice) AS 'Average List Price'
    FROM Production.Product
    WHERE ListPrice > @pmoney
    GROUP BY ProductModelID
    ORDER BY ProductModelID;
end
go
if exists(select name from sys.procedures where name='p_sel_group_by_w_expression')
begin
    drop procedure p_sel_group_by_w_expression
end
go
Create Procedure p_sel_group_by_w_expression
as
Begin
    SELECT AVG(OrderQty) AS 'Average Quantity',
```

```
    FROM Sales.SalesOrderDetail
    WHERE OrderQty > @i
    GROUP BY ProductID
    ORDER BY AVG(UnitPrice);
end
go
if exists(select name from sys.procedures where name='p_sel_product_by_quantity')
begin
    drop procedure p_sel_product_by_quantity
end
go
Create Procedure p_sel_product_by_quantity(@i int)
as
Begin
    SELECT ProductID
    FROM Sales.SalesOrderDetail
    GROUP BY ProductID
    HAVING AVG(OrderQty) > @i
    ORDER BY ProductID;
end
go
if exists(select name from sys.procedures where name='p_sel_order_by_tracking_partial')
begin
    drop procedure p_sel_order_by_tracking_partial
end
go
Create Procedure p_sel_order_by_tracking_partial(@i int)
as
Begin
```

```
    declare @ctNum nvarchar(25), @sqltext nvarchar(4000)
    set @ctnum=(select left(carriertrackingnumber, 4) from sales.SalesOrderDetail where SalesOrderDetailID=@i)

    set @sqltext='SELECT SalesOrderID, CarrierTrackingNumber
    FROM Sales.SalesOrderDetail
    GROUP BY SalesOrderID, CarrierTrackingNumber
    HAVING CarrierTrackingNumber LIKE ' + ''''+ @ctNum+  '%'+ ''''+'
    ORDER BY SalesOrderID ;'

    exec sp_executesql @sqltext
end
go
if exists(select name from sys.procedures where name='p_sel_product_by_price_and_quantity')
begin
    drop procedure p_sel_product_by_price_and_quantity
end
go
Create Procedure p_sel_product_by_price_and_quantity(@i int, @x int)
as
Begin


    SELECT ProductID
    FROM Sales.SalesOrderDetail
    WHERE UnitPrice < @i
    GROUP BY ProductID
    HAVING AVG(OrderQty) > @x
    ORDER BY ProductID;
end
```

```
go
if exists(select name from sys.procedures where name='p_sel_products_over_onemil_qlessthan3')
begin
    drop procedure p_sel_products_over_onemil_qlessthan3
end
go
Create Procedure p_sel_products_over_onemil_qlessthan3
as
Begin
    SELECT ProductID, AVG(OrderQty) AS AverageQuantity, SUM(LineTotal) AS Total
    FROM Sales.SalesOrderDetail
    GROUP BY ProductID
    HAVING SUM(LineTotal) > $1000000.00
    AND AVG(OrderQty) < 3;
end
go
if exists(select name from sys.procedures where name='p_sel_products_over_twomil')
begin
    drop procedure p_sel_products_over_twomil
end
go
Create Procedure p_sel_products_over_twomil
as
Begin
    SELECT ProductID, Total = SUM(LineTotal)
    FROM Sales.SalesOrderDetail
    GROUP BY ProductID
    HAVING SUM(LineTotal) > $2000000.00;
end
```

```
go
if exists(select name from sys.procedures where name='p_sel_sales_products_where_q_GT')
begin
    drop procedure p_sel_sales_products_where_q_GT
end
go
Create Procedure p_sel_sales_products_where_q_GT(@i int)
as
Begin
    SELECT ProductID, SUM(LineTotal) AS Total
    FROM Sales.SalesOrderDetail
    GROUP BY ProductID
    HAVING COUNT(*) > @i;
end
go
if exists(select name from sys.procedures where name='p_ins_temp_bicycles')
begin
    drop procedure p_ins_temp_bicycles
end
go
Create Procedure p_ins_temp_bicycles
as
Begin
if object_id('tempdb..#Bicycles') is not null
begin
    drop table #Bicycles
end

SELECT *
```

```
INTO #Bicycles
FROM Production.Product
WHERE ProductNumber LIKE 'BK%';

end
go
if exists(select name from sys.procedures where name='p_sel_get_sales_rollup_by_product_linetotal')
begin
    drop procedure p_sel_get_sales_rollup_by_product_linetotal
end
go
Create Procedure p_sel_get_sales_rollup_by_product_linetotal(@i int)
as
Begin
    SELECT ProductID, LineTotal, sum(linetotal), max(linetotal)
    FROM Sales.SalesOrderDetail
    WHERE UnitPrice < @i
    group by rollup(productid, linetotal)
     ORDER BY ProductID, LineTotal
end
go
if exists(select name from sys.procedures where name='p_sel_get_sales_cube_by_prod_ord_unit_line')
begin
    drop procedure p_sel_get_sales_cube_by_prod_ord_unit_line
end
go
Create Procedure p_sel_get_sales_cube_by_prod_ord_unit_line(@i int)
as
Begin
    SELECT ProductID, OrderQty, UnitPrice, LineTotal, sum(orderqty), sum(linetotal)
```

```
    FROM Sales.SalesOrderDetail
    WHERE UnitPrice < @i
    group by cube(ProductID, OrderQty, UnitPrice, LineTotal)
     ORDER BY ProductID, LineTotal
end
go
if exists(select name from sys.procedures where name='p_sel_prod_tble_discounts')
begin
    drop procedure p_sel_prod_tble_discounts
end
go
Create Procedure p_sel_prod_tble_discounts
as
Begin
    SELECT p.Name AS ProductName,
    NonDiscountSales = (OrderQty * UnitPrice),
    Discounts = ((OrderQty * UnitPrice) * UnitPriceDiscount)
    FROM Production.Product AS p
    INNER JOIN Sales.SalesOrderDetail AS sod
    ON p.ProductID = sod.ProductID
    ORDER BY ProductName DESC;
end
go

if exists(select name from sys.procedures where name='p_sel_select_into_union')
begin
    drop procedure p_sel_select_into_union
end
go
Create Procedure p_sel_select_into_union
as
```

```
Begin
IF OBJECT_ID ('dbo.ProductResults', 'U') IS NOT NULL
DROP TABLE dbo.ProductResults;

IF OBJECT_ID ('dbo.Gloves', 'U') IS NOT NULL
DROP TABLE dbo.Gloves;

-- Create Gloves table.
SELECT ProductModelID, Name
INTO dbo.Gloves
FROM Production.ProductModel
WHERE ProductModelID IN (3, 4);


SELECT ProductModelID, Name
INTO dbo.ProductResults
FROM Production.ProductModel
WHERE ProductModelID NOT IN (3, 4)
UNION
SELECT ProductModelID, Name
FROM dbo.Gloves;


SELECT ProductModelID, Name
FROM dbo.ProductResults;
end
go
if exists(select name from sys.procedures where name='p_sel_union_of_2_selects')
begin
    drop procedure p_sel_union_of_2_selects
```

```
end
go
Create Procedure p_sel_union_of_2_selects
as
Begin
IF OBJECT_ID ('dbo.Gloves2', 'U') IS NOT NULL
DROP TABLE dbo.Gloves2;


SELECT ProductModelID, Name
INTO dbo.Gloves2
FROM Production.ProductModel
WHERE ProductModelID IN (3, 4);


SELECT ProductModelID, Name
FROM Production.ProductModel
WHERE ProductModelID NOT IN (3, 4)
UNION
SELECT ProductModelID, Name
FROM dbo.Gloves2
ORDER BY Name;

end
go

---LEAVING OFF HERE!!!!---
```

4. Click on the file to load it into Management Studio and then click on **Execute** or press F5 to run the query.

```
/*
// Source via Bradley Ball :: braball@microsoft.com
// Credits - Jonathan Kehayias :: https://www.sqlskills.com/blogs/jonathan/the-adventureworks2008r2
// MIT License
// Permission is hereby granted, free of charge, to any person obtaining a copy of this software an
// The above copyright notice and this permission notice shall be included in all copies or substan
// THE SOFTWARE IS PROVIDED "AS IS", WITHOUT WARRANTY OF ANY KIND, EXPRESS OR IMPLIED, INCLUDING BU
*/

Use AdventureWorks2017
go
if exists(select name from sys.procedures where name='p_sel_SalesQuota')
begin
    drop procedure p_sel_SalesQuota
end
go
create procedure p_sel_SalesQuota
as
begin
    SELECT SalesQuota, SUM(SalesYTD) 'TotalSalesYTD', GROUPING(SalesQuota) AS 'Grouping'
    FROM Sales.SalesPerson
    GROUP BY SalesQuota WITH ROLLUP;
end
```

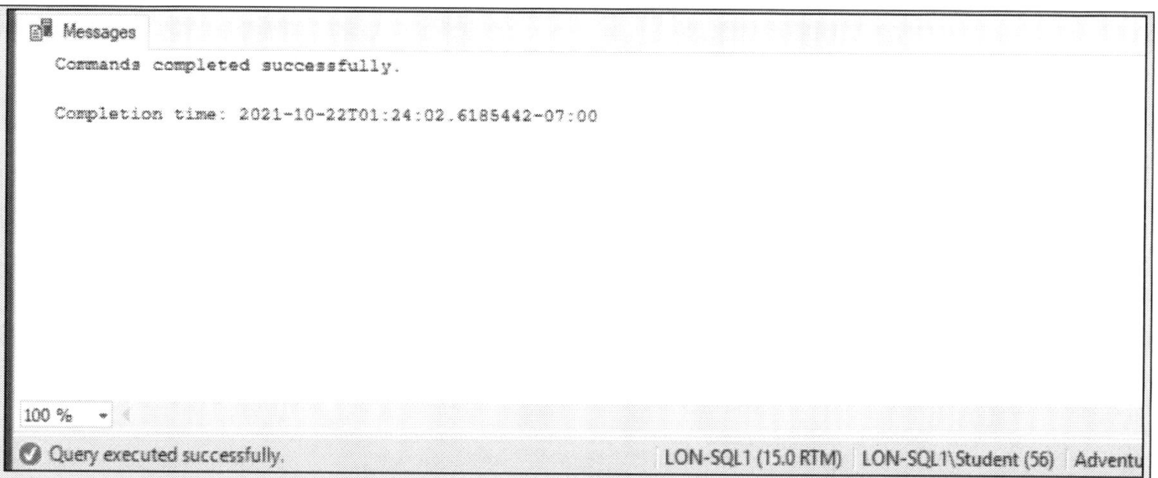

Messages

Commands completed successfully.

Completion time: 2021-10-22T01:24:02.6185442-07:00

100 %

Query executed successfully. LON-SQL1 (15.0 RTM) LON-SQL1\Student (56) Adventu

5. Click the **file** > **Open** > **File** menu in SQL Server Management Studio.

Microsoft SQL Server Management Studio Quick Launch (Ctrl+

File Project Tools Window Help

Connect Object Explorer...
Disconnect Object Explorer
New
Open
Close
Close Solution
Save Selected Items Ctrl+S
Save Selected Items As...
Save All Ctrl+Shift+S
Page Setup...
Print... Ctrl+P
Recent Projects and Solutions
Exit Alt+F4

Project/Solution... Ctrl+Shift+O
Folder... Ctrl+Shift+Alt+O
Merge Extended Event Files...
Merge Audit Files...
Vulnerability Assessment...
File... Ctrl+O
Analysis Services Database...
File with New Connection...
File Disconnected...
Policy

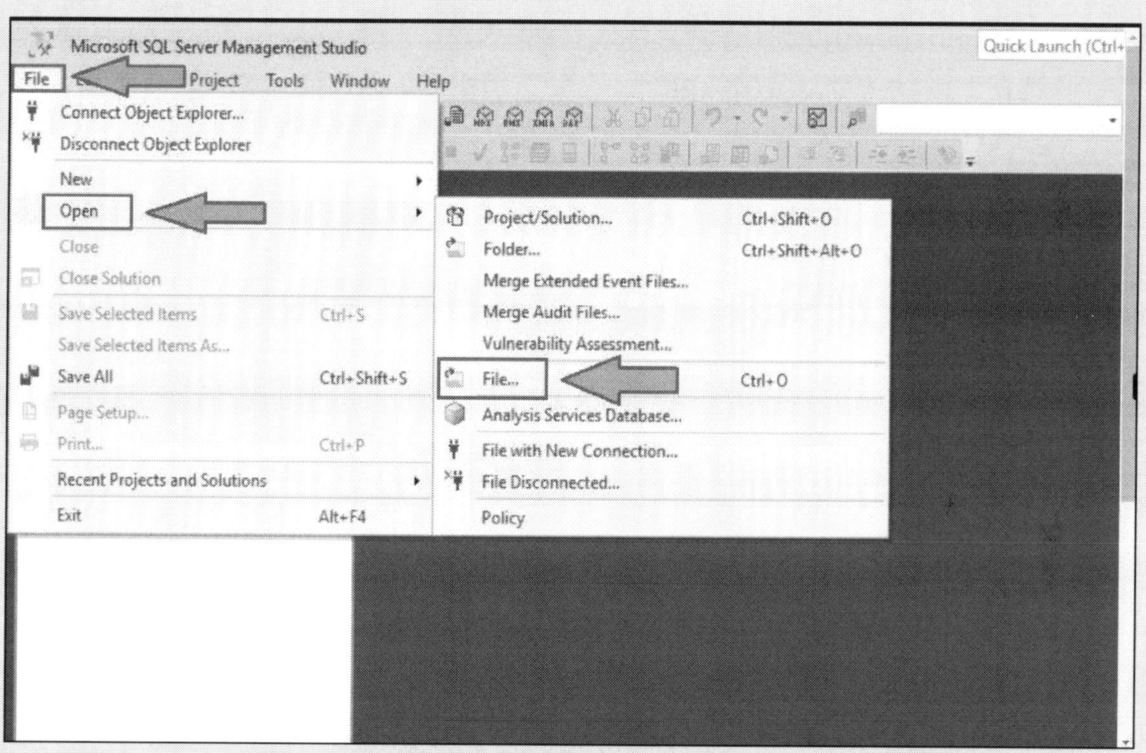

6. Go to the **D:\Labfiles\Query Performance\ExecuteRandomWorkload.SQL** script and open it.

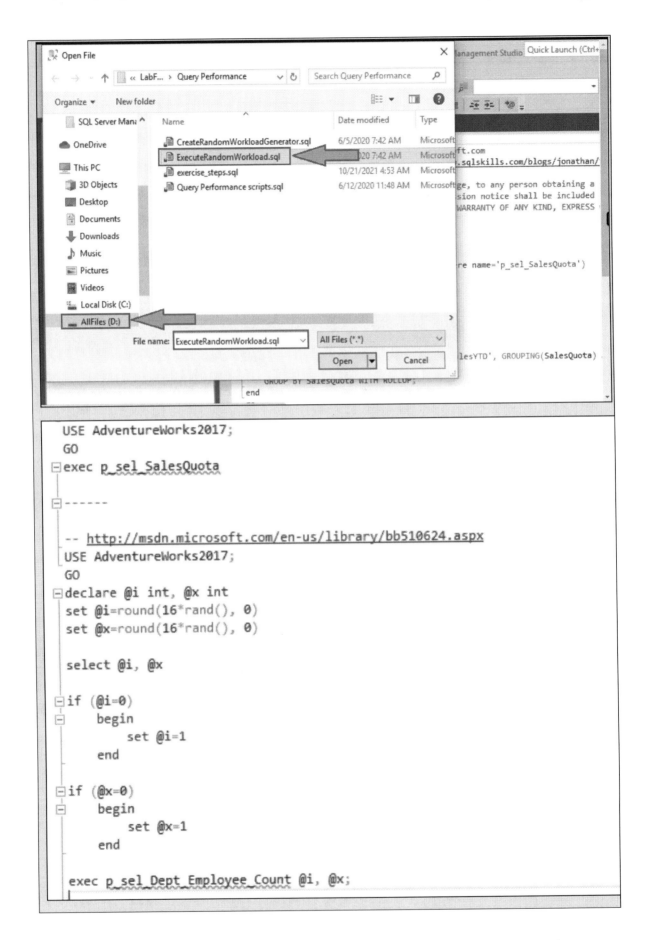


```
USE AdventureWorks2017;
GO
exec p_sel_SalesQuota

------

-- http://msdn.microsoft.com/en-us/library/bb510624.aspx
USE AdventureWorks2017;
GO
declare @i int, @x int
set @i=round(16*rand(), 0)
set @x=round(16*rand(), 0)

select @i, @x

if (@i=0)
    begin
        set @i=1
    end

if (@x=0)
    begin
        set @x=1
    end

exec p_sel_Dept_Employee_Count @i, @x;
```

```
-- http://msdn.microsoft.com/en-us/library/bb510624.aspx
USE AdventureWorks2017;
GO
declare @i int, @x int
set @i=round(16*rand(), 0)
set @x=round(16*rand(), 0)

if (@i=0)
    begin
        set @i=1
    end

if (@x=0)
    begin
        set @x=1
    end

exec p_sel_Dept_Employees_by_Job_Titles @i, @x;

------

-- http://msdn.microsoft.com/en-us/library/bb510624.aspx
USE AdventureWorks2017;
GO
declare @i int, @x int
set @i=round(16*rand(), 0)
set @x=round(16*rand(), 0)
```

```
if (@i=0)
    begin
        set @i=1
    end

if (@x=0)
    begin
        set @x=1
    end

exec p_sel_Dept_Employees_Count_By_Title @i, @x;

------

--http://msdn.microsoft.com/en-us/library/bb677202.aspx

USE AdventureWorks2017;
GO
declare @i int, @x int
set @i=round(290*rand(), 0)

if (@i=0)
    begin
        set @i=1
    end
```

```
exec p_sel_get_originization_by_employee @i;



------

-- http://msdn.microsoft.com/en-us/library/ms181708.aspx
USE AdventureWorks2017;
GO
GO
declare @i int, @x int
set @i=round(292*rand(), 0)

if (@i<274)
    begin
        set @i=274
    end
exec p_sel_get_sales_per_sales_person @i;
exec p_sel_get_sales_per_by_sales_person;
GO

------

-- http://msdn.microsoft.com/en-us/library/ms187731.aspx

/* http://msdn.microsoft.com/en-us/library/ms187731.aspx
A. Using SELECT to retrieve rows and columns
```

```
The following example shows three code examples. This first code
example returns all rows (no WHERE clause is specified) and all
columns (using the *) from the Product table in the
AdventureWorks2017 database.
*/

USE AdventureWorks2017;
GO
exec p_sel_aliased_select;
GO

/*
This example returns all rows (no WHERE clause is specified), and
only a subset of the columns (Name, ProductNumber, ListPrice) from
the Product table in the AdventureWorks2017 database. Additionally,
a column heading is added.
*/

USE AdventureWorks2017;
GO
exec p_sel_product_info;
GO

------

-- http://msdn.microsoft.com/en-us/library/ms187731.aspx
/*
```

```
This example returns only the rows for Product that have a product
line of Null and that have days to manufacture that is less than 4.
*/

USE AdventureWorks2017;
GO
declare @i int
set @i=round(4*rand(), 0)

if (@i>5)
    begin
        set @i=4
    end


exec p_sel_products_withDTM_Null @i
------

-- http://msdn.microsoft.com/en-us/library/ms187731.aspx
/*
This example returns only the rows for Product that have a product
line of R and that have days to manufacture that is less than 4.
*/

USE AdventureWorks2017;
GO
declare @i int
```

```
set @i=round(4*rand(), 0)

if (@i>5)
    begin
        set @i=4
    end

exec p_sel_products_withDTM_R @i

------

-- http://msdn.microsoft.com/en-us/library/ms187731.aspx
/*
This example returns only the rows for Product that have a product
line of M and that have days to manufacture that is less than 4.
*/

USE AdventureWorks2017;
GO
declare @i int
set @i=round(4*rand(), 0)

if (@i>5)
    begin
        set @i=4
    end
exec p_sel_products_withDTM_M @i
```

```
-- http://msdn.microsoft.com/en-us/library/ms187731.aspx
/*
This example returns only the rows for Product that have a product
line of S and that have days to manufacture that is less than 4.
*/

USE AdventureWorks2017;
GO
declare @i int
set @i=round(4*rand(), 0)

if (@i>5)
    begin
        set @i=4
    end
exec p_sel_products_withDTM_S @i
------

-- http://msdn.microsoft.com/en-us/library/ms187731.aspx
/*
This example returns only the rows for Product that have a product
line of T and that have days to manufacture that is less than 4.
*/

USE AdventureWorks2017;
GO
declare @i int
```

```
set @i=round(4*rand(), 0)

if (@i>5)
    begin
        set @i=4
    end
exec p_sel_products_withDTM_T @i

------

/* http://msdn.microsoft.com/en-us/library/ms187731.aspx
B. Using SELECT with column headings and calculations
The following examples return all rows from the Product table. The
first example returns total sales and the discounts for each product.
In the second example, the total revenue is calculated for each
product.
*/

USE AdventureWorks2017;
GO
exec p_sel_discount_sales;
GO


/*
This is the query that calculates the revenue for each product in
each sales order.
```

```
*/

USE AdventureWorks2017;
GO
exec p_calc_revenue_for_each_product;
GO
----LEAVING OFF HERE---
------

/* http://msdn.microsoft.com/en-us/library/ms187731.aspx
C. Using DISTINCT with SELECT
The following example uses DISTINCT to prevent the retrieval
of duplicate titles.
*/

USE AdventureWorks2017;
GO
p_sel_Employee_Jobtitles;
GO

------

/* http://msdn.microsoft.com/en-us/library/ms187731.aspx
D. Creating tables with SELECT INTO
The following first example creates a temporary table named
#Bicycles in tempdb.
*/
```

```
USE AdventureWorks2017;
GO
p_ins_temp_bicycles;
GO

/*
This second example creates the permanent table NewProducts.
*/

USE AdventureWorks2017;
GO
p_ins_NewProducts;
GO

------

/* http://msdn.microsoft.com/en-us/library/ms187731.aspx
  E. Using correlated subqueries
The following example shows queries that are semantically
equivalent and illustrates the difference between using the
EXISTS keyword and the IN keyword. Both are examples of a
valid subquery that retrieves one instance of each product
name for which the product model is a long sleeve logo jersey,
and the ProductModelID numbers match between the Product and
ProductModel tables.
*/
```

```
USE AdventureWorks2017;
GO
declare @i int
set @i=round(128*rand(), 0)

if (@i=0)
    begin
        set @i=1
    end

exec p_sel_all_products_like @i;

GO
------
/*
The following example uses IN in a correlated, or repeating,
subquery. This is a query that depends on the outer query for
its values. The query is executed repeatedly, one time for each
row that may be selected by the outer query. This query
retrieves one instance of the first and last name of each
employee for which the bonus in the SalesPerson table is 5000.00
and for which the employee identification numbers match in the
Employee and SalesPerson tables.
```

```
*/

USE AdventureWorks2017;
GO
declare @i int
set @i=round(290*rand(), 0)

if (@i<274)
    begin
        set @i=277
    end
exec p_sel_salesperson_by_bonus @i;
GO
------
/*
The previous subquery in this statement cannot be evaluated
independently of the outer query. It requires a value for
Employee.BusinessEntityID, but this value changes as the SQL
Server Database Engine examines different rows in Employee.

A correlated subquery can also be used in the HAVING clause of
an outer query. This example finds the product models for which
the maximum list price is more than twice the average for the
model.
```

```
USE AdventureWorks2017;
GO
exec p_sel_max_price_double_average_model;
GO

/*
This example uses two correlated subqueries to find the names
of employees who have sold a particular product.
*/
------
USE AdventureWorks2017;
GO
declare @i int
set @i=round(999*rand(), 0)

if (@i=0)
    begin
        set @i=777
    end
if (@i>5 and @i<316)
    begin
        set @i=4
    end
select @i
exec p_sel_employee_name_by_product_sales @i;
GO
```

```
------

/* http://msdn.microsoft.com/en-us/library/ms187731.aspx
F. Using GROUP BY
The following example finds the total of each sales order in
the database.
*/

USE AdventureWorks2017;
GO
exec p_sel_total_by_sales_order;
GO

------

/* http://msdn.microsoft.com/en-us/library/ms187731.aspx
Because of the GROUP BY clause, only one row containing the sum of all
sales is returned for each sales order.

G. Using GROUP BY with multiple groups
The following example finds the average price and the sum of
year-to-date sales, grouped by product ID and special offer ID.
*/

USE AdventureWorks2017;
GO
```

```
exec p_sel_group_by_clause;
GO

------

/* http://msdn.microsoft.com/en-us/library/ms187731.aspx
  H. Using GROUP BY and WHERE
The following example puts the results into groups after retrieving
only the rows with list prices greater than $1000.
*/

USE AdventureWorks2017;
GO
declare @i int
set @i=round(999*rand(), 0)

if (@i<513)
    begin
        set @i=716
    end
exec p_sel_results_by_price @i;
GO

------

/* http://msdn.microsoft.com/en-us/library/ms187731.aspx
I. Using GROUP BY with an expression
```

```
The following example groups by an expression. You can group
by an expression if the expression does not include aggregate
functions.
*/

USE AdventureWorks2017;
GO
exec p_sel_group_by_w_expression;
GO

------

/* http://msdn.microsoft.com/en-us/library/ms187731.aspx
J. Using GROUP BY with ORDER BY
The following example finds the average price of each type of
product and orders the results by average price.
*/

USE AdventureWorks2017;
GO
declare @i int
set @i=round(44*rand(), 0)

if (@i=0)
    begin
        set @i=41
    end
exec p_sel_get_avg_price_by_product @i;
```

```
GO


------

/* http://msdn.microsoft.com/en-us/library/ms187731.aspx
K. Using the HAVING clause
The first example that follows shows a HAVING clause with an
aggregate function. It groups the rows in the SalesOrderDetail
table by product ID and eliminates products whose average order
quantities are five or less. The second example shows a HAVING
clause without aggregate functions.
*/

USE AdventureWorks2017;
GO
declare @i int
set @i=round(44*rand(), 0)

if (@i=0)
    begin
        set @i=1
    end
exec p_sel_product_by_quantity @i;
GO
------
/*
```

```
USE AdventureWorks2017 ;
GO
declare @i int
set @i=round(121317*rand(), 0)

if (@i=0)
    begin
        set @i=1
    end
exec p_sel_order_by_tracking_partial @i;
GO

------

/* http://msdn.microsoft.com/en-us/library/ms187731.aspx
L. Using HAVING and GROUP BY
The following example shows using GROUP BY, HAVING, WHERE, and
ORDER BY clauses in one SELECT statement. It produces groups and
summary values but does so after eliminating the products with
prices over $25 and average order quantities under 5. It also
organizes the results by ProductID.
*/

USE AdventureWorks2017;
GO
declare @i int, @x int
set @i=round(3578*rand(), 0)
```

```
if (@i=0)
    begin
        set @i=1
    end
set @x=round(44*rand(), 0)

if (@x=0)
    begin
        set @x=1
    end
exec p_sel_product_by_price_and_quantity @i, @x;
GO

------

/* http://msdn.microsoft.com/en-us/library/ms187731.aspx
M. Using HAVING with SUM and AVG
The following example groups the SalesOrderDetail table by product
ID and includes only those groups of products that have orders
totaling more than $1000000.00 and whose average order quantities
are less than 3.
*/

USE AdventureWorks2017;
GO
exec p_sel_products_over_onemil_qlessthan3;
GO
```

```
/*
To see the products that have had total sales greater than
$2000000.00, use this query:
*/

USE AdventureWorks2017;
GO
exec p_sel_products_over_twomil;
GO

------
/*
create some temp tables and latch contention
*/

USE AdventureWorks2017;
GO
exec p_ins_temp_bicycles;
GO

/*
If you want to make sure there are at least one thousand five
hundred items involved in the calculations for each product, use
HAVING COUNT(*) > 1500 to eliminate the products that return totals
for fewer than 1500 items sold. The query looks like this:
*/
```

```
USE AdventureWorks2017;
GO
declare @i int
set @i=round(1500*rand(), 0)

if (@i=0)
    begin
        set @i=100
    end
exec p_sel_sales_products_where_q_GT @i;
GO

------

/* http://msdn.microsoft.com/en-us/library/ms187731.aspx
N. Calculating group totals by using COMPUTE BY
The following example uses two code examples to show the use
of COMPUTE BY. The first code example uses one COMPUTE BY with
one aggregate function, and the second code example uses one
COMPUTE BY item and two aggregate functions.

This query calculates the sum of the orders, for products with
prices less than $5.00, for each type of product.
*/
USE AdventureWorks2017;
GO
declare @i int
set @i=round(3579*rand(), 0)
```

```
if (@i=0)
    begin
        set @i=1000
    end
exec p_sel_get_sales_rollup_by_product_linetotal @i;
GO

------

/*  http://msdn.microsoft.com/en-us/library/ms187731.aspx
O. Calculating grand values by using COMPUTE without BY
The COMPUTE keyword can be used without BY to generate grand
totals, grand counts, and so on.

The following example finds the grand total of the prices and
advances for all types of products les than $2.00.
*/
USE AdventureWorks2017;
GO
declare @i int
set @i=round(3579*rand(), 0)

if (@i=0)
    begin
        set @i=1000
    end
exec p_sel_get_sales_cube_by_prod_ord_unit_line @i;
GO
```

```
------

/* http://msdn.microsoft.com/en-us/library/ms187731.aspx
The following examples return all rows from the Product table. The first example returns total sales and th
*/

USE AdventureWorks2017;
GO
exec p_sel_prod_tble_discounts
GO

------

/* http://msdn.microsoft.com/en-us/library/ms187731.aspx
Q. Using SELECT INTO with UNION
In the following example, the INTO clause in the second SELECT statement specifies that the table named Pro
*/

USE AdventureWorks2017;
GO

exec p_sel_select_into_union

------

/* http://msdn.microsoft.com/en-us/library/ms187731.aspx
```

```
------

/* http://msdn.microsoft.com/en-us/library/ms187731.aspx
The following examples return all rows from the Product table.
The first example returns total sales and the discounts for each product.
In the second example, the total revenue is calculated for each product.
*/

USE AdventureWorks2017;
GO
exec p_sel_prod_tble_discounts
GO

------

/* http://msdn.microsoft.com/en-us/library/ms187731.aspx
Q. Using SELECT INTO with UNION
In the following example, the INTO clause in the second SELECT statement specifies that the table
named ProductResults holds the final result set of the union of the designated columns of the
ProductModel and Gloves tables. Note that the Gloves table is created in the first SELECT statement.
*/

USE AdventureWorks2017;
GO
```

```
exec p_sel_select_into_union

------

/* http://msdn.microsoft.com/en-us/library/ms187731.aspx

R. Using UNION of two SELECT statements with ORDER BY
The order of certain parameters used with the UNION clause is important.
The following example shows the incorrect and correct use of UNION in two SELECT statements
in which a column is to be renamed in the output.
*/

USE AdventureWorks2017;
GO
exec p_sel_union_of_2_selects
```

7. Click on **Execute** or press F5 to execute the script.

```
/*
// Source via Bradley Ball :: braball@microsoft.com
// Credits - Jonathan Kehayias :: https://www.sqlskills.com/blogs/jonathan/the-adventureworks2008r2
// MIT License
// Permission is hereby granted, free of charge, to any person obtaining a copy of this software an
// The above copyright notice and this permission notice shall be included in all copies or substan
// THE SOFTWARE IS PROVIDED "AS IS", WITHOUT WARRANTY OF ANY KIND, EXPRESS OR IMPLIED, INCLUDING BU
*/
-- http://msdn.microsoft.com/en-us/library/ms178544.aspx
USE AdventureWorks2017;
GO
exec p_sel_SalesQuota

------

-- http://msdn.microsoft.com/en-us/library/bb510624.aspx
USE AdventureWorks2017;
GO
declare @i int, @x int
set @i=round(16*rand(), 0)
set @x=round(16*rand(), 0)

select @i, @x
```

	SalesQuota	TotalSalesYTD	Grouping
1	NULL	1252127.9471	0
2	250000.00	27370537.97	0
3	300000.00	7654925.9863	0
4	NULL	36277591.9034	1

	(No column name)	(No column name)
1	9	10

	Name	Job Title	Employee Count
1	Finance	Accountant	2
2	Finance	Accounts Manager	1
3	Finance	Accounts Payabl...	2

Query executed successfully. LON-SQL1 (15.0 RTM) LON-SQL1\Student (69) AdventureWor

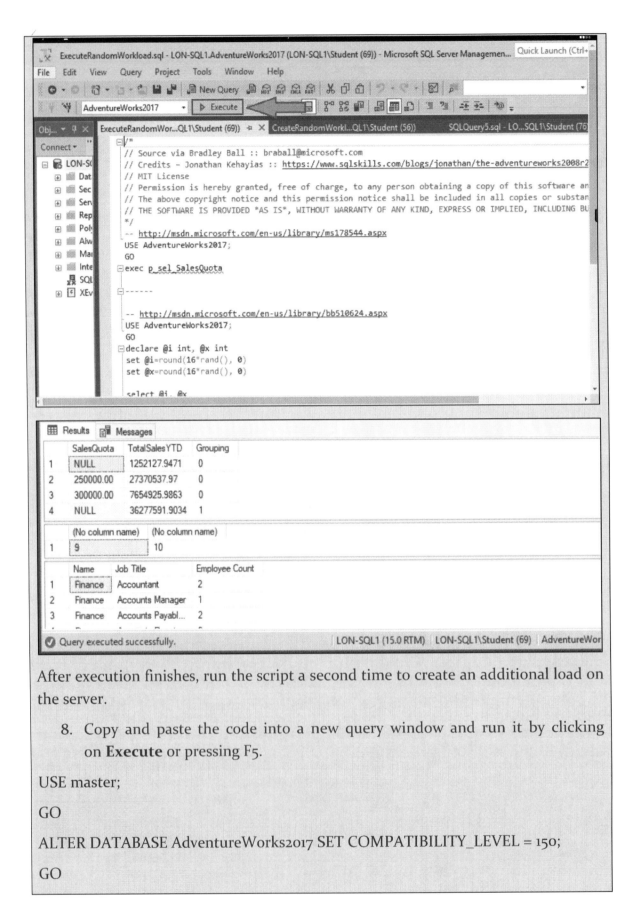

After execution finishes, run the script a second time to create an additional load on the server.

8. Copy and paste the code into a new query window and run it by clicking on **Execute** or pressing F5.

USE master;

GO

ALTER DATABASE AdventureWorks2017 SET COMPATIBILITY_LEVEL = 150;

GO

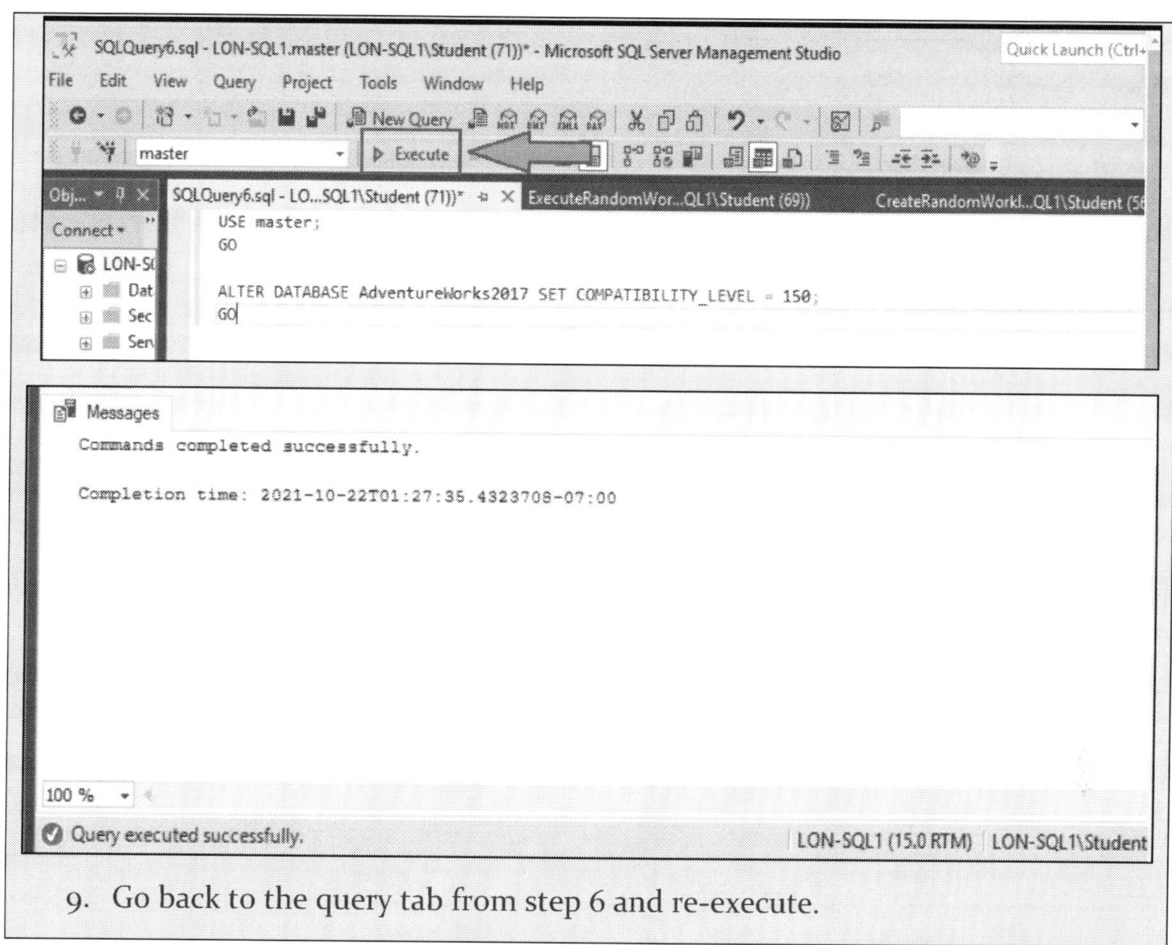

9. Go back to the query tab from step 6 and re-execute.

Examine Top Resource Consuming Queries to Identify Poor Performance

1. To view the Query Store node, you will have to refresh the database in Management Studio.

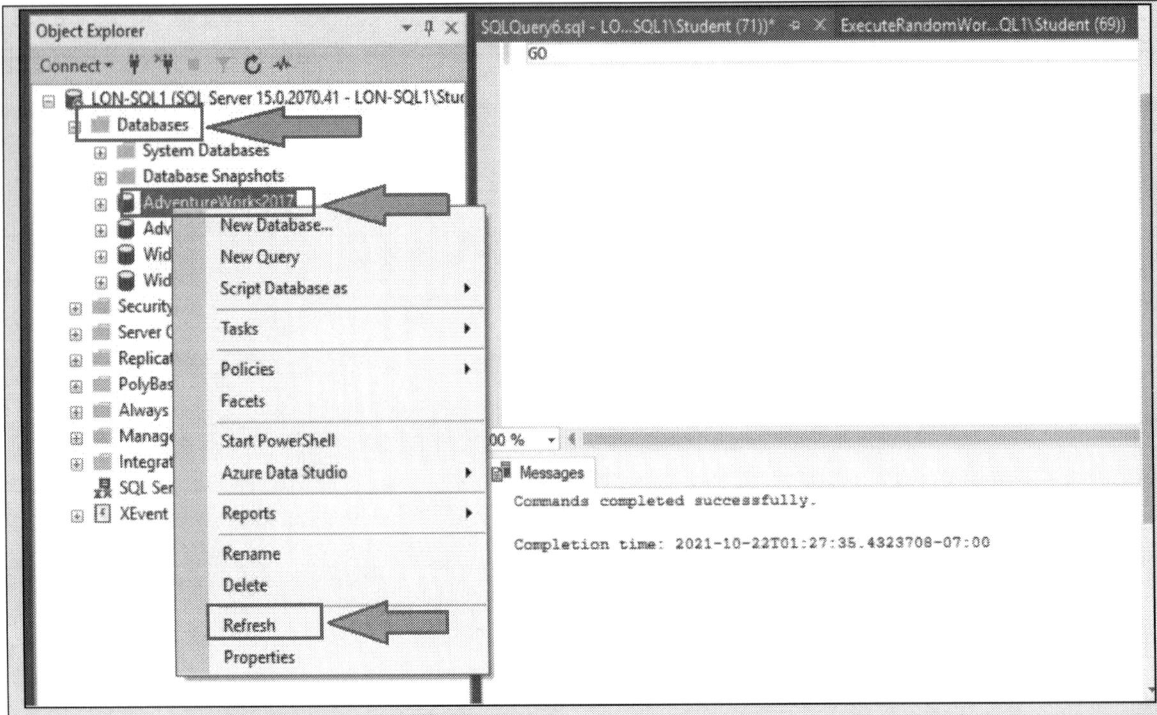

2. Expand the **Query Store** node to view all the available reports.

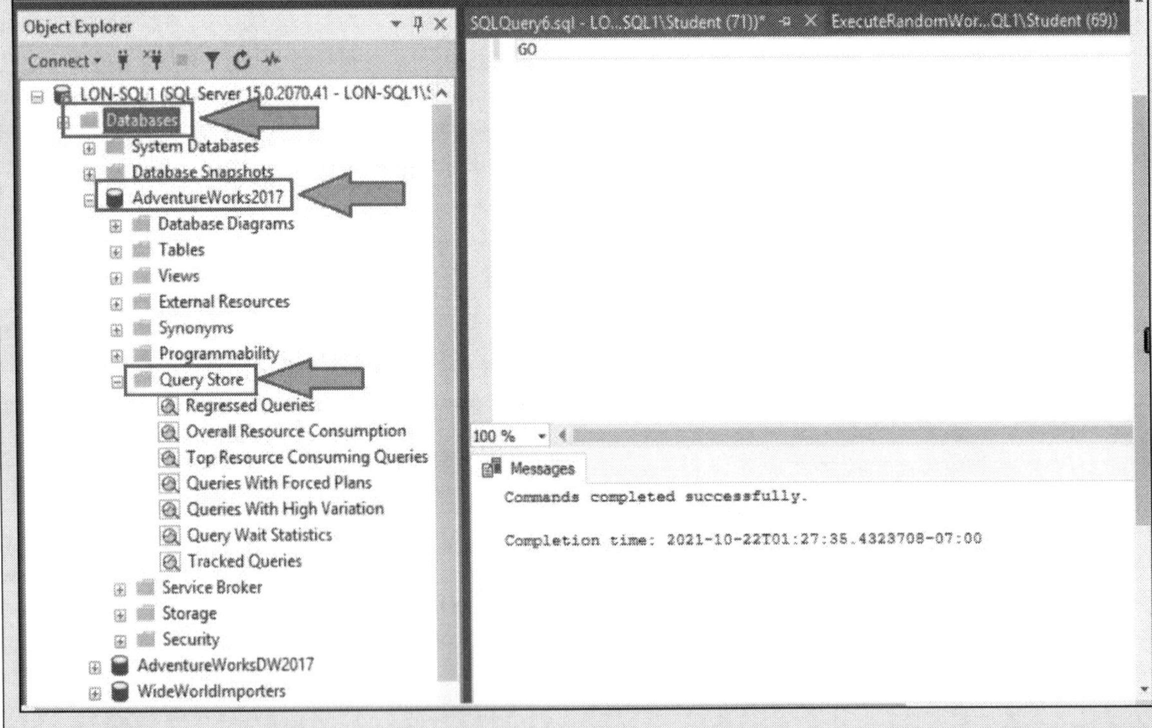

3. Click on **Top Resource Consuming Queries Report**.

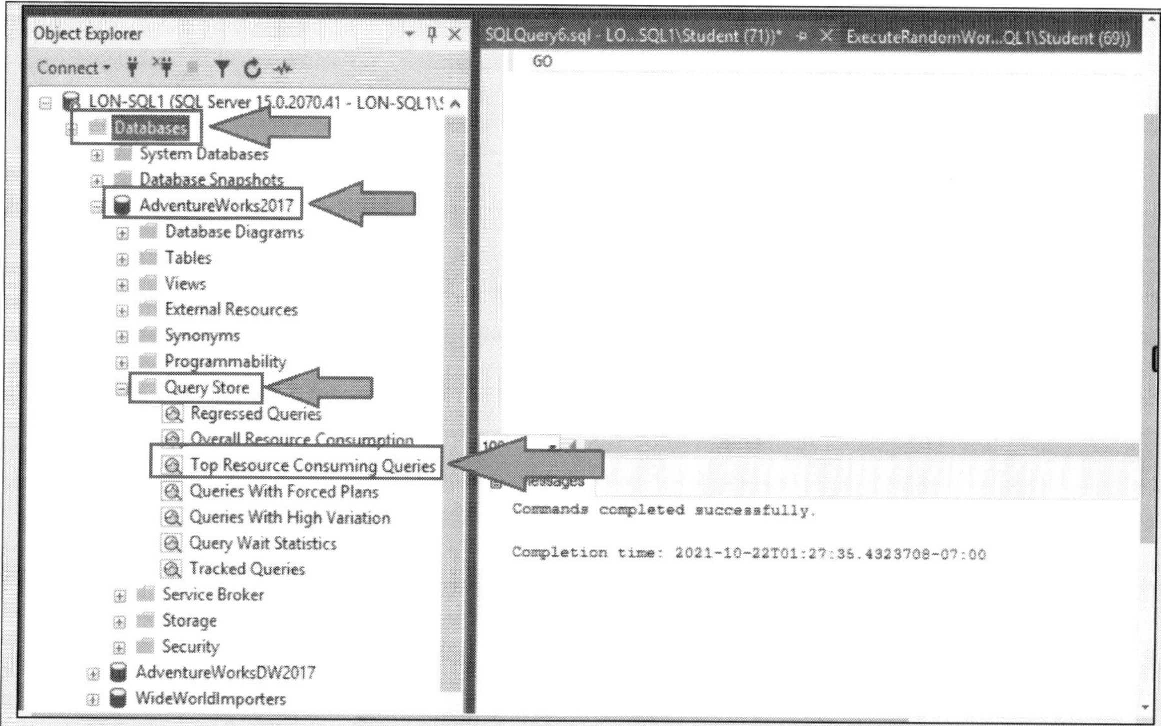

4. The report will open as shown below. On the right, select the menu dropdown, then click on **Configure**.

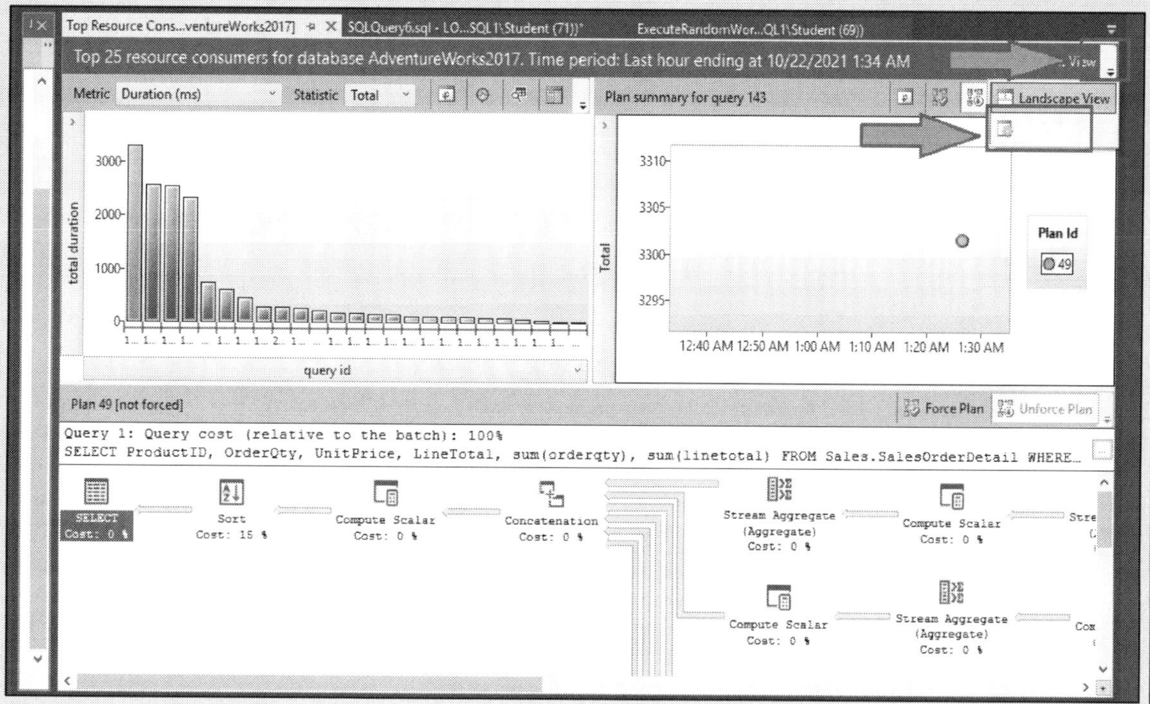

5. Change the filter for the minimum number of query plans to two in the configuration screen. Then click on **OK**.

Configure Top Resource Consu...

Resource Consumption Criteria

Check for top consumers of:

- Execution Count
- Duration (ms)
- CPU Time (ms)
- Logical Reads (KB)
- Logical Writes (KB)
- Physical Reads (KB)
- CLR Time (ms)
- DOP
- Memory Consumption (KB)
- Row Count
- Log Memory Used (KB)
- Temp DB Memory Used (KB)
- Wait Time (ms)

Based on:

- Avg
- Max
- Min
- Std Dev
- Total

Time Interval

Last hour From To

Time Format: Local UTC

Return

- All
- Top 25

Filters

Minimum number of query plans: 2

Ok Cancel Apply

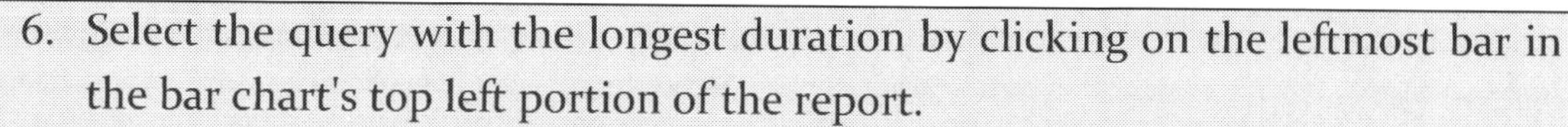

6. Select the query with the longest duration by clicking on the leftmost bar in the bar chart's top left portion of the report.

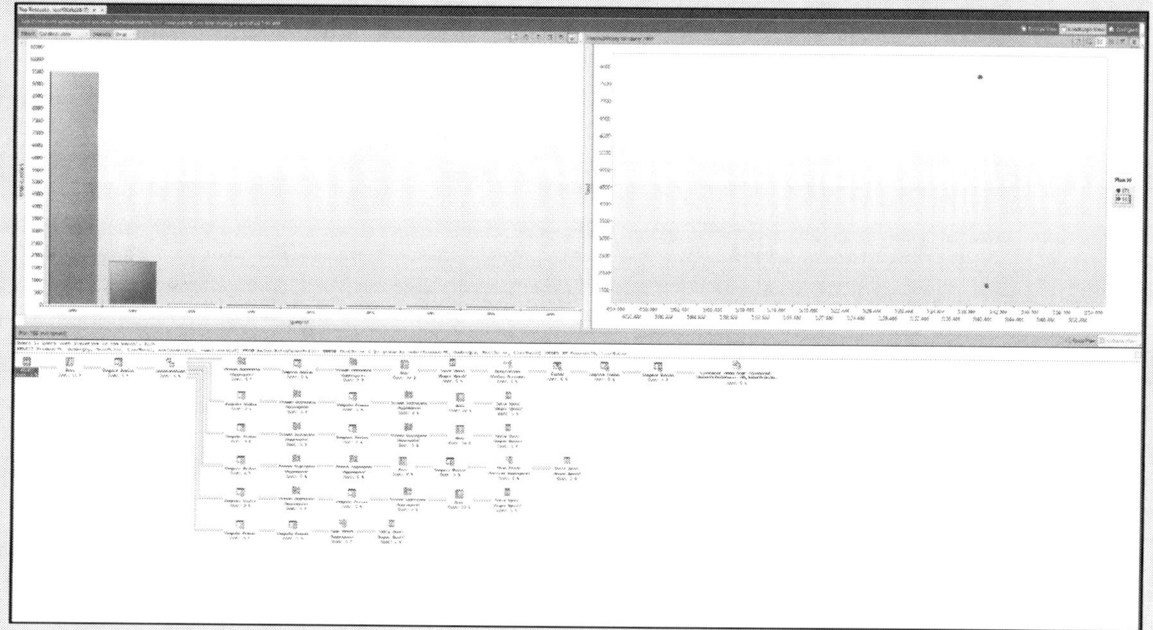

It will display the query and plan summary for the longest duration query in your query store.

Force a Better Execution Plan

1. Go to the plan summary portion of the report as displayed below.

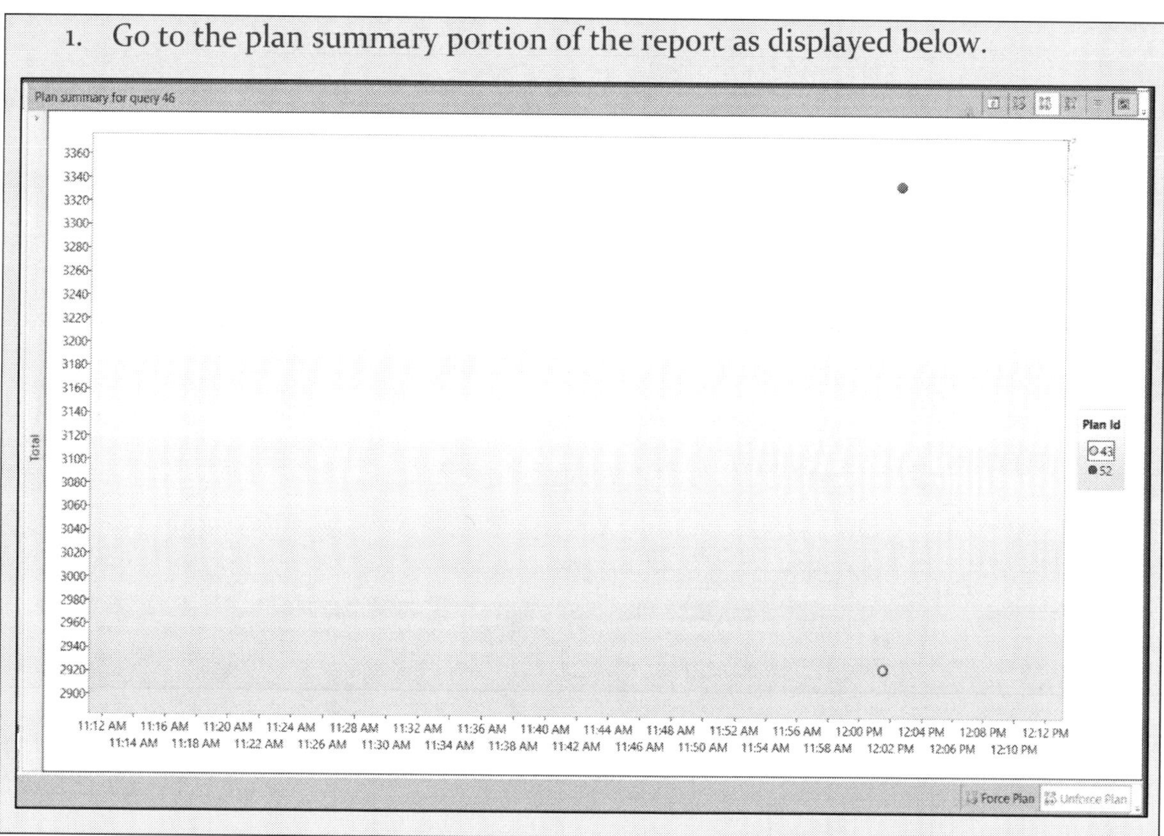

2. Select the Plan ID with the lowest duration in the top right window of the report.
3. Select **Force Plan** under the summary chart. A confirmation window will pop up; click on Yes to force the plan.

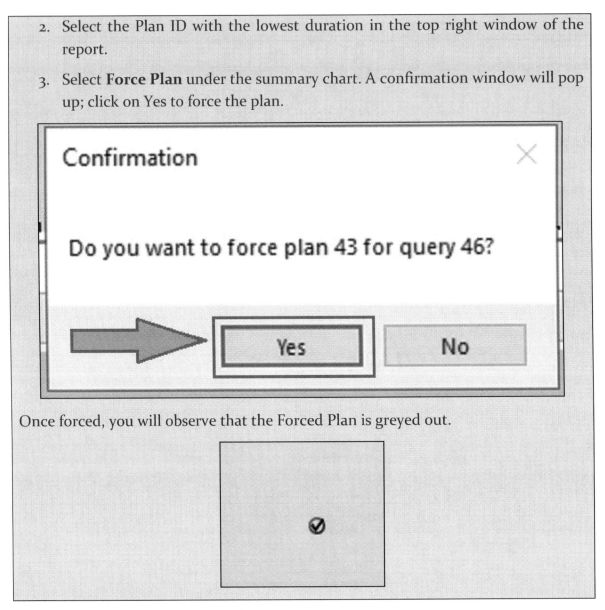

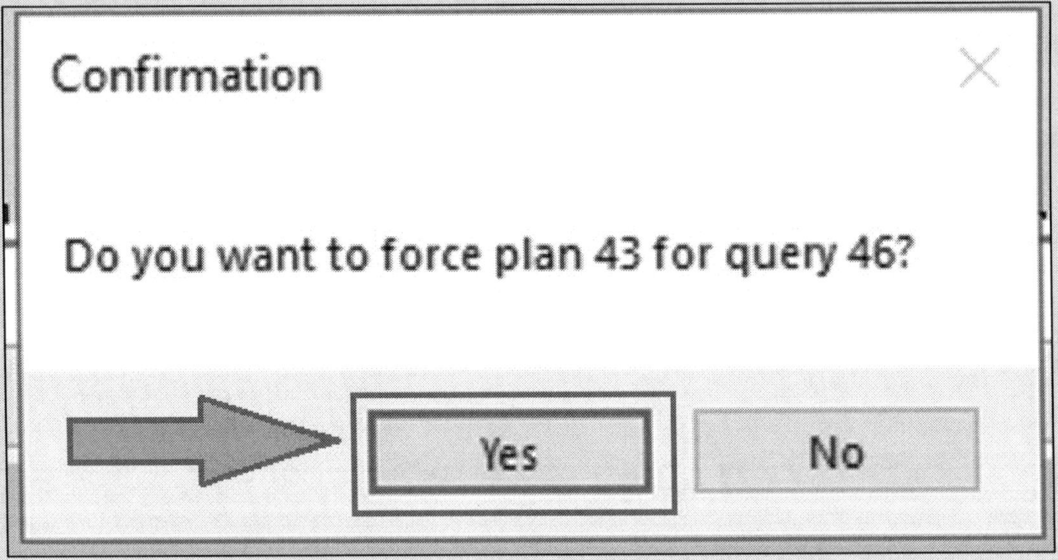

Once forced, you will observe that the Forced Plan is greyed out.

Use Query Hints to Impact Performance

Next, you will run a workload.

Run a Workload

Run the queries below, observe the Actual Execution Plan.

1. Select New Query and choose the **Include Actual Execution Plan** icon before executing the query or use CTRL+M.

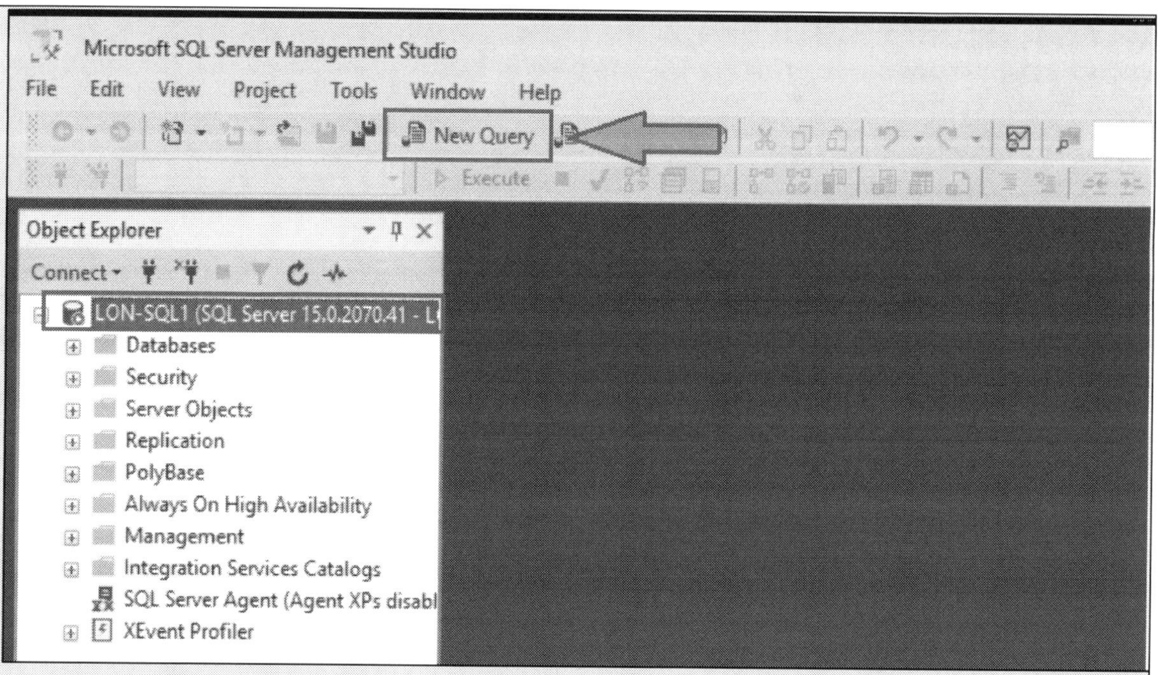

```
USE AdventureWorks2017;
GO
SELECT SalesOrderId, OrderDate
FROM Sales.SalesOrderHeader
WHERE SalesPersonID=288;
```

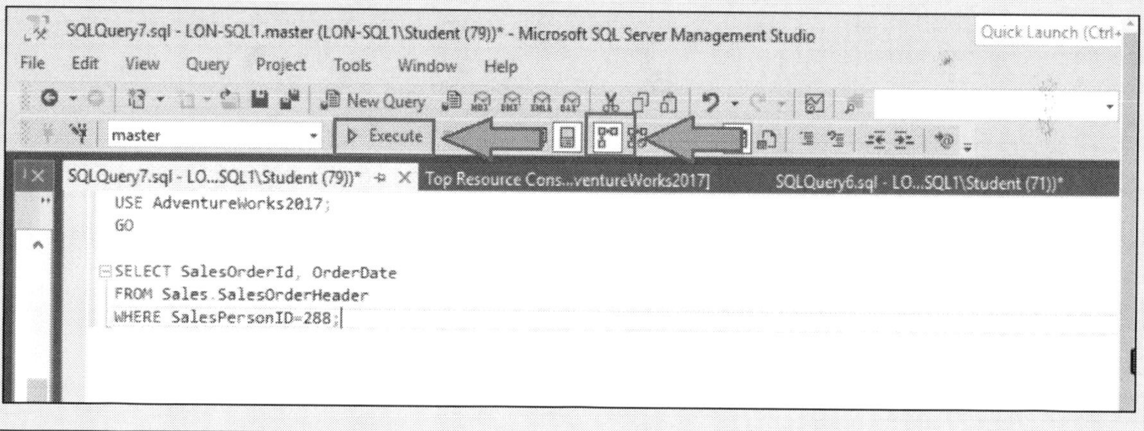

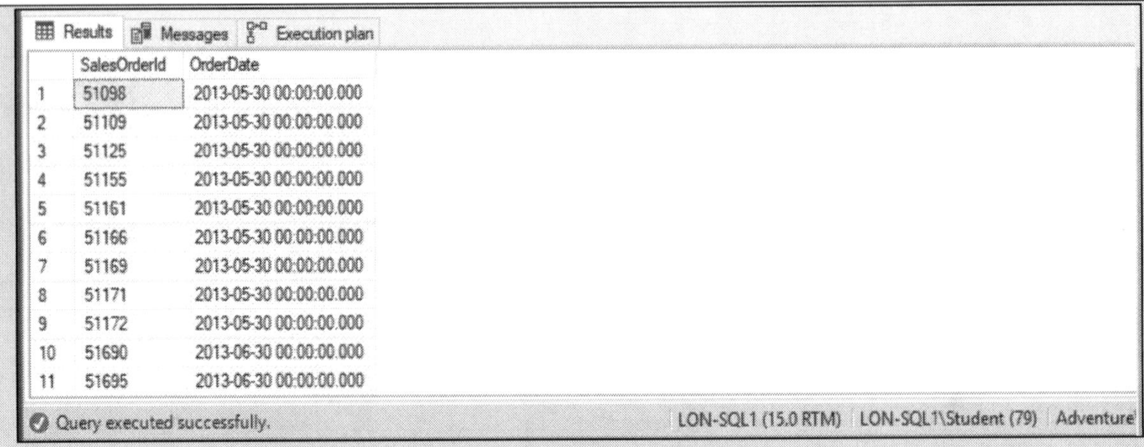

Results | Messages | Execution plan

	SalesOrderId	OrderDate
1	51098	2013-05-30 00:00:00.000
2	51109	2013-05-30 00:00:00.000
3	51125	2013-05-30 00:00:00.000
4	51155	2013-05-30 00:00:00.000
5	51161	2013-05-30 00:00:00.000
6	51166	2013-05-30 00:00:00.000
7	51169	2013-05-30 00:00:00.000
8	51171	2013-05-30 00:00:00.000
9	51172	2013-05-30 00:00:00.000
10	51690	2013-06-30 00:00:00.000
11	51695	2013-06-30 00:00:00.000

Query executed successfully. LON-SQL1 (15.0 RTM) LON-SQL1\Student (79) Adventure

2. Run the query. Note that the execution plan displays an index seek operator.

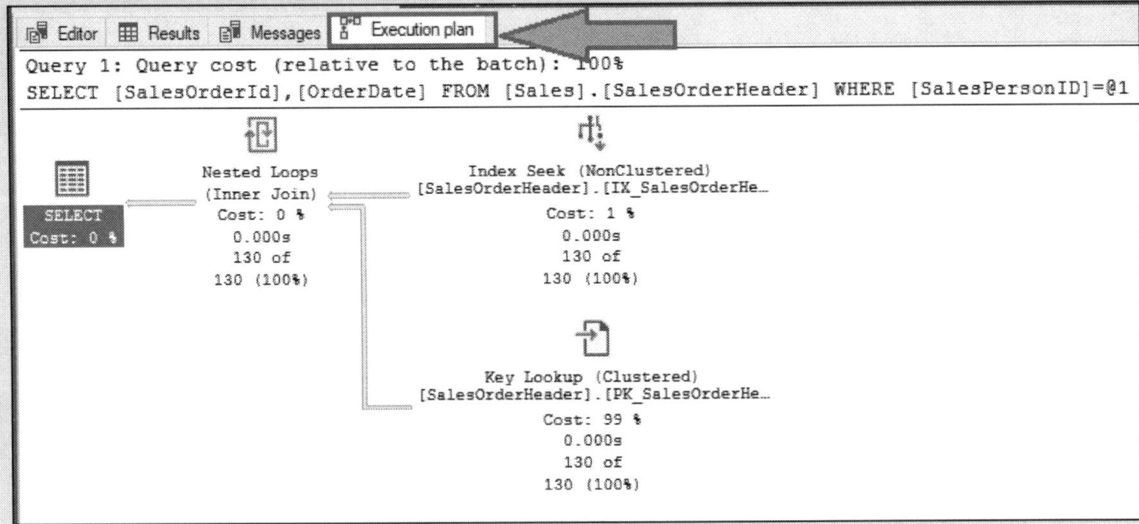

3. Now execute the next query.

```
USE AdventureWorks2017;
GO
SELECT SalesOrderId, OrderDate
FROM Sales.SalesOrderHeader
WHERE SalesPersonID=277;
```

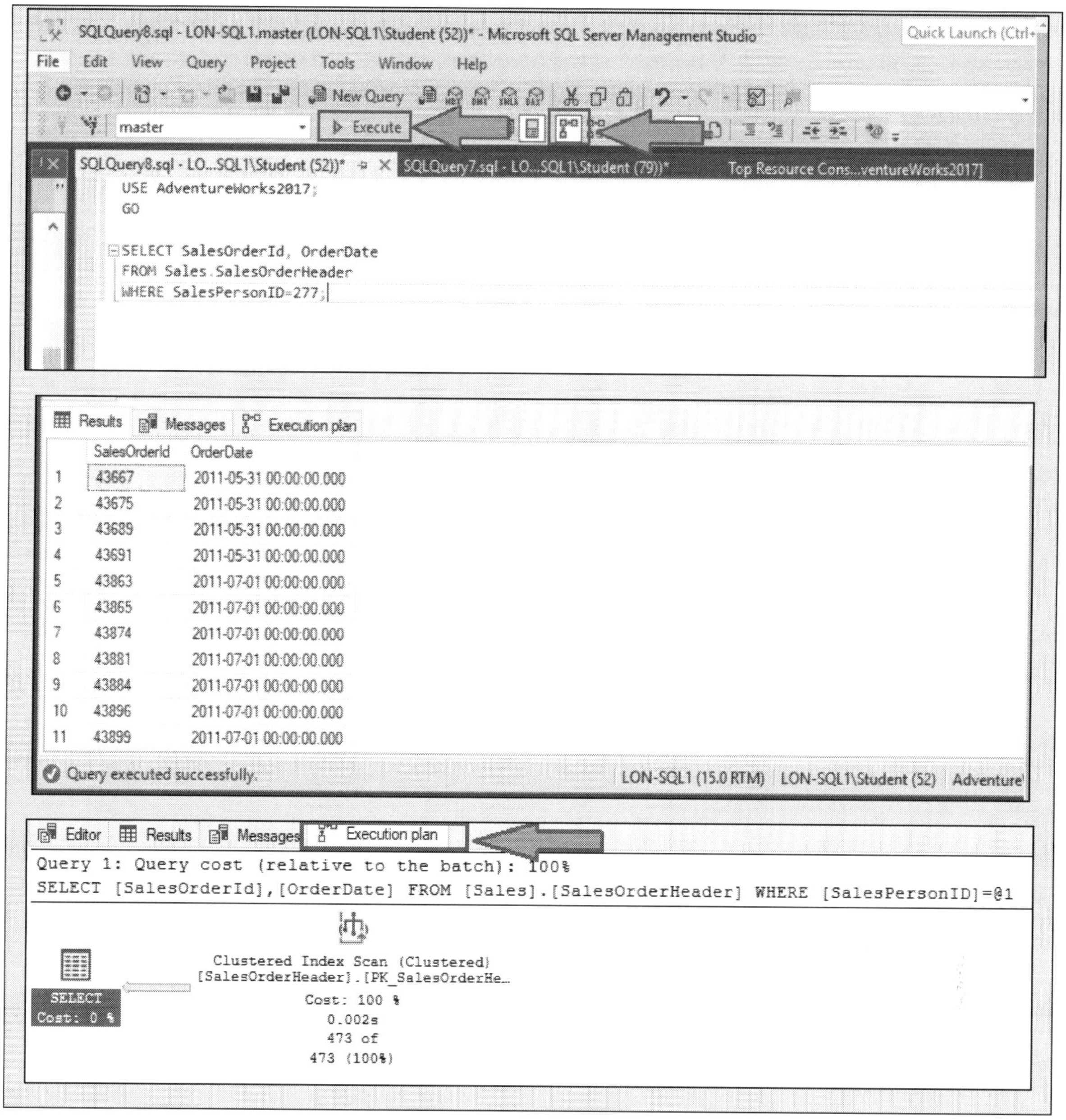

Change the Query to Use a Variable and Use a Query Hint.

1. Change the query to use a variable value for SalesPersonID.
2. Use the T-SQL **DECLARE** statement to declare **@SalesPersonID** so you can pass in a value instead of hard-coding the value in the **WHERE** clause.

```
USE AdventureWorks2017;

GO

SET STATISTICS IO, TIME ON;

DECLARE @SalesPersonID INT;

SELECT @SalesPersonID = 288;
```

SELECT SalesOrderId, OrderDate

FROM Sales.SalesOrderHeader

WHERE SalesPersonID= @SalesPersonID;

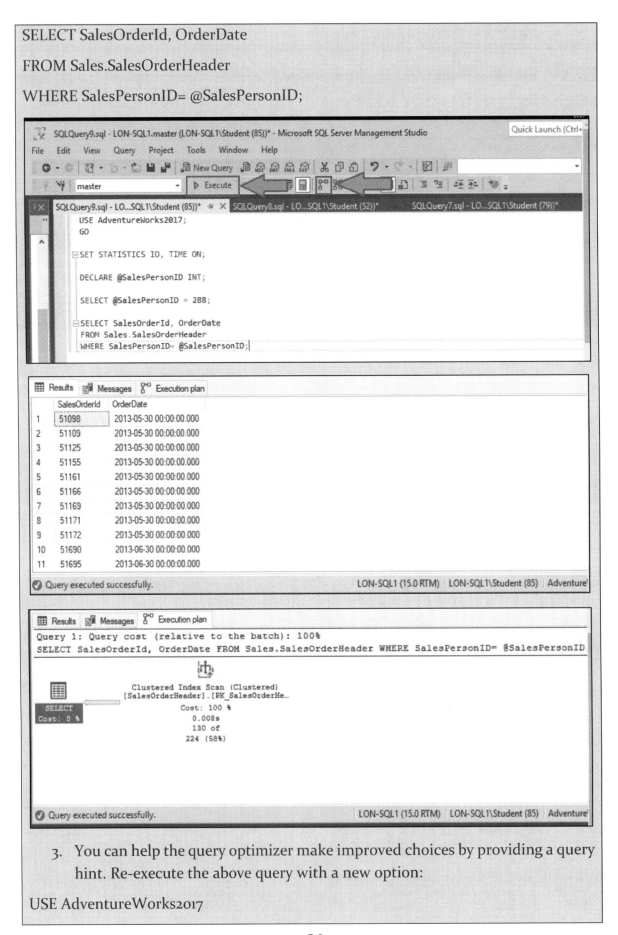

```
USE AdventureWorks2017;
GO

SET STATISTICS IO, TIME ON;

DECLARE @SalesPersonID INT;

SELECT @SalesPersonID = 288;

SELECT SalesOrderId, OrderDate
FROM Sales.SalesOrderHeader
WHERE SalesPersonID= @SalesPersonID;
```

	SalesOrderId	OrderDate
1	51098	2013-05-30 00:00:00.000
2	51109	2013-05-30 00:00:00.000
3	51125	2013-05-30 00:00:00.000
4	51155	2013-05-30 00:00:00.000
5	51161	2013-05-30 00:00:00.000
6	51166	2013-05-30 00:00:00.000
7	51169	2013-05-30 00:00:00.000
8	51171	2013-05-30 00:00:00.000
9	51172	2013-05-30 00:00:00.000
10	51690	2013-06-30 00:00:00.000
11	51695	2013-06-30 00:00:00.000

Query executed successfully.

Query 1: Query cost (relative to the batch): 100%
SELECT SalesOrderId, OrderDate FROM Sales.SalesOrderHeader WHERE SalesPersonID= @SalesPersonID

SELECT Cost: 0 % — Clustered Index Scan (Clustered) [SalesOrderHeader].[PK_SalesOrderHe... Cost: 100 % 0.008s 130 of 224 (58%)

Query executed successfully.

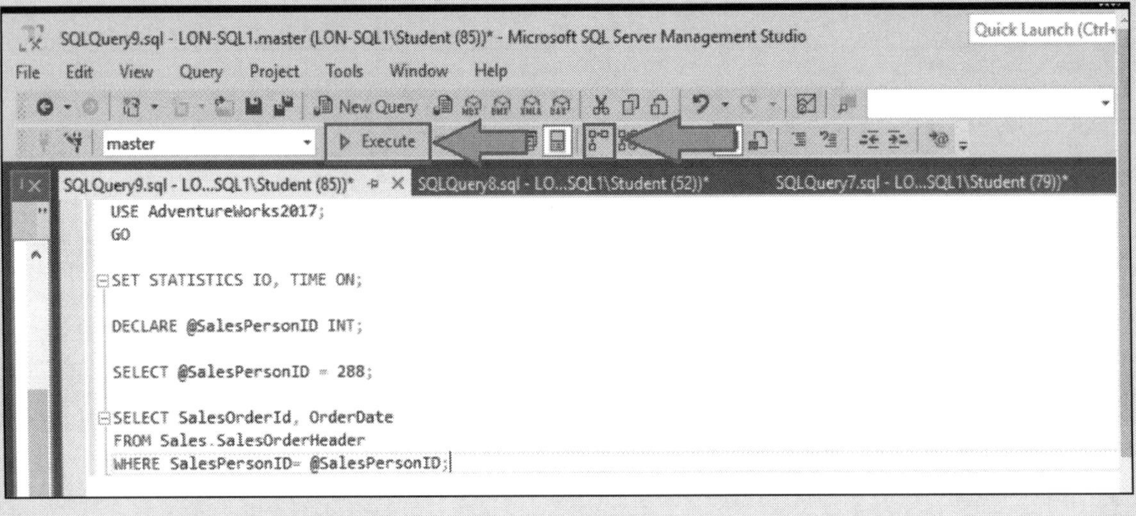

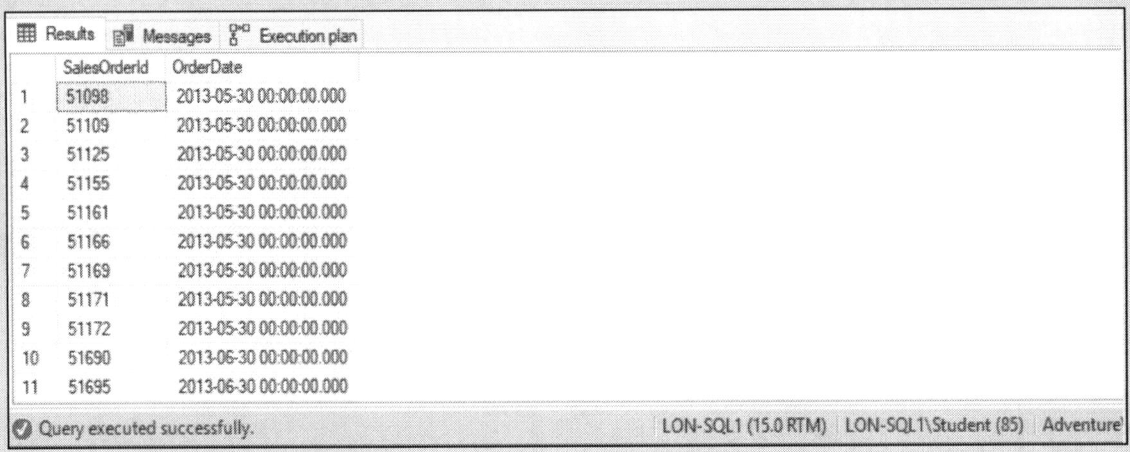

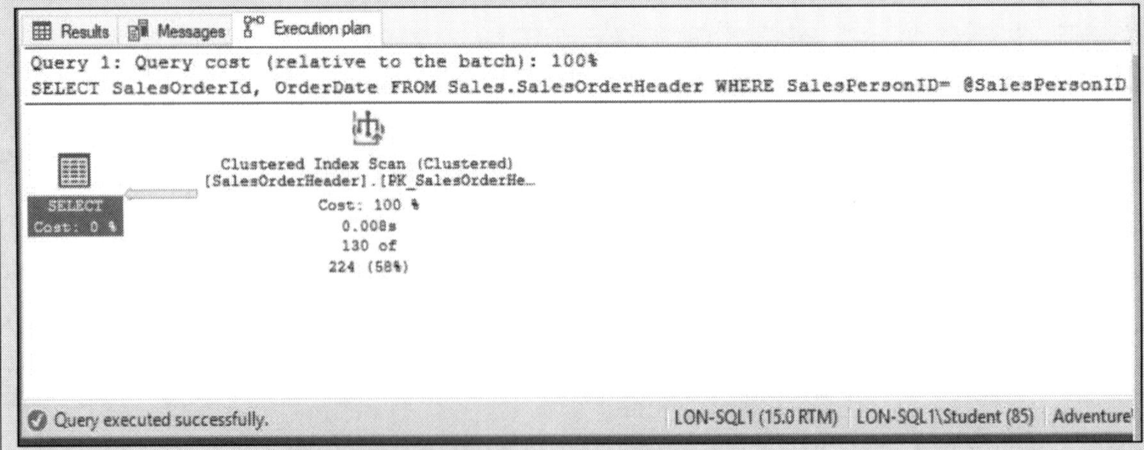

3. You can help the query optimizer make improved choices by providing a query hint. Re-execute the above query with a new option:

USE AdventureWorks2017

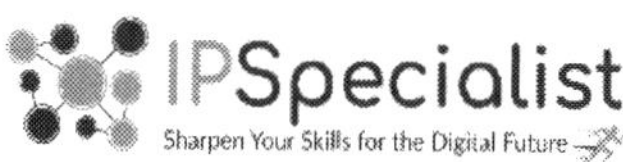

```
GO
SET STATISTICS IO, TIME ON;
DECLARE @SalesPersonID INT;
SELECT @SalesPersonID = 288;
SELECT SalesOrderId, OrderDate
FROM Sales.SalesOrderHeader
WHERE SalesPersonID= @SalesPersonID
OPTION (RECOMPILE);
```

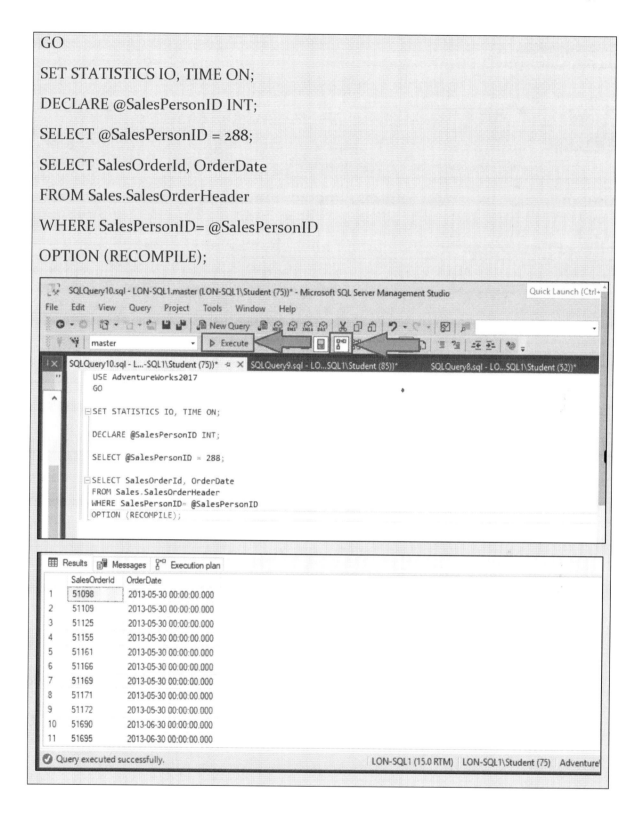

SQLQuery10.sql - LON-SQL1.master (LON-SQL1\Student (75))* - Microsoft SQL Server Management Studio
Quick Launch (Ctrl+
File Edit View Query Project Tools Window Help
New Query
master
Execute
SQLQuery10.sql - L...-SQL1\Student (75))*
SQLQuery9.sql - LO...SQL1\Student (85))*
SQLQuery8.sql - LO...SQL1\Student (52))*
USE AdventureWorks2017
GO
SET STATISTICS IO, TIME ON;
DECLARE @SalesPersonID INT;
SELECT @SalesPersonID = 288;
SELECT SalesOrderId, OrderDate
FROM Sales.SalesOrderHeader
WHERE SalesPersonID= @SalesPersonID
OPTION (RECOMPILE);
Results
Messages
Execution plan
SalesOrderId
OrderDate
1 51098 2013-05-30 00:00:00.000
2 51109 2013-05-30 00:00:00.000
3 51125 2013-05-30 00:00:00.000
4 51155 2013-05-30 00:00:00.000
5 51161 2013-05-30 00:00:00.000
6 51166 2013-05-30 00:00:00.000
7 51169 2013-05-30 00:00:00.000
8 51171 2013-05-30 00:00:00.000
9 51172 2013-05-30 00:00:00.000
10 51690 2013-06-30 00:00:00.000
11 51695 2013-06-30 00:00:00.000
Query executed successfully.
LON-SQL1 (15.0 RTM)
LON-SQL1\Student (75)
Adventure

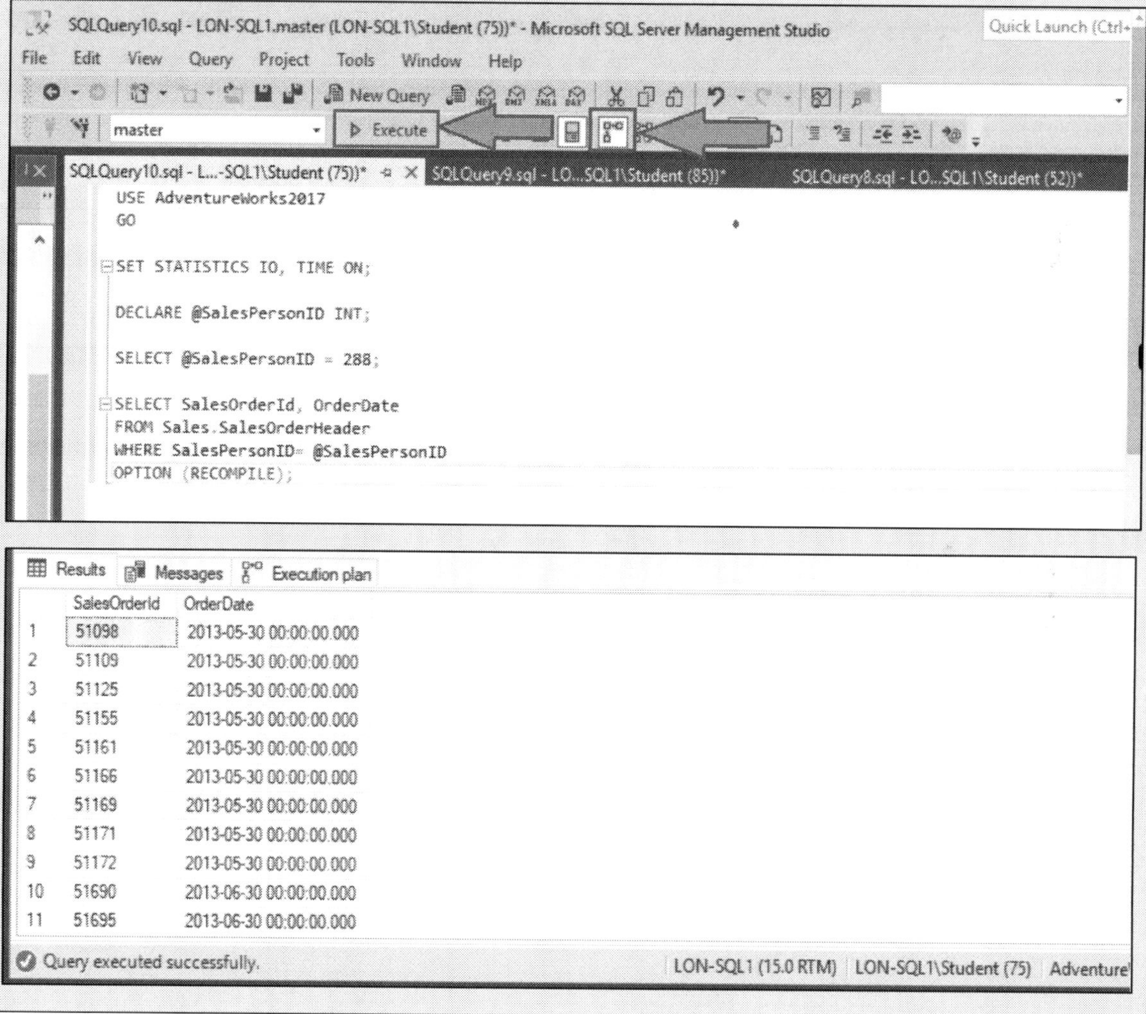

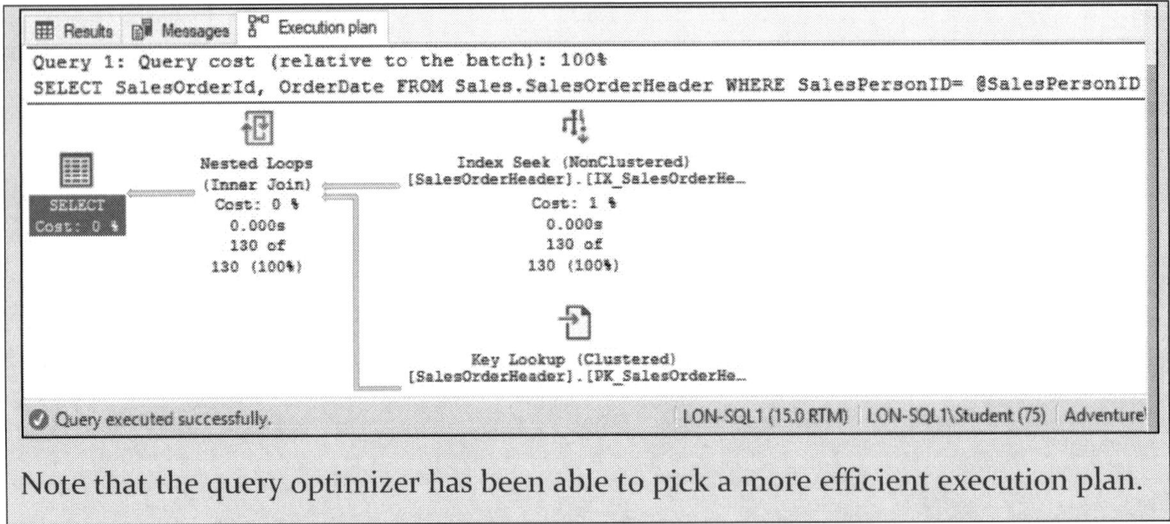

Note that the query optimizer has been able to pick a more efficient execution plan.

Mind Map

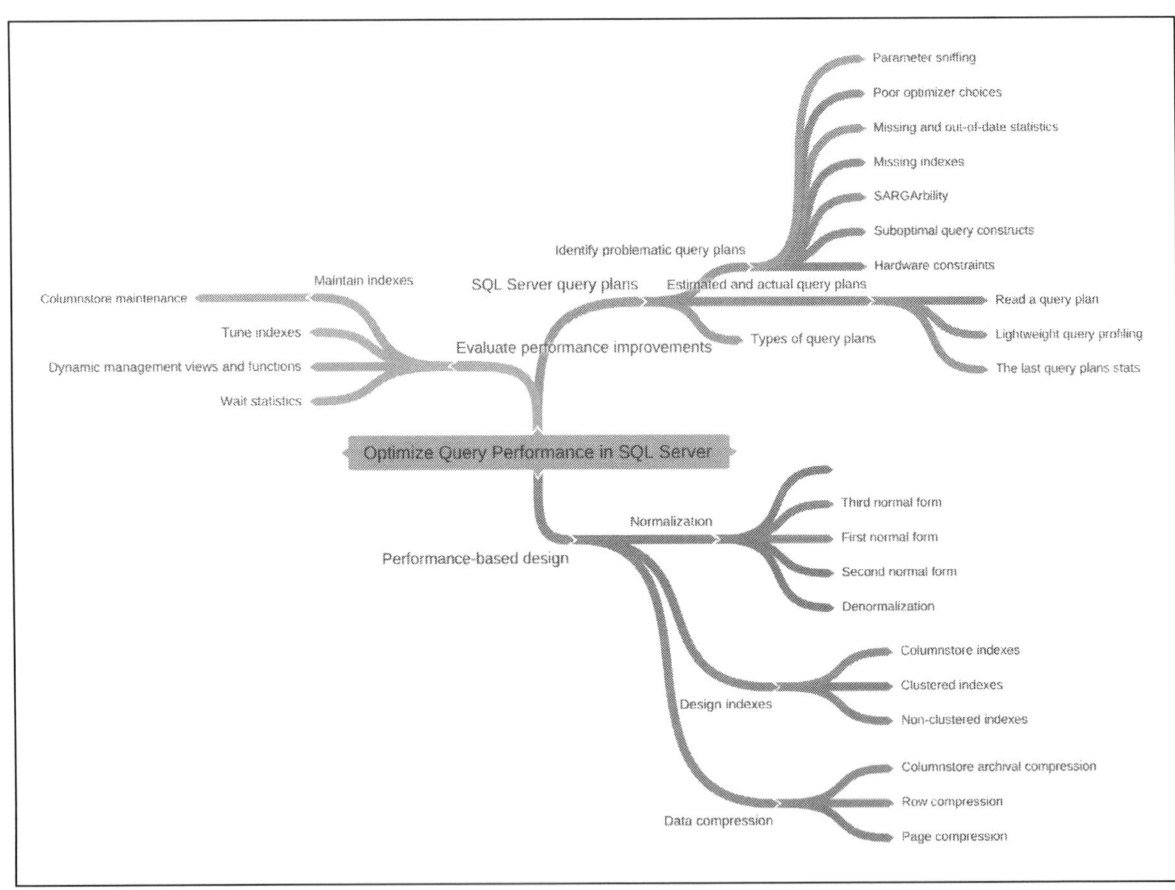

Figure 05-26: Mind Map

Practice Questions

1. Which type of execution plan is stored in the plan cache?

A. Estimated Execution Plan

B. Actual Execution Plan

C. Live Query Stats

D. None of the above

2. Which DMV should you use to find index utilization?

A. sys.dm_db_index_usage_stats

B. sys.dm_db_missing_index_details

C. sys.dm_exec_query_plan_stats

D. None of the above

3. Which of the following wait types would indicate excessive CPU consumption?

A. SOS_SCHEDULER_YIELD

B. RESOURCE_SEMAPHORE

C. PAGEIOLATCH_SH

D. None of the above

4. What type of index is best used on a data warehouse fact table?

A. Clustered Column store

B. Non-clustered Column store

C. Clustered b-tree

D. None of the above

5. Which DMV provides information about server-level wait statistics?

A. sys.dm_db_index_physical_stats

B. sys.dm_os_wait_stats

C. sys.dm_exec_session_wait_stats

D. None of the above

6. Which DMV can you use to capture the last Actual Execution Plan for a given query?

A. sys.dm_exec_cached_plans

B. sys.dm_exec_query_plan

C. sys.dm_exec_query_plan_stats

D. None of the above

7. What type of database design should you use for a data warehouse when you want to reduce the data volume of your dimensions?

A. Snowflake Schema

B. Star Schema

C. 3rd Normal Form

D. None of the above

8. What is the minimum number of rows you need to insert into a column-store index?

A. 102,400

B. 1,000,000

C. 1000

D. None of the above

9. Which compression type offers the highest level of compression?

A. Column Store Archival

B. Page Compression

C. Row Compression

D. None of the above

10. Query plans can be viewed in a ________ format.

A. Graphical Representation

B. Text-based

C. Both of the above

D. None of the above

11. There are ____ different types of execution plans that can be viewed.

A. One

B. Two

C. Three

D. Four

12. SQL Server has _______ types of table-valued functions.

A. One

B. Two

C. Three

D. Four

13. _____ data frequently requires multiple join operations to get all the necessary data returned in a single query.

A. Normalized

B. De-normalized

C. Both of the above

D. None of the above

14. Dimensions in a _______ schema are normalized to reduce redundancy, saving storage space.

A. Star

B. Snowflake

C. Both of the above

D. None of the above

15. Batch mode can provide up to a ______ performance increase over traditional row processing.

A. 10x

B. 100x

C. 1000x

D. None of the above

Chapter 06: Automate Tasks in SQL Server

Introduction

The Azure platform offers many options for deploying resources. You have the option to deploy either from Azure DevOps or through command line scripting options. Azure Resource Manager templates offer you the flexibility to granularly deploy Azure resources in a repeatable, consistent fashion. It is measured as a best practice to manage your infrastructure as code and implement source control. This has the side advantage of providing more consistent deployments.

The SQL Server Agent offers a robust mechanism for managing and keeping your SQL Server, and Azure SQL managed instance deployments. In addition to providing job scheduling, it also offers alerts and some monitoring options for your databases. Maintenance plans can be used to deliver backups, index and statistics maintenance, and log management activity. Finally, the essential thing you can do as a DBA is to guarantee that your databases are backed up and test your database backups regularly. Note that the SQL Server Agent is only available on SQL Server and Azure SQL Managed Instance, but not on Azure SQL Database.

The extended events engine in Azure SQL is a very powerful monitoring system that allows you to capture granular information about activity in your databases and servers. The monitoring solutions on the Azure platform let you easily configure powerful monitoring for your environment and provide automated responses to error conditions.

One of the advantages of cloud computing is that a framework for robust automation, monitoring, and tooling is part of the platform. In the on-premises world, a complex set of tools would be essential to be assembled just to match the built-in functionality available with Azure metrics, policy, and automation. Additionally, SQL Server offers an automation framework using SQL Agent and a very robust monitoring solution via Extended Events. You can take benefit of Azure automation and Azure elastic jobs to automate the management of your Azure resources.

Configure Automatic Deployment for Azure SQL Database

On-premises systems need cabling and racks of hardware to deploy a new database server. With cloud computing, this is not necessary. One of the key benefits of cloud computing is that system resources are abstracted behind an API. For Azure, this deployment and management layer is called Azure Resource Manager. Azure Resource Manager offers a consistent deployment mechanism called Resource Manager

Templates, JavaScript Object Notation (JSON) documents that can be used for parameterized deployment.

Describe Deployment Models in Azure

Azure Resource Manager Templates have the advantage of deploying a full set of resources in one single declarative template. You can form dependencies into the templates and use parameters to change deployment values at deployment time. Once you have a template, you can set it up in several ways, including using an Azure DevOps pipeline or through the custom deployments blade in the Azure portal. The benefit of these deployments is that they use a declarative model, which describes what should be created. The Azure Resource Manager framework then defines how to deploy it. The alternative to the declarative model is the imperative model. Imperative frameworks include PowerShell and the Azure CLI, which follow an authoritarian order of executing tasks.

A common term used around cloud computing deployments is "infrastructure as code," which means all your resources are well-defined as scripts stored in source control. They can simply be deployed to a new environment. While stateful resources like databases are not deployed as frequently as application code, by defining your infrastructure, you make sure that resources are deployed consistently, reducing the configuration risk and the impact of human error. As mentioned above, two programming models are used for cloud deployments: imperative and declarative.

In imperative programming, you are describing a set of prescriptive tasks for the target system to execute. A simple example of this model is using a batch script to install SQL Server and its prerequisites. In declarative programming, you define a set of resources, typically by a framework. A simple example is a CREATE TABLE statement, which refers to the columns and keys built by the SQL Server engine. The statement acts as the framework for building the table.

Azure Resource Manager Templates

Azure Resource Manager Templates let you create and deploy an entire infrastructure in a declarative framework. For example, you can set up not only a virtual machine but its network and storage dependencies in one document. Resource Manager also supports orchestration, which accomplishes the deployment of interdependent resources to create them correctly. For example, a VM is dependent on the existence of a virtual network, so the framework will deploy the network (or check for the existence of the network) before attempting to build the VM. Azure Resource Manager Templates also support extensibility, which lets you run PowerShell or Bash scripts on your resources after they are deployed.

PowerShell

PowerShell offers a core module known as Az, with child resource providers for nearly all Azure services. For example, 'Az.Compute' would cover Azure Virtual Machines. PowerShell is more commonly used for resource modification and status retrieval. While it is possible to create resources using PowerShell, it is not typically used for complex deployments. PowerShell can also be used to deploy Azure Resource Manager templates, so in a sense, it supports both declarative and imperative models.

Azure CLI

The Azure Command Line Interface, or CLI, is similar to PowerShell in the sense that it can be used either imperatively or declaratively. Like PowerShell and Azure Resource Manager templates, the Azure CLI offers a mechanism to deploy or modify Azure Resources. Some commands for Azure PostgreSQL and Azure MySQL Databases are only available in the Azure CLI.

Azure Portal

The Azure portal is a graphical interface to Azure Resource Manager. Any resources you form and deploy using the portal will have an Azure Resource Manager template that you can capture by clicking "Export Template" in the Settings blade:

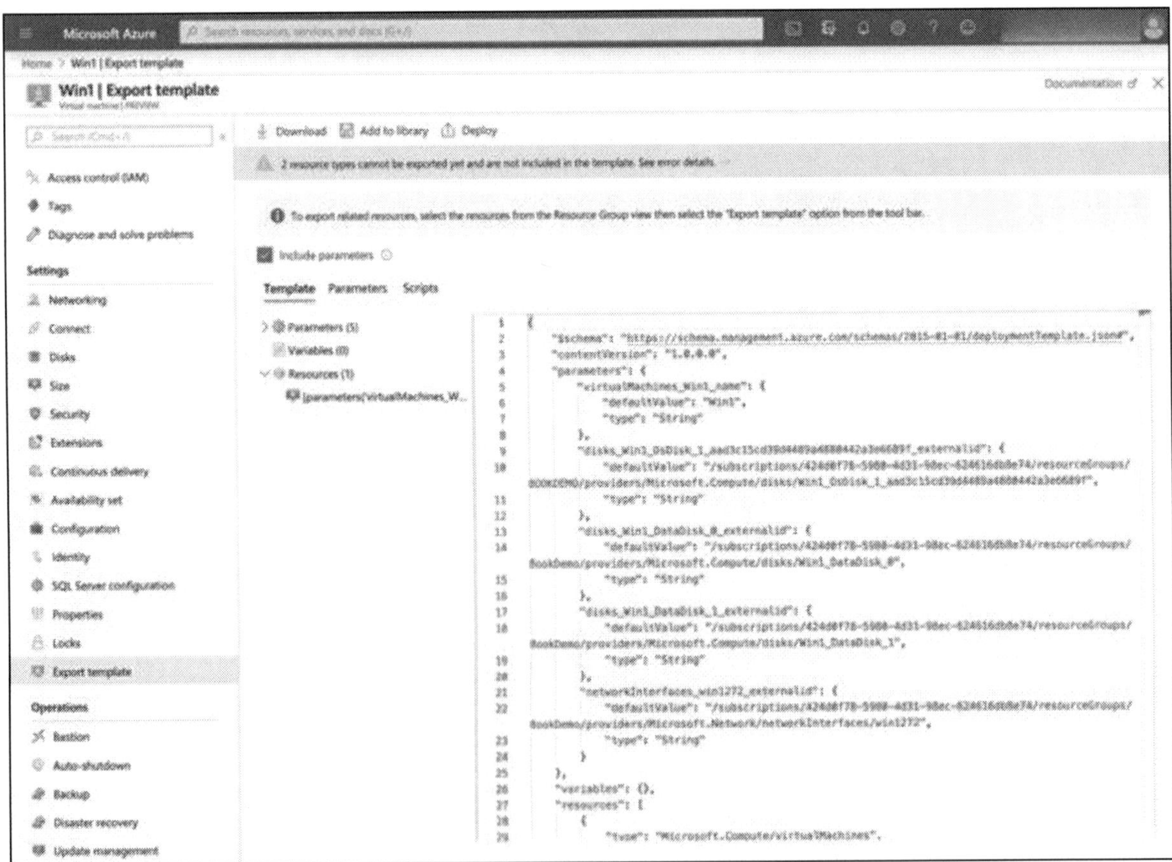

Figure 06-01: Azure Portal

The Azure portal is usually the easiest way to get on track when first learning about the Azure platform. Organizations (and DBAs) typically move into a more automated deployment model as their Azure estate and experience grows.

Deploying an Azure Resource Manager Template with PowerShell and CLI

With PowerShell, you have numerous options for the scope of your deployment. You can set up a resource group, a subscription, a Management Group (a collection of subscriptions under the same Azure template and commonly used in large enterprise deployments), or a tenant. Azure Resource Manager Templates are parameterized, and you want to pass in parameters, either inline or through the use of a parameter file, as shown in the example below.

```
New-AzResourceGroupDeployment -Name ExampleDeployment -ResourceGroupName ExampleResourceGroup `
 -TemplateFile c:\MyTemplates\azuredeploy.json `
 -TemplateParameterFile c:\MyTemplates\storage.parameters.json
```

Figure 06-02: Deploying an Azure Resource Manager Template with PowerShell

The parameter and template file can also be kept in a git repo, Azure Blob Storage, or any other place accessible from the deploying machine.

Deploying an Azure Resource Manager Template with Azure CLI

The Azure CLI lets the same options for deployment scope as you have with PowerShell. Also, like with PowerShell, you can use a local or remote parameter file and template, as shown in the example below.

```
az deployment group create --resource-group SampleRG --template-file '\path\template.json'
```

Figure 06-03: Deploying an Azure Resource Manager Template with Azure CLI

Using Azure DevOps to Deploy Templates

In Azure DevOps, deployments are approved using Azure Pipelines. Azure Pipelines are a fully-featured continuous integration and delivery service (CI/CD), letting you automate the build, testing, and deployment of your code. You can set up Azure resources using Azure Resource Manager templates in two ways. The first method calls a PowerShell script, as shown above. The second approach describes tasks that stage your artifacts (the templates themselves and any required secrets) and then deploy the templates. One task stages the artifacts, and the other tasks deploy the templates.

Continuous Integration

Continuous integration is a development methodology focused on making minor changes to code and frequent code check-ins to the version control system. Continuous

integration provides an automated way to form, package, and test applications. The framework facilitates frequent check-ins and allows better collaboration between developers to improve code quality. Continuous delivery builds on continuous integration automates the delivery of code changes to the underlying infrastructure.

Create an Azure Resource Manager Template

An Azure Resource Manager template is a JSON (JavaScript Object Notation) document that defines the resources deployed within an Azure Resource Group. The structure of these templates is shown below.

```
{
 "$schema": "https://schema.management.azure.com/schemas/2019-04-01/deploymentTemplate.json#",
 "contentVersion": "",
 "apiProfile": "",
 "parameters": { },
 "variables": { },
 "functions": [ ],
 "resources": [ ],
 "outputs": { }
}
```

Figure 06-04: Azure Resource Manager Template

The schema file, referenced on the first line of the above example, defines the template language's version—Microsoft provisions this file to define the Azure API. The content version number is only defined by you as needed and should align with your internal versioning standard. The API profile helps as a collection of API versions for this environment. This is especially beneficial when deploying resources to different national and commercial clouds with different resource providers. Parameters are values provided to the template to customize resources at deployment time, whereas variables are used as JSON fragments to simplify template language expressions. You can also include user-defined functions within the template. The resource component describes what resources are getting defined in the template. The resources are the resource types that you are deploying. The code sample below shows the example resources section from an Azure Resource Manager template to deploy an Azure SQL Database.

```
"resources": [
{
"name": "[variables('sqlServerName')]",
"type": "Microsoft.Sql/servers",
"apiVersion": "2014-04-01-preview",
"location": "[parameters('location')]",
"tags": {
"displayName": "SqlServer"
},
"properties": {
"administratorLogin": "[parameters('sqlAdministratorLogin')]",
"administratorLoginPassword": "[parameters('sqlAdministratorLoginPassword')]",
"version": "12.0"
},
"resources": [
{
"name": "[variables('databaseName')]",
"type": "databases",
"apiVersion": "2015-01-01",
"location": "[parameters('location')]",
"tags": {
"displayName": "Database"
},
"properties": {
"edition": "[variables('databaseEdition')]",
"collation": "[variables('databaseCollation')]",
"requestedServiceObjectiveName": "[variables('databaseServiceObjectiveName')]"
},
"dependsOn": [
"[variables('sqlServerName')]"
],
"resources": [
{
"comments": "Transparent Data Encryption",
"name": "current",
```

Figure 06-05 (a): Azure Resource Manager Template to deploy an Azure SQL Database

```
"type": "transparentDataEncryption",
"apiVersion": "2014-04-01-preview",
"properties": {
"status": "[parameters('transparentDataEncryption')]"
},
"dependsOn": [
"[variables('databaseName')]"
]
}
]
}
```

Figure 06-05 (b): Azure Resource Manager Template to deploy an Azure SQL Database

One of the most important things to note about the structure of the resources section of the above template is the **dependsOn** option. This option lets you build a dependency structure into your template. A simple example is in the template above; the Azure SQL Database is dependent on the existence of an Azure SQL Database server, and Transparent Data Encryption is dependent on the existence of the database. This option can be used to build even more complex dependency structures for complex application deployments.

It is significant to understand the difference between variables and parameters. Parameters can agree to take values outside the template by user interaction, a file, or CI/CD pipelines. Variables can be defined within the template and are used for simplification since you can describe a complicated expression once and then use it throughout the template. An example of variable definition in an Azure Resource Manager template is shown in the exhibit below.

```
"variables": {
 "storageName": "[concat(toLower(parameters('storageNamePrefix')), uniqueString(resourceGroup().id))]"
}
```

Figure 06-06: Azure Resource Manager Template

By defining this expression in the variables section of your template, you can again use it by referencing the variable in other parts of the template in the following manner: "[variables('storageName;)]." Variables allow you to avoid repeating a complicated expression throughout your template by using the variable name.

Source Control for Templates

Azure Resource Manager Templates are an example of infrastructure as code. Since all hardware resources are abstracted behind a set of APIs, your entire infrastructure can just be another component of your application code. Similar to the application or database code, it is essential to protect this code. In addition to the internal version in the template, your source control system must version your templates. You can also configure your templates to be automatically deployed from GitHub.

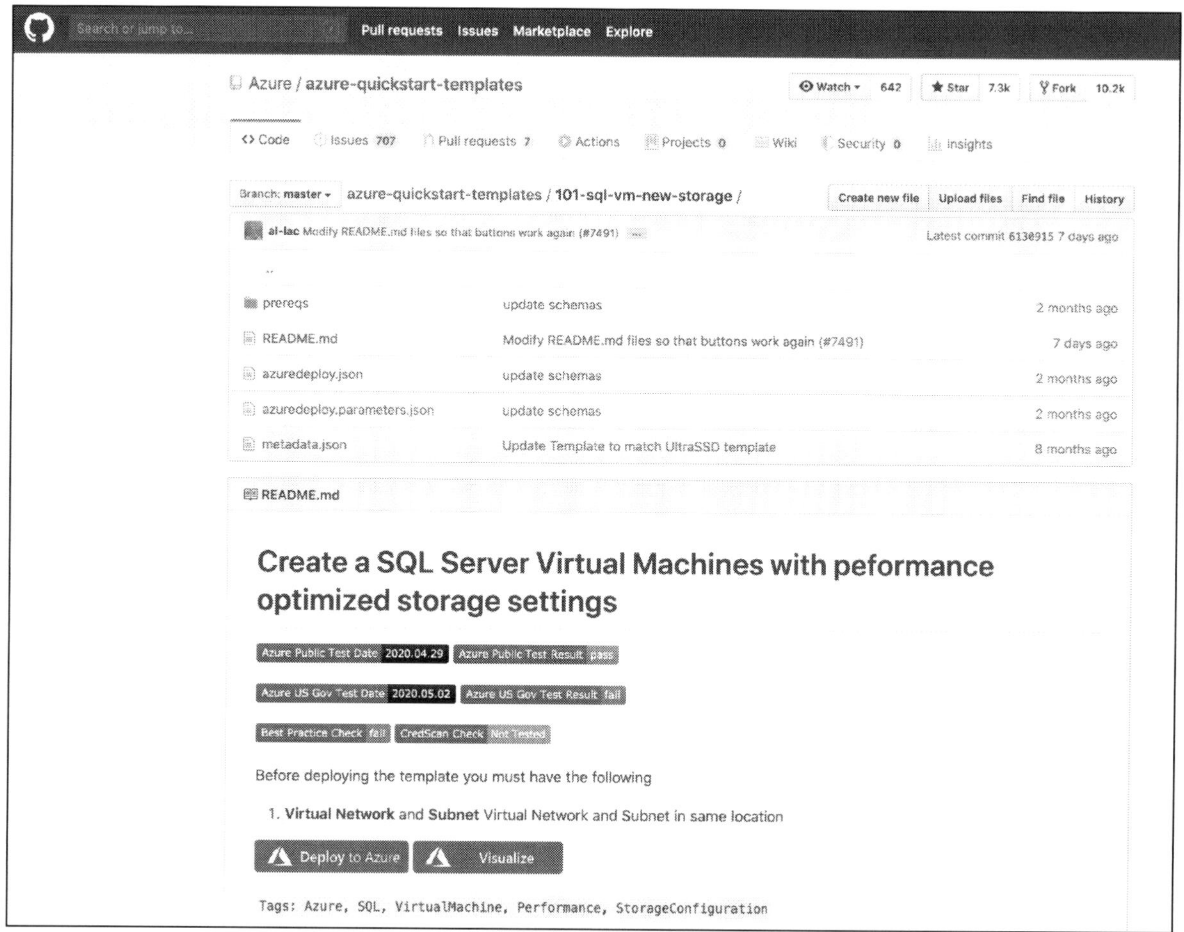

Figure 06-07: Source Control for Templates

Deploy an Azure Resource Manager Template

In most cases, the database administrator will not be writing their own Azure Resource Manager template from scratch. You may either form them from the Azure portal or use a template from the Quickstart templates provided by Microsoft on GitHub.

The template parameters are defined by the parameters section of the template file. There are only two VM sizes defined (the default value is a Standard_DS13_v2).

If you click the edit template button, you will get the JSON defining the template, which would let you change the values to meet your requirements.

```
"virtualMachineSize": {
 "type": "String",
 "defaultValue": "Standard_DS13_v2",
 "allowedValues": [
 "Standard_DS13_v2",
 "Standard_DS3_v2"
 ],
 "metadata": {
 "description": "The virtual machine size."
 }
 }
```

Figure 06-08: Deploy an Azure Resource Manager Template

After filling in the required parameters in the deployment screen, click Purchase and set up your template.

Schedule Tasks using SQL Server Agent

Database systems require regular maintenance, which contains tasks like making backups and updating statistics. Maintenance may also consist of regularly scheduled jobs that execute against a database. Common examples of these jobs would be extracting, transforming, and loading data into a data warehouse from a transaction processing system. In SQL Server and Azure SQL managed instances, the SQL Server Agent service lets you schedule jobs to perform these maintenance tasks (as well as provide other management functions). For Azure SQL Database and Azure Database for MariaDB/MySQL/Postgres, other options are available for scheduling maintenance operations, including Azure automation.

One of the ways you can take advantage of Azure is using the built-in resource monitoring that the platform provides. You can also take benefit of the Azure platform's options for handling and responding to events. In addition, it is essential to understand SQL Server's event handling system, called extended events, and be familiar with how you can use it to perform extensive monitoring of your systems.

Create a SQL Server Maintenance Plan

Typical activities that you can schedule for regular SQL Server maintenance include:

- Database and transaction log backups
- Database Consistency Checks
- Index maintenance
- Statistics updates

You should be attentive to the importance of backups, index, and statistics maintenance for all your databases. Database consistency checks, also known as CHECKDB (for the command DBCC CHECKDB), are of equal importance, as it is the only way to check an entire database for corruption. Depending on the size of your database and your uptime requirements, you may implement all of these activities overnight. Both index maintenance and consistency checks are I/O intensive operations and are typically done during weekend hours. More commonly, in production systems, the maintenance operations are built over the week.

Similarly, many DBAs stagger backups of large databases and only do one full backup a week. Differential and transaction log backups can then be utilized to manage recovery to a specific point in time. SQL Server provides a built-in way to manage all of these tasks using Maintenance Plans. Maintenance plans make a workflow of the tasks to support your databases. Maintenance plans are made as Integration Services packages, which let you schedule your maintenance activities.

EXAM TIP: Many DBAs also use open source scripts to perform database maintenance, allowing for more flexibility and control of maintenance activities.

Best Practices for Maintenance Plans

In addition to letting you perform database maintenance, maintenance plans offer options to let you prune data from the msdb database, which acts as the data store for the SQL Server Agent. Maintenance plans also let you specify that older database backups should be detached from the disk. Removing old backup files helps your SQL Server decrease the size of your backup volume and helps manage the size of the msdb database. Ensure that your backup retention period is longer than your consistency check window. This means if you run a consistency check weekly, you must retain eight days of backups. (Note: The backup operation will not notice corruption in a database, so it is possible to have corruption within a backup file). Maintenance plan activities are scheduled as SQL Server Agent jobs for execution.

Creating a Maintenance Plan

You can make a maintenance plan using SQL Server Management Studio, as shown below. Note that in the example below, multiple maintenance tasks are joined in one maintenance plan. The best practice would be to make a maintenance plan for each type

of task—and possibly even for a specific database on your server. For example, you might form a maintenance plan to back up system databases and another maintenance plan to back up user databases. You could also have another maintenance plan for special handling of the backup of one very large user database. The image below and the following examples show a maintenance plan using the maintenance plan wizard.

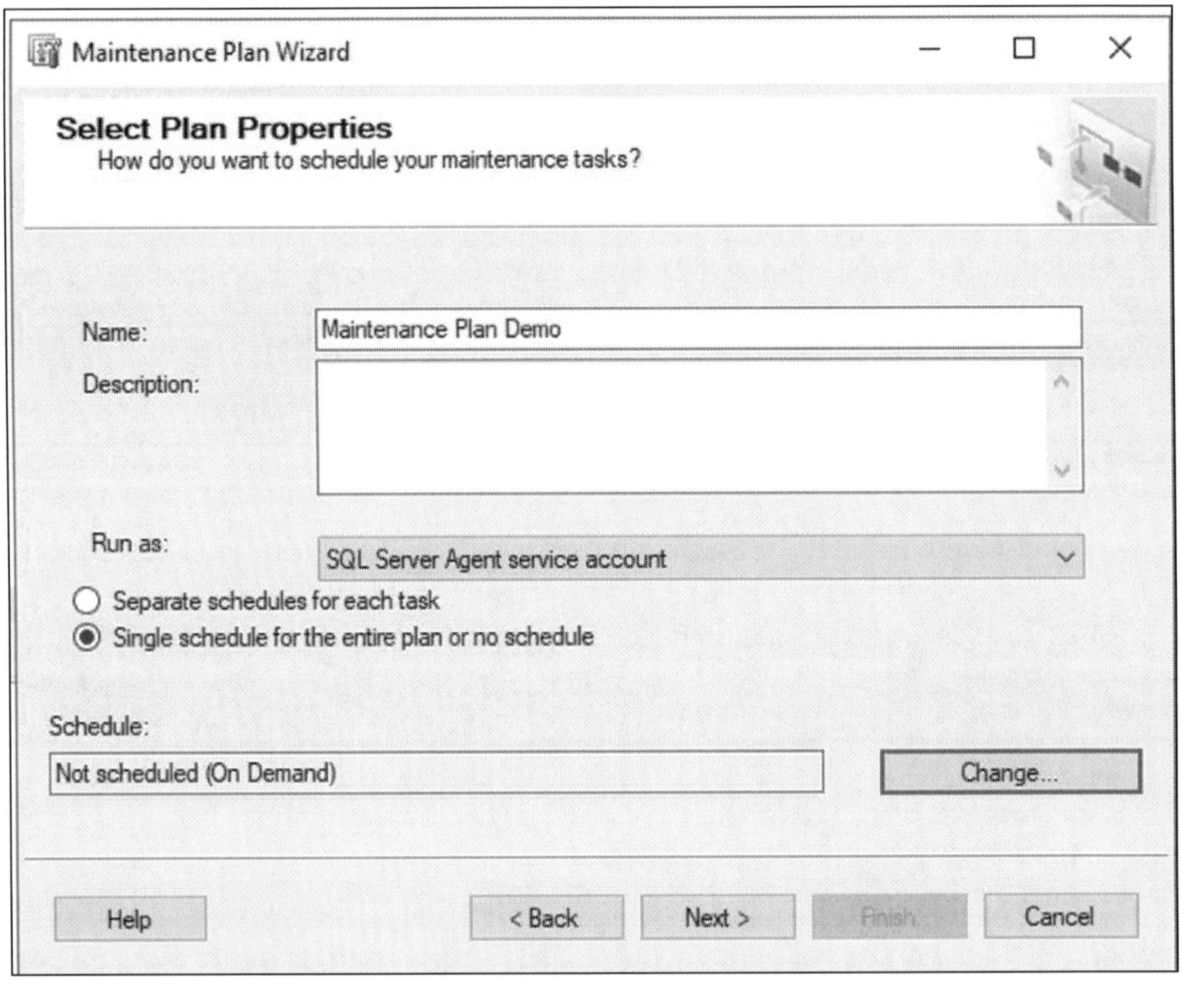

Figure 06-09: Creating a Maintenance Plan

The image above shows the first screen of the maintenance plan wizard from SQL Server Management Studio (SSMS). You must note a couple of things — you need to specify a name for your maintenance plan and select a run-as account from the dropdown menu. Typically, most maintenance operations will run as the SQL Server Agent service account, but you may want to run a task as a different account for security purposes. For example, if you need to back up to a file share that only a specific account has access to, you have to run that specific plan as a different user. This concept is known as a proxy user, which is another component of the SQL Server Agent.

What is a Proxy Account?

A proxy account is an account with stored credentials that the SQL Server Agent can use to implement the steps of a job as a specific user. The login information for this user is stored as a credential in the SQL Server instance.

> **Note:** Proxy accounts are typically used when granular security rights are needed for specific steps of a SQL agent job.

Job Schedules

Job schedules are a part of the job system in the msdb system database. SQL Server Agent jobs and schedules have a many-to-many relationship. Each job comprises multiple schedules, and the same schedule can be allocated to multiple jobs. The maintenance plan wizard, however, does not let the creation of independent schedules. It generates a specific schedule for each maintenance plan, as shown below:

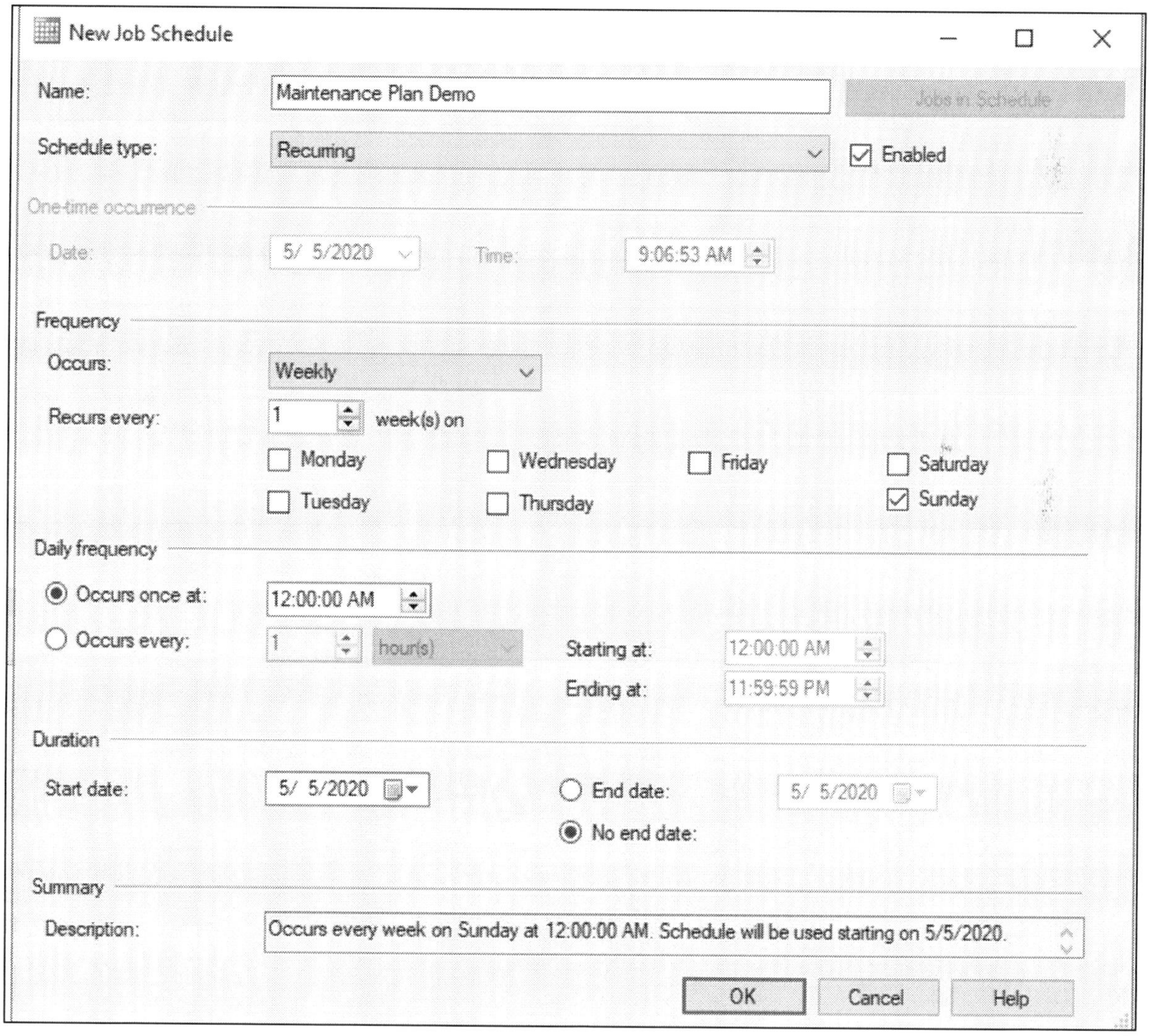

Figure 06-10: Job Schedules

The above schedule is for a weekly execution, but you can also make a schedule with hourly or daily recurrence. The next step in this process is to add maintenance tasks to the plan.

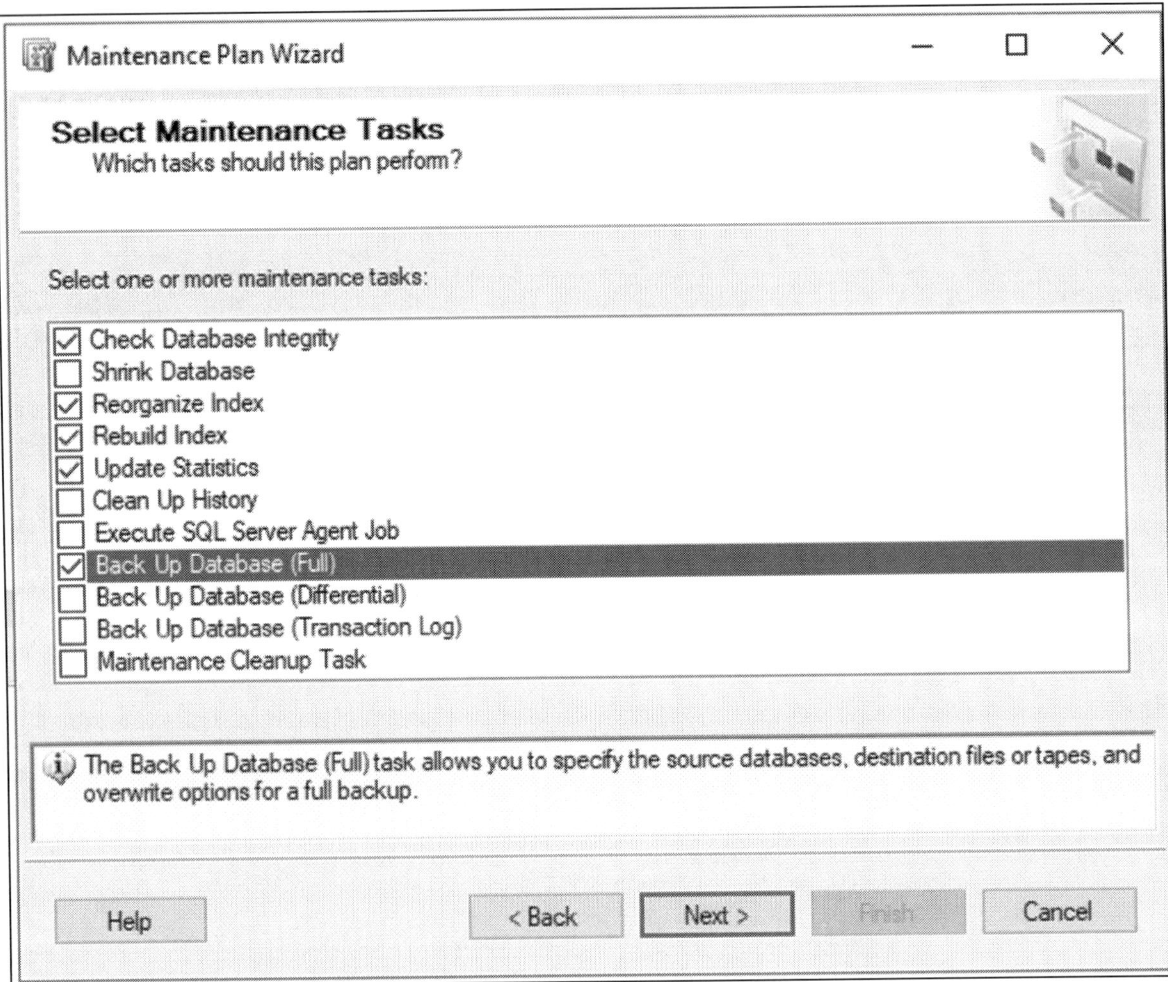

Figure 06-11: Add Maintenance Tasks to the Plan

The image above shows the maintenance tasks addition screen. This is where you choose the operations to be performed by your maintenance plan. The options are:

Check Database Integrity - This task performs the DBCC CHECKDB command, which authenticates the contents of each database page to ensure its logical and physical consistency. This task must be performed regularly (daily or weekly), aligning with your backup retention window. To ensure corruption is not passed over to your backups, ensure you complete a consistency check before leaving any prior backups.

Shrink Database - This task decreases the size of the database or transaction log file by moving data into free space on pages. When enough space is utilized, the free space can be reverted to the file system.

It is recommended that you never implement this action as part of any regular maintenance as it leads to severe index fragmentation, which can damage database

performance. The operation itself is also very I/O and CPU intensive and can severely impact your system performance.

Reorganize/Rebuild Index - This task will check the level of fragmentation in a database's indexes. It may also rebuild or reorganize the index based on the user-defined level of fragmentation. Note that rebuilding an index updates the statistics on the index.

Update Statistics - This task brings up-to-date column and index statistics that SQL Server uses to build query execution plans. It is essential that the statistics accurately reflect the data stored in tables so that the query optimizer can make the best decisions in building execution plans. This task lets you choose which tables and indexes are scanned and the percentage or number of rows scanned. The default sampling rate is satisfactory for most objects, though you may wish to capture more detailed statistics for specific tables.

Cleanup History - This task removes the history of backup and restores operations from the msdb database and the history of SQL Server agent jobs. This task is used to manage the size of the msdb database.

Execute SQL Server Agent Job - This task is used to implement a user-defined SQL Server Agent job.

Backup Database (Full/Differential/Log) - This task is used to back up databases on a SQL Server instance. A full backup backs up the complete database and is the starting point for a restore (you need a full backup to restore a database completely). Differential backups backup the pages in the database that have transformed since the last full backup and are typically used to provide an incremental restore point. Transaction log backups backup the active pages in your transaction log and let you define your recovery point objective. Transaction log backups cannot be performed on databases in SIMPLE recovery mode.

Here is an example of the use of different kinds of backups: If you took a full back up on Sunday and a differential each weeknight, and you desired to restore to your database to noon on Thursday, you would only have to restore Sunday's full backup and Wednesday's differential, followed by the transaction log backups from the point of Wednesday's differential backup until Thursday at noon.

Maintenance Cleanup Tasks - This removes old files related to maintenance plans, which includes text reports from maintenance plan execution and backup files. It only takes out backups on files in the folders specified, so any subfolders must be specifically listed, or they will be skipped.

Each task has a scope of user databases, system databases, or a custom selection of databases. Additionally, each task has its specific configuration options.

Once you finish creating the Maintenance Plan, you will be offered the details of the entire plan. You can get back to this view in SQL Server Management Studio by expanding the Management node, then expanding the Maintenance Plan node, right-clicking on the Maintenance Plan, and selecting Modify.

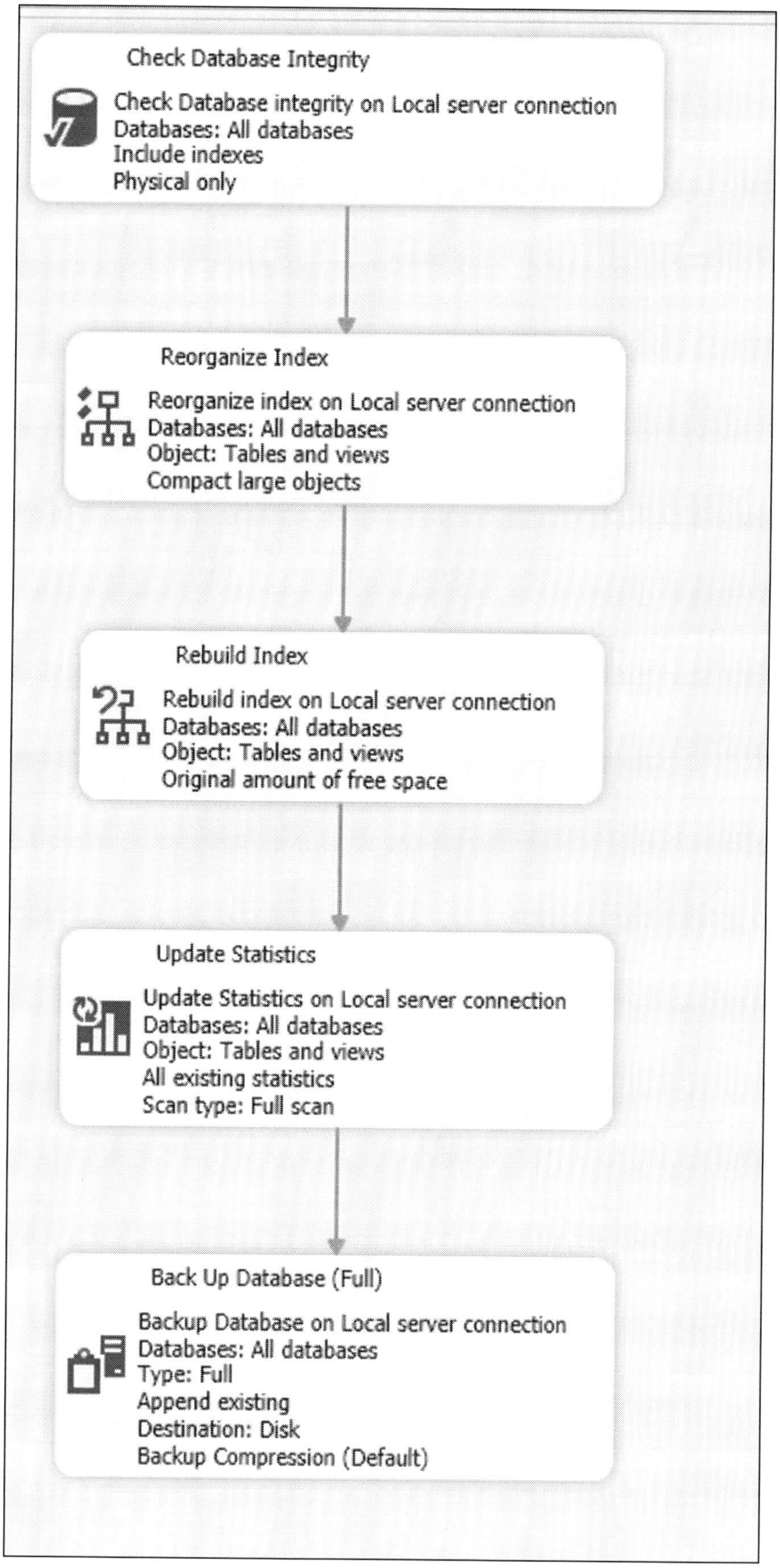

Check Database Integrity

Check Database integrity on Local server connection
Databases: All databases
Include indexes
Physical only

Reorganize Index

Reorganize index on Local server connection
Databases: All databases
Object: Tables and views
Compact large objects

Rebuild Index

Rebuild index on Local server connection
Databases: All databases
Object: Tables and views
Original amount of free space

Update Statistics

Update Statistics on Local server connection
Databases: All databases
Object: Tables and views
All existing statistics
Scan type: Full scan

Back Up Database (Full)

Backup Database on Local server connection
Databases: All databases
Type: Full
Append existing
Destination: Disk
Backup Compression (Default)

Figure 06-12: Maintenance Plan

Upon creation, the plan will look like a job in the SQL Server Agent. If you add a schedule during the creation process or after, that job will be implemented, and the maintenance tasks will be performed.

Multi-server Automation

In a multi-server environment, the SQL Server Agent offers the option of designating one server as a master server to implement jobs on other servers designated as target servers. The master server provisions a master copy of the jobs and allocates the jobs to the target servers. Target servers link to the master server periodically to update their schedule of jobs. This lets you define one job and deploy it across your enterprise. A good example of this would be configuring database maintenance across your environment.

> **Note:** You could generate a set of maintenance plan tasks once and let them be pushed out to a group of target servers to ensure consistent deployment.

Describe Task Status Notifications

One significant part of automation is providing notifications in job failure or if certain system faults are encountered. SQL Server Agent offers this functionality through a group of objects. Alerting is usually done via email using the Database Mail functionality of SQL Server. The other agent objects that are used in this workflow are:

- Operators—it is an alias for people or group who gets notifications
- Notifications—it is to notify an operator of the completion, success, or failure of a job
- Alerts—these are given to an operator for either a notification or a defined error condition

Operators

Operators act as an alias for a user or group of users that have been constructed to receive notifications of job completion or to be informed of alerts that have been directed to the error log. An operator is described as an operator's name and contact information. Typically, an operator will map to a group of people using an email group. Having multiple people in the email group offers redundancy so that a notification is not lost if someone is unavailable. Groups are also helpful if an employee leaves the organization; a single person can be detached from the email group. You do not have to update all of your instances. To send an email to an operator, you have to enable the email profile of the SQL Server Agent as shown below:

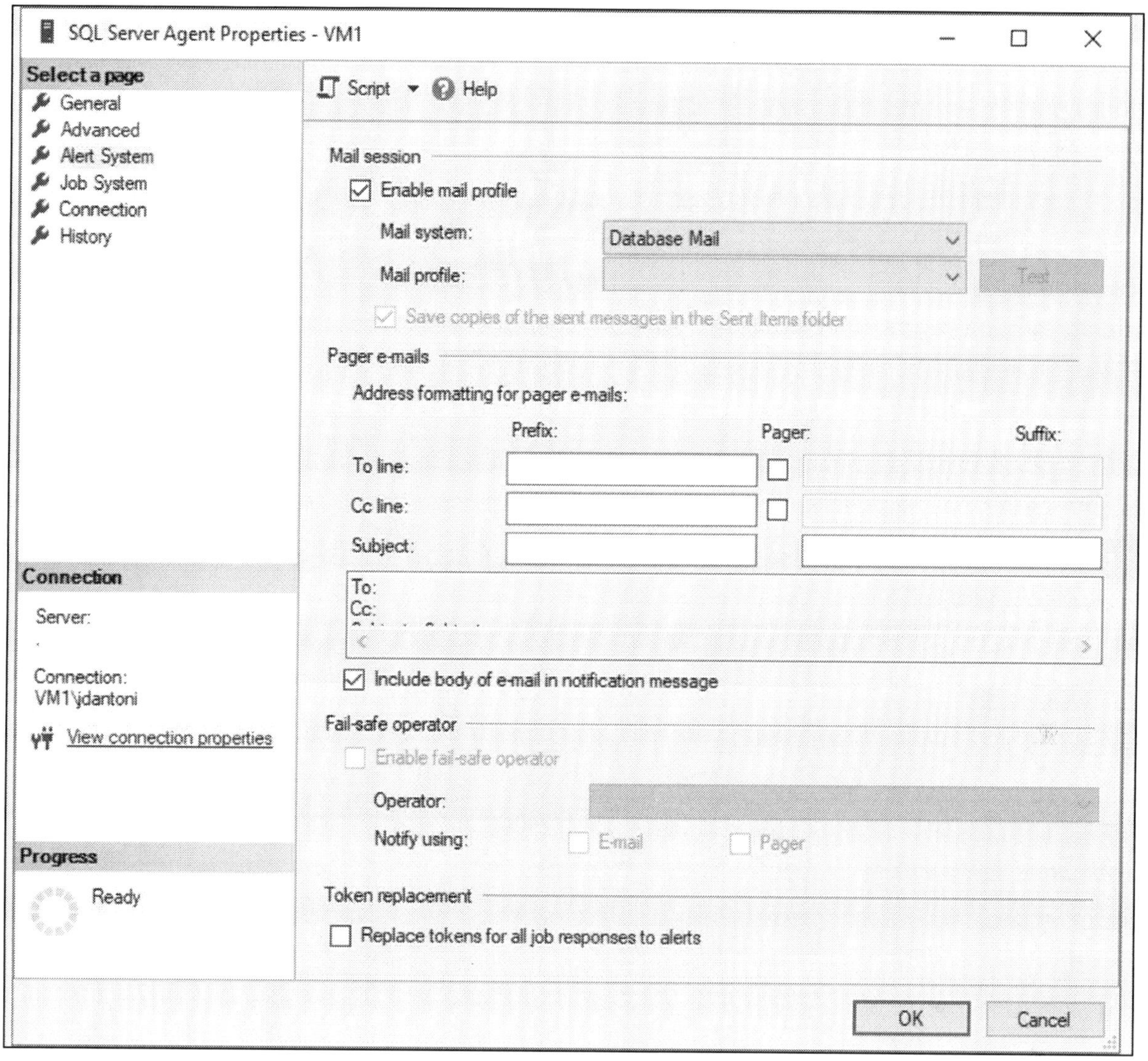

Figure 06-13: Describe Task Status Notifications: Operators

Notifications

You have the visibility of sending a notification on Job completion, failure, or success. Notification of completion is part of the job of each SQL Server Agent. Most DBAs notify on failure only to avoid an entry of notifications for successful jobs. Notifications have a dependency on an operator existing to send a notification as shown below:

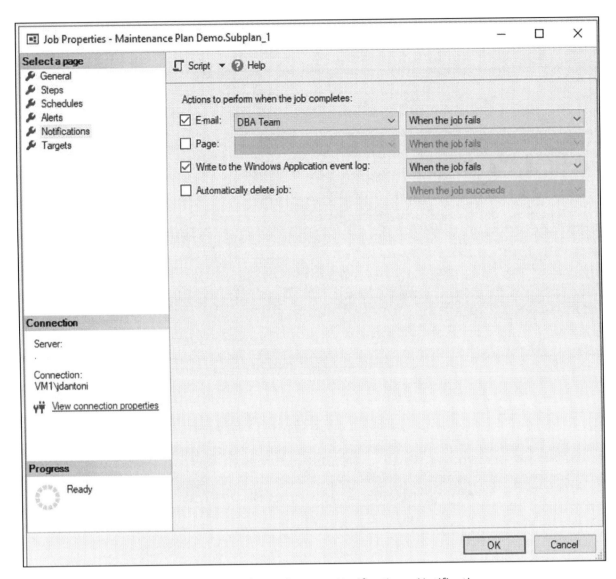

Figure 06-14: Describe Task Status Notifications: Notifications

Alerts

SQL Server Agent alerts let you be proactive with monitoring your SQL Server. The agent reads the SQL Server error log, and when it catches an error number for which an alert has been defined, it informs an operator. In addition to monitoring the SQL Server error log, you can set active alerts to monitor SQL Server Performance conditions, as well as Windows Management Instrumentation (WMI) events. You can identify an alert to be raised in response to one or more events. A common pattern is to increase an alert on all SQL Server errors of level 16 and higher and then add alerts for specific event types related to critical storage errors or Availability Group failover. Another example would be alert on performance conditions such as high CPU utilization or low Page Life Expectancy.

Another common use case for alerts is that DBAs may require to be notified in the event of certain server conditions. For example, if CPU utilization is over 90% for five minutes,

Page Life Expectancy decreases below a certain value. This is achieved by creating performance condition alerts. These conditions are created on the Windows Performance Monitor (perfmon) metrics tracked within the SQL Server database engine. You can spread the screen below by right-clicking **SQL Server Agent** (if it is running) and choosing **New|Alert**.

New Alert
Select a page
General
Response
Options
Script Help
Name: Low PLE Enable
Type: SQL Server performance condition alert
Performance condition alert definition
Object:
Buffer Node
Counter:
Page life expectancy
Instance:
000
Alert if counter
falls below Value: 3000
Connection
Server:
.
Connection:
DCAC\joey
View connection properties
Progress
Ready
OK Cancel

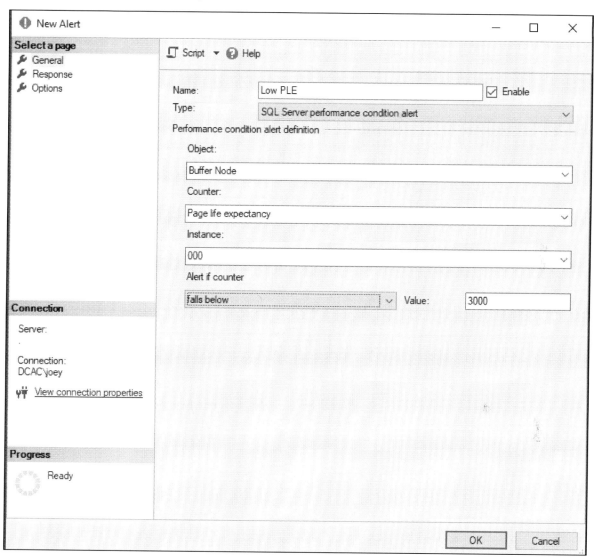

Figure 06-15: Describe Task Status Notifications: Alerts

You have options for responding to the performance condition — you can inform an operator via email, which is the most common approach, or you can implement another SQL Server Agent job, which could resolve the problem. Implementing another SQL Server Agent job is usually used when the condition is well-known and easily handled without manual intervention. A good example would be to generate an alert for SQL Server storage error conditions (errors 823, 824, 825) and then execute a job to achieve a database consistency check. The notifications for these alerts use the same SQL Server Agent subsystem.

Describe Extended Events

Extended events are a lightweight diagnostic system built into SQL Server and Azure SQL Database and managed instances. Extended events let you gather additional information about the internal operations of your databases. Historically, DBAs used a tool called Profiler to trace inbound queries and gather execution plans to identify problematic queries and their execution plans. Extended events form on the functionality of SQL Server Profiler by letting you trace queries and expose additional data (events) that you can monitor. Some examples of issues with Extended Events include:

- Troubleshooting blocking and deadlocking performance issues
- Identifying long-running queries
- Monitoring Data Definition Language (DDL) operations
- Logging missing column statistics
- Observing Memory Pressure in your database
- Long-running physical I/O operations

The extended event framework also lets you use filters to bind the amount of data you collect to decrease data collection overhead and effortlessly identify your performance problem by targeting your focus onto specific areas.

What can I Monitor with Extended Events?

Extended events cover the full surface area of SQL Server and are separated into four channels, which define the audience of an event.

- **Admin** - Admin events are targeted at end-users and administrators. These events indicate a problem within a well-defined set of actions, and these actions can be taen by an administrator. An example of this is the generation of an XML deadlock report to help recognize the root cause of the deadlock
- **Operational** - Operational events are used for investigation and diagnostics or common problems. These events can be used to trigger an action or task based on an occurrence of the event. An example of an operational event would be a database in an availability group changing state, indicating a failover
- **Analytic** - Analytic events are related to performance events and are issued in high volume. Tracing stored procedure or query execution would be an example of an analytic event
- **Debug** - Debug events are not essentially fully documented, and you should only use them when troubleshooting in conjunction with Microsoft support

EXAM TIP: Events are added to sessions that can host multiple events. Typically multiple events are grouped in a session to lock a related set of information.

Create an Extended Events Session

Here you will get the basic process of creating an Extended Events session using the New Session dialog from SQL Server Management Studio. You can get to this screen by expanding the Management node in SSMS, expanding the Extended Events node, right-clicking on Sessions, and choosing New Session.

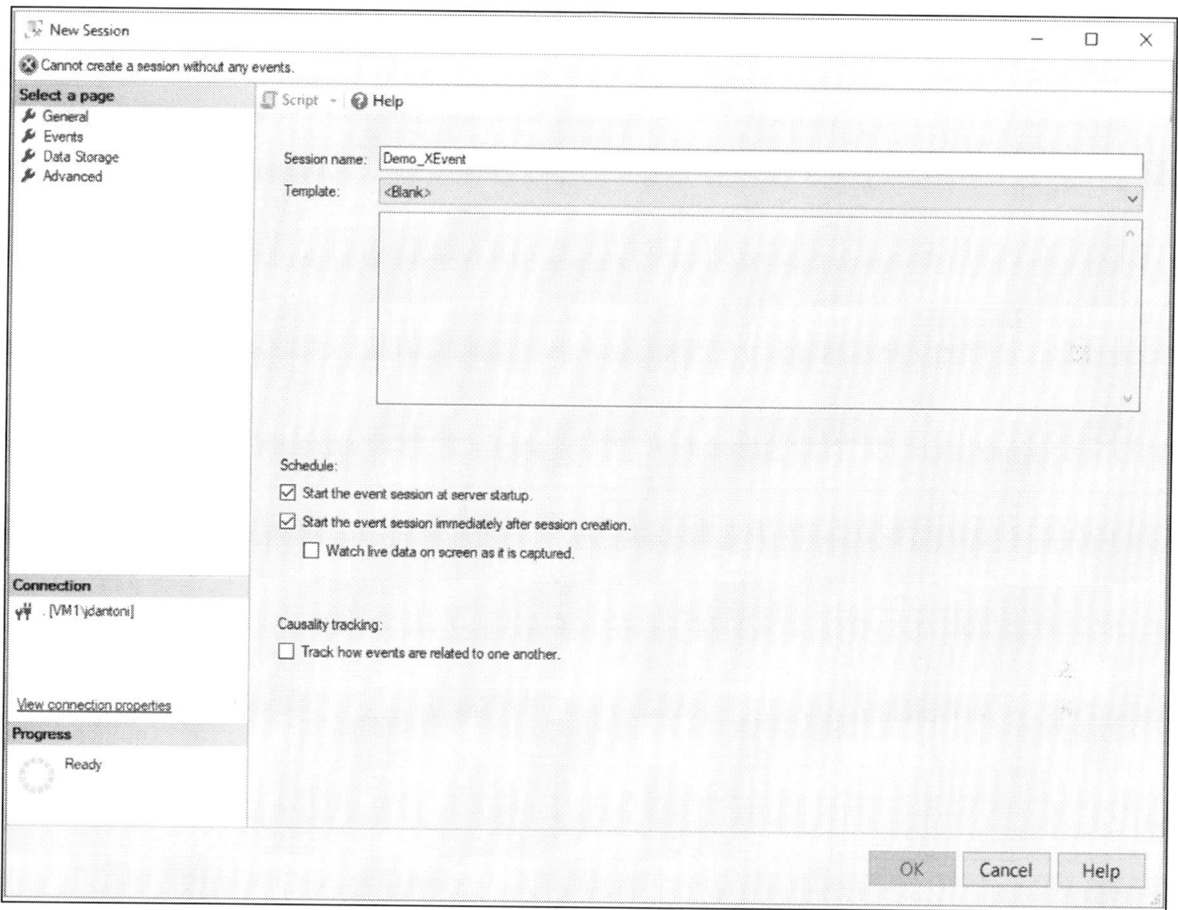

Figure 06-16: Create an Extended Events Session

The image above displays the first creation screen in the new Extended Events session. You should first name the session. SQL Server provides many templates, which are grouped into the following categories:

- Locks and Blocks
- Profiler Equivalents
- Query Execution
- System Monitoring

These predefined templates can get you started with using Extended Events for quick monitoring. In this example, you will understand how events, can be manually added to the session and walk through all of the provided options. You have a couple of check box options for when to start this session. You can select to start your new session whenever the server starts, and you can also pick to start the session as soon as it has been created. The administrator can start and stop event sessions through the Extended Events node in SQL Server Management Studio. You also have the option of allowing causality tracking, which adds a globally unique identifier (GUID) and sequence number to the output of each event, which lets you step through the order that the events occurred easily.

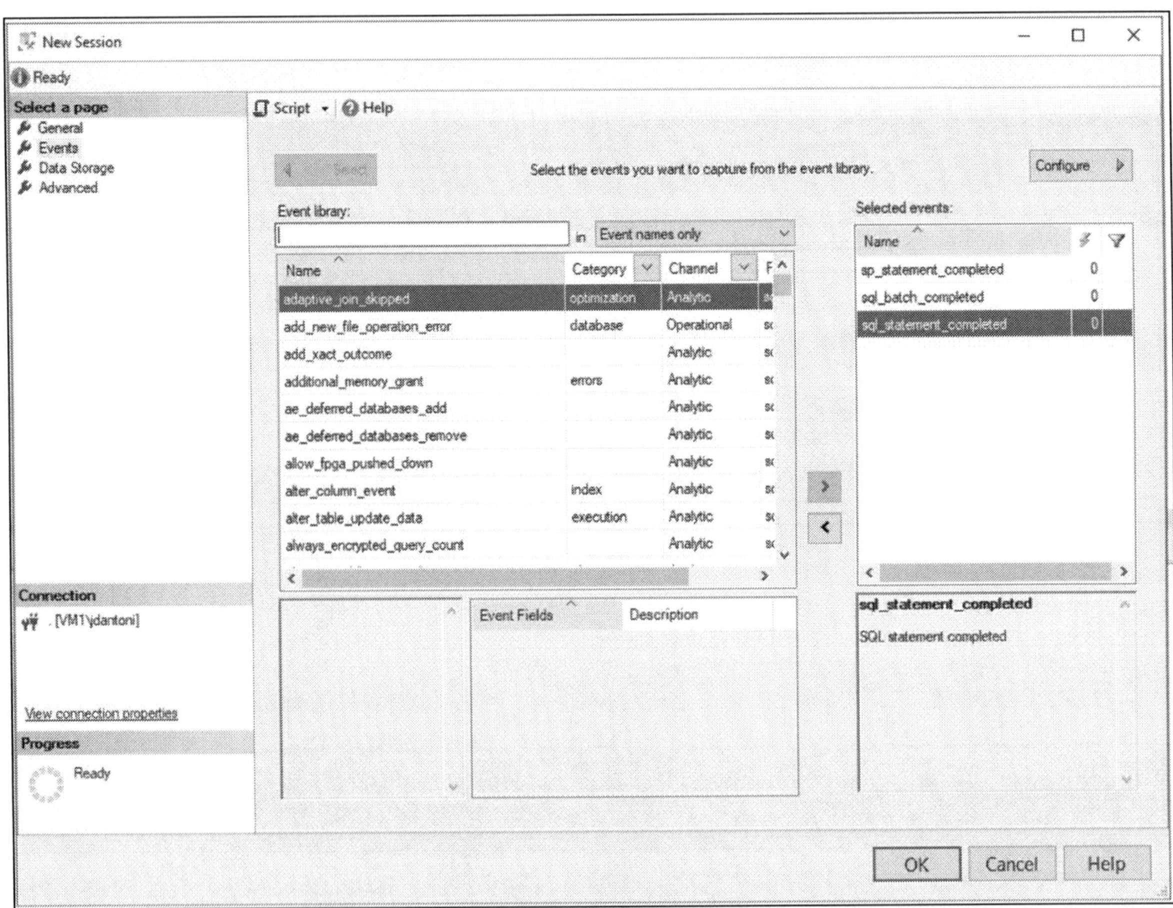

Figure 06-17: Create an Extended Events Session: Events

The image above shows the screen where you add the events to your session. An event signifies a point of interest within the database engine code — these can denote purely internal system operations or be associated with user actions like query execution. In the above example, three events (sp_statement_completed, sql_batch_completed, sql_statement_completed) have been added to the event session. By default, this session would capture all instances of these events taking place on your instance. You can limit collection by checking the configure button.

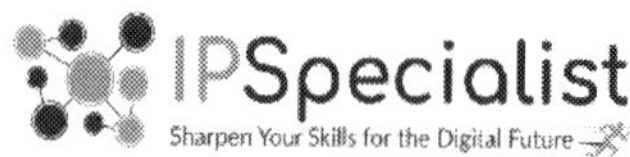

Event configuration options:

Global Fields (Actions) | Filter (Predicate) | Event Fields

Name	Description
callstack	Collect the current call stack
client_app_na...	Collect client application name
client_connec...	Collects the optional identifier provided at conne...
client_hostna...	Collect client hostname
client_pid	Collect client process ID
collect_cpu_c...	Collect the current CPU's cycle count
collect_curren...	Collect the current Windows thread ID
collect_syste...	Collect the current system time with 100 microse...
compile_plan...	Collect compiled plan guid. Use this to uniquely i...
context_info	Collect the same value as the CONTEXT_INFO(...
cpu_id	Collect current CPU ID
create_dump...	Create mini dump including all threads
create_dump...	Create mini dump for the current thread
database_id	Collect database ID
database_name	Collect current database name
datapool_ddl_...	Collect guid datapool DDL query
debug_break	Break the process in the default debugger
distributed_pl...	Collect distributed plan step

Figure 06-18: Event Configuration Options

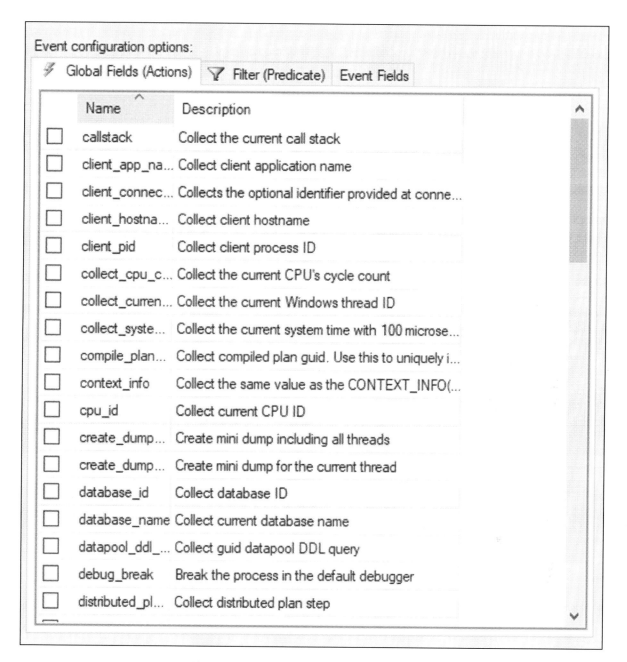

The event configuration screen lets for define what data you are collecting as it relates to your events. Global fields let you choose the data you are gathering when your event occurs. Global fields are also known as actions, as the action is to add additional data fields to the event. These fields signify the data collected when the extended event occurs and are common across most extended events. The image below shows the Filter options for an extended event.

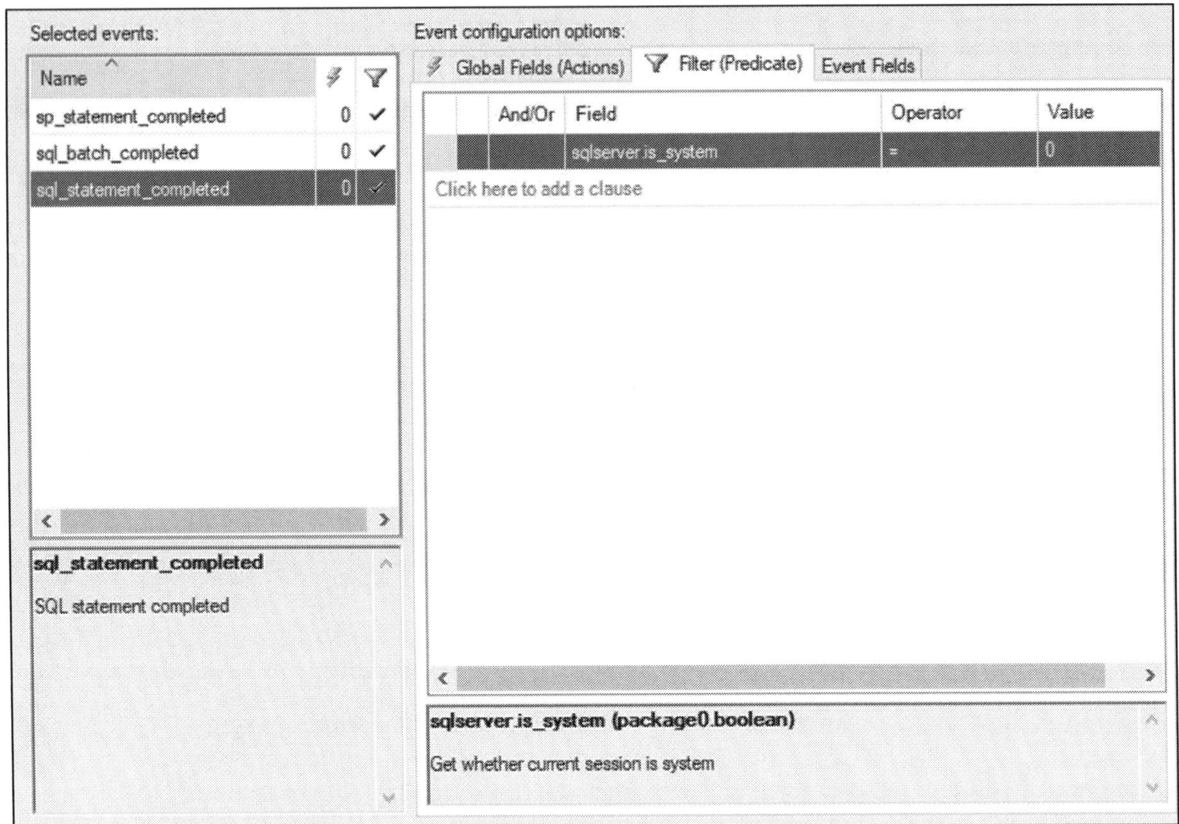

Figure 06-19: Filter Options

Filters are a dominant feature of Extended Events that lets you use granular control to capture only the specific occurrences of the event you need to capture. In this example, you can see that filter is being applied on the field sqlserver.is_system where it is equal to zero, which shows that the query is not an internal operation. In other words, the session will not capture the end of statements submitted by system connections. You only want to capture statements submitted by users or user applications.

Filters apply to a single field on a single event. If you need to make sure that you are not tracing system activities for any events, you will make a separate filter for each: for the sql_statement_completed event (shown), for the sql_batch_completed event, and for the sp_statement_completed event (which is a statement run inside a stored procedure).

It is recommended that you organize a filter for each event that you are capturing. This helps recover the efficiency of data collection and lets you narrow the focus of your search.

The image below shows the event fields that are collected. These are precise to the event being triggered and can include optional fields for collection. In the above event, you can see the collection options are statement and parameterized_plan_handle. In this example, the statement field has been chosen for the collection.

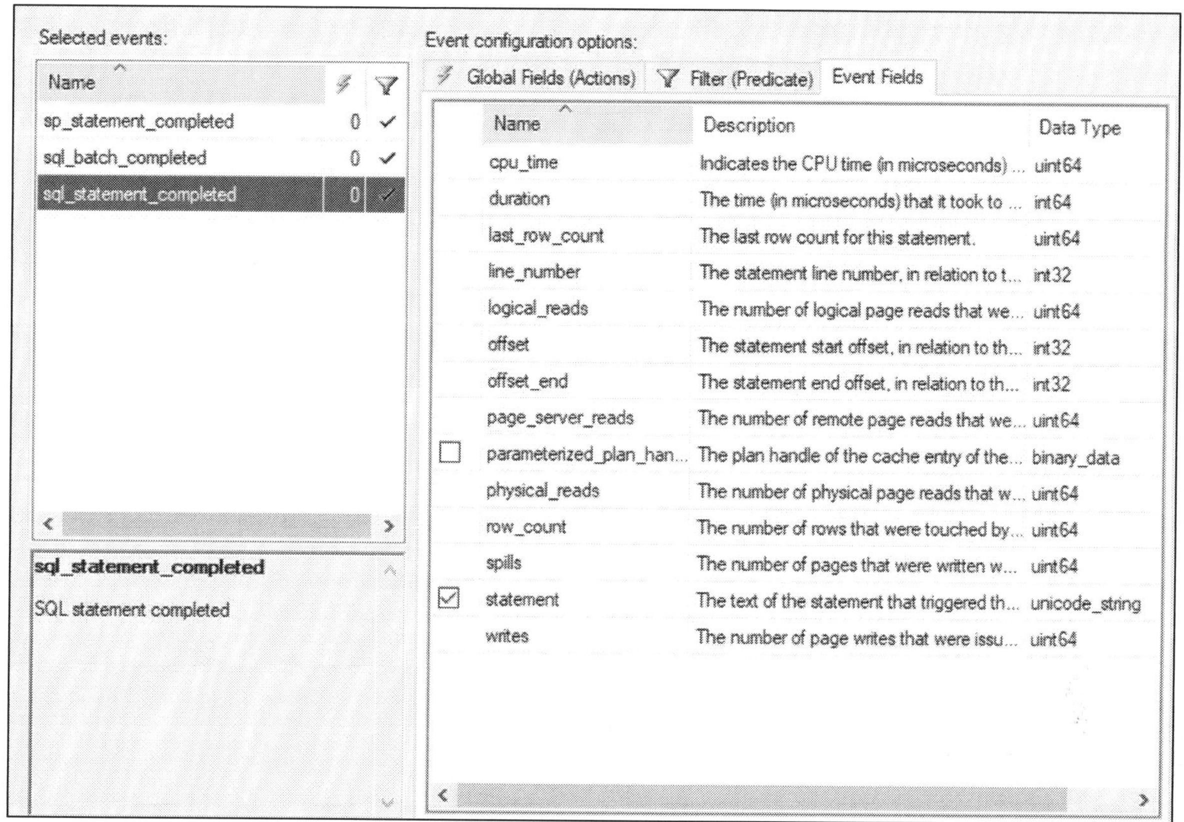

Figure 06-20: Events Fields

Once you have defined an event session, you will describe a storage target, as shown in the image below.

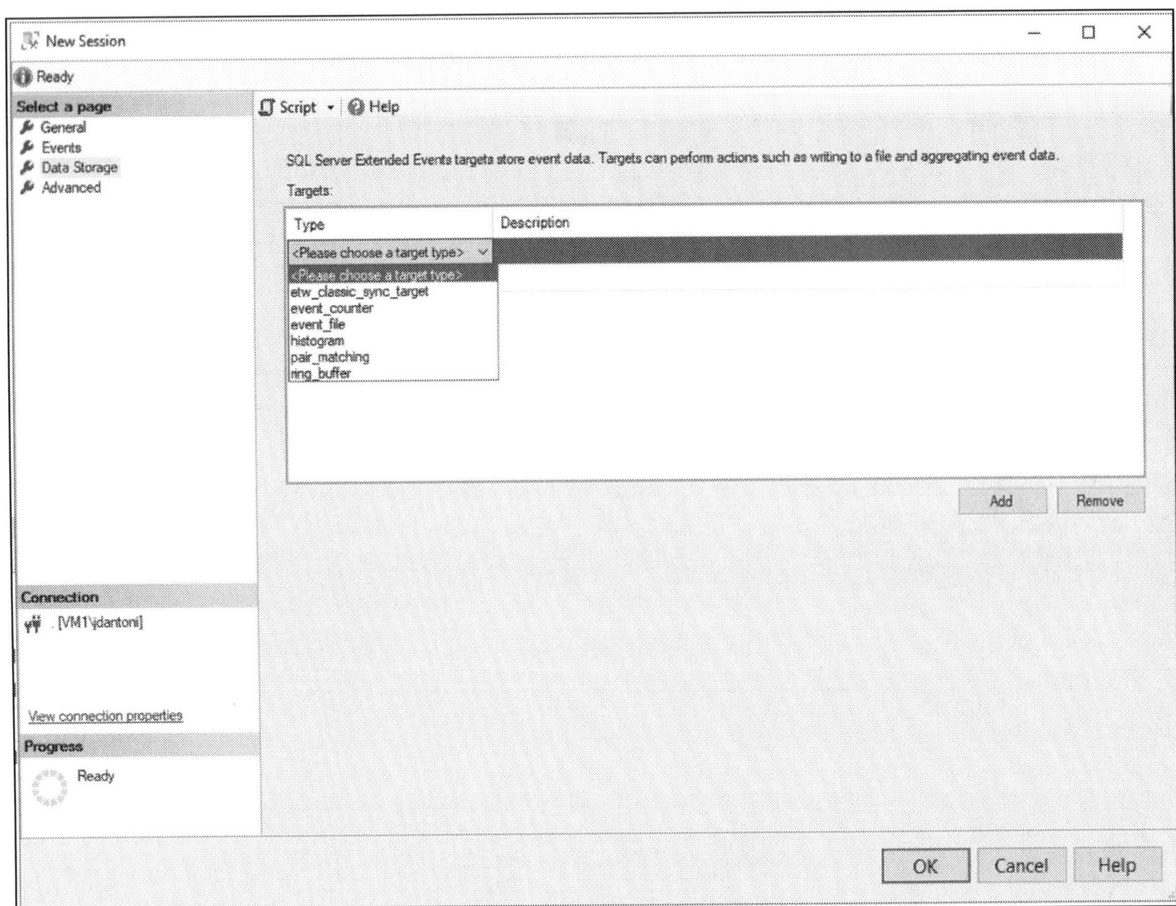

Figure 06-21: Storage Target

An extended event session has a target — a target can only be thought of as a place for the engine to record an event's occurrences. Two of the more common targets are *the event* file on the file system that can use events (the size and the number of files are configurable to control runaway growth). In Azure SQL PaaS offerings, this data is written to blob storage. Another common target is the *ring buffer* which is within SQL Server's memory. The *ring buffer* is usually used for live observation of an event session, as it is a circular buffer, and data does not persevere beyond a session. Most targets process data asynchronously, which means that the event data is written to memory before being persisted to disk. The exception is the Event Tracing for Windows target (ETW) and Event Counter targets handled synchronously.

The following table contains information and uses for each type of Extended Events target:

TABLE 1		
Target	**Description**	**Processing**
Event Counter	Counts all events that happened during an Extended Event session. This is used to get information about	Synchronous

	workload characteristics without the overhead of a full event collection.	
Event File	Writes event session output from memory onto a persistent file on disk.	Asynchronous
Event Pairing	Many events commonly occur in pairs (e.g., lock acquire, lock release), and this collection can classify when those events do not occur in a matched set.	Asynchronous
Event Tracing for Windows (ETW)	Used to link SQL Server events with Windows Operating System event data.	Synchronous
Histogram	This is related to the event counter, which counts the occurrences of an event. The difference is that the histogram can count based on a specific event column or action.	Asynchronous
Ring Buffer	Used to hold data in memory. Data is not persisted to disk and maybe often flushed from the buffer	Asynchronous

Table 06-01: Information and Uses for Each Type of Extended Events Target

Creating Extended Events Sessions with T-SQL

There are two options for forming an Extended Event session. You can make it programmatically using T-SQL or use the GUI in SQL Server Management Studio. However, using T-SQL to set up event sessions is repeated and should be part of automation routines. The T-SQL for a sample event session is shown below:

```
IF EXISTS (SELECT * FROM sys.server_event_sessions WHERE name='test_session')
 DROP EVENT session test_session ON SERVER;
GO
CREATE EVENT SESSION test_session
ON SERVER
 ADD EVENT sqlos.async_io_requested,
 ADD EVENT sqlserver.lock_acquired
 ADD TARGET package0.etw_classic_sync_target
 (SET default_etw_session_logfile_path = N'C:\demo\traces\sqletw.etl' )
 WITH (MAX_MEMORY=4MB, MAX_EVENT_SIZE=4MB);
GO
```

Figure 06-22: Creating Extended Events Sessions with T-SQL

Event sessions can be scoped to a server or a database. You add two events in the example shown above and practice the Event Tracing for Windows (ETW) path with a file location. After you form the session, you will have to start it. You can do this using T-SQL and ALTER the session using the STATE option or enable the Extended Events | Session node in SQL Server Management Studio. You can also have the session enabled at server startup, common for lightweight event sessions that monitor over time.

Manage Azure PaaS Resources using Automated Methods

You have learned about some of the competencies of the SQL Server Agent. However, suppose you are using Azure SQL Database or Azure Database for MariaDB/MySQL/PostgreSQL. In which case, you will require an alternative scheduling mechanism, as both the msdb database and the SQL Server agent are unavailable.

Implement Azure Policy

Group Policies, or GPOs, have been used by Windows server administrators for a long time to manage security and provide consistency across your organization's Windows Server environment. Some group policies include applying password complexity, mapping shared network drives, and configuring networked printers.

Azure provides similar features in Azure Resource Manager using Azure policy. A policy offers a level of governance over your Azure subscriptions. The policy can impose rules

and controls over your Azure resources. Examples include limiting the regions you can deploy a resource to, enforcing naming standards, or monitoring resource sizes. Azure offers many example policies that you can use, or you can describe custom policies using JSON.

Policies are allocated to a specific scope: a management group (a group of subscriptions that are managed together), a subscription, a resource group, or even an individual resource. Generally, the policy will be applied at the subscription or resource group level. Individual policies can be grouped using a structure known as initiatives, which are also called policy sets. Policies have a scope of assignment that can be described at the individual resource, the resource group, the subscription, management group (a group of subscriptions managed together), or all of the subscriptions in a given tenant.

Another example of how you should implement Azure Policy is tagging of resources. Azure tags defined below store metadata about Azure resources in key-value pairs and are usually used to highlight environment type (test, QA, or production) or cost center for a given resource. A policy is essential for all resources to have a tag for the environment, and the cost center would create an error and block the deployment of an Azure resource that did not have the required tags.

Use Azure Subscriptions and Tag Azure Resources

Organizations use several subscriptions for numerous reasons, including budget management, security, or isolation of resources. These subscriptions may be handled together in a management group, allowing you to manage policy and compliance across subscriptions. One example of this would be an organization that has both internal and customer-facing resources. The internal resources could be in one subscription and the customer resources in another for easier billing separation and internal resources isolation.

Tags are simply metadata that are used to define your Azure resources better. These tags are stored as key-value pairs and appear in the Azure portal associated with your Azure resources. Since they are associated with the resource, you can filter your commands built on tags using PowerShell or Azure CLI commands. In that sense, you can reflect them like a WHERE clause in a SQL query. A basic example is shown below:

```
$rg=(get-AzResourceGroup)

$rg=($rg|where-object {($_.tags['Use'] -ne 'Internal')}).ResourceGroupName
```

Figure 06-23: Azure Subscriptions and Tag Azure Resources

In this code sample on the second line, you can get that the list of resource groups is filtered by the tag called 'Use' and will return only those resource groups where that tag

does not have a value of 'Internal.' Tags can be utilized in the Azure portal programmatically via PowerShell, Azure CLI, or Azure Resource Manager template deployment. Tags can also be utilized at the subscription, resource group, or individual resource level. In addition, tags can be improved at any time. Azure supports applying up to 15 tags to each Azure resource.

Tags are also involved in Azure billing information, so tagging by the cost center makes it easier for management to break down the Azure charges. Tags are in the overview section of the blade for every Azure Resource. To add tags to a resource using the Azure portal, click tags and enter the key and value for your tag. Click save after you apply the tags to your resources.

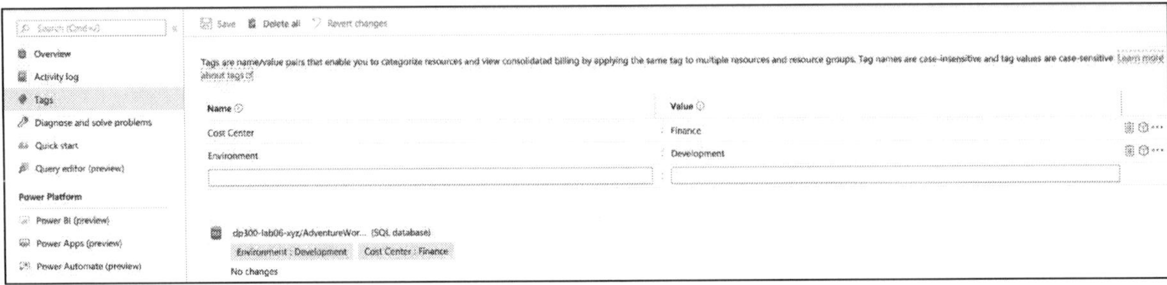

Figure 06-24: Tag Azure Resources

You can also use PowerShell or the CLI to add tags. The PowerShell example is below:

```
$tags = @{"Dept"="Finance"; "Status"="Normal"}

$resource = Get-AzResource -Name demoStorage -ResourceGroup demoGroup

New-AzTag -ResourceId $resource.id -Tag $tags
```

Figure 06-25: Use PowerShell to Add Tags

The Azure CLI example is below:

```
az resource tag --tags 'Dept=IT' 'Environment=Test' -g examplegroup -n examplevnet `

 --resource-type "Microsoft.Network/virtualNetworks"
```

Figure 06-26: Use CLI to Add Tags

Describe Azure Automation

Azure provides numerous ways to automate processes. Azure Functions and Logic Apps are both Azure services that allow serverless workloads. Both services generate workflows that are a collection of steps to run complex tasks. For example, a Logic App

can populate a table in an Azure SQL Database when an entry is made in a SharePoint list. A full description of these services is beyond the scope of this course.

For complete control and granularity of your automation, Azure Automation allows process automation, configuration management, full integration with Azure platform options (such as role-based access control and AAD), and can accomplish Azure and on-premises resources. One of the unique benefits of Azure Automation is that it can manage resources within Azure or on-premises VMs. For example, suppose you have a VM typically kept down for cost savings (except when it needs to be used). In that case, you have the ability within Azure Automation, using a feature called hybrid runbooks, to run a script to start the VM, kick off a SQL Server backup from within the VM, and finally turn off the VM.

Overview of Azure Automation Components

Azure Automation supports both automation and configuration management activities. This module will look at the automation components, but you should be aware that automation can also manage server updates and desired state configuration. The components of automation you will need to use to execute automated tasks are as follows:

Runbooks - Runbooks are the unit of execution in Azure automation. Runbooks can be described as one of three types: a graphical runbook based on PowerShell, a PowerShell script, or a Python script. PowerShell runbooks are usually used to manage Azure SQL resources.

Modules - Azure Automation describes an execution context for the PowerShell or Python code you run in your runbook. To run your code, you need to import the supporting modules. For example, if you want to run the Get-AzSqlDatabase PowerShell cmdlet, you must import the Az.SQL PowerShell module into your automation account.

Credentials - Credentials save sensitive information that runbooks or configurations can use at runtime.

Schedules - Schedules are connected to runbooks and trigger a runbook at a specific time.

Build an Automation Runbook

To build an automation runbook, you have to first generate an automation account. The image below shows this process in the Azure portal after selecting Azure Automation from the Azure Marketplace.

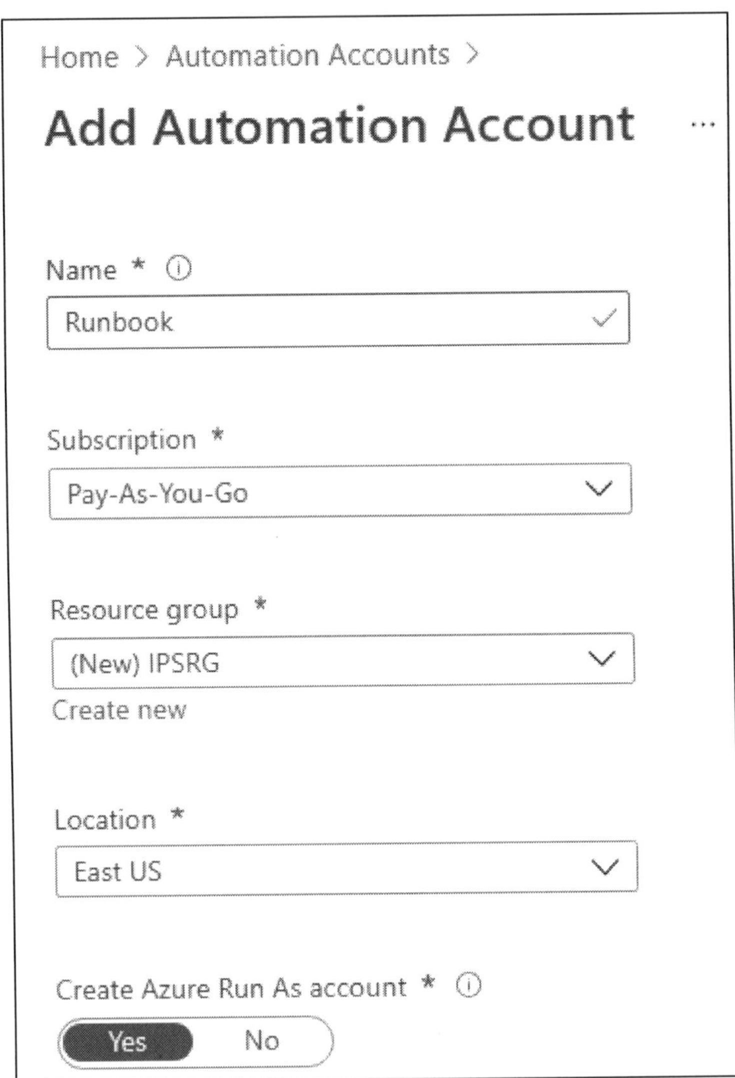

Figure 06-27: Build an Automation Runbook

This procedure can create an Azure Run As account, which produces a service principal in your Azure Active Directory. This service principle offers authentication for Azure Automation to use Azure Resources.

In this example runbook, you will connect to an Azure SQL Database using PowerShell. This means you have to import modules to support those cmdlets. Before you form your runbook, you will import modules into your Azure Automation account. Navigate to the Shared Resources section of the main blade for your automation account and click Modules Gallery to do this import. The first module you will import is **Az. Accounts** as the **Az.SQL** module is dependent on it.

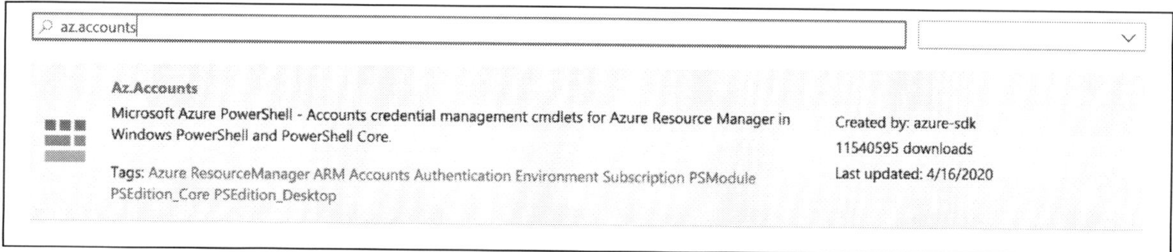

Figure 06-28: Azure Accounts

You will look for the module in the gallery and search for the module you are looking for, as shown in the image above. After you check on the module, you will have the option to import it, as shown in the image below.

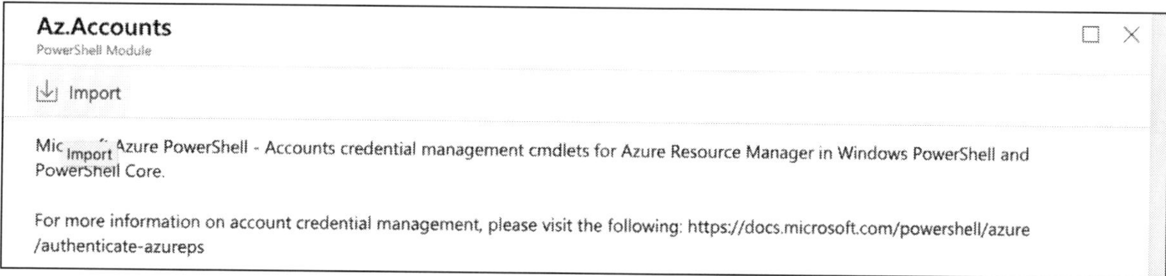

Figure 06-29: Azure Accounts

This will import the module into your account. In this example, the process was repeated for the Az.SQL and SqlServer PowerShell modules.

Next, you can optionally generate a credential that your runbook can use. You can create a credential by clicking on Credentials in the Shared Resources of your automation account, as shown in the image below. You do not have to generate a credential to use Azure Automation, but this example refers to one.

New Credential

Name *

DemoDp300

Description

User name *

sqluser

Password *

••••••••

Confirm password *

••••••••

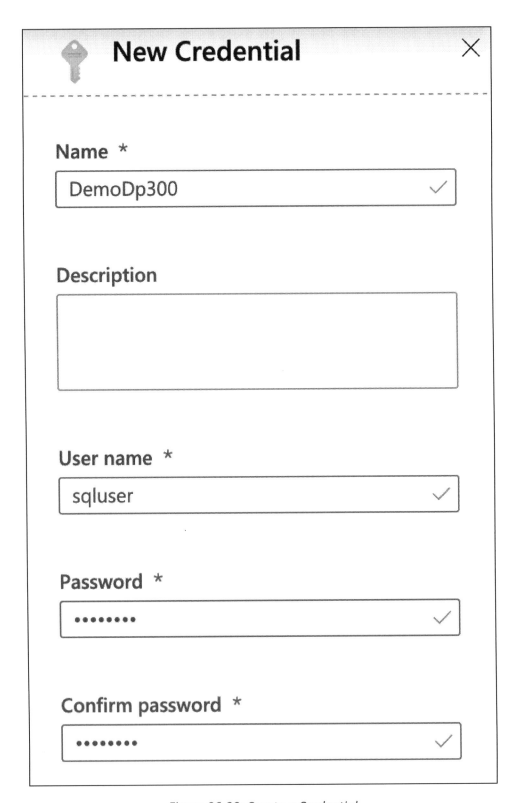

Figure 06-30: Create a Credential

Next, you will form a runbook, navigae to the Process Automation section of the automation blade and click Runbooks. Your account will come with three sample runbooks (one for each type of runbook).

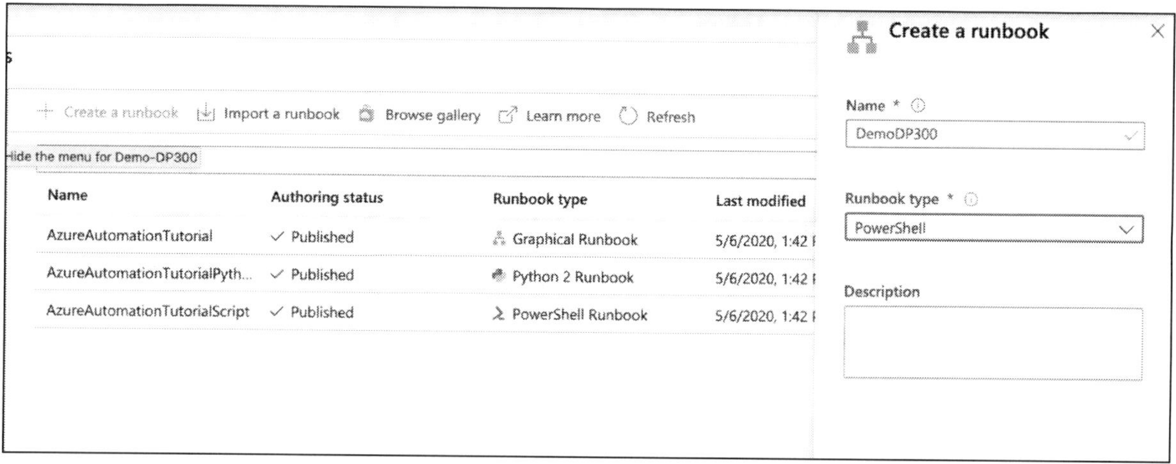

Figure 06-31: Create a Runbook

When creating the runbook, you will give a name, the type of runbook, and optionally a description. Since this example specified PowerShell as the type, a PowerShell editor opens.

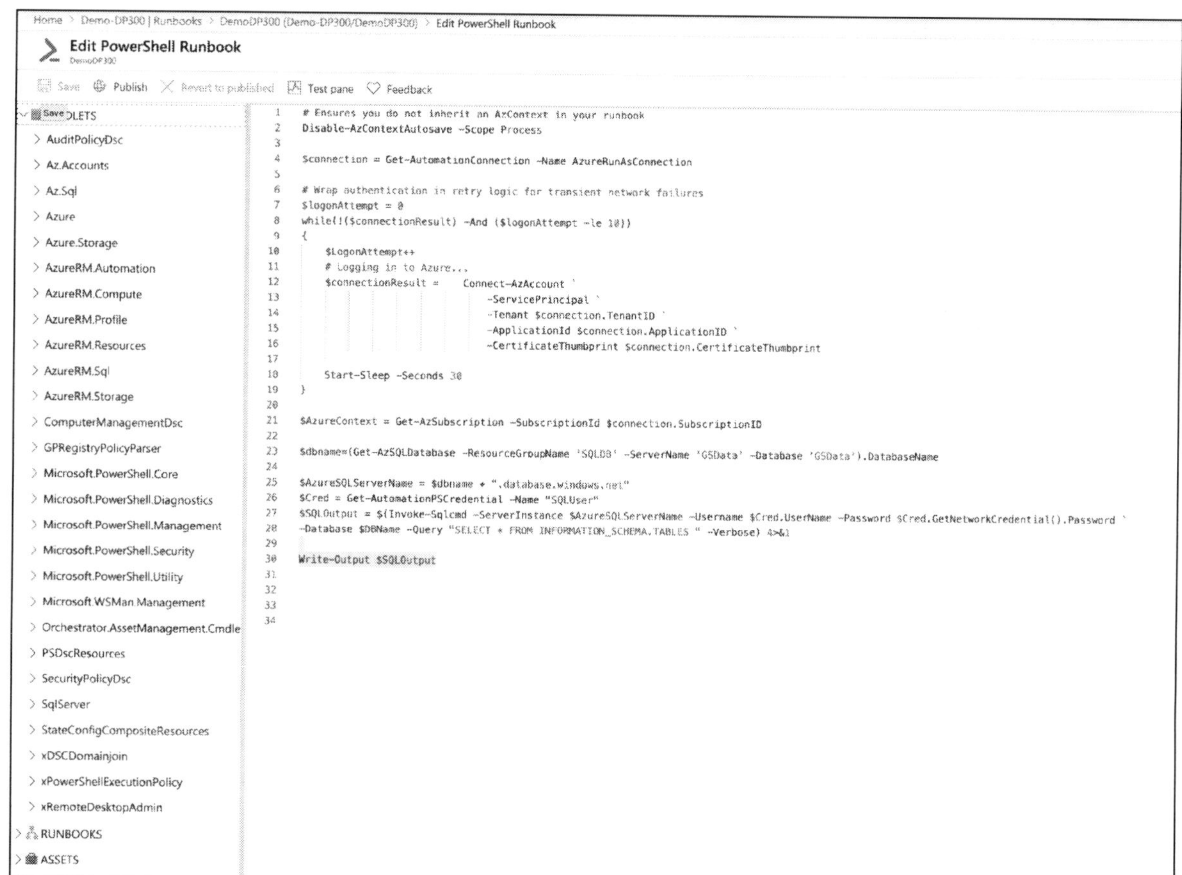

Figure 06-32: PowerShell Editor

The image above shows the edit runbook screen, where you describe the code you are executing. In this example, in lines 1-21, you are executing a series of cmdlets to connect to the Azure account. You get the database name from the Get-AzSQLDatabase cmdlet

and then use the get-AutomationPSCredentail cmdlet to allocate your credential to a variable. Finally, you assign the invoke-sqlcmd cmdlet to run a query against the Azure SQL Database and use the write-output cmdlet to return the query results.

After you have finished your code in the portal, you click on "Test Pane" in the code editor in the Azure portal. This lets you test your code in the context of Azure Automation. A typical development process is to form your PowerShell code locally and then test it within the automation environment. This lets you separate any PowerShell errors from errors generated from the context of automation execution. Always test your code within automation to confirm there are no errors in the code itself.

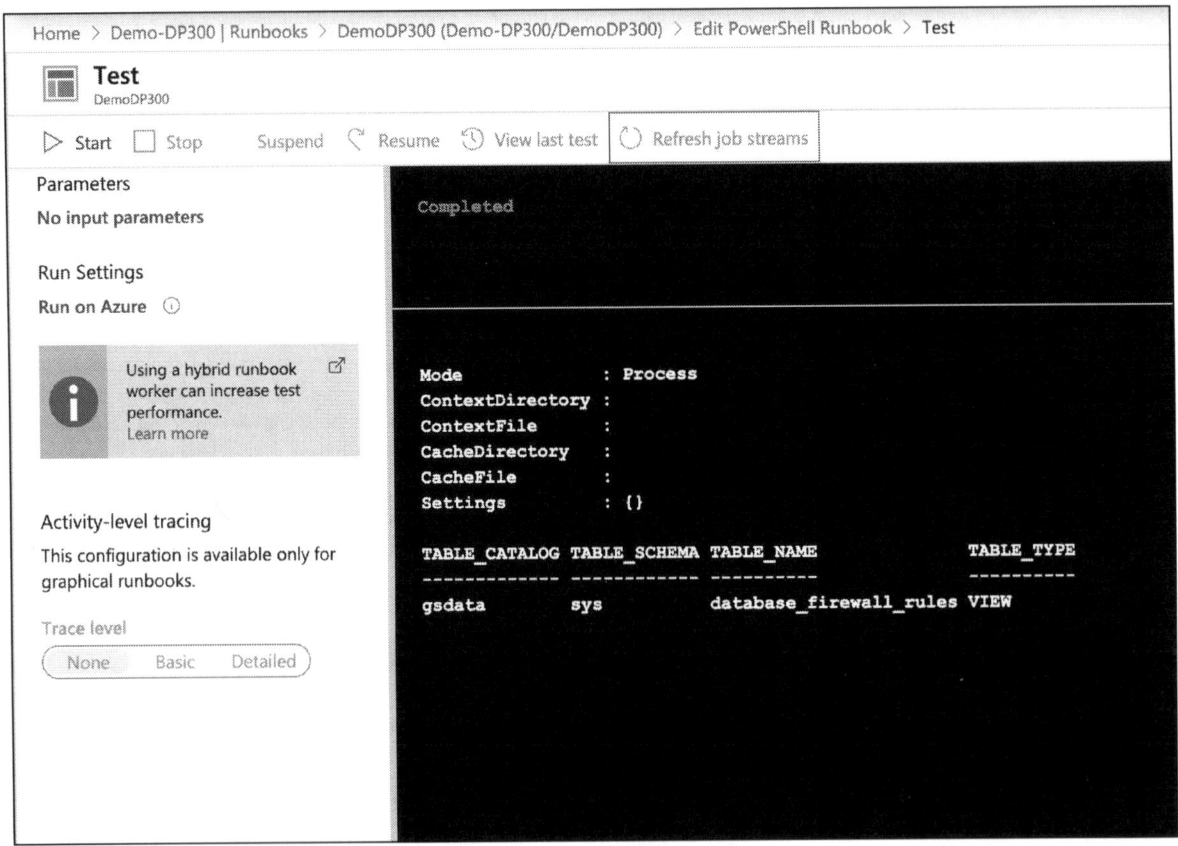

Figure 06-33: Test your Code

The image above displays the results of the completed runbook. Note the informational bubble on the left side of the screen referring to hybrid runbooks. Hybrid runbooks are used when you want to execute cmdlets inside of a virtual machine. You will want a configuration on the virtual machines and in the Azure Automation account. This concept can be unclear, but the easiest way to understand it is to think of Azure resources as boxes that Azure Resource Manager manages. Without a hybrid runbook, you can achieve the state of those boxes, but you cannot use or manage anything within the boxes. Hybrid runbooks provide you the option to control what is inside of the box.

After you have productively tested your runbook, you can then click publish in the runbook editor screen. A runbook should be published to be executed by the service. After you have published the runbook, you can generate a schedule by clicking on schedules in the Shared Resources section of the automation account blade.

New Schedule

Name *

Runbook Schedule

Description

Starts *

05/06/2020 4:30 PM

Time zone

United States - Eastern Time

Recurrence

Once Recurring

Recur every *

1 Day

Set expiration

Yes No

Expires

Never

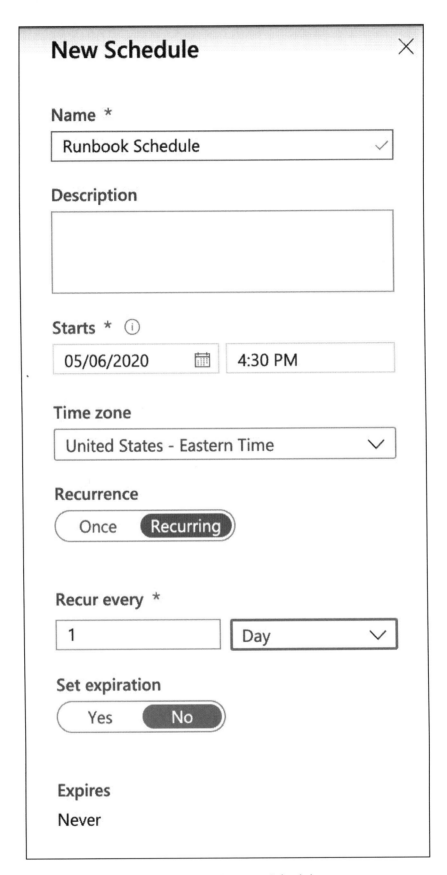

Figure 06-34: Create a Schedule

The image above displays the creation process for a new schedule. The default settings are there to make sure there is no recurrence of the job. In the above example, the job has been configured to run once daily at 4:30 pm Eastern Time. Once you have produced a schedule, you can connect it to a runbook by navigating back to the runbook and clicking link to the schedule on the runbook page, as shown in the image below.

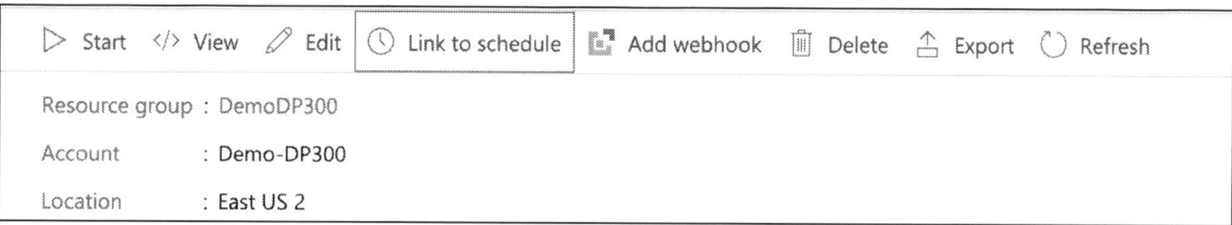

Figure 06-35: Link Schedule to a Runbook

Configuration Management

Azure Automation also supports using PowerShell Desired State Configuration (DSC) to manage variations in configuration across VMs in your environment. DSC works as an extension to VMs and provides a consistent configuration state across all VMs that the configuration is applied to. Azure Automation integrates with DSC, automatically updating configuration across physical and virtual machines and reporting capabilities.

Describe Elastic Jobs in the Azure SQL database

One of the reasons many DBAs became so aware of Azure automation is that Azure SQL Database initially lacked capabilities for scheduled jobs. The introduction of elastic jobs lets you run a set of T-SQL scripts against a collection of servers or databases as a one-time job or by using a defined schedule. Elastic jobs work similar to SQL Server Agent jobs, except that they are limited to executing T-SQL. The jobs work across all tiers of Azure SQL Database (excluding managed instance, which has a SQL Server Agent). To form Elastic Jobs, you require a Job Agent and database dedicated to managing your jobs. The agent is free, but the database is required to be a paid database. The recommended service tier is S1 or higher, and the optimum service tier will be dependent on the number of jobs you are executing and the frequency of those jobs.

You must describe a target group in elastic jobs consisting of a SQL Database server, an elastic pool, or one or more single databases. Suppose a server or elastic pool is the target; in that case, a credential within the master database of the server or pool must be created so that the job agent can count the databases within. For a single database, a database credential is all that is needed. The execution of T-SQL scripts by elastic jobs must be idempotent. If the job is run multiple times, whether accidentally or because of job failure, the job would not fail or produce unintended results. You will be able to run the same script multiple times without failure.

Lab 06-01: Deploy an Azure SQL Database using an Azure Resource Manager Template

Introduction

Azure Resource Manager Templates allow you to describe your infrastructure as code and set up your solutions to the Azure cloud for Azure SQL Database and Azure SQL Managed Instance.

Problem

You have been promoted as a Senior Data Engineer to help in the day-to-day operations of database administration. This automation is to make sure that the databases continue to work at peak performance and provide methods for alerting based on certain criteria.

Solution

Azure SQL Database is one such offering. This solution must integrate closely with Azure services and require as little hands-on maintenance as possible, letting your team focus on other tasks. Performing the actions of this lab will help you become aware of how to provision an Azure SQL database.

Step 01: Deploy an Azure SQL Database

1. In the virtual machine, open the "**Microsoft Edge**" browser, and on the https://portal.azure.com page, sign in to Microsoft Azure using the Azure portal username and password.

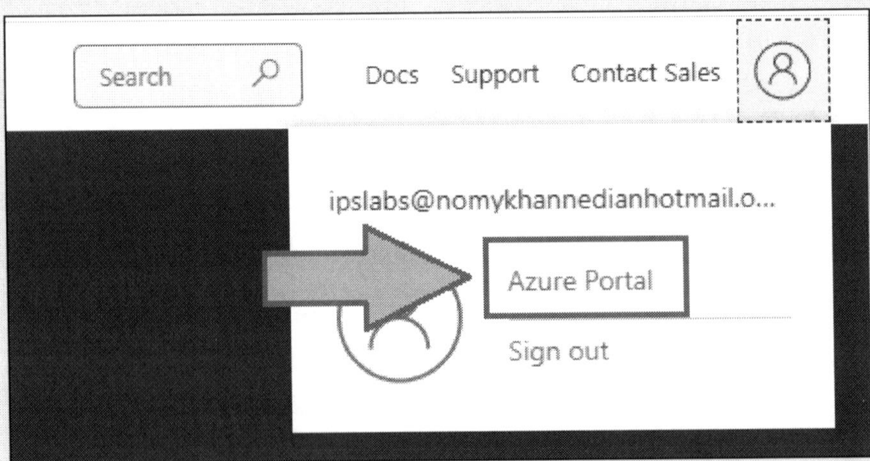

2. In Microsoft Edge, open a new tab and navigate to the following path in a GitHub repository containing an ARM template to deploy a SQL Database resource.

https://github.com/Azure/azure-quickstart-templates/tree/master/quickstarts/microsoft.sql/sql-database

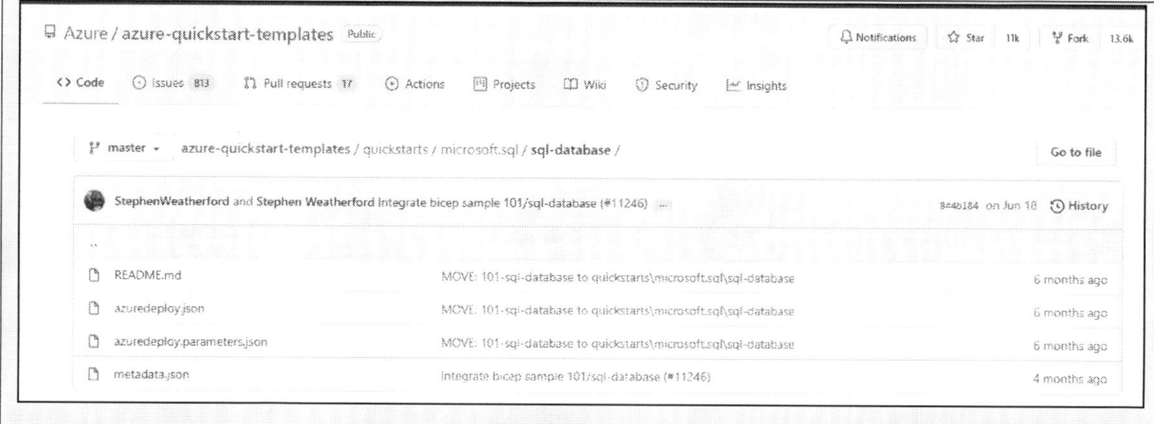

3. Right-click "**azuredeploy.json**" and choose "**Open link in the New Tab to View the ARM Template**," which should look similar.

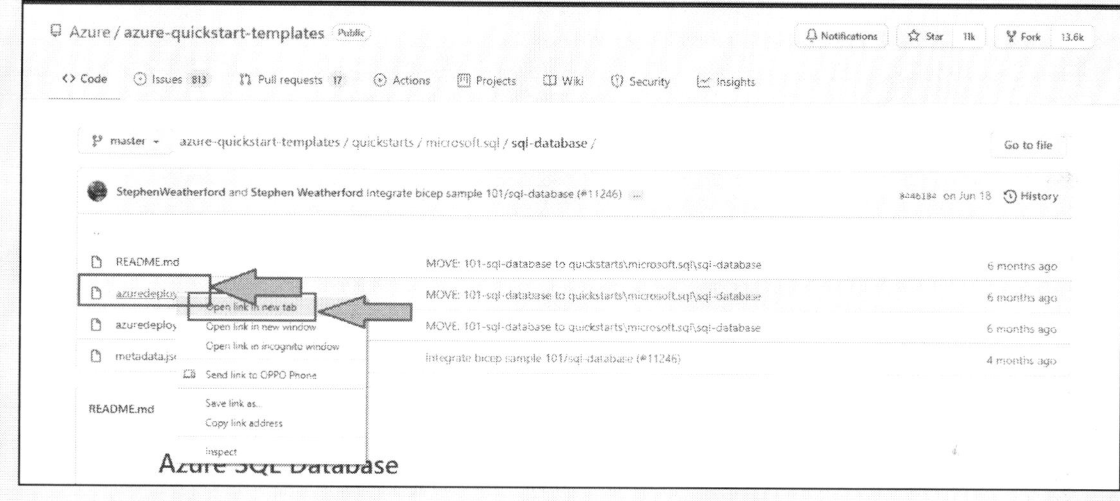


```
{
"$schema":                "https://schema.management.azure.com/schemas/2019-04-01/deploymentTemplate.json#",
"contentVersion": "1.0.0.0",
"parameters": {
  "serverName": {
  "type": "string",
  "defaultValue": "[uniqueString('sql', resourceGroup().id)]",
  "metadata": {
    "description": "The name of the SQL logical server."
  }
  },
```

```
    "sqlDBName": {
    "type": "string",
    "defaultValue": "SampleDB",
    "metadata": {
       "description": "The name of the SQL Database."
    }
    },
    "location": {
    "type": "string",
    "defaultValue": "[resourceGroup().location]",
    "metadata": {
       "description": "Location for all resources."
    }
    },
    "administratorLogin": {
    "type": "string",
    "metadata": {
       "description": "The administrator username of the SQL logical server."
    }
    },
    "administratorLoginPassword": {
    "type": "securestring",
    "metadata": {
       "description": "The administrator password of the SQL logical server."
    }
    }
},
"variables": {},
"resources": [
```

```
  {
  "type": "Microsoft.Sql/servers",
  "apiVersion": "2020-02-02-preview",
  "name": "[parameters('serverName')]",
  "location": "[parameters('location')]",
  "properties": {
    "administratorLogin": "[parameters('administratorLogin')]",
    "administratorLoginPassword": "[parameters('administratorLoginPassword')]"
  },
  "resources": [
    {
    "type": "databases",
    "apiVersion": "2020-08-01-preview",
    "name": "[parameters('sqlDBName')]",
    "location": "[parameters('location')]",
    "sku": {
      "name": "Standard",
      "tier": "Standard"
    },
    "dependsOn": [
      "[resourceId('Microsoft.Sql/servers', concat(parameters('serverName')))]"
    ]
    }
  ]
  }
]
}
```

```
{
"$schema": "https://schema.management.azure.com/schemas/2019-04-01/deploymentTemplate.json#",
"contentVersion": "1.0.0.0",
"parameters": {
    "serverName": {
    "type": "string",
    "defaultValue": "[uniqueString('sql', resourceGroup().id)]",
    "metadata": {
        "description": "The name of the SQL logical server."
    }
    },
    "sqlDBName": {
    "type": "string",
    "defaultValue": "SampleDB",
    "metadata": {
        "description": "The name of the SQL Database."
    }
    },
    "location": {
    "type": "string",
    "defaultValue": "[resourceGroup().location]",
    "metadata": {
        "description": "Location for all resources."
    }
    },
    "administratorLogin": {
    "type": "string",
    "metadata": {
        "description": "The administrator username of the SQL logical server."
    }
    },
    "administratorLoginPassword": {
    "type": "securestring",
    "metadata": {
        "description": "The administrator password of the SQL logical server."
```

```
        }
        }
},
"variables": {},
"resources": [
    {
    "type": "Microsoft.Sql/servers",
    "apiVersion": "2020-02-02-preview",
    "name": "[parameters('serverName')]",
    "location": "[parameters('location')]",
    "properties": {
        "administratorLogin": "[parameters('administratorLogin')]",
        "administratorLoginPassword": "[parameters('administratorLoginPassword')]"
    },
    "resources": [
        {
        "type": "databases",
        "apiVersion": "2020-08-01-preview",
        "name": "[parameters('sqlDBName')]",
        "location": "[parameters('location')]",
        "sku": {
            "name": "Standard",
            "tier": "Standard"
        },
        "dependsOn": [
            "[resourceId('Microsoft.Sql/servers', concat(parameters('serverName')))]"
        ]
        }
    ]
    }
]
}
```

4. Review the JSON in the ARM template.
5. Close the "**azuredeploy.json**" tab and back to the tab containing the "**sql-database**" GitHub folder.

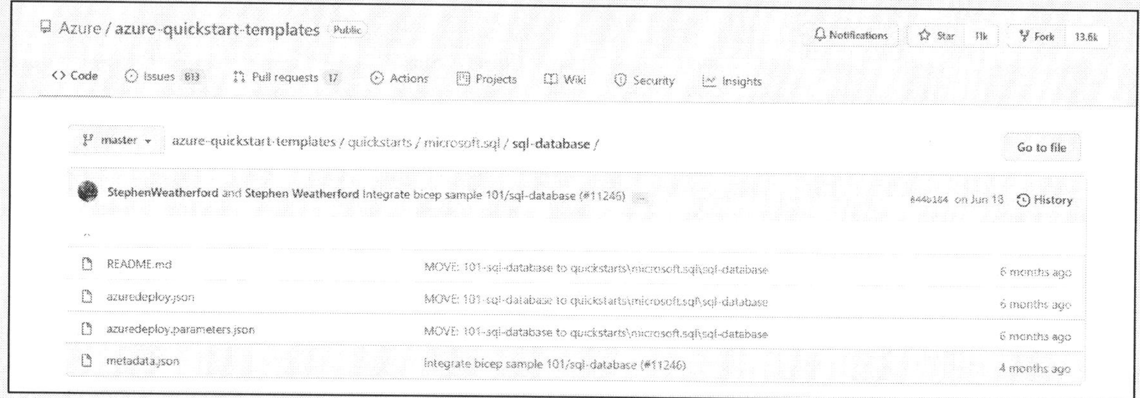

6. On the GitHub web page, scroll down and select "**Deploy to Azure.**"

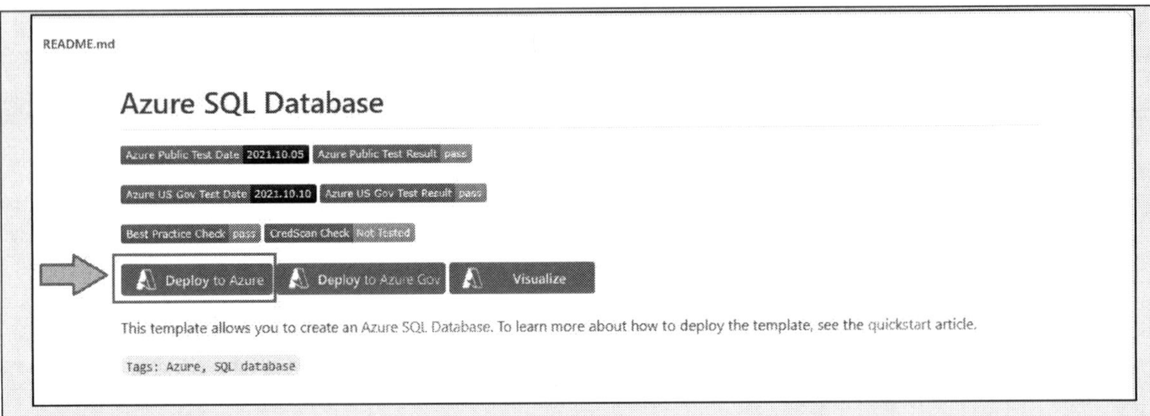

7. The Azure portal will open at the deployment details page for a "**SQL Server and Database**" resource with resource details partially filled in from the ARM template. To deploy this resource, complete the blank fields with this information:
   - Resource group: *Select the existing resource group*
   - Sql Administrator Login: "**ipsadmin**"
   - Sql Administrator Login Password: Enter a strong password

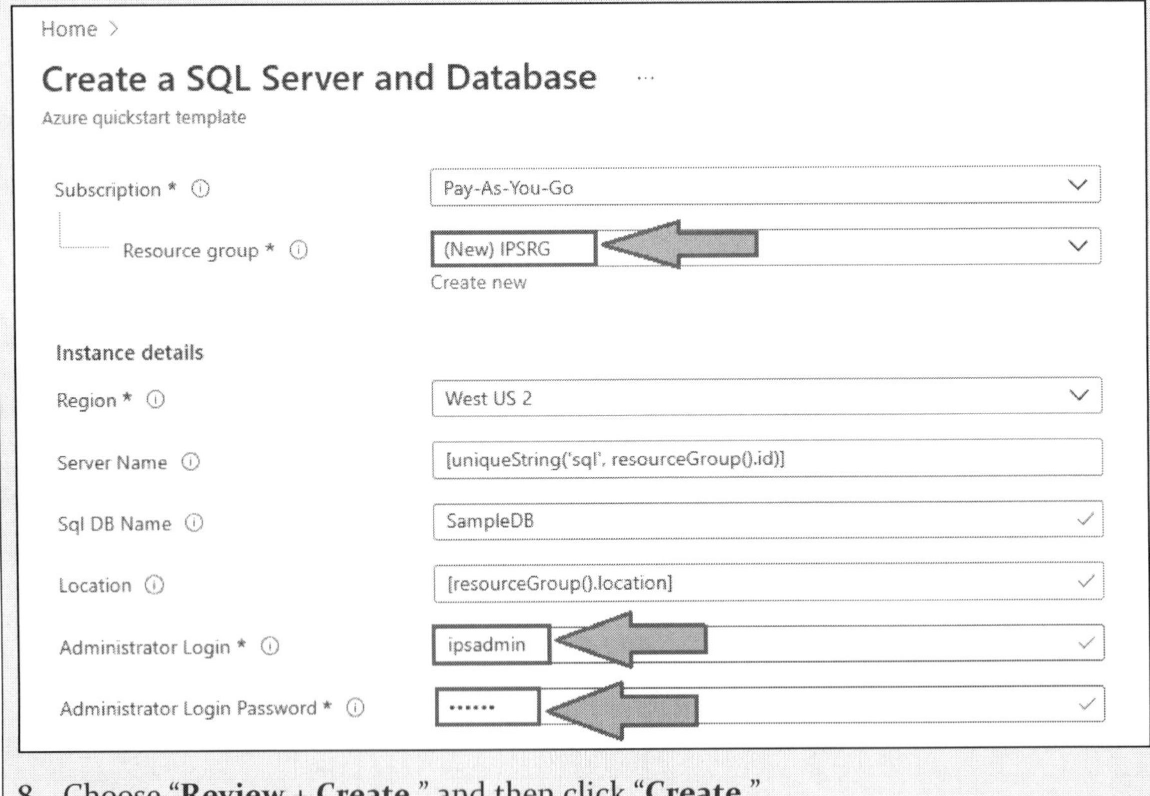

8. Choose "**Review + Create**," and then click "**Create**."

Home >

Create a SQL Server and Database ...

Azure quickstart template

Subscription * Pay-As-You-Go

Resource group * (New) IPSRG

Create new

Instance details

Region * West US 2

Server Name [uniqueString('sql', resourceGroup().id)]

Sql DB Name SampleDB

Location [resourceGroup().location]

Administrator Login * ipsadmin

Administrator Login Password * ••••••

Review + create | Next : Review + create >

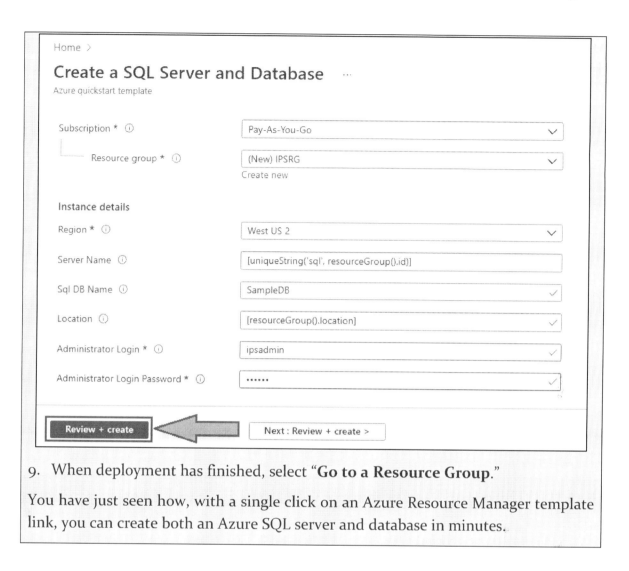

9. When deployment has finished, select "**Go to a Resource Group**."

You have just seen how, with a single click on an Azure Resource Manager template link, you can create both an Azure SQL server and database in minutes.

Step 02: Create a CPU Status Alert for a SQL Server

Create an Alert when a CPU Exceeds an Average of 80 percent

1. Type SQL and select SQL databases in the search bar at the top of the Azure portal. Select the "**SampleDB (km4q0765iiha2/SampleDB)**" database name.

sql

Services See all

SQL databases

SQL servers

SQL elastic pools

SQL managed instances

SQL Server registries

Marketplace See all

SQLstream 6.0.0.1

Azure Synapse Analytics

Azure SQL

SQL Server 2017 Web on SUSE Linux Enterprise Server (SLES) 1...

Documentation See all

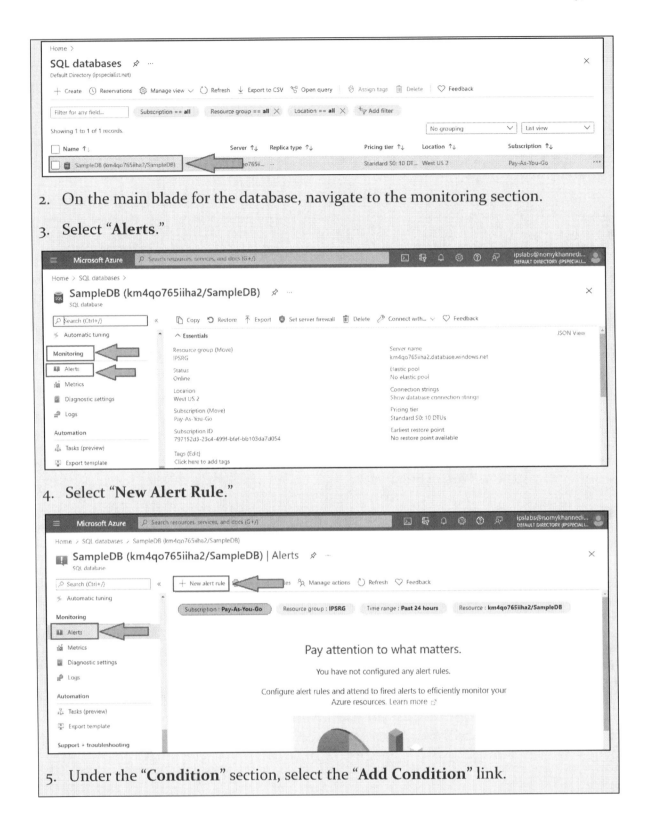

2. On the main blade for the database, navigate to the monitoring section.
3. Select "**Alerts.**"
4. Select "**New Alert Rule.**"
5. Under the "**Condition**" section, select the "**Add Condition**" link.

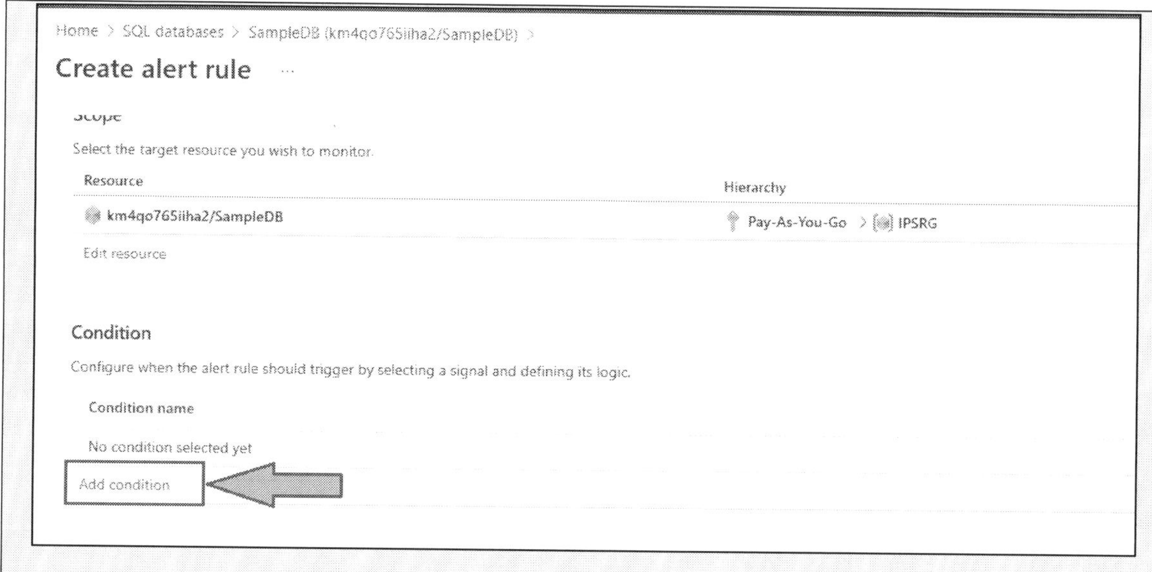

6. In the Configure signal logic slide out, choose "**CPU Percentage**."

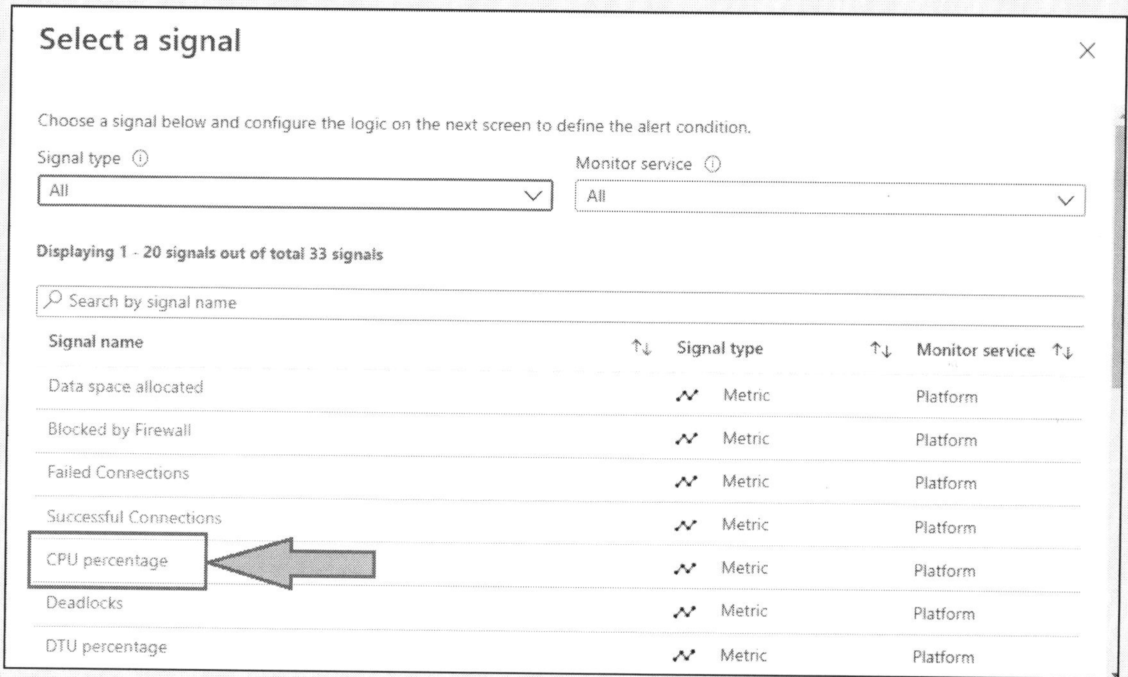

7. Check that the Operator is "**Greater than**" the Aggregation type is "**Average**." Then in the "**Threshold Value,**" enter a value of "**80**." Click on "**Done**."

Configure signal logic

km4qo765iiha2/sampledb
0.05 %

Alert logic

Threshold
Static | Dynamic

Operator: Greater than
Aggregation type *: Average
Threshold value *: 80 %

Condition preview

Whenever the average cpu percentage is greater than 80%

Evaluated based on

Aggregation granularity (Period) *: 5 minutes
Frequency of evaluation: Every 1 Minute

Done

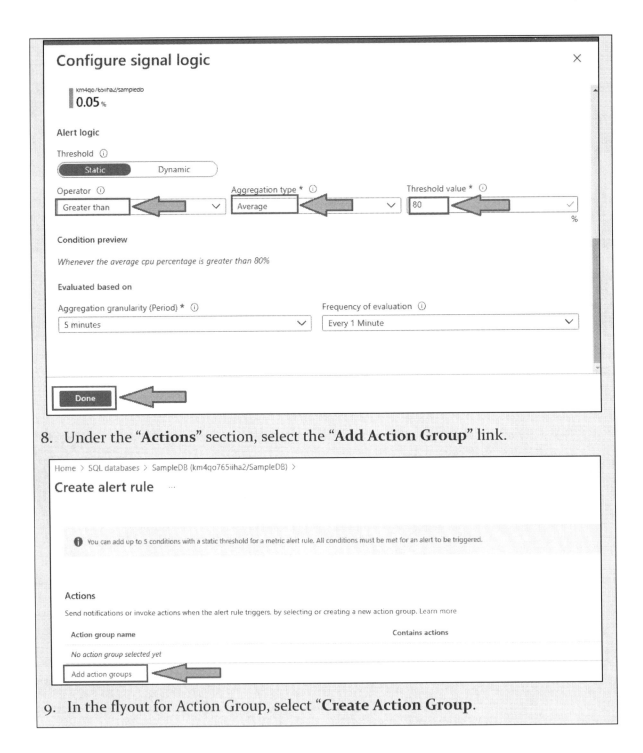

8. Under the "**Actions**" section, select the "**Add Action Group**" link.

Home > SQL databases > SampleDB (km4qo765iiha2/SampleDB) >

Create alert rule ...

You can add up to 5 conditions with a static threshold for a metric alert rule. All conditions must be met for an alert to be triggered.

Actions

Send notifications or invoke actions when the alert rule triggers, by selecting or creating a new action group. Learn more

Action group name	Contains actions
No action group selected yet	

Add action groups

9. In the flyout for Action Group, select "**Create Action Group**.

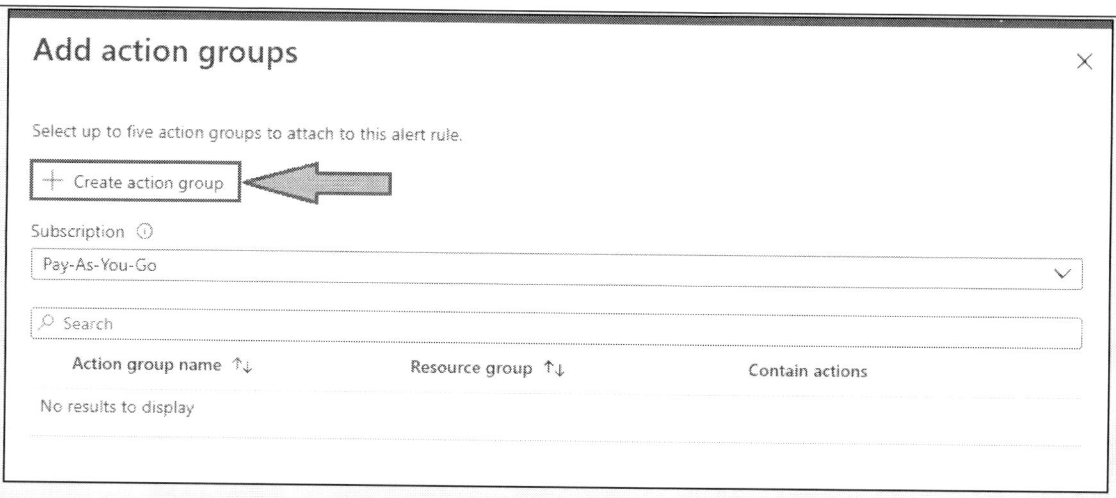

Add action groups

Select up to five action groups to attach to this alert rule.

+ Create action group

Subscription

Pay-As-You-Go

Search

Action group name | Resource group | Contain actions

No results to display

On the Action Group screen, type "**emailgroup**" in the "**Action Group Name**" field.

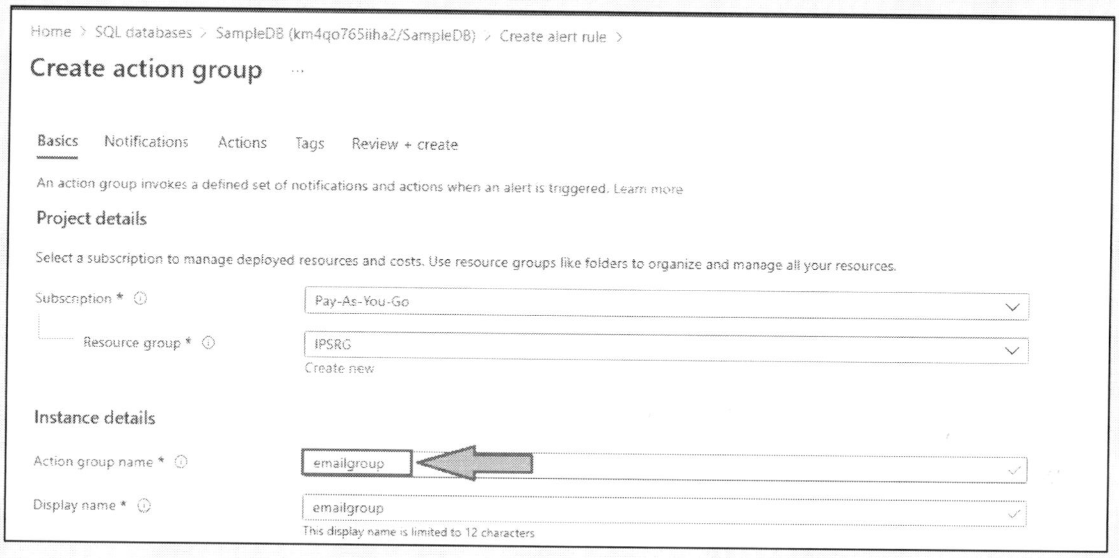

Home > SQL databases > SampleDB (km4qo765iiha2/SampleDB) > Create alert rule >

Create action group

Basics Notifications Actions Tags Review + create

An action group invokes a defined set of notifications and actions when an alert is triggered. Learn more

Project details

Select a subscription to manage deployed resources and costs. Use resource groups like folders to organize and manage all your resources.

Subscription * Pay-As-You-Go

Resource group * IPSRG

Create new

Instance details

Action group name * emailgroup

Display name * emailgroup

This display name is limited to 12 characters

10. Choose "**Next: Notifications**."

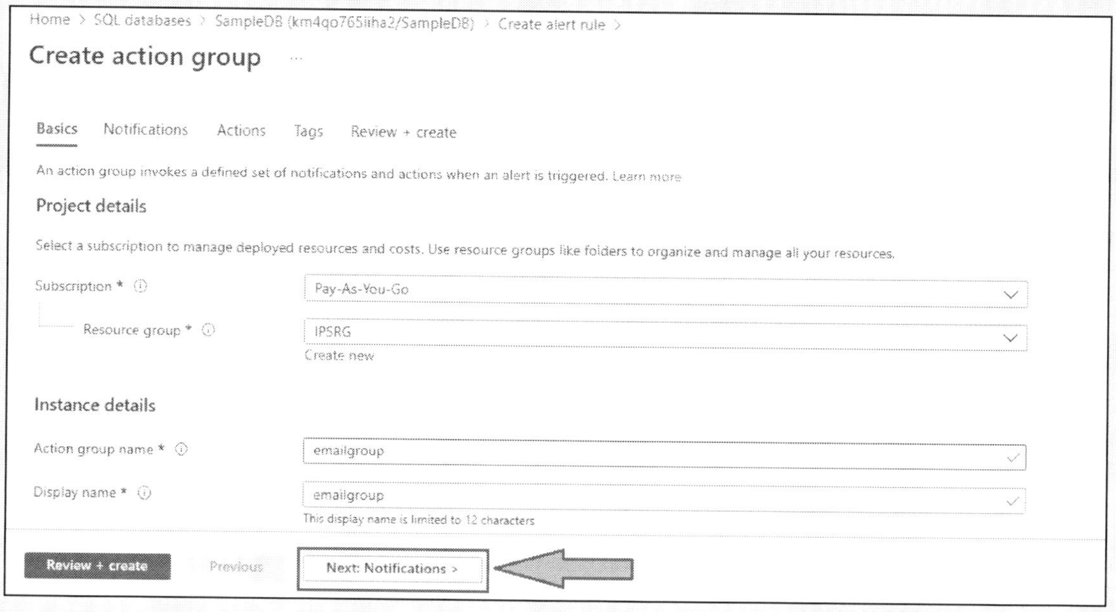

Home > SQL databases > SampleDB (km4qo765iiha2/SampleDB) > Create alert rule >

Create action group

Basics Notifications Actions Tags Review + create

An action group invokes a defined set of notifications and actions when an alert is triggered. Learn more

Project details

Select a subscription to manage deployed resources and costs. Use resource groups like folders to organize and manage all your resources.

Subscription * Pay-As-You-Go

Resource group * IPSRG

Create new

Instance details

Action group name * emailgroup

Display name * emailgroup

This display name is limited to 12 characters

Review + create Previous Next: Notifications >

Enter the following information:

- Notification type: "**Email/SMS message/Push/Voice**"
- Name: "**IPSLab**"
- Email: You can use the Azure Username you signed in with

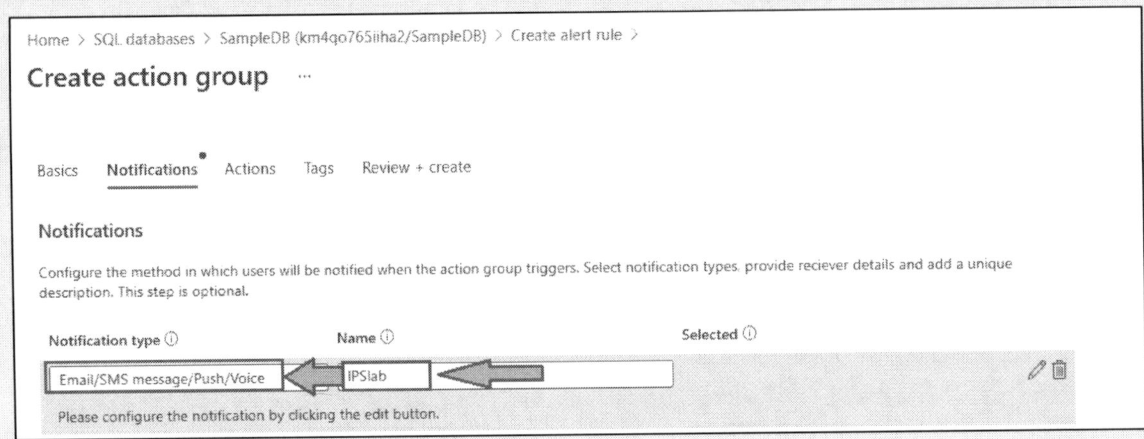

11. Select "**OK** "in the Email/SMS message/Push/Voice flyout.
12. Select "**Review + Create**," then click on "**Create**."

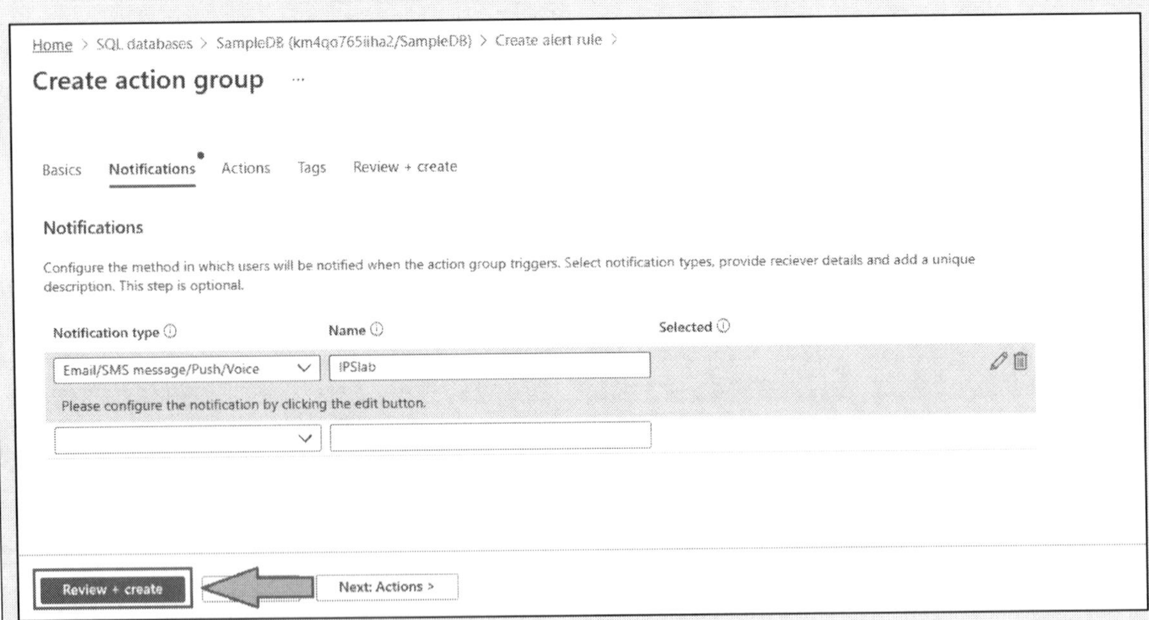

13. On the Create alert rule screen, add an "**Alert Rule Name**" of "**DemoAlert**," and then select "**Create Alert Rule**."

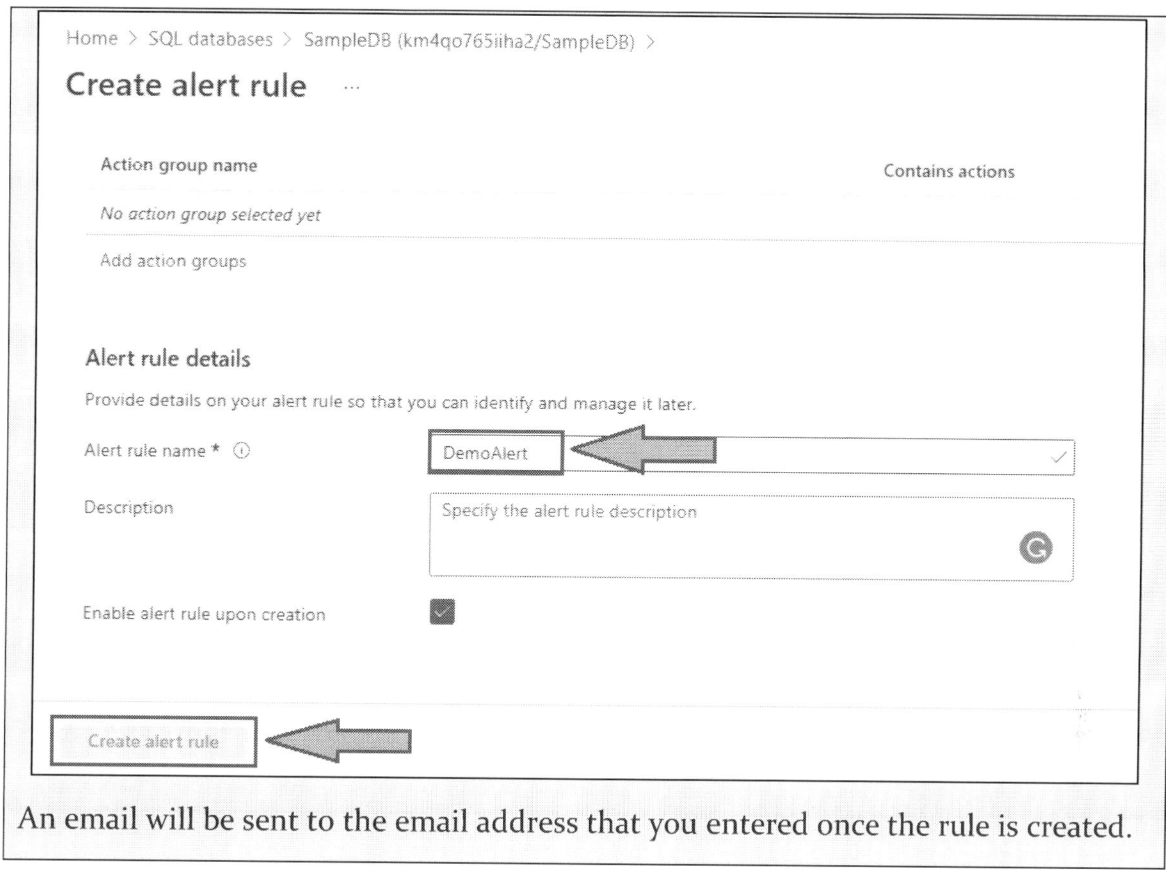

An email will be sent to the email address that you entered once the rule is created.

Step 03: "Deploy an Automation Runbook to Automatically Rebuild Databases Indexes

Create an Automation Account

1. Type automation in the Azure portal and then select Automation Accounts from the search results in the search bar.

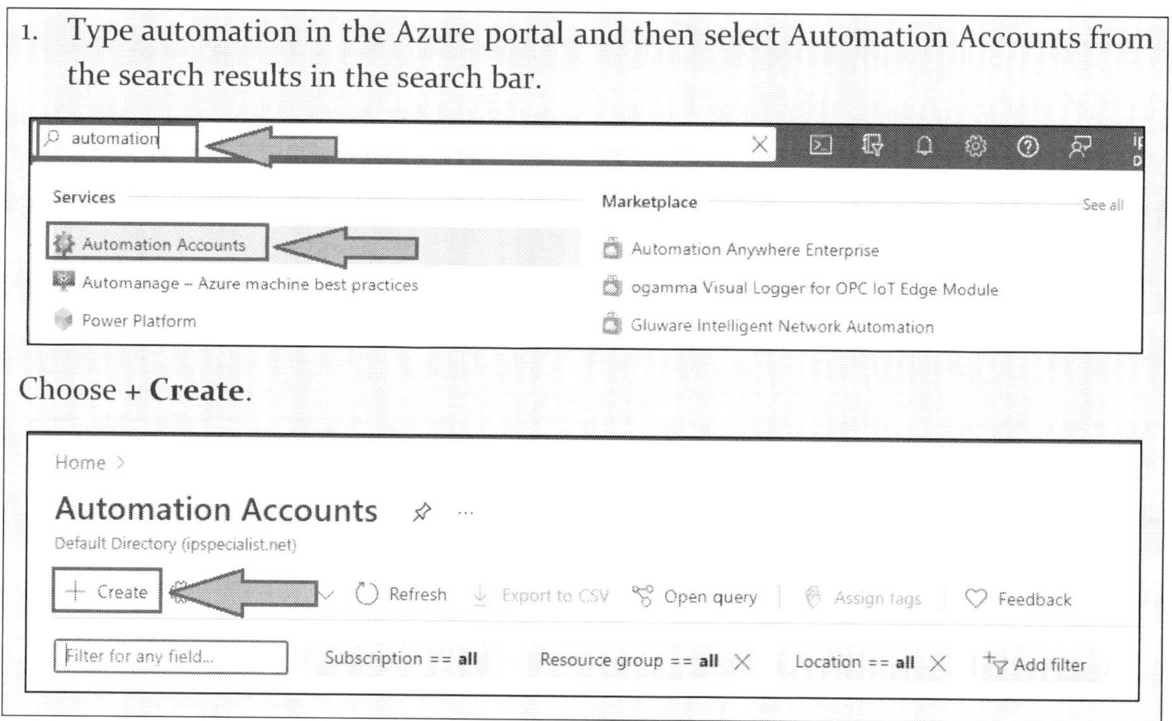

Choose + **Create**.

2. On the "**Add Automation Account**" page, enter this information:
    - Name: "**autoAccount**"
    - Resource Group: "**IPSRG**"
    - Location: Use the default.

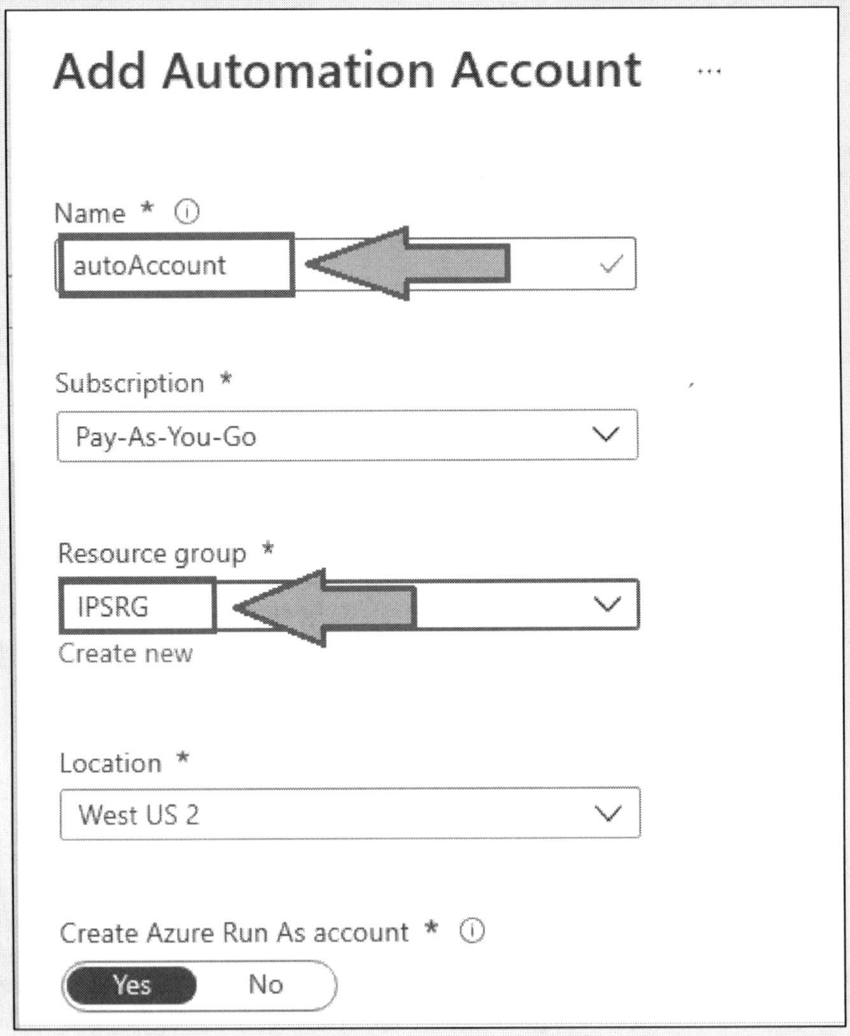

Add Automation Account ...

Name * ⓘ
autoAccount

Subscription *
Pay-As-You-Go

Resource group *
IPSRG
Create new

Location *
West US 2

Create Azure Run As account * ⓘ
Yes No

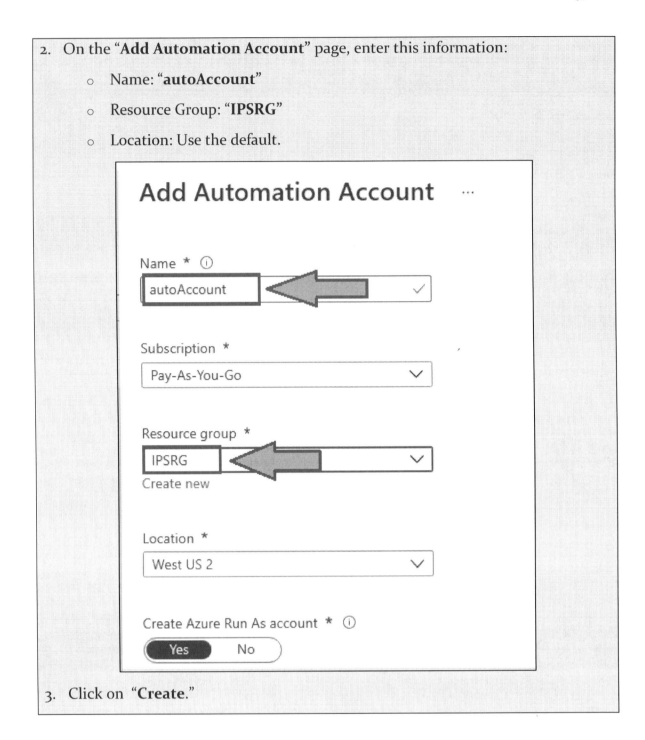

3. Click on "**Create.**"

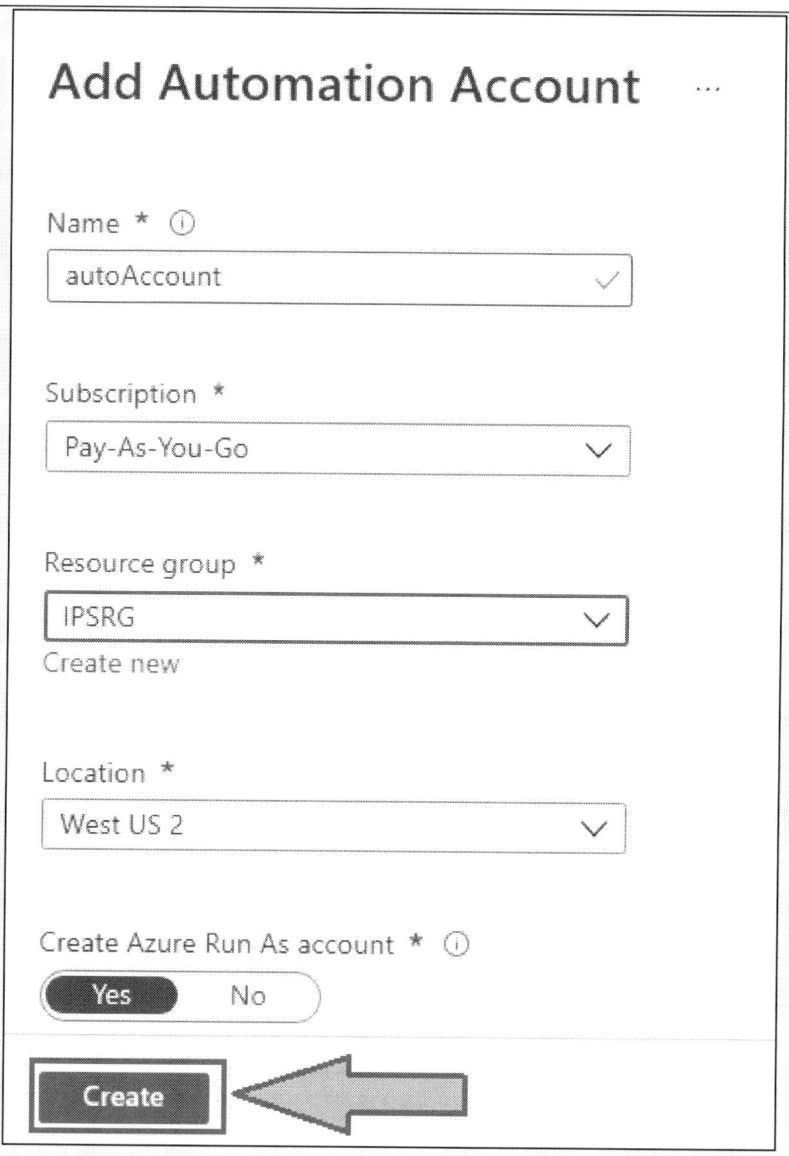

Add Automation Account ...

Name * ⓘ

autoAccount

Subscription *

Pay-As-You-Go

Resource group *

IPSRG

Create new

Location *

West US 2

Create Azure Run As account * ⓘ

Yes No

Create

Your automation account should be created in around three minutes.

Connect to an Existing Azure SQL Database

1. In the Azure portal, navigate to your database by searching for "**sql databases**."

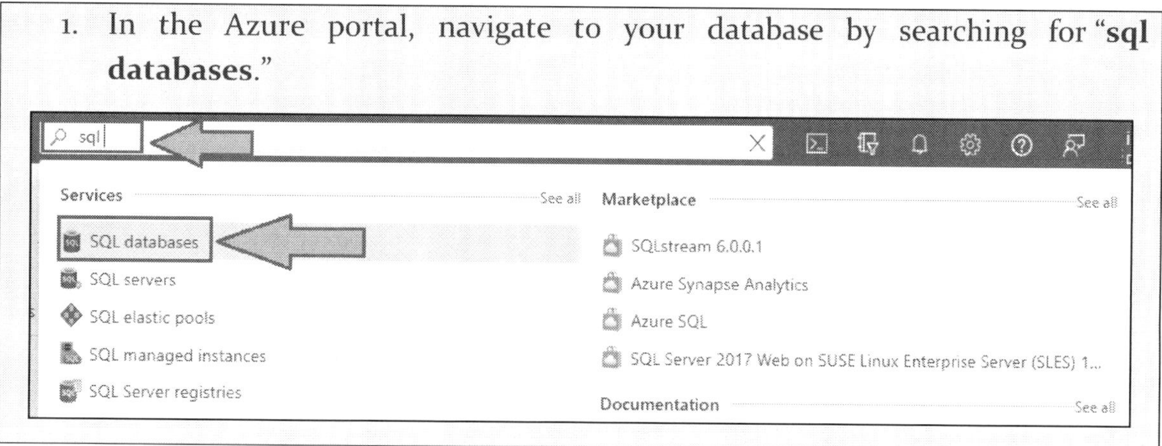

Then select the SQL database.

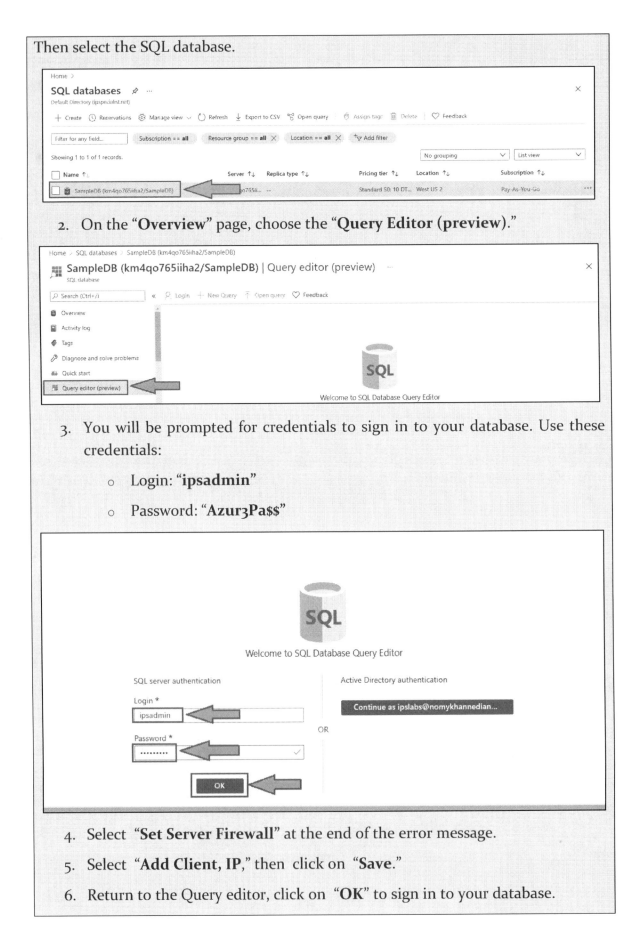

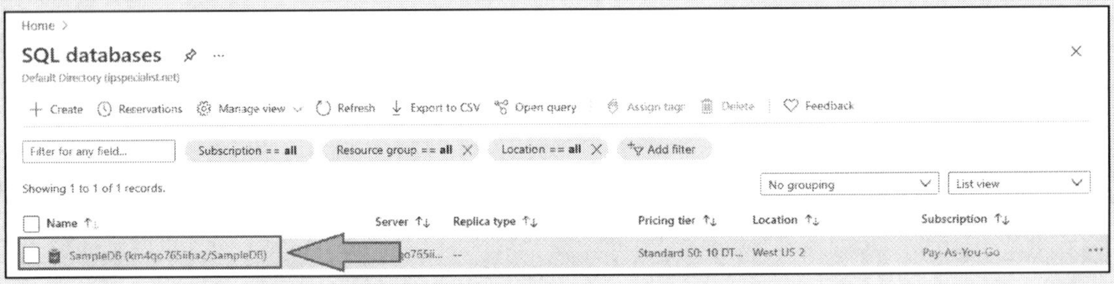

2. On the "**Overview**" page, choose the "**Query Editor (preview)**."

3. You will be prompted for credentials to sign in to your database. Use these credentials:
    - Login: "**ipsadmin**"
    - Password: "**Azur3Pa$$**"

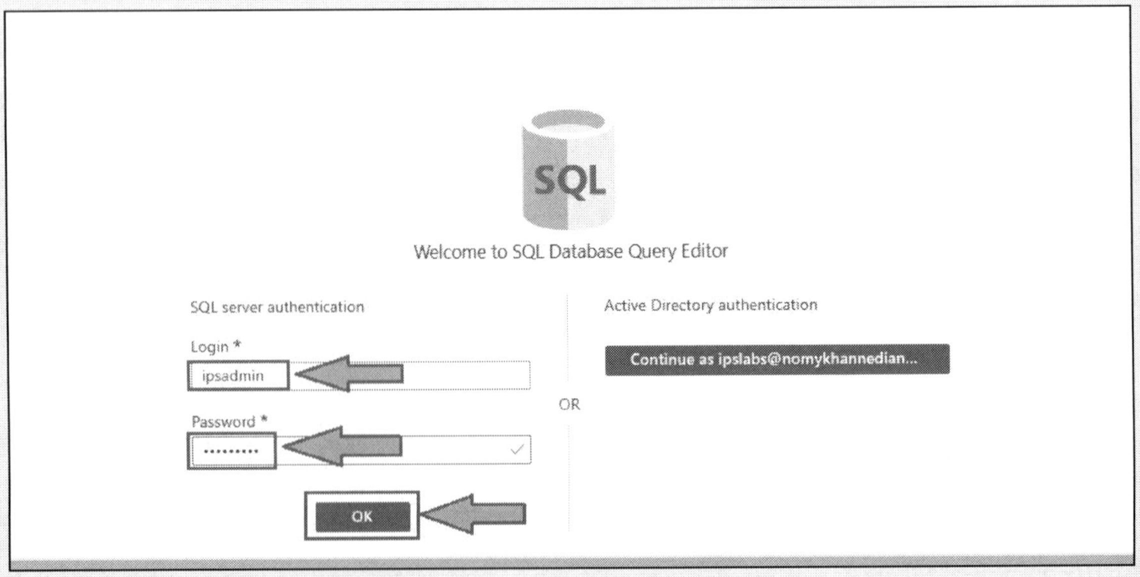

4. Select "**Set Server Firewall**" at the end of the error message.
5. Select "**Add Client, IP**," then click on "**Save**."
6. Return to the Query editor, click on "**OK**" to sign in to your database.

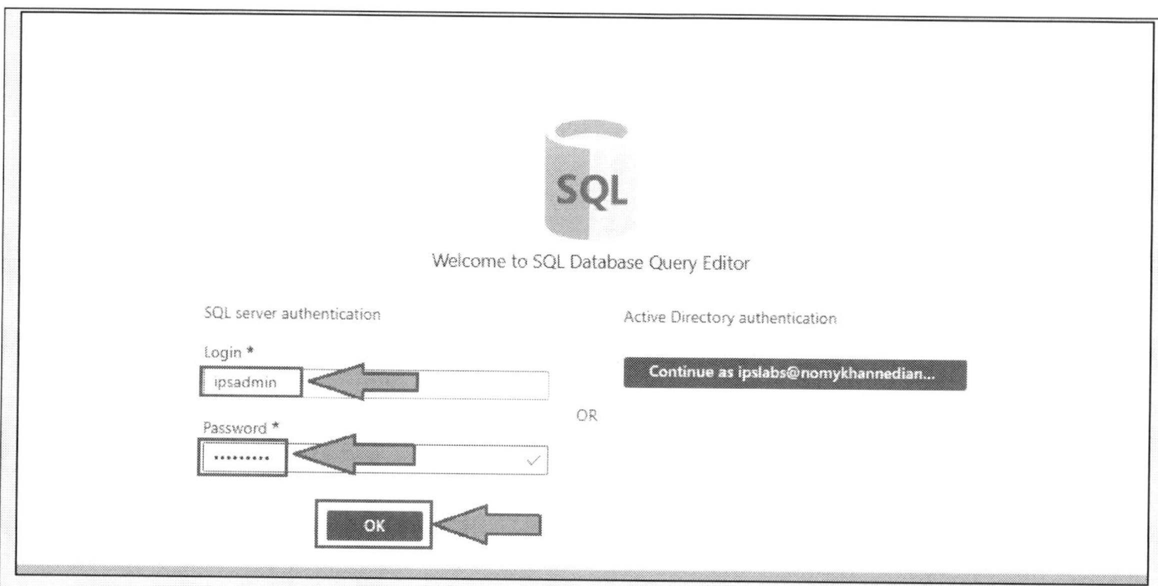

7. Open a new tab in your browser and navigate to the GitHub page for "**AdaptativeIndexDefragmentation**." https://github.com/microsoft/tigertoolbox/blob/master/AdaptiveIndexDefrag/usp_AdaptiveIndexDefrag.sql

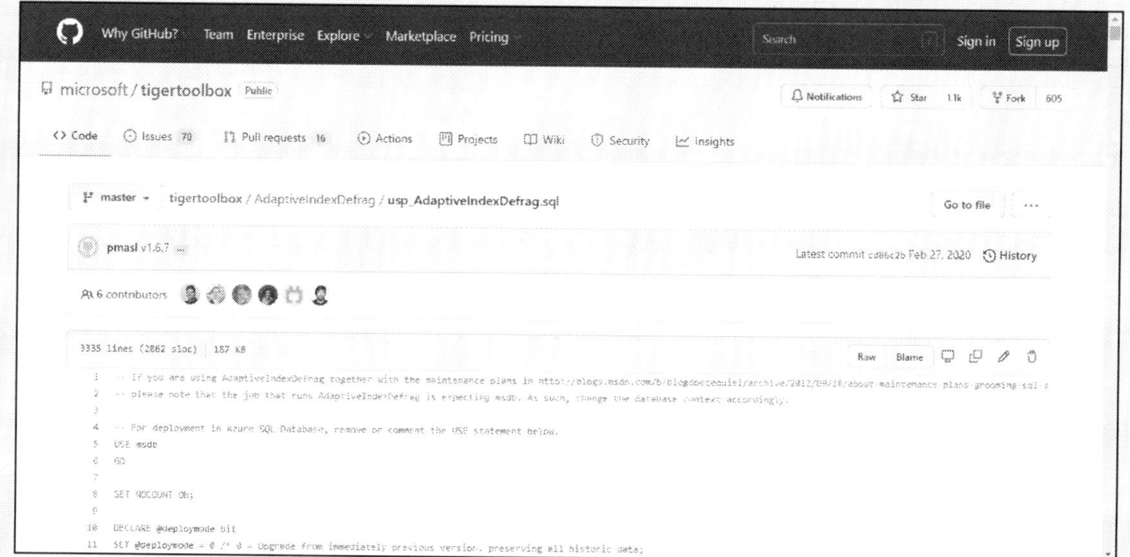

Select "**Raw**." This will provide the code in a format where you can copy it. Select all text (CTRL + A) and copy it to your clipboard (CTRL + C).

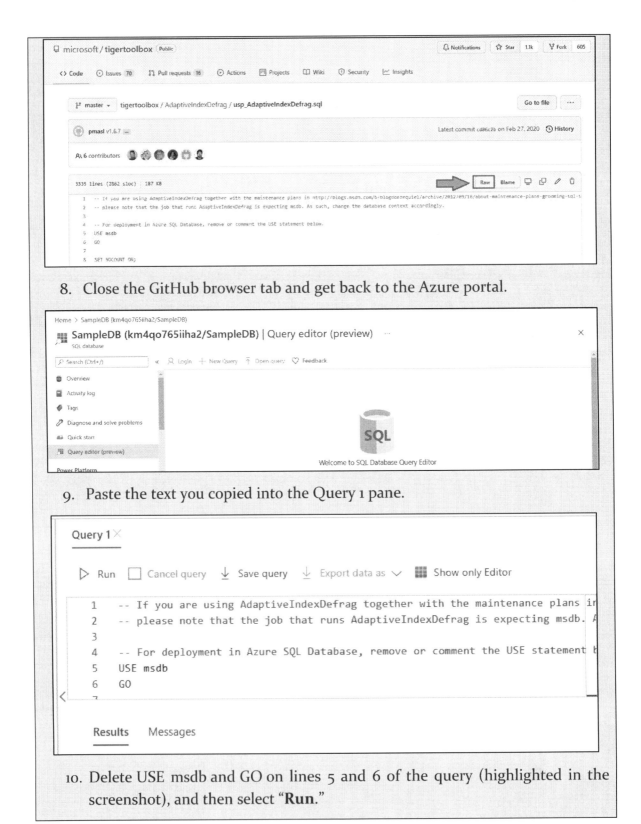

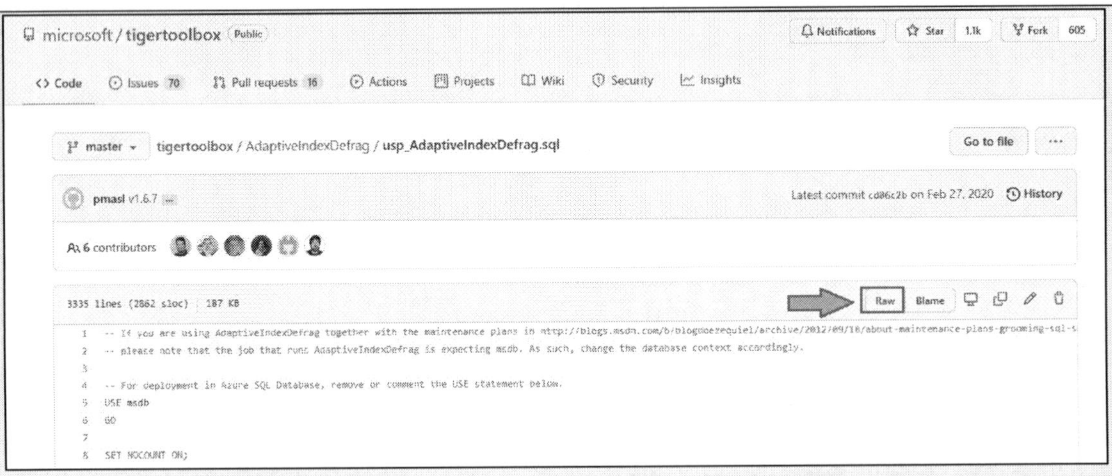

8. Close the GitHub browser tab and get back to the Azure portal.

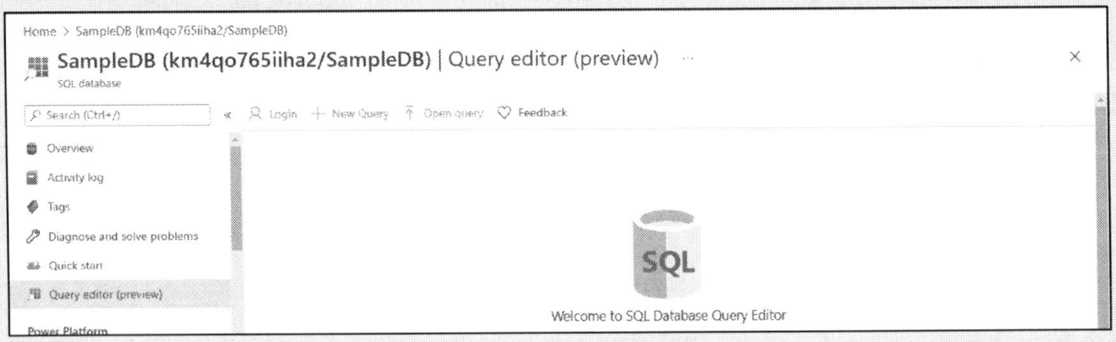

9. Paste the text you copied into the Query 1 pane.

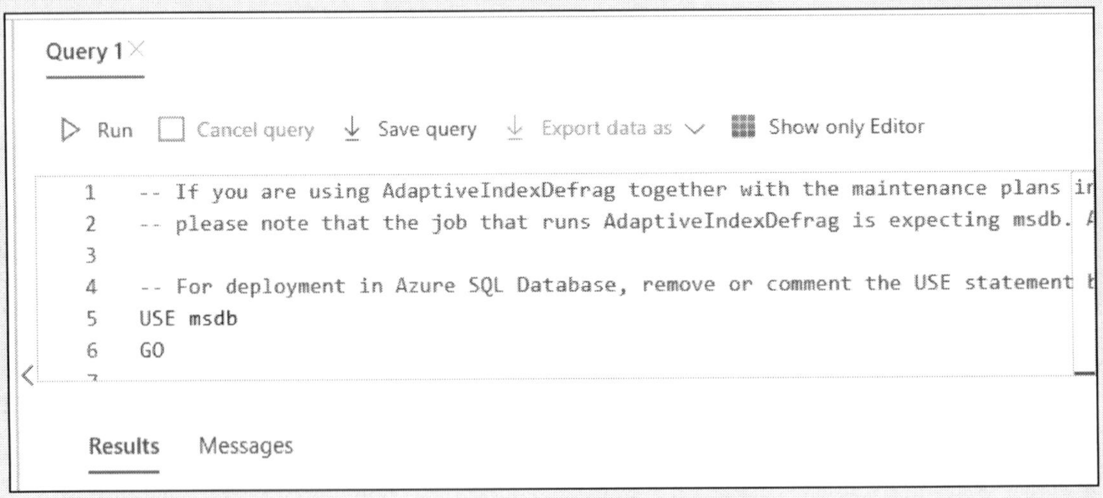

10. Delete USE msdb and GO on lines 5 and 6 of the query (highlighted in the screenshot), and then select "**Run**."

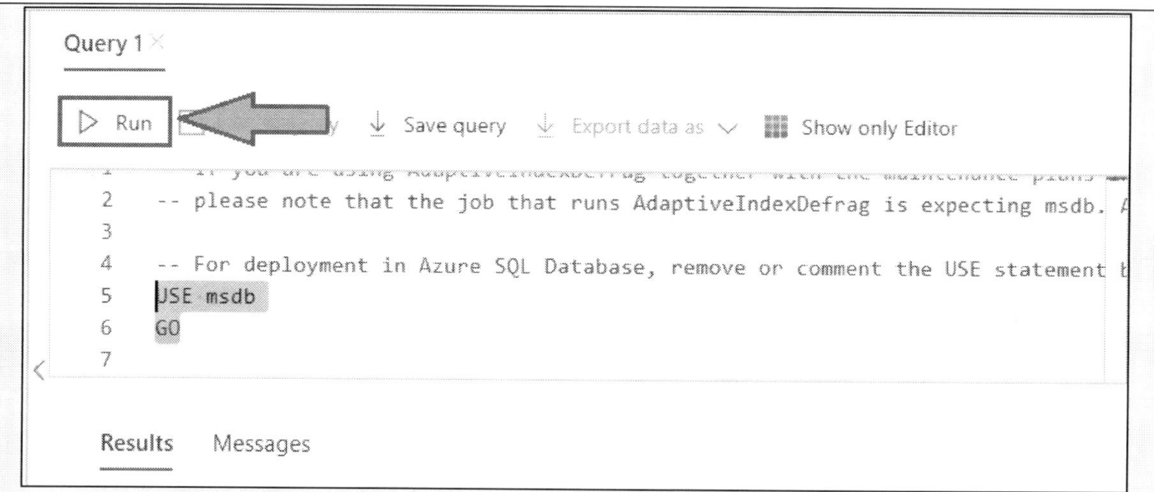

The purpose of running this code is to form stored procedures on a SQL database that can perform intelligent defragmentation on one or more indexes. The code will also update statistics if needed.

11. Expand the "**Stored Procedures**" folder to see what was created.

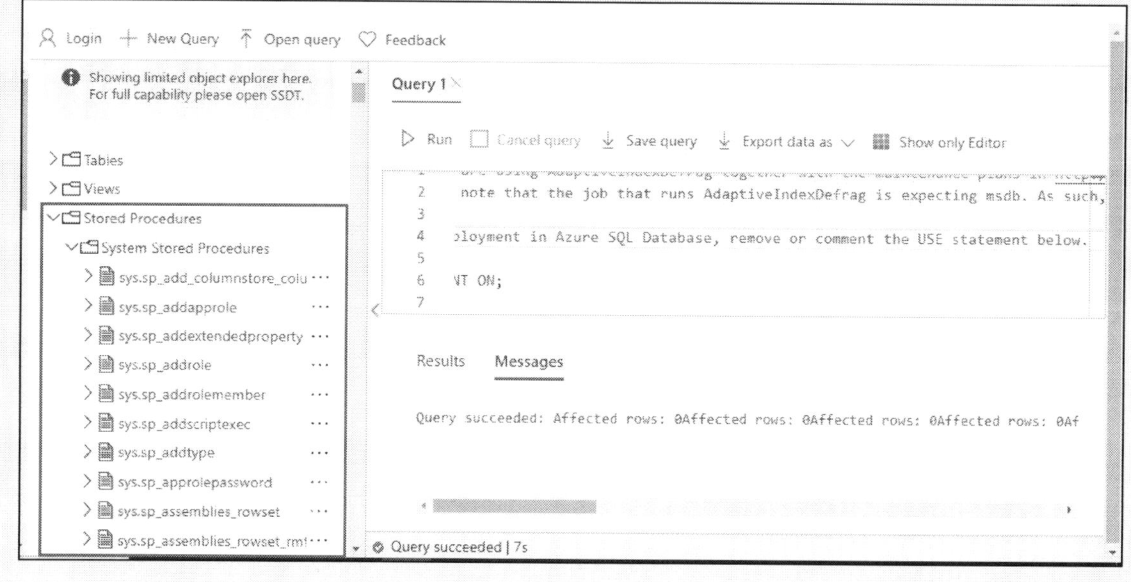

Add Automation to an Automation Account

1. On the Azure portal, in the top search box, type "**Automation**." Then choose "**Automation Accounts**."

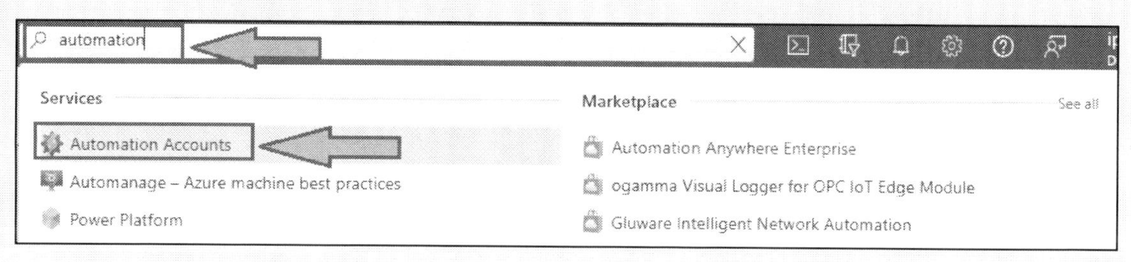

2. Select the automation account that you created.

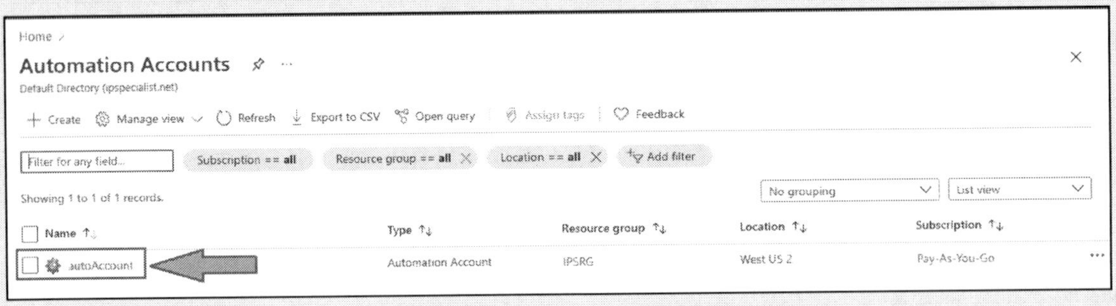

3. Select "**Modules**" from the Shared Resources section of the Automation blade.

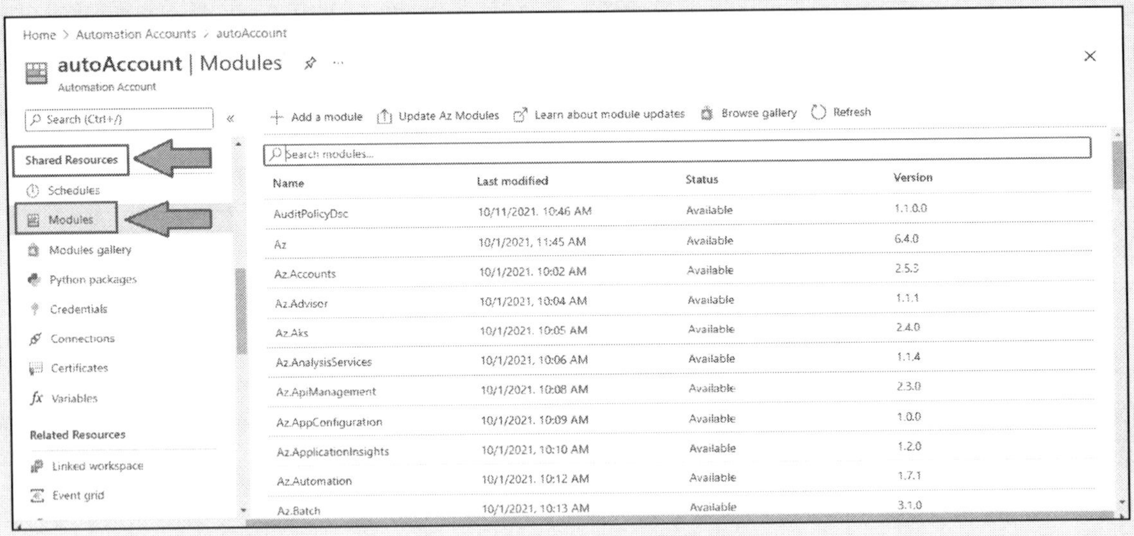

4. Select "**Browse Gallery**."

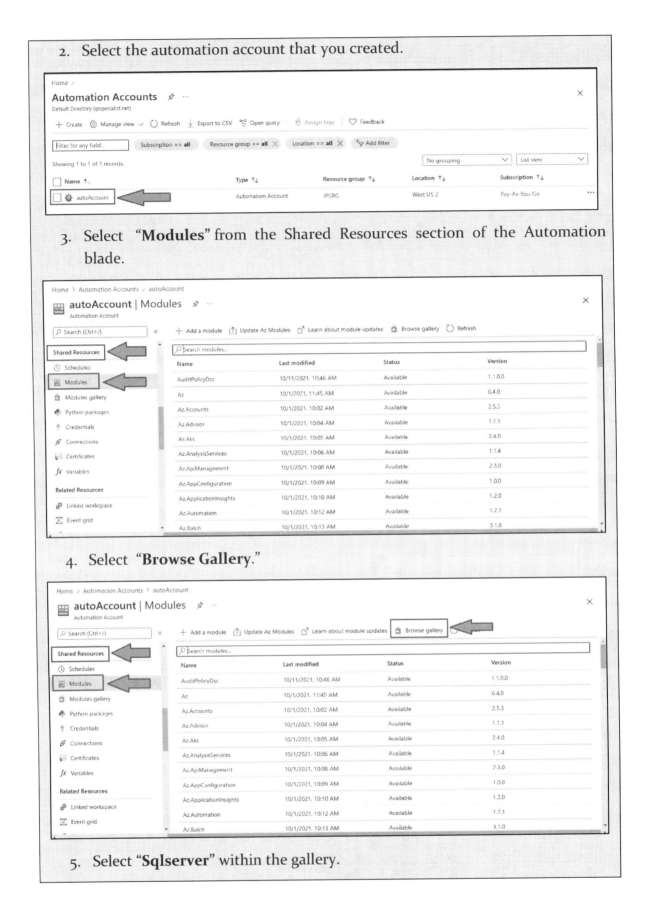

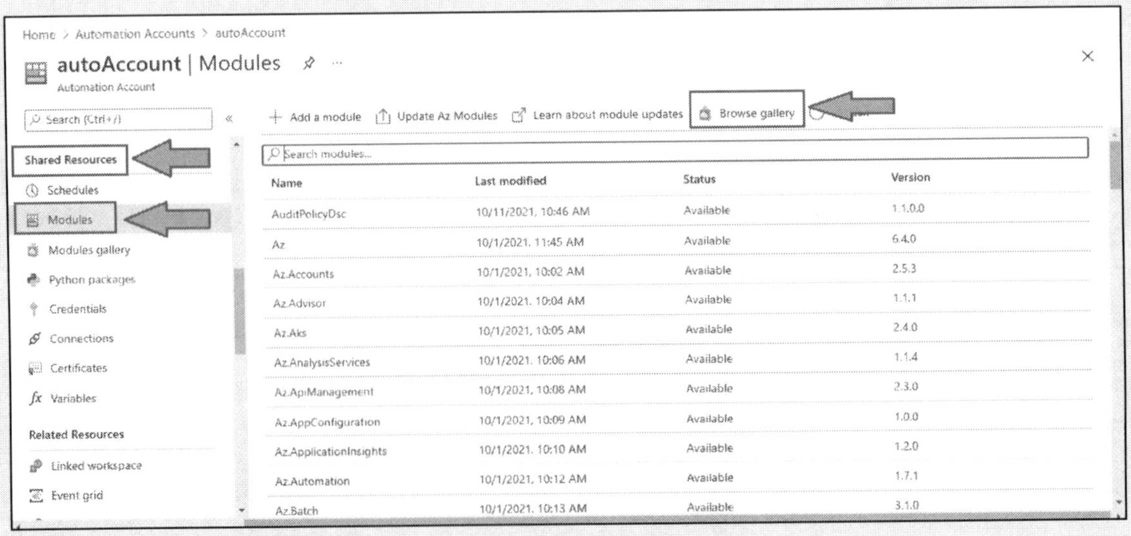

5. Select "**Sqlserver**" within the gallery.

Home > Automation Accounts > autoAccount >

Browse Gallery ...

sqlserver

SqlServer

This module allows SQL Server developers, administrators and business intelligence professionals to automate database development and server administration, as well as both multidimensional and tabular cube processing.
Tags: SQL SqlServer SQLPS Databases SqlAgent Jobs SSAS AnalysisServices Tabular Cubes SSIS ExtendedEvents xEvents VulnerabilityAssessment DataClassification PSModule

Created by: matteot_msft
23416782 downloads
Last updated: 7/14/2021

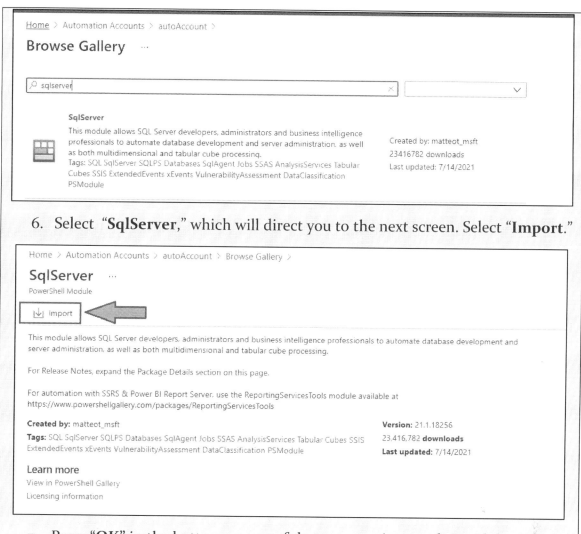

6. Select "**SqlServer**," which will direct you to the next screen. Select "**Import**."

Home > Automation Accounts > autoAccount > Browse Gallery >

SqlServer ...

PowerShell Module

Import

This module allows SQL Server developers, administrators and business intelligence professionals to automate database development and server administration, as well as both multidimensional and tabular cube processing.

For Release Notes, expand the Package Details section on this page.

For automation with SSRS & Power BI Report Server, use the ReportingServicesTools module available at https://www.powershellgallery.com/packages/ReportingServicesTools

Created by: matteot_msft
Tags: SQL SqlServer SQLPS Databases SqlAgent Jobs SSAS AnalysisServices Tabular Cubes SSIS ExtendedEvents xEvents VulnerabilityAssessment DataClassification PSModule

Version: 21.1.18256
23,416,782 **downloads**
Last updated: 7/14/2021

Learn more
View in PowerShell Gallery
Licensing information

7. Press "**OK**" in the bottom corner of the screen to import the module.

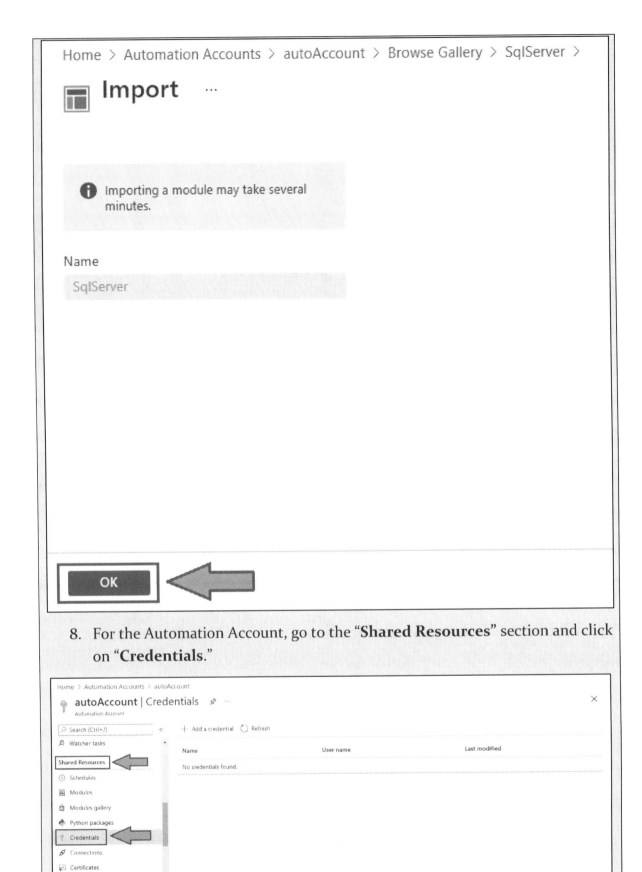

8. For the Automation Account, go to the "**Shared Resources**" section and click on "**Credentials**."

Select "+ **Add a Credential**," and then create a credential with these properties:

- Name: "**SQLUser**"
- User name: "**ipsadmin**"
- Password: "**Azur3Pa$$**"
- Confirm password: "**Azur3Pa$$**"

Then click on "**Create**."

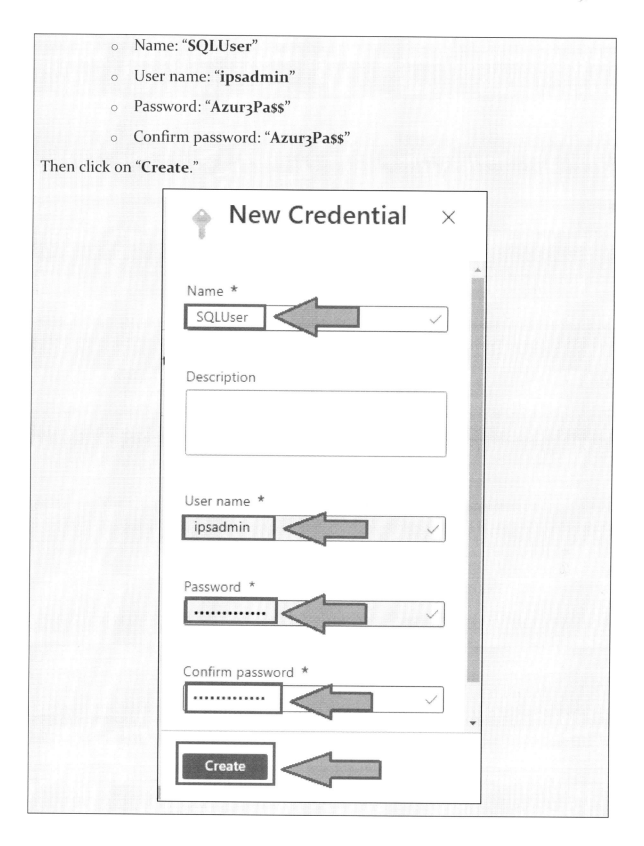

Create a PowerShell Runbook

1. In the Azure portal, navigate to your database by searching for "**sql Databases**."

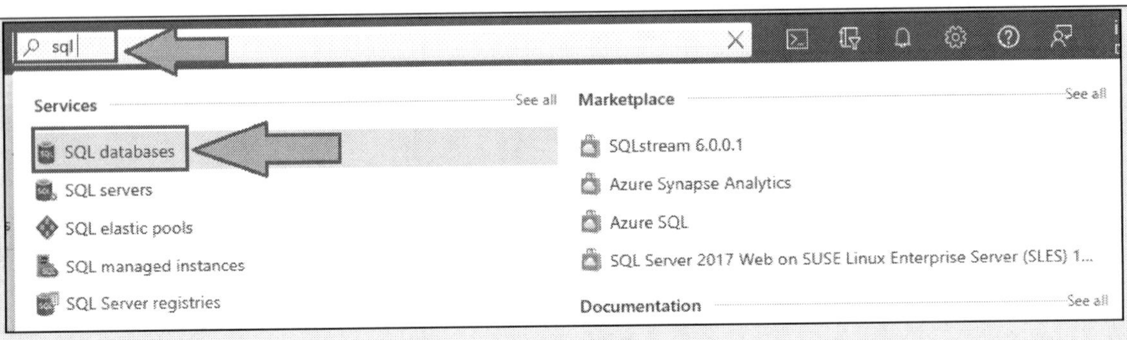

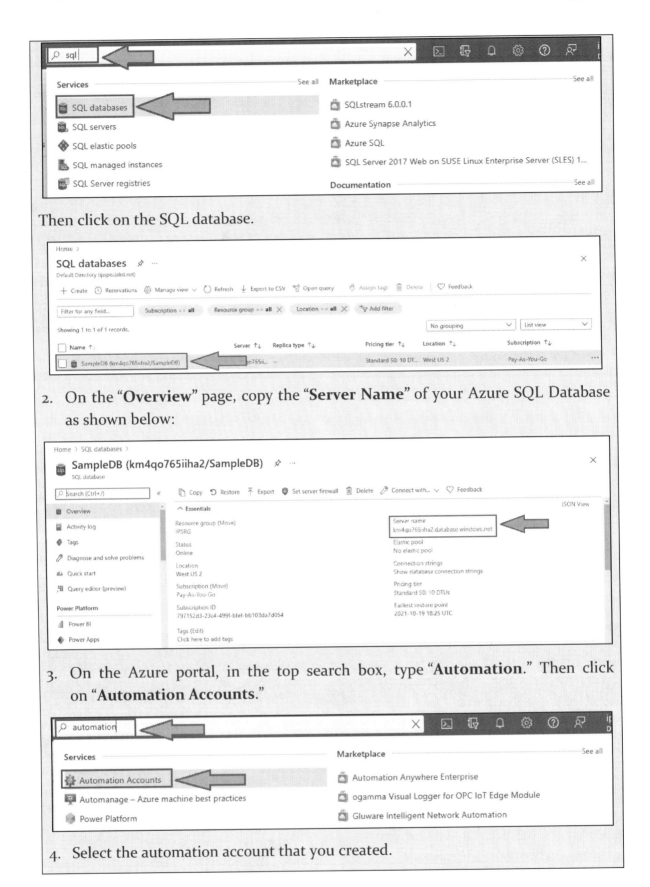

Then click on the SQL database.

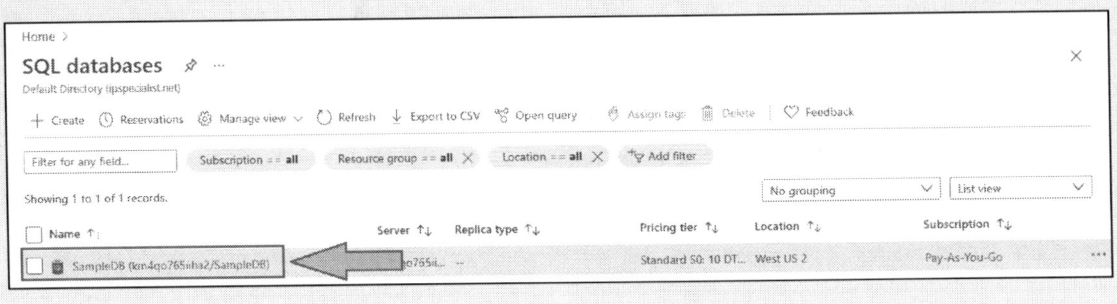

2. On the "**Overview**" page, copy the "**Server Name**" of your Azure SQL Database as shown below:

3. On the Azure portal, in the top search box, type "**Automation**." Then click on "**Automation Accounts**."

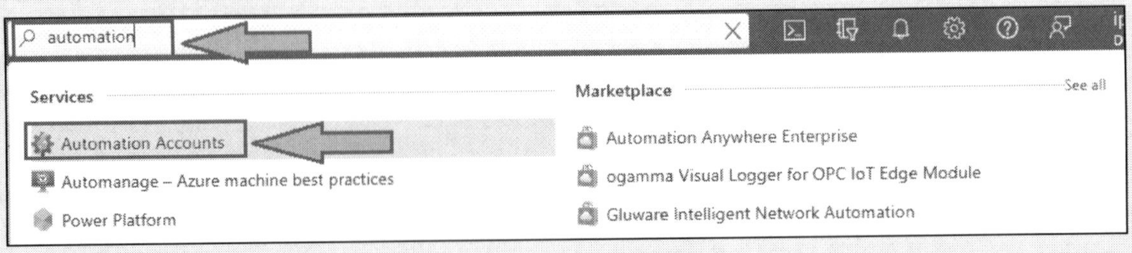

4. Select the automation account that you created.

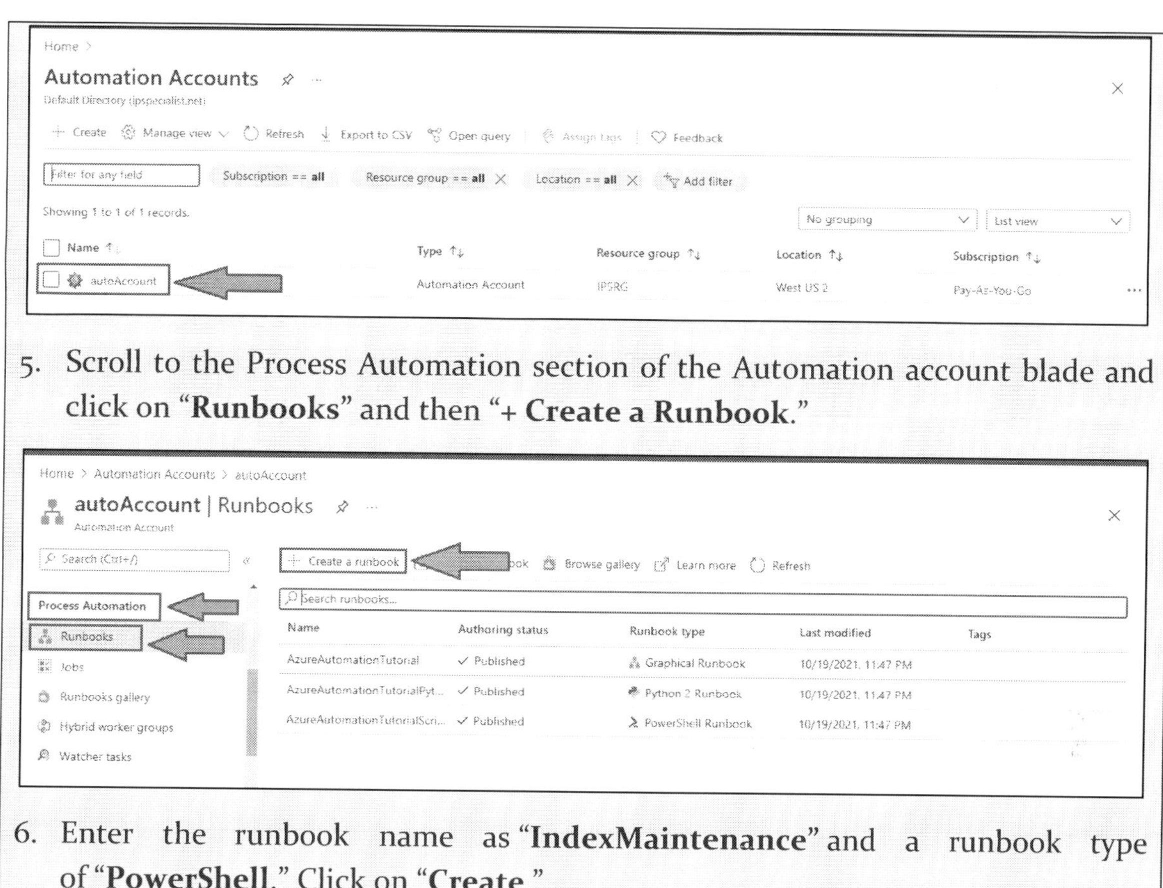

5. Scroll to the Process Automation section of the Automation account blade and click on "**Runbooks**" and then "+ **Create a Runbook**."

6. Enter the runbook name as "**IndexMaintenance**" and a runbook type of "**PowerShell**." Click on "**Create**."

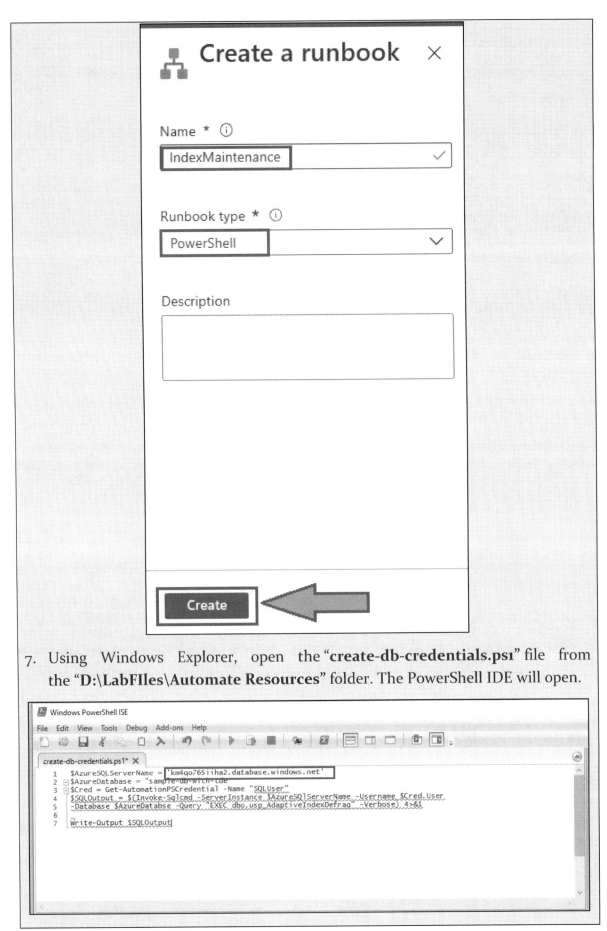

7. Using Windows Explorer, open the "**create-db-credentials.ps1**" file from the "**D:\LabFIles\Automate Resources**" folder. The PowerShell IDE will open.

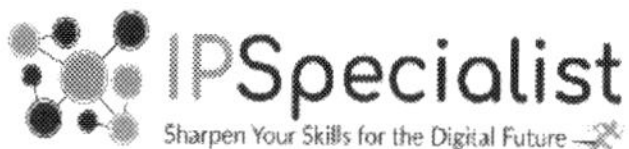

8. On-Line 1 of the file, paste in the "**Server Name**" you copied in the steps above. Please select all text (CTRL + A) and copy it to your clipboard (CTRL + C).
9. Navigate to your automation runbook in the Microsoft Edge browser, and paste the PowerShell code.

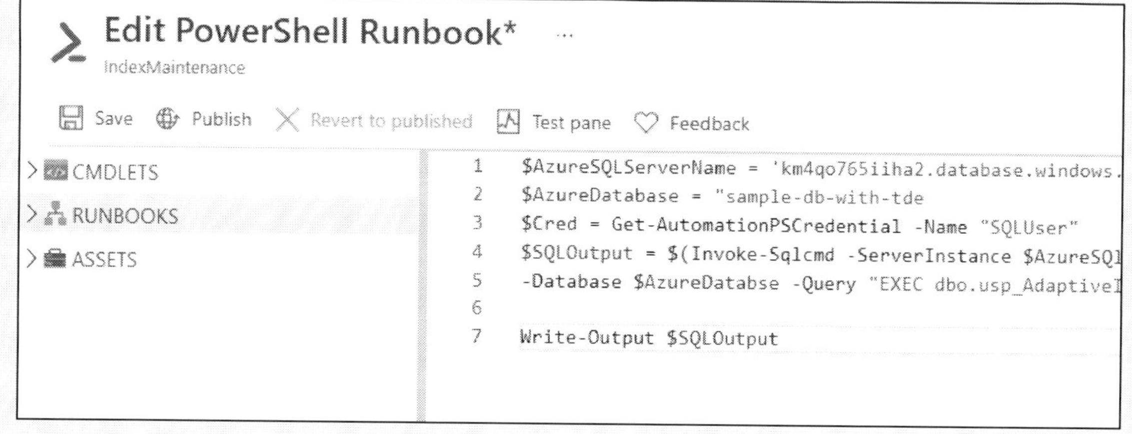

10. Click on "**Save**," and then click on "**Publish**."

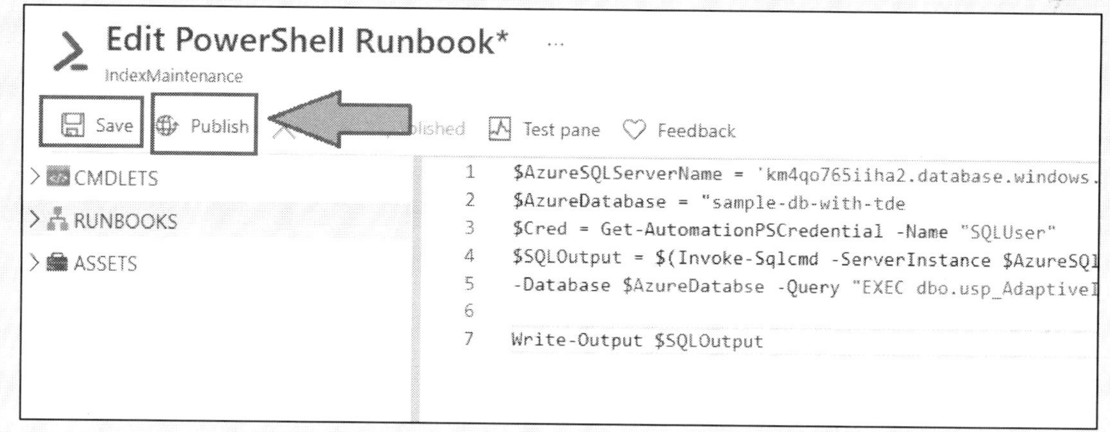

Create a Schedule for a Runbook

Next, you will schedule the runbook to execute regularly.

1. Under Resources in the left-hand navigation, select "**Schedules**." Then click on "+ **Add a Schedule**."

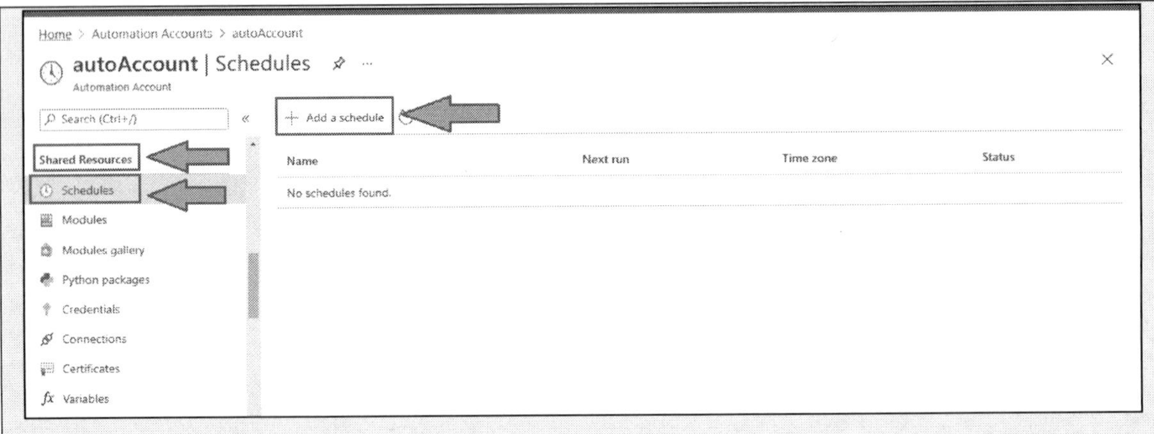

2. Select "**Link a Schedule to your Runbook**."
3. Click on "**Create a New Schedule**."

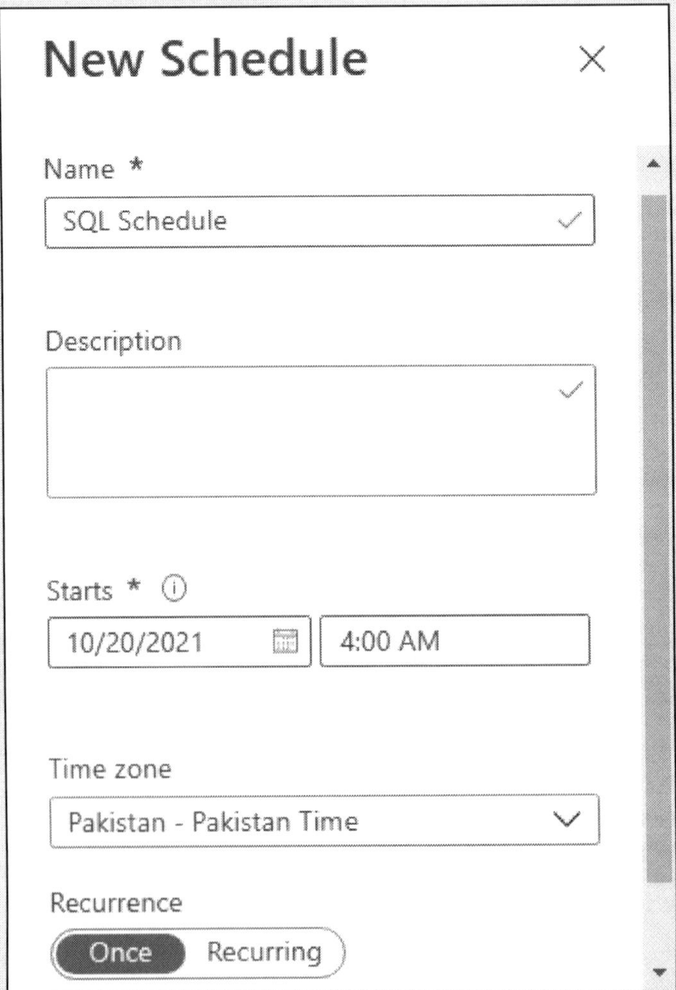

4. Supply a descriptive schedule name and a description if desired.
5. Define the start time of "**4:00 am**" of the following day and in the "**Eastern Time Zone**." Configure the reoccurrence every "**1** "day. Do not set an expiration.

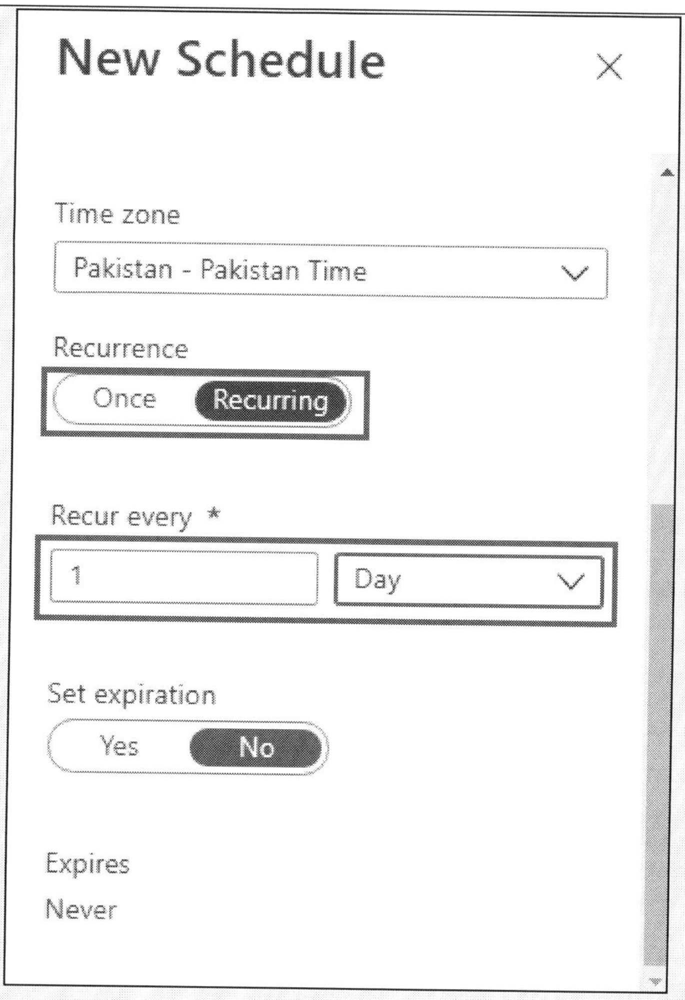

New Schedule

Time zone

Pakistan - Pakistan Time

Recurrence

Once Recurring

Recur every *

1 Day

Set expiration

Yes No

Expires

Never

6. Click on “**Create**,” and then select “**OK**.”

New Schedule

Time zone

Pakistan - Pakistan Time

Recurrence

Once Recurring

Recur every *

1 Day

Set expiration

Yes No

Expires

Never

Create

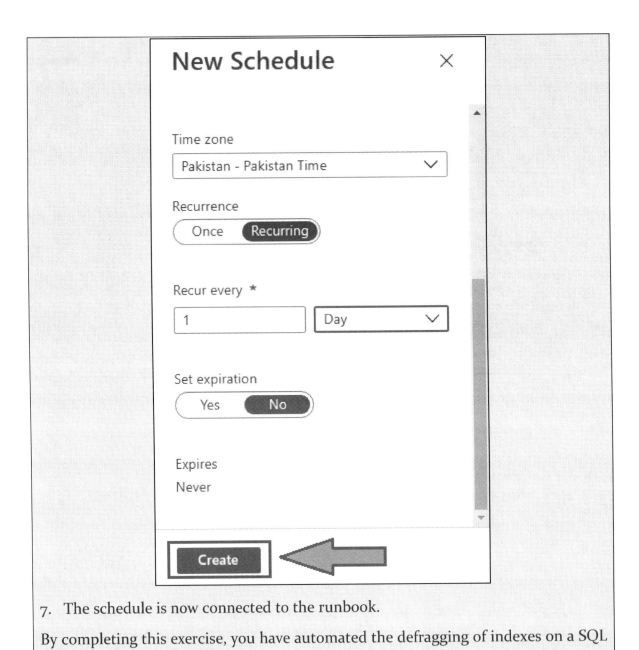

7. The schedule is now connected to the runbook.

By completing this exercise, you have automated the defragging of indexes on a SQL server database every day, at 4 am.

Mind Map

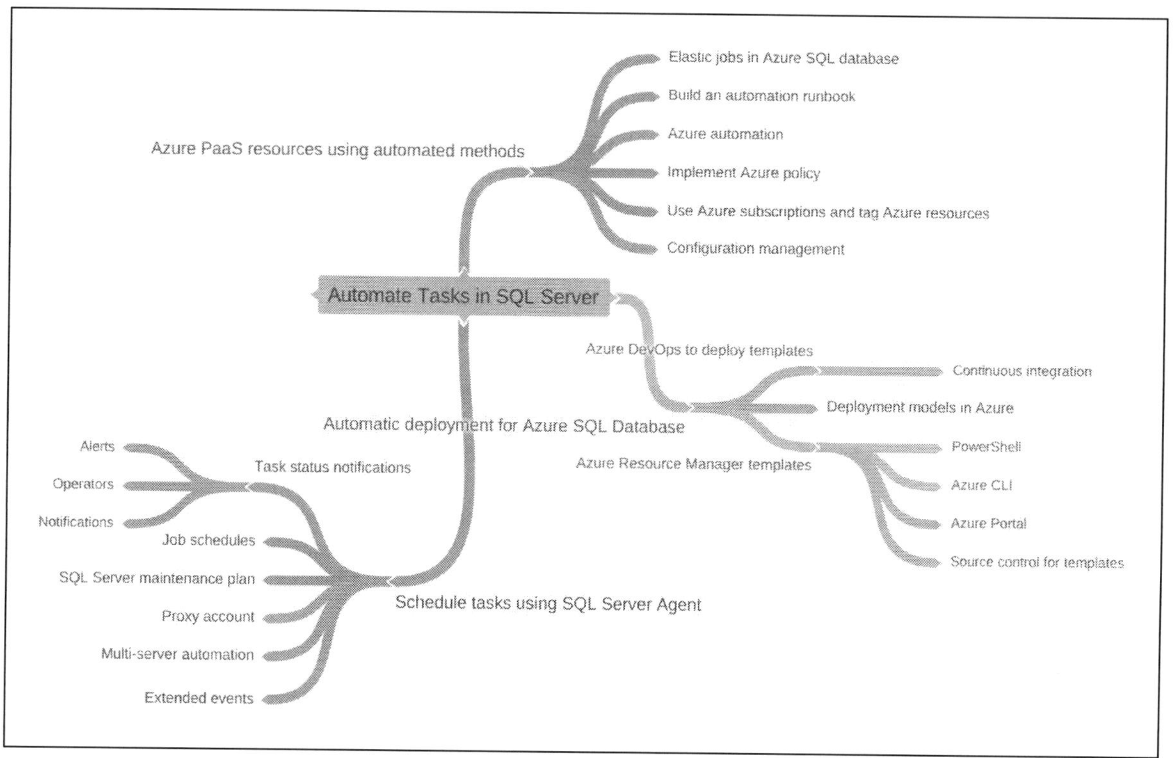

Figure 06-36: Mind Map

Practice Questions

1. What language are Azure Resource Manager templates written in?

A. JSON

B. C#

C. T-SQL

D. None of the above

2. If you want to specify the region for a resource group deployment, which option should you include in your template?

A. Parameter

B. Variable

C. Output

D. None of the above

3. Which element of a template allows you to build dependencies into resources?

A. dependsOn

B. concat

C. apiVersion

D. None of the above

4. What has to be configured before the SQL Server Agent can send an email?

A. A mail profile

B. An agent job

C. An alert

D. None of the above

5. Which system database stores SQL Server Agent jobs and their information?

A. msdb

B. Master

C. Model

D. None of the above

6. Which operation recalculates the statistics on an index?

A. Rebuild

B. Reorganize

C. Shrinking a file-group

D. None of the above

7. Which Extended Events target only writes to memory?

A. Ring Buffer

B. Target File

C. ETW

D. None of the above

8. Where do you implement a filter in your Extended Event Session?

A. On the Event

B. On the Storage Target

C. On a Global Field

D. None of the above

9. What is the unit of execution for your Azure Automation Account?

A. Runbook

B. Schedule

C. Container

D. None of the above

10. What scope can Azure Policy be deployed to?

A. Tenant

B. Subscription

C. User

D. None of the above

11. What is the name for the scope that you must define for a SQL Elastic Job?

A. Target Group

B. Management Group

C. Resource Group

D. None of the above

12. __________ provides a core module known as Az, which has child resource providers for nearly all Azure services.

A. Azure PowerShell

B. Azure CLI

C. Azure Portal

D. None of the above

13. SQL Server Agent _______ allows you to be proactive with monitoring your SQL Server.

A. Alerts

B. Notification

C. Both of the above

D. None of the above

14. _________ are a powerful feature of Extended Events that allow you to use granular control.

A. Filters

B. Tables

C. Files

D. None of the above

15. _______ are simply metadata that are used to describe your Azure resources better.

A. Tags

B. Files

C. Tables

D. None of the above

Chapter 07: Plan and Implement a High Availability and Disaster Recovery Environment

Describe Recovery Time Objective and Recovery Point Objective

Understanding recovery time and recovery point objectives is critical for any High Availability and Disaster Recovery (HADR) plan since they serve as the foundation for any availability solution.

Recovery Time Objective

The greatest amount of time available to put resources back online after an outage or incident is referred to as the Recovery Time Objective (RTO). If the process takes longer than the RTO allows, there may be implications such as financial fines, work that cannot be completed, and so on. RTO can be configured for the entire system, including all resources, as well as for individual components like SQL Server instances and databases.

Recovery Point Objective

The Recovery Point Objective (RPO) is the point in time at which a database should be recovered. It corresponds to the greatest amount of data loss that the company is willing to allow. Assume an IaaS VM containing SQL Server goes down at 10:00 a.m. and the databases within the SQL Server instance have an RPO of 15 minutes; no matter what feature or technique is used to restore that instance and its databases, it is expected that no more than 15 minutes of data would be lost. That means the database can be restored at 9:45 a.m. or later to assure minimum to no data loss while fulfilling the RPO. There may be elements that affect whether or not that RPO is attainable.

Defining Recovery Time and Recovery Point Objectives

RTOs and RPOs are driven by business requirements, but they are also based on different technological and other aspects like the administrators' skills and talents (not just DBAs). While the company may desire no downtime or data loss, this may not be feasible or attainable for a variety of reasons. Determining the RTO and RPO of your solution should be an open and honest dialogue amongst all parties involved.

Understanding the cost of downtime is critical for both RTO and RPO. It is easier to create solutions if you define that number and the entire impact of being down or unavailable has on the business. For example, if a corporation can lose $10,000 per hour or face a fine from a government agency if something cannot be processed, it is a measurable way to help define RTO and RPO. The cost of the solution should be proportional to the amount of downtime. If your HADR solution costs $10,000 per hour or is subject to a fine from a government body if something cannot be processed, this is a quantitative technique to assist in defining RTO and RPO. The cost of the solution

should be proportional to the amount of downtime. If your HADR solution costs X but only affects you for a few seconds rather than hours or days when a problem occurs, it has paid for itself.

RTO should be defined at the component level (for example, SQL Server) as well as for the complete application architecture from a non-business aspect.

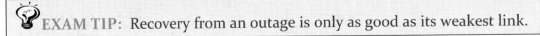

EXAM TIP: Recovery from an outage is only as good as its weakest link.

For example, if SQL Server and its databases can be brought online in five minutes, but application servers require 20 minutes, the entire RTO would be 20 minutes rather than five. The SQL Server environment could still have an RTO of five minutes; however, this will have no effect on the overall time to recover.

RPO focuses on data and has a direct impact on the design of any HADR solution as well as administrative rules and processes. The features utilized must support both the required RTO and RPO. For example, if transaction log backups are scheduled every 30 minutes but the RPO is 15 minutes, a database can only be recovered to the most recent transaction log backup available, which in the best-case scenario is 30 minutes ago. This timing implies that there are no additional difficulties and that the backups have been tested and are known to be reliable. While testing every backup made for each database in your environment is difficult, backups are simply files on a file system. There is no guarantee that they are in good condition unless they are restored on a regular basis. Running checks during the backup process can provide you with some assurance.

Your RTOs and RPOs will be affected by the features you utilize, such as an Always On Availability Group (AG) or an Always On Failover Cluster Instance (FCI). IaaS or PaaS systems may or may not instantly failover to another site, depending on how the features are configured, which may result in prolonged downtime. By specifying RTO and RPO, the technological solution that supports that requirement can be created with time and data loss tolerances in mind. If those prove to be unreasonable, RTOs and RPOs must be revised correspondingly. For example, if the desired RTO of two hours is set, but a backup takes three hours to replicate to the destination server for restoration, the RTO has already been missed. These kinds of considerations must be made while setting your RTOs and RPOs.

RTOs and RPOs should be defined for both HA and DR. HA are regarded as a more localized event that is easier to recover from. An AG automatically failing over from one replica to another inside an Azure region is an example of high availability. That could take a few seconds, and at that time, you would need to make sure the application can reconnect after the failover. The downtime for SQL Server would be low. Depending on the criticality of the solution or system, a local RTO or RPO could be assessed in minutes.

DR would be equivalent to constructing an entirely new data center. The puzzle has many components, and SQL Server is simply one of them. It could take hours or even days to get everything online. This is why RTOs and RPOs are distinct. Even if many of the technologies and features utilized for HA and DR are similar, the amount of effort and time required may not be.

All RTOs and RPOs should be fully documented and updated on a regular basis, as needed. After they have been documented, you can think about what technologies and features you might employ for the architecture.

Explore High Availability and Disaster Recovery Options

To visualize a virtual machine (VM) solution, you must first grasp the availability options for IaaS-based deployments.

Infrastructure-as-a-Service Versus Platform-as-a-Service

When it comes to availability, whether you choose IaaS or PaaS matters, you have a virtual machine with IaaS, which means there is an operating system and SQL Server installed. The SQL Server administrator or group would have a choice of high availability and disaster recovery (HADR) options, along with a considerable level of control over how that solution was configured.

HADR solutions are embedded into PaaS-based deployments such as Azure SQL Database and often only need to be enabled. There are only a few configuration choices.

Because of these distinctions, the decision between IaaS and PaaS may have an impact on the ultimate design of your HADR system.

SQL Server HADR Features for Azure Virtual Machine

When using IaaS, you can use SQL Server's functionality to boost availability. They can be used with Azure-level features in some circumstances to boost availability even further.

The features of SQL Server are listed in the table below.

Feature Name	Protects
Always On Failover Cluster Instance (FCI)	Instance
Always On Availability Group (AG)	Database
Log Shipping	Database

Table 07-01: Features of SQL Server

An instance of SQL Server is the whole SQL Server installation (binaries, all the objects inside the instance including things like logins, SQL Server Agent jobs, and databases).

EXAM TIP: Instance-level protection means that the availability feature takes into account the entire instance.

In SQL Server, a database contains the data that end-users and applications use. SQL Server relies on system databases as well as databases developed for end-users and applications. SQL Server instances always have their own system databases. Database-level protection means that anything in the database or captured in the transaction log for a user or application database is taken into account as part of the availability feature. Anything that exists outside of the database or is not captured in the transaction log, such as SQL Server Agent jobs and linked servers, must be dealt with manually to guarantee the destination server can function as the primary in the case of a planned or unexpected failover event.

FCIs and AGs both necessitate an underlying cluster mechanism. It is a Windows Server Failover Cluster (WSFC) for SQL Server deployments running on Windows Server and Pacemaker for Linux.

Always On Failover Cluster Instances

When SQL Server is installed, an FCI is configured. A standalone SQL Server instance cannot be converted to an FCI. The FCI is given a distinct name as well as an IP address that differs from the underlying servers or nodes in the cluster. In addition, the name and IP address must be distinct from the underlying cluster mechanism. For access, applications and end-users would use the FCI's unique name. Because of this abstraction, apps do not need to know where the instance is operating. One significant distinction between Azure-based FCIs and on-premises FCIs is that Azure requires an internal load balancer (ILB).

EXAM TIP: The ILB is used to ensure that applications and end-users may connect to the unique name of the FCI.

When an FCI fails over to another cluster node, whether it is initiated voluntarily or as a result of a failure, the entire instance restarts on the new node. That is, the failover procedure involves a complete shutdown and restart of the SQL Server. During failover, all applications or end-users connected to the FCI will be unplugged, and only programs that can handle and recover from this interruption will be able to reconnect automatically.

The instance goes through the recovery process when it starts up on the other node. The FCI will be consistent to the point of failure, so there will be no data loss theoretically. However, any transactions that need to be rolled back will be done so as

part of the recovery process. Since it is the instance-level protection, everything required (logins, SQL Server Agent jobs, etc.) is already in place, allowing businesses to resume as usual once the databases are ready.

FCIs requires only one copy of a database, but that copy also serves as the single point of failure. FCIs require some type of shared storage to ensure that another node can access the database. For Windows Server-based systems, this can be accomplished through an Azure Premium File Share, iSCSI, Azure Shared Disk, Storage Spaces Direct (S2D), or a third-party solution such as SIOS DataKeeper. FCIs that use SQL Server Standard Edition can have up to two nodes. FCIs also necessitates the usage of Active Directory Domain Services (AD DS) and Domain Name Services (DNS), implying that AD DS and DNS must be implemented someplace in Azure for an FCI to function.

Note: FCIs can leverage Storage Replica to create a native disaster recovery solution for FCIs using Windows Server 2016 or later, without the need for functionality such as log shipping or AGs.

Always On Availability Groups

AGs first appeared in SQL Server 2012 Enterprise Edition, and as of SQL Server 2016, they are also available in Standard Edition. An AG in Standard Edition can only have one database, but an AG in Enterprise Edition can have several databases. While AGs and FCIs have certain similarities, they are fundamentally distinct.

The most significant distinction between an FCI and an AG is that AGs give database-level protection. The primary replica is the instance in an AG containing the read/write databases. To keep it synced, the primary sends transactions through the log transport to a secondary replica. A primary replica's data movement can be synchronous or asynchronous. Any secondary replica's databases are in a loading state, which means they can receive transactions but cannot be completely writeable copies until that replica becomes the primary. An AG in Standard Edition can only have two replicas (one primary and one secondary), but Enterprise Edition can have up to nine replicas (one primary, eight secondary). A secondary replica is started either from a backup of the database or, starting with SQL Server 2016, via a function called 'automatic seeding.' The log stream transport is used by automatic seeding to stream the backup to the secondary replica for each database in the availability group using the configured endpoints.

An AG provides an abstraction to the listener. The listener is similar to the unique name issued to an FCI in that it has its own name and IP address that is distinct from everything else (WSFC, node, etc.). The listener likewise requires an ILB and goes through a stop and start the procedure. Applications and end-users can utilize the listener to connect; however, unlike an FCI, the listener is optional. Direct connections to the instance are possible. Secondary replicas in Enterprise Edition can also be

configured for read-only access and used for other features like database consistency checks (DBCCs) and backups if required.

AGs have a shorter failover time than FCIs, which is one of the reasons why they are appealing. While AGs do not require shared storage, each replica contains a copy of the data, increasing the total number of database copies and overall storage expense. Each duplicate has its own storage; for example, if the primary replica's database data footprint is 1 TB, each replica will have the same. Thus, if there are five clones, you will require 5 TB of storage.

Any item that exists outside of the database or that is not captured in the database's transaction log must be manually created and accounted for on each SQL Server instance that needs to become the new primary replica. SQL Server Agent jobs, instance-level logins, and linked servers are examples of items for which you would be responsible. It will be easier to gain access if you can utilize Windows authentication or contained databases with AGs.

Many enterprises may experience difficulties in developing highly available architectures and may just require the high availability provided by the Azure platform or a PaaS solution like Azure SQL Managed Instance. Before we go into Azure platform solutions, there is one more SQL Server function you should be aware of: log shipping.

Log Shipping

Log shipping has been around since SQL Server's early days. The capability is built on backup, copy, and restore and is one of the most basic ways to achieve HADR for SQL Server. Log shipping is mostly used for disaster recovery, although it can also be utilized to improve local availability.

Because log shipping like AGs provides database-level security, you must still care for SQL Server Agent jobs, related servers, instance-level logins, and so on. Because log shipping does not provide any native abstraction, a switch to another server participating in log shipping must be able to withstand a name change. If it is not possible, there are methods, such as DNS aliases, that can be configured at the network layer to try to reduce name change concerns.

The log shipping technique is straightforward: first, backup the source database on the primary server and then restore it in a loading state (STANDBY or NORECOVERY) on another instance known as a secondary server or warm standby. This new database copy is referred to as a secondary database. An automated process included in SQL Server will then back up the transaction log of the primary database. Then copy the backup to the standby server and ultimately restore the backup to the standby.

EXAM TIP: SQL Server HADR features are not the only way to improve IaaS availability. There are certain Azure features that should be evaluated as well.

Describe Azure High Availability and Disaster Recovery Features for Azure Virtual Machines

Azure offers three major solutions for improving availability for IaaS deployments:

- Availability Sets
- Availability Zones
- Azure Site Recovery

All three of these solutions exist outside of the virtual machine (VM) and have no idea what kind of workload is executing within it.

Availability Sets

Availability settings protect a single data center against Azure-related maintenance and single points of failure. This was one of the initial availability features added to the Azure platform, and it functions similarly to anti-affinity rules for your VMs. This means that if two SQL Server VMs were in an availability set or log shipping pair, they would never run on the same physical server.

To support both changes to the underlying Azure Infrastructure, availability sets are divided into fault domains and update domains. Fault domains are groups of servers within a data center that share a common power source and network. A data center can have up to three fault domains, as shown in the figure below by FD 0, 1, and 2. Update domains, marked by the letter UD in the figure below, are groups of virtual computers and underlying physical hardware that can be rebooted simultaneously. Separation is ensured by using different update domains.

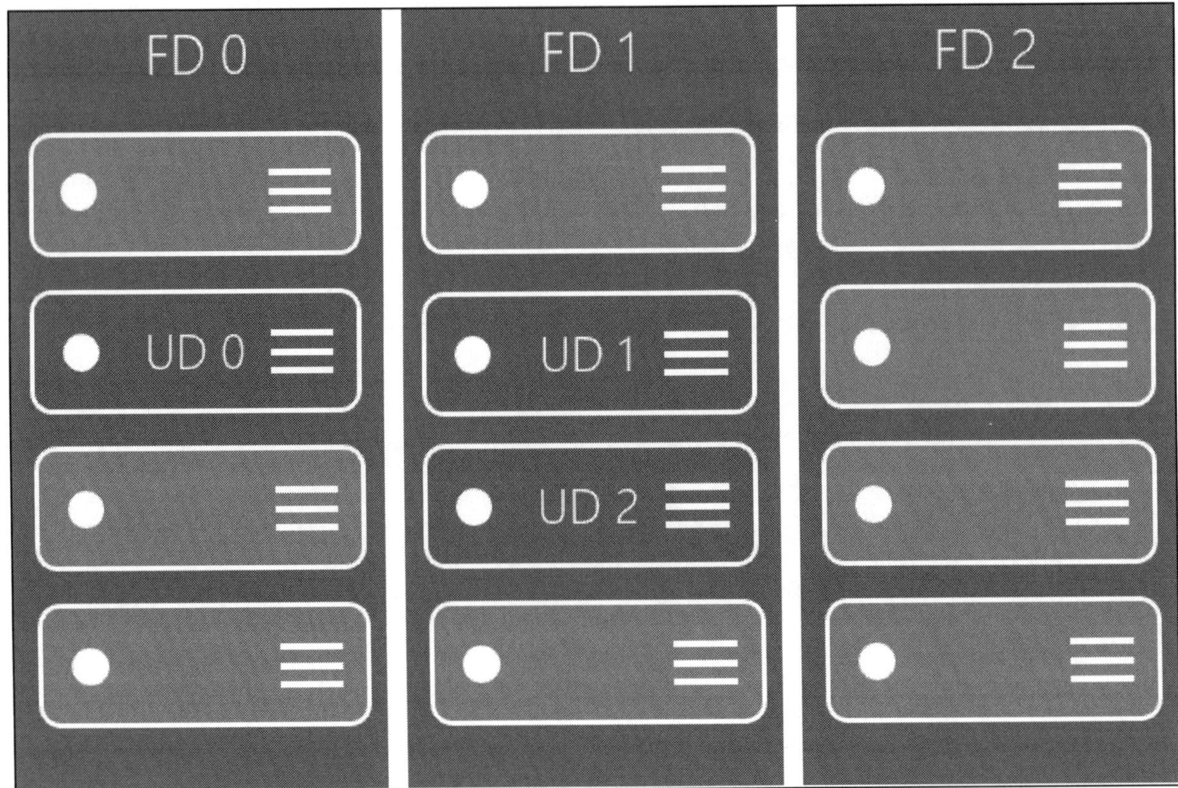

Figure 07-01: Availability Sets

Because availability sets and zones do not guard against in-guest failures such as an OS or RDBMS crash, you must use additional solutions such as AGs or FCIs to fulfill RTOs and RPOs. Both availability sets and zones are intended to mitigate the impact of environmental issues on the Azure level, such as datacenter failure, physical hardware failure, network outages, and power outages.

If you have a multi-tiered application, each tier should have its own availability set. For instance, if you were developing a web application with a SQL Server backend and Active Directory Domain Services (AD DS), you would define the availability set for each tier (web, database, and AD DS).

The use of availability settings is not the only method for separating IaaS VMs. Availability Zones are likewise provided by Azure, although they cannot be combined, and you can choose between the two.

Availability Zones

In Azure, availability zones account for data center-level failure. Each Azure region is made up of a number of data centers linked together by low-latency network links. When you install VM resources in a location that supports Availability Zones, you can choose from Zones 1, 2, and 3. A zone is a distinct physical location within an Azure region, such as a data center.

Zone numbers are logical representations. For example, just because two Azure subscribers deploy a VM into Zone 1 in their respective subscriptions, it does not imply that both VMs are located in the same physical Azure data center. Furthermore, due to the distance, some additional latency may be introduced into zonal deployments. You should evaluate the latency between your VMs to ensure that it matches your performance goals. Round-trip latency will be less than one millisecond in most circumstances, allowing for synchronous data transfer in features such as availability groups. Azure SQL Database can also be deployed into Availability Zones.

Azure Site Recovery

Azure Site Recovery improves VM availability at the Azure level and can be used with SQL Server-hosted VMs. Azure Site Recovery replicates a virtual machine (VM) from one Azure region to another in order to provide a disaster recovery solution for that VM. As previously stated, this feature is unaware that SQL Server is running in the VM and has no knowledge of transactions. Azure Site Recovery's monthly RTO is stated to be two hours. While most database experts prefer a database-based disaster recovery technique, Azure Site Recovery works well if it fits your RTO and RPO requirements.

Describe High Availability and Disaster Recovery Options for PaaS Deployments

When it comes to availability, PaaS is different; you can only configure the options that Azure provides.

Active geo-replication (Azure SQL Database only) and auto-failover groups are available for the SQL Server-based options of Azure SQL Database and Azure SQL Database Managed Instance (Azure SQL Database or Azure SQL Database Managed Instance).

Azure Database for MySQL includes a service level agreement that assures availability of 99.99 percent, which means there should be almost no downtime. If a node-level fault like hardware failure occurs in Azure Database for MySQL, a built-in failover method will take effect. Upon commit, all transactional changes to the MySQL database are written synchronously to storage.

> EXAM TIP: When a node-level interruption occurs, the database server generates a new node and attaches the data storage.

Because all connections are terminated as part of spinning up the new node, and any in-flight transactions are lost, you will need to implement the necessary retry logic from an application standpoint. This procedure is considered a best practice for any cloud application since it should be designed to tolerate transitory outages.

In its conventional deployment strategy, Azure Database for PostgreSQL is identical to MySQL. However, Azure PostgreSQL also offers a scale-out hyperscale solution called

Citus. Citus provides a server group with both scale-out and enhanced high availability. If enabled, a standby replica is configured for each node in a server group, which increases the cost by doubling the number of servers in the group. If the primary node experiences difficulty, such as becoming unresponsive or failing completely, the backup node takes its place. PostgreSQL synchronous streaming replication keeps the data in sync.

As with Azure Database for MySQL, PostgreSQL solutions must include retry logic in the application due to failed connections and loss of in-flight transactions.

The option for a read replica is available in both Azure Database for MySQL and PostgreSQL. This means that a replica can be used to offload tasks from the primary database, such as reporting. Because it exists in another region, a read replica improves availability.

Explore an IaaS High Availability and Disaster Recovery Solution

There are numerous feature combinations that might be deployed in Azure for IaaS. This topic will go through five common High Availability and Disaster Recovery (HADR) architectures for SQL Server in Azure.

Single Region High Availability Example 1 – Always On availability groups

If you only need high availability and not disaster recovery, setting an (availability group) AG is one of the most widely used techniques, regardless of where SQL Server is used. The figure below depicts an example of one conceivable AG in a single region:

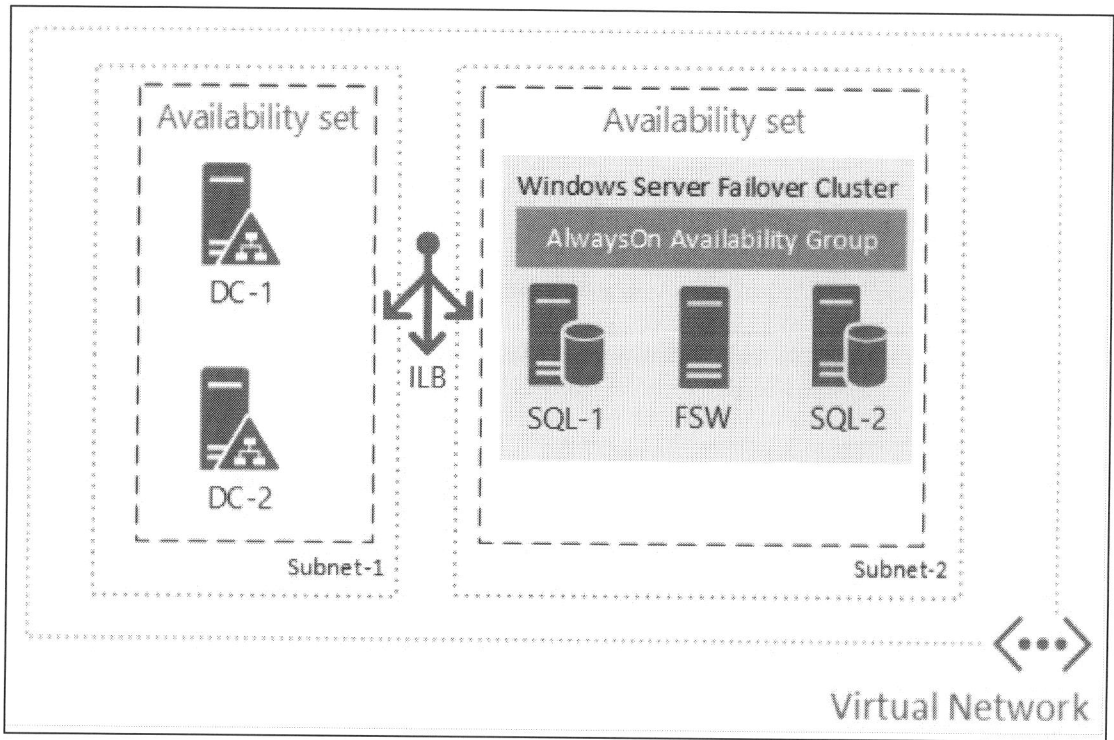

Figure 07-02: AG in a Single Region

Why should this architecture be considered?

- This design safeguards data by storing several copies on distinct virtual machines (VMs).
- If properly built, this architecture allows you to satisfy recovery time objectives (RTO) and recovery point objectives (RPO) with little to no data loss.
- This design gives programs a straightforward and standardized way to access both primary and secondary replicas (if things like read-only replicas will be used).
- This architecture improves availability in patching settings.
- Because this architecture does not require shared storage, it is less complicated than employing a failover cluster instance (FCI).

Single Region High Availability Example 2 – Always On Failover Cluster Instance

FCIs were the most popular approach to create SQL Server high availability prior to the introduction of AGs. FCIs, on the other hand, was created during a time when physical deployments were the norm. Because a VM rarely has a problem, FCIs in a virtualized world do not provide any of the same protections as they would on real hardware. FCIs were meant to defend against network card failure and disk failure, both of which are unlikely to occur in Azure.

FCIs, on the other hand, have a place in Azure. They function, and as long as you have realistic expectations about what will and will not be delivered, an FCI is a perfectly

acceptable option. The figure below depicts a high-level perspective of an FCI deployment utilizing Storage Spaces Direct:

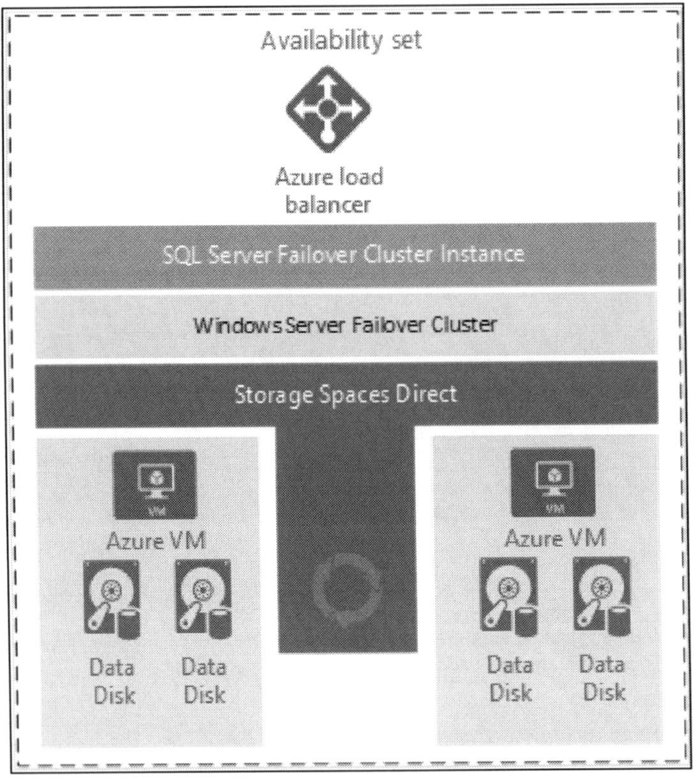

Figure 07-03: FCI Deployment

Why should this architecture be considered?

- FCIs are still a popular solution for availability.
- With features like Azure Shared Disk, the shared storage story is improving.
- This design meets the majority of RTO and RPO requirements for HA (although DR is not handled).
- This design gives programs an easy and standardized way to access the clustered instance of SQL Server.
- This architecture improves availability in patching situations.

Disaster Recovery Example 1 – Multi-Region or Hybrid Always On Availability Group

If you use AGs, you have the option of configuring the AG across several Azure regions or as hybrid architecture. This signifies that all nodes containing replicas are members of the same WSFC. This implies strong network connectivity, especially if the configuration is hybrid. One of the most important aspects of the WSFC would be the witness resource. This architecture will necessitate the availability of AD DS and DNS in each region, as well as perhaps on-premises if this is a hybrid solution. The figure below depicts a single AG configured across two locations using Windows Server:

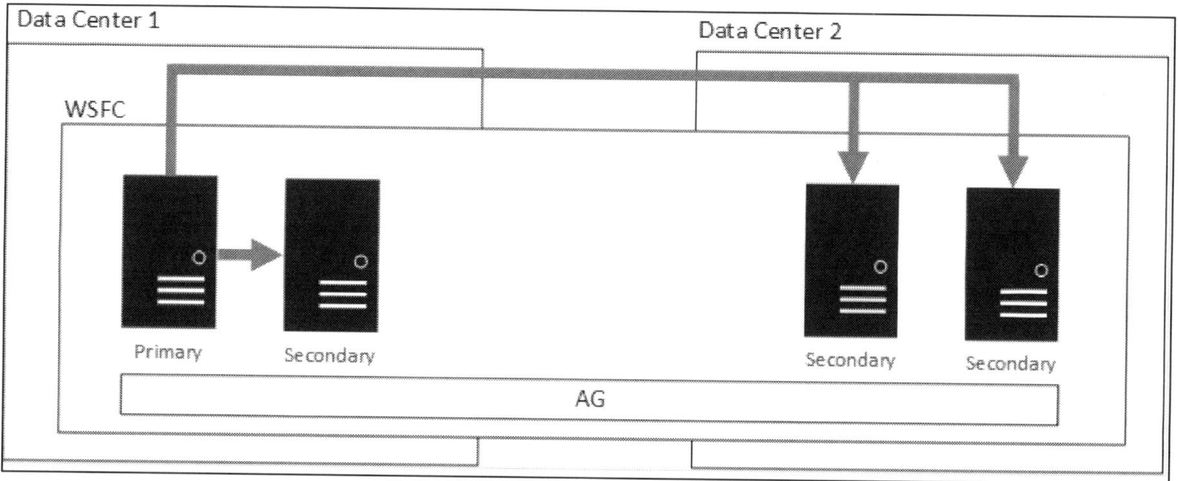

Figure 07- 04: Single AG Configured Across Two Locations

Why should this architecture be considered?

- This architecture is a tried-and-true solution; it is no different than having two data centers in an AG topology today.
- This design is compatible with SQL Server Standard and Enterprise editions.
- AGs naturally provide redundancy by storing multiple copies of data.
- This architecture makes use of a single feature that supports HA as well as D/R.

Disaster Recovery Example 2 –Distributed Availability Group

A distributed AG is a SQL Server 2016 Enterprise Edition-only feature, which is not like a regular AG. A distributed AG is made up of numerous AGs rather than having one underlying WSFC, with all nodes containing replicas participating in one AG, as indicated in the previous example. The global primary is the primary replica that contains the read-write database. The primary replica of the second AG is known as a forwarder, which is responsible for keeping the secondary replica(s) of that AG in sync.

This architecture makes dealing with issues like quorum easier because each cluster maintains its own quorum, which means it also has its own witness. A distributed AG would work whether you use Azure for all of your resources or a hybrid architecture.

The figure below depicts an example of a distributed AG architecture. There are two WSFCs in operation. Assume that each is in a different Azure region or that one is on-premises and the other is in Azure. Every WSFC has an AG and two replicas. The global primary in AG 1 keeps the secondary of AG 1's duplicate synchronized, as well as the primary of AG 2 called forwarder. That replica keeps AG 2's secondary replica synchronized.

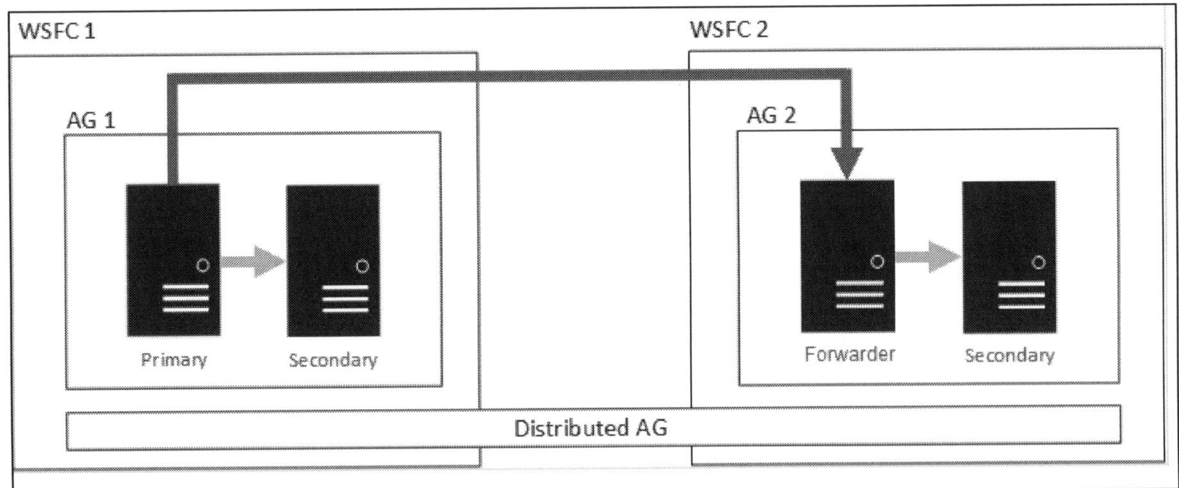

Figure 07-05: Distributed AG Architecture

Why should this architecture be considered?

- If all nodes lose communication, this architecture isolates the WSFC as a single point of failure.
- One primary replica does not synchronize all secondary replicas in this architecture.
- This architecture allows for failover from one place to another.

Disaster Recovery Example 3 – Log shipping

Log shipping is one of the older HADR approaches for establishing SQL Server disaster recovery. The transaction log backup is the unit of measurement, as previously stated. Data loss is almost certain unless a switch to warm standby is planned to assure no data loss. When it comes to disaster recovery, it is usually preferable to anticipate some data loss, even if it is minor. An example of log shipping architecture is shown in the figure below:

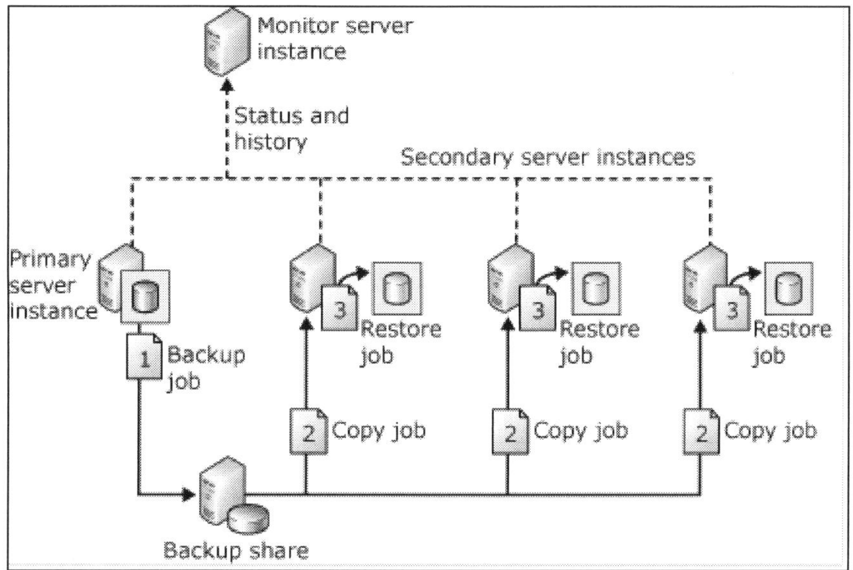

Figure 07-06: Log Shipping Architecture

Why should this architecture be considered?

- Log shipping is a tried-and-true feature that has been in use for more than 20 years.
- Because it is based on backup and restoration, log shipping is simple to deploy and manage.
- Log shipping is tolerant of unstable networks.
- Most RTO and RPO goals for disaster recovery are met through log shipping.
- Log shipping is an effective method of protecting FCIs.

Disaster Recovery Example 4 – Azure Site Recovery

Azure Site Recovery is an option for individuals who do not wish to adopt a SQL Server-based disaster solution. Most data professionals, however, favor a database-centric approach because it has a lower RPO.

Why should this architecture be considered?

- Azure Site Recovery will support more than SQL Server.
- RTO and perhaps RPO may be met with Azure Site Recovery.
- Azure Site Recovery is a feature of the Azure platform.

Describe Hybrid Solutions

You should now understand recovery time objectives (RTOs) and recovery point objectives (RPOs), as well as the various features available in SQL Server and Azure to increase availability. You can now combine all of this knowledge and design a solution to meet your high availability and disaster recovery (HADR) requirements.

While architecture can be deployed in one or more Azure regions, many organizations will require or prefer solutions that span both on-premises and Azure, or even Azure to another public cloud. A hybrid solution is a name given to this type of architecture.

By definition, PaaS systems are not intended to support traditional hybrid solutions. The Azure infrastructure provides HADR, but there are a couple of exceptions. For example, SQL Server's transactional replication functionality can be enabled from an on-premises (or other clouds) publisher to an Azure SQL Database Managed Instance subscriber, but not the other way around.

Because hybrid solutions rely on existing infrastructure, they are IaaS-based. Hybrid solutions are beneficial since a hybrid architecture can be utilized to aid the transition to Azure. However, it is most commonly employed to construct a solid disaster recovery solution for an on-premises system. In Azure, for example, a secondary replica for an AG can be added. It means that any accompanying infrastructure like AD DS or DNS must exist.

Networking is arguably an essential factor for a hybrid HADR solution that extends to Azure. If you do not have enough bandwidth, you can miss your RTO and RPO. ExpressRoute is a rapid networking option available in Azure. If your organization cannot or will not install ExpressRoute, create a secure site-to-site VPN so that the Azure VMs serve as an extension of your on-premises infrastructure. It is not recommended to expose IaaS VMs directly to the public internet.

EXAM TIP: Although Azure is not typically thought of as a hybrid platform, it can be utilized as the destination for a database backup as well as cold and archival storage for backups.

Explore IaaS and PaaS Platform Tools for High Availability and Disaster Recovery

Describe Failover Clusters in Windows Server

An underlying cluster is required for all availability settings of availability groups (AGs). There are numerous aspects of cluster setup that you should be aware of.

Considerations for a Windows Server Failover Cluster in Azure

Deploying a Windows Server Failover Cluster (WSFC) in Azure is identical to setting one up on-premises. There are several Azure-specific considerations, which will be addressed in this section.

Choosing what to use as a witness resource is one of the most crucial components. A witness is an essential part of the quorum method. Quorum is what ensures that

everything in the WSFC stays operational. If the quorum is lost, the WSFC will collapse, taking an AG or FCI with it. A disk, file share (SMB 2.0 or later), or cloud witness can be used as the witness resource. It is suggested that you utilize a cloud witness because it is entirely Azure-based, particularly for applications that span multiple Azure regions or are hybrid. Windows Server 2016 and later include the cloud witness functionality.

The Microsoft Distributed Transaction Coordinator (DTC or MSDTC) is the next point to consider. Some apps make use of it, although the vast majority do not. If you need DTC and you are deploying an AG or FCI, you need to cluster DTC. Clustering DTC requires a shared disk to function effectively even if you do not need one otherwise, as in the case of an AG.

Most WSFC implementations necessitate the usage of both AD DS and DNS, as do FCIs. AGs can be configured without AD DS but still require DNS. In Windows Server 2016, there is a Workgroup Cluster variation of a WSFC that can only be used with AGs.

The WSFC requires a unique name in the domain (and DNS) and an object in AD DS known as the Cluster Name Object (CNO). Anything with a name generated in the context of the WSFC will require a unique name as well as at least one IP address. IP addresses will be in a single subnet if the configuration remains in a single area.

EXAM TIP: If the WSFC spans numerous regions, more than one IP address, as well as an AG, will be linked with the WSFC.

A basic Azure-based WSFC will only necessitate the use of a single virtual network card (vNIC). Unlike an on-premises physical or virtual server, the IP address for the vNIC must be defined in Azure rather than in the VM. As expected, it will appear as a dynamic (DHCP) address inside the VM. However, cluster validation will produce a warning that may be safely disregarded.

Considerations for the WSFC's IP address differ from those on-premises. Because the IP address is fully preserved within the guest configuration, there is no way to reserve it at the Azure level. This implies that you must check for conflicts if later Azure resources that utilize an IP address employ DHCP.

The Failover Clustering Feature

Before a WSFC can be configured, the underlying Windows feature on each node that will participate in the WSFC must be enabled. This can be accomplished in one of two ways:

- Through the Server Manager
- Through PowerShell

Failover Clustering must be configured in the Add Roles and Features Wizard in Server Manager.

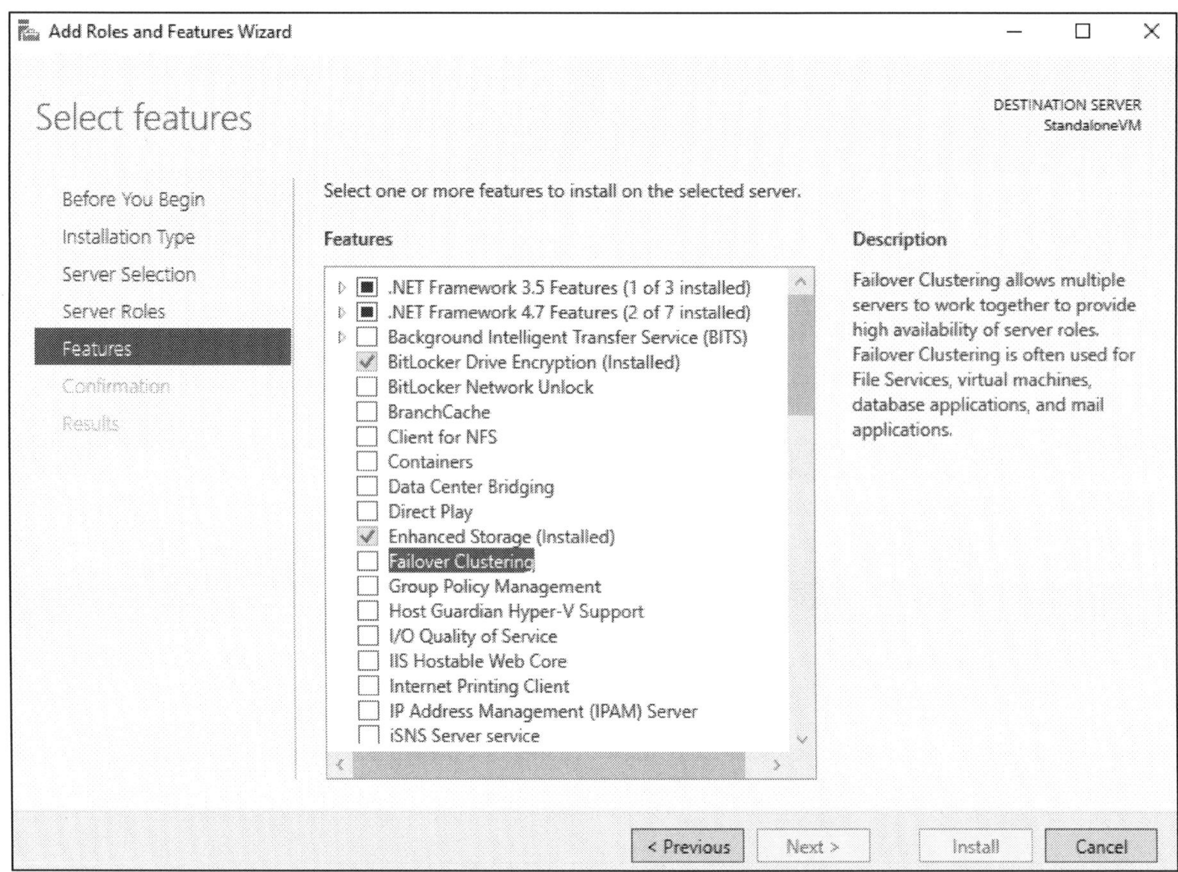

Figure 07-07: Add Roles and Features Wizard

Use the following command to enable the capability through PowerShell, which will also install the utilities required to administer a WSFC:

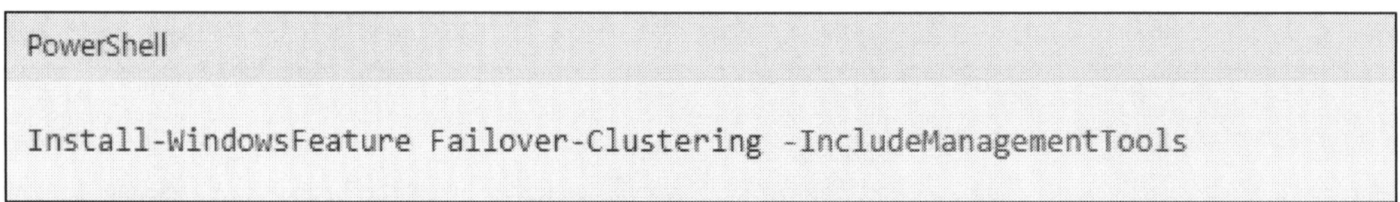

```
PowerShell

Install-WindowsFeature Failover-Clustering -IncludeManagementTools
```

Figure 07- 08: Sample Code

EXAM TIP: Once the functionality has been installed on the servers designated as WSFC nodes, the configuration must be validated.

Cluster Validation

A WSFC must pass cluster validation in order to be considered supported. Cluster validation is a built-in process that runs a number of tests on the nodes to confirm that the overall setup is adequate for clustering. Following validation, each of the tests will return an error, warning, pass, or a message indicating that the test is not applicable. If the condition is expected in your environment, warnings are permissible. If this is not the case, it should be addressed. All inaccuracies must be corrected.

Validation can be performed using Failover Cluster Manager or the Test-Cluster PowerShell cmdlet.

These tests additionally check the shared storage for FCIs to confirm that the discs are properly configured. In Windows Server 2016 and later, the results for AGs with no shared storage will be returned as not applicable. When there are no shared disks, the disk tests in Windows Server 2012 R2 will display a warning. This is to be expected.

After the cluster validation procedure has determined that the configuration is valid, you can proceed to establish the WSFC.

Create a Windows Server Failover Cluster

You cannot utilize the Wizard in Failover Cluster Manager for FCIs or AGs deployed with Windows Server 2016 or earlier to successfully construct a WSFC in Azure. Because of the DHCP issue noted previously, the only option to construct the WSFC at the moment is to use PowerShell and specify the IP address. This could change in future Windows Server versions.

Use the following syntax for a shared storage configuration:

```
PowerShell

New-Cluster -Name MyWSFC -Node Node1,Node2,…,NodeN -StaticAddress w.x.y.z
```

Figure 07-09: Sample Code

Here MyWSFC is the name you desire for the WSFC, Node1, Node2,..., NodeN are the names of the nodes that will participate in the WSFC, and w.x.y.z is the WSFC's IP address (for example: 10.252.1.100.) If you are constructing a WSFC that spans multiple subnets, you can give multiple IP addresses separated by commas for -StaticAddress.

Add the -NoStorage option to a configuration that does not have shared storage.

```
PowerShell

New-Cluster -Name MyWSFC -Node Node1,Node2,…,NodeN -StaticAddress w.x.y.z -NoStorage
```

Figure 07-10: Sample Code

The syntax is also slightly different for a Workgroup Cluster that will just use DNS.

```
PowerShell                                                                                   Copy
New-Cluster -Name MyWSFC -Node Node1,Node2,…,NodeN -StaticAddress w.x.y.z -NoStorage -AdministrativeAccessPoint
```

Figure 07-11: Sample Code

For IaaS, Windows Server 2019 will use a dispersed network name by default. A distributed network name generates only a network name, but the IP address is associated with the underlying nodes. If an IP address is not required or required, you do not need to specify it as stated above. A distributed network name can only be used with the name of a WSFC, as it cannot be used with the name of an AG or FCI.

Unless you tell it otherwise, the WSFC creation mechanism in Windows Server 2019 identifies whether it is running in Azure and creates the cluster with a distributed network name. Distributed network names are currently incompatible with FCIs, and while they do work with AGs, you may want to consider deploying a WSFC conventionally using PowerShell if you face a problem. You must add a new option: -ManagementPointNetwork with the value Singleton. As an example, consider the following:

```
New-Cluster -Name MyWSFC -Node Node1,Node2,…,NodeN
-StaticAddress w.x.y.z -NoStorage
-ManagementPointNetwork Singleton
```

Figure 07-12: Sample Code

You must guarantee that the name and IP address(es) for any name or IP address formed in the context of the WSFC, such as the WSFC itself, an FCI name and IP address, and an AG listener name and IP address are in DNS for a Workgroup Cluster.

Microsoft modified the way WSFCs are built by default in Azure with Windows Server 2019. It uses a distributed network name rather than a network name and an IP address. This is not yet supported by either of the Always-On features. Thus, the WSFC must still be created using the technique mentioned above.

Test the Windows Server Failover Cluster

You have to test that the WSFC is operational once it has been formed but before configuring FCIs or AGs. For clusters that require shared storage, like those that support a SQL Server Failover Cluster Instance, it is critical to validate the ability of all nodes in the cluster order to access any shared storage and take ownership of the storage as they would in a failover. In Failover Cluster Manager, click on **Storage** and then **Disks**, as seen in the figure below. You can move available storage by right-clicking on each clustered disc device.

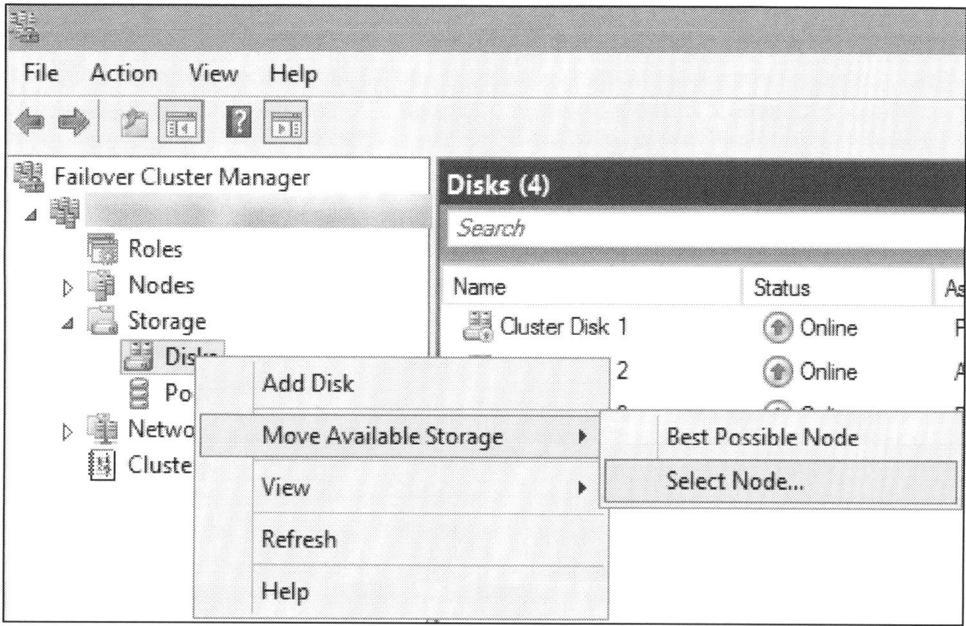

Figure 07-13: Failover Cluster Manager

Configure Always-on Availability Groups

An underlying cluster is necessary for all availability configurations of availability groups (AGs), whether or not they use AD DS. You will understand the factors for implementing an AG in Azure by the end of this section.

Considerations for Always On Availability Groups in Azure

Configuring an AG in Azure is virtually identical to doing it on-premises, as are the majority of the considerations, such as how to initialize secondary replicas. The majority of the Azure-specific factors, like the requirement for an ILB, have already been explored. As with the WSFC, you cannot reserve the listener's IP address in Azure. Therefore, you must ensure that nothing else comes along and grabs it, or else there may be a network conflict causing availability issues.

Place no permanent databases on ephemeral storage. All virtual machines (VMs) involved in an AG should have the same storage configuration. Depending on the application workload, drives must be adequately sized for performance.

The AG feature must be enabled before an AG can be configured. This can be done via SQL Server Configuration Manager (as seen in the figure below) or with PowerShell's Enable-SqlAlwaysOn cmdlet. Enabling the AG feature necessitates a restart of the SQL Server service.

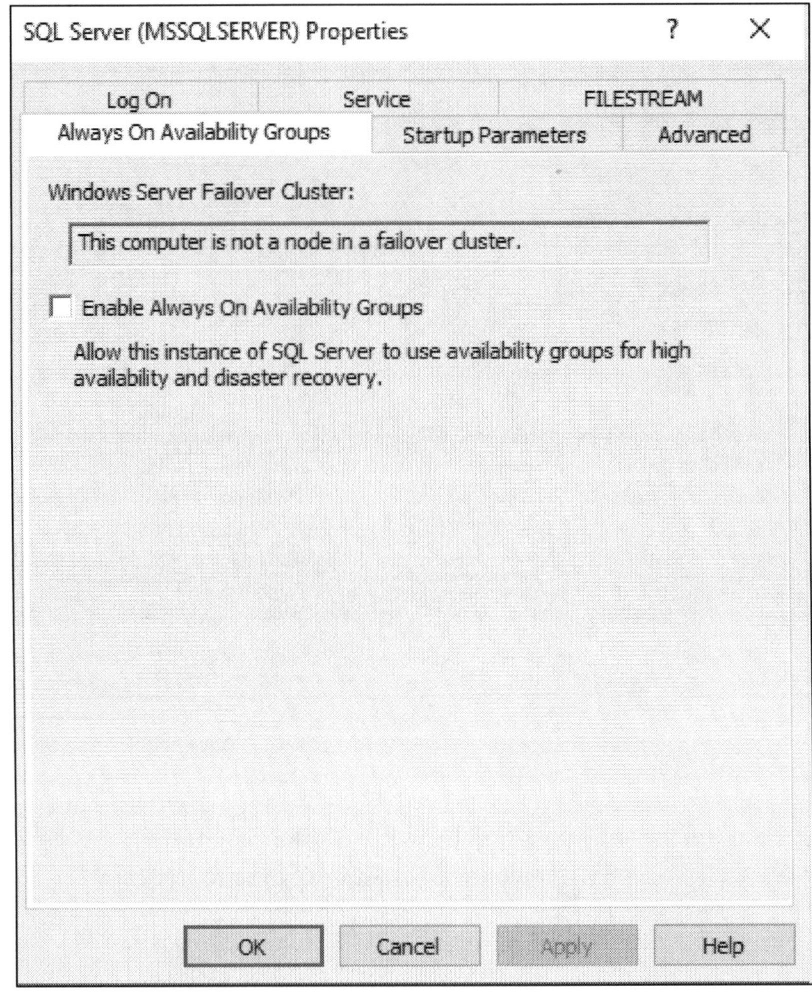

Figure 07-14: SQL Server Configuration Manager

Create the Availability Group

Creating an AG in Azure is identical to creating one on-premises. SQL Server Management Studio (SSMS), T-SQL, and PowerShell are all possible options.

The only difference is whether or not you build the listener as part of the original AG configuration because the listener necessitates the creation of an Azure load balancer and requires some further configuration in the WSFC relating to the load balancer.

Create an Internal Azure Load Balancer

After creating the listener, an internal load balancer (ILB) must be employed. Applications, end-users, administrators, and others cannot utilize the listener without configuring an ILB unless they are connected to the VM that contains an AG's primary replica.

Depending on your requirement or configuration, you can utilize a basic or standard load balancer. Availability Zone deployments necessitate the usage of a standard load balancer. The load balancer is set up with the listener's IP address and the port utilized for the listener.

EXAM TIP: Because a single load balancer can support more than one IP address, you may not need a separate load balancer for each AG setup on those nodes, depending on your standards.

The probe port is another factor to consider for the load balancer. The listener will not function properly without the probe port because simply creating the load balancer is insufficient. A unique probe port is required for each IP address that will use the load balancer. There must be two probe ports if there are to be two listeners. The probe ports have large numbers, such as 59999.

The probe port is configured with the following syntax on the IP address(es) connected with the listener:

```
PowerShell

Get-ClusterResource IPAddressResourceNameForListener | Set-ClusterParameter ProbePort PortNumber
```

Figure 07-15: Sample Code

Adding the probe port will necessitate a stop and start of the listener's IP address, which will also momentarily bring the AG offline. Therefore, it is advisable to get this configured before deploying it in production.

If you have a multi-subnet configuration, you must establish a load balancer in each subnet (whether or not the other subnet is deployed in a different region) and associate the probe port for that region with the IP resource for that subnet in the WSFC.

The only way to confirm that the listener is properly configured without physically connecting to it is to use the PowerShell cmdlet 'Test-NetConnection' with the particular port. The following is the syntax:

```
PowerShell

Test-NetConnection NameOrIPAddress -Port PortNumber
```

Figure 07-16: Sample Code

This command should be executed from a location other than the VM holding the primary replica.

Some situations may also need that the WSFC's IP address and specific ports (such as 445) be available for administration or other purposes. This may necessitate configuring those as part of the same or a different load balancer.

Once the load balancer has been verified to be operational, you may begin testing AG failover and listener access to the AG.

Distributed Availability Groups

Planning and configuring distributed AG on-premises is the same as it is on Azure, with the exception of any Azure-specific considerations for particular AGs. The key difference between an on-premises and an Azure configuration for a distributed AG is that the endpoint port for the AG must be added as part of the load balancer configuration in each region.

 EXAM TIP: The default port number is 5022.

Azure Site Recovery

Azure Site Recovery is a recovery option that works with the Virtual Machine regardless of whether SQL Server is operating inside of it. It is compatible with SQL Server, but it is not designed to account for nuances that may be necessary when you have a certain RPO. A VM's discs are replicated to another region when it is configured to use Azure Site Recovery. This replication is indicated by the "Data flow" arrow in the figure below.

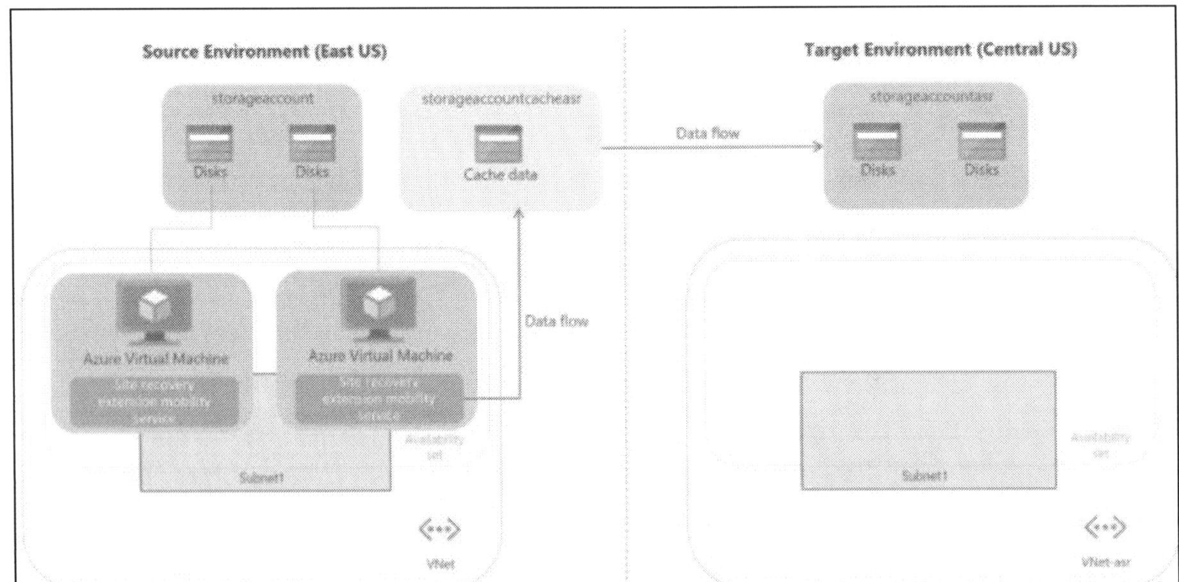

Figure 07-17: Azure Site Recovery

This means that all disk changes are replicated as soon as they happen, but this process is unaware of database transactions. As a result, recovering to a specific data point with Azure Site Recovery may not be achievable in the same manner that it is with a SQL Server-centric solution, such as when utilizing an AG.

If one of the in-guest choices for IaaS solutions cannot be deployed, Azure Site Recovery is a feasible option for disaster recovery management.

Additionally, Azure Site Recovery may be able to defend you from ransomware. If the VM becomes infected, you can roll it back to a point before the infection was introduced. From a SQL Server standpoint, this could result in data loss. Although some

data loss, especially in this scenario, may be more than acceptable, as up and running is often preferable to being out for hours, days, or weeks while attempting to eradicate ransomware from your network.

When you enable replication on a VM, you should be aware of the following:

- The VM is configured with a Site Recovery Mobility extension.
- Unless Azure Site Recovery is not configured or replication is deactivated, changes are sent continuously.
- Every five minutes, crash-consistent recovery points are generated, while application-specific recovery points are generated based on the replication strategy.

To reduce RPO, you may want to alter the 'App consistent snapshot frequency' parameter in SQL Server. However, as Azure Site Recovery uses Volume Shadow Service (VSS), reducing this value may cause problems for SQL Server because there is a brief freeze and thaw of I/O when snapshots are taken. If other options, such as an AG, are configured, the impact of the freeze and thaw could be amplified. Most will not have any problems; however, if Azure Site Recovery interferes with SQL Server, you may want to examine other choices for availability.

If many VMs are part of a larger solution, they can be replicated to establish a shared crash- and application-consistent recovery point. This is known as multi-VM consistency, and it has an effect on performance. It is not recommended to configure this option unless VMs must be restored in this manner.

EXAM TIP: One significant advantage of Azure Site Recovery is that you can test disaster recovery without interrupting production.

One thing to keep in mind with Azure Site Recovery is that when failover to another region occurs, the replica VMs are not protected when they are brought online. They will have to be protected again.

Describe Temporal Tables in Azure SQL Database

Temporal Tables is a feature of Azure SQL Database that allows you to track and evaluate changes to your data. This functionality necessitates the conversion of the tables themselves to temporal, which implies the table will have unique attributes and a related history table. You can utilize the Temporal Table functionality to recover data that has been deleted or updated by using the history table. Data recovery from the history table is a manual operation utilizing Transact-SQL. Although, it may be useful in some instances, such as if a user deletes essential data that the organization requires.

Describe Active Geo-replication for Azure SQL Database

Active geo-replication is another approach for increasing Azure SQL Database availability. Active geo-replication creates a replica of the database in another region that is kept up-to-date asynchronously. That replica, like an AG in IaaS, is also readable. Azure uses the same methods as an AG beneath the surface, which explains why some of the language and functionality are identical (primary and secondary logical servers, read-only databases, etc.).

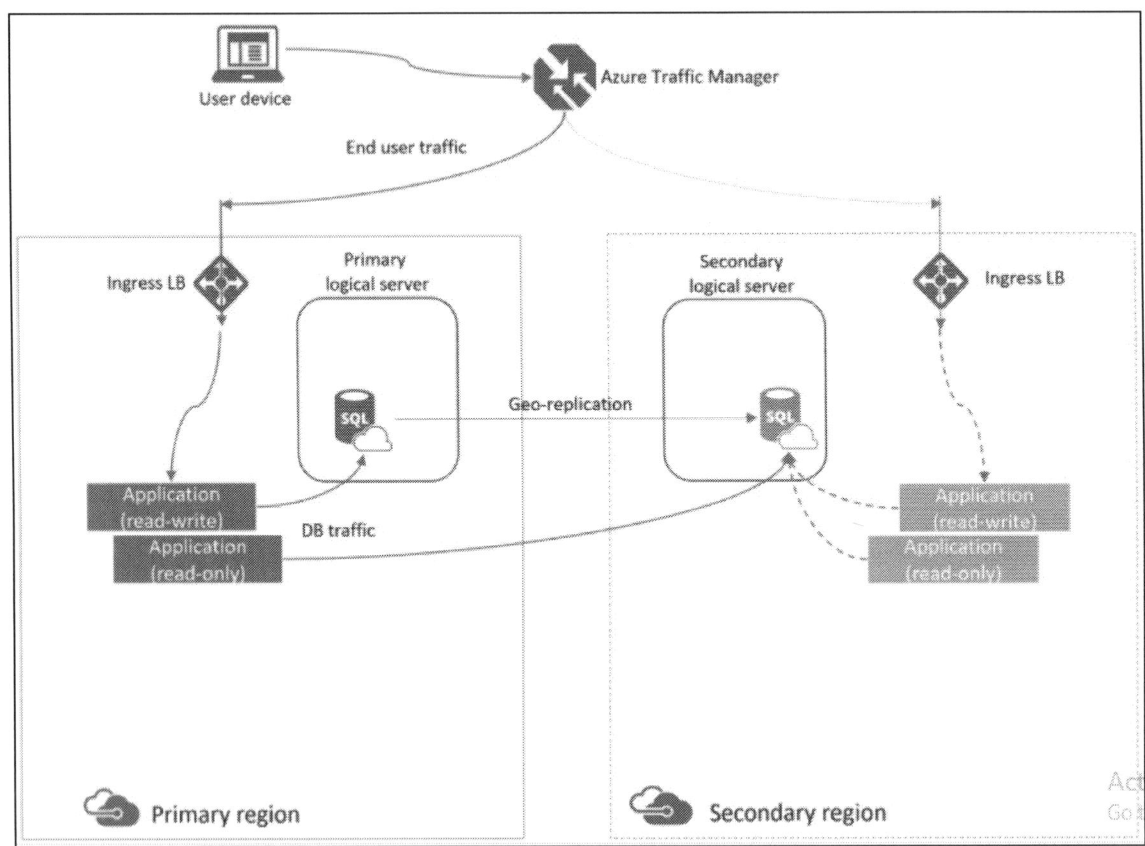

Figure 07-18: Active Geo-Replication for Azure SQL Database

Explore Auto-failover Groups for Azure SQL Database and Azure SQL Database Managed Instance

An auto-failover group is a type of availability feature that is available in both Azure SQL Database, and Azure SQL Database Managed Instance. Autofailover groups allow you to control how databases on an Azure SQL Database server or Azure SQL Database Managed Instance are replicated to another region and how failover occurs. The autofailover group's name must be unique within the *.database.windows.net domain. Only one autofailover group is supported by Azure SQL Database Managed Instance.

A listener, which permits both read-write and read-only activity, is provided by autofailover groups and provides AG-like capability. This functionality is depicted in the

figure below, which differs slightly from the one for active geo-replication. There are two types of listeners: one for read-write traffic and one for read-only traffic. DNS is adjusted behind the scenes during a failover so that clients can point to the abstracted listener name without knowing anything else. The primary is the database server that has the read-write copies, while the secondary is the server that receives transactions from the primary.

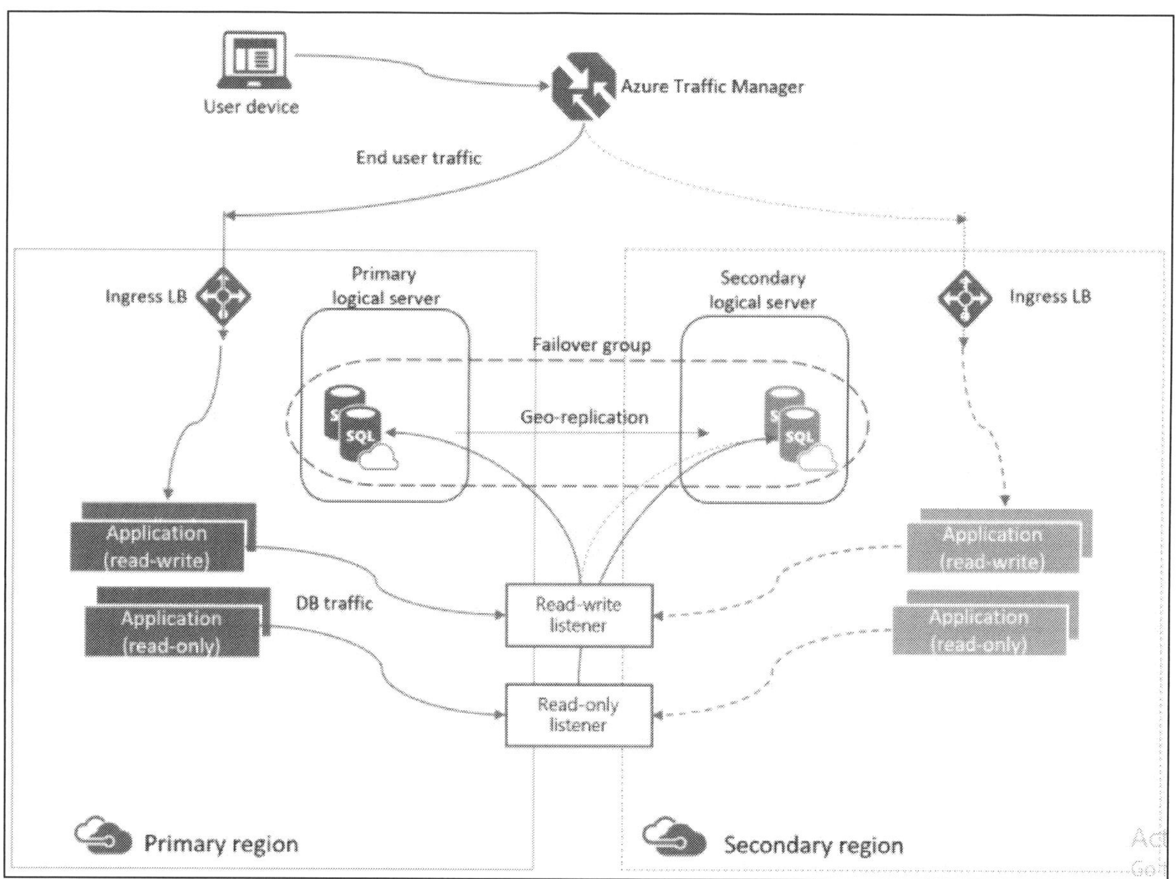

Figure 07-19: Auto-failover Groups for Azure SQL Database

When it comes to failover, autofailover groups can be configured with two different policies.

Automatic

When a failure occurs and it is decided that failover is required, the autofailover group will switch regions by default. The ability to automatically failover can be disabled.

Read-Only

When a failover occurs, the read-only listener is deactivated by default to ensure the new primary's performance while the secondary is down. This behavior can be adjusted such that following a failover, both forms of traffic are enabled.

Even if automated failover is permitted, failovers can be conducted manually. Data loss may occur depending on the type of failover. If forced and the secondary is not fully

synchronized with the primary, unplanned failovers may result in data loss. The GracePeriodWithDataLossHours configuration determines how long Azure waits before failing over. The timer is set to one hour by default. If you have a low RPO and cannot afford considerable data loss, increase the amount so that Azure waits longer before failing over, ideally resulting in less data loss.

One or more databases can be included in a single autofailover group. The primary and secondary databases will have the same size and edition. The database is automatically created on the secondary through a procedure known as seeding. Depending on the size of the database, this may take a while. Be careful to plan ahead of time, taking into consideration factors such as network speed.

Backup and Restore Databases

Backup and Restore SQL Server Running on Azure Virtual Machines

SQL Server has two database types: system and user. System databases, such as master and msdb, are used by SQL Server. User databases are those that are built by users to store data for applications. Both must be considered while developing a backup and recovery strategy. However, there are a few exceptions to consider. The nature of most system databases is that they are updated less regularly. System databases, as a general rule, are not recovered from one SQL Server instance to another.

EXAM TIP: Backing up the user databases should be your primary concern.

Full, differential, and transaction log backups are the most typical types of backups made for SQL Server deployments. Not all of these may be available, depending on the deployment technique.

A full database backup is a single database backup. When a backup is created, all of the database's pages are copied to the backup device. The backup provides enough information to restore the database to the point at which it was backed up. If you need to restore to a specific point in time to meet your RPO, you can do it via differential and/or transaction log backups. The transaction log is not flushed (or backed up) during a full backup. Only a transaction log backup accomplishes this, as detailed further below:

A differential backup includes all database pages that have changed since the last full backup.

A transaction log backup is utilized not only to achieve RPO and get to a more granular point in time but also to clear the transaction log and maintain its manageable size. Backups of transaction logs can be made as regularly as every 30 seconds, though this is impracticable.

Other backup choices include copy-only, file, filegroup, partial, and others.

After restoring a full database, a differential or log backup can be restored if the database RESTORE command includes the WITH NORECOVERY or WITH STANDBY options. If neither option is selected, the database RESTORE will perform a database recovery, after which no subsequent backups can be applied.

Every SQL Server database employs one of three recovery strategies: FULL, BULK LOGGED, or SIMPLE. The recovery model is configured as a database option and determines the kind of backups and restores that can be performed on the database. The majority of databases are configured to FULL or SIMPLE. FULL supports all forms of backups, while SIMPLE does not support transaction log backups. As a result, if you have a lower RPO, SIMPLE may not suit your needs because you cannot restore to a specific point in time.

Backup a SQL Server Virtual Machine

VMs comprising of SQL Server can be backed up using Azure Backup. These backups would include more than just SQL Server databases. They would include everything in the VM so that it could be restored as a whole. While this method may not be suitable for everyone, it has the ability to protect against issues such as ransomware.

Because VM-level backups are SQL Server-aware, also known as application-aware, they provide an application-consistent backup. This means that restoring a VM-level backup will not 'break' SQL Server. If you choose this option, you will notice in the SQL Server log that the I/O has been frozen for a brief period of time and then resumes when completed. If this causes problems with availability features such as AGs, you might want to reconsider your backup plan.

Combining SQL Server backups and snapshots may result in problems. Set the following registry key if snapshot delays cause backup failures:

```
[HKEY_LOCAL_MACHINE\SOFTWARE\MICROSOFT\BCDRAGENT]
"USEVSSCOPYBACKUP"="TRUE"
```

Figure 07-20: Registry Key

Use Local Disks or a Network Share for Backup Files

Databases like on-premises SQL Server instances can be backed up to disks attached to the VM or network shares (including the Azure Files file share) that SQL Server has access to. If you backup to disks on the VM, be sure they are not written to ephemeral storage, which is wiped upon shutdown or restart. You should also ensure that backups are replicated to a secondary place to avoid creating a single point of failure.

Backup Databases to and Restore from URL

Another alternative is to configure the SQL Server instance deployed in the VM to backup to a URL. Unlike on-premises backups, backup and restore from URL for an IaaS VM is essentially a local option.

Backup to URL necessitates the usage of an Azure storage account and the Azure blob storage service. Containers are located within the storage account, and blobs are saved within them. The path to a backup file, unlike a path on your local disc, will appear something like: https://ACCOUNTNAME.blob.core.windows.net/ContainerName/MyDatabase.bak. Additional folder names can be added to your container for easier backup identification (for example, FULL, DIFF, LOG).

Authentication must be established between the SQL Server instance and Azure in order to backup to or restore from a URL. Remember that SQL Server within an Azure VM is unaware that it is operating on Azure. A SQL Server Credential is made up of the Azure storage account's name and access key authentication, or it might be a Shared Access Signature. The backup will be stored as a page blob if the former is utilized and as a block blob if the latter is used. Because only block blobs are available starting with SQL Server 2016, you need to utilize a Shared Access Signature.

> EXAM TIP: Block blobs are also less expensive, while Shared Access Signature tokens provide better security control.

Restoring from a URL is just like restoring from a disk or a network share. Select URL from the backup media type in the Wizard of the SQL Server Management Studio UI. Instead of FROM DISK, you would use FROM URL with the appropriate location and backup file name if using Transact-SQL (s). Given below are a few examples of statements:

The following statement would serve as a backup for a transaction log.

```
Transact-SQL

BACKUP LOG contoso
TO URL = 'https://myacc.blob.core.windows.net/mycontainer/contoso202003271200.trn'
```

Figure 07-21: Sample Code

The following line will restore a full database backup without recovering it, allowing you to use differential or transaction log backups.

Transact-SQL

```
RESTORE DATABASE contoso
FROM URL = 'https://myacc.blob.core.windows.net/mycontainer/contoso20200327.bak'
WITH NORECOVERY
```

Figure 07-22: Sample Code

Automated Backups Using the SQL Server Resource Provider

The SQL Server resource provider can be used by any IaaS VM that has SQL Server installed. One of its features is the ability to configure automated backups so that Azure handles SQL Server database backups. It necessitates the creation of a storage account.

One advantage of deploying backups in this manner is that you may control backup retention times. Another advantage is that you can ensure RPO by storing database and transaction log backups in a single, easy-to-configure location. The figure below depicts an example of configuring an automated backup in the Azure portal.

AUTOMATED BACKUP

Configure backups for databases in your virtual machine. All your SQL Server databases in this virtual machine will be backed up automatically per the settings you choose. If you decide to change settings via SQL Server Managed Backup in the future, the new settings will override the Automated Backup settings.

Automated backup	Disable **Enable**
Retention period (days)	30
Storage account *	**module7storage (Standard_RAGRS)** https://module7storage.blob.core.windows.net/ Select storage account
Encryption	**Disable** Enable
Backup system databases	Disable **Enable**
Configure backup schedule	Automated **Manual** Specify the schedule for full and log backups
FULL BACKUP SCHEDULE	
Backup frequency	**Daily** Weekly Take full backups every day at the specified start time
Backup start time (local VM time)	15:00 (3:00 p.m.)
Full backup time window (hours)	1
LOG BACKUP SCHEDULE	
Backup frequency (minutes)	10

Figure 07-23: Configuring an Automated Backup

Backup and Restore a Database Using Azure SQL Database

Backing up and restoring an Azure SQL Database is not the same as IaaS.

Backups for Azure SQL Database are generated automatically. All backups are stored as read-access, geo-redundant (RA-GRS) blobs that are replicated to a datacenter paired, according to Azure criteria. That implies backups are safe from a single data center outage.

As indicated in the image below, backup policies can be specified per database. With retention policies, Azure SQL Database can help you stay compliant with necessary backups for regulatory purposes.

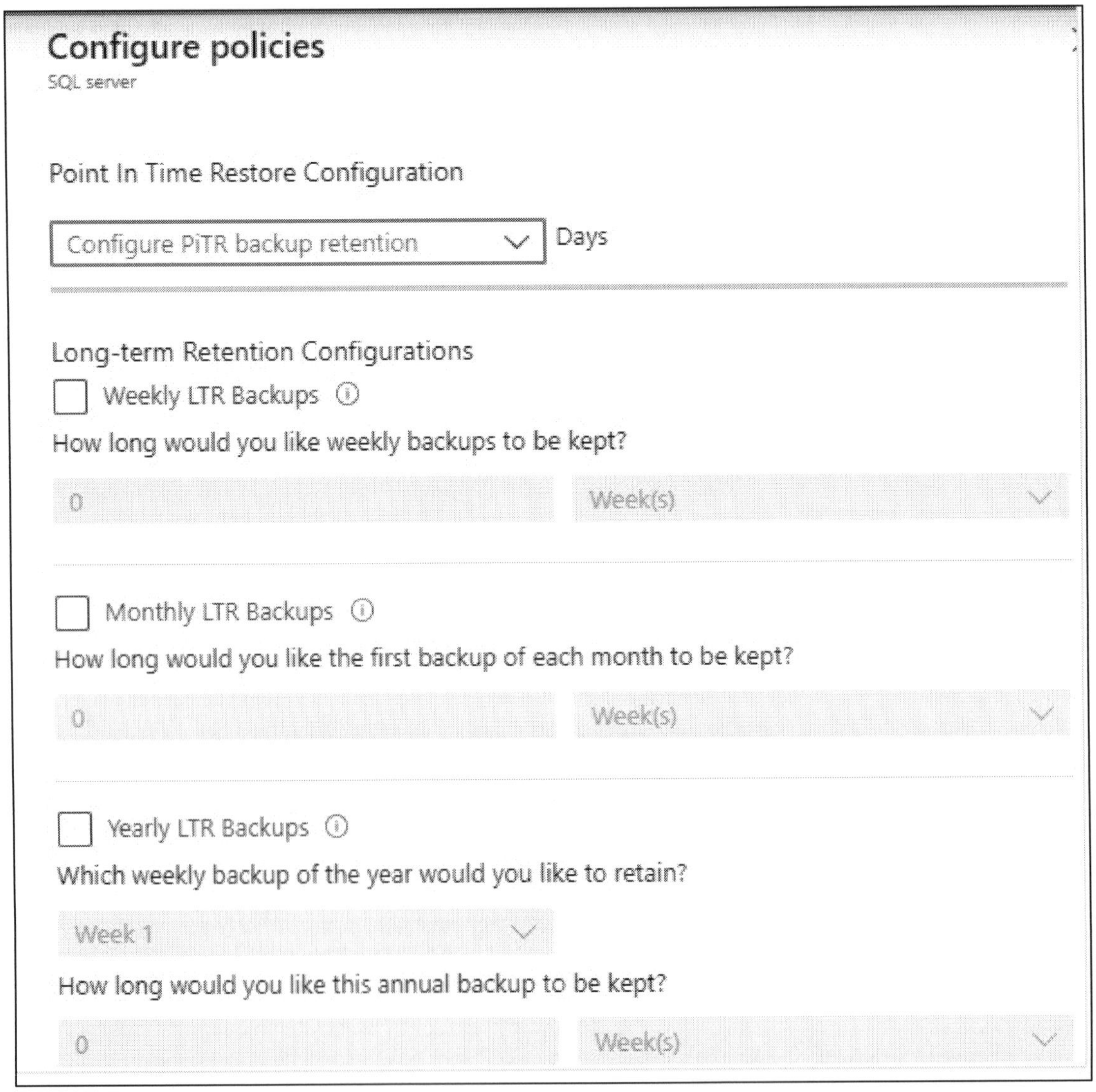

Configure policies
SQL server

Point In Time Restore Configuration

Configure PiTR backup retention | Days

Long-term Retention Configurations

Weekly LTR Backups

How long would you like weekly backups to be kept?

0 | Week(s)

Monthly LTR Backups

How long would you like the first backup of each month to be kept?

0 | Week(s)

Yearly LTR Backups

Which weekly backup of the year would you like to retain?

Week 1

How long would you like this annual backup to be kept?

0 | Week(s)

Figure 07-24: Configuring Policies

EXAM TIP: If the database server is erased, all backups are deleted at the same time, and there is no way to retrieve them. If the server is not removed, but the database is, the database can be normally restored.

Accelerated Database Recovery (ADR) is a feature available in both Azure SQL Database, and Azure SQL Database Managed Instance. Its goal is to reduce the time required to deal with long-running transactions so that they do not affect recovery time. Although ADR was designed for Azure and was originally an Azure-only feature, it was also included in SQL Server 2019.

Note: Backups created for Azure SQL Database are incompatible with Azure SQL Database Managed Instances or any version of SQL Server.

Database Backup and Restore for Azure SQL Database Managed Instance

Azure, by default, produces backups for databases in Azure SQL Database Managed Instance and performs functions similar to Azure SQL Database.

You may also back up and restore databases manually using Azure SQL Database Managed Instance, utilizing the same backup to URL/restore from URL capabilities that were previously discussed in SQL Server. This necessitates the usage of credentials to gain access to Azure Blob Storage.

There is one significant difference: for full backups, you can only create a COPY ONLY backup since Azure SQL Database Managed Instance keeps the log chain. A sample backup statement would be as follows:

```
Transact-SQL

BACKUP DATABASE contoso
TO URL = 'https://myacc.blob.core.windows.net/testcontainer/contoso.bak'
WITH COPY_ONLY
```

Figure 07-25: Sample Code

Backups produced by the Azure SQL Database Managed Instance cannot be used to restore a SQL Server or Azure SQL Database.

Database Backup and Restore for Azure Database for MySQL

Backups of the data files and transaction log are made automatically in either locally or geo-redundant storage for Azure Database for MySQL. The backups are encrypted and have a retention period of seven days by default, with a maximum of 35 days. One advantage of backups is that they are free; if a server is supplied with 100 GB of storage, an equal amount of backup space is included in the price you are already paying. However, there will be a fee if backup storage surpasses 100 GB.

Restores can be done to a specific point in time or as a geo-restore, which recovers the database in another region if geo-redundant storage is enabled.

These backups, like Azure SQL Database and Azure SQL Database Managed Instance, can only be utilized by Azure Database for MySQL and not by a conventional MySQL installation.

Database Backup and Restore for Azure Database for PostgreSQL

The Azure Database for PostgreSQL backup and restoration process is similar to that of MySQL. Backups are performed automatically, where both data files and transaction logs are saved. The retention and encryption settings are the same, as are the options for local or geo-redundancy, pricing, and restoration. The main difference is that Azure will create complete and differential backups (up to 4 TB) or snapshot backups based on the specified maximum storage size (up to 16 TB).

These backups, like all other Azure PaaS products, can only be used by Azure Database for PostgreSQL and not by a conventional PostgreSQL installation.

Lab 7-01: Plan and Implement a High Availability and Disaster Recovery Environment

Introduction

Active geo-replication is another approach for increasing Azure SQL Database availability. Active geo-replication creates a replica of the database in another region that is kept up-to-date asynchronously.

Unlike on-premises backups, backup and restore from URL for an IaaS VM is essentially a local option.

Backup to URL necessitates the usage of an Azure storage account and the Azure blob storage service. Containers are located within the storage account, and blobs are saved within them.

Problem

Your Organization has given you the task to set up geo-replication for Azure SQL Database and backup a database to an Azure URL.

Solution

You are working as a DBA for your Organization. You must understand how to set up geo-replication for Azure SQL Database, confirm that it is operational, and manually fail it over to another region via the portal.

As a DBA, you must back up a database to an Azure URL and restore it after a human error.

Pre-requisites:

To perform this lab, you must have the following:

- Azure SQL Server
- Azure SQL Database
- SQL Server Management Studio

Step 1: Enable geo-replication

1. Select the **Menu** and then **SQL databases** from the Home screen.

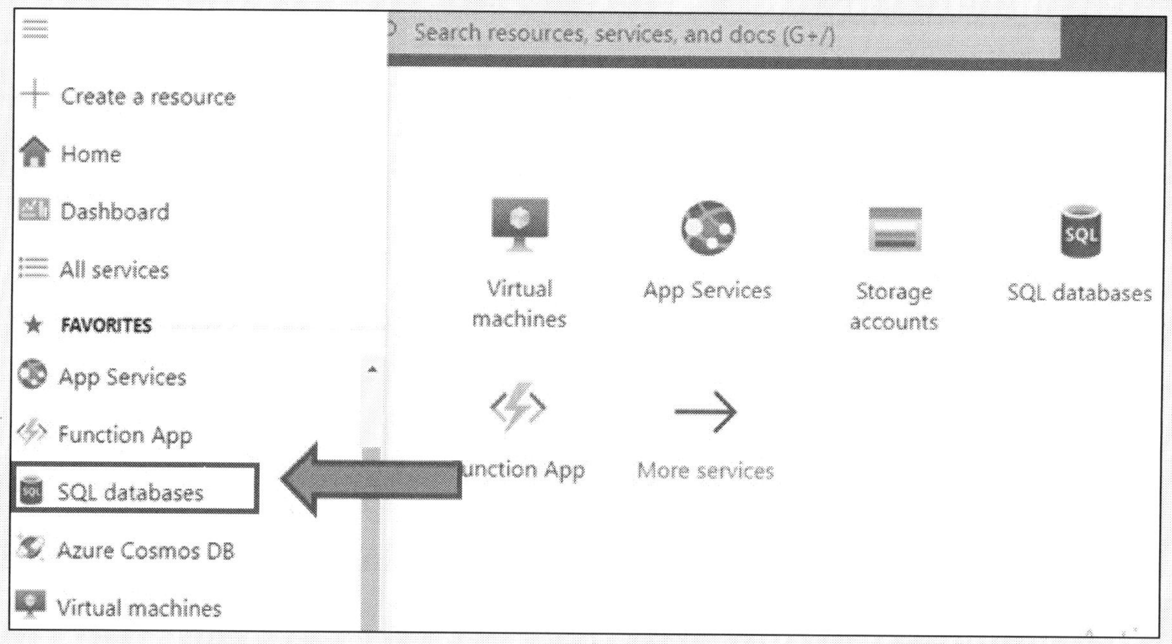

2. Select your **Azure SQL Database**.

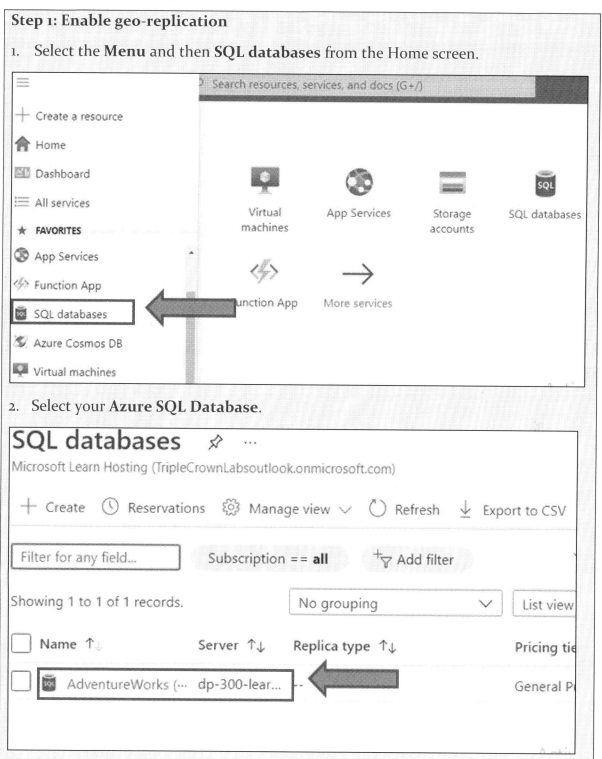

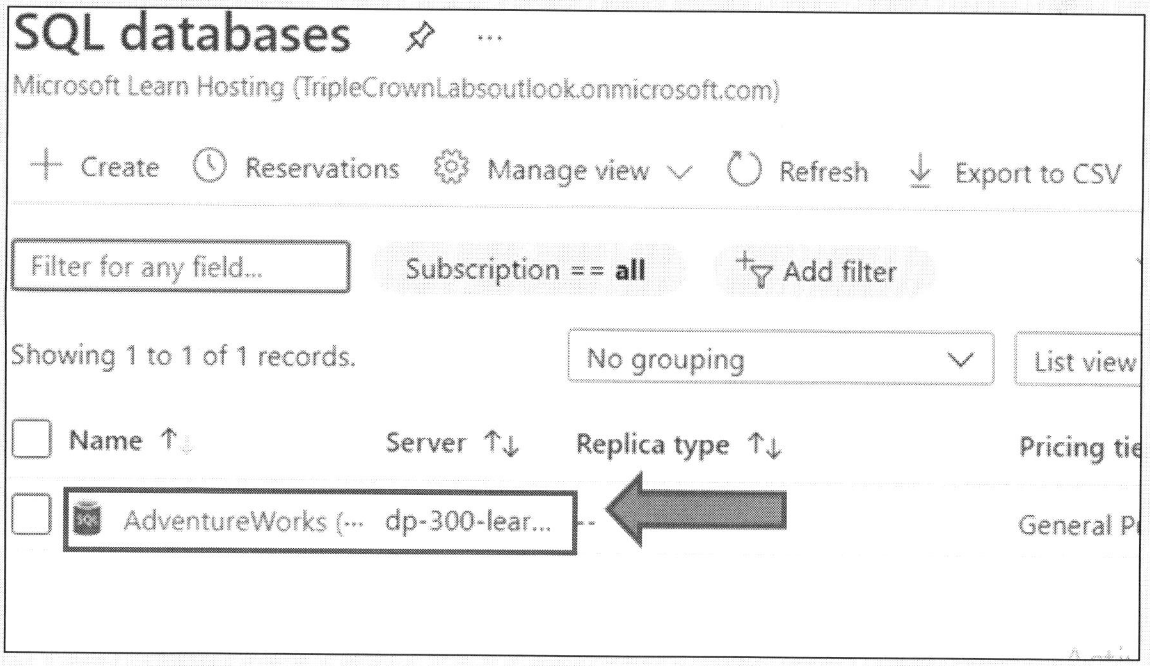

3. Select **Geo-Replication** from the Database blade's Settings.

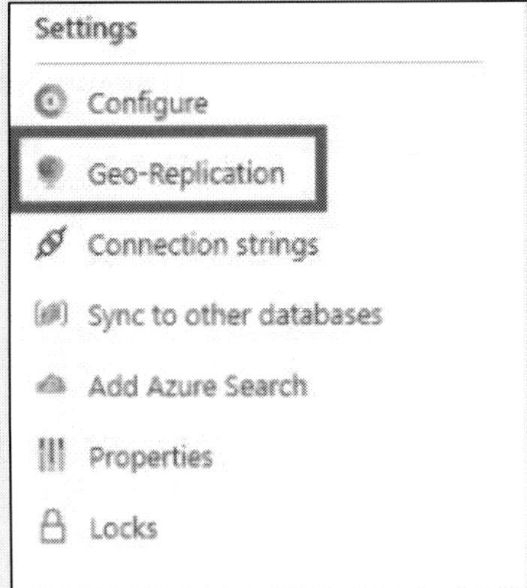

4. Choose one of the Target locations at the bottom of the blade. A hexagon with a green outline will be drawn around all available regions.
5. West US 2 was chosen in this example, as seen on the Create secondary blade.

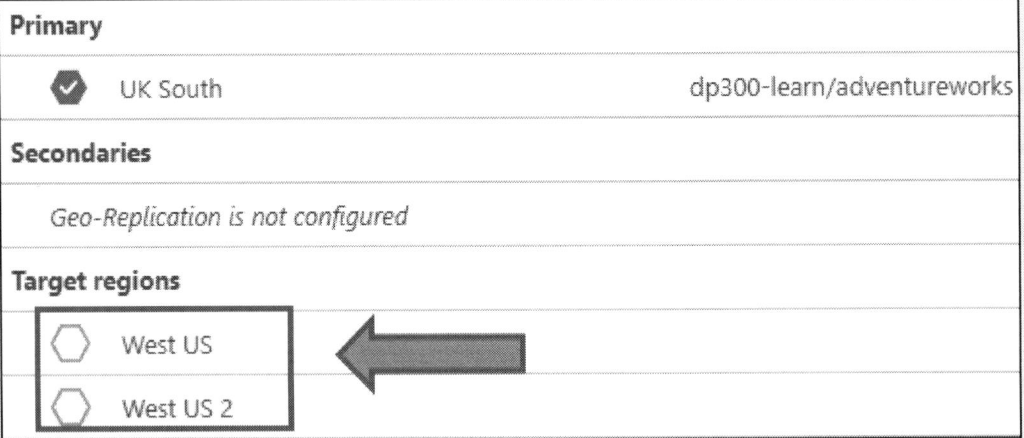

6. Choose the target server.

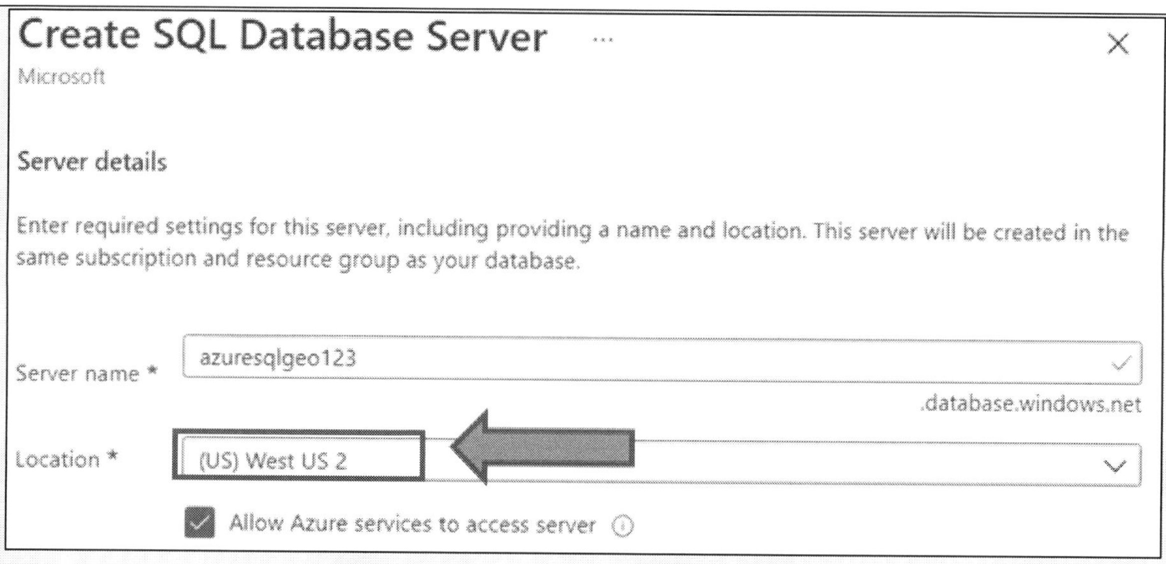

Create SQL Database Server ...
Microsoft

Server details

Enter required settings for this server, including providing a name and location. This server will be created in the same subscription and resource group as your database.

Server name * azuresqlgeo123 .database.windows.net

Location * (US) West US 2

Allow Azure services to access server

7. Enter a server name and a server admin login on the new server blade. Enter and validate a safe password. When you are finished, click **Select**.

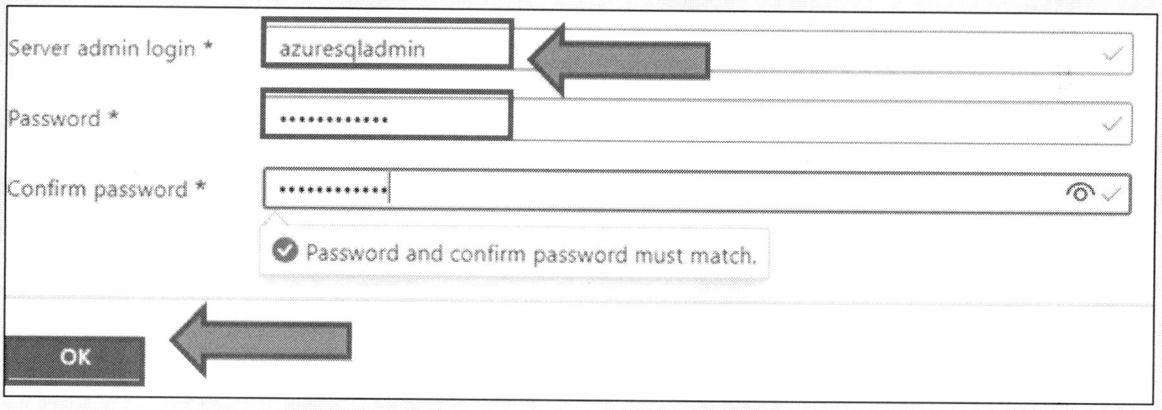

Server admin login * azuresqladmin

Password * ••••••••••••

Confirm password * ••••••••••••

Password and confirm password must match.

OK

8. On the Create secondary blade, click **OK**. The secondary server and database will be established now. To check the status, go to the top of the site and click the Notifications icon. If it is successful, it will move from Deployment in Progress to Deployment Successful.

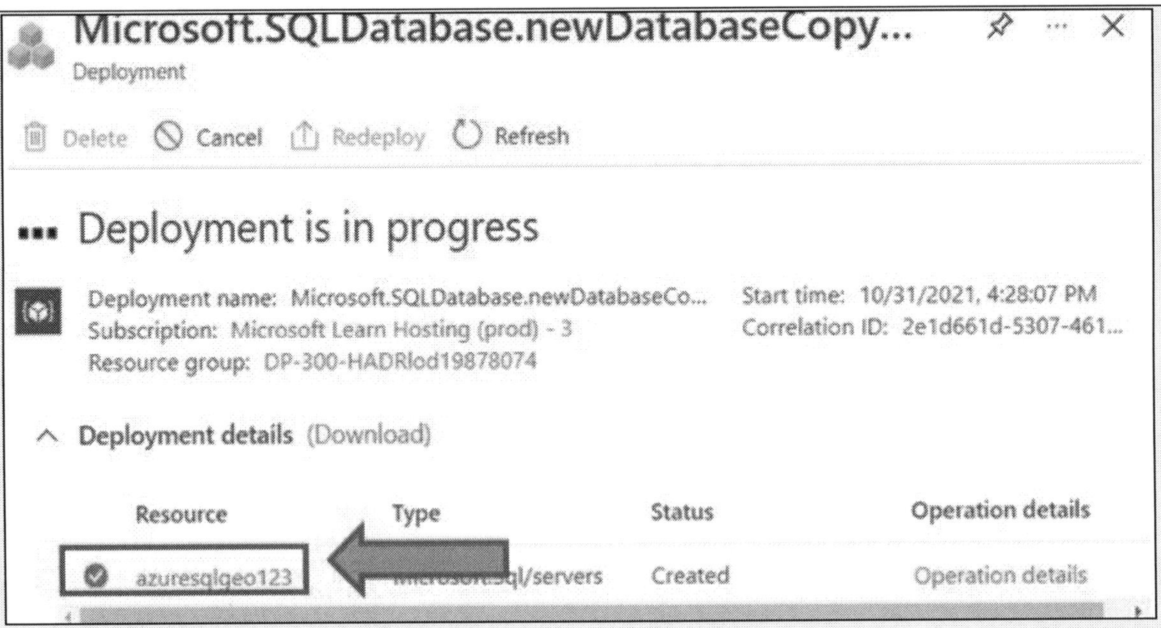

Microsoft.SQLDatabase.newDatabaseCopy...

Deployment

Delete Cancel Redeploy Refresh

Deployment is in progress

Deployment name: Microsoft.SQLDatabase.newDatabaseCo...
Subscription: Microsoft Learn Hosting (prod) - 3
Resource group: DP-300-HADRlod19878074

Start time: 10/31/2021, 4:28:07 PM
Correlation ID: 2e1d661d-5307-461...

Deployment details (Download)

Resource	Type	Status	Operation details
azuresqlgeo123	...l/servers	Created	Operation details

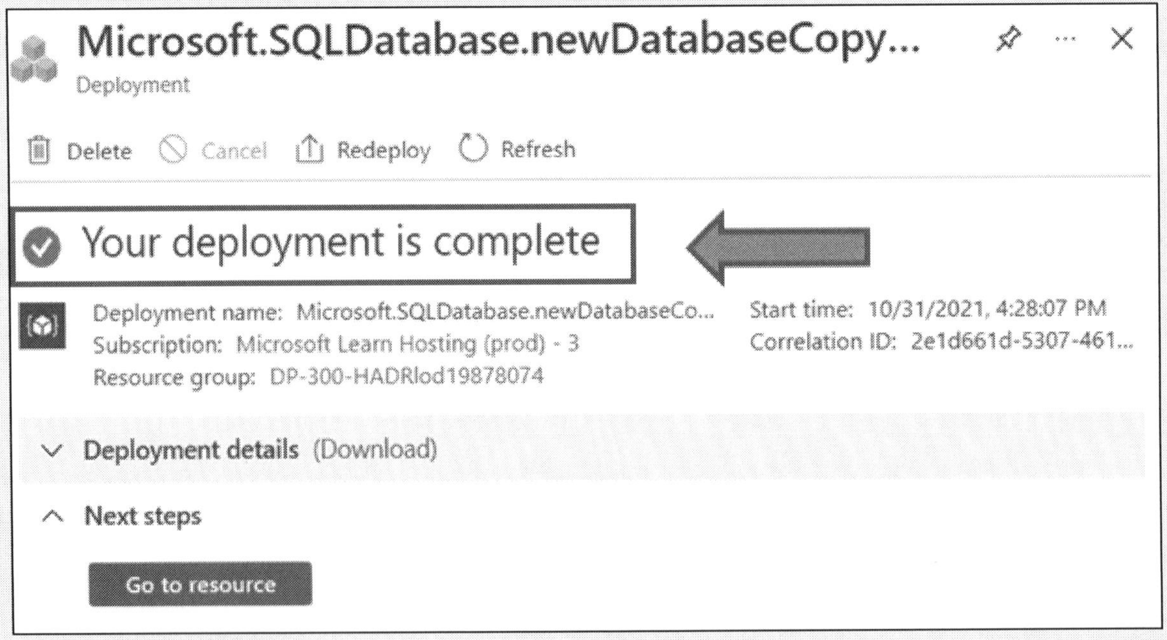

Microsoft.SQLDatabase.newDatabaseCopy...

Deployment

Delete Cancel Redeploy Refresh

Your deployment is complete

Deployment name: Microsoft.SQLDatabase.newDatabaseCo...
Subscription: Microsoft Learn Hosting (prod) - 3
Resource group: DP-300-HADRlod19878074

Start time: 10/31/2021, 4:28:07 PM
Correlation ID: 2e1d661d-5307-461...

Deployment details (Download)

Next steps

Go to resource

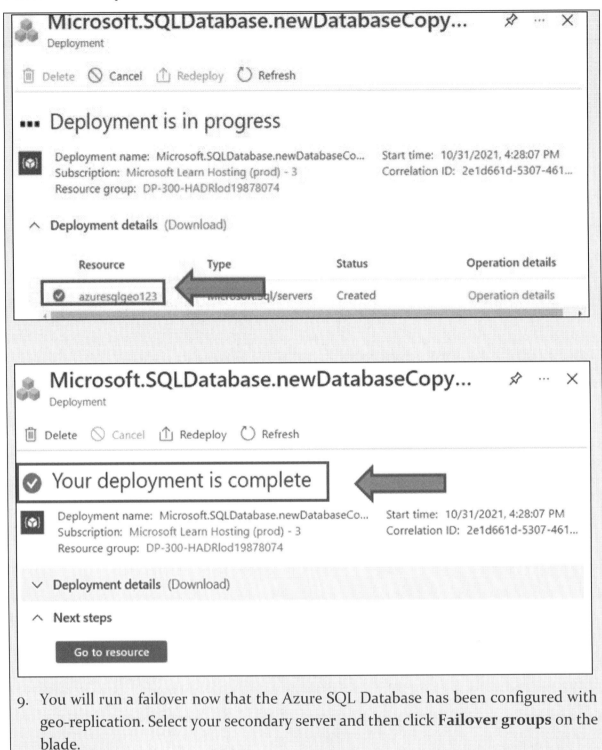

9. You will run a failover now that the Azure SQL Database has been configured with geo-replication. Select your secondary server and then click **Failover groups** on the blade.

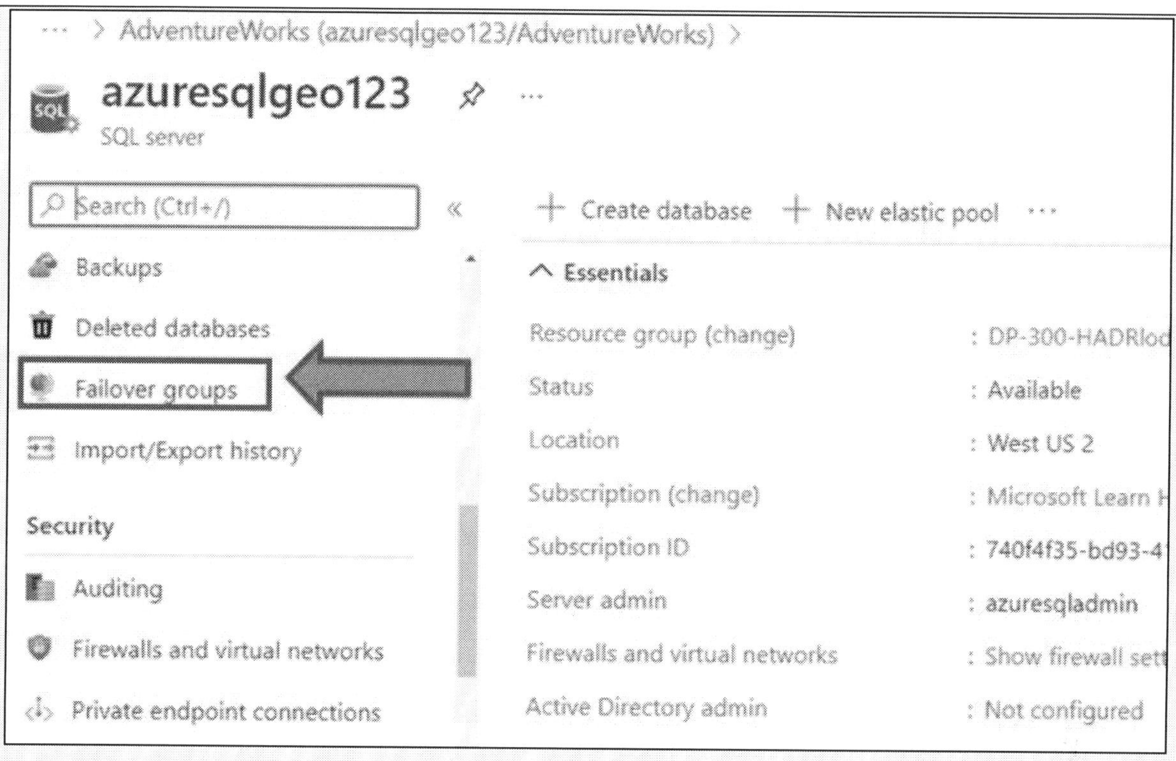

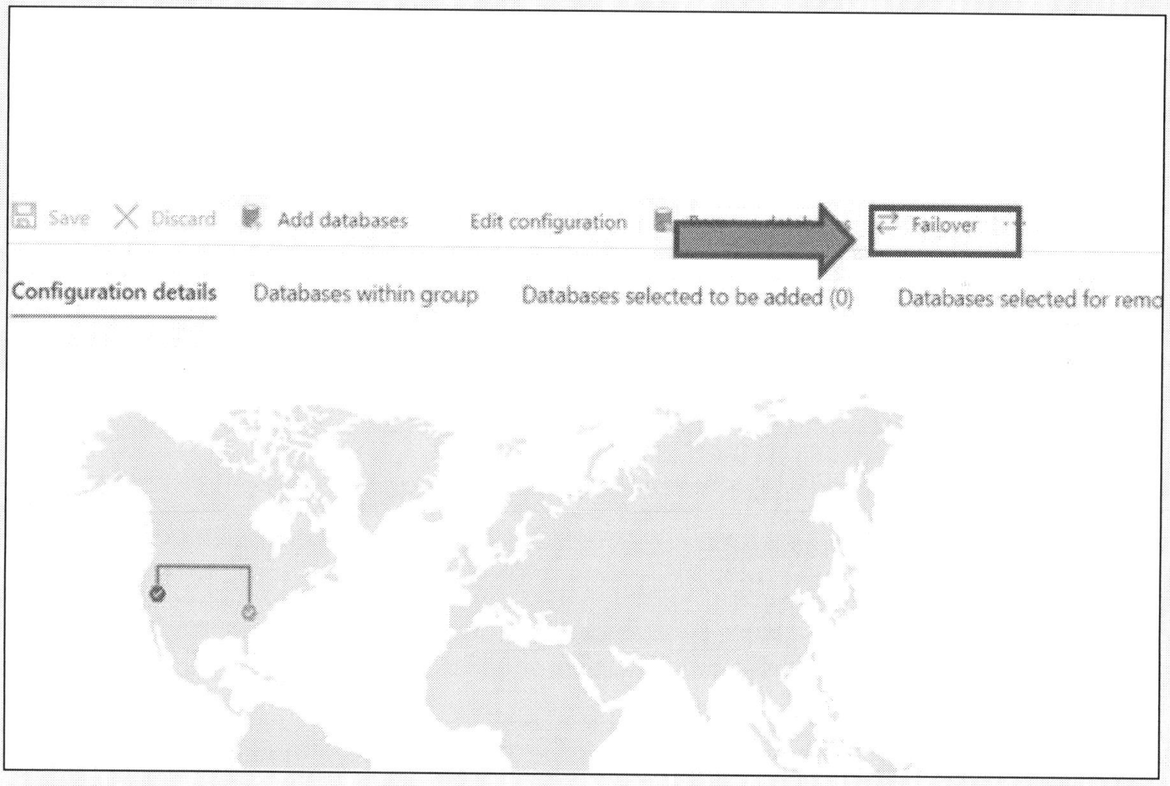

10. When prompted, choose the **Yes** button.

11. The primary replica's status will change to Pending and the secondary to Failover. It will only take a few minutes to complete the procedure. When the project

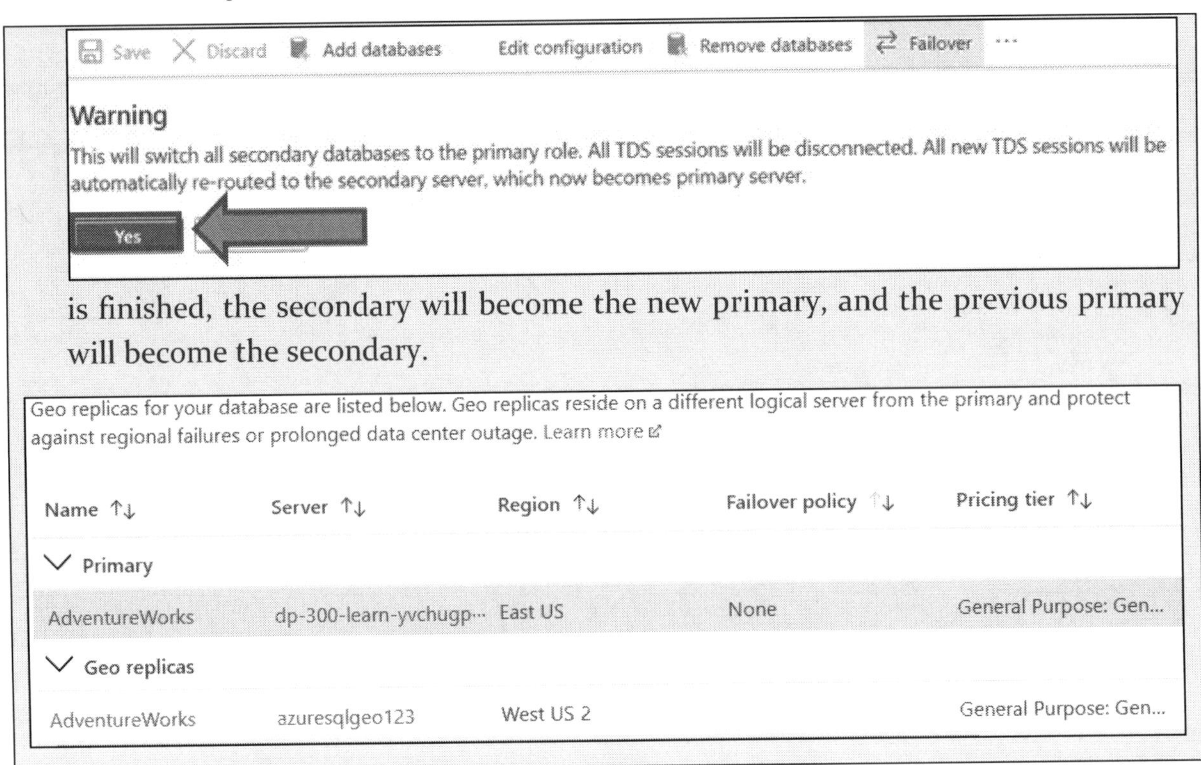

Save
Discard
Add databases
Edit configuration
Remove databases
Failover
Warning
This will switch all secondary databases to the primary role. All TDS sessions will be disconnected. All new TDS sessions will be automatically re-routed to the secondary server, which now becomes primary server.
Yes
is finished, the secondary will become the new primary, and the previous primary will become the secondary.
Geo replicas for your database are listed below. Geo replicas reside on a different logical server from the primary and protect against regional failures or prolonged data center outage. Learn more
Name
Server
Region
Failover policy
Pricing tier
Primary
AdventureWorks
dp-300-learn-yvchugp···
East US
None
General Purpose: Gen...
Geo replicas
AdventureWorks
azuresqlgeo123
West US 2
General Purpose: Gen...

Step 2: Backup to URL

Configure Backup to URL

1. Select the icon shown below to launch a Cloud Shell prompt.

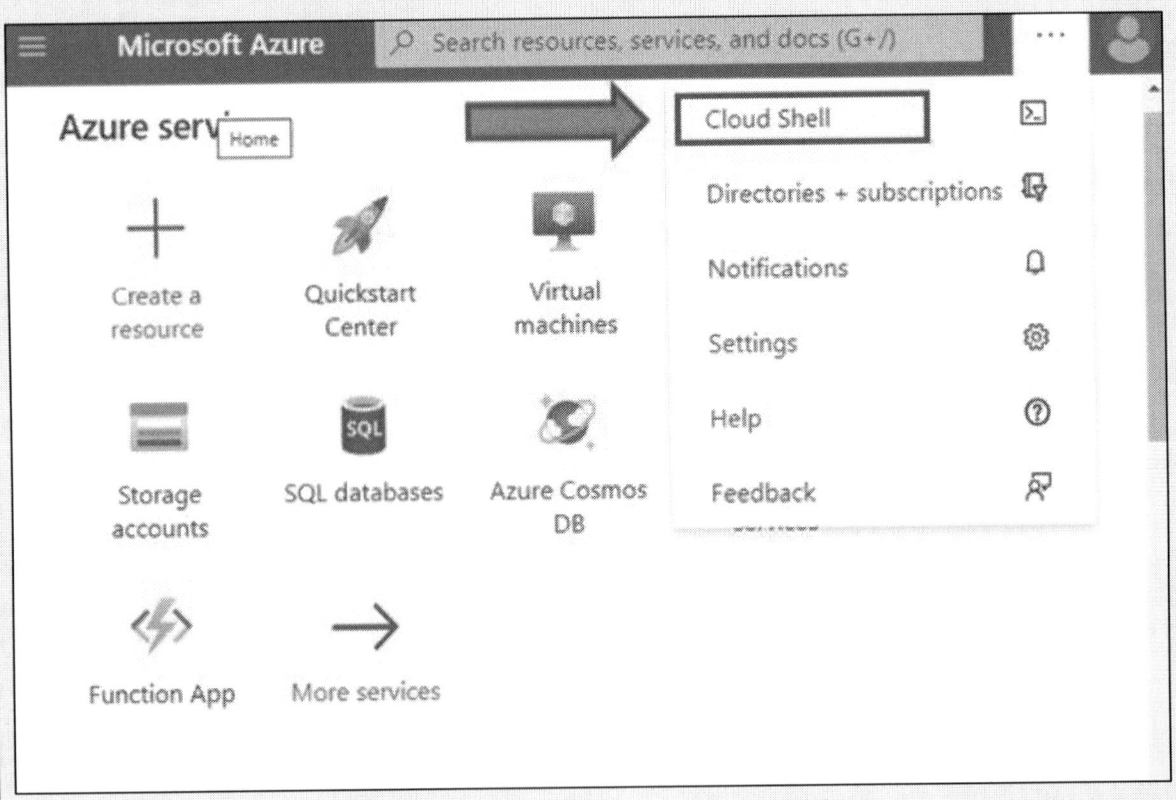

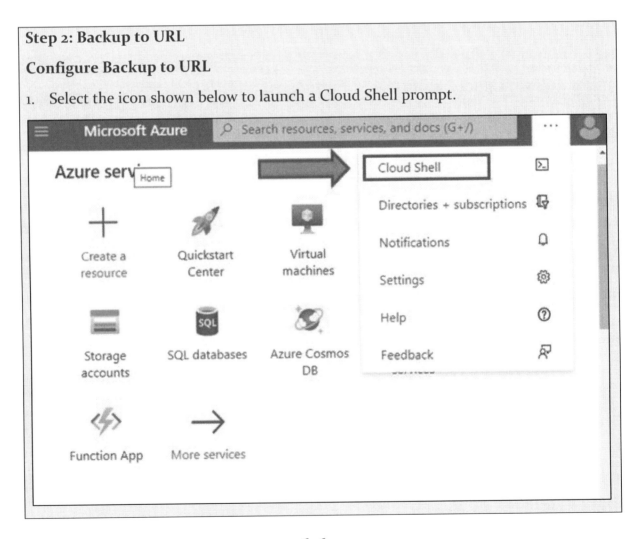

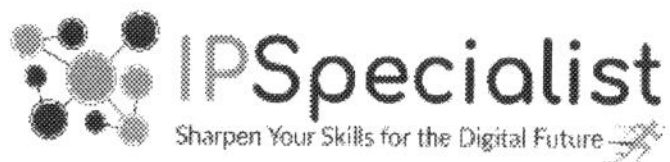

2. If you have not used a Cloud Shell before, you could see a message at the bottom of the portal. Choose **Bash**.

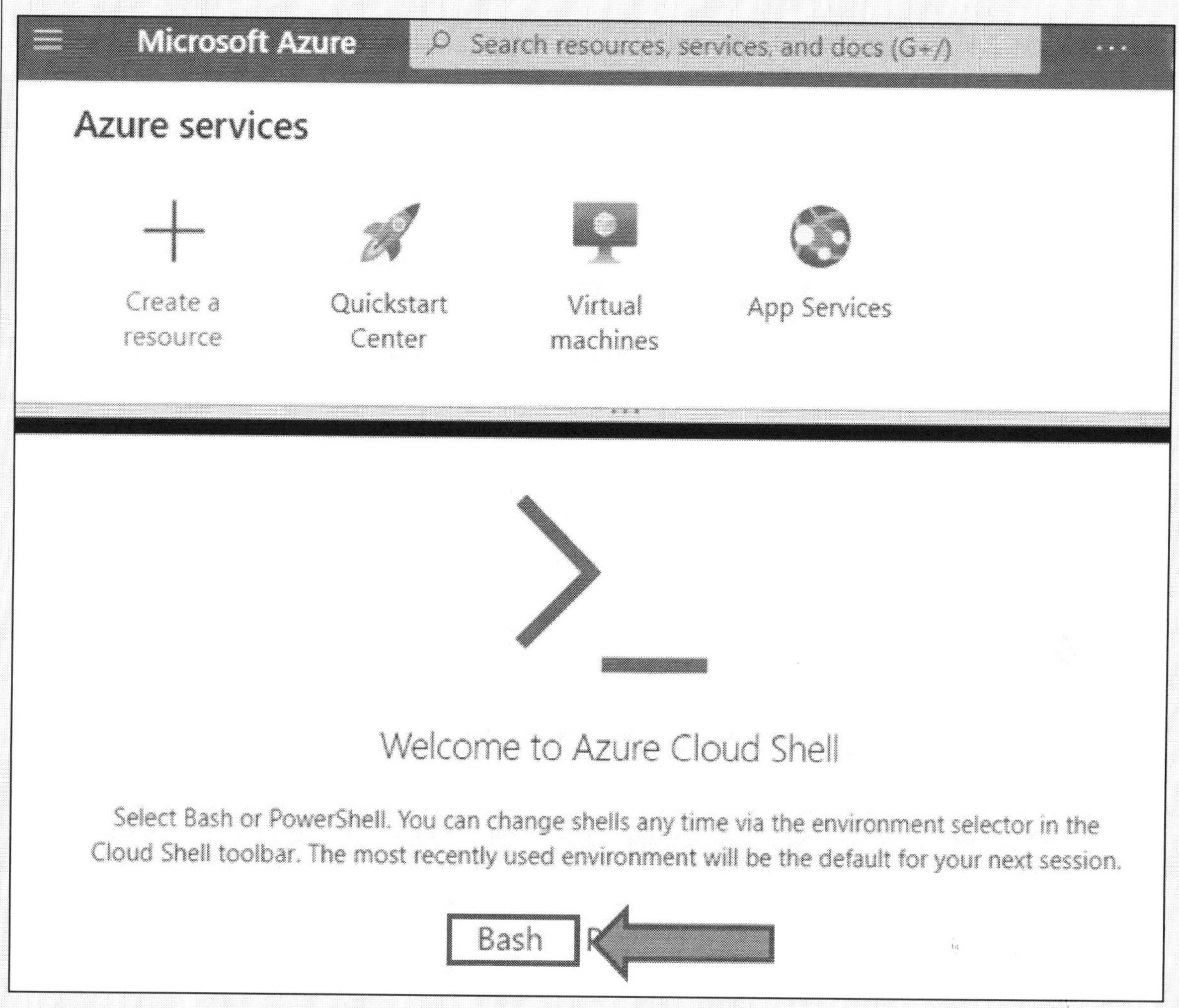

Microsoft Azure
Search resources, services, and docs (G+/)
Azure services
Create a resource
Quickstart Center
Virtual machines
App Services
Welcome to Azure Cloud Shell
Select Bash or PowerShell. You can change shells any time via the environment selector in the Cloud Shell toolbar. The most recently used environment will be the default for your next session.
Bash

3. If you have never used a Cloud Shell before, you must provide it storage. In the window that appears, click **Show advanced settings**:

You have no storage mounted
Azure Cloud Shell requires an Azure file share to persist files. Learn more
This will create a new storage account for you and this will incur a small monthly cost. View pricing
* Subscription
Microsoft Learn Hosting (prod) - 3
Show advanced settings
Create storage

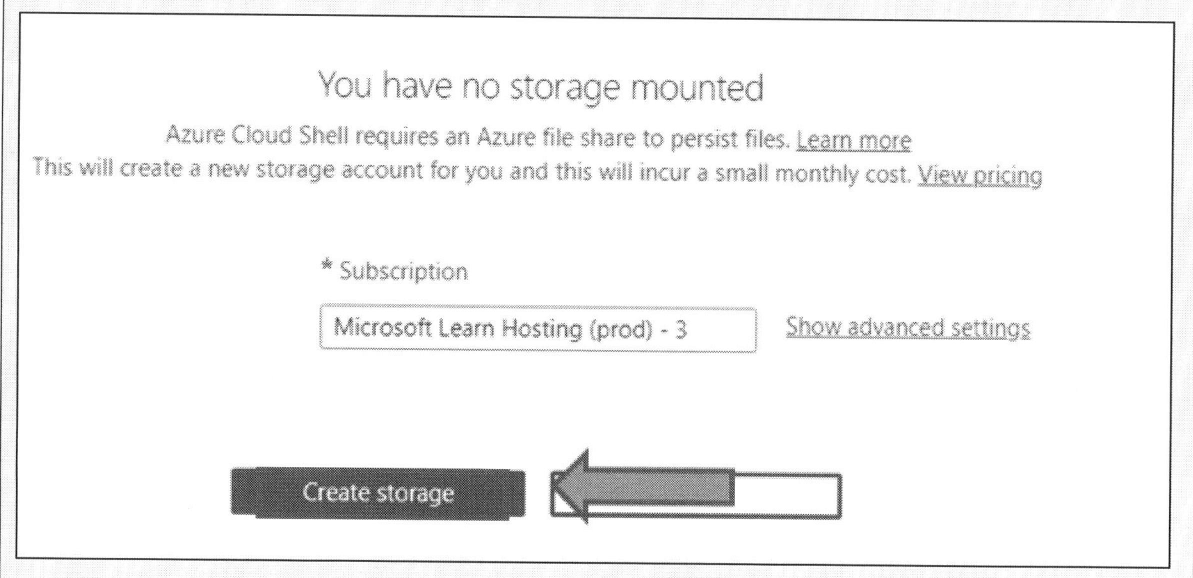

4. Use a Resource group and give the Storage account and File share new names. Then click the **Create storage button**.

You have no storage mounted

* Subscription	* Cloud Shell region	Hide advanced settings
Microsoft Learn Hosting (prod) - 3	West US 2	Show VNET isolation settings
* Resource group: Create new / Use existing (selected)	* Storage account: Create new (selected) / Use existing	* File share: Create new (selected) / Use existing
DP-300-HADRlod19878376	ipsrg	ipsfileshare

Further information about Cloud Shell storage and VNET isolation.

Create storage | Close

5. Check that Bash is visible in the upper left corner of the Cloud Shell screen.

When you are finished, you will see a prompt similar to the one below:

```
Bash
Requesting a Cloud Shell.Succeeded.
Connecting terminal...
```

6. By performing the following command in Cloud Shell, you can create a new storage account from the CLI.

```
user1-19878376@Azure:~$ az storage account create -n dplabstorage123 -g DP-300-H
ADRlod19878376 --kind StorageV2 -l eastus2
{
```

Following that, you will receive your account keys, which you will use in the following steps. In Cloud Shell, run the following code with your storage account's unique name:

```
user1-19878376@Azure:~$ az storage account keys list -g DP-300-HADRlod19878376 -
n dplabstorage123
[
```

The output of the above command will contain your account key. Copy the received value for key1 (without the double quotes) as follows:

```
  {
    "creationTime": "2021-11-01T00:18:44.413567+00:00",
    "keyName": "key1",
    "permissions": "FULL",
    "value": "ChSRhZ4Omyd+qSS6uiRzNELSfHLzupLbPMZVEPkqrE2cRrA3DBKdH5fBFl+2HQDh2F
aUGW5kYS/D41KwZPv0bA=="
  },
  {
    "creationTime": "2021-11-01T00:18:44.413567+00:00",
    "keyName": "key2",
    "permissions": "FULL",
    "value": "/OSCrS9D9DZdy7g/9tVXnbaG9prEe6+wdWHiBRB/FrSiaqaT2jLThZnnMS85/HnrN3
JUJXQLcbeUFZ02ssViNg=="
```

7. Backing up a SQL Server database to a URL makes use of a storage account and a container within it. In this step, you will establish a container specifically for backup storage. To do so, follow these steps:

```
user1-19878376@Azure:~$ az storage container create --name "backups" --account-n
ame "dplabstorage123" --account-key "ChSRhZ4Omyd+qSS6uiRzNELSfHLzupLbPMZVEPkqrE2
cRrA3DBKdH5fBFl+2HQDh2FaUGW5kYS/D41KwZPv0bA==" --fail-on-exist
{
  "created": true
}
```

8. To confirm that the container backups have been made, run:

```
user1-19878376@Azure:~$ az storage container list --account-name "dplabstorage12
3" --account-key "ChSRhZ4Omyd+qSS6uiRzNELSfHLzupLbPMZVEPkqrE2cRrA3DBKdH5fBFl+2HQ
Dh2FaUGW5kYS/D41KwZPv0bA=="
```

The output should look something like this:

```
{
  "deleted": null,
  "encryptionScope": {
    "defaultEncryptionScope": "$account-encryption-key",
    "preventEncryptionScopeOverride": false
  },
  "metadata": null,
  "name": "backups",
  "properties": {
    "etag": "\"0x8D99CCE511D6E1E\"",
    "hasImmutabilityPolicy": false,
    "hasLegalHold": false,
    "lastModified": "2021-11-01T00:26:58+00:00",
    "lease": {
      "duration": null,
      "state": "available",
      "status": "unlocked"
    },
```

9. For security, a shared access signature (SAS) at the container level is necessary. This can be accomplished using Cloud Shell or PowerShell. Carry out the following:

```
user1-19878376@Azure:~$ az storage container generate-sas -n "backups" --account
-name "dplabstorage123" --account-key "ChSRhZ4Omyd+qSS6uiRzNELSfHLzupLbPMZVEPkqr
E2cRrA3DBKdH5fBFl+2HQDh2FaUGW5kYS/D41KwZPv0bA==" --permissions "rwdl" --expiry "
2021-12-30T00:00Z" -o tsv
```

The output should look something like this. Copy and paste the entire shared access signature into Notepad because it will be used in the next task:

```
user1-19878376@Azure:~$ az storage container generate-sas -n "backups" --account
-name "dplabstorage123" --account-key "ChSRhZ4Omyd+qSS6uiRzNELSfHLzupLbPMZVEPkqr
E2cRrA3DBKdH5fBFl+2HQDh2FaUGW5kYS/D41KwZPv0bA==" --permissions "rwdl" --expiry "
2021-12-30T00:00Z" -o tsv
se=2021-12-30T00%3A00Z&sp=rwdl&sv=2018-11-09&sr=c&sig=3xek5N0I9bogOw2evv5r7OlE4N
zVcS4g0bKIx97zQCY%3D
user1-19878376@Azure:~$
```

Generate a Backup File as a Blob in Azure

1. Start up SQL Server Management Studio (SSMS).
2. The connection to SQL Server will be requested. Make sure Windows Authentication is enabled, then click **Connect**.

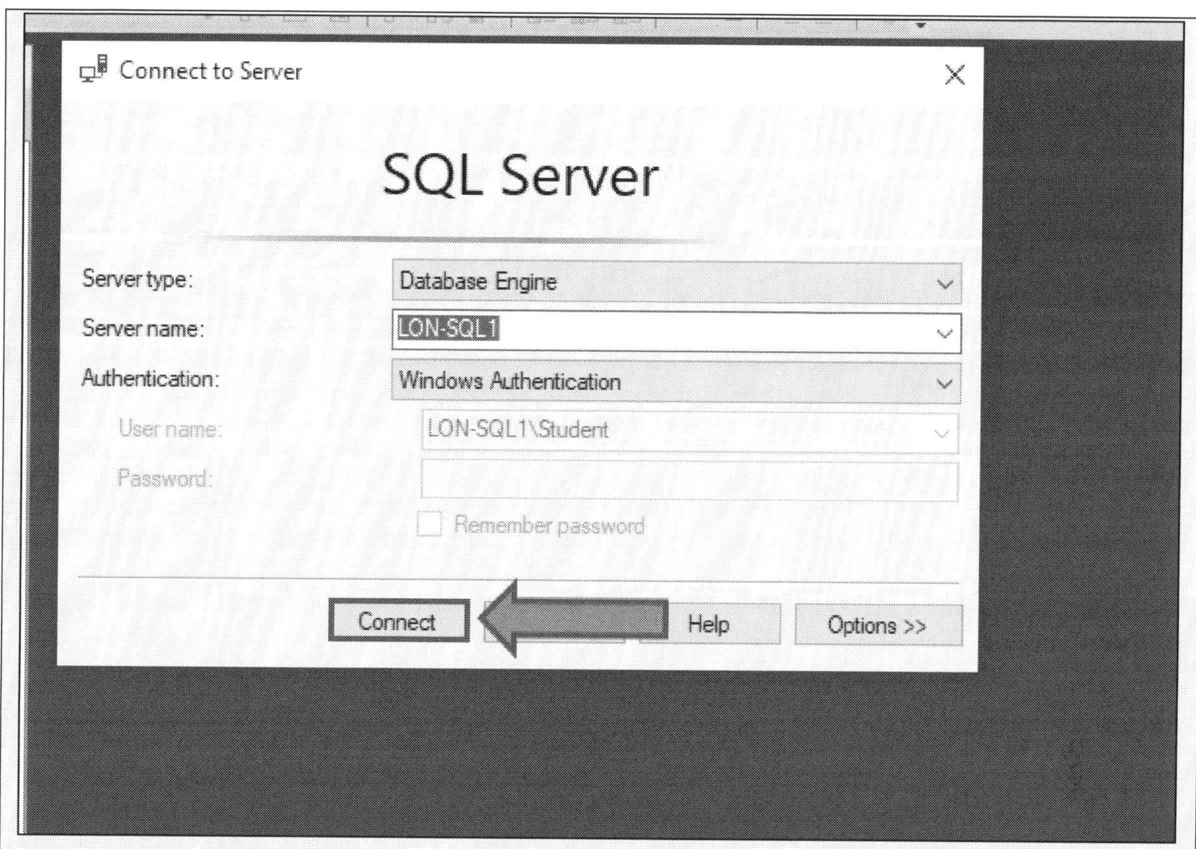

3. Select **New Query**.

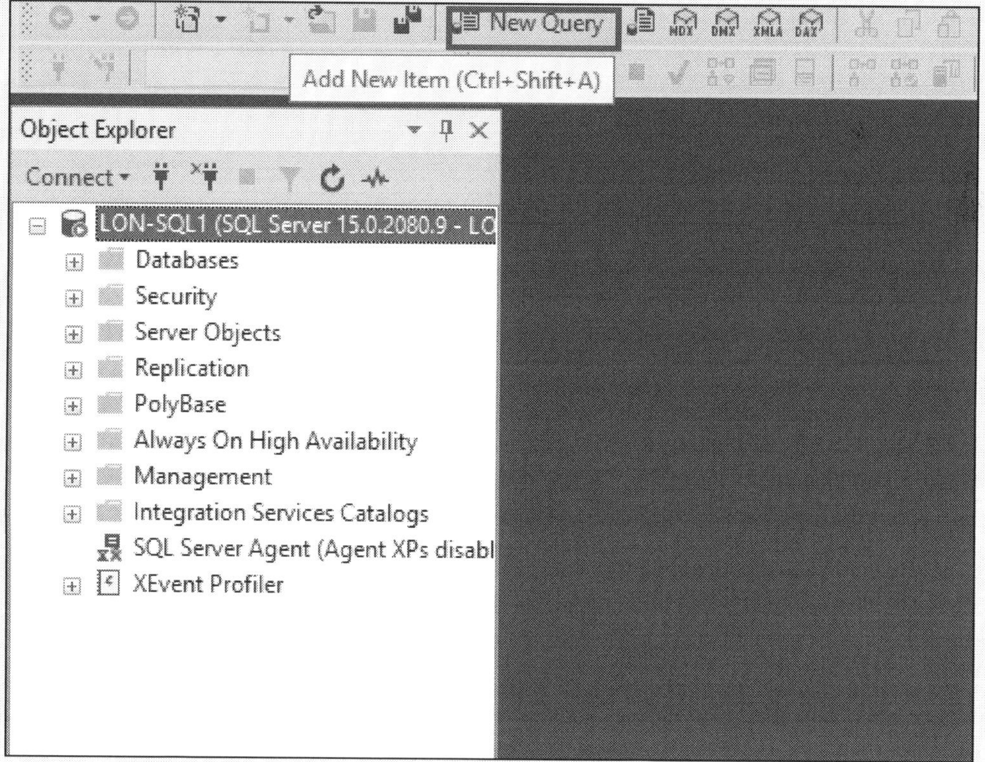

4. With the following Transact-SQL, create the credential that will be used to access cloud storage. Fill in the blanks with the proper values:

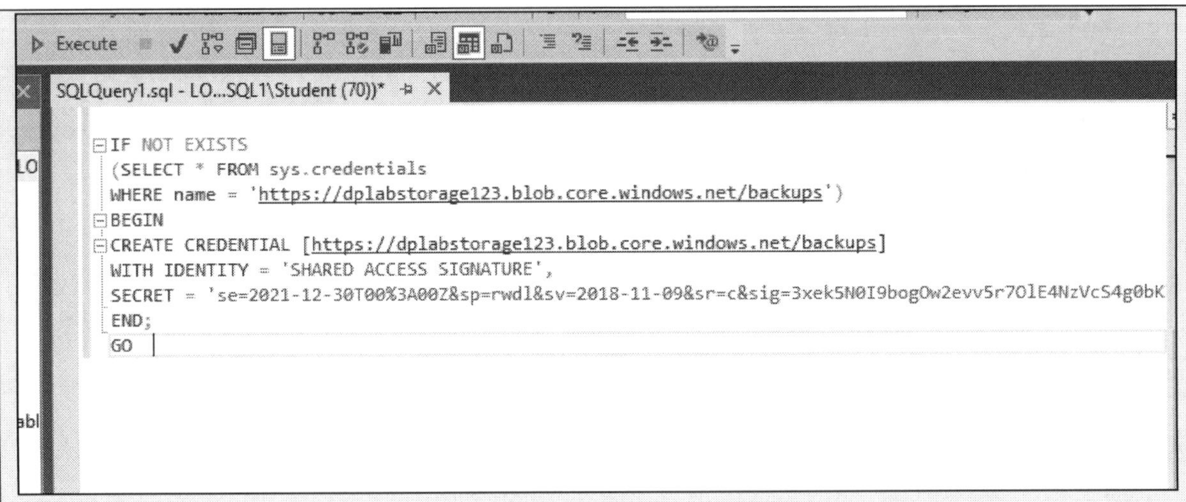

```
IF NOT EXISTS
(SELECT * FROM sys.credentials
WHERE name = 'https://dplabstorage123.blob.core.windows.net/backups')
BEGIN
CREATE CREDENTIAL [https://dplabstorage123.blob.core.windows.net/backups]
WITH IDENTITY = 'SHARED ACCESS SIGNATURE',
SECRET = 'se=2021-12-30T00%3A00Z&sp=rwdl&sv=2018-11-09&sr=c&sig=3xek5N0I9bogOw2evv5r7OlE4NzVcS4g0bK
END;
GO
```

5. Click the **Execute** button. This ought to be a success.

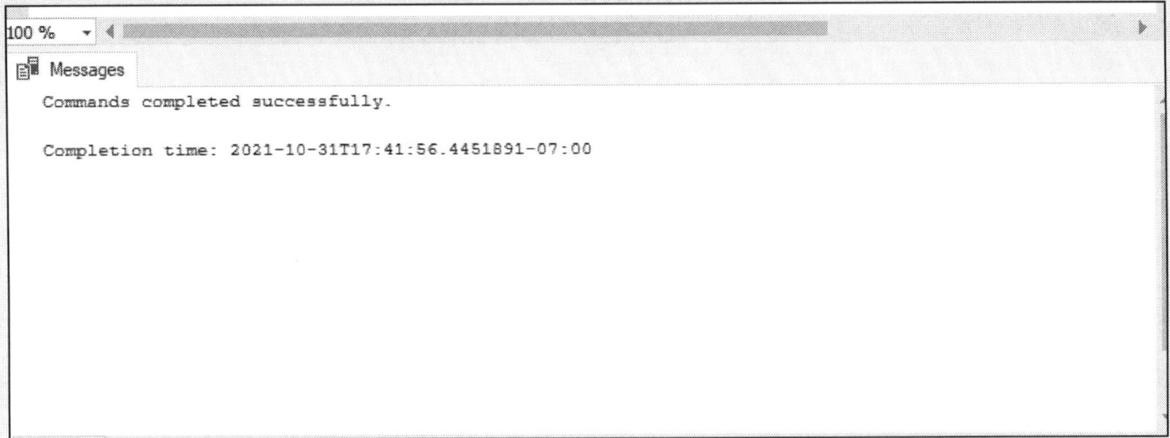

```
Commands completed successfully.

Completion time: 2021-10-31T17:41:56.4451891-07:00
```

6. Back up the database to Azure using the Transact-SQL command:

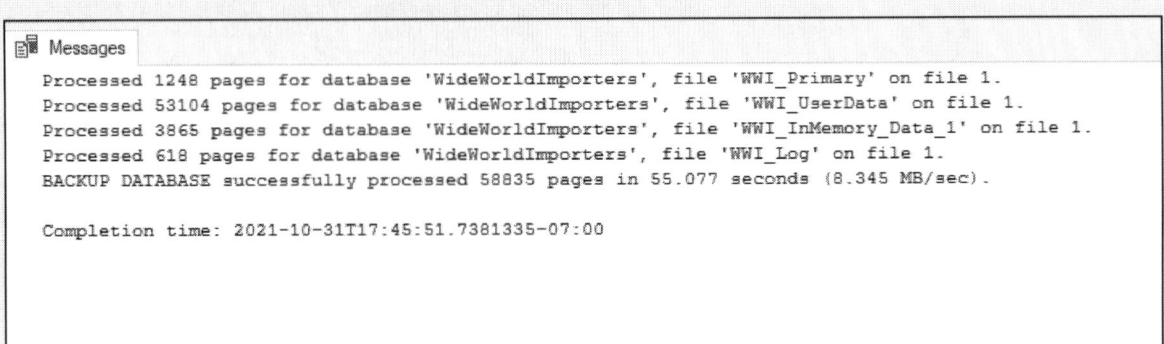

```
BACKUP DATABASE WideWorldImporters
TO URL = 'https://dplabstorage123.blob.core.windows.net/backups/WideWorldImporters.bak';
GO
```

```
Processed 1248 pages for database 'WideWorldImporters', file 'WWI_Primary' on file 1.
Processed 53104 pages for database 'WideWorldImporters', file 'WWI_UserData' on file 1.
Processed 3865 pages for database 'WideWorldImporters', file 'WWI_InMemory_Data_1' on file 1.
Processed 618 pages for database 'WideWorldImporters', file 'WWI_Log' on file 1.
BACKUP DATABASE successfully processed 58835 pages in 55.077 seconds (8.345 MB/sec).

Completion time: 2021-10-31T17:45:51.7381335-07:00
```

7. If something is configured improperly, you will receive an error message.

Validate the Backup

You can use Storage Explorer (preview) or Azure Cloud Shell to verify if the file is indeed on Azure.

1. Navigate to https://portal.azure.com using the Microsoft Edge browser from the toolbar.
2. To run this Azure CLI command, use the Azure Cloud Shell:

```
user1-19879761@Azure:~$ az storage blob list -c "backups" --account-name "dplabstor
age123" --account-key "D/ZayN/Ruy3U7ZJQpAPqSJBDb3zRiiIZ7gns8FhaODbDRusN/lDzewHD1SSW
J49cQ2DppxS5GWyEGhvUf3eNWA=="
[
```

3. To use the Storage Explorer (preview), go to the Azure portal's home page and click **Storage accounts**.

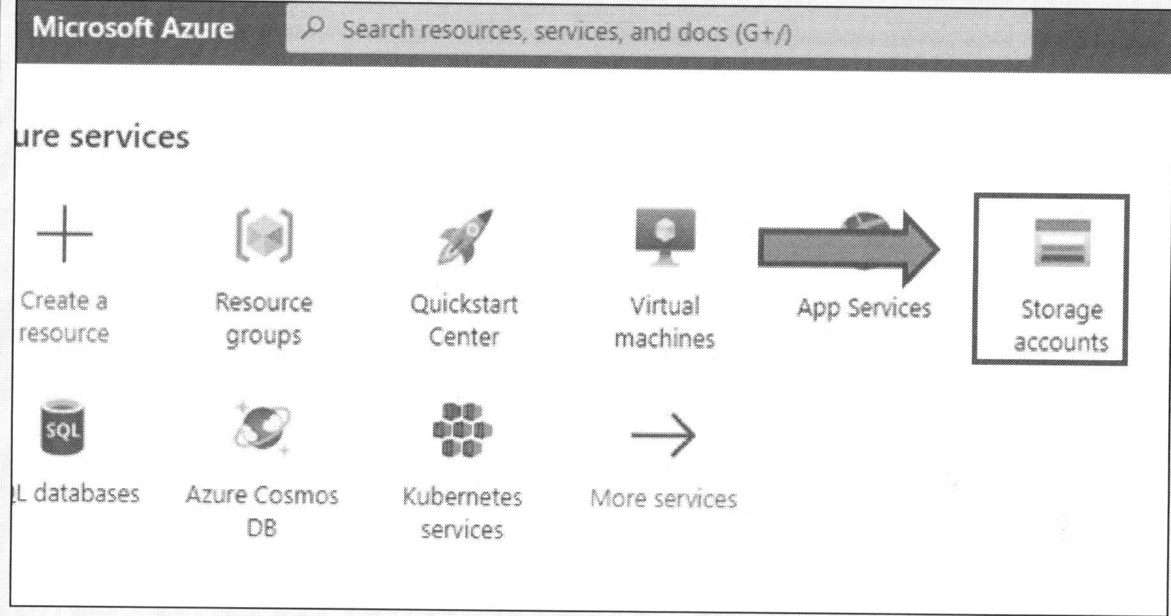

4. Choose your **storage account**.

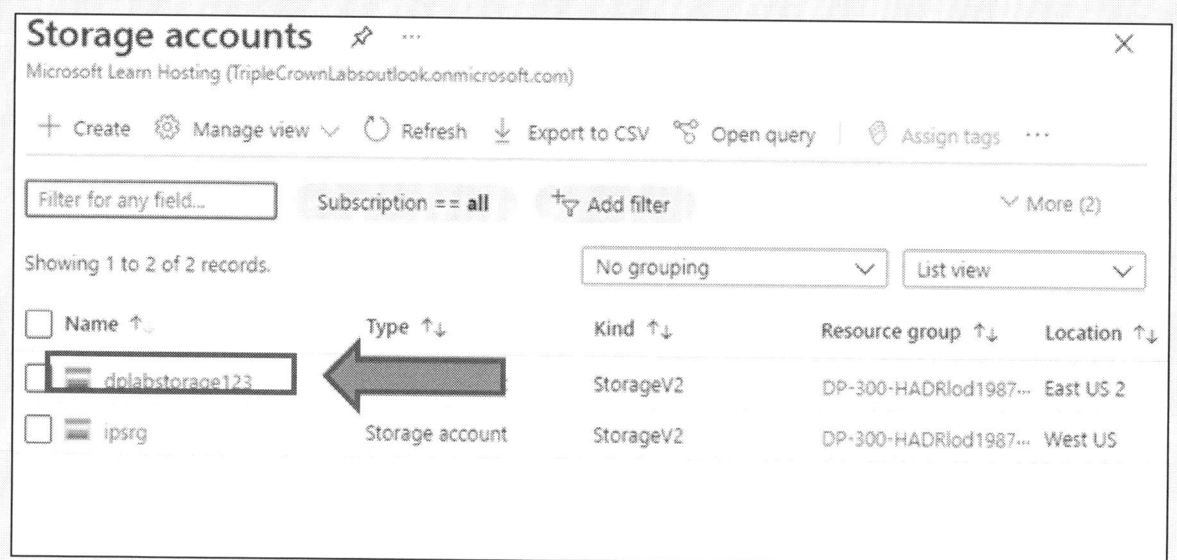

5. Select **Storage browser** from the left navigation (preview). Expand BLOB CONTAINERS and then backups.

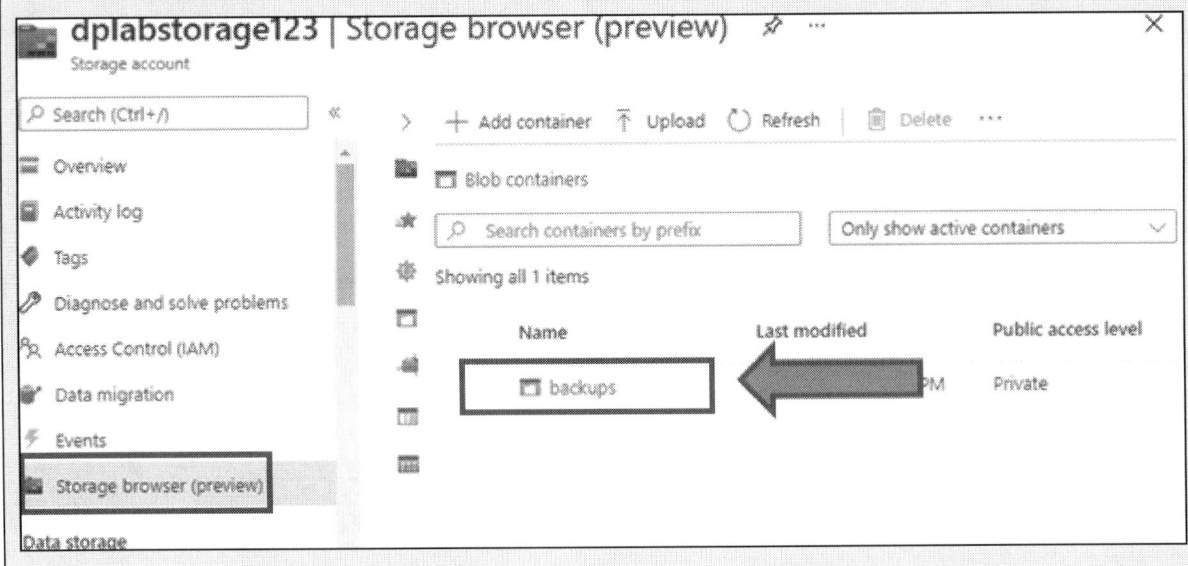

Restore a Database

1. Run the following query in a query window:

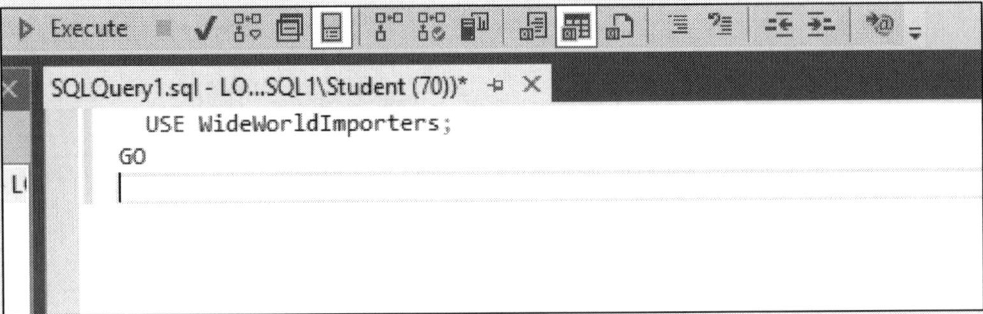

2. Now run the following statement to get the first row of the Customers database which has a CustomerID of 1. Take note of the customer's name:

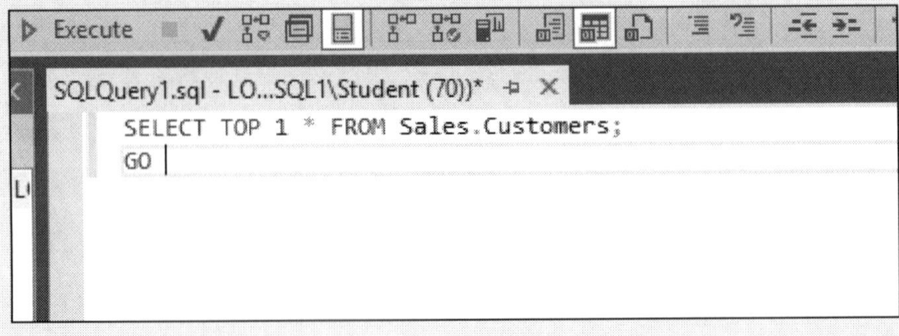

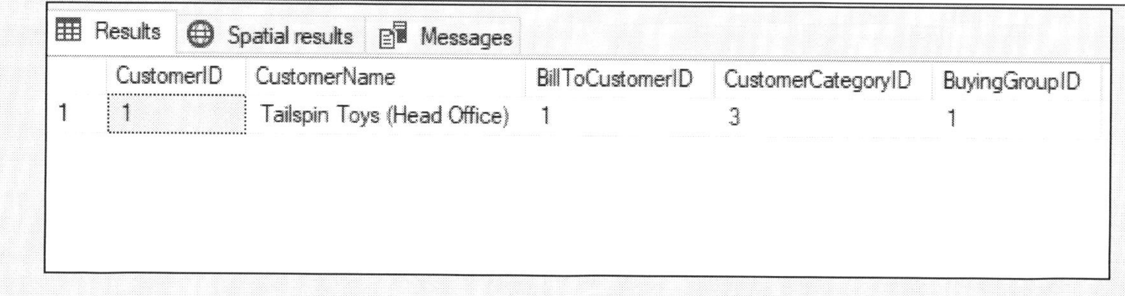

	CustomerID	CustomerName	BillToCustomerID	CustomerCategoryID	BuyingGroupID
1	1	Tailspin Toys (Head Office)	1	3	1

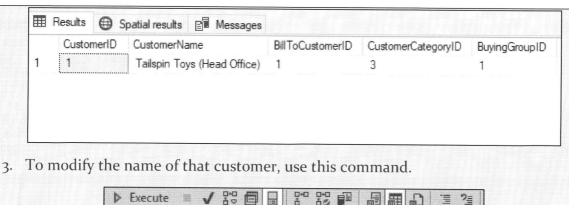

3. To modify the name of that customer, use this command.

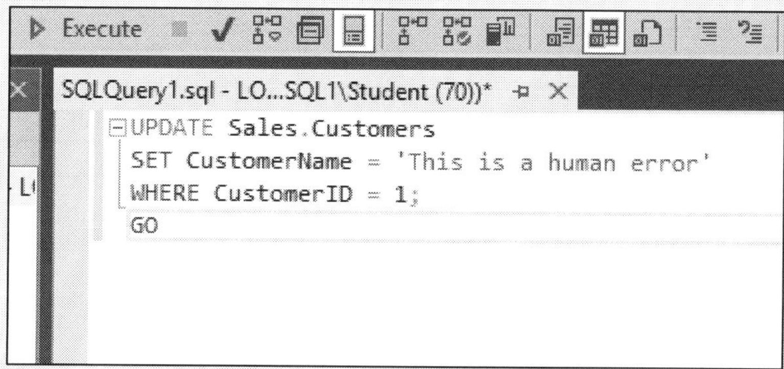

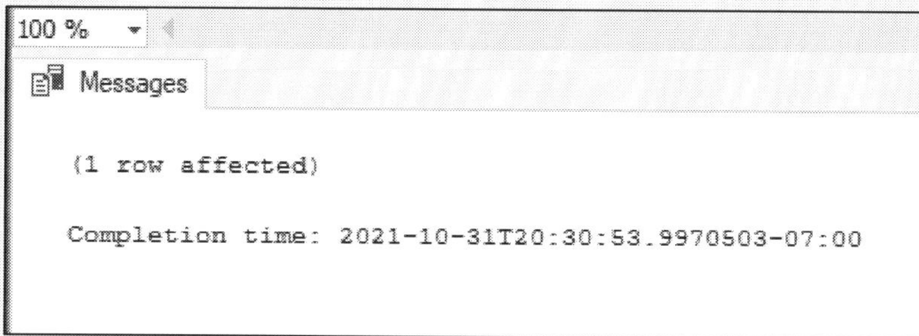

4. Step 2 should be repeated to ensure that the name has been changed. Consider what would happen if thousands or millions of rows were altered without a WHERE clause — or with the incorrect WHERE clause.
5. To get the database back to where it was before you made the update in Step 3, do the following.

```
USE master;
GO

RESTORE DATABASE WideWorldImporters
FROM URL = 'https://dplabstorage123.blob.core.windows.net/backups/WideWorldImporters.bak';
GO
```

6. The output should look like this:

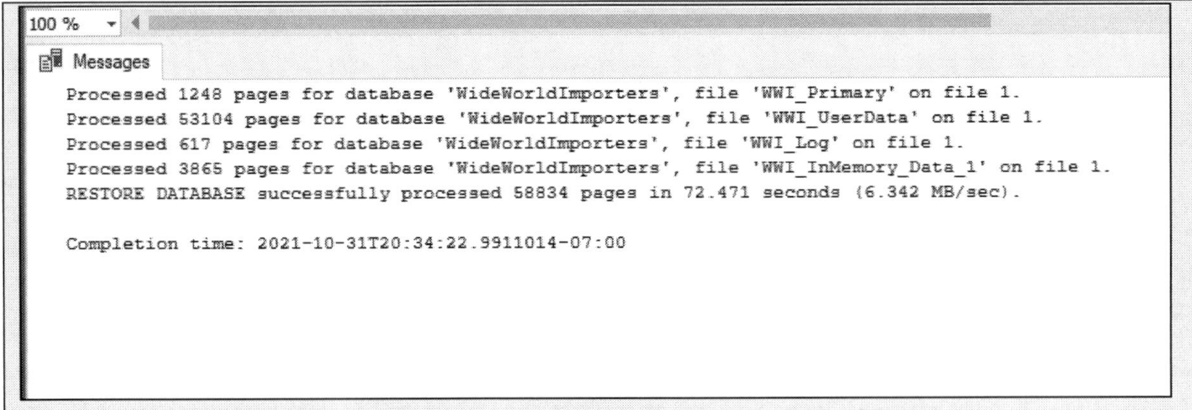

```
Processed 1248 pages for database 'WideWorldImporters', file 'WWI_Primary' on file 1.
Processed 53104 pages for database 'WideWorldImporters', file 'WWI_UserData' on file 1.
Processed 617 pages for database 'WideWorldImporters', file 'WWI_Log' on file 1.
Processed 3865 pages for database 'WideWorldImporters', file 'WWI_InMemory_Data_1' on file 1.
RESTORE DATABASE successfully processed 58834 pages in 72.471 seconds (6.342 MB/sec).

Completion time: 2021-10-31T20:34:22.9911014-07:00
```

7. Step 2 should be repeated to ensure that the data has been restored.

Mind Map

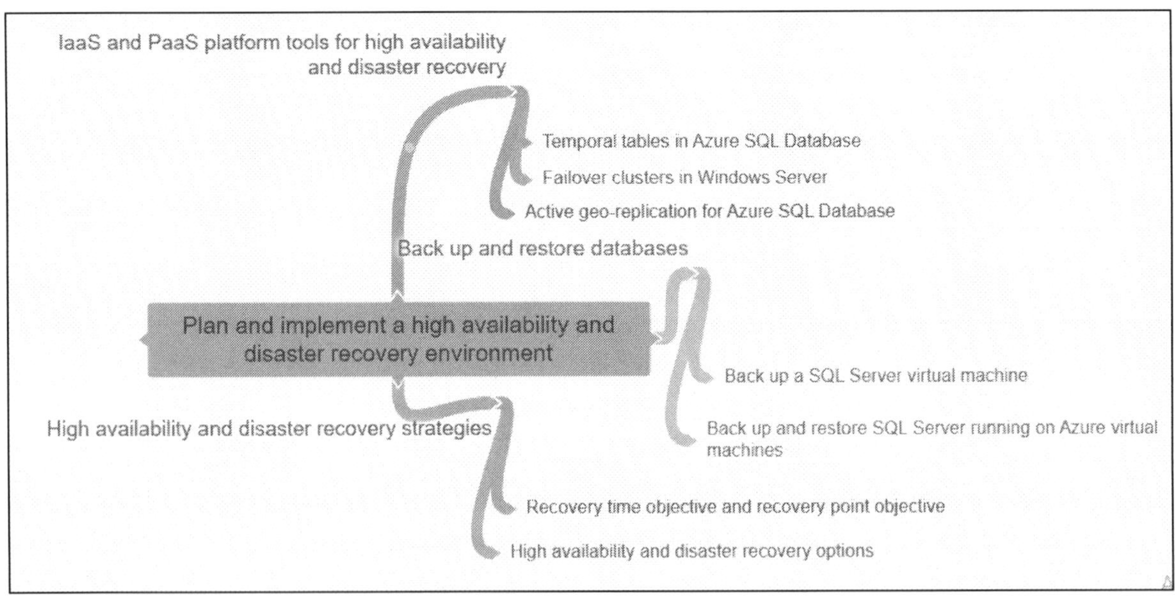

Figure 07-26: Mind Map

Practice Questions

1. Backup to URL in SQL Server or Azure SQL Server Database Managed Instance stores the backup file in what format?

A. As a URL

B. As a blob

C. As a pointer

2. To which platforms may an Azure Database backup of a PostgreSQL database be restored?

A. PostgreSQL only

B. Azure Database for PostgreSQL only
C. PostgreSQL or Azure Database for PostgreSQL

3. How much does backup storage cost for Azure Database for MySQL and Azure Database for PostgreSQL?
A. Free up to the size of the database
B. Double the cost of the service
C. Half the cost of the service

4. What Azure component must be configured in order for the listener in an AG to function properly?
A. The NIC
B. The NSG
C. A load balancer

5. What tool may be utilized in Azure to establish a WSFC for AGs and FCIs?
A. Wizard in Failover Cluster Manager
B. PowerShell
C. WMI

6. What Azure feature allows you to test disaster recovery without affecting the production system?
A. Azure Site Recovery
B. Azure SQL Database
C. Azure Load Balancer

7. What functionality provides an asynchronously updated replica of the database in another region?
A. Failover group
B. Secondary replica that is readable
C. Active geo-replication
D. All of the above

8. What features do Temporal Tables offer in Azure SQL Database?
A. Recover deleted data
B. Scale-out reads
C. Temporarily process additional data

9. What auto-failover group settings must be altered to get a low RPO?
A. RPOZero
B. AlwaysBeInSync
C. GracePeriodWithDataLossHours

10. What is RPO?
A. The number of nodes in a cluster
B. The point to which data needs to be recovered after a failure
C. A partial database restore

11. What is a hybrid solution?

A. A solution that includes resources from both Azure and on-premises or from another cloud provider.

B. A solution that employs two distinct database engines, such as MySQL and SQL Server.

C. A solution that spans two different SQL Server versions.

12. What is available in SQL Server following a failover with database-level protection?

A. Logins, Databases, and SQL Server Agent Job

B. Databases and SQL Server Agent jobs

C. Whatever is in the databases; anything outside must be dealt with manually

13. Which Azure service acts as a resource firewall?

A. Network Security Group

B. Virtual Network

C. Virtual Machine

D. Azure Resource Manager

14. What is the lowest priority rule that is applied in every Network Security Group?

A. Allow Rule

B. Deny Rule

C. None of the above

IPSpecialist
Sharpen Your Skills for the Digital Future

Answers

Chapter 01: Azure SQL Fundamentals

1. **A** (SQL server in an Azure virtual machine)

Explanation

Only SQL Server in an Azure virtual machine provides you access to the underlying OS. The OS is abstracted away from you in the PaaS deployment options, meaning Azure manages it, but you cannot access it.

2. **B** (Azure SQL Managed instance)

Explanation

Azure SQL Managed Instance is the only PaaS service that gives instance-scoped features like CLR and Service Broker. The first answer choice is also correct, but it does not provide PaaS's benefits.

3. **C** (Azure SQL Database, single database)

Explanation

Azure SQL Database, a single database, is currently the only deployment option supporting databases of that size, specifically with the Hyperscale service tier. If Azure SQL Managed Instance supports Hyperscale in the future, because the application does not currently need any instance-scoped features, Azure SQL Database might still be the right option.

4. **B** (Azure will pause your database to stop compute costs and charge you only for storage.)

Explanation

To reduce your costs during inactivity, Azure will pause the compute resources and charge only for storage during this time.

5. **D** (All of the above)

Explanation

Resource limits include memory, max log size, size of tempdb, max concurrent workers, and backup retention.

6. **B** (SELECT * FROM sys.dm_user_db_resource_governance)

Explanation

This option will return the configuration and capacity settings.

7. **B** (3 GB)

Explanation

The transaction log is managed over and above the data size, and the log's maximum size is always 30 percent of the Data max size.

8. **D** (Proxy for connections outside Azure and redirect for connections within Azure)

Explanation

Redirect can be used by default because the ports needed are open within Azure.

9. **D** (SQL Server on an Azure VM and Azure SQL Managed Instance)

Explanation

In an Azure VM, it is just SQL Server, so it is supported. In Azure SQL Managed Instance, native restore from a URL is supported.

10. **C** (Use simple recovery mode)

Explanation

This capability is not currently supported in Azure SQL Database or Azure SQL Managed Instance. Full recovery mode is required to meet the SLA.

11. **D** (Private link)

Explanation

This will create a DNS hierarchy without information related to the Azure SQL Database logical server and create a truly private endpoint.

12. **D** (All of the above)

Explanation

In Azure SQL Database, you can form Azure SQL auditing and apply DMVs, metrics, and alerts to monitor security-related events.

13. **C** (Increasing the number of vCores through the Azure portal)

Explanation

Increasing the number of vCores can give you additional tempdb files.

14. **B** (Choose a deployment option that meets your I/O requirements)

Explanation

Resource limits for specific deployment options have I/O performance commitments.

15. **A** (You can create, rebuild, and reorganize indexes in Azure SQL just like SQL Server)

Explanation

Azure SQL supports all options to create, rebuild, and reorganize indexes, just like SQL Server.

Chapter 02: Plan and Implement Data Platform Resources

1. A (Ultra)

Explanation

Ultra Disk gives the lowest latency of the three storage types.

2. A (Two)

Explanation

Each VM will have at least two disks: the operating system disk and the temporary disk.

3. A (Two)

Explanation

There are two service tiers available when creating an Azure SQL Managed Instance, and they are the same as the Azure SQL Database vCore model.

4. C (Data Migration Assistant)

Explanation

The data migration assistant provides both tooling to assess and execute a migration.

5. B (Azure Reserved VM Instances)

Explanation

Azure Reserved VM Instance can offer significant cost savings over pay as you go licensing.

6. B (99.9%)

Explanation

A single Azure Virtual Machine provides three nines (99.9%) of high availability when used with Azure-managed storage.

7. B (Availability zones)

Explanation

To spread workloads across data centers in a region, you should choose availability zones.

8. A (Azure Site Recovery)

Explanation

Azure Site Recovery is a low-cost solution that will perform block-level replication of your Azure virtual machine.

9. C (Azure SQL managed instance)

Explanation

Azure SQL managed instance is the only offering here that provides cross-database transactions.

10. C (Azure SQL Database Hyperscale)

Explanation

Azure SQL Database Hyperscale is the only option that offers 50 TB of data.

11. An (Azure SQL Database Serverless)

Explanation

Serverless will lower the cost significantly for a database that is only used during business hours.

12. B (Every 12 hours)

Explanation

With Azure SQL managed instances, differential backups occur every 12 hours.

13. A (Connection resiliency)

Explanation

Connection resiliency should be built into your application to handle transient failures, like failover or database resizing.

14. A (Managed automated backups)

Explanation

Automated backup is a feature of the service.

15. B (Create a dump and restore to a server at the higher version)

Explanation

It is required to create a backup and restore to upgrade to a new major version.

Chapter 03: Implement a Secure Environment for a Database Service

1. **B** (In the catalog view sys.sensitivity classifications.)

Explanation: The data from data classification is stored in n the sys.sensitivity_classifications catalog view in SQL Server 2019.

2. **C** (SQL Injection)

Explanation: SQL Injection inspection is one of the key features of ATP.

3. **A** (SQL Injection)

Explanation: SQL injection attacks are widespread when dynamic SQL is poorly designed.

4. **C** (OAuth)

Explanation: For authentication, Azure Active Directory employs HTTPS protocols like SAML and OpenID Connect, and for permission, it employs OAuth.

5. **A** (master)

Explanation: Login information is saved in the master database.

6. **B** (db_accessadmin)

Explanation: Access admin can add and create users in the database.

7. **A** (Control)

Explanation: The ability to control allows the user to drop or modify an object.

8. **B** (Tables)

Explanation: Data can be inserted into tables.

9. **A** (Ownership chaining)

Explanation: Ownership chaining essentially provides the user with temporary access to the objects referenced by the process.

10. **B** (Master Key)

Explanation: Encrypting databases requires the use of a master key.

11. **A** (Always Encrypted)

Explanation: Always Encrypted only keeps encrypted data in SQL Server, so the data is never available to a database user without the column key which the application has.

12. **A** (Azure Key Vault)

Explanation: Always Encrypted and TDE keys can be stored in Azure Key Vault.

13. **B** (Private Link)

Explanation: A private IP address in an Azure vNet for an Azure SQL Database is provided by a private link.

14. **A** (Network Security Group)

Explanation: Network Security Group (NSG) has a private resource firewall that allows the connection of VNet, subnet, or another network interface with VM.

15. **C** (Executing a T-SQL statement)

Explanation: The only way to construct a database firewall rule is to execute a T-SQL statement.

Chapter 04: Monitor and Optimize Operational Resources in SQL Server

1. A (Log Analytics)

Explanation

Storing data in Azure Log Analytics allows you to gain further intelligence on the events in your database.

2. A (Page Life Expectancy)

Explanation

PLE is how long the engine expects a given page to live in memory.

3. A (The SQL VM Resource Provider)

Explanation

The SQL VM resource provider has an agent in your SQL Server VM, which provides this information.

4. B (Read Committed Snapshot Isolation)

Explanation

The level allows each reader to have their version of the data and prevents readers from blocking writers.

5. B (Sys.dm_tran_locks)

Explanation

This DMV shows the active locks in a given database at the point of time in the query.

6. C (Sys.query_store_queries)

Explanation

This view contains the queryID and can be joined to other views for other information.

7. C (Disk storage)

Explanation

Disk storage is designed for VMs and is the best storage option.

8. B (Write IOPs)

Explanation

Write RG can control IOPS.

9. A (Storage configuration)

Explanation

The resource provider will configure your storage pool.

10. A (Batch mode on row store)

Explanation

Batch mode is most efficient in aggregation queries.

11. C (Resource pools)

Explanation

Resource pools are where resources are allocated in resource governor.

12. C (Compatibility level)

Explanation

This setting affects the way the plan is created based on some engine factors.

13. B (Azure SQL Database)

Explanation

SQL Database does support automatic indexing creation and removal.

14. C (Auto Update Statistics Asynchronously)

Explanation

The 'Auto Update Statistics Asynchronously' option lets statistics be updated during query execution.

15. A (sys.dm_db_tuning_recommendations)

Explanation

This DMV displays the recommendations and the status.

Chapter 05: Optimize Query Performance in SQL Server

1, An (Estimated Execution Plan)

Explanation

The estimated execution plan is stored in the plan cache.

2. A (sys.dm_db_index_usage_stats)

Explanation

Sys.dm_db_index_usage_stats shows the read and write operations against each index.

3. A (SOS_SCHEDULER_YIELD)

Explanation

The SOS_SCHEDULER_YIELD wait is the only one of these wait types associated with the CPU.

4. A (Clustered Column Store)

Explanation

A clustered column-store index will provide the best performance for a data warehouse fact table.

5. B (sys.dm_os_wait_stats)

Explanation

It shows the wait stats across the server.

6. C (sys.dm_exec_query_plan_stats)

Explanation

In SQL Server 2019, you can query sys.dm_exec_query_plan_stats to get a query's final execution plan.

7. A (Snowflake Schema)

Explanation

Snowflake schema would reduce the data volume.

8. A (102,400)

Explanation

102,400 is the minimum number of rows to bulk insert into a column-store index; fewer rows will use a normal insert operation.

9. A (Column store Archival)

Explanation

Column store archival provides the highest level of compression in SQL Server.

10. C (Both of the above)

Explanation

Query plans can be viewed either in a graphical representation or text-based format.

11. C (Three)

Explanation

There are three different types of execution plans that can be viewed.

12. B (Two)

Explanation

SQL Server has two types of table-valued functions, inline and multi-statement.

13. A (Normalized)

Explanation

Normalized data usually needs multiple join operations to get all the required data returned in a single query.

14. B (Snowflake)

Explanation

Dimensions in a snowflake schema are normalized to decrease redundancy, saving storage space.

15. A (10x)

Explanation

Batch mode can provide up to a 10x performance increase over traditional row processing.

Chapter 06: Automate Tasks in SQL Server

1. A (JSON)

Explanation

An Azure Resource Manager template is a JSON (JavaScript Object Notation) document that describes the resources deployed within an Azure Resource Group.

2. A (Variable)

Explanation

Parameters are values that are provided to the template to customize resources at deployment time.

3. A (dependsOn)

Explanation

DependsOn allows you to build a dependency structure into your template.

4. A (a mail profile)

Explanation

To send an email to an operator, you need to enable the email profile of the SQL Server Agent.

5. A (msdb)

Explanation

The msdb database acts as the data store for the SQL Server Agent.

6. A (Rebuild)

Explanation

Rebuilding an index updates the statistics on the index.

7. A (Ring Buffer)

Explanation

Ring Buffer is used to hold data in memory. Data is not persisted to disk and may be frequently flushed from the buffer.

8. A (On the Event)

Explanation

It is recommended that you configure a filter for each event that you are capturing.

9. A (Runboook)

Explanation

Runbooks are the unit of execution in Azure Automation.

10. B (Subscription)

Explanation

A policy provides a level of governance over your Azure subscriptions, which enforce rules and controls your Azure resources.

11. A (Target Group)

Explanation

You must define a target group in elastic jobs: a SQL Database server, an elastic pool, or one or more single databases.

12. A (Azure PowerShell)

Explanation

Azure PowerShell provides a core module known as Az, which has child resource providers for nearly all Azure services

13. A (Alerts)

Explanation

SQL Server Agent alerts allow you to be proactive with monitoring your SQL Server.

14. A (Filters)

Explanation

Filters are a powerful feature of Extended Events that allows you to use granular control to capture only the specific occurrences of the event you want to capture.

15. A (Tags)

Explanation

Tags are simply metadata that are used to describe your Azure resources better.

Chapter 07: Plan and Implement a High Availability and Disaster Recovery Environment

1. B (As a blob)

Explanation: Backup to URL necessitates the usage of an Azure storage account and the Azure blob storage service.

2. B (Azure Database for PostgreSQL only)

Explanation: These backups, like all other Azure PaaS products, can only be used by Azure Database for PostgreSQL and not by a conventional PostgreSQL installation.

3. A (Free up to the size of the database)

Explanation: One advantage of backups is that they are free. If a server is supplied with 100 GB of storage, an equal amount of backup space is included in the price you are already paying.

4. C (A load balancer)

Explanation: The listener necessitates the creation of an Azure load balancer and some additional WSFC settings relating to the load balancer.

5. B (PowerShell)

Explanation: Server Manager or PowerShell can be used to enable the Failover Cluster feature.

6. A (Azure Site Recovery)

Explanation: One significant advantage of Azure Site Recovery is that you can test disaster recovery without interrupting production.

7. C (Active geo-replication)

Explanation: Active geo-replication creates a replica of the database in another region that is kept up to date asynchronously.

8. A (Recover deleted data)

Explanation: You can utilize the Temporal Table functionality to recover data that has been deleted or updated by using the history table.

9. C (GracePeriodWithDataLossHours)

Explanation: The GracePeriodWithDataLossHours setting determines how long Azure waits before failing over.

10. B (The point to which data needs to be recovered after a failure)

Explanation: The recovery point objective (RPO) is the point in time at which a database should be recovered and is the greatest amount of data loss that the organization is willing to accept.

11. A (A solution that includes resources from both Azure and on-premises or from another cloud provider)

Explanation: Hybrid solutions cover on-premises and Azure, as well as Azure and another public cloud.

12. C (Whatever is in the databases; anything outside must be dealt with manually)

Explanation: Database-level protection means that anything collected in a user or application database's transaction log is accounted for as part of the availability feature. Anything that exists outside of the database or is not captured in the transaction log, such as SQL Server Agent jobs and linked servers, must be dealt with manually. This guarantees that the destination server can function as the primary in the case of a planned or unplanned failover event.

13. A (Network Security Group)

Explanation: Network Security Group (NSG) has a private resource firewall that allows the connection of VNet, subnet, or another network interface with VM.

14. B (Deny Rule)

Explanation: Deny rule explicitly blocks all traffic that matches the rule. The lowest priority rule is always the "Deny all" rule. This is the default rule added to every security group for in-bound and out-bound traffic with a priority of 65500. Therefore, to allow the traffic to pass through the security group, you must have an allow rule. Otherwise, all the traffic will be blocked due to denying rule.

Acronyms

AAD	Azure Active Directory
ACI	Azure Container Instances
ACL	Access Control List
AD	Active Directory
ADC	Application Delivery Controller
ADF	Azure Data Factory
ADLS	Azure Data Lake Storage
ADR	Accelerated Database Recovery
AES	Advanced Encryption Standard
AG	Availability Group
AHB	Azure Hybrid Benefit
AI	Artificial Intelligence
AIP	Azure Information Protection
AKS	Azure Kubernetes Service
API	Application Program Interface
APU	Accelerated Processing Unit
ARM	Azure Resource Manger
ASB	Azure Security Benchmark
ASG	Application Security Group
AWS	Amazon Web Service
AZ	Availability Zone
Azure ATP	Azure Advanced Threat Protection
B2B	Business-to-Business
CapEx	Capital Expenditure
CDN	Content Delivery Network
CLI	Command Line Interface
CLR	Common Language Runtime

CPE	Customer Premises Equipment
CPU	Central Processing Unit
DB	Database
DC	Domain Controller
DC/OS	Distributed Cloud Operating System
DDoS	Distributed Denial of Service
DevOps	Development and Operations
DMS	Database Migration Services
DNS	Domain Name System
DoS	Denial of Service
DR	Disaster Recovery
DRS	Default Rule Set
DSA	Dynamic Site Acceleration
DTU	Database Transaction Unit
DWUs	Data Warehouse Units
EAI	Enterprise Application Integration
ETL	Extracting, Transforming, and Loading
EU	European Union
FaaS	Function as a Service
FCI	Failover Cluster Instance
FIPS	Federal Information Processing Standards
GCP	Google Cloud Platform
GDPR	General Data Protection Regulation
GPU	Graphics Processing Unit
HA	High Availability
HDD	Hard Disk Drive
HDFS	Hadoop Distributed File System
HDI	HDInsight
HSM	Hardware Security Model
HTTP	Hypertext Transfer Protocol

HTTPS	Hypertext Transfer Protocol Secure
IaaS	Infrastructure as a Service
IOPS	Input/Output Operations per Second
IoT	Internet-of-Things
IP	Internet Protocol
ISO	International Standardization Organization
IT	Information Technology
JSON	JavaScript Object Notation
KEDA	Kubernetes-based Event Driven Autoscaling
MAXDOP	Max Degree of Parallelism
MCU	Micro-Controller Unit
MFA	Multi-Factor Authentication
ML	Machine Learning
MPLS	Multiprotocol Label Switching
MSDTC	Microsoft Distributed Transaction Coordinator
NIST	National Institute of Standards and Technology
NSG	Network Security Group
OpEx	Operational Expenditure
OS	Operating System
PaaS	Platform as a Service
PCI	Payment Card Industry
PITR	Point in Time Restore
POC	Proof of concept
POP	Point of Presence
POS	Point of Scale
PVS	Persisted Version Store
RBAC	Role Based Access Control
RCAs	Root Cause Analyses
RDDS	Resilient Distributed Datasets
RDMA	Remote Direct Memory Access

SaaS	Software as a Service
SAQL	Stream Analytics Query Language
SDKs	Software Development Kits
SLA	Service Level Agreement
SOC	Standard Occupational Classification
SQL	Structured Query Language
SSD	Solid State Drive
SSE	Storage Service Encryption
SSH	Secure Shell
SSIS	SQL Server Integration Services
SSL	Secure Sockets Layer
SSMS	SQL Server Management Studio
SSO	Single Sign-On
SSTP	Secure Socket Tunneling Protocol
TCO	Total Cost of Ownership
TCP	Transmission Control Protocol
TFS	Team Foundation Server
TFVC	Team Foundation Version Control
TVF	Table-Valued Functions
UDF	User Defined Functions
UDR	User-Defined Routes
UIDs	Unique Identifiers
URL	Uniform Resource Locator
US	United State
VM	Virtual Machine
VMs	Virtual Machines
VNet	Virtual Network
VPN	Virtual Private Network

References

https://docs.microsoft.com/en-us/learn/certifications/exams/dp-300

https://docs.microsoft.com/en-us/learn/paths/implement-secure-environment-database-service/

https://www.simplilearn.com/tutorials/azure-tutorial/azure-virtual-network-vnet

https://www.varonis.com/blog/azure-virtual-network/

https://www.simplilearn.com/tutorials/azure-tutorial/azure-virtual-network-vnet

https://www.varonis.com/blog/azure-virtual-network/

https://k21academy.com/microsoft-azure/az-304/virtual-networks-in-microsoft-azure-vnet-peeringexpressroutevpn-gateway/

https://www.coursera.org/projects/introduction-to-virtual-networks-in-microsoft-azure

https://aviatrix.com/learn-center/cloud-networking/azure-networking-fundamentals/

https://www.azureguru.org/what-is-azure-virtual-networking/

https://www.eginnovations.com/documentation/Microsoft-Azure/Azure-Virtual-Network-classic-Test.htm

https://docs.microsoft.com/en-us/learn/paths/plan-implement-data-platform-resources/

https://docs.microsoft.com/en-us/learn/modules/deploy-mariadb-mysql-postgresql-azure/

https://docs.microsoft.com/en-us/learn/modules/deploy-azure-sql-database/

https://docs.microsoft.com/en-us/learn/modules/deploy-sql-server-virtual-machine/

https://docs.microsoft.com/en-us/learn/paths/optimize-query-performance-sql-server/

https://docs.microsoft.com/en-us/learn/modules/describe-sql-server-query-plans/?ns-enrollment-type=LearningPath&ns-enrollment-id=learn.wwl.optimize-query-performance-sql-server

https://docs.microsoft.com/en-us/learn/modules/evaluate-performance-improvements/?ns-enrollment-type=LearningPath&ns-enrollment-id=learn.wwl.optimize-query-performance-sql-server

https://docs.microsoft.com/en-us/learn/modules/explore-performance-based-design/?ns-enrollment-type=LearningPath&ns-enrollment-id=learn.wwl.optimize-query-performance-sql-server

https://k21academy.com/microsoft-azure/az-304/virtual-networks-in-microsoft-azure-vnet-peeringexpressroutevpn-gateway/

https://docs.microsoft.com/en-us/learn/certifications/exams/dp-300

https://docs.microsoft.com/en-us/learn/paths/plan-implement-high-availability-disaster-recovery-environment/

https://docs.microsoft.com/en-us/learn/modules/describe-high-availability-disaster-recovery-strategies/

https://docs.microsoft.com/en-us/learn/modules/explore-iaas-paas-platform-tools-for-high-availability-disaster-recovery/

https://docs.microsoft.com/en-us/learn/modules/backup-restore-databases/

https://docs.microsoft.com/en-us/learn/modules/backup-restore-databases/5-exercise-backup-url/?ns-enrollment-type=LearningPath&ns-enrollment-id=learn.wwl.plan-implement-ha-dr-environment

https://www.coursera.org/projects/introduction-to-virtual-networks-in-microsoft-azure

https://aviatrix.com/learn-center/cloud-networking/azure-networking-fundamentals/

https://www.azureguru.org/what-is-azure-virtual-networking/

https://www.eginnovations.com/documentation/Microsoft-Azure/Azure-Virtual-Network-classic-Test.htm

https://docs.microsoft.com/en-us/learn/paths/plan-implement-data-platform-resources/

https://docs.microsoft.com/en-us/learn/modules/deploy-mariadb-mysql-postgresql-azure/

https://docs.microsoft.com/en-us/learn/modules/deploy-azure-sql-database/

https://docs.microsoft.com/en-us/learn/modules/deploy-sql-server-virtual-machine/

https://docs.microsoft.com/en-us/learn/paths/automate-tasks-sql-server/

https://docs.microsoft.com/en-us/learn/modules/configure-automatic-deployment-azure-sql-database/

https://docs.microsoft.com/en-us/learn/modules/schedule-tasks-using-sql-server-agent/

https://docs.microsoft.com/en-us/learn/modules/manage-azure-paas-resources-using-automated-methods/

https://acloudguru.com/hands-on-labs/deploying-an-azure-sql-database

https://docs.microsoft.com/en-us/learn/modules/configure-database-authentication-authorization/

https://www.simplilearn.com/tutorials/azure-tutorial/azure-virtual-network-vnet

https://www.varonis.com/blog/azure-virtual-network/

https://k21academy.com/microsoft-azure/az-304/virtual-networks-in-microsoft-azure-vnet-peeringexpressroutevpn-gateway/

https://www.coursera.org/projects/introduction-to-virtual-networks-in-microsoft-azure

https://aviatrix.com/learn-center/cloud-networking/azure-networking-fundamentals/

https://www.azureguru.org/what-is-azure-virtual-networking/

https://www.eginnovations.com/documentation/Microsoft-Azure/Azure-Virtual-Network-classic-Test.htm

https://docs.microsoft.com/en-us/learn/paths/plan-implement-data-platform-resources/

https://docs.microsoft.com/en-us/learn/modules/deploy-mariadb-mysql-postgresql-azure/

https://docs.microsoft.com/en-us/learn/modules/deploy-azure-sql-database/

https://docs.microsoft.com/en-us/learn/modules/deploy-sql-server-virtual-machine/

https://docs.microsoft.com/en-us/learn/paths/monitor-optimize-operational-resources-sql-server/

https://docs.microsoft.com/en-us/learn/modules/describe-performance-monitoring/

https://docs.microsoft.com/en-us/learn/modules/explore-causes-performance-issues/

https://docs.microsoft.com/en-us/learn/modules/configure-sql-server-resources-optimal-performance/

https://docs.microsoft.com/en-us/learn/modules/configure-databases-performance/

https://docs.microsoft.com/en-us/learn/modules/describe-performance-related-maintenance-tasks-sql-server/

https://docs.microsoft.com/en-us/learn/modules/protect-data-transit-rest/

https://docs.microsoft.com/en-us/learn/modules/implement-compliance-controls-sensitive-data/

https://docs.microsoft.com/en-us/learn/modules/configure-database-authentication-authorization/2-describe-active-directory/?ns-enrollment-type=LearningPath&ns-enrollment-id=learn.wwl.implement-secure-environment-database-service

https://docs.microsoft.com/en-us/learn/modules/configure-database-authentication-authorization/4-describe-security-principals/?ns-enrollment-type=LearningPath&ns-enrollment-id=learn.wwl.implement-secure-environment-database-service

https://docs.microsoft.com/en-us/learn/modules/configure-database-authentication-authorization/5-describe-database-object-permissions/?ns-enrollment-type=LearningPath&ns-enrollment-id=learn.wwl.implement-secure-environment-database-service

https://docs.microsoft.com/en-us/learn/modules/protect-data-transit-rest/2-describe-role-firewalls/?ns-enrollment-type=LearningPath&ns-enrollment-id=learn.wwl.implement-secure-environment-database-service

https://docs.microsoft.com/en-us/learn/modules/protect-data-transit-rest/4-describe-role-azure-key-vault-transparent-data-encryption/?ns-enrollment-type=LearningPath&ns-enrollment-id=learn.wwl.implement-secure-environment-database-service

https://docs.microsoft.com/en-us/learn/modules/implement-compliance-controls-sensitive-data/3-describe-advanced-threat-protection/?ns-enrollment-type=LearningPath&ns-enrollment-id=learn.wwl.implement-secure-environment-database-service

https://docs.microsoft.com/en-us/learn/modules/implement-compliance-controls-sensitive-data/2-describe-data-classification/?ns-enrollment-type=LearningPath&ns-enrollment-id=learn.wwl.implement-secure-environment-database-service

https://docs.microsoft.com/en-us/learn/paths/azure-sql-fundamentals/

https://docs.microsoft.com/en-us/learn/modules/azure-sql-intro/

https://www.simplilearn.com/tutorials/azure-tutorial/azure-virtual-network-vnet

https://www.varonis.com/blog/azure-virtual-network/

https://k21academy.com/microsoft-azure/az-304/virtual-networks-in-microsoft-azure-vnet-peeringexpressroutevpn-gateway/

https://www.coursera.org/projects/introduction-to-virtual-networks-in-microsoft-azure

https://aviatrix.com/learn-center/cloud-networking/azure-networking-fundamentals/

https://www.azureguru.org/what-is-azure-virtual-networking/

https://www.eginnovations.com/documentation/Microsoft-Azure/Azure-Virtual-Network-classic-Test.htm

https://docs.microsoft.com/en-us/learn/paths/plan-implement-data-platform-resources/

https://docs.microsoft.com/en-us/learn/modules/deploy-mariadb-mysql-postgresql-azure/

https://docs.microsoft.com/en-us/learn/modules/deploy-azure-sql-database/

https://docs.microsoft.com/en-us/learn/modules/deploy-sql-server-virtual-machine/

https://docs.microsoft.com/en-us/learn/modules/azure-sql-deploy-configure/

https://docs.microsoft.com/en-us/learn/modules/azure-sql-performance/

https://docs.microsoft.com/en-us/learn/modules/azure-sql-case-studies/

https://www.sentryone.com/products/sentryone-platform/db-sentry/azure-sql-database-monitoring

https://intercept.cloud/en/news/azure-sql-sql-managed-instance-or-sql-server/

https://www.pluralsight.com/courses/azure-sql-course

https://cloudacademy.com/course/implementing-azure-sql-databases-1208/introduction/

https://www.semanticscholar.org/paper/Microsoft-Azure-SQL-Database-Step-by-Step-Lobel-Boyd/4834064e69f217fad1f078434d35699018b34f09

https://clc.newhorizons.com/training-and-certifications/course-outline/id/80/c/sql-querying-fundamentals-part-1

https://githubmemory.com/repo/mokoweb/mslearn-azure-sql-fundamentals

About Our Products

Other products from IPSpecialist LTD regarding CSP technology are:

 AWS Certified Cloud Practitioner Study guide

 AWS Certified SysOps Admin - Associate Study guide

 AWS Certified Solution Architect - Associate Study guide

 AWS Certified Developer Associate Study guide

 AWS Certified Advanced Networking – Specialty Study guide

 AWS Certified Security – Specialty Study guide

 AWS Certified Big Data – Specialty Study guide

 Microsoft Certified: Azure Fundamentals

 Microsoft Certified: Azure Administrator

 Microsoft Certified: Azure Solution Architect

 Microsoft Certified: Azure DevOps Engineer

 Microsoft Certified: Azure Developer Associate

 Microsoft Certified: Azure Security Engineer

 Microsoft Certified: Azure Data Fundamentals

 Microsoft Certified: Azure AI Fundamentals

 Microsoft Certified: Azure Database Administrator Associate

 Microsoft Certified: Azure Data Engineer Associate

 Microsoft Certified: Azure Data Scientist

Oracle Certified: Foundations Associate

Oracle Certified: Developer Associate

Google Certified: Professional Network Engineer

Google Certified: Associate Cloud Engineer

Other Network & Security related products from IPSpecialist LTD are:

- CCNA Routing & Switching Study Guide
- CCNA Security Second Edition Study Guide
- CCNA Service Provider Study Guide
- CCDA Study Guide
- CCDP Study Guide
- CCNP Route Study Guide
- CCNP Switch Study Guide
- CCNP Troubleshoot Study Guide
- CCNP Security SENSS Study Guide
- CCNP Security SIMOS Study Guide
- CCNP Security SITCS Study Guide
- CCNP Security SISAS Study Guide
- CompTIA Network+ Study Guide
- Certified Blockchain Expert (CBEv2) Study Guide
- EC-Council CEH v10 Second Edition Study Guide
- Certified Blockchain Expert v2 Study Guide